ST JAMES'S PALACE

ST JAMES'S PALACE

From Leper Hospital to Royal Court

EDITED BY SIMON THURLEY

RUFUS BIRD
SIMON THURLEY
MICHAEL TURNER

YALE UNIVERSITY PRESS, NEW HAVEN AND LONDON
in association with ROYAL COLLECTION TRUST

First published by Yale University Press 2022
302 Temple Street, P.O. Box 209040, New Haven CT 06520-9040
47 Bedford Square, London WC1B 3DP
yalebooks.com | yalebooks.co.uk

Unless otherwise stated, text and all works reproduced are Royal Collection Trust /
© Her Majesty Queen Elizabeth II 2022

All rights reserved. Except as permitted under current legislation no part of this work may be photocopied, stored in a retrieval system, published, performed in public, adapted, broadcast, transmitted, recorded or reproduced in any form or by any means, without the prior permission of the copyright owner.

The authors assert their moral rights to be identified as the authors of this work in accordance with the Copyright, Designs and Patents Act 1988.

ISBN 978-0-300267-46-4

10 9 8 7 6 5 4 3 2 1
2026 2025 2024 2023 2022

Library of Congress Control Number: 2022931577

A catalogue record for this book is available from the British Library.

FOR ROYAL COLLECTION TRUST

Publisher: Kate Owen
Project Manager: Polly Fellows
Copyeditor: Alison Tickner
Designer: Laura Parker
Reconstruction drawings: Bob Marshall
Indexer: Nicola King
Production Manager: Sarah Tucker

Colour reproduction: Alta Image
Typeset in Andulka Pro and printed on Arctic Volume 150 gsm
Printed and bound in Wales by Gomer Press

FRONTISPIECE: Abraham Allard, *State Entry of George I and the Prince of Wales into London*, 1714 (detail of Fig. 3.4)

PAGE VI: Ceiling in the Chapel Royal

ENDPAPERS: 'Mallow' wallpaper, 1879, designed by Kate Faulkner for Morris & Co. (V&A, E.811-1915)

CONTENTS

vii   Foreword
         HRH THE PRINCE OF WALES

viii   Acknowledgements

ix   Notes for the Reader

1   Introduction
         SIMON THURLEY

13   **1. From the Hospital of St James to the Civil War**
         SIMON THURLEY

13   The Hospital of St James
17   Henry VIII and the Rebuilding of St James's
27   The Later Tudors
30   The Early Stuarts
53   The Civil Wars
60   The Commonwealth and Protectorate
63   The Bailiwick of St James's before 1660

71   **2. The Restoration to Queen Anne**
         SIMON THURLEY

71   St James's House at the Restoration
74   The District of St James's after 1660
78   The Queen's Chapel
88   The Duke and Duchess of York
94   James II and Mary Beatrice of Modena
97   William and Mary
102   Princess Anne
105   Queen Anne: St James's Becomes a Palace
111   The Fringes of St James's

119   **3. The Georgian Court**
         RUFUS BIRD

119   George I, 1714–27
131   George II and Queen Caroline, 1727–60
146   George III and Queen Charlotte, 1760 to the 1790s
160   The Princes and their Apartments, 1790s–1809
167   Fire and Dilapidation, 1809–20

175   **4. George IV to the Second World War**
         MICHAEL TURNER

175   George IV, 1820–30
190   William IV, 1830–37
193   Queen Victoria, 1837–1901
212   Edward VII, 1901–10
215   George V, 1910–36
219   Edward VIII, 1936
223   George VI, 1936–52

227   **5. The Palace Today**
         SIMON THURLEY

238   Notes
255   Abbreviations and Bibliography
274   Index
281   Illustration Credits
284   Plans A–D

CLARENCE HOUSE

St James's Palace is perhaps the least well known of all the official royal residences. The principal seat of the British monarchy since 1698, it was at St James's that Her Majesty The Queen was proclaimed monarch on 8 February 1952. Despite its rich history, it surprises me to learn that little has been written about this quietly splendid building just minutes from Buckingham Palace.

St James's retains an active life today. It is here that ambassadors present their credentials, before travelling to Buckingham Palace for an audience with the Sovereign. Each year more than one hundred official events and receptions take place within its walls, many for charities supported by the Royal Family. As well as this public-facing role, St James's remains the home of several members of the Royal Family and many happy family occasions, such as weddings and christenings, have taken place here since the eighteenth century – most recently of the children of The Duke and Duchess of Cambridge.

Over the past 900 years, the palace has had many different roles. First as a place of sanctuary for the sick, then as a remote and secure nursery for the royal children and, eventually, as the official royal residence until the reign of Queen Victoria. The continual reinvention of this relatively unassuming building provides fascinating insights into the history of our nation.

One of the Royal Collection Trust's primary aims is to ensure that the Royal Collection and Palaces are valued and enjoyed by everyone. I am delighted that this unprecedented publication will enable the Trust to fulfil that objective by finally telling the whole story of this charming building and those who have shaped its history.

ACKNOWLEDGEMENTS

The publication of this book owes thanks to the contribution of a great many willing and endlessly helpful colleagues, experts and friends. The authors have drawn heavily on documents held in various archives and they are grateful to the archivists and staff at All Souls College, Oxford, the British Library, the British Museum, the National Archives, Historic England Archive, Swindon, Northamptonshire Record Office, the Royal Institute of British Architects and Sir John Soane's Museum, and to Allison Derrett from the Royal Archives for painstakingly checking our references.

Within the Royal Household we are grateful to the following past and present members of staff who provided help and support during the compilation of the book: Philip Rhodes, Senior Page of the Chambers and Custodian of the State Apartments, St James's Palace, for his help and assistance with access to the State Apartments for research and photography; Alistair Harrison, Marshal of the Diplomatic Corps, and Georgina Harford; The Reverend Canon Paul Wright, Sub-Dean of Her Majesty's Chapels Royal, and Jon Simpson, Sergeant of the Vestry; as well as Lauren Briant, Sarah Drysdale, Laura Hobbs, Hannah Howard, Louis Randall and Bridget Wright. We are also indebted to Chris Savage and the Yeomen of the Guard and Tim Rayson and the Honourable Corps of the Gentlemen-at-Arms' mess.

We would like also to thank the many historians, architectural specialists and other experts who provided information and advice or who reviewed and commented on sections of the book at various stages, including Dr Andrew Barclay and Dr Anthony Geraghty (expert readers) for their invaluable guidance and advice in shaping the text; as well as the Rt Hon the Earl of Airlie, Dr Thomas P. Campbell, Dr Anna Keay, Dr Simon Neale, the late Jane Roberts, former Royal Librarian and Curator of the Print Room at Windsor Castle, the Rt Hon the Earl of Rosslyn, James Edgar, Allyson McDermott, and Dr Timothy Wilks.

For the visual content of the book, our thanks go to Juan Jose Fuldain and Tracy Wellman (Museum of London Archaeology) for drawing the maps and plans, to Bob Marshall for creating the historical reconstruction drawings, and to Peter Smith for the new photographs of the palace.

During the editorial and production process, we were assisted by Alison Tickner (copyeditor), Laura Parker (designer), Stephen Hebron (typesetter), Bev Zimmern, Catherine Best and Kate Bell (proofreaders), Nicola King (indexer) and Sarah Tucker (Production Manager). Within the Royal Collection, particular thanks are due to Polly Fellows and Kate Owen for their efforts to create this book and manage the editorial and production processes. They were ably assisted by Hannah Bowen, Wilhelmina Castelijns van Beek, Nina Chang, Stephen Chapman, Carly Collier, Alexander Collins, Abigail Field, Sophie Gordon, Lisa Heighway, Kathryn Jones, Karen Lawson, Isabella Manning, Anna McGee, Fiona Norbury, Stella Panayotova, Daniel Partridge, Shruti Patel, Clara de la Peña Mc Tigue, Alice de Quidt, Rosie Razzall, Jemima Rellie, Desmond Shawe-Taylor, Bill Stockting, Nicola Turner Inman, Lucy Whitaker, Richard Williams and Eva Zielinska-Millar. Thanks are also owed to Directors of the Royal Collection, past and present, Tim Knox, Sir Jonathan Marsden and Sir Hugh Roberts, for the inception of this project and their support along the way.

NOTES FOR THE READER

Measurements
For historical references, imperial measurements are given where relevant (with metric equivalents in parentheses). In all other cases, metric measurements only are stated.

Life dates
Life/active dates are given in the text for key figures, including artists and makers, with regnal dates given for English/British monarchs. Where life/active dates are available for other individuals, these are given in the index.

New Style and Old Style dates
In 1752, Britain adopted the Gregorian calendar in place of the Julian calendar. As a result, the start of the year was changed from 25 March (Lady Day) to 1 January. Some historians referring to events occurring before 1752 use the contemporary or Old Style date found on the documents of the time, whereas others prefer to change the date to its Gregorian or New Style form. Thus, although according to contemporary records, Henry VIII's death occurred on 28 January 1546, most modern historians cite it as occurring on 28 January 1547. To avoid the confusion that sometimes arises from using the two systems in parallel, dates in this book occurring before 1752 and falling within the period 1 January to 24 March have been carefully checked and rendered in an unambiguous dual form where appropriate. It should be noted that the Gregorian calendar was adopted by some European countries as early as the sixteenth century and by others as late as the twentieth century. In addition, in implementing the changeover, each country had to remove a number of years from its calendar for that year, with the result that the dates occurring on foreign documents may be at variance with those of the contemporary British calendar.

Queen Victoria's Journal
References to Queen Victoria's Journal, covering the period 1832–1901, take the form RA VIC/MAIN/QVJ. The references may differ, however, depending on which version of the Journal is cited. There are four versions of the Journal in total: the original, written by Queen Victoria herself; Lord Esher's typescripts, covering 1 August 1832 to 16 February 1840; a transcript written by Princess Beatrice for the period 1 January 1837 to 13 January 1901; and Queen Victoria's drafts for the period 2 September 1843 to 10 December 1855. The complete online collection of Queen Victoria's Journal in the Royal Archives can be consulted at www.queenvictoriasjournals.org.

Maps and plans
The maps and plans featured in this book were prepared in 2019 on the basis of information then available. The three reconstruction drawings depicting the palace at key points in its development are based on archaeological and historical evidence, but where there is no direct evidence, conjectural details have been drawn from a range of historical sources to make them as representative of the period concerned as possible. The most detailed drawings are Plans A–D, which appear as fold-outs at the end of the book and can be viewed in tandem with the text. Plan D is a phased plan of the palace: it includes colours and tones to show the different phases of construction only, not the decorative linings or refacings. Unless otherwise stated, historical maps and plans are orientated with north at the top.

To see more images and details of Royal Collection material included in this book, please visit
www.rct.uk/st-james-palace

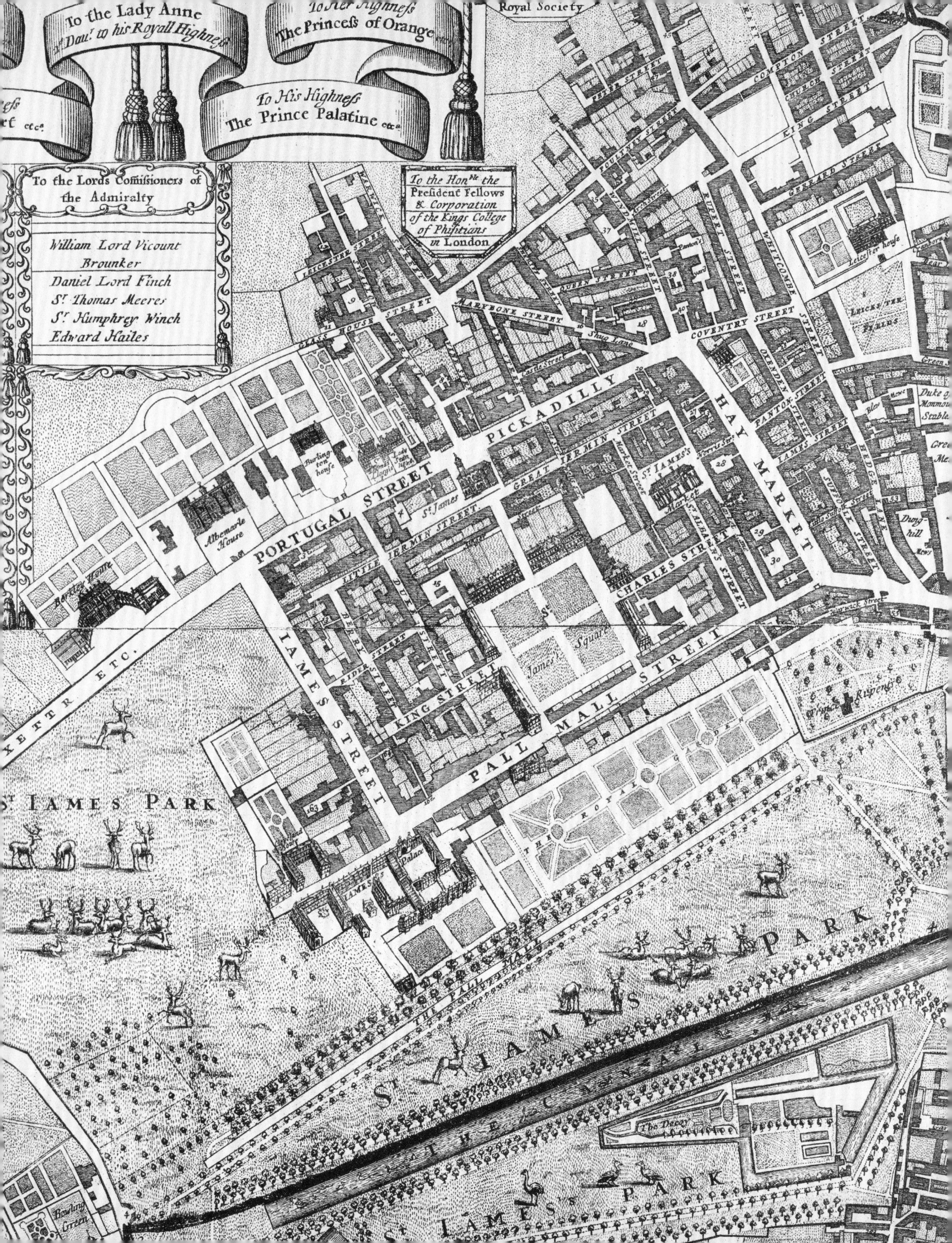

Introduction

SIMON THURLEY

For most people, St James's Palace is a mysterious and confusing place. Unlike its near neighbour, Buckingham Palace, whose role is clear and appearance famous, St James's is an odd, messy-looking building whose purpose and use are not well understood. This was not always the case. Until Queen Victoria (r. 1837–1901) moved into Buckingham Palace in 1837, St James's had been, for more than a hundred years, the principal seat of the British monarchy, and before a quarter of it burnt down in 1809, it was much more architecturally coherent.

As the palace remains in intensive royal use, it is difficult casually to visit its brick-built precincts, and this adds to a sense of the unknown. However, looked at from above (Fig. 0.1), the overall disposition of the palace can be simply explained. The Tudor main gate, its most recognisable feature, is at the end of St James's Street and leads into what is now called Colour Court, once the outer courtyard of the palace. To the east of this, on the other side of Marlborough Road, is the Queen's Chapel, well-known to architectural aficionados as being one of Inigo Jones's (1573–1652) few surviving buildings.

Opposite the chapel, on the west side of Marlborough Road, is what looks like an open parade ground, called Friary Court. Its Victorian name refers to the Roman Catholic friary that was once attached to the chapel. The court is, in fact, two sides of a Tudor inner courtyard which burnt down in 1809. The Household guardsmen parade here, and when a new monarch is proclaimed, it is from a balcony on the open court's west side.

Along The Mall is the palace garden, still in use, and on the other side of this, glimpsed through the trees, is a long, red-brick range which contains the State Apartments, some Tudor, some Stuart, and all altered by the Georgians and Victorians. At the far western end of the State Apartments is a white stuccoed building, Clarence House. Often thought of as a separate building, it is, in reality, an integral part of St James's, and the London residence of HRH The Prince of Wales (b. 1948).

On the north side of the palace, along Cleveland Row, is another long range of red-brick buildings, once home to various members of the royal family, but now mainly Royal Household offices. Behind this, viewed from above, are two other courts, Engine Court and Ambassadors Court; these are not formal spaces like Colour Court and are made up of buildings from all periods in the palace's history. They now contain residences, more offices and the guardsmen's mess. The far western part of the palace is the old stable yard and contains Lancaster House, a large, stone-built mansion owned by the government.

0.1

William Morgan, *London Actually Survey'd*, 1682. Although Morgan's detailed mapping of St James's gives, perhaps, a more ordered impression of the area than actually existed in the 1680s, his map is the first accurate survey of the area. The palace buildings are representative rather than a faithful image, but it shows the park and gardens with reasonable accuracy (detail of Fig. 2.4)

0.2
Map of Westminster today

Remarkably, there has been no modern history of this extensive royal building. The late Kenneth Scott's history, published in connection with the Duke of Edinburgh's Award Scheme in 2010, is a short, popular account. Neither this, nor Charles Graves's *Palace Extraordinary* published in 1963, nor Bruce Graeme's *The Story of St James's Palace* published in 1929, consulted primary sources. All of them rely on Edgar Sheppard's two-volume *Memorials of St James's Palace* published in 1894, the only history to be referenced. Compiled by a former Sub-Dean of the Chapel Royal, this antiquarian compilation is far less thorough than the near-contemporary histories of Hampton Court by Ernest Law, or of Windsor Castle by Sir William St John Hope, both of which were great scholarly achievements based on detailed archival research.

Up until now, for a reliable account of the palace's architectural history, the reader would turn to the relevant sections in Sir Howard Colvin's monumental *History of the King's Works*. This book, whilst the basis of all modern scholarship on royal building, is the official story of the royal Office of Works, and while it chronicles, in some detail, changes to the fabric of the building, they are not put into the context of the life of the court, the history of English architecture or the topography of the West End (Fig. 0.2). But for St James's, the problem is deeper. Because the palace was occupied by the sovereign's children and consorts, much building work was accounted for in the Privy Purse accounts of members of the royal family and not by the Office of Works. This means that some work falls outside the scope of the *King's Works*. Moreover, the *King's Works* account ends in the mid-nineteenth century and does not cover the important and interesting Victorian and Edwardian history of the palace.

All of this is to say that, despite some valuable recent periodical literature, the story of St James's has never been properly told. Despite it being the palace from which the emergent British Empire was run, and the place to which

0.3
The accession of Her Majesty The Queen, proclaimed from the balcony in Friary Court, 8 February 1952

ambassadors are still accredited, it is the least understood and appreciated of all royal buildings.

The historian of English royal buildings is blessed with nearly one thousand years of bureaucracy. For St James's there are untold of pages of warrants, accounts, bills and official correspondence. Added to this are private archives of letters, memoirs, diaries and financial accounts. The challenge is too much information rather than too little. Cutting through a mountain of paper to identify what is significant in the history of St James's has been the challenge for the present authors. We have set out not just to write an architectural story, though the architecture is in the lead, but to cover the wider social and cultural significance of the place. And to do this, it is necessary to introduce the subject in the wider context of royal building, and to highlight some of the important themes that will emerge.

When King George VI (r. 1936–52) died at Sandringham House on 6 February 1952, Princess Elizabeth was more than 4,000 miles away in Kenya. In her absence, the Privy Council met at St James's Palace to make arrangements for her accession as Queen Elizabeth II (r. 1952–). Two days later, her accession was proclaimed from the balcony in Friary Court (Fig. 0.3), the monarch and her consort watching from the window of the Tapestry Room. The new Queen then chaired her Accession Council at the palace, taking the oath of succession.

The chain of events that led to the 1953 ceremonies of accession taking place at St James's is long and complex, but ultimately conditioned by the status of the palace as the official seat of the monarchy – its principal palace. Although the term 'palace' is now indiscriminately applied to any residence of a sovereign or, indeed, any large mansion occupied by a person of rank, the term

INTRODUCTION 3

originally had a very specific meaning. It derives from the residence of the Roman emperors on the Palatine Hill in Rome and came to be applied to a monarch's principal residence. As such, monarchs only had one palace; other residences were houses, castles or manors. In the Middle Ages, the official residence of English kings was the Palace of Westminster, and the term 'palace' was exclusively applied to this. After its destruction by fire in 1512, and the subsequent conversion and extension of York Place to form Whitehall, Henry VIII (r. 1509–47) passed an Act of Parliament to extend the term 'palace' to embrace not only the remains of the medieval buildings at Westminster, but also Whitehall.[1] This remained the situation until 1698, when Whitehall Palace was also destroyed by fire. At this point, the machinery of the English state split in two. Parts of the permanent administration, such as the Treasury, remained in the undamaged areas of Whitehall on the west side of the road, while the sovereign and the court moved to nearby St James's.

From around 1700, without any official instrument, the royal manor of St James's started to be known as St James's Palace, and as various plans to rebuild Whitehall were abandoned, the palace became acknowledged as the principal seat of the British Crown. As early as 1825, in the midst of George IV's (r. 1820–30) improvements to Buckingham House, it, too, started to be known as a palace, to signify that it was a royal residence.[2] However, this was, and remains, in a technical sense, a courtesy title, because the official seat of the British monarchy remains at St James's Palace. It is there, in Friary Court, that the Garter King of Arms proclaims a new sovereign, and where a new monarch holds their Accession Council. Ambassadors are accredited to the Court of St James's, although they are likely to present their credentials at Buckingham Palace.

Buckingham Palace is thus the administrative seat of the monarchy; St James's is its official seat; and the Palace of Westminster, which retains seniority amongst all royal residences, contains not only the upper and lower chambers of the British legislature, but also a royal palace from which the sovereign processes to open Parliament.

For almost everyone, these are technical niceties, and the perception is that Her Majesty The Queen lives at Buckingham Palace, while St James's, if it is noticed at all, is an old building hiding behind a high wall off The Mall. Remarkably, despite the unexpected promotion which that 'old building' received in 1698, when it became, by default, the seat of the monarchy, it also retains today its original function – the official home of the heir to the throne. HRH The Prince of Wales lives in Clarence House, an integral part of St James's, and there, before him, lived The Queen when she was Princess Elizabeth. This historic usage goes right back to the origins of the palace as a royal residence.

St James's was conceived as a winter home for the heir to the throne and was used by Henry VIII's illegitimate son, Henry Fitzroy, Duke of Richmond (1519–36), and by Prince Edward, the future Edward VI (r. 1547–53). Under James I (r. 1603–25), it was home to Prince Henry (1594–1612) and Prince Charles, and when the latter became King (Charles I, r. 1625–49), to Prince Charles and Prince James. After the Restoration, James, as Duke of York and heir presumptive, lived at St James's, and his daughters, Princess Mary (r. 1689–94), and Princess Anne (r. 1702–14), were brought up there. After the death of Mary, it became Anne's official residence as next in line to the throne.

For the parade of Stuart heirs that lived at St James's, there were few alterations or additions to the Tudor royal manor house, at least, none that qualified as being architecturally significant – except one. This was the Roman Catholic chapel, which was begun in 1623 as part of the negotiations for a marriage between Charles, Prince of Wales, and the Spanish Infanta, and then completed as part of the marriage treaty between Charles I and Henrietta Maria (1609–69). This was the single most important addition to the palace in its history, not primarily because it was designed by Inigo Jones (although this was significant) but because it came to play a key part in the decisive constitutional events of the seventeenth century.

The chapels of St James's are thus one of the most prevalent themes in this book. The Tudor chapel, which, after 1698, became the home to the Chapel Royal, the monarch's personal religious establishment, remains its headquarters today. Here, weddings and christenings take place and members of the royal family have lain in state. This chapel, built for Henry VIII, has always (apart from five years under Mary I, r. 1553–8) been Anglican, but Inigo Jones's Queen's Chapel was, from its completion until 1688, Roman Catholic. Confusingly, the Queen's Chapel was not part of St James's and was legally owned by the Queen Consort for life. It thus belonged to Henrietta Maria from 1626 to 1662, then to Catherine of Braganza (1638–1705) from 1662 to 1685, and to Mary of Modena (1658–1718) from 1685 until 1688. Neither Henrietta Maria nor Catherine of Braganza lived at St James's, dividing their time in London between their apartments at Whitehall and their jointure house – Somerset House on the Strand.[3] Mary of Modena was the only consort who lived at St James's for part of her reign.

In the build-up to the Civil War, the Queen's Chapel became part of the Catholic iconography of the royal family, which was hated by a few and distrusted by most. After the Restoration, this was magnified by the construction of, first, a friary, then a monastery attached to the chapel. St James's thus became a target of both polemical and physical abuse during the turbulent period of the Popish Plot, the Exclusion Crisis, accession of the Catholic James II (r. 1685–8) and the Glorious Revolution. This book places St James's and the Queen's Chapel in their proper place in our understanding of the constitutional twists and turns of the period 1630–88 and its aftermath.

In exactly the same period, it can be argued that St James's played a critical role in the genesis of the royal art collection. Although monarchs and their families had collected what we would call works of art before the reign of James I, the collecting activities of James's eldest son, Henry, Prince of Wales, were of a different order and for a different purpose. At St James's he brought together easel paintings, coins, medals, bronzes, books and manuscripts, which would be added to, after his early death, by his brother, the future Charles I. Although Charles I kept his best, or at least his favourite, paintings at Whitehall, St James's remained the location for the Royal Cabinet and library, and contained some of the best classical sculpture and many fine paintings. The magnificent three-sided picture gallery was one of the great wonders of early Stuart London.

It has been suggested that, as at Nonsuch, where Henry VIII provided a classical education on the walls of the inner courtyard for Prince Edward, he may have done the same in the galleries of St James's – hanging them with portraits of European royalty.[4] This is difficult to prove, given the paucity of evidence, but the acquisition and construction of a library for Prince Henry at St James's was certainly part of an educational programme, and may explain the retention of the royal library at the royal nursery house until 1707. It is also likely that the picture hang in the Stuart galleries had an educational aspect to it and was not purely decorative.

After 1698, when St James's became the principal royal residence, the nature of the art collections began to change; inventories show that, although paintings and other works of art may have been chosen for their artistic merit, their dynastic significance was much more important. The palace became a celebration of the legitimacy of the Hanoverian dynasty, and in the heady days after the defeat of Napoleon, George IV added canvasses celebrating the military victories of the British to the dynastic portraits. But in 1863, when a picture gallery was created out of a new passageway to ease congestion during levees, it was again hung with more dynastic pictures. If the paintings at St James's were now principally reflective of family history and national glory, the libraries continued to represent more vibrant intellectual thought. St James's remained a bookish place throughout the eighteenth century, and Queen Caroline's (1683–1737) library (Fig. 0.4), the only significant architectural addition to the palace of the century, marked the culmination of this tradition.

0.4
George II in the anteroom to Queen Caroline's library at St James's, c.1738. The empty chair of state may refer to the Queen's death in 1737 (English Heritage, Marble Hill, J920095)

The problem suffered by St James's after 1698 was that it was never designed to be an impressive architectural symbol of either the monarchy or the nation. It was built to safeguard the monarch's children, and as such had never had a principal public façade. There was thus a gulf between any public understanding of a 'palace' and the reality of a modest building that had been converted to undertake a magnificent task. When Baron Bielfeld (1717–70) visited George II's court at St James's in 1741, he thought it 'a lodging hous [sic]; crazy, smoky and dirty'.[5] In 1823, the *Morning Post* stated bluntly that 'The outside will never look like a royal palace until the brick walls shall have been covered with a stone facing ornamented with pillars and porticoes'. The following year, an MP said in the House of Commons that 'St James's palace looked more like an almshouse than a kingly residence, and was a disgrace to the country'.[6]

Although voices were raised against the palace by Britons who had travelled abroad and thought St James's a pale reflection of the might of the British Crown, there were others who saw it as an appropriate expression of the monarch's constitutional role. When the poet and diplomat Matthew Prior was shown around Versailles by one of Louis XIV's household officials, he was asked whether William III's (r. 1689–1702) achievements were celebrated in English royal houses. Prior piously proclaimed that 'the monuments of my master's actions are to be seen everywhere but in his own house'.[7] In response to criticisms of St James's by Baron Bielfeld, the translator of his letters, William Hooper, sprang to the defence of St James's in 1770. He thought that 'the glory of the monarch consists, not in a handful of tinsel courtiers, or in expensive and pompous festivals; but in the … ease and affluence … the freedom, the dignity and the happiness of his people'. Those people were reflected, he thought, in the Royal Crown, which was given lustre far superior to the 'blaze of the court of an absolute monarch'.[8] For him and many of his contemporaries, absolutism was expressed in brick, stone and oil paint. Prior thought Versailles 'the foolishest in the world', where Louis XIV was shown 'galloping in every ceiling'.[9] St James's could thus be seen as the ideal expression of a limited monarchy, as constituted after 1689 in the Bill of Rights.

The Georgian monarchy, ensconced, for ceremonial purposes, at St James's, displayed an architectural carapace that was, in fact, deliberately understated. George I (r. 1714–27), who disliked ceremonial and courtly formality, rejected Sir John Vanbrugh's (1664–1726) plans for replacing St James's, extending Kensington Palace and completing Hampton Court. Even when offered the means of financing a rebuilding of Whitehall by the creative financial genius of Sir Robert Walpole (1676–1745), he did not take up the offer.[10] Instead, he supported extremely modest alterations and adaptations at Kensington and Hampton Court.

In typical Hanoverian fashion, George I's disdain for ceremony encouraged his son's passion for it. Lord Hervey famously observed, 'all the pageantry and splendour, of badges and trappings of royalty, were as pleasing to the son as they were irksome to the father'.[11] This did, at first, make a material difference to the appearance of the court. Daniel Defoe, in his *Tour thro' … Great Britain*, published in the mid-1720s, drew a contrast between the splendour of the court and its official seat:

ST JAMES'S PALACE

The Palace of *St James's*, tho' the Winter Receptacle of all the Pomp and Glory of this Kingdom, is really mean, in Comparison of the glorious Court of *Great Britain*. The Splendor of the Nobility, the Wealth and Greatness of the Attendants, the Oeconomy of the House, and the real Grandeur of the whole Royal Family, outdo all the Courts of *Europe*; and yet this Palace comes beneath those of the most petty Princes in it.[12]

George II's (r. 1727–60) burst of courtly glory came to a crushing end with the death of Queen Caroline in 1737. After this, the devastated King withdrew from public ceremonial as much as he could, and ceased to take the court to Hampton Court. Neither he nor his father had much used Windsor, and as a result, the British monarchy shuttled between St James's, Kensington and a variety of summer residences in Kew and Richmond. The importance of St James's, as the only royal house of any size in regular use, was thus further enhanced.[13]

The sovereign's appropriation of St James's as the principal seat of the monarchy deprived the heir to the throne of their traditional seat. With no separate official residence for the Prince of Wales, monarch and heir began to share the same residence after 1714. Even if it had not been for the rivalries, jealousies and disagreements between the Georgian monarchs and their sons, this would have been a bad arrangement. St James's did not have three full suites of state rooms, and accommodation for the Prince of Wales was inadequate. After a furious row in 1717, George I expelled the Prince of Wales from St James's, and he and the Princess took a lease on Leicester House, the Jacobean mansion on the north side of Leicester Square. Here they lived for a decade, boosting accommodation by linking Leicester House with neighbouring Savile House by means of a covered corridor.

In 1727, when George, Prince of Wales, became King, father and eldest son lived together at St James's once more. George II firmly believed that the King's palace was 'the only proper place … for the heir apparent to the crown'.[14] But all the practical inadequacies of this arrangement soon became evident again, and in 1737, in an almost exact repetition of the events of 1717, George expelled Frederick, Prince of Wales (1707–51), from St James's. In the summer of 1743, Leicester House again became the residence of the Prince of Wales and his family. In 1756, in a lull in hostilities between father and son, the Prince was offered Kensington Palace as a home, but the offer was turned down.[15]

Soon after his accession, George III (r. 1760–1820) acquired the freehold of Buckingham House (later Buckingham Palace), a large, aristocratic mansion built on the western edge of St James's Park, a stone's throw from the palace. The purpose was to provide a suitable residence for the Queen, as Somerset House, the Queen's official historic London residence, was now not only very old, but also in a quarter of London that was unfashionable and down at heel. It had been used only sporadically by Caroline of Ansbach (consort of George II), and in 1760, it was deemed impossibly old and uncomfortable by George III's consort, Charlotte of Mecklenburg-Strelitz (1744–1818).[16]

Buckingham House (Fig. 0.5), which had been built in 1702–5, had brilliantly appropriated the royal landscape of St James's Park, being sited on an axis with the avenues and canal. St James's Palace was side-on to these, and after the destruction of Whitehall, it seemed to the uninformed observer that the park was aligned on Buckingham House. Its prime location and relative modernity compared to venerable St James's made it an obvious acquisition for the Crown, especially as part of it was built on Crown land. After its purchase by the King in 1762, improvements were made to make it fit for royal occupation, and in 1775, George, by Act of Parliament, settled the house on the Queen for life, relinquishing Somerset House for government use. Buckingham House now became known as the Queen's House.[17]

For centuries, sovereigns had used the lodgings of their consorts as a way of avoiding the restrictive etiquette of the King's apartments, and George III was only following a long tradition as he increasingly used the Queen's House as his own residence. Kensington Palace, which had previously been

0.5

*Buckingham House, c.*1710. The house was bought by George III for use by Queen Charlotte, but it soon became the royal family's favourite London seat (BM, 1880,1113.2384)

the more domestic pendant to St James's, was now completely abandoned, and the King and Queen split their time, when in London, between familial informality at their private residence, Buckingham House, and official and state grandeur at St James's.[18]

It was also George III who solved the issue of a residence for the Prince of Wales by granting, in 1783, Carlton House to Prince George as his official London seat (Fig. 0.6). Carlton House had been built in the royal gardens in St James's Park after the Restoration, and had been purchased by the King's father, Frederick, Prince of Wales, in 1732. On being granted an independent establishment, Prince George immediately set about improving and extending the property, which became his home for some 40 years.[19] Soon after, the King also made arrangements for the accommodation of his next two sons. In 1825, Frederick, Duke of York (1763–1827), was granted Godolphin House, lying immediately to the west of St James's; and, encouraged by his spendthrift brother, he began to replace it with a magnificent stone mansion now known as Lancaster House.[20] George's third son, the Duke of Clarence (later William IV, r. 1830–37), was also granted apartments on the west side of St James's, amongst various seventeenth-century buildings that had grown up near the kitchens.

George III redrew the royal topography of Westminster, establishing a new modus vivendi for the royal family. St James's, Buckingham House and Carlton House worked as a trio that differed little in function and spatial relationship from the separate elements of the medieval palace of Westminster. Yet there was an important difference, because after 1700, St James's may have become a palace, but it was one that contained a separate entity – the Court of St James's. This was a new way of describing the royal court and one that separated it from the person of the monarch. After 1688, there were potentially multiple courts: the court of St Germain near Paris, where the deposed James II received ambassadors as sovereign of England and Scotland, with all the trappings but none of the powers of a monarch; and

0.6

The South Front, Carlton House, c.1819. St James's being occupied by the monarch, the house was granted to George IV, when Prince of Wales in 1783, as his official London residence (RCIN 922169)

William III's two courts: the English court, and his court at The Hague. After 1714, when the Elector of Hanover became George I, there were courts in Britain and in Hanover, a situation that lasted until 1837.[21] It thus became necessary to specify geographically to which court reference was being made. The Court of St James's, to which ambassadors are still accredited, therefore became something that had an independent existence from the person of the sovereign and an official seat at St James's Palace.

After a long wait to accede to the throne, George IV finally became King in 1820 at a time of great national triumph. In the aftermath of the Napoleonic Wars, with Britain mastering the oceans and transforming the world economy with its industrial might, there was a sense that the monarch and his palaces should reflect the power and prestige of the state. Indeed, in Parliament, the Chancellor of the Exchequer, granting the King what was eventually to be a million pounds to rebuild Windsor, observed that the investment was necessary to create 'a degree of splendour that was becoming the sovereign who ruled over the country, and also the country over which he ruled'.[22] It was this shift in parliamentary attitude towards royal residences being reflective of the state of the nation that led to public funding for the rebuilding of Buckingham Palace and Windsor Castle.

In early 1826, George IV decided to abandon Carlton House, strip it of its fittings and embark on the expansion of Buckingham House. At the end of that year, with everything ready for his reception, he moved into St James's. The King's plans for Buckingham House were not for a palace of state, but for what he termed a pied-à-terre, with no suite for a Queen or offices for Household departments. For a private residence it was an extremely large undertaking, and when the King died in 1830, he was still using St James's as his London residence. The cost of extending Buckingham House had spiralled upwards, and on George IV's death, John Nash (1752–1835), its architect, was under investigation for

INTRODUCTION

0.7

Queen Victoria's Levee for Volunteer Officers, St James's Palace, 7 March 1860, c.1860. Queen Victoria's final levee was in 1861. After the death of Prince Albert, levees at St James's Palace were held by the Prince and Princess of Wales (RCIN 916813)

incompetence and mismanagement.[23] The Treasury wondered whether the building was intended for a private or a state residence, but in 1832 William IV insisted that St James's should continue to be 'the royal residence of the King of England'.[24]

The fact was that William liked his comfortable apartments at St James's and was reluctant to move into the vast palace started by his brother. When the Houses of Parliament burnt down in 1834, he even suggested that it should become a new home for Parliament. Parliamentarians, however, had their own plans for the state functions of the Crown. In 1822–4, at the request of George IV, Sir John Soane (1753–1837) had designed a series of improvements to the royal entrance, gallery and anterooms to the House of Lords, to enhance the magnificence of the State Opening of Parliament. When the old Houses of Parliament burnt down, the debate about the architectural presence of the monarchy in Parliament intensified. Although the Houses of Parliament were built into and around the remains of the old medieval palace of Westminster, they were not commonly referred to as a 'palace'. In 1836, it was announced that the Houses of Parliament would henceforth be known as 'Westminster New Palace', and were to contain a suite of royal rooms of extreme magnificence – in fact, no less than an entirely new royal palace. Westminster thus became the theatre of state and the principal setting for much royal ceremonial.[25] This inevitably led to questions as to why St James's, which *The Times* called 'That Dingy Mausoleum of Departed Grandeur', was necessary at all.[26]

From the early 1660s, St James's Palace became the kernel around which the West End of London was to grow. It attracted courtiers, ambassadors and members of Charles II's family. After it became the principal royal seat in 1698, the status of the area rose still further, and it became a political and social quarter as well as a residential one. In fact, although Queen Victoria shifted her principal residence to Buckingham Palace in 1837, society still regarded St James's as its centre. Court drawing rooms and levees continued to be held at St James's (Fig. 0.7), the Queen leaving Buckingham Palace and travelling the short distance to preside at the Court of St James's. Victoria's insistence on using St James's for formal events had deep roots, because she, like her predecessors, regarded Buckingham Palace as a private residence. Even today, Buckingham

Palace retains an air of being a country house set privately in parks and gardens, while St James's is structurally and socially part of the West End.

With the accession of Queen Victoria, St James's became home to successive members of the royal family, but did not resume its role as home to the sovereign's heir, the Prince of Wales. At the age of nine Prince Albert Edward (later King Edward VII, r. 1901–10) was assigned Marlborough House in 1850; he eventually took possession of it in 1860.[27] St James's did not reassume its original purpose as the home of the heir to the throne until 1919, when the then Prince of Wales (later King Edward VIII) moved into York House. He never liked it much and eventually used it as more of an office than a home. After an interlude during the Second World War, in 1947 the heir to the throne was once more quartered at St James's when, at King George VI's suggestion, Princess Elizabeth moved into Clarence House. Between 1953 and 2002, St James's became the dower house of Queen Elizabeth The Queen Mother (1900–2002), before HRH The Prince of Wales took up residence.

In the history of European royal residences, few have a story as unlikely as that of St James's. In the sixteenth and seventeenth centuries, it was an unexceptional royal manor, though unusual in European terms, as few other monarchies provided independent residences for the heir. For some 70 years, its interest and notoriety came from the associated but independent Roman Catholic chapel and monastery belonging to a parade of foreign Catholic consorts. But in 1698, it became, by default, the official seat of the British Crown.

In the eighteenth century, the contrast between St James's and its European equivalents is much starker and more interesting, and provides a commentary on the British monarchy's long, slow passage from sovereign rule to sovereign reign. From as early as 1702, a combination of constitutional shifts and the destruction of Whitehall meant that St James's epitomised the question of whether the sovereign embodied the nation in all their deeds (*L'état, c'est moi*) or only the ceremonial part of it. In the former state, the sovereign's residence would be expected to be of great magnificence; in the latter, only suitable to the needs of the royal family. From the accession of Anne in 1702 until the accession of Victoria in 1837, St James's was the representation in brick and stone of the political and constitutional debate over the role and powers of the monarchy. Some felt it a national disgrace, and others the appropriate home for a constitutional monarch.

This dilemma was only partially solved in the reign of Queen Victoria. The Queen, who inherited the magnificent palaces built by her uncle, was certainly housed in buildings suitable to the status of an empress, though she had little inclination to exploit them for the theatre of state. The Prince Consort saw the monarchy as an instrumental device rather than a theatrical institution, and even setting aside the 20 years of royal seclusion after Albert's death in 1861, Queen Victoria had little taste for the ceremonial aspects of her role. Victoria's vision of monarchy was closer to the domesticity of George III than to the chutzpah of George IV.[28]

It was left to King Edward VII to exploit fully the architectural stage left to him by his great-uncle. He came to the throne determined to be publicly magnificent: the redesign of The Mall, the construction of Admiralty Arch and the Victoria Memorial, and the refronting of Buckingham Palace created a big stage for state ceremonial, centred on the corpulent person of the monarch himself. Edward repackaged and polished the monarchy for the twentieth century. In this, the politicians were complicit, for upholding the dignity and magnificence of the monarchy bolstered the authority and legitimacy of the state. Without respect for the institutions of state, there would be no respect for the rule of law. All political parties recognised the legitimising power of the Crown, and also, increasingly, its importance as a symbol of international power. The stage was set in the Gothic halls of the Palace of Westminster, the castellated ramparts of Windsor and the imperial topography of Buckingham Palace, rather than in the mellow Tudor brickwork of St James's.[29]

INTRODUCTION 11

1. From the Hospital of St James to the Civil War

SIMON THURLEY

The Hospital of St James, Westminster

Leprosy and the plague were the twin terrors of the early Middle Ages. No less than a death sentence, leprosy was often seen as a punishment from God, although from an early point it was known that it could be caught by human contact.

The medieval eye made little or no distinction between leprosy (technically speaking, Hansen's disease) and other disfiguring diseases of the flesh, and sufferers were immediately proclaimed outcasts, driven from towns and villages and excluded from any sort of normal existence. This systematic victimisation was eased by a Church ruling in 1179 that authorised lepers to form communities with a church and priest, as long as they remained completely isolated. This softening of attitude was prefigured by Henry I's (r. 1100–35) queen, Matilda (1079–1118), who was sympathetic to sufferers and founded a hospital for lepers at St Giles's Fields, north of Westminster, in around 1118.[1]

Unusually for such a prominent foundation, it is not known for certain when the twin Hospital of St James, Westminster, was founded. However, charters of Henry II (r. 1154–89) and John (r. 1199–1216) might suggest that St James's was also a foundation either by, or in honour of, Queen Matilda.[2] Certainly, when the right to appoint the master was contested in 1339–40, a jury found in favour of the King, and Richard II (r. 1377–99) subsequently referred to the house as 'the foundation of our progenitors'.[3]

While St Giles's hospital was founded to care for leprous men, the Hospital of St James was established for a maximum of 16 leprous women, one of whom would be prioress. There were also up to eight brothers, living under the rule of St Augustine, several of whom were priests. They were needed to say Masses for the hospital's wealthy benefactors, who would attend the church on feast days and holydays. The brothers elected one of their number to be master of the house, and in the thirteenth century, he was inducted into his position by the abbot of Westminster.

The site for the new hospital was chosen with great care. It was built on the lower of two flat gravel terraces that line the lower Thames valley. Modern Piccadilly runs along the upper terrace and Pall Mall along the lower one. Between the two is steeply falling ground, still very apparent on St James's Street. The hospital was sited on the lower terrace, where one of the branches of the Tyburn stream flowed over it into what is now St James's Park. Evidence for the Tyburn tributary has been found under Colour Court, and the hospital's location must have been influenced by the presence of fast-flowing clean water – essential for the treatment

1.1

Tudor fireplace in the Tapestry Room. One of the quatrefoils above the fireplace contains the initials 'HA', thought to stand for Henry VIII and Anne Boleyn, and a true lover's knot, suggesting that it was carved before the Queen's execution in 1536. Others feature a Tudor rose, a fleur-de-lis, a portcullis and a crowned 'H'. The spandrels are filled with foliage and beasts' heads

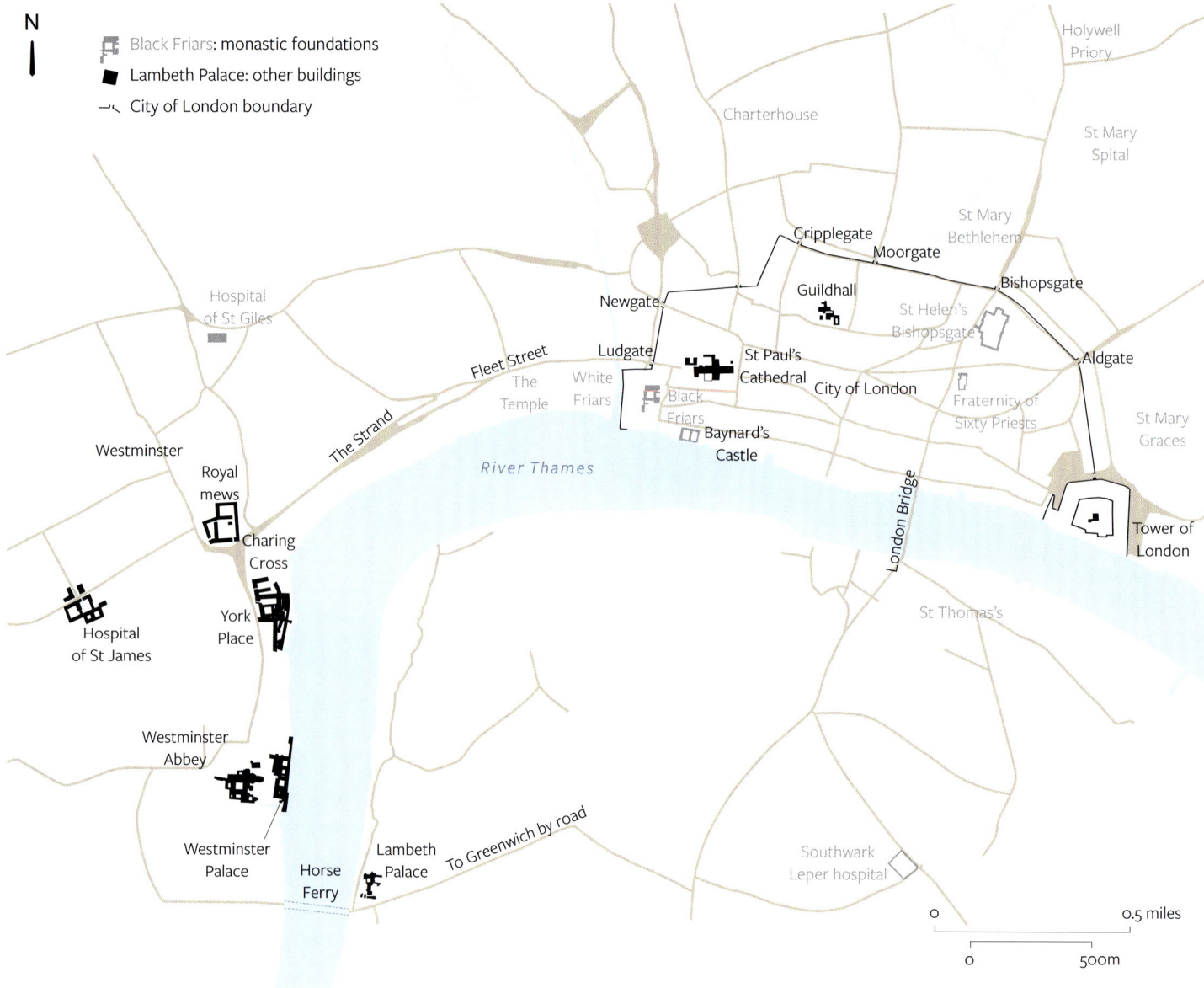

1.2

Map of medieval Westminster, the City of London and surrounding area, showing the relation of the Hospital of St James to the principal buildings and settlements

of skin conditions.[4] Other tributaries of the Tyburn flowed over land that was eventually to be owned by the hospital, and the hospital's mill was built on one of these.

The surrounding area was almost completely undeveloped. Roads ran along the flat of both terraces as they do today, but the site of the new hospital was a good ten minutes' walk from Charing Cross to the east, and perhaps 15 minutes' walk across uneven ground to Westminster in the south. Isolation was crucial to the purpose of the hospital, as it was to all ten leper hospitals that eventually were to ring London and Westminster.

Topography was important (Fig. 1.2), but so was jurisdiction. Although it is likely that the hospital was, in fact, a royal foundation, it lay within the overlapping ecclesiastical and royal jurisdictions of Westminster Abbey and Westminster Palace. While Queen Matilda had been careful to exclude the Hospital of St Giles from the authority of the abbot of Westminster, no such provisions seem to have been enacted at St James's, and this led to competing authorities involving themselves in hospital affairs, a confusing situation exploited by the brethren. Its early history bears this out, as the master and the brothers and sisters of

St James's were censured several times for their laxity, immorality and neglect of their assets. The dereliction of their original purposes reached a peak in the 1320s, with their lands uncultivated, their rents dilapidated and the roof of their church caved in.

In 1331, there was a new master, John de Sydenham, and for the next five years he instituted a programme of reform and consolidation, neatly set out in surviving financial accounts now amongst Westminster Abbey's muniments. There is little evidence as to the extent or disposition of the hospital buildings before the 1330s, but the restoration of the house under de Sydenham provides, for the first time, an idea of what the hospital comprised.

The hospital was a remote institution set in a rural landscape and was thus walled and entered by a gate; in 1332–3, a new wall was built between this and the brothers' dormitory. In the same year, a new hall was begun for the brothers; built of stone, with chalk foundations, it was roofed with tiles, painted within and contained a pulpit from which Psalms could be read at mealtimes. Next to the hall was a chamber furnished with a heavy lock and lead-lined shutters. A covered walkway led from the hall to a new kitchen, also of stone, with a tiled roof and containing a fireplace and oven. Water was supplied to this, and to a washing place in the hall, by brass pipes. Next to the kitchen were two 'solars', or private rooms. The following year, the brothers were built a new bakehouse.

In 1333–4, it was the turn of the sisters to have a new hall, also of stone; it was entered by a porch, had three windows, and iron crosses stood on its gable ends. The adjoining kitchen was furnished with a new oven, fireplace and lead vat. New gutters were made for the infirmary building, which stood beside the sisters' hall. These buildings, together with a mill, dovecote, barns, a walled vineyard and other structures, give the impression of a comfortable residence: the brothers' dormitory was divided into individual rooms with beds, and the great hall was fitted with a lavabo, fireplace and chimney.[5]

The energetic regime of John de Sydenham did not herald greater discipline at St James's, and as a result of continuing turmoil, the Crown and Westminster Abbey went to court in 1339–40, over the right to approve the position of master. The Crown claimed the hospital as a royal foundation, while the abbot stressed his absolute ecclesiastical jurisdiction in Westminster. Appointment of the master mattered because the post, and offices attached, were valuable patronage for whoever had the right to dispense it. Though the outcome of the case was ambiguous and disputed, from 1340 it was accepted that the hospital was, in fact, a royal foundation.[6]

From the 1340s, the mastership of the Hospital of St James thus became a royal sinecure. Masters appointed by successive monarchs treated the hospital as a comfortable residence close to the royal court at Westminster. One such was Thomas Orgrave, who had been made treasurer clerk in the Receipt in 1369 and was promoted to Chamberlain of the Exchequer, right-hand man to the royal treasurer, in 1385.[7] In the inner circle of Richard II's court, Orgrave built, or at least strengthened and embellished, a stone tower at St James's, without the necessary licence from the Crown. This was issued, in retrospect, in 1379.[8]

The house was subsequently held by Richard Clifford, sometime Bishop of London, who was also in Richard II's inner circle, first as his personal chaplain, and then as Keeper of the Great Wardrobe.[9] In October 1399, Henry IV (r. 1399–1413) ratified not only his post at St James's, but also his tenure of the Deanship of York, the Archdeaconry of Canterbury and four prebends. The next master was Louis Recouchez, Henry IV's French physician, who was rewarded not only with the wardenship of the hospital, but with the lucrative keepership of the Tower Mint.[10] Under Henry V (r. 1413–22), the master was William Kynwolmersh, who had been in France with the King as cofferer of the Household before being promoted to Treasurer of England, acting, in the King's last years, as one of his closest advisers.[11] After Kynwolmersh's death, William Alnwick became master for life. He had risen to prominence as Henry V's confessor and secretary, and in the following reign, he became Keeper of the Privy Seal and first Bishop of Norwich and then of Lincoln, garnering, along the way, a long list of benefices. As bishop, he was a great builder, although there is no record of him embellishing the Hospital of St James.[12]

The hospital was thus a rich man's plaything, a perk won through a close personal relationship with the sovereign. How many of these great men actually resided at the hospital, or for how long, is not known. Orgrave, for instance, was happy to rent it out (apart from a recently built cellar containing his personal wine).[13]

In 1449, possibly on the suggestion of William Alnwick, the Hospital of St James was granted by Henry VI (r. 1422–61, 1470–71) to Eton College, as part of its vast landed endowment. Thomas Kemp, who had been appointed master in 1443, had become Bishop of London in 1448 and resigned his post at the hospital in favour of the college. In order not to lose the perk, Kemp rented back the 'principal hospice with the tower' from the college for £6 13s 4d a year. Kemp had no personal use for this and allowed Henry Beaufort, Bishop of Winchester, to use the house instead.[14]

Eton College was, for nearly a century, an appreciative owner of the estate. Most of its assets were rented out, bringing in a handsome income of some £100 a year while the hospital was retained in hand. In the mid-fifteenth century, there were four alms-sisters living there, maintained at the college's expense. They welcomed pilgrims, heard Mass said by their two chaplains, and took their pews on holy days in the church. The college supplied the church with books, candles, vestments and refreshments for St James's Day and at Rogationtide. The provost, meanwhile, retained rooms in the house and used it as a convenient headquarters in Westminster. The best rooms, including the tower, were still let out to a succession of courtiers.[15]

The female inhabitants who rubbed shoulders with the fashionable tenants of the master's house were not suffering from leprosy, nor, indeed, were they needy or abandoned. The almswomen were well-off widows, with comfortable lodgings in a fashionable institution. One of their number, Dame Catherine Vampage, the widow of a wealthy Westminster merchant, left substantial possessions in her will and asked to be buried in the chancel of St Margaret's, Westminster.[16]

Although the medieval hospital contained architectural components that are very familiar in conventual terms, with the current state of knowledge it is impossible to work out their plan. This is largely because, unlike other types of monastery, leper hospitals had no prescribed plan or standardised design.[17] Yet records kept by both Westminster Abbey and Eton College, together with a little archaeology, do give some indication of the size and layout of the hospital in the late fifteenth century. The first useful document in this respect dates from the grant of the hospital by Thomas Orgrave to Lady Despenser in 1386. The patent that confirmed this transaction describes its extent at this point:

> all the houses and buildings in the said hospital within the gate of the long entrance before the door of the principal hall of the hospital, as well the said hall and the upper and lower chambers at each end of the same hall, and the stone tower with its appurtenances, as well as the chamber over the said entrance, the kitchen and bakery …, and all other houses and buildings with appurtenances which are assigned within the gate, as the master's house, with all the gardens, open spaces and vineyards within the said gate[18]

It is likely that these are the buildings of the 1330s erected by John de Sydenham, plus Orgrave's tower. The fifteenth-century Eton College accounts describe the main house, or 'great place', as having a tower, hall, chamber and parlour, and being surrounded by a great garden and a great orchard. It is probable that this, the most prestigious part of the complex, formed an inner court on the southern part of the site, because the accounts describe a gatehouse on what is now Pall Mall and an outer court to its south. To the west of the outer court was the sisters' house, and to its east, the church and churchyard, with an inner and an outer cemetery.[19]

The church was clearly a building of some substance. Churches at the larger leper hospitals were like substantial parish churches, and this must have been what stood at St James's, given the prestige and location of the foundation. References exist to its chancel, its pillars, bells and possibly a tower. It is likely that it was the remains of this church that were found by workmen excavating in Colour Court in 1925. The long buttressed north wall of a building with a tiled floor was discovered in a trench. The encaustic tiles are of the Westminster type and can be dated to the late thirteenth century (Fig. 1.3). Beneath the floor of the building and outside its walls were five burials.[20]

The outer court also contained what were described as the 'houses of husbandry', a barn and a granary, joined by a 'longhouse', plus a dovecote, and somewhere nearby, a mill. There was also a kitchen garden and a herb garden.

In 1529, this elegant, fashionable and peaceful enclave on the periphery of Westminster was to catch the eye of Henry VIII, as he began to contemplate his first, and ultimately largest, building project.

Henry VIII and the Rebuilding of St James's

Henry VIII, like his predecessors, regarded Westminster Palace, the ancient seat of the English monarchy, as his prime residence. It adjoined the administrative offices of the Crown, abutted the law courts and was integrated with Westminster Abbey, the royal coronation church and mausoleum. It had grown over the centuries into a dense, complex mass of building, where vast public audience halls led to a warren of more intimate spaces. The palace contained a private area for the King and Queen known as the Privy Palace, and another for the Prince of Wales, known as the Prince's Palace.

In 1512, there was a serious fire in the Privy Palace, leaving Westminster unusable by the royal family. Henry showed no interest in rebuilding the venerable edifice of his ancestors, relocating his headquarters to the royal manor of Greenwich, and staying south of the river at Lambeth Palace when he needed to be close to Westminster. In 1521, he began a new residence just outside the walls of the City of London at Bridewell, and Parliament was summoned to Black Friars, the Dominican friary next door, instead of meeting at Westminster.

This might have remained the arrangement had it not been for the fact that Henry fell in love with Anne Boleyn (1501/7–36) and decided to divorce his wife, Katherine of Aragon (1485–1536). The repercussions of this event were, of course, far greater than anyone at the time could have imagined, but one of the first casualties was the King's chief minister, Cardinal Wolsey (1473–1530), who took the blame for failing to secure the King's divorce.

Wolsey was the last of the great pluralists to hold a large number of high Church offices, the most powerful of which was that of Archbishop of York. With the archbishopric came York Place, the archdiocese's London residence, sited midway on King Street between Westminster Palace and Charing Cross. Wolsey moved into York Place in 1515 and proceeded to extend and modernise it, in a series of building campaigns that were still unfinished at the time he fell from power in 1529. Nevertheless, it was a large,

1.3
Westminster tiles dating from c.1260–80, excavated in Colour Court in 1925. Such tiles were used in secular as well as ecclesiastical buildings, but their proximity to burials is suggestive of these being the floor of a chapel

modern and comfortable house within a short distance of Westminster. In the autumn of 1529, the King and his mistress decided to turn York Place into their new home, and only two days after Wolsey's disgrace, they came down river from Greenwich to inspect it. Delighted with what they found, Henry and Anne spent November and December 1529 with the King's architect, James Nedeham, devising a scheme for a hugely ambitious new royal residence.

Henry VIII had not shown much interest in architecture up to this point. He had championed a great gatehouse at Windsor Castle, and stables, an armour factory and a tiltyard at Greenwich, but had not given serious consideration to domestic architecture. Now, with the prospect of a new wife, and, he hoped, a son and heir, he became obsessively engaged in the new project. Plans were drawn and brought to the King wherever he might be staying, for comment and approval, and he made dozens of short visits to Westminster to inspect the site.

The location was problematic. Unlike Greenwich, which was set within a royal park with plenty of scope for expansion and embellishment, York Place was in the middle of a densely inhabited town and the King owned none of the land. Most of it was the freehold of Westminster Abbey, but there were other freeholders and many leaseholders with long leases and valuable real estate. Beyond the built-up areas, Westminster was still very rural. Although in 1513 there were some 608 residences in the town and a population of perhaps 2,500, its boundaries were very tightly drawn, with dense development round the abbey and along the streets running north and west, but farmland immediately beyond. It was in this farmland that the Hospital of St James lay.

The King's plan was to purchase not only the urban properties close to York Place, but to acquire all the land west of it, including the Hospital of St James and beyond. The conception was not for an urban palace like Westminster, but for a country estate set in a large landholding, including parkland for hunting. Cardinal Wolsey's former land agent, Thomas Cromwell (c.1485–1540), was recruited by the King to manage the complex legal work required to achieve this. He began in February 1530 by securing York Place and the freehold of all the properties along King Street, plus 100 acres (40.5 hectares) of land from Westminster Abbey. Next, Eton College made over the Hospital of St James and all its land, and then Abingdon Abbey, the Hospital of Burton Lazars (Leics) and the Mercers' Company transferred their Westminster estates to the King. Other land transfers followed, including Covent Garden, the manors of Neate and Ebury to the west of Westminster Abbey, and the vast manor and park of Hyde. By 1536, the King had acquired almost all the land that today covers the area from Ebury Bridge in the west to Oxford Street in the north and St Martin's Lane in the east, some 1,200 acres (485.6 hectares) in all.

By 1531, the King had begun not one, but two residences within the new estate: the principal mansion house at York Place – soon to be known as Whitehall – and a subsidiary residence at St James's. Neither was complete in 1536, but nevertheless, that year the King passed an Act of Parliament that transferred to Whitehall all the legal privileges that Westminster Palace had enjoyed time out of mind, thus formally creating Whitehall as the principal palace of the realm. In 1544, Henry added to his already enormous Westminster estate substantial lands to the north, including Marylebone (now Regent's) Park. A second Act of Parliament that year erected an honour within the City of Westminster. This ancient legal mechanism recognised the sovereign as lord over all the manors in the estate and identified Whitehall Palace as its centre.[21]

The dissolution of the monasteries allowed one final act. The suppression of Westminster Abbey in 1540 abolished the power of the abbot over Westminster and enabled Henry to create the new post of High Steward, which, in future, was to dispense patronage and represent the City to the Crown. The stewardship was presented to Sir Anthony Denny, the keeper of Whitehall Palace. The King then declared that Westminster was a city with the power to nominate two MPs, and legislated to transform the abbey into a cathedral. The new Bishop of Westminster was to be Thomas Thirlby, his own Dean of the Chapel Royal. Thus, in the short period of 15 years, the face of Westminster was transformed; the Crown not only owned a huge residential and recreational estate, but also the governance of the manor, the City and the cathedral was completely in royal hands.[22]

Henry's pursuit of his new project was single-minded, particularly as, by the end of 1532, he knew that Anne was pregnant. Convinced that she was bearing a son, an integral and urgent part of their project was providing accommodation for a Prince of Wales. Since the thirteenth century, Westminster Palace had housed the Prince's Palace, where the heir to the throne lived, but Henry and Anne had a slightly different concept for Whitehall: they envisaged a separate residence, which they had identified as St James's.[23]

In this way, the Hospital of St James became part of the King's vision for Westminster. The comfortable residence with a fashionable church attached was no longer a serious charitable or religious enterprise, and few could have regretted its absorption into the King's new estate.

Royal children were always established in separate residences, remote from the hazards of dense population, where contagion quickly spread. Henry himself had been largely brought up at Eltham, a few miles from Greenwich, where Henry VII had rebuilt the royal manor. St James's was in the same relationship to Whitehall, remote and secure, but close to the King and Queen.

That St James's was built for Henry's children was a fact well understood at the time. In 1553, the Spanish Ambassador described the house as 'built by the late King Henry VIII as a residence for the Royal Children', and in 1584, a German visitor to England was told that it was where 'in former times young English Kings were brought up'; many later references confirm this intention.[24]

Though the hospital buildings were in good order, Henry decided to rebuild them completely. There is no evidence that any of the former hospital was incorporated into the new royal residence, other than as rubble foundations and wall core.[25] Yet it is likely that, as at Whitehall, existing buildings were utilised by the workforce and potentially remained standing into the late 1530s. The architect for the new building was almost certainly James Nedeham, who was appointed Surveyor of the King's Works in October 1532. From his office at Scotland Yard to the north of Whitehall, Nedeham was able to direct operations both there and at St James's. Day-to-day control of the works was delegated to Thomas Heritage, another of Wolsey's former agents and a close associate of Thomas Cromwell.

Despite St James's today retaining substantial amounts of Tudor fabric, not enough remains to determine the original plan of the house without the use of documentary evidence. The key to understanding what Henry VIII completed is the earliest surviving accurate plan, dating from *c.*1703–14, drawn by William Dickinson (d. 1724), a surveyor in Sir Christopher Wren's office (Fig. 1.4).[26] By a process of elimination, using the unbroken sequence of repair accounts that start early in Elizabeth I's reign (r. 1558–1603), it is possible to determine the parts of this plan that pre-date 1603. As nothing of significance was built by either Edward VI or Mary, this can be taken to be the house as built by Henry VIII.

The house that stood in 1547 was built around four courtyards: an outer court entered by the existing great gate from the north; the Kitchen Court to the west; and on the south, two inner courts around which the royal lodgings were ranged (see Plan A). While the plan of the inner quadrangle is largely what would be expected of a royal residence of the 1530s, the eastern and outer quads show some anomalies which suggest that at some stage there was a break in building or a change of plan.

The first thing that is striking is that the gatehouse is positioned off-centre in the north façade, something quite unexpected in Tudor entrance fronts, which are normally symmetrical; the western arm of the entrance façade also oddly lies at an angle to the gatehouse rather than being in alignment with

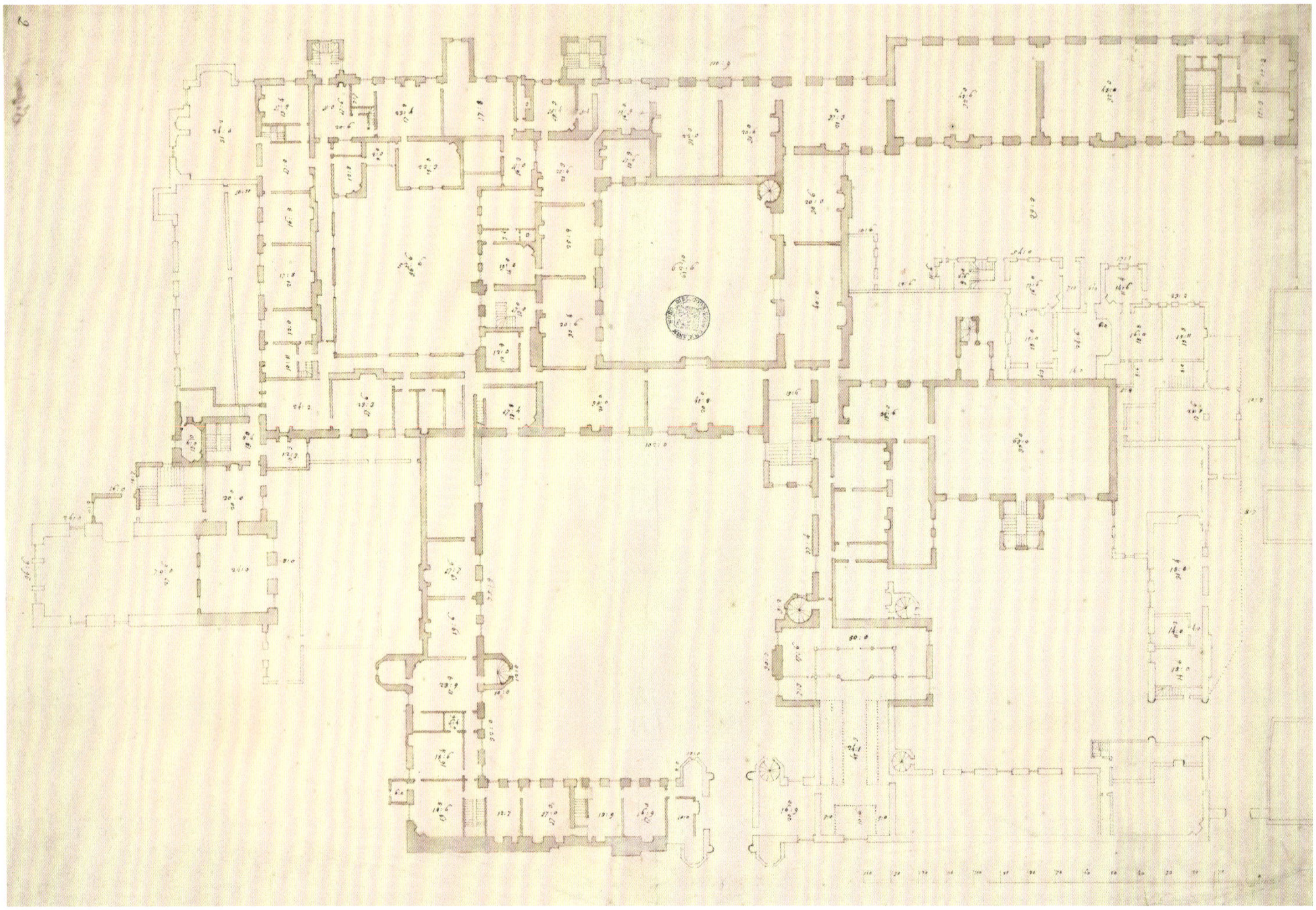

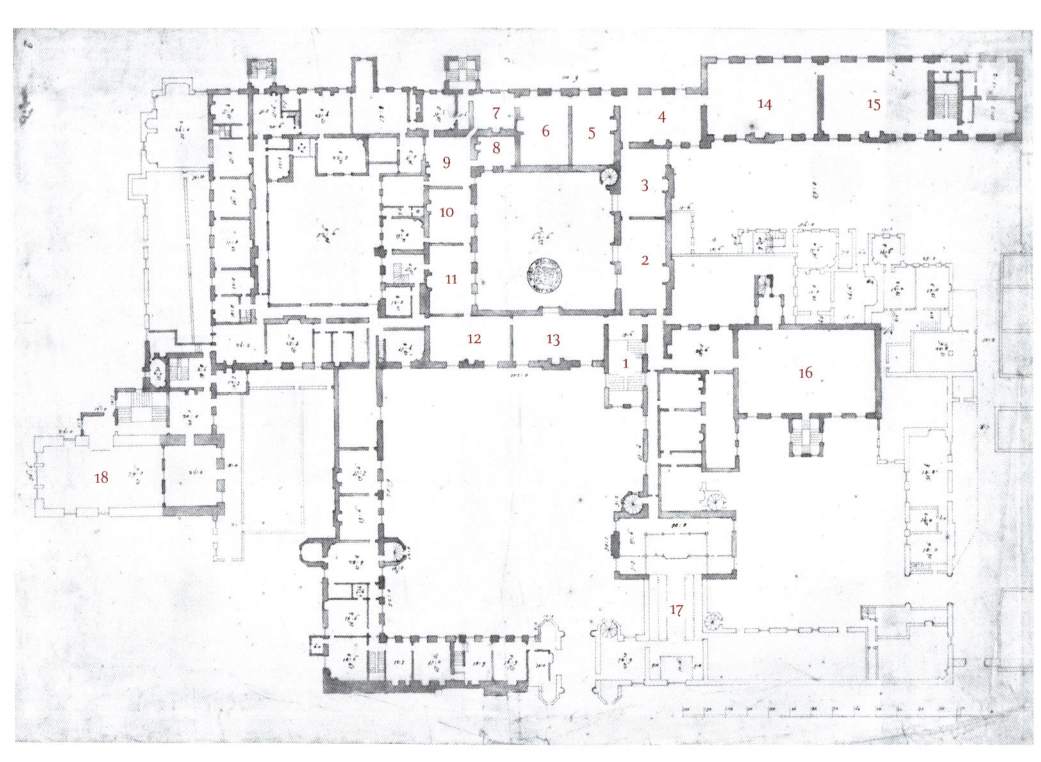

1.4
Plan of the first floor of
St James's by William Dickinson,
c.1703–14 (AS, I:2)

1. Great stairs
2. Guard chamber
3. Presence chamber
4. Privy chamber
5. Great bedchamber
6. Little bedchamber
7. Dressing room
8. Closet
9. Bedchamber
10. Privy chamber
11. Drawing room
12. Presence Chamber
13. Consort's guard chamber
14. Drawing Room / Audience Chamber
15. Council Chamber
16. Ballroom
17. Chapel Royal
18. Former Queen's Chapel

the eastern arm. The chapel, most unusually, is built directly beside the gate, facing north. The east side of the outer court is built in two thicknesses, the northern section much wider than the southern part; the south-east junction between the inner and eastern courts shows different wall thicknesses. These are all anomalous and irregular features, not what would be expected in a new house planned on a virgin site.

Understanding exactly what went on in the 1530s and 1540s is hampered by an almost total lack of building records. St James's is amongst the most poorly documented of Henry VIII's many construction projects. Only two structures are mentioned in the surviving fragmentary accounts of the early 1530s: a gallery and a bill for great hooks for the gate.[27] It is very likely that the gate mentioned in the accounts was, in fact, the Great Gatehouse that still stands. It must have been built in the first phase because the spandrels of one of its doorways contains the initials 'H&A', presumably for Henry and Anne. This, and the documentary reference, suggests that the gatehouse and the range to its east, which is integral with it, was completed in 1533.

The eastern part of the entrance range is now covered with eighteenth-century accretions (see Plan D), but a drawing of the house taken from the north, and attributed to Wenceslaus Hollar (1607–77), shows it as it appeared in the 1650s (Fig. 1.5), and reveals that the gate and its eastern flank wall were conceived as part of the outer perimeter of what is now St James's Park. There are no ground-floor windows on the palace's north front, making it essentially an extension of the adjacent park wall.

The park wall was built in 1532–3 and was eventually 1.7 miles (2.7 km) long, completely enclosing what is now St James's Park.[28] Access to the Park was only from the west side of Whitehall Palace or through St James's. The wall prominently appears in an equestrian portrait of Henry, Prince of Wales (Fig. 1.6), a later occupant and owner of St James's. The fact that the gatehouse was, in fact, part of the security precautions of the Whitehall precinct probably explains the priority given to its construction.

To the west of the gatehouse, tucked in close to its western turrets, is the chapel. While the plan of the chapel itself can find parallels in the plans of chapels at Eltham, Hampton Court and elsewhere, its position in the outer court, facing north, is unique. There is no evidence to suggest that it was a later addition or afterthought, so this must have been the original intention. Previously, household chapels had been built at two of Henry VIII's houses, Greenwich and Richmond. At Richmond, there was a symmetrical arrangement, with the great hall and chapel balancing each other either side of the outer court. At Greenwich, the chapel was also arranged in relation to a parallel great hall, and was sited at the east end of the

1.5

Attributed to Wenceslaus Hollar, *The Manor of St James's, Whitehall Park and Westminster from the north*, c.1650. This is a key document for understanding the Tudor building, as it shows that the whole of the north façade acted as part of the northern boundary of the Whitehall enclave. The entrance range is shown in its original state with no windows at ground-floor level, emphasising the secure nature of the house (RCIN 913264)

1.6
Robert Peake the Elder (c.1551–1619), equestrian portrait of Henry, Prince of Wales, c.1606–8. The Prince is shown in front of a substantial wall, almost certainly the wall of St James's Park. Set into the wall is a stone plaque containing the Prince of Wales's feathers (Parham Park, Pulborough, West Sussex)

principal waterfront range, butted up against a gatehouse. It is possible that the original intention at St James's was to follow this arrangement and balance the chapel with a hall on the east side of the outer court. This might explain the anomalies in the thickness of the range in this area (see Fig. 1.4).

It has often been said that the chapel was completed in 1540 on the basis of the comprehensive painted heraldic programme on its ceiling that celebrates the marriage of Henry VIII and Anne of Cleves (1515–57). As well as Anne's coat of arms, badge and the ducal arms of Cleves, there are the inevitable conjoined 'H&A's, which appear eight times; there are 20 panels that name possessions of the Cleves family – Berg, Gulick, Juliers, LaMarck and Mons – and 12 dates in 1540. Even by Tudor standards, this heraldic celebration gives unusually heavy prominence to the king's consort, and the parts relating to Anne of Cleves can only have been painted between 6 October 1539, when the marriage treaty with Cleves was signed, and February 1540, when Henry decided to divorce her. Indeed, it is more realistic to suppose that the heraldic painting had been completed by their marriage, which the King was most reluctant to conclude, on 6 January, that is, within three months.[29]

The union had been promoted by Thomas Cromwell, and it was Henry's intense disappointment in the marriage that was a major cause of Cromwell's fall from power. During 1538–9, Cromwell frequently lodged at St James's (see below), and it must have been he who proudly ordered the decoration of the chapel ceiling in anticipation of Anne's arrival. If the chapel, which is of one build with the gatehouse, had been started in 1531–2, it must have been completed and the ceiling installed long before late 1539. The panels in the ceiling are, in fact, removable and simply slot into the suspended timber framework. It is likely, therefore, that after October 1539, Cromwell ordered a number of existing panels to be extracted and new ones inserted for Anne. This kind of heraldic retro-fitting became common in Henry's buildings after 1532.[30]

The design of the ceiling (Fig. 1.7; see Fig. 2.17) is illustrated by Sebastiano Serlio (1475–1554) in his *Fourth Book of Architecture*, published in Venice in 1537 and probably available in England by the end of that year. This is normally assumed to be the source of the design at St James's, and, indeed, it might be. However, the design was not the invention of Serlio: the pattern was quite a common ancient Roman one, most easily seen in the fourth-century church of Santa Costanza in Rome. It had been used by Serlio's teacher, Baldassare Peruzzi (1481–1536), in 1520, in the Palazzo della Cancelleria, the vast Roman palace that housed the Papal Chancellery. Subsequently, it was used by Giulio Romano (c.1499–1546) at the Palazzo Te in Mantua, which Serlio had admired and which was completed in 1534. Thus it is not safe to assume that the published version was the source of the design, since both English travellers and Italian architects working in England were familiar with it before 1537. Indeed, the design had been used in the screen

1.7
The ceiling of the Chapel Royal at St James's, published by Charles James Richardson in 1840. Although probably completed before 1537, it was decorated for the marriage of Henry VIII and Anne of Cleves in 1540. The 'H&A' monograms probably relate to Henry and Anne Boleyn
(RCIN 506602)

at the chapel of King's College, Cambridge, in 1536, the year before its publication by Serlio.[31] Thus the ceiling could date from as early as 1534–5, in which case the 'H&A's would refer to Anne Boleyn, not Anne of Cleves. This would fit the thesis that Cromwell adapted a pre-existing ceiling for the disastrous Cleves marriage.[32]

Most of the large royal houses in the Thames valley had household chapels, and most also had great halls. By the 1530s, great halls were no longer used on a daily basis by the monarch and their family, but were principally large dining rooms for the royal household, only being brought into polite usage if there was a particularly important reception. In such a case, the hall would be hung with tapestry and used as the first and largest of the outer reception rooms. Henry VIII built only one great hall, at Hampton Court, in 1532–5. In many of his building projects of the later 1530s and 1540s, the King dismantled existing great halls, and at his only new house, Nonsuch, he never planned to have one.[33]

Whatever the original intention, there was never a great hall at St James's, but the house was furnished with a large household kitchen south of the western Kitchen Court, so provision was made for feeding a resident domestic household. Evidence for this comes from William Dickinson's plan (see Fig. 1.4), and from a slightly later survey of the kitchen areas, also in Dickinson's hand.[34] The kitchens cannot have been located far from a suitable room where the household could dine. The inventory of goods taken on Henry VIII's death lists 47 livery tables with their trestles which were used for dining. Various dining rooms are mentioned in the financial accounts in following reigns, including the grooms' dining room under Elizabeth. At Nonsuch in the early 1540s, there was a room described as the 'dining room in the outer court', and there may have been a similar arrangement at St James's, perhaps located near the chapel on the east or south side of the service court.[35]

It is very likely that work was also under way, in the first phase, on the principal lodgings on the south front. These rooms must have been well advanced in 1537, because we know that Thomas Cromwell was allowed to occupy the

1.8

J.C. Buckler (1793–1894), *Chimney piece lately discovered in the Guard Room at St James's Palace, 24 May 1822*. The drawing shows the fireplace in the present Tapestry Room (see also Fig. 1.1). The date 1538 is unusually placed and may not be reliable (BL, Add. MS 36370, fol. 120)

house as a convenient base near Whitehall; in cataloguing his list of achievements in the King's service, in around 1536, Cromwell was able to record that he had masterminded the building at St James's of 'a magnificent and goodly house'. His domestic accounts for 1537 are full of references to the house being prepared for his arrival, for hanging rooms with textiles and paying tips to the keeper and wages to the gardener. The state papers also contain many letters and documents that he signed there while using it as a base for undertaking royal business.[36]

An original fireplace survives in what is today called the Tapestry Room (see Fig. 1.1), originally the Consort's presence chamber, and one of its carved quatrefoils contains 'HA' and a true lover's knot, showing it was carved before the fall of Anne Boleyn in 1536. A reference in the financial accounts to 'charcoal for the gallery' at St James's refers to charcoal for braziers lit to dry the plaster in a recently completed gallery. It may have been this gallery in which the Bishop of Lincoln and Cromwell had a conversation in June 1537.[37]

It thus seems that in the first phase of building, an L-shaped range containing the gatehouse was completed, securing the site from the street. To one side of this was the chapel; to the south there was an inner court containing the principal lodgings. The Kitchen Court, built on a different alignment, the eastern side of the outer court, built to a different width, and the second inner court are likely to have been constructed in a second phase which may have envisaged a great hall on the east of the outer court.

If there had been a change in plan or a break in building as is suggested here, the most obvious point for this would have been the fall of Anne Boleyn. If work had begun in a rush of expectation in 1531, it might have been halted in 1536, as Henry, still without a male heir, furiously ordered the execution of his wife. When the following year, his third wife, Jane Seymour, was pregnant, the King's focus had moved to Hampton Court, where, at breakneck speed, in only six months, a nursery wing was built for Edward, Prince of Wales.[38] In the meantime, St James's was given to Thomas Cromwell for his use. Cromwell was not the only person to occupy the half-finished manor; Henry Fitzroy, the King's bastard son, also seems to have been allowed to stay there.

In the absence of a legitimate male heir, Fitzroy had been created Duke of Richmond in 1525 and he was granted various residences, including Baynard's Castle in the City of London. St James's was never given to him, but he was certainly living there at the time of his death in July 1536. He had recently started to cohabit with his wife, Mary Howard, and both suites of lodgings at St James's were hung with tapestry and furnished with a state bed. The Duke's presence chamber contained his own canopy and chair of estate of cloth of gold.[39]

The extremely fragmentary financial records for St James's seem to indicate that work had either restarted or regained pace after 1537; with Cromwell still in residence, work was continuing. An antiquarian drawing shows the fireplace in what was the Queen's guard chamber, bearing the date 1538 (Fig. 1.8). After Cromwell's execution in July 1540, money continued to be spent on the house, but after 1541 it seems to have diminished to a dribble and the main works must have been complete by then.[40]

Until 1542, Henry VIII himself seems to have taken little interest in the house. He is recorded as having stayed there for three nights in June 1538, but apart from that he can only ever have paid fleeting day visits to view the works. That he made use of the house more regularly after Christmas 1542 probably reflects the fact that it had now been completed. He stayed for a week in December 1542, the Privy Council meeting there several times, and the following year made two longer stays of ten days in March, and a fortnight over Easter, when he participated in the Maundy Thursday liturgy in the chapel, his robes being delivered to St James's specially. In June 1544, he stayed again for a little over a week, and in 1545, he stayed a number of nights in April and May. There were, no doubt, shorter visits, as the state papers refer to meetings of the Privy Council there on a number of other occasions.[41]

It is likely that Henry used St James's during the early 1540s because works at Whitehall made it inconvenient to stay there. In the last years of his reign, the King did not use the house at all. The inventory of all his goods taken after his death records its furnishings in the early part of Edward VI's reign, and the impression is of a place rarely visited and poorly equipped. The chapel was the only part of the house adequately furnished, containing fine altar frontals, vestments and an organ. The rest of the house was littered with low-grade furniture, some of it broken or damaged, and without any carpets or tapestries. There were not even any beds. The main items of value in the house were 55 paintings, most of which were portraits of European royalty, with a small number of pictures of members of the King's own family. The inventory is not specific as to whether these paintings were distributed round the house or whether, perhaps, they were all concentrated in the privy gallery.[42]

St James's in 1547

St James's was built by the King's Office of Works, and the office and its successor bodies retained responsibility for maintaining the palace until 1991, when it was assumed by the Royal Household property section. Although the financial records for its early history are extremely defective, there is an almost complete run of account summaries from 1603 up until the Civil War. These, together with William Dickinson's plan (see Fig. 1.4) and a small number of other maps and views, enable us to reconstruct the layout of the rooms built for Henry VIII in the decade after 1531.

In common with most royal residences, there were two entrances to St James's. There was the Great Gatehouse in the north, which provided access to the outer court, and on the south front was a privy entry guarded by a porter; this allowed the monarch to ride across the park from Whitehall and ascend, via a private staircase, directly into the royal lodgings on the first floor.[43] From the outer court, there was a great staircase that led up to the royal lodgings. The great stair shown on Dickinson's plan is not a Tudor form and the original was probably a single flight, 15 ft (4.6 m) wide, similar to the exactly contemporary stair beneath Anne Boleyn's gateway at Hampton Court.

The royal lodgings were disposed around two courts (see Plan A). The inner court had east, west and north ranges a uniform 20 ft (6.1 m) deep, and the south, garden, range was a little wider, at 31 ft (9.5 m). The original configuration of the eastern court is unclear. St James's shared the standard arrangement of two sides, one for the sovereign and the other for the consort. Generally speaking, the suite with the larger rooms was the sovereign's, or, perhaps in the case of St James's, that of the Prince of Wales. The larger and more elegantly disposed of the two suites ran along the north and east sides of the inner court.

At the top of the great stair a landing led, as it does now, to two guard chambers: the one to the east was the sovereign's, and the one to the south, the consort's. In the guard chambers stood the Yeomen of the Guard; a partition on the sovereign's side enabled the straw mattresses upon which they slept at night to be neatly stowed during the day.[44] There was a fireplace on the north wall and a bay looking into the inner court. Over the fireplace of this room, and most of the rooms in the inner court, was a terracotta roundel. These roundels of fruit and leaves,

1.9

Le Cercle De Leurs Magestes Dans La Chambre De Presence: A: S. Iames. Print showing Charles I, Henrietta Maria, their children and Marie de' Medici, surrounded by attendants, in the Presence Chamber at St James's Palace. The walls are decorated with fleurs-de-lis and a terracotta roundel can be seen over the fireplace (Metropolitan Museum of Art, New York, 17.3.3580)

containing the heads of Roman emperors, were in vogue during the early 1530s and were used at Whitehall and Greenwich, as well as several lesser houses. A similar set adorns the gatehouses at Hampton Court today, but the roundels are not in their original positions.[45]

When, in 1638–41, St James's was lent to Marie de' Medici (1573–1642), Charles I's mother-in-law and Dowager Queen of France, a series of prints was made, illustrating the rooms that she inhabited. Although not entirely reliable, these show the roundels above each fireplace, including in the Presence Chamber (Fig. 1.9) – information corroborated by Charles Wild's (1781–1835) watercolour of the King's presence chamber of *c.*1816 (see Fig. 3.50).

In Tudor royal houses, a passage led from the Presence Chamber to the Privy Chamber. Off this was a private oratory and a chapel for the monarch. There was also normally a stair that connected to the wardrobe of the robes below. The passage certainly existed at St James's, but there is no plan that indicates exactly how the closets were arranged.[46] The passage led to the Privy Chamber, which was on the east side of the inner court, and beyond this was the bedchamber in the corner of the court.[47] A door led from the bedchamber into the innermost chambers on the south front.

The consort's lodgings, which are, as is normally the case, less well documented in the financial accounts, were similarly arranged: from the Guard Chamber there was a presence chamber, still partially surviving as the Tapestry Room. Beyond this was a privy chamber on the corner of the courtyard. On the south front, the Privy Chamber led to a withdrawing chamber, bedroom and closet. A spiral stair connected the consort's inner rooms to service rooms and wardrobes below.

The sovereign and consort's innermost chambers met on the south front in a tall, slender, tower.[48] It is just possible that this tower was, in some way, part of the fifteenth-century master's house, but it is more likely to have been built for Henry VIII at the point where the lodgings joined, providing a privy stair leading down to the gardens and a prospect chamber above, looking over the park towards Whitehall and Westminster. This was the precise arrangement in the contemporary lodgings built at Hampton Court, for instance.[49]

From the 1530s, royal houses had a private or privy gallery, entered from the royal bedchamber and innermost rooms. St James's conforms to this norm: Elizabeth I had a privy bedchamber beyond her principal bedroom, and this led onto the south-facing, privy gallery, 65 ft (19.8 m) long and 17 ft 8 in. (5.5 m) wide.[50] Its north wall was windowless and designed to be hung with tapestries. In contrast, the south façade was well fenestrated, with views over the garden. At the east end a staircase led down to the gardens, and in the middle, a small private chamber; such stairs and gallery chambers were also typical of the period.[51] The fireplace was set between two windows; its tall chimney was on the south façade. This was an unusual arrangement, but one that allowed the entire north wall to be devoted to wall hangings.

The south elevation of the privy gallery was built around a foot (30 cm) in advance of the rest of the south front, and at the point where it joins it, there are anomalies in wall thickness. This suggests either that the privy gallery was added later or that plans changed during construction. At the east end of the gallery was the privy kitchen, to serve the sovereign's table.[52] References in the fragmentary accounts of the early 1540s suggest that this might only have been completed by then.[53] If so, the privy gallery may have been added in the early 1540s, after the fall of Thomas Cromwell.

The privy gallery formed the southern side of an eastern court, which is here called the Privy Court. The east and north ranges were, like the privy gallery, 17 ft 8 in. (5.5 m) deep, and by the early eighteenth century they contained lodgings accessed by galleries that ran round the inside of the Privy Court (see Plan A). This was not the original arrangement; the uniformity of depth of the ranges suggests that the courtyard was planned as a single conception; the walls on all sides were windowless, containing chimney flues. It is possible that the eastern range, as at Hampton Court, was originally set aside as a nursery wing, served by a privy kitchen. This is speculative, and the original arrangement is uncertain, if indeed it was ever completed. We do know that by the early seventeenth century, all three sides of the Privy Court contained galleries (below), and that by the time we have a plan of the area, it had been divided up into lodgings.[54]

The household chapel was reached from the landing at the top of the main stairs from the outer court. A narrow access gallery led to the royal holyday closet in a pew that looked down into the body of the chapel below. The extremely narrow gallery cannot have been the original intention, as normally the sovereign's Sunday procession to the holyday closet was a state occasion, with much pomp and many spectators. That it was tolerated until the reign of Anne (see p. 111) demonstrates the private nature of St James's, where monarchs must have attended chapel in relative privacy.

A notable feature of the royal lodgings at St James's is that, with the exception of the rooms on the south front, they looked inwards. The consort's rooms in the west range had no western windows, and the main view was of the inner court; all the sovereign's rooms also looked out onto the inner and outer courtyards. This arrangement was extremely unusual in a royal house, where great efforts were normally taken to provide fine views from as many rooms as possible. It emphasises the extremely secure nature of the building, in both design and, as will emerge, in future use.

The state and privy rooms at St James's were stage sets for furniture and soft furnishings that were delivered when the monarch or members of the royal family came to stay. Like other royal houses, the floors of the main rooms were boarded and then plastered, before being laid with mats. The Great Stairs, Council Chamber and royal rooms were given fretwork ceilings. These were geometrically arranged, gilded timber battens, with cast lead or leather maché enrichments. At the points where the battens met, there were gilded lead balls with oak leaves. Such ceilings survive in the contemporary holyday closet at Hampton Court, and lead embellishments are still to be found on the St James's chapel ceiling. In the more important rooms there were also cornices of gilded and painted moulded work, containing grotesquework and heraldry.[55]

In 1547, Henry VIII had left a house that was to be barely altered for more than a century. It was a place started in a burst of optimism and anticipation, but one that never fulfilled its potential in his lifetime. On Henry's death, the throne passed to his children in succession, none of whom themselves had children, so St James's was not used for its intended purpose until the early seventeenth century.

The Later Tudors

The manor of St James had been conceived by Henry VIII for his son and heir, but when, in

1547, the nine-year-old Prince Edward acceded the throne as King Edward VI, he had not used it much. Most of his life had been spent in a series of lesser houses to the north of London, with his sisters, Mary and Elizabeth. On the death of a monarch, it was traditional for the heir to move directly to the Tower of London, and it was there that Edward received the nobility of England who came to pay him homage.

Henry VIII's will had established a council that would rule until Edward reached his majority, but, perhaps inevitably, one of their number, the King's uncle, Edward Seymour (c.1506–52), established himself as 'Lord Protector' of the realm. Seymour, who took the title Duke of Somerset, had as his first duty the care of the boy king, and realising that Whitehall was too large and insecure, chose to lodge him at St James's. Thus the court was established at St James's, and Somerset and the Council ruled across the park from Whitehall.[56]

St James's may have been secure from the populace, but not from a determined court insider. Thomas Seymour (1508–49), brother to the Lord Protector and uncle to the King, aggrieved by a perceived lack of status, called to see the King at St James's at 9 o'clock one morning. John Fowler, one of Edward's Privy Chamber, described that Seymour had come 'into the gallery where I was playing the lute. He said that there was slender company about the king, no-one in the presence chamber and not a dozen in the whole house'; he then went on to say, 'a man might steal away the King now if he came with more men than were in the house'. This is exactly what he then tried to do.

With the complicity of Henry Fitzalan, Earl of Arundel and Lord Chamberlain (1512–80), Seymour obtained a pass key to the privy garden and the privy lodgings. He got all the way to the King's bedchamber door armed with a loaded pistol and was only foiled by the furious barking of the King's dog. Seymour was sent to the Tower, where he was executed in March 1549. Fitzalan, responsible for security at court, was accused of neglect, of removing 'bolts and locks' and not properly securing the doors of the Privy Chamber: he was heavily fined. Orders were immediately given to tighten security: more guards were stationed in the watching chamber at St James's, and at Whitehall, door locks were reinforced.[57]

Little is known about Edward's life at St James's, although he enjoyed watching troops drilling in the park and took an interest in the rebuilding of the royal mews at Charing Cross.[58] His reign is notable for the importance of the Council, and it may have been in the late 1540s that a Council Chamber was built at St James's, located on the west side of the outer court, between the Great Stairs and the chapel. That the Council Chamber was a later addition to the original plan is suggested by the awkward narrowness of the gallery to the chapel. From 1551, the young King regularly attended meetings there himself.[59]

Edward's reign ended in tragedy: the 15-year-old boy, so full of promise, died, probably of tuberculosis, in July 1553. His eldest sister, the Roman Catholic Mary, successfully defeated a plot to put the Protestant Lady Jane Grey (1537–54) on the throne, and entered London as Queen in early August. Edward was still lying in state at Whitehall, so Mary moved upriver to Richmond, where she first began to establish her court. This was far from the epicentre of power, and she soon realised that she needed to be in Westminster, so was rowed back upriver, establishing herself at St James's.[60]

Security was no less a problem for Mary than it had been for Edward; many of her subjects were appalled by the thought of someone whom they regarded as a heretic on the throne. St James's provided a secure and secret place for her to make plans for her coronation and marriage, the Spanish ambassador coming and going clandestinely across the park.[61] It soon became known that the Queen's intention was to marry Philip II, King of Spain (1527–98), son of her cousin, the Emperor Charles V (1500–58). This announcement added xenophobia to the already toxic atmosphere, and a rebellion, starting in Kent and led by Sir Thomas Wyatt (c.1521–54), set out to force the Queen to give up her marriage plans, and perhaps, even to remove her from the throne. Some 3,000 rebels successfully routed a force of Household guards and Whitecoats (London militia) at Rochester and made for London Bridge. Finding the gates there barred to them, they moved south of the river, crossing at Kingston, and made their way towards Westminster.

Mary was at Whitehall, where she had assembled as many troops as she could muster in St James's Park. The rebels came to the great gate of St James's and found they could not gain access to the park there, so followed the park wall all the way down to Charing Cross, where they skirmished with more Household guards. Wyatt was seized, but his men got to the very gates of Whitehall, the Queen watching anxiously from the privy gallery above.[62]

Wyatt's rebellion demonstrated that St James's house, integrated with the mighty park walls, could stand firm against civil unrest and violence. This was possibly part of the attraction of the place for Mary, who used the house a great deal, preferring it to Whitehall. She would often stay at St James's, and would cross the park and enter Whitehall, only to emerge at the waterside and board her barge at the privy stairs. In 1555, she rode from St James's to Whitehall, before going to Westminster Abbey to open Parliament.[63]

Various events took place in the state rooms: in April 1554, Mary created Sir John Bridges baron in the Presence Chamber, and in 1557, William Harvey Clarenceaux was made King of Arms in the withdrawing room.[64] In 1554, the Queen celebrated the feast day of St George, with its traditional processions, in the chapel, and a few days later she joined the rogation processions round the parish of St Margaret's, setting off from St James's and circumnavigating the whole park, with the royal heralds, sergeants-at-arms and four bishops in full vestments.[65]

As a wife and queen, Mary's life was dominated by the necessity to become pregnant and thus prevent her Protestant sister, Elizabeth, next in line to the throne, from becoming queen. In March 1558, for a second time, the 42-year-old Queen was convinced that she was with child, but this was no pregnancy; she was ill, and in August, moved from Hampton Court, where she had been staying, to St James's. It was to be the last remove of her reign: early on 17 November, she died in the Great Bedchamber, surrounded by her household.

Royal protocol determined that until a monarch was buried, they were not dead, and their Household and government continued. Thus, while Elizabeth prepared to take the reins of power at Hatfield House, her residence at the time, in the bedchamber at St James's, the embalmers were removing Mary's heart and bowels and stuffing her torso with preservative herbs and spices. Her body was then taken to the Privy Chamber next door, where, in a lead casket enclosed in a timber coffin, she lay in state. It was not until 10 December that preparations were complete for the funeral and her body was moved through the black-draped state rooms to the chapel. Three days later, a solemn procession left the Great Gatehouse and trundled down what is now Pall Mall, along the park wall to Charing Cross, eventually arriving at Westminster Abbey.[66]

Elizabeth knew St James's well; indeed, she had sometimes been granted permission to use the house during the reigns of her siblings.[67] Yet Elizabethan St James's was far from the centre of court life. Over the course of her long reign, the Queen rarely visited, and then only briefly. Only one of the many visitors who came to the Elizabethan court and recorded their impressions gained access to St James's, and he thought it disappointing, noting 'the Queen does not often stay there'.[68] But there were good reasons for her to use the house, especially when she wanted to be isolated or safe. At least two of her longer stays were triggered by fear of military action. Once in 1588, with the Spanish Armada off the English coast, Elizabeth returned in a hurry from Richmond to London, not to Whitehall, but to the more secure and easier to defend St James's; she remained there until October, when it was clear that all danger had passed. Then, in 1599, Philip III of Spain (1578–1621) sent a fourth Spanish armada of 180 ships and there was panic across southern England and London. The Queen was driven at high speed in her coach to St James's, where she remained until the crisis subsided.[69]

In April 1593, with plague rife in London, the Queen was at St James's, away from the crowds at Whitehall, and gave special instructions for roads in the surrounding area to be kept clean, so she could safely take the air in the park. She celebrated Easter there in the chapel, descending from her closet and receiving communion on her knees in the body of the chapel.[70] The house was not only used as a refuge; in 1581–2 it had been spruced up and the grounds improved, in order to play a part in accommodating the entourage of the Duke of Alençon, one of the Queen's suitors.[71] In 1592, the Queen celebrated St George's Day at St James's: a dais with a curtain was set up in the chapel; a buffet was constructed of timber to lay out the plate; and a new communion table was installed.[72]

The house was used often enough for most of the important courtiers to be assigned lodgings there. The Queen's favourites, the Earl of Leicester (1532/3–88) and the Earl of Essex (1565–1601), both had suites of rooms, as did her secretary, Lord Burghley (1520–98), and Lord Howard of Effingham (1536–1624), the Lord Admiral. Leicester's household accounts show that he brought nine carts full of household furnishings when he stayed at St James's in 1584, and the following year he had a new bed delivered to the house.[73]

Despite the slim usage, the house was well maintained by the Office of Works, and evidence of its diligence remains in the unbroken run of annual account summaries. These valuable rolls show that no alterations of significance were made to the royal lodgings under Elizabeth I, although parts of the kitchens were extended and enlarged.

On coming to the throne, surveys were made of the condition of the many royal houses that Elizabeth had inherited. St James's had been well used by Mary, and the only observation made by the royal surveyors was that the water supply was deficient and the pipes 'rotten'. In 1570–71, a new supply was run from Hyde Park. Small brick conduit heads collected water from natural springs and channelled it to a conduit house in the vicinity of modern Hyde Park Corner. The conduit house, much like the surviving Tudor house on Coombe Hill, Kingston, contained settling tanks to remove sediment, before piping the water, via lead pipes, to a cistern in the house. It is not known where this was, but references to a conduit court might suggest that any overflow powered a fountain. The Elizabethan Office of Works liked to mark its buildings, and the conduits bore the Queen's arms and the date.[74]

The dissolution of the monasteries, the royal supremacy and the reform of religion that began in Henry VIII's reign had little effect at first on the Chapel Royal. Henry VIII's chapel at his death was much the same as it had been in the 1520s. The accession of Edward VI brought sweeping changes in the Church and these were reflected in the royal chapels. Altars were removed and replaced by communion tables, and the liturgy was reformed and simplified. These changes were reversed by Mary, and it is certain that whatever alterations were made in the chapel at St James's by Edward VI were abandoned after his death. It was left to Elizabeth, in the first years of her reign, to establish the Church of England, and at the same time, to lay down new norms for the Chapel Royal.

The Queen had strong views about royal religion and believed that it was necessary for the Chapel Royal to maintain a degree of magnificence that was not tolerated in the Anglican Church at large. In 1586–7, when the Queen decided to use the chapel at St James's, a new organ was installed, as well as a pulpit,[75] and it was not until 1591/2 that a communion table was made, either replacing a previous model or substituted for a stone altar that had been installed by Queen Mary.[76]

The Early Stuarts: James I

In 1603, England once again had a royal family: James I and Queen Anne had three children: nine-year-old Prince Henry, his three-year-old brother Charles, and Elizabeth (1596–1662), their sister, aged seven. It had been such a long time since this had been the case that

Sir Robert Cecil (1563–1612) was asked to investigate what arrangements should be made for accommodating and financing multiple households. Immediately, three separate households were established, for the King, the Queen and the royal children.[77]

St James's was assigned to the royal children, and alterations were promptly put in hand to accommodate them.[78] Prince Henry was set up in the sovereign's side, and presumably Charles, Duke of York, was given the consort's side, though this is nowhere confirmed. The boys had a 'school chamber' near Prince Henry's bedchamber, for which two bookcases, 12½ ft (3.8 m) long and 7½ ft (2.3 m) high, were made.[79] While Princess Elizabeth does not seem to have had lodgings at the house, in April 1605, after the birth of Princess Mary, a nursery was built for her at St James's. It was a stand-alone building, 60 ft (18.3 m) long and 15 ft (4.6 m) wide, of two storeys, with eight rooms. It is not clear where this structure was, but it had a little garden fenced around it. The Princess died in December 1607, aged only two.[80]

Lodgings were also distributed to courtiers who would be in charge of the boys' welfare. Key amongst these was Sir Thomas Chaloner, Prince Henry's governor and later his Lord Chamberlain, Adam Newton, the Princes' tutor, and Sir Roger Aston, a former groom of the

1.10

Richard Newcourt (surveyor; d. 1679) and William Faithorne (engraver; 1616–91), *An Exact Delineation of the Cities of London and Westminster and the Suburbs Thereof* (detail). The survey dates from the mid-1640s, although this image is from a printing of *c*.1658. The original scale was 14 inches to a mile, so the level of detail could be quite high. Unfortunately, the detailed representation of St James's is inaccurate, despite the overall disposition of buildings being correct (BL, Maps, Roll 17.a.3)

1.11

Adriaen van de Venne (1589–1662), 'A game of Pell-Mell, from an album of 102 drawings; the Winter King about to strike a ball along the alley'. The St James's 'pell-mell' alley would have been just like this (BM, 1978,0624.42.30)

bedchamber to the King in Scotland, and the King's eyes and ears in the Princes' household. Rooms close to the Princes were also allocated to the three young noblemen chosen to be Prince Henry's special companions: Robert Devereux, 3rd Earl of Essex (1591–1646), William Cecil, Lord Cranborne (1591–1668), and John Harington, 2nd Baron Harington of Exton (1592–1614). Other young men were given more peripheral lodgings in the house.[81]

Provision was made for the amusement of the little household: a table was provided for the musicians, a shovelboard table, 13 ft (4 m) long, was constructed, and archery butts were set up in the garden, as were two decorative pheasant houses with little domes – the pheasant keeper was built a comfortable house nearby.[82] In due course, an area in St James's Fields (see p. 64) was set aside as a recreation ground. As at Whitehall, this was on the other side of a public highway and contained a tennis court. The court is shown in this position on Faithorne's survey of c.1658 (Fig. 1.10). What is not shown is the elevated gallery that took players over the road to the upper balcony in the court. Henry was obsessed with tennis and 'neither observed moderation, nor what appertained to his dignity and person', playing tennis in just a shirt. He used the courts at Whitehall but, in 1619, Gideon Lozer built a court on the corner of St James's Street for Prince Charles. There was a keeper's house and garden, and in this, the court. Its dimensions were 110 by 35 ft (33.5 by 10.7 m), and as such, was a larger court than that built by Henry VIII at Whitehall, but similar in size to the large tennis court built by Charles I at Hampton Court in 1625.[83] It continued in use until the Civil War and Charles lost large sums of money when he was beaten by the keeper of the court.

Next door to the tennis court was the 'pell mell' (a game which later became known as Pall Mall). This consisted of a hard surface made of crushed cockle shells rolled into the loam and laid out in a narrow strip half a mile (0.8 km) long. On either side there were boards to prevent balls, whacked with a croquet-like mallet, from going astray (Fig. 1.11). The balls had to go through hoops positioned at points along the alley. The 'pell mell' was laid out between a double avenue of 140 lime trees.[84] Although the first documentary evidence for the 'pell mell' dates from 1630, it was one of the games that James I encouraged Prince Henry to play, and it is likely that the alley was built for him. In 1635, one Archibald Lumsden was given a monopoly for supplying equipment for the game, which Charles I was recorded as playing in 1639.[85]

Other personal interests of the Prince were also coming to the fore at St James's: he was obsessed with warships, military hardware, riding and jousting. As well as butts for archery, the Prince ordered an artillery house in the orchard. This stout platform supported an ordnance that could be fired at a 'stronge large board of elme'.[86] But above all, he loved great horses upon which he could practise *haute école*, the art of schooling a horse to make supple and agile movements in a confined space. These equine acrobatics were transferrable to the tiltyard and enabled riders to perform remarkable feats for the watching crowds. James I's interest in horses was confined to hunting, but Henry, Prince Charles, and Charles's friends, Essex, Cranborne and William Cavendish, later Duke of Newcastle, devoted themselves to *haute école*.[87]

In 1605–6, a new, brick-built stable, barn, straw house, oat house and coach house were built for Henry at the royal mews at Charing Cross.[88] This large complex of stables, the headquarters of royal equestrian activity, had been rebuilt in the 1550s by another royal teenager, Edward VI, and then adapted by Elizabeth I to take the newly fashionable coaches. The stables were not suitable for practising *haute école*, and in 1607–9, a new building was constructed at St James's for the purpose. The site was on the west side of the Kitchen Court, where a riding house, 124 ft (37.8 m) long and 42 ft (12.8 m) wide, was built, at a cost of nearly £150. The building, the first purpose-built of its type in England, was of great interest at the time and was carefully surveyed by the architect Robert Smythson, whose drawing survives (Fig. 1.12).[89]

By 1607, Prince Henry's household had become a magnet for the young, fashionable and ambitious; it had swollen to many times its intended size and its cost was enormous. In fact, it was a rival centre to that of the King, in fashion, if not in power.[90] But expenditure at St James's was still controlled by the Office of Works, and other than the substantial new buildings for Henry's equestrian interests,

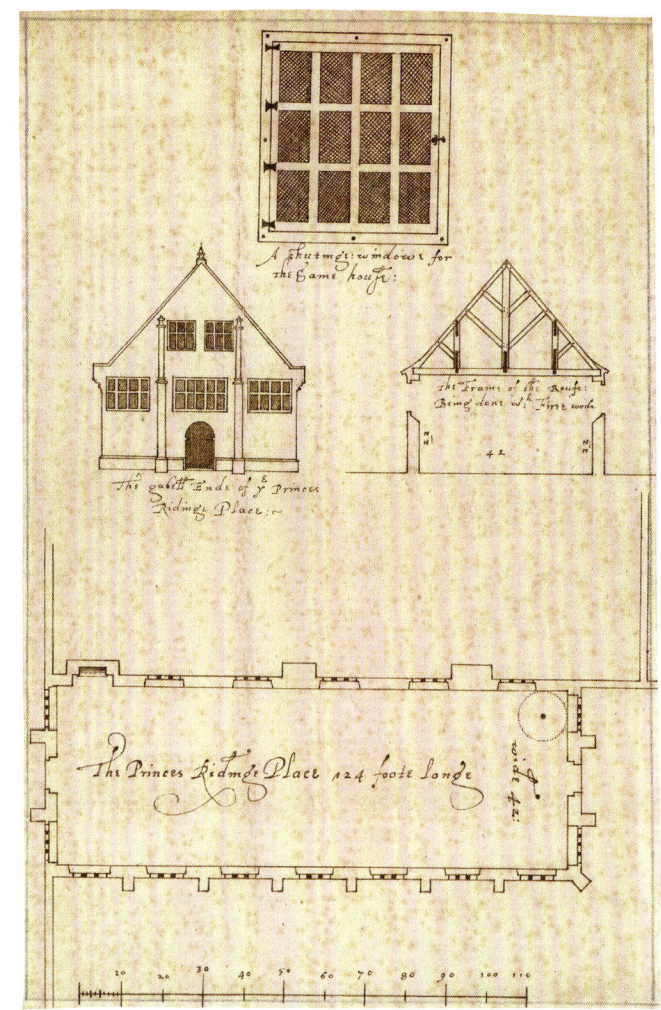

most changes to St James's thus far had been ephemeral.

Prince Henry was formally created Prince of Wales in June 1610, but his gradual transition to princely manhood and independence had been marked, at St James's, by a series of important improvements. The first of these was the acquisition of a library. A fine library was an important part of the equipage of a gentleman and a vital part of the education of a prince. Bookish James I was clear about this and so was the Archbishop of Canterbury, Richard Bancroft, who was actively looking for a way to provide Henry with one. As discussion continued about how to furnish the Prince with a suitable library, Lord Lumley, the owner of one of the two greatest private libraries in England, died, and his library was acquired for Prince Henry. On the advice of Adam Newton, it was transferred, in October 1609, to St James's. Patrick Young,

1.12

Robert Smythson (1534/5–1614), *The Riding House at St James's*, as surveyed in 1609. Constructed for Prince Henry in 1607–9, this was the first purpose-built riding house in England (RIBA Smythson SC229/I/14)

1. FROM THE HOSPITAL OF ST JAMES TO THE CIVIL WAR

1.13
Drawing in the hand of Sir Christopher Wren of the library at St James's, 1706. The room was fitted out for Prince Henry, and the central stack with its responds is likely to be from this date. The fireplace and floor-to-ceiling shelving are probably later (TNA, T1/100, fol. 184v)

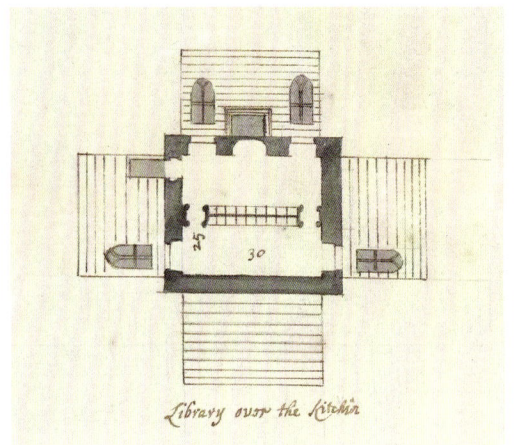

the son of one of the Prince's tutors, was made librarian, a position he continued to hold throughout most of Charles I's reign.[91]

Such a library, with more than 2,000 volumes, required a suitable space and it was decided to fit up a room over the privy kitchen, at the eastern end of the privy gallery. Not only was this in the heart of the Prince's privy lodgings; its location above a kitchen meant it would be kept dry and warm. It is not clear what the room had previously been used for, but it was necessary to insert a new window (probably in the north wall and in Tudor style) to let in more light.

The interior was fitted out by Maximilian Colt, who had made his name carving Elizabeth I's monument in Westminster Abbey. He was a Fleming from Arras, who had come to England in the mid-1590s via Utrecht and had been promoted by Robert Cecil, 1st Earl of Salisbury, for whom he worked in a private capacity. In 1608, he became the King's master carver, and it was obvious that the job of building the library would fall to him.[92] The bookcases were made in the prevailing Mannerist style of Hans Vredeman de Vries and decorated with 81 terms – tapering pedestals that melded into human busts or beasts at the top. There were also four great arches, with the Prince's arms in the spandrels, forming part of a vault over the room, and smaller arches on the book cupboards – the latter contained, in all, 620 shelves.[93] On the east wall there was a massive fireplace, with a vigorous chimney surround framed by two giant terms, Corinthian pilasters and the upper section with tall pierced pyramids, satyrs and Doric columns. Such virtuoso chimneys were all the rage and Colt was working on such a piece, in stone, at exactly the same time, for Robert Cecil's library at Hatfield.[94] The library was furnished with desks and 'drawing boxes' before the books were delivered.

In 1706, Sir Christopher Wren (1632–1723) was asked to review the St James's library in light of the 1701 purchase of the famous collection of books and manuscripts amassed by Sir Robert Bruce Cotton (1571–1631). Wren described the library as a 'lofty room and shelved as full as it can well be', providing a plan and elevations of the room. By this date, many of the Jacobean fittings, including the fireplace, had been removed, but the central stack, with arches connecting it to the outer walls, was still there (Fig. 1.13).[95] Wren's plan (see Fig. 2.18) shows that by this date the room was not approached from the gallery, but by a staircase, which gave separate access to it from the ground floor. The history of this room, and its collections (see pp. 98–9), suggest this was unlikely to have been the original arrangement.

At the same time that the library was fitted out, the long gallery was panelled. Previously, it must have been plastered and hung with tapestry, and the new panelling was to enable the Prince to hang paintings there. Clement Chapman, the joiner, provided the huge quantity of 859 square yards (718.2 m²) of panelling to the pattern, 'cipher and square', with fluted pilasters every 10 ft (3 m).[96] The whole was finished with a freeze and cornice. Whatever the original arrangement, by 1609 there was a continuous gallery that ran round the eastern court, described in the accounts as the 'three long galleries adjoining there together'.[97] This important point has not been previously understood. The south front privy gallery and the northern gallery overlooking the outer court were both exactly 100 ft (30.5 m) long end to end; the eastern gallery, known as the 'crosse gallery', was 125 ft (38.1 m) long. These might seem very long, but it must be remembered that there were several galleries at Whitehall more than 400 ft (121.9 m)

long, and the Queen's Gallery at Hampton Court was 150 ft (45.7 m) long. It is impossible now to calculate precisely how much of this great U-shaped gallery was panelled in 1609, but allowing for windows, doors and fireplaces, the 859 square yards does seem to represent the panelling of the entire space.[98]

An analysis of the monthly disbursements for St James's shows that expenditure reached a peak in October, November and December 1610. The Prince was rushing to complete his improvements for a great coming-out.[99] On Twelfth Night, he launched his public life with a magnificent court festival. At Christmas, challenges were issued to all comers to fight at the barriers. On 6 January, the tournament took place indoors, in the Banqueting House at Whitehall, with the young men of the court fighting with swords and pikes. The public spectacle, with speeches by Ben Jonson and scenery by Inigo Jones, continued until three in the morning. The next day, Henry rode to Whitehall from St James's, escorting his parents and sister back to his house. There, in his brand new gallery, he provided them, his brother and the cream of the court with supper on a table that was reported to be 120 ft (36.6 m) long – almost the full length of the eastern section; the company then went to see a play (probably in the old Council Chamber), before returning to be feasted in the gallery, no doubt served from the privy kitchen at its end.[100]

The spectacular opening-night party for his new gallery was a prelude to a hugely ambitious programme of building planned for both St James's and his summer residence at Richmond; with remarkable self-knowledge, the young Prince told Lord Salisbury that 'I am like enough to prove an unthrift'.[101] The following May, the Prince appointed his own works establishment that would, in due course, take over the design, procurement and execution of building works at his residences. Inigo Jones was surveyor, William Smith his paymaster, and Francis Carter clerk of works.[102] As far as everyone could see, the stage was set for him to become a major new patron of architecture and the arts. The Venetian ambassador reported that he was paying particular attention to his houses and had already ordered some new fountains and buildings.[103]

Although the Prince's new office contained men of both promise and ability, they did not, at first, take over full control. The Office of Works continued to execute and pay for improvements at St James's, and although the Prince's office also spent some £1,625 on the library, gallery and other miscellaneous improvements in 1610–11, the work was commissioned by the King's Office of Works, not by Inigo Jones. In the last months of his life, the Prince's office did spend some £1,586 at St James's on works that were unspecified in William Smith's accounts, and at his death, there were further sums, as then unpaid, signed off by Inigo Jones.[104]

The gallery was a spectacular setting for the Prince's picture collection and one that was

1.14

Jan Porcellis, *A Storm at Sea*, before 1612. This painting was almost certainly used as an overdoor in the gallery at St James's. It bears the 'HP' brand on the reverse, identifying it as one of the Prince's paintings (RCIN 402633)

1. FROM THE HOSPITAL OF ST JAMES TO THE CIVIL WAR

deliberately conceived in conjunction with his library. The late sixteenth century had seen an explosion of collecting across the princely courts of Europe: galleries and cabinets were filled with Old Master paintings, sculptures, coins and medals, manuscripts and books. Through those in his close circle and household, Henry knew of the great collections of the Medici and of the Emperor Rudolph II (1552–1612) in Prague; his mother, Anne of Denmark (1574–1619), was also interested in collecting, and the Prince and his advisers deliberately set out to establish a collection worthy of his position.[105]

The first evidence we have for Prince Henry buying paintings is in January 1611, at exactly the time that the gallery was completed, and soon after it was public knowledge that the Prince had set out to create a great gallery of painting. The same month, the Venetian ambassador, Marc Antonio Correr, wrote that the Prince was 'paying special attention to the adorning of a most beautiful gallery of very fine pictures, ancient and modern'.[106] A few months later, with work still in progress in the library, Sir Thomas Chaloner gave a tour of the rooms to Ottaviano Lotti, the Grand Duke of Tuscany's representative in London, asking him to send works of art to the Prince to be displayed there. As far as we know, this led to nothing,[107] but in late April or early May that year, he was presented with two paintings by the States General of the Dutch Republic as a diplomatic gift. These were a large canvas by Hendrick Vroom (1566–1640), depicting a battle off Gibraltar which is now in the Rijksmuseum, and a 'great sea peece' sold at the time of the Commonwealth, and now lost, by Jan Porcellis (1583/5–1632); both were described as being for the gallery at St James's and specially framed for it.

Henry had a taste for such marine paintings, for he commissioned three further paintings from Porcellis, each on panel and painted to a very specific size, 16¼ by 49 in. (41.3 by 124.5 cm), and thus almost certainly for overdoors (Fig. 1.14). These were not the only new arrivals, as a request, this time to Vincenzo Salviati, the Florentine ambassador, led to the receipt in June 1611 of a large shipment of paintings that was delivered by the architect Constantino de' Servi, at Richmond. As the paintings were unpacked, Henry asked the Italian 'about the decoration of their Highnesses galleries and if there were subject pictures and what kind of statues, and he confirmed his intention of using the foresaid pictures for his new gallery'.[108]

The trickle of Italian paintings had turned into a deluge: *Prometheus Chained to the Caucasus* by Palma Giovane was given to the Prince by Robert Cecil, Earl of Salisbury, and then a major shipment of paintings from Venice arrived, for which the Prince paid more than £400. Other paintings once hanging in the gallery at St James's in Henry's time can be identified in later inventories, although no comprehensive list survives from before the Civil War. What is certain, though, is that quickly and decisively, Henry, Prince of Wales, created what was, at the time, the largest picture gallery in England, more than 325 ft (99 m) long, and hung with perhaps as many as 50 paintings.[109]

In 1611, work was under way on the Prince's cabinet, a small room set aside for collections of antique coins, medals and bronzes, all of which he started collecting avidly in 1610. One purchase for this was a famous collection of antiquities from a Dutch collector, for which he paid a colossal £2,200 in 1611. The cabinet was unfinished at the time of the Prince's death and its location cannot now be pinpointed.[110] The combined costs of building the library and cabinet, and panelling the gallery, were a very substantial £2,800 and represented an extraordinary undertaking.[111]

Henry VIII had combined galleries with cabinets of treasures before, but what Prince Henry was doing was deliberately creating a comprehensive collection of contemporary knowledge, in imitation of, and potentially in rivalry with, the cabinets of other European princes. Neither Elizabeth I nor the Prince's father were interested in such an enterprise, but his brother Charles was to continue his endeavours with vigour later in the century.

At only 18 years of age, this princely architectural patron succumbed to what was probably typhoid, and after a horrible illness, made infinitely ghastlier by the ministrations of his doctors, he died at St James's on 6 November 1612. His embalmed body was sealed in a lead-lined coffin and placed on trestles in his bedchamber. The room was hung with black velvet and a matching canopy of state hung over the coffin. On the coffin were placed the Prince's coronet, robes of state, sword and golden sceptre. While the bedroom was hung with valuable velvet, his Privy Chamber, Presence Chamber and Guard Chamber were also hung with black textiles of decreasing richness and value. In the Privy Chamber, each morning and evening, the Prince's senior household officials gathered and said prayers, led by his chaplains.

After nearly a month, the coffin was brought from the bedchamber into the Privy Chamber, where it rested a night, and then to the Presence Chamber for another night. The following day it was ceremoniously carried, with suitable dignified pauses, through the guard chamber into the chapel, where it was placed beneath another canopy in the nave. Services were held, sermons were preached and, eventually, an effigy of the young Prince was placed on top of the coffin in preparation for the procession to Westminster Abbey. On Monday 7 December, exactly a month after his death, the cortège left St James's, making its morbid way along modern Pall Mall, via Charing Cross, to Westminster.[112]

Charles I, when Prince of Wales

Charles, Duke of York, had looked up to Henry, as younger brothers often do, and Henry was cool about his brother's overtures of friendship, as is often the response. Yet the two boys did live, study and play together, and as Henry lay dying, his bother touchingly visited him and attempted to comfort his expiring sibling. For Charles, the loss of his elder brother was followed by what was, perhaps, an even harsher blow – the marriage of his beloved sister, Elizabeth, to Frederick, the Elector Palatine (1596–1632; known as the Winter King). Charles adored his sister and formed a strong bond of friendship with his brother-in-law, but the couple, who married at Whitehall in February 1613, left soon after for their new home in Heidelberg, leaving Charles feeling very alone.

On the death of the Prince of Wales, James I was eager for the Duke of York to leave St James's and relocate to Whitehall, where he was not yet to have a full independent household.[113] From at least 1610, Charles's household had been a subset of his elder brother's: Prince Henry's cofferer paid the wages of the Duke's master of horse, cupbearer, carver, sewer, gentleman usher and grooms of the bedchamber. Charles had a keeper of his withdrawing room, a groom of his great chamber and two pages of the bedchamber; he also had a barge master and his own kitchen establishment. With his brother's household dissolved, the Duke's household became a subset of the King's, and under close scrutiny.[114]

In June 1613, the King finally agreed to appoint chamber and bedchamber officers to Charles's household, but he only acquired a full suite of household officers and financial independence when he was created Prince of Wales in November 1616.[115]

In 1619, John Smythson produced a drawing of a 'newe building' at St James's (Fig. 1.15). This has been tentatively identified with a rather

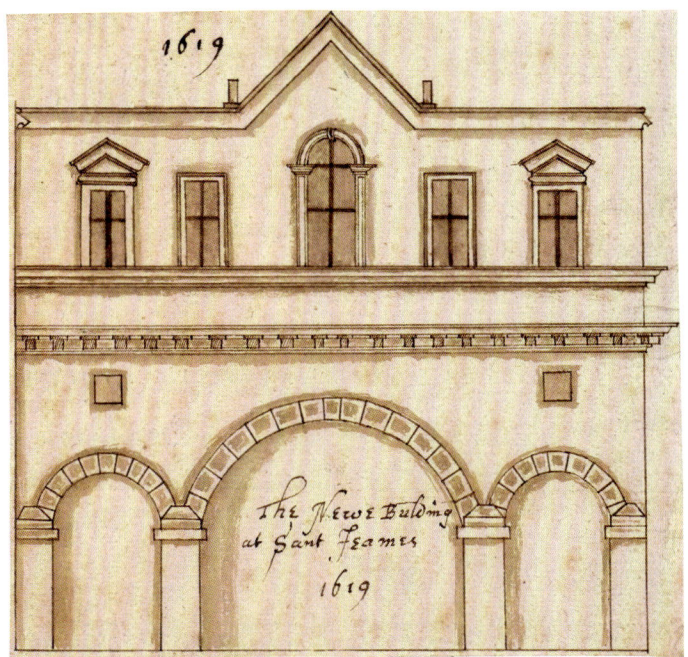

1.15

John Smythson (d. 1634), elevation of the 'newe building' at St James's, identified as the buttery and housekeeper's lodgings, built in 1617–19. It may have formed an entrance gateway to the outer court (see Fig. 1.33 for its conjectural location) (RIBA, Smythson SC237/III/8 (1))

1. FROM THE HOSPITAL OF ST JAMES TO THE CIVIL WAR

pretentious-sounding buttery built on the west side of the palace, facing Cleveland Row. This building, raised up on pillars and arches, contained a large and luxurious lodging on the first floor, possibly the new lodging of the housekeeper mentioned in the accounts.[116]

From 1621, there is greater evidence for the use of the house by the Prince; we know, for instance, that the former Council Chamber near the chapel was set up with staging for plays in both 1622–3 and 1623–4.[117] Charles also began to take up some state duties: in January 1621, six commissioners from the United Provinces were received by him at St James's; as they were about to enter the Presence Chamber, they realised that they had given the letters intended for the Prince to the King, and retained in their hands the letters intended for James – deeply embarrassed, they blamed their secretary's eyesight. In April 1622, Prince Charles received, with greater success, the son of the Landgrave of Hesse in the Privy Chamber at St James's. On these occasions, ambassadors arrived by coach, driving through the gatehouse into the outer court and mounting the principal stairs.[118]

In February 1623, the Duke of Buckingham (1592–1628) and the Prince of Wales left England in disguise, to ride across Europe to Madrid, where Charles hoped to win the hand of the King of Spain's daughter, the Infanta Maria Anna (1606–46). Their mission was so secret that, at first, not even the Secretary of State knew of the plan, but it had deep roots in the close friendship that had grown up between James I and the Spanish ambassador in London, Count Gondomar (1567–1626). Such a plan could not be kept secret for long, and soon, all Europe knew of the audacious 600-mile gallop that delivered Charles and Buckingham to the British ambassador in Madrid on 7 March.

Negotiations for a marriage between a Protestant Prince and a Catholic Princess were never going to be straightforward, nor were the European power-politics that lay behind the proposed dynastic alliance. Discussions were detailed, vexed and lengthy, and as negotiations dragged on in Spain, and while Charles and Buckingham consumed the £30,000 that they had brought with them, preparations were afoot in England to receive the Infanta. The day after Charles and Buckingham arrived in Madrid, the Secretary of State, Edward, Viscount Conway (c.1564–1631), consulted the Lord Chamberlain, William Herbert, 3rd Earl of Pembroke (1580–1630), on which houses would be most suitable for receiving the Infanta and her entourage. Inigo Jones, now Surveyor of the King's Works, was also consulted. He thought Denmark House would be the cheapest and easiest to prepare, but St James's was the seat of the Prince of Wales and it was decided that this would be the Infanta's 'constant seat', although Denmark House would also be assigned to her as her own London residence in due course. However, Conway was told that St James's was not up to standard; Secretary Sir George Calvert thought the Princess's side too small, the furniture 'far too mean' and the whole palace out of date. The rooms at St James's were, after all, much as they had been finished nearly a century before.[119]

Interior decoration may have been vexing the Privy Council, but religion was the key to the marriage treaty. For the Catholic powers, a Roman Catholic Queen of England was to be a Trojan horse for the reconversion of the apostate English, but more specifically, there was a deal to be done over the Princess's own religious practice when Queen. In April 1623, the Pope granted a dispensation for the marriage on the condition that the Princess's religion could be freely practised in her own establishment by her, and by Londoners who wished to attend, and that her children should be brought up as Roman Catholics.

This necessitated new chapels at both Denmark House and St James's, and the refitting of the old Savoy Chapel for the Princess's household. The two residences were inspected by Don Carlos Coloma, the Spanish ambassador, who asked for various improvements and was insistent on the importance of both chapels.[120] These were required, by an advisory panel of Spanish theologians, to be 'public churches', which were 'sufficiently large in which all the divine offices may be celebrated … there may be a number of altars, crosses, images, holy water, indulgences

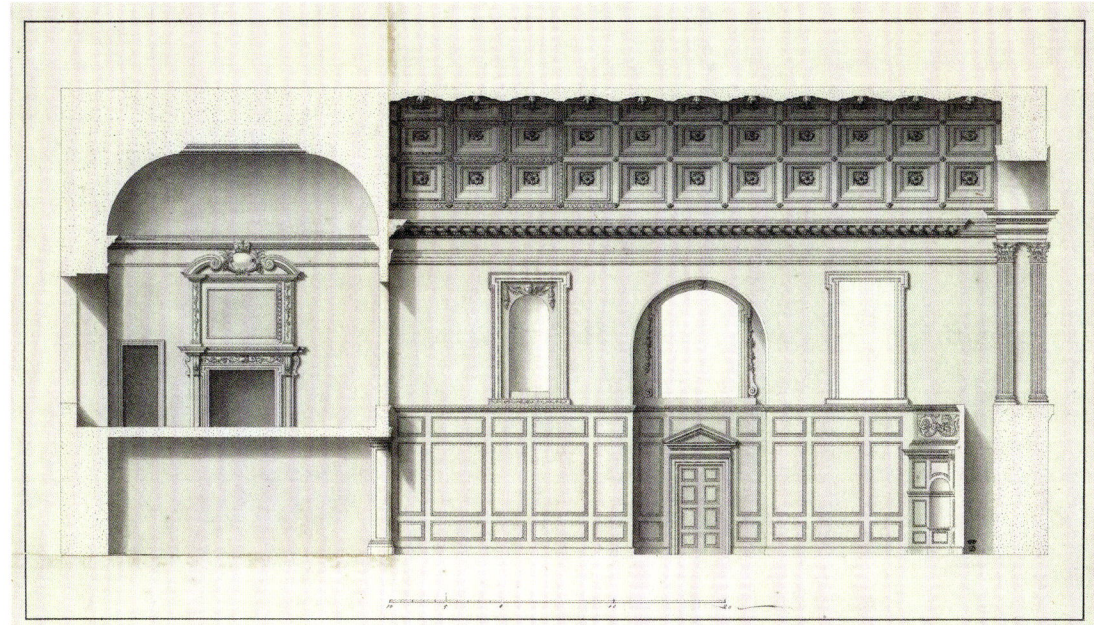

1.16

Henry Flitcroft (1697–1769), long section (west–east) of the Queen's Chapel, St James's, c.1720. Although drawn (at the command of Lord Burlington) after the chapel had been modified many times, Flitcroft's section shows the simplicity and elegance of Jones's design. The chimneypiece in the royal pew is Jones's design. The niche in the north hall was inserted in 1673–4. The central door on the ground floor led to the sacristy (RIBA, SC198/JoI&WeJ[29])

where Catholics may be buried with the ceremonies that are customary'.[121]

On May 3 it was reported that Inigo Jones had been ordered to prepare designs for a chapel for St James's, 'with great state and costliness'. He must have worked fast, for on 14 May, 'a plot of the chapel at St James' was sent to Spain by Secretary Calvert for approval. Not waiting for a reply, the following day Jones submitted an estimate for £5,475 11s 11d, covering the construction of two chapels and fitting up rooms at St James's and Denmark House. The day after that, the Spanish ambassador laid the foundation stone, marking it with a cross and saying a (French) prayer. Things were moving very quickly.[122]

The Tudor chapel at St James's faced north, and it seems as that part of Jones's brief was not to repeat this solecism, but to place the chapel on the east side of the palace so it could be correctly orientated. On the east side was the pheasant yard, a walled enclosure containing pheasant and pigeon houses, built in 1605–9, for Prince Henry, and it was here that the new chapel was to be located.[123] Orientation was one determining factor, but there were others. Key to locating the chapel was to be access both for the princess-to-be, and for her Roman Catholic household. The former required convenient access at first-floor level from the royal lodgings; the latter a passage from the outside. The galleries round the eastern court were the obvious solution to providing a route to the new royal pew, and Jones thus placed the chapel at the north-east corner of the Privy Court, where access was provided by a door at the north end of the cross gallery (see Plans B and C); this led to an antechamber seen on early plans and views. The antechamber led to an outer room, still remaining, with bold acanthus-clad ceiling brackets, and then to the royal pew.

Ground-floor access was more controversial. Under the terms of the marriage treaty, the chapel, or perhaps more accurately, church, was to be open to Roman Catholics at large; thus it had to be possible to enter the west door of the chapel from the street. It was also possible to enter from St James's Park; this was particularly useful for any Catholics at court, who could cross the park from Whitehall and enter the chapel unseen from the street. To make this easy, there was a pathway, eventually walled on both sides, from the park to the south door of the chapel (see Fig. 2.23).

There were no convenient English models for the design of the new chapel. It had been nearly a hundred years since a church had been built for Roman Catholic worship in England,

1. FROM THE HOSPITAL OF ST JAMES TO THE CIVIL WAR

1.17

Anonymous, St James's Palace and the Queen's Chapel from the park, looking west, *c.*1630. The Great Gatehouse can be seen in the background, and the park wall is to the right (London Metropolitan Archives, SC/PZ/WE/01/3048)

1.18

The Curia and Arch of Septimius Severus in the Forum, Rome, from Dupérac 1575, fol. 3. Inigo Jones would have seen the Curia and it may have influenced his design for the chapel at St James's (British School at Rome, Thomas Ashby Print Collection, tapir-L611.D9.003)

and Jones had to balance what would satisfy the Spanish bride and her advisers with what would be acceptable in Protestant London. Jones was also his own man and had clear ideas about how such a building might be designed (Fig. 1.16).

Only two of Inigo Jones's drawings for the chapel survive, for the chimneypiece and overmantel in the chapel closet. Their survival is probably because Jones's pupil, John Webb (1611–72), retained them to use as models for fireplaces in his own buildings at Greenwich.[124] Other than these, we have no contemporary record, yet the basic building-blocks are clear. Jones's chapel was a double cube, a proportion much loved by him and used at the Banqueting House at Whitehall. The west end contained the

40 ST JAMES'S PALACE

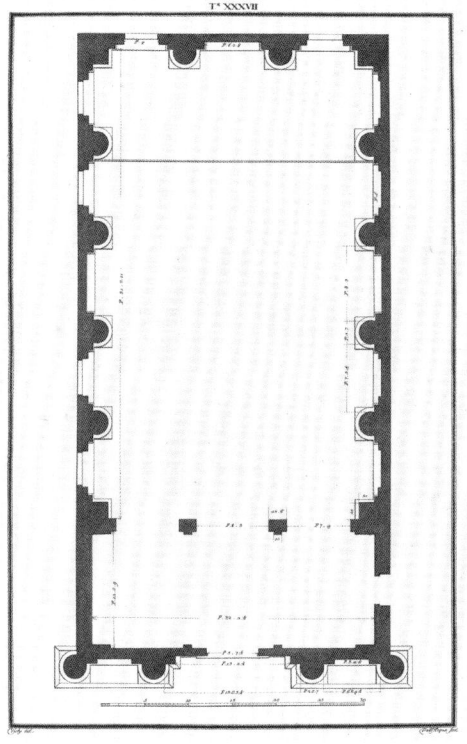

1.19

Plan and elevation of the church of Santa Maria Nova in Vicenza, probably designed by Andrea Palladio (1508–80), 1578–90. Inigo Jones would have seen this building during his visit in September 1613, and it is the most obvious Palladian inspiration for the Queen's Chapel at St James's in terms of both form and function (Bertotti Scamozzi 1776–83, I, pls 37 and 38)

royal closet, elevated and separated from the body of the chapel by a screen with Corinthian pilasters and festoons. The building is astylar externally and relies on the bold use of quoins, cornice, window architraves and pediments to achieve a sense of proportion and architectural articulation. Inside, the ceiling is barrel-vaulted with square coffers, based on Palladio's reconstruction of the Temple of the Sun and Moon in Rome; and the east window is the first use in England of what became known as a Serlian or Venetian window. This can be seen on the earliest surviving image of the chapel, a print from *c*.1630 (Fig. 1.17). Although there was no structural chancel, the presbytery was marked by the gilding of the 28 coffers above.[125]

In designing the chapel, Jones was clearly adhering to the (lost) specification from the Spanish royal household, but he was also drawing on other sources. Some of these were ancient models, and the late Giles Worsley pointed out that one may have been the Curia in the Forum, Rome, a building of similar dimensions to the Queen's Chapel and with an identical modillion cornice (Fig. 1.18).[126]

More significantly, perhaps, Jones had seen the most up-to-date ecclesiastical architecture in his two trips to Italy; in fact, he had probably studied more contemporary Roman Catholic churches than any living Englishman. Of these, perhaps the most relevant to the St James's commission was the small church of Santa Maria Nova, attached to the Augustinian convent of the same dedication in Borgo Porta Nuova on the west side of Vicenza (Fig. 1.19). The convent was patronised by the wealthy of the city and nearby towns; some sent their daughters there as nuns. In 1578, the Vicentine nobleman, Lodovico Trento, commissioned a church that was almost certainly designed by Andrea Palladio and completed by 1590. It was a simple rectangle of very similar dimensions to the St James's chapel, with a hipped roof and a heavy modillion cornice; at the west end there was a raised gallery. The design owed much to the Roman temple at Nîmes that Palladio had illustrated in his *Quattro Libri*. As a chapel attached to a convent for aristocratic patrons, this church may have been in Jones's mind as he considered his response to the commission in London.[127]

His response to the brief, however, was very much in an English vein. The austere and astylar west front of the St James's chapel was

1. FROM THE HOSPITAL OF ST JAMES TO THE CIVIL WAR   41

1.20

Inigo Jones, detail of a design for Prince Charles's lodgings at Newmarket, 1619 (RIBA, SC200/JoI&WeJ[61]2)

1.21

The Queen's Chapel from Marlborough Road. The impression of the western elevation given today is quite different from its historical appearance, as its west end was embedded in a cloister and the whole front was therefore never visible as it is today (see Plans B and C)

a variation on Jones's unbuilt design for the Prince's new lodgings at Newmarket of c.1619 (Figs 1.20 and 1.21). The tripartite division of the west front, articulated, as at Santa Maria Nova, by Corinthian columns, was achieved at St James's by plain, but boldly moulded fenestration, constrained by corner quoins and a string course.[128]

Despite the rush to construct the new chapel for the Spanish bride, in early October 1623, Charles and Buckingham returned to England empty-handed. Though the mission was a failure in terms of its original objectives, everyone was delighted; the heir to the throne had safely returned, and without an unpopular Spanish bride. The bells in the City rang out and the streets surged with rejoicing citizens. In the King's privy chamber at Royston, father, son and favourite hugged and kissed and rejoiced, happy to be together again. At St James's, there was the carcass of a large chapel.

At this point, just who, apart from the architect himself, was interested in the design of the chapel is not clear, because, as will be explained, just as the Spanish match collapsed and was replaced by a French one, James I died and Charles became King. Thus, when Henrietta Maria arrived in England in 1625, it was as Queen Consort, not Princess of Wales, and her attention turned to designing a new chapel at Denmark House, one in which Jones had an active, informed and engaged patroness.[129]

The St James's chapel was thus born of circumstances very different from those pertaining at Denmark House. That chapel owed much more to Counter-Reformation influences introduced by the Queen; at St James's, while the design was influenced by both ancient Rome and Renaissance Italy, its execution was what Jones was to call 'masculine and unaffected' – his own response to Antique and Renaissance sources.[130] In plan and function, it should be noted, the chapel was intensely traditional. A rectangular chapel with an elevated royal closet at the west end was the age-old formula for a royal chapel.

Perhaps influenced by the splendour of the Spanish court and palaces, soon after Charles's return from Spain in the autumn of 1623, it was decided to redecorate his rooms at St James's. The Tudor blue and gold battened ceilings were repainted and gilded with great care, at a cost of some £87, but nothing was done in the consort's lodgings, so recently damned as unfashionable by Lord Pembroke.[131] Back in his redecorated lodgings and seething with animosity against the perfidious Spaniards, Charles opened negotiations for the hand of Henrietta Maria, the 15-year-old sister of the King of France. This was despite his father's continuing hopes for a Spanish match. A treaty was rapidly concluded, allowing Henrietta Maria and her servants to practise their religion, a guarantee for a Roman Catholic chapel open to the public, a promise to bring up her children as Catholics until they were 13, and the relaxation of English recusancy laws.

While detailed arrangements to achieve all this were being made, James I died. He had been in decline for several years, and in the end, he was a pathetic figure, in thrall to his son and to his favourite, the Duke of Buckingham. On 28 March 1625, the day after the old King's death, the Privy Council assembled at St James's and kissed the hand of Charles I. As a mark of respect, Charles kept to his bedchamber at first, but presently dined in his privy chamber (dressed all in black), and after dinner, went to chapel. The body of James I was not taken to Whitehall, but lay in state at Denmark House, so, on 5 April, Charles I slipped through St James's Park and took up residence at Whitehall.[132]

Charles I and Queen Henrietta Maria

The new French queen-to-be arrived in England on 12 June 1625. The only concrete preparation for the practice of her religion was the half-built chapel at St James's. But this had been started on two assumptions: first, that there would be a Princess of Wales living there, and that this would be her chapel before she became Queen; second, that as both the Spanish and French marriage treaties required children of the union to be brought up as Roman Catholics, there would have to be a Catholic chapel at the house of the official royal nursery. In 1625 it was clear that Henrietta Maria would live at the official residence of the Queen Consort, Denmark House, not St James's, and that there was, as yet, no heir to be accommodated. Work on the chapel at St James's thus proceeded extremely slowly. In the summer of 1625, Henrietta Maria was using her closet at Whitehall to hear Mass, and she begged Charles to accelerate the completion of the chapel, but if one contemporary is to be believed, the King told her that if her closet was not large enough she should use her great chamber, that if they could not all fit in there they should use the garden, and if that was proving too small she should move into the park.[133]

The French, like the Spanish, must have been given details of the chapel as designed by Inigo Jones, for Henrietta Maria's extensive trousseau contained everything that was needed to furnish two chapels and equip their staff. Jones's drawings would have indicated, for instance, the number, position and size of the altars, and the Queen's trousseau contained several altarpieces to fit them: three large ones for the chapel and a smaller one for the sacristy.[134] It is likely that the three large paintings were intended for the high altar and two side altars, but in 1625, a crucifixion was commissioned for the high altar at St James's from Francis Cleyn (1582–1658), at a cost of £60, so one of those brought from France must have been deemed unsatisfactory.[135]

The 12 Oratorian priests sent over to serve in the Queen's Chapel were supplied with 12 matching sets of furniture, beds, woollen bedding, tables, chairs and other necessaries – each priest furnished at a cost of 200 livres. But it seems as if they were not stationed at St James's, for Henrietta Maria made Denmark House the centre of her religious life, and the chapel at St James's seems to have been mainly used by her household.[136] The chapel

1.22

Sir Anthony van Dyck (1599–1641), *The Five Eldest Children of Charles I*, 1637 (RCIN 404405)

must have been completed by Easter 1626, however, because that year the Queen and her ladies walked there from Denmark House on Holy Thursday, visiting the Easter Sepulchre they had made there before being driven back by carriage.[137] This was an unusual visit, and after the Queen's Oratorians were expelled and replaced by Capuchin friars in 1630, they were all based at Denmark House. In 1630, a chapel and friary were completed there and the St James's chapel became peripheral to the Queen's religious interests.[138]

After a rocky start to their marriage, Charles and Henrietta Maria gradually reached an accommodation, and then fell in love. The Queen gave birth to a stillborn child in 1629, but in early 1630, the Queen was pregnant again, and Charles, extremely fastidious and eager to maintain the utmost decorum and tradition, ordered the clerk of the wardrobe to consult his department's records to ascertain the etiquette used by Henry VII and Henry VIII for the lying-in of a queen.[139] It was decided that St James's would be the place where she should give birth; this had always been part of its intended role, being close to Whitehall, but far enough away to be free from the infections that made the more crowded royal residences unsafe. Indeed, the Venetian ambassador explained that it had been chosen because 'of its better air and convenience'. Between 1630 and 1637, Henrietta Maria eventually gave birth to five children at the house (Fig. 1.22), coming to believe that it was her lucky place for childbirth.[140]

Each time the Queen neared her due date, the Office of Works would prepare her bedchamber and withdrawing room, and the Great Wardrobe would hang the rooms with rich textiles and beds. The Queen's own lying-in bed was, of course, magnificent, but there was also the lavish royal cradle, with all its bedclothes, as well as beds for the child's nurses and attendants. In the bedroom, the bed was surrounded by a rail, and screens kept off draughts and unwanted observers.[141]

To great national rejoicing, the Queen's first lying-in resulted in the birth of a healthy son, Charles, who was christened at the palace on 27 June 1630. For this important occasion, the court assembled in the privy gallery and the Prince's governess and nurses bore him into the waiting throng. He was then carried through the galleries and the King's presence and guard chambers, down the stairs into the Chapel Royal. The passage through the first court was railed to keep away crowds, who pressed to get a first glimpse of the royal child. The christening party of aristocrats, City aldermen and clergy were admitted to the chapel, where a font had been erected on a dais. Two galleries had been built to make more space for musicians, and the King occupied one side of the holyday closet, looking down on the scene from the glazed window to his pew. After the Prince had been baptised, by the richly coped Bishop of London, trumpets and drums were the signal to hoist a flag on the roof of the gatehouse; this being spied by a lookout on the Banqueting House at Whitehall, a flame was lit that was visible from the Tower of London. The signal spotted, an order was given to fire the Tower's cannon and to let off ordnance from the naval vessels in the Pool of London. The child was then carried back up to the royal lodgings and taken to his mother's bedroom on the south front.[142]

It was during the Queen's pregnancy that orders were given to make improvements to her lodgings and chapel. Various alterations, impossible to identify now, were made to the Roman Catholic chapel and its interior. The Queen's bedchamber was modernised by the addition of a painted frieze above the hangings, with swags of fruit painted to look like marble. In the adjacent drawing room, a large balcony was added, with a handsome balustrade of green-painted turned balusters. This latter improvement brought St James's into line with the consort's withdrawing rooms at all the other royal houses where balconies already existed.[143]

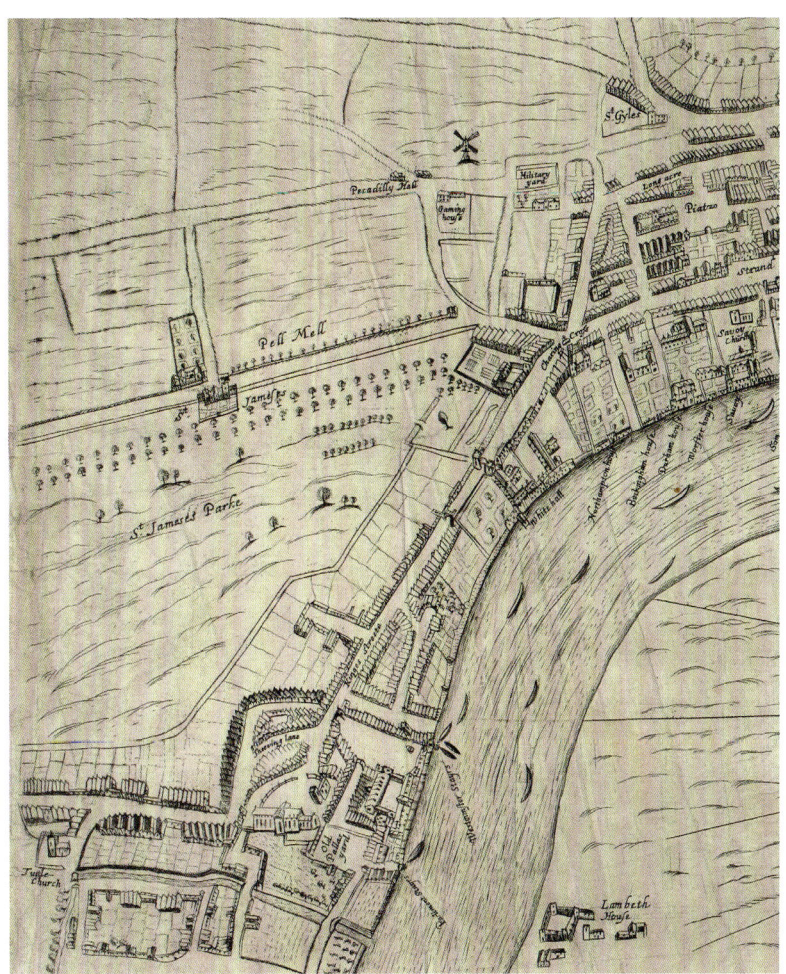

THE GARDENS

The internal decoration and improvements made to the house were minor compared to the extremely ambitious laying-out of a new garden undertaken around 1630–33. To understand exactly what was commissioned, it is necessary to take a few steps back and consider the wider setting of the house.

The park was, from the start, integral to the conception and setting of the house, but the park was always also a public place; not in the sense that it was open to everyone, but in the sense that it was used by the court and household at the King's pleasure. Thus part of the original Henrician construction was a walled private, or privy, garden on the south side of St James's that could be used by the royal family. This is seen on a map of Westminster, dated to 1642–52, amongst the Gough Maps in Oxford (Fig. 1.23). The privy garden, which remains a garden to this day, was used by the royal family

1.23

Map of Westminster in an unknown hand (north is at the bottom), appended to *The Countrymans or Strangers Ready helpe, in his finding of our streeyts, lanes or Places in London* of c.1642–52. The privy garden is clearly shown to the south of the palace (Bodl., Gough Maps London 5)

until the late eighteenth century; stairs from the royal lodgings on the south front provided direct access to it, and a passage on the ground floor allowed it to be approached from the inner courtyards.

Anne of Denmark and Prince Henry were both extremely interested in gardens, and the Queen built a remarkable garden at Denmark House, while the Prince commissioned ambitious gardens at his country house at Richmond-upon-Thames.[144] In May 1609, Alphonsus Fowle, the keeper of the garden at St James's, was granted money to make repairs and alterations there. Fowle had succeeded his father to the post and had built a house, Tart Hall, on the western edge of St James's Park (see pp. 67–9).[145] By this time there were two gardens. The first was the walled privy garden to the south of the house – the exclusive domain of the royal family, accessed either directly from stairs from the royal lodgings or from a ground-floor gate in the middle of the south front. To the east was another walled enclosure known as the orchard. In Tudor and early Stuart garden terminology, this was a pleasure garden, not a garden devoted to arboriculture, though there were trees in it. In 1610–11, stairs with elaborately carved rails, balusters and heraldic beasts were installed, presumably to give access to terraces that ran round the orchard's outer walls. One of the orchard terraces can be seen on an early eighteenth-century view (see Fig. 2.7) and was an essential feature of such a garden, allowing its geometry to be appreciated from above. The orchard also contained a railed walk and an aviary.[146] There is no accurate survey of the orchard before William Morgan's map of 1682, as William Faithorne and Richard Newcourt's map (see Figs 1.10 and 2.4) is inaccurate and fanciful in its depiction of St James's and its gardens. Yet sandwiched between the park boundary to the north and on the alignment of the privy garden to the south, the Tudor and Jacobean orchard must have been the same width as shown by Morgan, and descriptions in 1638 and 1640 state it to have been square, that is to say, of 400 square ft (37.2 m²).[147]

In 1611–12, a wall 10 ft (3 m) high enclosed an irregularly shaped parcel of land in the north-east corner of the park known as the Spring Garden. This was ground that had been fenced by Henry VIII as a plantation, to contain and breed game of various sorts – especially exotic birds.[148] During the reign of Elizabeth I, it acquired the character of a garden with walks and rose-beds, a usage that continued under James I.[149] Enclosing it with a wall, the Prince started to make it a private pleasure garden, a retreat from the main gardens at St James's containing fruit trees and exotic birds. It is possible that it was in front of this new wall, embellished with the Prince of Wales's feathers, that Prince Henry was painted by Robert Peake (see Fig. 1.6). Responsibility for maintaining it, and looking after the wildlife, seems to have remained with the keeper of Whitehall Palace.[150]

Following the death of Prince Henry, one of Prince Charles's first commissions (in 1616–17) was the construction of a tiltyard, 300 ft (91.4 m) long, in the park adjacent to the orchard. One side of this was against the long, high orchard wall; the other was boarded with timber planks and posts. This enclosed tilt was his private practice ground, where he ran at the ring and, in due course, practised jousting, a long course of training that finally bore fruit at his debut tournament in the Whitehall tiltyard in 1620.[151] In 1621–2, the Prince ordered a new sundial for the garden, set on a base of Portland stone, on two stone steps.[152]

This is what is known of the gardens at St James's before 1630, when Henrietta Maria and the King began an ambitious new plan. It is quite certain that this was a joint project because specific references in the accounts refer to their personal participation in its design and procurement.[153] Indeed they both brought elements of their own taste and interest to the project. Henrietta Maria had already been interested in gardens before her arrival in England. After all, she was the daughter of one of the greatest artistic patrons in Europe and had been brought up partly at Saint-Germain-en-Laye, where Marie de' Medici had laid out a famous garden. It is also very likely that the Earl of Danby (1573–1644), Charles I's close friend and the keeper of St James's from 1625, was involved in planning the gardens. He was a great patron of horticulture, and founder of the Oxford Botanic Garden; and his brother, Sir John Danvers, had built a celebrated garden at his house in Chelsea.

Henrietta Maria was a patron of John Parkinson (1567–1650), James I's apothecary, who was the most brilliant botanist of his day. In 1629, Parkinson dedicated his book, the first in English on gardening, *Paradisi in sole Paradisus Terrestris. Or, A Garden of all sorts of pleasant flowers*, to Anne of Denmark, 'knowing your majesty so much delighted with all the fair flowers of a garden'. As a reward, he was appointed *Botanicus Regius Primarius* to Charles I, and provided plants 'for his majesty's use and delight', including fruit trees and vines grown in a small walled garden north of the tennis courts.[154]

Not satisfied with what Parkinson could supply, Henrietta Maria sent to France for trees and plants; she also sent for one of the most fashionable gardeners of his day, André Mollet (d. 1665).[155] The grand old man of French gardening was Claude Mollet (d. 1649), who had laid out gardens for Henry IV at Saint-Germain-en-Laye, Fontainebleau and the Tuileries; he had four sons, all of whom followed in his profession. The most successful was to be André, who, as garden designer and writer of a hugely successful book of designs, *Le jardin de plaisir* (1651; Figs. 1.24 and 1.25), spread their family style across northern Europe. While his father dominated the court of France, André sought patronage elsewhere, and through the agency of Henrietta Maria, was brought to England, appointed chief gardener in December 1627, and asked to redesign the gardens at St James's. It is possible that a survey of St James's, commissioned by the Queen from Richard Hayward, was to furnish him with an accurate survey for the purpose.[156]

Mollet laid out the privy garden as an elaborate scrolling parterre in box, quite a novelty in England at the time. It was described in 1639 as 'parterres of different figures, bordered on every side by a hedge of box'; the walls of the garden were sown with 'all sorts

1.24 and 1.25

Two plates from André Mollet's *Le jardin de plaisir* (1651, pls 8 and 20), illustrating the garden designs laid out at St James's for Henrietta Maria and Charles I, c.1630–33. The top design is for a *parterre de broderie* such as was in the privy garden; the bottom design is for a *compartiment de gazon* and may be the one that was laid out in the orchard

1. FROM THE HOSPITAL OF ST JAMES TO THE CIVIL WAR

1.26
Andrea Palladio, the Tuscan order in a colonnade (Palladio 1570, I, pl. VIII)

1.27
Inigo Jones, design for a gateway for St James's Park, 1627. The gateway was probably erected in 1631–2 (RIBA, SC198/JoI&WeJ[30])

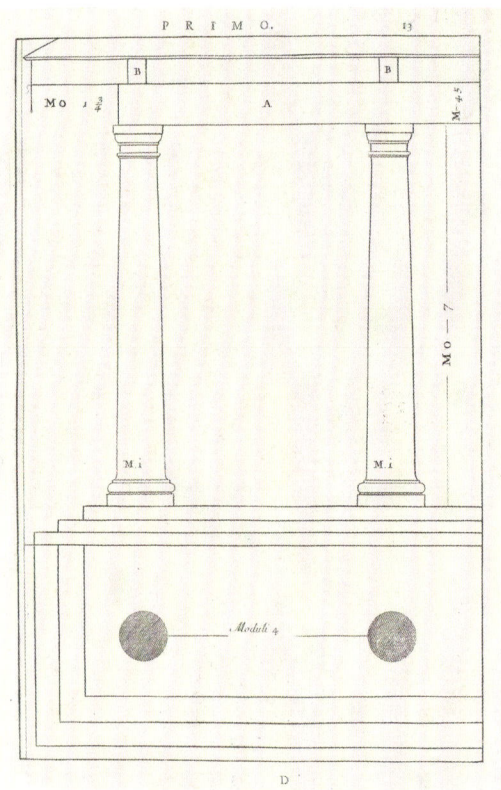

of fine flowers', carefully planted to keep the garden in colour all year round. The orchard next door was in a different style, with 'divers walks, some sanded and others of grass, but both bordered on each side by an infinity of fruit trees'; another description in 1640 characterised it as 'an orchard of fruit trees, planted in a checker pattern, with a big wooden post in the middle, which spouts water'.[157] He must have been quite proud of the work because he published the design in his book, *Le jardin de plaisir* (see Figs 1.24 and 1.25).

In 1629–30, to the walks and trees in the orchard was added a long, low gallery to contain sculpture. This was not England's first sculpture gallery – the Earl of Arundel had already created one at Arundel House on the Strand, where he was painted by Daniel Mytens (c.1590–1647) in 1621 – but it was the first royal one. The gallery was an open colonnade built against the south wall, the section against which the King, when Prince, had built his practice tiltyard. The wall was raised in height by 8 ft (2.4 m), and cleverly, the roof of the gallery was cantilevered over it to provide a deep awning on the park side,

creating a covered way on which the King and his companions could run at the ring.[158] On the garden side, the gallery presented a Tuscan colonnade of oak columns, 10 ft (3 m) high, on stone bases. Palladio, whose villas contain many such atria, states that the pillars should be spaced at four times the column's diameter (Fig. 1.26). The columns were 15 in. (38.1 cm) diameter, so would have been spaced 5 ft (1.5 m) apart, giving a total length for the gallery of around 70 ft (21.3 m). The garden was linked to the park by a new gate, also of the Tuscan order; a drawing in Inigo Jones's hand survives for such a gate, dated 1627 (Fig. 1.27), a couple of years before it was accounted for by the Office of Works. Assuming that the drawing is, in fact, the gate that was built in 1631–2, and that the entablature of the gate would have protruded above the wall-top, it seems as though the wall was 21 ft (6.4 m) high. This would confirm that the sculpture atrium must have been built on top of one of the raised terraces that are shown in later depictions of the gardens, and explains why the spaces between the columns were filled with a balustrade.[159] In 1633–4, the space towards the garden, above the balustrade, was covered in by a timber lattice, presumably for security.[160]

The sculptures, which began to arrive at St James's in 1630, were part of the famous collections of the Gonzaga dukes of Mantua, assembled in the sixteenth century and enriched in the early years of the seventeenth. By 1620, the ducal family was in a state of collapse and desperate for money, and through intermediaries, Charles I bought, first, a large number of the paintings, and then, in a second transaction completed in 1628, more paintings and much sculpture. It is no exaggeration to state that this was one of the most spectacular art purchases of all time, immediately transforming the royal art collection in quantity and quality.

As the works of art arrived in England, they were distributed amongst the royal houses, with Whitehall and Hampton Court receiving many of the largest and most important pieces, but Denmark House and St James's had a role too. In 1634, the writer and commentator Henry Peacham noted Charles I's enthusiasm for antique sculpture, describing 'a whole army of old foreign Emperors, captains and senators all at once to land on his coasts to come and do him homage and attend him in his palaces of St James's and Somerset [Denmark] House'.[161]

As the statues arrived at St James's and were unpacked, some were damaged, and new arms and legs had to be provided; as most of the full-length sculptures were nude, a painter was paid for 'covering the naked places of divers figures'.[162] The consignments from Mantua fed the King's lust for sculpture, and he commissioned the French sculptor and former armourer, Hubert Le Sueur (*c*.1580–1658), to make bronze casts of some of the most important sculptures that he could not get his hands on. For instance, bronzes of the *Farnese Hercules*, '*Spinario*' and the *Borghese Gladiator* (Fig. 1.28) were made for the privy garden at St James's, and marble plinths installed to bear them.[163]

From the inventory of the King's possessions taken in 1649, at that time St James's contained 292 sculptures, 95 statues described under the

1.28
Hubert Le Sueur, the *Borghese Gladiator*, made for St James's privy garden, *c*.1631–2. Le Sueur was sent by Charles I to Italy to make a mould of the original, and its pedestal was made in 1629–30. It was later moved from the privy garden to the end of the 'long water' in the park, where it remained until 1701, when it went to Hampton Court. George IV later moved it, and the other bronzes at Hampton Court, to Windsor, where the statue remains (RCIN 71436)

heading of 'whole figures', 157 'single heads', 51 of which were on pedestals and 40 more busts then kept in the Armoury. It is known that a number of bronzes by Le Sueur were in the privy garden, and certain 'Grecian' busts were sited at the end of alleys in the orchard. There must have been more, for in 1651, the council of state moved 12 statues from the garden at St James's to that at Whitehall. Which sculptures, or how many, were in the garden gallery is uncertain, but it is possible that the 40 oak pedestals, 5 ft (1.5 m) high, painted green and made for marble busts, were placed there, and perhaps another 20 pedestals, also made in 1632–3.[164]

In around 1627–8, the Spring Garden was officially made part of St James's and assigned its own keeper, separate from Whitehall. Improvements were immediately put in hand: the archery butts that had been set up for the King in his youth were relocated, and ground was levelled to make a bowling green within a railed enclosure. A new garden house was built for 'his majesty to repose in'. In 1630, probably to the designs of Mollet, work was under way planting trees, making broderie, planting flowers and building terraces; as well as the bowling green, we learn of 'the bathing

1.29

An engraving by Wenceslaus Hollar, after a painting by Van Dyck. It shows Prince Charles in 1638, when he was eight, at which time he was given his own household and became a Knight of the Garter (he is depicted wearing the Garter sash). Hollar, who published the print in 1649, may have included the Banqueting House in the background as a reference to Charles I's execution; the viewpoint is from St James's (BM, 1856,0607.58)

house pond and fountain'. In 1640, the garden was described as 'a small wood, which contains some quite pleasant avenues'.[165]

THE ROYAL NURSERY AND TREASURE HOUSE

Charles and Henrietta Maria's joint interest in the gardens at St James's was reflected in the rather unusual status of the house itself. The Queen had her own residences – in London, specifically, Denmark House – but St James's became a special sphere of interest for her. In 1628, the King decided to ease the Queen's overstretched finances by granting her additional lands worth £6,000 a year. About half of these had been the King's while he was Prince of Wales, and included most of the royal land to the north of St James's known as the bailiwick.[166] So although she was not granted the house of St James's, its lands, mainly to its north, were now part of her jointure. Modifications and repairs to the house, however, continued to be undertaken by the King's Office of Works, although the Queen did sometimes pay for items from her Privy Purse accounts.

From 1630, the young Prince Charles was the principal resident of St James's. It was here during the winter and autumn that he spent most of his time; in summer he was based at Richmond, in the old Tudor manor. He was joined at St James's by his eldest sister, Mary, in 1631 and by his brother, James, who was born there in November 1633. In due course there were three more children: Princesses Elizabeth (b. 1635) and Anne (b. 1637), and Henry, Duke of Gloucester (b. 1640). Each time the Queen lay in at St James's, the house was refurnished by the Great Wardrobe: hangings, beds, carpets and other furniture were imported from other houses, and a rail brought to surround the Queen's bed.[167] At each birth, more rooms were brought into use as nursery rooms, all furnished richly and in the latest fashion, but there are no records to suggest that the house had to be extended or rooms altered to make space.[168] The children were served by their own kitchen in the complex of workhouses to the west of the house, and Prince Charles had his own flower garden next to the Queen's Chapel.[169] The Prince was also given a chapel establishment, which was supplied with fine vestments, linen and plate. The children used the Tudor Chapel Royal, which was maintained and furnished for them.[170] With each child came a large number of staff: for Prince Charles, for instance, as well as his dry nurses, there were seven rockers who waited on him, each furnished with a gown of 'coronation satin' with a silver lace trimming. These people all required their own lodgings.[171]

The house thus became dedicated to children. In 1645, the thresholds in the doors in the privy lodgings were cut down 'to avoide tumbling' by the toddlers, and a swing was erected. To make it more comfortable at mealtimes, a little bench was made to put beneath the table for Charles and James to rest their feet on. Young Prince Charles, like his father and long-dead uncle, Prince Henry, enjoyed war games, and the Armoury at St James's was full of military models, companies of toy soldiers with their wagon trains and equipment, as well as models of artillery and forts. Some of the miniature brass cannon, made for the Prince in 1638 and 1639, remain in the Royal Armouries, and were probably shot in the park. The King and Queen paid regular visits, and proudly brought visiting relatives and dignitaries to see the children.[172] Plays became a regular feature of family life at the house, and for the King's birthday in 1633, a play called *The Young Admiral* was acted by the Queen's players. During the plague of 1636–7, the royal family all retreated to St James's, where they were kept amused by the Queen's players.[173]

Life at St James's was not all fun for the royal children – they had to attend to their lessons under their tutors and practise riding and archery in the park. Ambassadors were sent to be received by the two Princes: in 1638, the Moroccan ambassador formally took his leave of the boys in the Presence Chamber. That same year, when he was eight (Fig. 1.29), Prince Charles's household was formalised and the Duke of Newcastle made his governor; under Newcastle was a household in miniature, with grooms, ushers, gentlemen and servers – 50 people in all. A set of regulations, an 'establishment book', was issued, setting out the duties and entitlements of household members, and how they should conduct themselves appropriately in the presence of the boy-prince.[174]

St James's was not simply the royal nursery house. When Charles came to the throne, he had not stripped the paintings from the great U-shaped gallery, nor denuded the library of books, nor even extracted the bronzes, medals and coins in the cabinet. In fact, he reinforced St James's as the centre of royal connoisseurship by appointing Prince Henry's collections curator, the Dutch artist and expert in coins and medals, Abraham van der Doort (*c.*1575–1640), as both keeper of the cabinet room and, soon after, surveyor of his pictures – the latter an entirely new post.[175] To the existing collections at St James's, Charles the King added royally. Just as the Mantuan

1.30

Sir Anthony van Dyck, *King Charles I and M. de St Antoine*, 1633. The painting was commissioned for the privy gallery at St James's, where it hung between 1633 and 1649. The King would have appeared to be riding in from St James's Park, which could be seen from the windows of the gallery. It is unclear whether it was given a frame to match the other paintings in the gallery (RCIN 405322)

1. FROM THE HOSPITAL OF ST JAMES TO THE CIVIL WAR

purchase brought statues to the garden, so came great paintings to the gallery. In 1639, it was described admiringly. It was still the three-sided gallery of the Tudor period and retained many pictures from Prince Henry's time, but there were important additions from Mantua, including 12 heads of Caesar by Titian (c.1488/90–1576; one was actually by Van Dyck), and seven smaller portraits of mounted emperors by Giulio Romano.[176]

As far as we know, only one painting had actually been commissioned for the room: Sir Anthony van Dyck's equestrian portrait of *King Charles I and M. de St Antoine* (Fig. 1.30). This painting is one of only a handful of its period that we know were commissioned for a particular location. In 1639, the French traveller Sieur de la Serre described it hanging at the junction of two of the galleries, most likely at the end of the privy gallery on the east wall of the cross gallery – the only gallery end without a door or window. It was a big canvas, 12 ft (3.7 m) high and more than 8 ft (2.7 m) wide; it must have hung more or less floor to ceiling, dominating the long view down the privy gallery, 18 ft (5.5 m) wide. With this in mind, Van Dyck created an architectural setting for the mounted King that could have been part of the panelled gallery itself. The deep perspective and illusionistic effect of the archway must have given the impression that the King was riding in from the park.[177]

A second enormous canvas was placed in the gallery, measuring 13 ft by 7 ft (4 by 2.1 m), much the same size as the Van Dyck, and possibly to balance it. This was *Daedalus and Icarus*, a painting by Giulio Romano, now lost, but valued during the Commonwealth at £500, a vast sum. At that time, it was at Greenwich, apparently in a ceiling, but in 1631–2 it hung at St James's.[178] This painting, together with the other Mantuan paintings, was furnished with a matching frame by the Office of Works, and painted 'sad lute colour' with a gilded 'small fillet' by the sergeant painter. In 1634–6, eight more 'large' frames were made for the gallery, en suite with the earlier set. Together, they must have presented an extremely coherent and carefully composed hang, arranged between the pilasters of the gallery, while over the doors were already the panels of seascapes acquired by Prince Henry. In 1633, more frames were made for paintings in the Queen's rooms, including a large frame for the overmantel in her bedchamber in black and gold.[179]

The cabinet room was in the innermost royal lodgings and of very restricted access. Its precise location is unclear, but it was most likely in the south-east corner of the inner court. After its contents had been relocated to Whitehall in 1638/9, Abraham van der Doort made a comprehensive list of the 'pictures and rarities' that it contained. It is not clear how much of this ever-expanding collection had come from St James's, but the list gives the impression of a room crammed with paintings, miniatures, drawings, books, bronzes, reliefs, jewels, minerals, plate, coins and medals. Marginal notes suggest that the room at St James's was fitted out with cupboards and drawers in which at least part of the collection was housed.[180]

When the contents of St James's was inventoried by the parliamentary surveyors, in 1649–50, it was still full of artworks: some 550 paintings, 300 pieces of sculpture, more than 100 hangings, plus beds and carpets. The intensity of Charles's collections at St James's suggests an interest in and use of the house that is not paralleled in the record of the royal itinerary. As far as can be told, the King rarely spent the night there, so he must have visited on day trips, crossing the park from Whitehall and returning afterwards. Indeed, during the late 1630s, the house was full of children and their attendants, and Prince Charles may have been using the sovereign's side. The rich collections at St James's were thus not only for the King's private delectation, but also for the edification and education of his children – material for historical, artistic and cultural instruction. Just as James I established a library for Prince Henry, so Charles I ensured that books, paintings, sculpture and antiquities were available for the Princes Charles and James.

There is no record of why the King decided to move his cabinet from St James's to Whitehall in 1638/9, but it is likely to have been a consolidation of the cream of his collection in the inner rooms of the Whitehall privy gallery. Here they could be enjoyed by the King, shown to his guests, and guarded by his curator, Van der Doort. At any rate, in the autumn of 1638, the Dowager Queen of France, Henrietta Maria's mother, Marie de' Medici, arrived in England. For most Englishmen, she was an unwanted and embarrassing guest. Exiled from France, and shooed away from the Spanish Netherlands, she disembarked with six coaches, 70 horses and a retinue of 160. She expected her son-in-law to provide for her, and he, dutifully but reluctantly, ordered, in November, that she was to receive £100 a day from the Exchequer. It was also decided that Marie should be given St James's as her residence – a place that the Venetian ambassador thought 'the usual lodging for royalty in this city'. The house was in the midst of being prepared for the Queen's lying-in, and furniture already delivered had to be quickly relocated, as furnishings were assigned from the Great Wardrobe for the Queen Mother and her attendants.[181]

While the Queen Mother was in residence, one of her retinue, the Sieur de la Serre, had the opportunity to view the state rooms and record what he saw. His description is essentially of the Tudor chambers, hung with the best tapestry the Great Wardrobe could supply. As expected, the presence and privy chambers had cloths and chairs of estate. The bedchamber contained a bed of black velvet, gold-fringed, with chairs and stools to match. The walls were hung with new silk tapestries of the Nine Worthies, upon which were mounted silver sconces; a crystal chandelier hung from the middle of the room. Near the Queen Mother's closet was her private chapel, and this opened onto the great gallery that has already been described. The gallery, de la Serre tells us, led to the 'Great Chapel', which, being Roman Catholic, was assigned to the Queen Mother.[182]

The Civil Wars

Charles I was King in two countries, and in Scotland he came to believe that there was a conspiracy to subvert his rule. This was because the Scottish Church refused to accept any kind of conformity with the Church of England, and indeed, declared its opposition both to the King's prayer book and to the authority of bishops. Charles saw this as a direct challenge to his right to rule and resolved to bring the Scots to heel by military action. In 1639–40, there were two military expeditions to Scotland, known as the Bishops' Wars. Both resulted in humiliation for the King, and the Treaty of Ripon, which concluded the second 'war', committed the Crown to pay the Scots a substantial daily subsidy.

Before the Scottish wars, Charles had ruled in England without Parliament for 11 years, but the necessity to raise finance for his army and to pay the Scots' subsidy forced him to call Parliament to vote him supply. On 3 November 1640, what became known as the Long Parliament met; nobody could have known at the time that it was to sit intermittently for 20 years and was to go to war against its sovereign.

In 1640, London was in a febrile state. There was widespread anxiety about a Roman Catholic conspiracy, fed by a loathing of Henrietta Maria's Capuchin Friary at Denmark House and her Roman Catholic chapel at St James's. London crowds demonstrated at the gates of Lambeth Palace, Denmark House and in the streets of Westminster. The Queen Mother at St James's became a target, the protesters believing she was sheltering the 'Pope and the Devil' there. Marie, terrified, was granted a protective guard of 50 men.[183]

The Queen Mother was now more than an unwanted guest, she was a political liability and a drain on resources that Charles could ill afford. Her monthly allowance of £3,000 was first reduced and then, eventually, stopped. Marie had to dismiss many of her household, sell some of her horses, and drastically reduce the state in which she lived. In the end, it was not the King's views that were important, but those of the Long Parliament; in May 1641, the House of Commons requested her to leave the country due to the disquiet caused by 'the flowing of Priests and Papists to her House; and, by the Use and Practice of the Idolatry of the Mass, and Exercise of other superstitious Services of the Romish Church'.[184]

The problem was that nobody wanted her – she was unwelcome in both France and the Low Countries, and to boot, she had no money to move. As the very soldiers who guarded her asked to be relieved of their dreary responsibilities, Parliament granted her £3,000 with which to take herself to the continent, and in August 1641, she left St James's for Cologne.[185] St James's was vacated not a moment too soon, for Charles I urgently needed to move his children there from Whitehall, which had been the focus of popular demonstrations against the King's leading minister, the Earl of Strafford (1593–1641). Prince James, Princess Elizabeth and Henry, Duke of Gloucester, were settled at St James's amidst tight security.

In January 1642, after a botched attempt to arrest five members of Parliament, whom Charles regarded as opposition ringleaders, the King, Queen and Prince of Wales fled to Hampton Court and then to Windsor, leaving the younger children at St James's. The Queen was sent abroad to Holland, and despite Parliament's attempts to secure Prince Charles, father and son made their way north to York. In due course, the King sent for James, Duke of York, leaving Princess Elizabeth and her baby brother, Henry, Duke of Gloucester, at St James's, under the care of Jane, Countess of Roxburghe (c.1585–1643), a committed Roman Catholic and Henrietta Maria's closest confidante and companion. The Wardrobe, meanwhile, was ordered to take items from St James's and send them on for Prince Charles's use.[186]

Frustrated by all attempts to reach a consensus with Parliament, Charles I raised his standard at Nottingham Castle on 22 August 1642, and for three years and eight months the British Isles descended into the chaos of civil war. London was in the hands of Parliament and here the mob propelled anti-Catholic sentiment to fever pitch. Even before the King had declared war, the House of Commons was debating legislation to curb what it saw as popish practices in parish churches, but these were nothing compared to the alleged idolatry at the Queen's chapels.

In November 1642, the Commons ordered the sheriffs of London and Middlesex to 'reform' the royal chapels at Denmark House and St James's, and the Queen's Capuchin friars at Denmark House were given notice to quit the country.[187] The French ambassador protested, citing the Queen's marriage treaty, which guaranteed her freedom of worship in her two chapels. This diplomatic protest was effective enough to stay the hand of the iconoclasts, but not for long. In April 1643, Parliament set up the Committee for the Demolition of Monuments of Superstition and Idolatry, under the chairmanship of Sir Robert Harley, Master of the Mint, with a zeal for purifying churches that he considered to have fallen victim to idolatry. The following month, he issued an order to London churchwardens requiring, amongst other reforms, all images and crucifixes to be removed and destroyed.[188] This seems to have triggered a move to burn all the 'Romish Rubbish and Superstitious Trumperie' at Denmark House and St James's on 23 May (Fig. 1.31). This, it seems, probably only included Mass books and other small items, because the House of Lords had prohibited any direct attacks on royal property.[189]

But St James's was too important to be left alone. Two royal children lived there and it was still entirely possible that one or other of them might, one day, reign in place of their father (Fig. 1.32). With the King on the field of battle, Parliament effectively took the children as wards. As there was no formal mechanism for funding their household, Lady Roxburghe, in a state of desperation, petitioned Parliament for an allowance, and it was agreed that £800 a month would be provided. Traumatically for the children, Lady Roxburghe died in May 1643, and Parliament appointed a Committee under Cornelius Holland, MP (1600–?71), for the 'Regulating of the Household of Saint James's'. From Parliament's point of view, Holland was a shrewd choice. He was of a family long in court service, and had himself risen to be paymaster and Clerk of the Green Cloth to the Prince of Wales. He had left royal service in 1641 and had become one of the most radical of the MPs opposing the Crown – indeed, eventually, one of the regicides. Holland thus understood both how to run the little household and how to reform it. As well as controlling resources, his committee was asked 'to inform themselves, what Papists, and other disaffected Persons to the Parliament, are Attendants upon or Servants to the Children at St James'; and 'to inform themselves, what disaffected Ministers do preach there; and to appoint able Divines to preach there in their stead; and to see defaced any superstitious Pictures at the Chapel at St James'.[190]

In early 1644, it was still felt that the servants of the King's children were a focus of opposition and a conduit for royalist communications, and a general purge was enforced at St James's, with 11 servants thrown out. In March, a list of approved servants and a new set of household regulations were published. The new houschold was mainly female and comprised rockers for the baby prince, chamber ladies and a laundress. The men included a physician, French master, pages, a wardrobe keeper, tailor, cap-maker and shoemaker. There were also footmen, a chariot-man and a small contingent who worked in the kitchen. Most notable were the six resident chaplains under Samuel Torshell, the household chaplain. This platoon of ministers conducted prayers and exposition of the scriptures for an hour each morning and each afternoon, with two sermons on Sundays. Security was tight: the gates were locked at sunset and nobody was permitted entry after 10pm. New sets of master keys were made and issued to household staff.[191]

1.31

The burning of 'superstitious' books and images at St James's and Somerset House [Denmark House] on 23 May 1643, from Vicars 1648, p. 19 (BL, Prints and Drawings, G.4099)

1.32

In 1643, London was enclosed within defences thrown up against a possible attacking Royalist army. William Stukeley (1687–1765) sketched this plan of the remaining ramparts at the Restoration. St James's was near the largest of the peripheral artillery positions, as marked by ∆ on the plan (Corpus Christi College, Cambridge, MS 613)

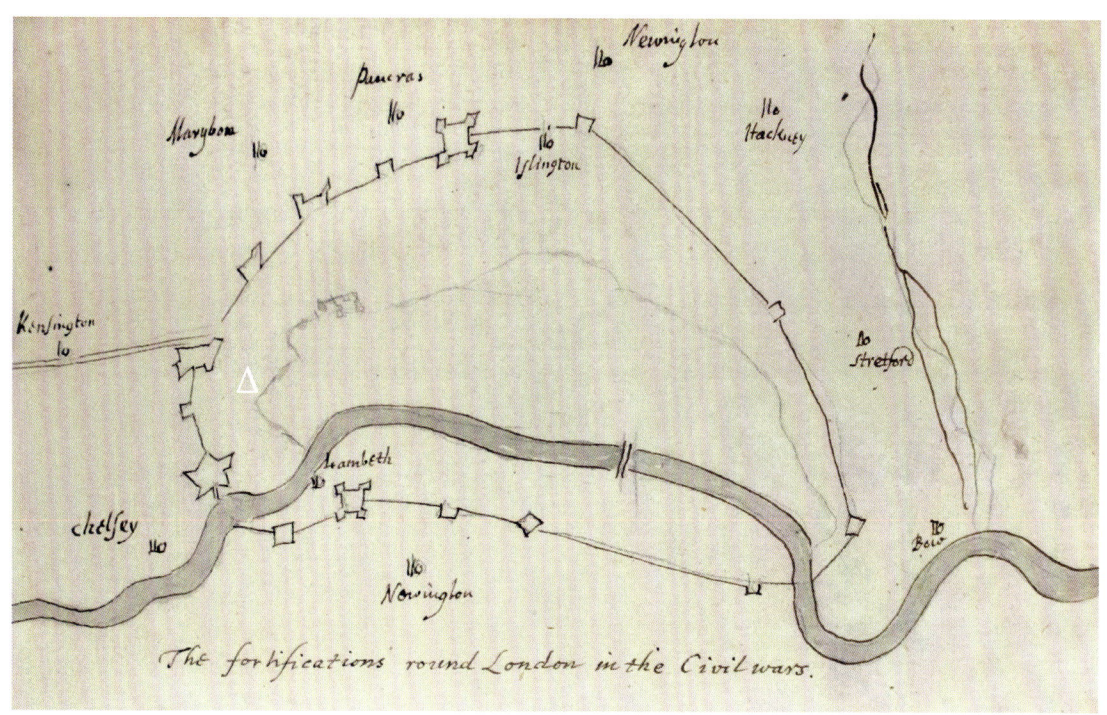

1. FROM THE HOSPITAL OF ST JAMES TO THE CIVIL WAR

The death of Lady Roxburghe gave the opportunity for Parliament to appoint Mary, Lady Vere (1581–1671), in her stead. In complete contrast to Roxburghe, Vere was a Calvinist Presbyterian and in an inner circle of Puritan opponents to the Crown. She had introduced Sir Robert Harley to his future wife, Brilliana, and in 1642, the Harleys sent their daughter, also called Brilliana, to live with Lady Vere to be at her house in Hackney. Parliament wanted Lady Vere in charge of the royal children to ensure they were brought up under godly guidance. The appointment found little favour with Princess Mary, the King or the House of Lords, and her appointment by the Commons was never confirmed by the upper house; indeed, in July 1643, it was decided that Mary Sackville, Countess of Dorset (1586–1645), should become governess of the children's household instead. As a Protestant and former governess to both the Prince of Wales and the Duke of York, she seems to have been acceptable to all concerned.[192]

Although Lady Vere had not been accepted, Harley and Holland were still in charge of the household at St James's, and Harley himself inspected both chapels to ensure their suitability for the children's religious improvement. Inevitably, he was outraged by both the Roman Catholic and the Anglican chapels and drew up a detailed specification for the reformation of both. Holland was asked to supervise, and the parliamentary workmen duly started work in April 1644. In the Roman Catholic chapel, the altar rails and side chapels were demolished and the whole chapel floor was levelled, removing all altar steps. In the Tudor chapel, the Communion rail and a tapestry depicting the Virgin Mary were removed, while wall paintings of the Virgin were whitewashed and sculptures of the Sacred Wounds of Christ (hands, feet and heart) were destroyed.[193] Some thought the Catholic chapel should simply be demolished, 'for it was full of adultery and idolatory', and was where the Queen 'committed all her sin in this kingdom, and the iniquity cannot but sink deeply into the walls'.[194]

Harley's orders give a remarkable picture of the Anglican chapel in Charles I's time. From the start of his reign, the King had embarked on a programme of enforcing order, decorum and dignity in the royal chapels, but had also embellished them to reflect the beauty of holiness. At St James's, he had regilded the ceiling of his closet, but Harley's list shows that the chapel also contained overtly Catholic images, in particular the tableaux of the Sacred Wounds.[195]

In early 1645, the Countess of Dorset fell ill, and in March, as she was dying, Algernon Percy, Earl of Northumberland (1602–68), was appointed governor to the royal children in her stead. Formerly in command of the navy and in high office in the Cavalier army, he was now a moderate Parliamentarian. The Commons authorised Northumberland to draw on royal possessions from any residence to accommodate suitably the children.[196]

In 1646–7, the children spent some time at the Earl of Northumberland's Syon House to the west of London, but their headquarters remained at St James's, where, after the surrender of Oxford to the Parliamentarians in the spring of 1646, they were joined by their elder brother, James, Duke of York. The return of Prince James was the most magnificent royal event in London since Charles's return from Scotland in 1641. He arrived in the City with a large train of coaches and was given a warm welcome by both people and aldermen, before being conveyed, in state, to St James's. The welcome was an ambiguous one. While, on the one hand, some were speaking of placing James on the throne instead of his father, on the other, his servants and attendants were dismissed by Parliament and replaced with those deemed to be suitable and reliable. The Earl of Northumberland had the unenviable job of looking after the petulant teenager, and discovering that the £600 granted to him for setting up the Prince had to be supplemented by substantial amounts of his own cash.[197]

As Charles I's rule imploded, so the various offices of the Royal Household were taken over by men appointed by Parliament. In the summer of 1642, Inigo Jones left his post as Surveyor of the King's Works in the hands of his deputy, John Webb, and joined the King in the field. In his absence, he was declared a delinquent and a fine of £1,000 set on his estate. Soon, Webb was expelled from office too, and replaced by Edward Carter, Jones's former executive officer at St Paul's. Carter was an experienced administrator and an architect in his own right, and from 1643 he began to receive monies from Parliament's Committee for the Revenue, for maintaining central government buildings at Westminster and the King's houses in and around London. For six years he received annual disbursements in the region of £1,800.[198]

Throughout the period, other than Whitehall, which was requisitioned by Parliament as an administrative headquarters, St James's saw the lion's share of works expenditure (Fig. 1.33). The surviving particulars are almost all for repairs rather than alterations, but the accounts make it clear that the royal children had separate lodgings and their governors their own apartments.[199] One interesting anomaly in this period concerns the heading used in the accounts for 1644–5, where the house is called 'the palace of St James'. Up to this point, the house was always referred to as the manor of St James, and later, the house of St James. Whether this single instance was a slip of the clerk's quill or a pointed reference to the regality of the place will never be known.[200]

In the summer of 1646, the King gave himself up to the Scots; then, as prisoner of Parliament, and subsequently of the army, he was moved between various royal houses, ending up at Hampton Court in August 1647. Here, the royal children were allowed to visit, and on one of those visits, Charles told the Duke of York that he should escape and join his mother in France.[201] James made various attempts to give his guards the slip, and Parliament angrily threatened him with being taken to the Tower before coercing him to swear an oath not to escape. The fact that he did eventually successfully steal away from St James's suggests that, at the very least, the Earl of Northumberland turned a blind eye. The children were allowed the run of the house and grounds, and the Duke had taken to playing hide and seek each evening with his siblings.

One night in April 1648, the Duke slipped away to a waiting accomplice in the middle of a game. He donned a wig and they walked through the park to the Spring Garden, from where they took a coach to the City. Dressed as a woman in a specially made outfit, James took a barge to a waiting ship and sailed for Holland.[202] The immediate consequence of the Duke's escape was that Northumberland was instructed to move the children from St James's to Syon House, dismiss their servants and keep them under close guard.[203]

At the end of 1648, when some believed there was a chance that the King and Parliament would finally come to some kind of accommodation, the army took matters into its own hands. Expelling MPs who supported an agreement with the King, they pushed for a trial at which Charles would be held to account for making war on his people. Events moved quickly, and the King was brought in the royal coach from Windsor to St James's, and taken to the sovereign's rooms to await trial.

The army had already reduced the number of attendants accompanying him and had passed a resolution that he should not dine in state, but be served privately. So when Charles arrived at St James's on 19 January, he was confined to his bedchamber and was not allowed to leave to eat, pray or even relieve himself. Soldiers were posted on rota in the room, and drank and smoked in his presence. The following day, the King was moved across the park to Whitehall, and then to the house of Sir Thomas Cotton (1594–1662), on the river, next to Westminster Hall, where his trial took place. The proceedings over, he was conveyed in a closed sedan chair back to St James's. Here, he spent his last days in his bedchamber, closely attended by the Bishop of London, William Juxon.

The Duke of Gloucester and Princess Elizabeth were brought from Syon House to say goodbye, the emotional scene recorded by the King's valet, Sir Thomas Herbert. After the official sentence was pronounced in Westminster Hall, it was proposed to station two musketeers in the condemned King's bedchamber, but Herbert and Juxon won the King his last night in peace and contemplation.

1.33

St James's as it may have appeared in 1640, reconstructed using surviving building and topographical sources. By this date the building's isolation had been reduced by the construction of Berkshire House opposite the kitchen yards, yet its location was still remote and secure; the gardens were safe within St James's Park, but the tennis court, physic garden and pell mell lay outside the secure zone. The layout of the kitchens is the most conjectural part of this reconstruction

On the day of his execution, the army was determined to prevent any attempted disruption, and the way across the park from St James's to Whitehall was lined by foot soldiers. On the morning of 30 January, Charles I walked between two companies of halberdiers, their great drums beating, to Whitehall, where he was taken to his bedchamber for his last prayers before walking onto the scaffold. The King's decapitated body was at first put on show at Whitehall, then entombed in a coffin and taken back to St James's, before being moved to Windsor for burial.[204]

The Commonwealth and Protectorate

While the sprawling galleries and halls of Whitehall had been used by both Parliament and the army since 1642, St James's had remained an operating royal residence. In June 1644, Parliament had seized some jewels and plate from there to pay for shot for the army, but other than this, the royal art collection and all other furnishings in the house and grounds remained intact.[205] Indeed, as Whitehall filled up with troops in 1647–8, Parliament ordered that all the most important books, manuscripts and antiquities be moved from there, for safe keeping, to St James's, by the King's librarian, Patrick Young. As this order was being carried out, Young received another, this time by the hand of the King himself. Charles, incarcerated at Carisbrooke Castle, asked Young to consult the antiquary, Sir Simonds D'Ewes, and organise his coin collection, placing specimens in date order and removing duplicates.[206]

But St James's was no longer under royal control. In August 1648, Parliament had appointed the Independent minister and arch-critic of the King, Hugh Peter (1598–1660), to be in charge of the house. At the Restoration, he was accused of stealing, or at least selling, coins and manuscripts from the library. Although Peter denied it, in 1649 it was believed that items had gone missing and that there had been a plan afoot to sell everything. The more sophisticated members of the Council of State recognised that the collection, with the exception of that in the Vatican Library, was the finest in Europe, and one of the Commissioners of the Great Seal, Bulstrode Whitelocke (1605–75), claimed that its loss 'would be a dishonour and damage to our nation, and to all scholars therein'. The Council duly appointed Whitelocke as library keeper, giving him lodgings at St James's and authority to appoint a deputy. Anxious about the security of the collection, he appointed John Durie (1596–1680) as deputy and holder of the keys. He was instructed to collaborate with Patrick Young, the former royal librarian and an old friend of Whitelocke's, in compiling a full catalogue of books and manuscripts, as well as the coin and medal cabinet.[207]

Soon, there was pressure to bring the whole collection to Whitehall, where it would be safer, but despite several orders to this effect, the library and cabinet stayed put. Indeed, it was proposed that they should be moved from the former privy lodgings and placed in the Roman Catholic chapel, which would be set up as a public library. The Surveyor of Works was instructed to start converting the chapel immediately, and John Durie was told to move the books the moment it was completed. In fact, this ambitious idea may have been Durie's. A former Church of Scotland minister, who had lived in the Netherlands and Germany and returned to be tutor to the royal children, Durie was a promoter of educational reform as a way of creating a New Jerusalem in the English Commonwealth. In 1650, he published a tract entitled *The Reformed Library Keeper*, in which he argued that libraries were 'a public stock of learning'. There were several in the Council of State who also believed in widening educational opportunities beyond the social and economic elite, and a public library would further this ambition.[208]

The army coup that had led to the trial and execution of the King saw London under military occupation and many public buildings were requisitioned. Colonel John Berkstead's regiment was billeted at Whitehall, and Colonel Thomas Pride's at St James's. One month after the King's death, Whitehall was declared to be the headquarters of the Council of State and repairs were put in hand to accommodate this. The palace was besieged by petitioners, clamouring for rewards, justice, patronage or redress of personal grievances, and there were also ill-intentioned royalists who had scores to settle and who would have liked to overthrow the regime.[209]

Security was the primary concern and St James's was the obvious place to station a large force to protect Whitehall. The St James's regiment, initially under Thomas Pride, had responsibility for securing the park and providing a 24-hour rotating guard for Whitehall. As time passed, the Council of State tried to demilitarise Whitehall and find alternative billets for the soldiers and prisoners lodged there. More prisoners were moved to St James's, as command of the garrison was passed over to Major General Thomas Harrison.[210] In December 1651, a young gentleman in the train of an embassy from the States General of the Dutch Republic visited London and found Whitehall dingily occupied by the Council of State, and St James's completely inaccessible, heavily garrisoned and full of prisoners.[211]

Of the many problems that the Council of State faced the most pressing was that of the royal debts. The Civil War had left a large number of former royal servants and suppliers with substantial unpaid bills, and there was a widespread view that for justice to be done, these should be paid. The Council of State resolved that the best way to do this would be to sell royal property, at least that part which the Council would not require itself. Acts were passed in 1649, and again in 1651, to give the powers and establish the mechanisms for the sale of both the buildings and their contents.

In 1649, the King owned around 20 private residences, in addition to the uninhabited royal castles. Most of these would be sold, but in May 1649, Parliament decided to reserve Greenwich, Hampton Court, St James's, Theobalds, Windsor, Whitehall and Somerset House for state use. Ultimately, Greenwich and Theobalds would be sold, but the others were kept, and St James's, as in royal times, remained a pendant to Whitehall.[212] Somerset House was cleared to create an art repository and saleroom, and the process of inventorying the vast Royal Collection began. It was slow, chaotic and expensive. The market was flooded, buyers were reluctant to come forward and there was confusion over what the Council of State wished to reserve for its use. In all, the sales failed to yield anything approaching what had been predicted.

At St James's, the priority was to prevent the embezzlement of royal treasures; an order was issued in February 1649 to safeguard the 'Publick Library', statues in the garden and works of art. The former royal librarian, Patrick Young, was instructed immediately to make a full inventory of the 2,755 books held in the library. Meanwhile, the process of inventorying the other contents began in the summer of 1649, but it seems that most of the furniture had already been moved to Somerset House for safe keeping. The parliamentary surveyors arrived at St James's and found some 300 items of statuary that were still there, a collection of more than 550 paintings and the contents of the Armoury.[213]

The statues have already been mentioned, and 12 were chosen from amongst these that would be moved to Whitehall and placed in the privy garden, while the plinths of others were moved to the Whitehall privy gallery.[214] The list of paintings is split between those recorded *in situ* and those already moved to Somerset House. Around 270 were still hanging in various (unidentified) rooms and these can be taken as an indication of the picture hang in St James's while a royal residence. There were landscapes and scenes from classical mythology, but the largest number were portraits, a few of British and European royalty, but mainly of courtiers and individuals whom those drawing up the list could not identify.

The second largest category of paintings was of religious subjects, more than 70 in all. A large number of these (22) were paintings of the Virgin Mary. These covered her entire life, from childhood to the Annunciation, through her marriage to the birth and adulthood of Christ, and the Assumption. It is not clear where any of these were hung, but there were enough of them to assume that they were in all the principal suites occupied by the royal children, who had clearly been exposed to their mother's tastes. There is a single reference to a painting in a specific location: a canvas of St Agnes by Antiveduto Grammatica (1571–1626), over the chimney in 'the bedroom'. St Agnes was the virgin martyr of ancient Rome, and Grammatica worked in the highly dramatic style of Caravaggio. It was thus probably a striking image of female martyrdom hung in one of the principal bedrooms.

Prince Charles and Prince James grew up in the vast three-sided gallery hung with the two series of heads of Roman emperors, one by Titian and the other by Giulio Romano (see p. 52). Like Henry VIII's choice of stucco and terracotta moulded Roman emperors at Nonsuch, set out as a tutorial for his son, Prince Edward, these heroic figures in the house of Charles I's sons were surely part of his programme of education for the boys.

Other than paintings, we learn of an armoury that contained a collection of military toys, presumably belonging to the various Stuart children, and a collection of Japanese armour. Apart from a bedchamber and the Armoury, the only precise location specified in the parliamentary surveyors' lists was Colonel Pride's room. It seems as though he may have been lodging in part of the library or cabinet, as various books of prints and drawings are listed, including a book of prints with 'cats' faces'. Hanging on the walls were a moonlight scene and a still life, but, most interestingly, he also enjoyed a silver table and silver andirons, the most valuable items listed in the house.[215]

While all these items were removed and sold, the library remained. Always referred to as the 'Public Library at St James's', it, like so much in the Interregnum, was put under the control of a committee, and Whitelocke handed the keys to administer the library on a day-to-day basis. The library remained important to the new power elite at Whitehall, and while Whitelocke was away on a diplomatic mission in Sweden, Henry Lawrence (1600–64), Cromwell's future Lord President of the Council, was appointed keeper in his stead. He ordered that the books be moved to a larger room.[216]

In September and October 1654, the remaining Royalist prisoners were removed from the house, and in December 1654, St James's was one of the former royal houses vested in the Lord Protector. Cromwell (1599–1658) showed no personal interest in it, and throughout the Protectorate it was used as a barracks for a foot regiment which was guarding Whitehall.[217]

As Cromwell assumed his new role, so responsibility for state buildings was transferred from Edward Carter, as Surveyor of Works, to the former royal sergeant plumber, John Embree. Embree was more in tune with the new regime, purchasing a large quantity of former royal artworks at the Somerset House sales. He speculated in church lands and even bought former royal buildings in Scotland Yard. He was an active surveyor whose focus was the buildings occupied by Cromwell as Protector: Whitehall, the Charing Cross mews and Hampton Court. In this very poorly documented period, it is likely that nothing beyond basic maintenance was undertaken at St James's.[218]

Oliver Cromwell died in 1658, and in the May of the following year, Parliament reconstituted a Council of State, one of whose immediate tasks was not only to safeguard the public library at St James's, but also to consider the sale of the remaining paintings and statues there. The sale of the house itself was contemplated, but in the end, it was resolved that it should be presented to Mrs Cromwell as a dower house. This was a handsome gift, together with a £20,000 annual allowance. The soldiers were ordered out and work began on cleaning up the place.[219] But in the end, it was not for Cromwell's widow that the house was to be prepared, but for the commander-in-chief of the army, George Monck (1608–70).

In the chaotic period after Cromwell's death and the deposition by the army of his son, Richard (1626–1712), there was a struggle for power between Parliament and the army; St James's became the headquarters of the army, with Richard Cromwell living at Whitehall.[220] Eventually, General Monck, whom Cromwell had made commander-in-chief in

Scotland, marched south at the head of an army, to defend Parliament against the radicals in the English army. Parliament offered him £1,000 and St James's as his base if he would consent to come to London to safeguard the Commons. Thus, from March 1660, it was from St James's that Monck choreographed the Restoration, and as he made his way to Dover to welcome Charles II (r. 1660–85), the last of the troops were ejected from St James's and preparations began to restore it to the Crown.[221]

The Bailiwick of St James's before 1660

The process by which Henry VIII acquired St James's and several thousand acres of land around it has already been described (see p. 18). These land purchases created not only the topographical context for St James's, but its social and political environment. When Lord Burghley, as High Steward of Westminster, introduced a measure of local government into Westminster in 1584, the Act of Parliament that gave powers to the new Court of Burgesses described Westminster as 'the seat of Royalty, the Receipt of the Nobles and Estate of the Honourable Council, the sanctuary of all justices, the place of Parliament, the Show of all the Nobles and Ambassadors coming from Foreign Parts'.[222] This sense of Westminster being a place that reflected the majesty of the sovereign was strongly held by the Tudor and Stuart monarchs.

The detailed maps and surveys that must have been commissioned by Thomas Cromwell during the acquisition of the honour are long lost, but there are a number of late sixteenth- and early seventeenth-century maps that allow the lands around St James's to be reconstructed on a modern plan.

The copperplate map normally known as Agas shows Westminster Abbey and Palace and Whitehall, but only the corner of St James's Park and Charing Cross. It also shows the Royal Mews on the site of what is now the National Gallery.[223] So the starting point has to be the map entitled *An Exact Delineation of the Cities of London and Westminster and the Suburbs Thereof* (see Fig. 1.10), drawn by the surveyor, Richard Newcourt, who conducted a survey of London and its suburbs in the 1640s.[224] It gives an impression of Westminster at the end of the early Stuart period, but the details are problematic. His depiction of St James's, for instance, is completely made up. He also invented a number of houses on the west side of the park, and the palaces of Whitehall and Westminster themselves can only be described as diagrammatic.

Yet William Faithorne is the first to map Westminster and clearly shows the relationship of St James's to the park, to Westminster and to the as yet undeveloped bailiwick to its north. Faithorne's map can be cross-referenced with a sketch map in the Bodleian Library, Oxford (see Fig. 1.23). The sheet showing Westminster was pasted on to a map of the early 1640s, originally printed as *The Countrymans or Strangers Ready helpe, in his finding of our streeyts, lanes or Places in London*. The added section shows Westminster immediately before the Civil War and depicts St James's much more accurately.[225]

Both maps make clear the complete isolation of St James's on the far side of the park. The Elizabethan mapmaker, John Norden, described St James's in 1572, as 'standing from other buildings about 2 furlong [402.3 m], saving a farmhouse opposite against the north gate … on the south the stately buildings of Westminster with the pleasant parks and delights thereof; on the north the green fields'.[226]

The maps show the road now known as Pall Mall, which had run from Charing Cross to the leper hospital of St James since the early Middle Ages. This road continued westwards across what is now Green Park, fording the River Tyburn and eventually crossing the Westbourne river at Knightsbridge. They also show the new road built by Henry VIII to link the gatehouse of St James's with what is now Piccadilly (known as St James's Street after 1660).[227] As for the rest of the land, it was mostly common fields when it was acquired. Henry VIII enclosed the 45 acres (18.2 hectares) of St James's Field, translating the arable land to meadow, but the remainder of the bailiwick was let. The bailiff responsible for these lands was, throughout the

1.34

Ralph Treswell (c.1540–1616/7), map of the lands in the bailiwick of St James's relating to a legal dispute, 1585. St James's is off the map at the bottom left-hand corner (TNA, MPB1/1)

OPPOSITE

1.35

Unknown hand, map of the Davies estate in the parishes of St Martin's and St Margaret's, Westminster, c.1665, but based on an earlier map of c.1615. This shows the vast Crown landholding west of St James's. On the right-hand side of the map is St James's Park (BL, Add. MS 38104)

sixteenth and early seventeenth centuries, the keeper of St James's, who also had oversight of St James's Field, upon which an annual fair had been held on the Feast of St James (25 July). This rowdy four-day affair was a popular feature of Westminster life, and Henry moved it to the new St James's Street, where it was tolerated because of the tolls that it brought the bailiwick. St James's Field was also used for the more orderly mustering of royal troops, particularly in times of crisis.[228]

Under the early Stuarts, St James's Field became a royal recreation ground. Faithorne accurately shows the tennis court on the corner of St James's Street (see p. 31). North of that, not properly shown on either map, was the physic garden established by John Parkinson; the pell mell, however, is accurately depicted. The early Stuarts thus gave St James's Field something of the character of a private enclosure – indeed, it became known as Pell Mell Field. In 1630, Charles I ordered that all entrances into it be closed, except the door from the tennis court, 'which is to be for the King's private use and ye admittance of whom his majesty shall please'.[229] When it was surveyed by the parliamentary commissioners in 1650, it appears that as well as the physic garden, there was another orchard (see p. 47), well-stocked with apples, pears, cherries, quinces and other fruits, and a pigeon house. At that time, 44 acres (17.8 hectares) of the field remained undeveloped.[230]

In 1585, there was a dispute over land boundaries between two tenants in the bailiwick, and the legal proceedings resulted in a map by the surveyor, Ralph Treswell, which covers much of the area (Fig. 1.34), in fact, all the land from St Martin's Lane in the east to Bond Street in the west, and from Oxford Street in the north to Charing Cross in the south. It shows in detail the fields and closes let out by the Crown, and the three large fields: St James's, St Martin's and St Giles's.[231]

In 1617, James I granted the whole bailiwick (less the Royal Mews and St James's Park) to Prince Charles. The land was to be held in trust on a 99-year lease, for the Prince's benefit. To release value from the grant, the trustees were permitted to let leases of fewer than 31 years.

The bailiwick remained a source of revenue for Charles as King, but in 1629, he instructed his trustees to pass the bailiwick, and its annual revenues of £3,000, to the Queen's trustees for her benefit.[232]

Treswell's map does not show St James's Street, but it is evident from the survey of Crown freeholds ordered by Parliament in 1650 that Crown leases and some freeholds had been granted along modern St James's Street by then.[233] There were around 15 houses on the west side of the street and a smaller number of less prestigious houses on the east side.

The level of detail which Ralph Treswell's map provides for the bailiwick is replicated by another map related to a similar legal dispute. This is of the Davies estate (Fig. 1.35), which would later become the Grosvenor estate, and which stretched between the Thames and Hyde Park, covering all the land in the manor of Eye bought by Henry VIII. It was drawn by lawyers in around 1665, who were copying an earlier survey of 1614.[234]

It seems likely that the village of Eye, such as it was, was located at the west end of what became St James's Park, on the site of Buckingham Palace.[235] This small settlement may have limped on into the early seventeenth century, but in 1609–10, as part of his scheme to create a home-grown silk industry, James I enclosed four acres (1.6 hectares) of land at the west end of the park and planted it with mulberry trees. The mulberry garden, clearly shown on the Davies map, was roughly on the site of the south wing of Buckingham Palace today, and was a significant investment in which the King hoped to lead the nation: the new garden cost nearly a thousand pounds, the trees £435, and the annual outlay on silkworms was to be £120.[236]

To the north, the map also shows part of the huge manor of Hyde, bought by Henry VIII in 1636.[237] This became one of the hunting parks attached to Westminster and St James's, and in the early 1540s, Henry built a new road linking St James's with Hyde Park, so he could conveniently take carts and wagons there. There was also a banqueting house built in 1546, and it is probably this that is indicated

1. FROM THE HOSPITAL OF ST JAMES TO THE CIVIL WAR

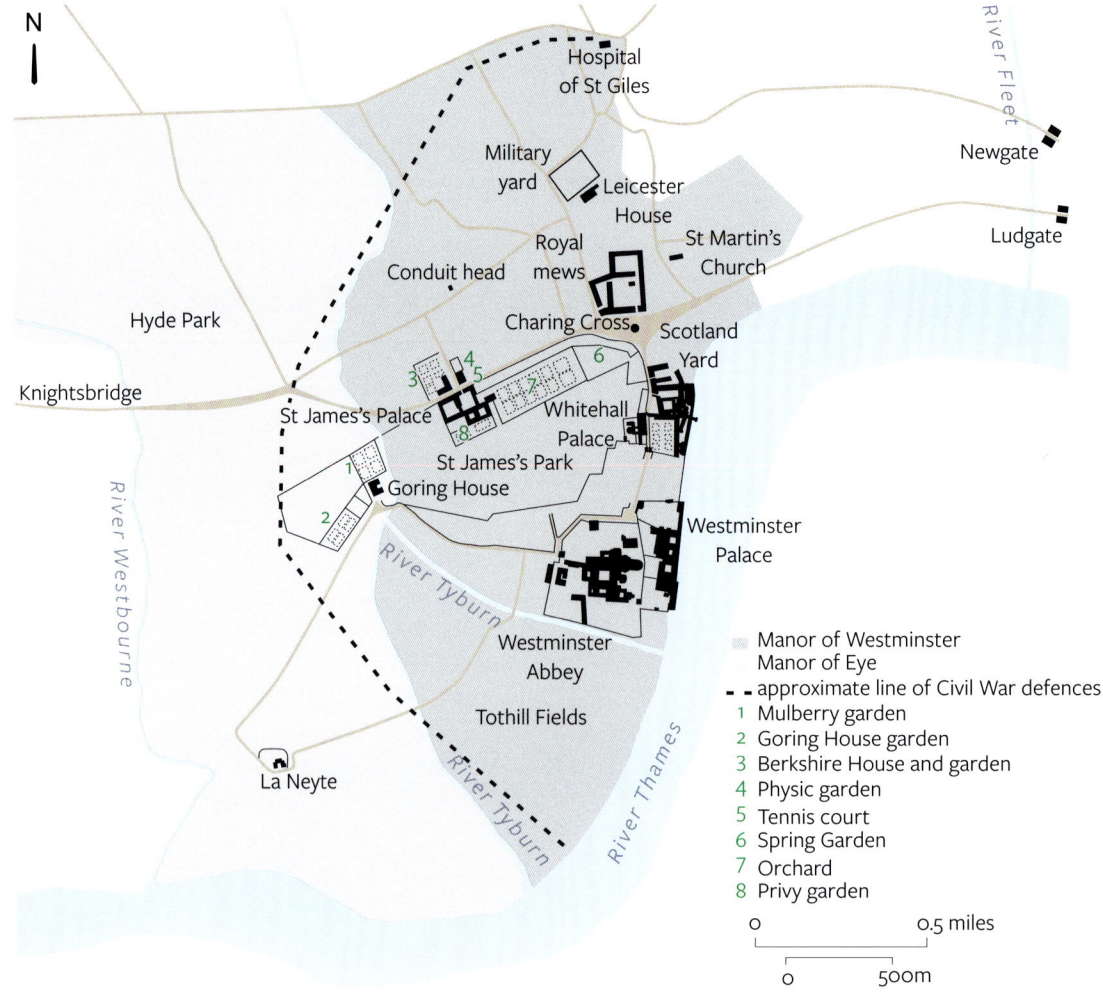

1.36
The Westminster lands of the Crown, 1536–1660. This map shows the locations of all the places mentioned in the text, but does not represent Westminster at any one point in time, and some of the places identified did not co-exist

on the Davies plan. The Tudors and Stuarts used Hyde Park for the shooting of both deer and wildfowl, and the banqueting house and a number of lodges were used for refreshment and entertaining.[238]

The information on these various maps can be combined to give a good picture of the royal estates in Westminster (Fig. 1.36). The geographical centre of them was the park. Because it lay on the edge of one of the terraces of the River Thames, the park sloped steeply down from St James's to a marshy area now occupied by the lake. This area was drained by various streams and a pool, formerly part of a sub-manor called Rosamunds. There was little formal tree planting, but there were coverts for birds and a long avenue at the edge of the terrace in front of St James's. Prince Henry and Prince Charles both shot waterfowl that congregated there, and driven deer that were bred and presented as gifts.[239] The park also contained a royal menagerie, with specimens of rare birds brought from America and elsewhere for James I, including a cassowary and other beasts that were given as royal and diplomatic gifts. After Prince Charles's return from his Spanish trip, for instance, it was home to an elephant and five camels, furnished with a special house. The elephant, who had its own keeper, drank a gallon of wine a day.[240]

Because the park was a rural space so close to the densely packed streets of Westminster, it was a favourite place for royal picnics and strolls. But access to it was strictly controlled: Charles I enforced regulations that restricted access to the park only through the Whitehall

66 ST JAMES'S PALACE

stairs and through St James's; the park was definitively not open to all comers.[241]

A major reason for the purchase of land around Westminster was to preserve the environs of the royal enclave. A series of proclamations, first issued in 1580, but repeated and reinforced many times, attempted to restrict the growth of London and the build-up of Westminster – James I had famously regarded the growth of London as 'a general nuisance to the whole kingdom'.[242] Yet although, on the face of it, royal policy was to throttle London's growth, Charles I, in particular, was happy to grant licences to individual peers to build in the environs of Westminster. The best-known example of this was his encouragement of the Earl of Bedford to develop a residential area in Covent Garden. This was allowed only on condition that the buildings were of a quality of which the King and his Surveyor of Works, Inigo Jones, approved. In fact, the royal aspiration to increase both the quality of buildings in Westminster, and the class of people living there, had been initiated by James I and was a consistent royal ambition before the Civil War.[243]

Wealthy courtiers obviously wanted to live in the old Westminster, near the abbey and palace, but during Charles I's reign in particular, they started to build and buy houses in the parish of St Martin's. It has been calculated that between 1625 and 1641, more than 750 people with a claim to gentility owned or occupied property in the parish; this compares to 71 people in 1614. In 1640, there were 20 English peers, 57 knights and 51 esquires as residents.[244]

This is not what Charles wanted. His concern was to ensure that the aristocracy and gentry resided in their country seats to govern the kingdom, as was their duty. But there were exceptions, for during the 1630s, special permission was given to close friends to build houses in the orbit of the royal palaces.

These all can be seen on Faithorne's map (see Fig. 1.10). First was Berkshire House, begun by Sir Thomas Howard (1587–1669), who was in the equestrian circle of Henry, Prince of Wales, and, in 1614, became Master of the Horse to Prince Charles. Howard went to Madrid with Prince Charles and Buckingham, and in 1622 was created Lord Howard of Charlton; on Charles I's coronation, he became the Earl of Berkshire. Sometime in the early 1620s, he built a house opposite the riding house at St James's, on the other side of the highway. It was a substantial place, with a great hall and a long gallery; it had a garden, 253 ft (77.1 m) long, to the north and was in an excellent position for access both to St James's and for the court at Whitehall.[245]

To the south of the mulberry garden, at the west end of St James's Park, was a half-acre (0.2 hectare) plot on which a successful lawyer, Sir William Blake, had built a modest house in 1623. Blake died in 1630 and his house was sold to Sir George Goring (1585–1663) in 1633. Goring was a courtier and a soldier, but more importantly, he was vice chamberlain to Henrietta Maria and her Master of the Horse. He spent a huge amount on extending the mansion, building outhouses, stables and a series of beautiful walled gardens facing St James's Park.[246]

To the north of the mulberry garden was a house, built from 1633 by Thomas, Earl of Arundel (1585–1646), Earl Marshall, one of Charles I's closest advisers and a Catholic sympathiser. Seen on a seventeenth-century map and in the background of an engraving, it appears to have been a large, U-plan, three-storey mansion, densely fenestrated. Nobody now knows why it was called Tart Hall, but it was designed by Nicholas Stone, master mason to the Crown. Tart Hall, the mulberry garden and Goring House can all be seen on Faithorne's map (see Fig. 1.10);[247] as can another large mansion, Leicester House, built in the northern part of the bailiwick, by Robert Sidney, 2nd Earl of Leicester (1595–1677). Sidney was a leading Caroline diplomat who bought four acres (1.6 hectares) of St Martin's Field. Prohibited from developing it by royal decree, in August 1631, he acquired a licence from Charles I to build a house 'with necessary outhouses buildings and gardens', on the condition that 'the forefronts and all the utter walls and windows of the premises bee wholly made of brick and stone or one of them, the forefronts to be made in that uniform sort and

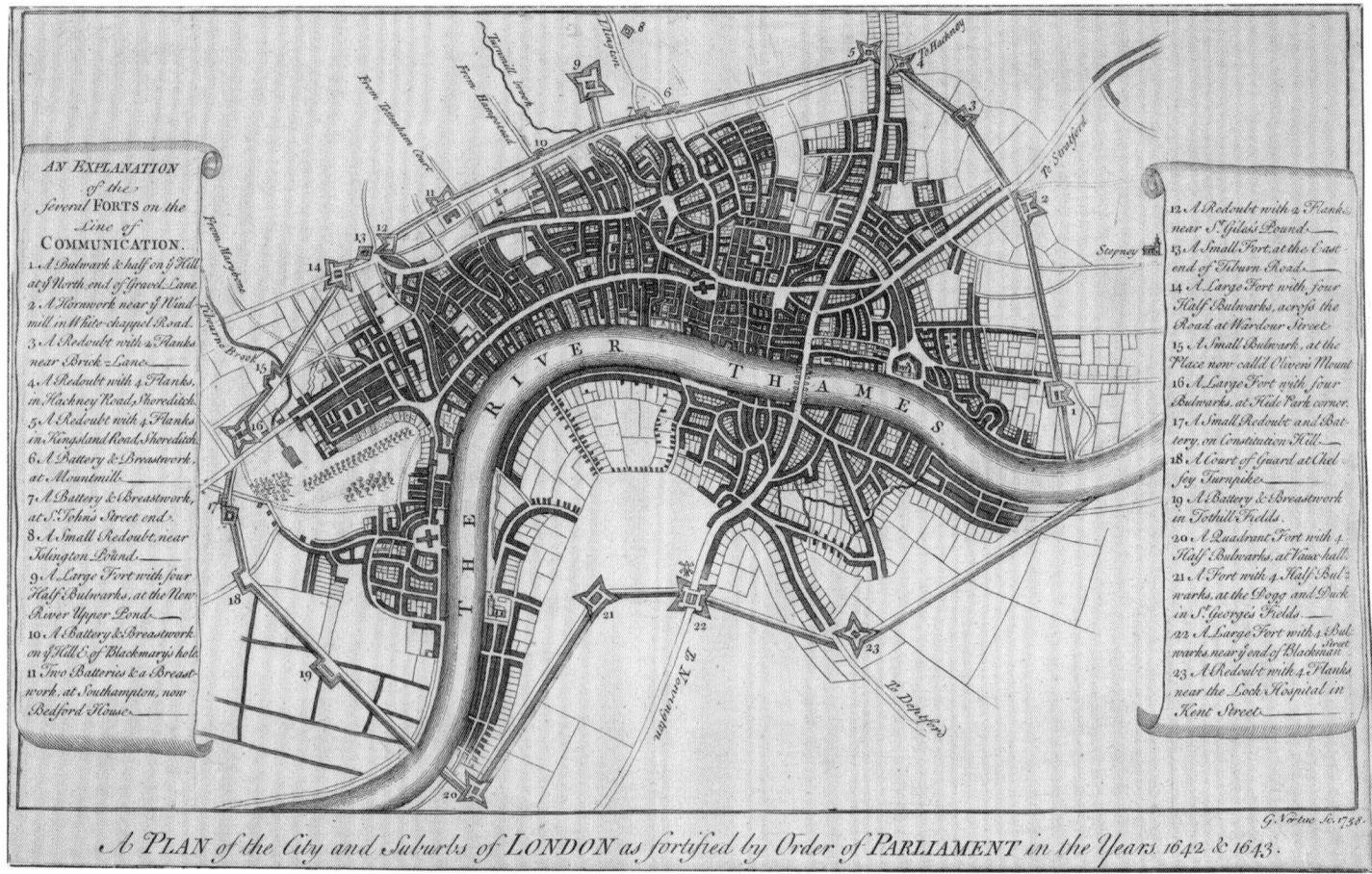

1.37

Map of London's Civil War defences, engraved by George Vertue (1684–1756) for Maitland's *History of London* (1739). The survey was based on an examination of the earthworks surviving at the time and it shows streets and roads as they were a century after the war (BL, Maps, Crace Port., 1.39)

order as may best beautify the place'.²⁴⁸ Nearby, to the north west, was the house (begun in 1627) of Sir William Howard, Viscount Stafford (1612–80), a crypto-Catholic close to Henrietta Maria.²⁴⁹ Both these houses also appear prominently on William Morgan's map of 1682, by which time they had been engulfed by terraces of houses built since the Restoration (see Fig. 2.4).

One other development that took place in the bailiwick of St James's requires notice: this is the military ground – a parade ground laid out sometime soon after 1615, for the trained bands of Westminster to practise upon. The ground was enclosed by a wall, 9 ft (2.7 m) high, and contained the armoury house, a large building comprising a hall, library, parlour and upstairs meeting room. The King's arms were prominently displayed in the hall, which housed an armoury of ordnance and weapons. Close to the royal mews, and in the bailiwick of St James's, this was most likely the initiative of Prince Henry, though the licence to establish an independent military company was only granted after his death.²⁵⁰

All this shows that by the outbreak of the Civil War, although there had been considerable building in old Westminster and in the parish of St Martin's, with the exception of a small number of aristocratic mansions licenced by the King in order to enhance the environs of the royal lands, and a royal parade ground, St James's and the lands around it were still remarkably undeveloped. Hollar's view of Westminster from the north (see Fig. 1.5) shows an uninterrupted view across St James's Field, apart from the Tudor brick conduit house.

The Civil War changed all this. In 1642 and 1643, Parliament ordered the fortification of London (Fig. 1.37).²⁵¹ The City of London was still walled, ditched and fortified with gates, but Westminster was extremely vulnerable to attack. At first, there were hurriedly erected, stand-alone defences, small earthwork forts, short trenches, bars and chains across roads. But in 1643, with the real prospect that Charles I's forces could make an assault on London, it was resolved to construct a comprehensive defensive line around the city and its suburbs, which enclosed the bailiwick and park of St James's. The line of the fortifications ran from St Giles's in an arc across St James's Field towards Hyde Park Corner, where it ran south past Goring House, round the south side of Westminster to Tothill, and so to the Thames.

The lines comprised ramparts 9 ft wide and 18 ft high (2.7 by 5.5 m) on the outer ditch side. These were studded with earthwork forts, including three in the bailiwick of St James's. These were particularly strongly defended, as St James's was an obvious target and the falling land would give an attacking army an advantage there. The house was home to the King's children, and they must have watched the construction of the fortifications with apprehension. The Hyde Park Corner fort was one of the largest on the whole circuit, defending the way to Westminster. It was a double bastion, with 17 angles and 19 cannon. Within this ring of defence, described at the time as 'wonderful strong and of great bounds', were further security measures: turnpikes were set up on the principal routes, including crucial roads past St James's towards Charing Cross.[252]

After the execution of the King, with London under military occupation, all the large buildings round Westminster fell under parliamentary scrutiny. St James's was taken over as a barracks and a prison (see p. 61); Goring House and the mulberry garden were regarded as Crown land and sold; Leicester House and Tart Hall were requisitioned for the army; and Berkshire House, at the gates of St James's, was taken over for the use of visiting ambassadors. While the leases in the bailiwick held good, freehold Crown land in hand in 1649 was gradually sold off by Parliament.

The most important sale was that of St James's Field. This was under the control of the keeper of St James's, who was, *ex officio*, also bailiff. In 1625, the keepership had been taken over by Henry, Lord Danvers (1573–1644), created Earl of Danby the following year, who had appointed one Hugh Woodward as his deputy. It was Woodward who purchased the land from Parliament in 1651 for nearly £2,000, with a view to building houses on it, and immediately began digging for brick earth. However, after an outcry, Cromwell was forced to halt building works, but not before Woodward had built some houses on the edge of the field, ten of which were recognised as being legitimate in 1661. The development, on the south-east corner of the field, is shown on an important map by the cartographer, Jonas Moore (1617–79), from *c*.1662–3.[253] The map also shows the extent of development on the west side of St James's Street.

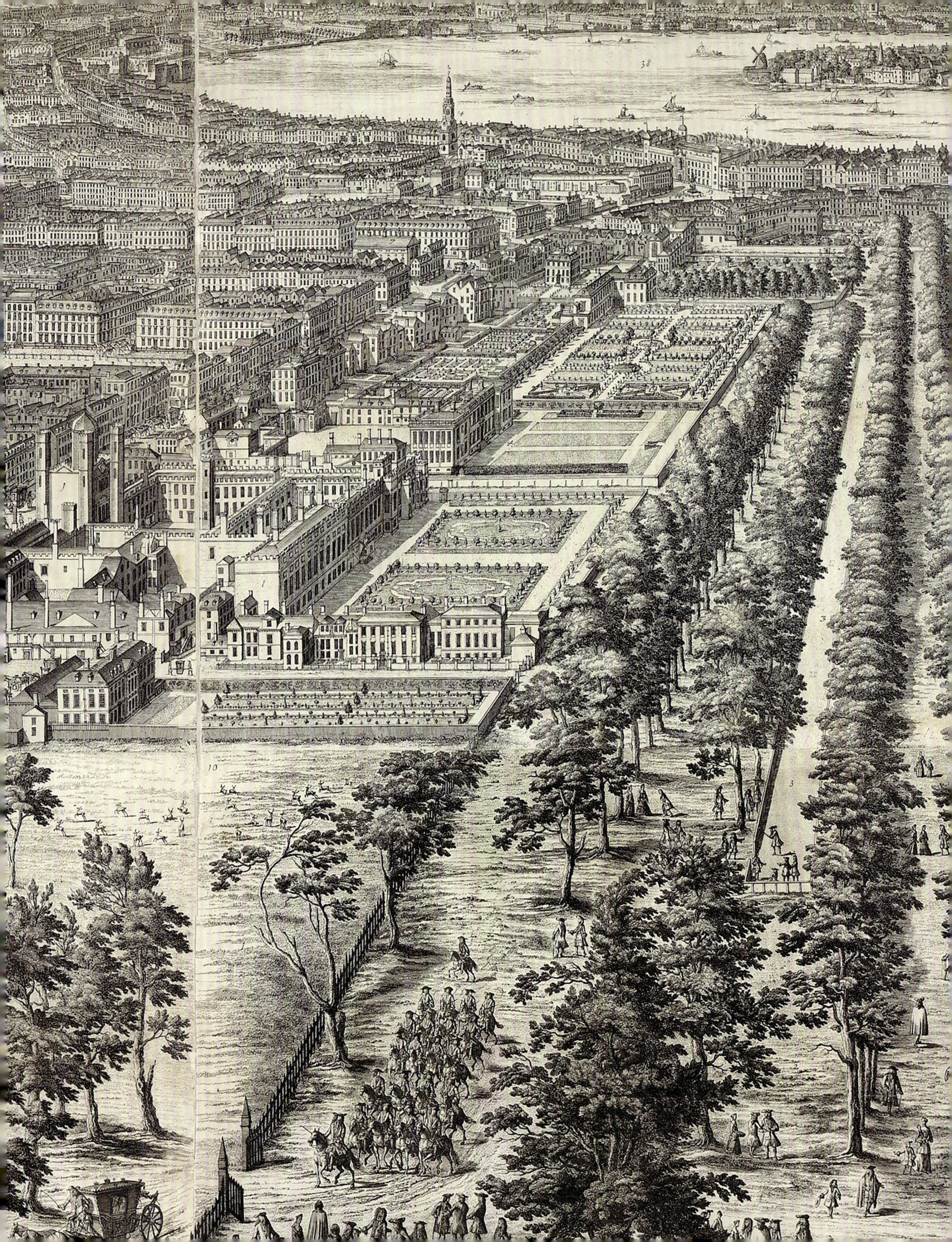

2. The Restoration to Queen Anne

SIMON THURLEY

St James's House at the Restoration

The moment it was clear that the monarchy was to be restored, there was fevered activity to repair the principal London residences of Whitehall, Somerset House and St James's.[1] St James's had remained a barracks right up to the moment when General Monck took possession in March 1660. In order to accommodate more troops, the riding house and former royal larders had been converted into barrack rooms and temporary sheds, and timber structures had been built in and around the courtyards. Meanwhile, the pastry house had been converted into the officers' coach house. Several of the principal rooms of state had been subdivided, and both chapels had been stripped of their fittings.[2]

The chapels were quickly restored. The Anglican (Tudor) chapel had been converted into a plain preaching box, the elevated royal closet dismantled and the antechapel partitioned off. The closet and antechapel were reinstated, the pews were removed, the pulpit altered and stalls reintroduced, with a canopy over the Dean's seat.[3] The Catholic chapel was still the property of Henrietta Maria and had been cleared in anticipation of converting it into a library. The closets were repaired and an altar and altar rail re-erected.[4]

This work was undertaken under the auspices of the Office of Works, which, like all the other departments of the Royal Household, was reconstituted in 1660. Some of Charles I's officers simply reclaimed their former posts, while positions that were vacant, including that of surveyor, formerly held by Inigo Jones, were quickly granted by Charles II. The new surveyor was Sir John Denham (1615–69), a fervent Royalist who had been handy not only with his sword, but with his pen during the Civil War and Interregnum. Unlike Jones, he was no architect, but he was an effective and efficient administrator, who employed others to undertake any design work. The new paymaster, in contrast, was a designer. Although Hugh May's (1621–84) official duty was to look after the money, in due course he was to win the biggest royal architectural commission of the reign – the remodelling of Windsor Castle. Day-to-day responsibility at the various houses was delegated to a clerk of works. Responsibility for St James's was part of a wider brief, covering the old Palace of Westminster, Whitehall and St James's Park. In 1660, Thomas Rotherham took up responsibility for the Westminster district, a role he later combined with a personal appointment to Catherine of Braganza at Somerset House. On his death in 1681, he was replaced by Leonard Gammon, who, as a young man, had assisted his father, Richard, repairing St James's at the Restoration. Despite having great responsibilities, Gammon was, according to Sir John Vanbrugh, 'a drunken sot'.[5]

OPPOSITE

Detail of Johannes Kip's perspective of London, c.1727 (see Fig. 2.28)

It is clear from the detailed accounts of the Office of Works that once the temporary partitions were removed from the royal lodgings, the rooms were in precisely the same configuration they had been a decade or so before. But there were scars: much of the panelling of the great three-sided privy gallery had been removed, and in 1660–61, the remaining wainscot was dismantled and there was only enough in good condition to repanel the south gallery next to the privy garden; the cross gallery and north gallery were whitewashed with a black skirting.[6] A large ceiling canvas in the cross gallery was taken down and the ceiling painted white. The doors in the privy lodgings had been broken and removed, and these were restored and painted 'cedar colour'.[7]

While these defects were being remedied, discussions were under way about the future of the house. In 1660, Charles had appointed John Grenville (1628–1701; soon to be Earl of Bath, and already Charles's groom of the stool) keeper of St James's Park and house. He received lodgings in the outer court, in the north-east corner near the Queen's Chapel, which he occupied until his death.[8] St James's was the house of the heir to the throne, and as, in 1660, Charles was unmarried and childless, the heir presumptive was his brother, James, Duke of York. In 1659, to the dismay of his mother and brother, James had contracted to marry Anne Hyde (1637–71), the daughter of Sir Edward Hyde (1609–74), whom Charles II was to make his Chancellor. James thus returned to England a married man, with a pregnant wife, and it must have been they who instructed Sir John Denham to modernise St James's in preparation for their use.

Anne was a commoner and her rise to be the sovereign's sister-in-law seemed to many to be the product of unacceptable family ambition. Gilbert Burnet, Bishop of Salisbury and chronicler of Charles II's reign, noted that 'she was a very extraordinary woman … She soon understood what belonged to a princess, and took state upon her, rather too much'.[9] Her father, who was made Earl of Clarendon by Charles II in 1661, also, it was felt, took too much state upon himself, becoming the greatest architectural patron of his day. Clarendon House, erected in the 1660s and designed by Sir Roger Pratt (1620–85), was ostentatiously positioned at the north end of St James's Street, facing his daughter's new home at St James's (see Fig. 2.4). It was described by John Evelyn as a 'palace' – 'the best contrived, the most useful, graceful and magnificent house in England'.[10]

The Duke and Duchess had their own income, derived, as was traditional, from lands, excise and duties, and income from the Post Office granted by Parliament in 1663. In addition, the Duke had been granted one-off sums of £10,000 in 1660 and £120,000 in 1665. It is difficult to compute his normal annual income, but it was not less than £100,000 a year. James was thus the richest subject in the kingdom and was able to finance works himself, but in the early 1660s, the restoration and modernisation of St James's were financed by the Crown through the Office of Works.[11] Although the Crown funded the architectural shell, it was down to the Duke and Duchess to pay for furniture and fittings. This means that, unlike the houses occupied by the King and Queen, the Wardrobe accounts do not reveal how St James's was furnished.

It is certain, though, that the Duke and Duchess regarded the royal lodgings as old-fashioned, and in the early 1660s, they did much to make rooms symmetrical, replaced stone casements and introduced fashionable features. The sequence and number of rooms available was also now inadequate, and within the existing carcass, rooms were reconfigured. Both James and Anne were provided with a great bedchamber, reserved for ceremonial, and a little bedchamber in which they normally slept. This was an architectural formalisation of practices that had been adopted before the Civil War and had probably been commonplace in exile.

With her father building a palace in sight of the gates of St James's, the Duchess's efforts to create a fashionable suite of apartments had a benchmark to be superseded; her rooms were given a more thoroughgoing modernisation than the Duke's, whose principal lodgings were at Whitehall. A French visitor in 1663 thought the Duchess 'better lodged than the King or the Queen', her chambers being larger and cleaner.[12] In 1660, Anne ordered that her bedchamber be rebuilt in order to accommodate a bed alcove. This fashionable French feature was simultaneously being built in Charles II's principal bedchamber at Whitehall, and, like the King's, the Duchess's was elaborately carved with coats of arms and wooden swags over the opening. A rail was inserted with turned balusters, 18 in. (45.7 cm) high, and a bed placed behind. The chimney was moved into the centre of the wall and given a modern marble surround, and the room was panelled and painted to look like white marble, with mouldings highlighted in gold leaf.[13]

Next door was the new little bedchamber, with windows looking into the inner court; on the garden front, next to it, was the Duchess's closet, with a chimney on the window wall.[14] The room is identifiable in a plan of c.1703–14 (see Fig. 1.4), because one door to it was cut in an angle through the corner of the room. The room to which the closet led to the north was said to be Charles I's former closet, and there, shelves and cupboards were taken out and a chimneypiece dismantled and carried to Hampton Court. It was replaced by one brought from Greenwich.[15]

The precise geography of the rooms at the head of the Duchess's backstairs is not now possible to discern. There was a passage that led to the stairs from the little bedchamber, facilitating access to the wardrobe and service rooms below. The Duchess had a dressing room here that communicated with the Duke's closet, and nearby was her private oratory that in 1663–4 had an altar step built in it. In all, by 1665, the Duchess had five rooms in her privy lodging.[16]

The Duke was assigned the sovereign's side, and at first, the priority was to construct new privy lodgings for him on the south front. This was done by cannibalising part of the southern gallery to form a new bedchamber and withdrawing room. The Jacobean panelling in the gallery was dismantled and three partitions were built across it. Chimneys were formed, not on the northern wall facing the courtyard, but on the southern window wall. At first, the Tudor fenestration was retained, but in 1666, the Tudor casements were removed and timber windows substituted. A sliver of a room was carved out next to the bedchamber as a WC, with its own fireplace and window. The drawing room, which lay beyond the bedchamber, was linked by a passage to the Duke's backstairs (see Plan C).[17]

In 1662, attention turned to the Duke's outer chambers. The Tudor Presence and Guard Chambers were remade into symmetrical rooms by moving the partition that divided them.[18] The sixteenth-century terracotta roundel over the fireplace in the Presence Chamber (see p. 25, and Fig. 1.9) was taken down and the chimney's flues reconstructed so the mantelpiece could be in the middle of the north wall. A new Portland stone chimneypiece with black marble shelf was inserted, and another was installed in the Guard Chamber next door. The Presence Chamber was not panelled, but hung with tapestry, as was traditional.[19]

The reconfigured Presence Chamber led, via a passage, to the Duke's great bedchamber, and beyond that were his privy lodgings, interconnecting with those of the Duchess. By 1665, he had seven rooms, two passages and a closet in his privy lodgings.[20] Some of the rooms now looked into the Privy Court, which, in 1660, was planted with topiary bay trees and became known as the Bay Court.[21]

The Duke's household had a substantial stable that required accommodation, and the King agreed that this should be based at St James's, in the area of the old riding house, where a new stable yard was created. The riding house was converted to the Duke's stables, a barn was built for hay, and three coach houses erected in a building 113 ft (34.4 m) long. A wall enclosed the new yard and this opened both onto the highway and, via new gates, through the wall into the park.[22]

In 1660–61, St James's briefly became home to several other members of the royal family. Henrietta Maria returned to England in October 1660, accompanied by her youngest daughter, Princess Henrietta (1644–70). Rooms were prepared for the Princess and she was joined by her mother, who was escaping the smallpox that had claimed the lives of two of her other children, the Duke of Gloucester (1640–60) and Mary, Princess of Orange (1631–60). Devastated, Henrietta Maria soon left England for good with Princess Henrietta, and by early 1661, the principal resident at St James's was the Duchess of York. The chapel, however, remained under the nominal control of the Dowager Queen, and once restored, it was once again open to London's Roman Catholics. Charles II, in an echo of his father's attempts to control access to the royal chapel in the 1630s, forbade people who were not officers of one of the royal households from attending.[23]

In June 1661, Charles signed a treaty for his marriage to the Portuguese princess, Catherine of Braganza. Like her mother-in-law, Henrietta Maria, she was a Roman Catholic and her marriage treaty guaranteed her freedom to enjoy Roman rites and maintain a Roman chapel wherever she lived. As the bride was expected to arrive at Whitehall in June 1662, the Duke of York, who seems, up until then, to have had the use of the consort's lodgings there, relocated on a more permanent basis to St James's. From this point onwards, until he became King, James used St James's as his London summer residence.[24]

In 1666–7, reflecting his increased use of the house, James commissioned three new rooms in his inner lodgings. A room was to be built in the inner court, now known as Bay Court, for the gentleman of his bedchamber, which would connect to James's drawing room. This room, clearly seen on William Dickinson's plan of c.1703–14 (see Fig. 1.4), was the first of a number of structures built out into the court. The other new rooms were a dressing room with a wardrobe below (built against the privy kitchen, at the far east end of the old privy gallery) and a closet at the head of the backstairs. Construction work was undertaken by the Office of Works, but James contributed £300 to the cost.[25] Other rooms mentioned in the accounts in the later 1660s include the Duke's chapel and antechapel, his supping room and his library, although it has not been possible to identify their location.[26]

The District of St James's after 1660

Amongst the former lands restored to Henrietta Maria after the Restoration were the freeholds of the bailiwick of St James's, which was in turn granted to Henry Jermyn, Earl of St Albans (c.1605–84). Jermyn had entered Henrietta Maria's household in 1627 and had risen to be her favourite, inevitably causing gossip about their relationship. After fighting for the King during the Civil War, he went into exile, becoming the Queen's Lord Chamberlain and her closest companion through the Interregnum. During this time, Jermyn had raised 647,416 *livres tournois* for the royal family (about £20–£25 million in modern terms) and had incurred vast debts. At the Restoration, to repay him, Charles II confirmed him as co-proprietor of the Northern Neck of Virginia, and granted him leases of the former royal houses of Byfleet, Oatlands and Weybridge, Surrey, while the Queen Mother granted him the bailiwick of St James's, Westminster.

It was as the owner of the bailiwick that Jermyn effectively founded the West End of London. And as he did so, he also brought into reality Charles I's dream of an aristocratic quarter that complemented the royal estate of Westminster. In a petition to Charles II, requesting the freehold of the land on which he wanted to build, he pointed out 'ye beauty of this great Town and the convenience of ye court are defective in point of houses fit for the dwellings of Noble men and other persons of quality, and that your Majesty hath thought fit for some Remedy hereof to appoint it the Place in St James field should be built in great and good houses'.[27] The centrepiece of the development was St James's Square, known, in 1677, as the 'Place Royal'. It was recognised that the houses there were intended for 'the conveniency of the Nobility and Gentry who were to attend upon his Majestie's Person, and in Parliament'.[28] Just as at Covent Garden, royal control was to be exercised over the design of the new houses, a condition built into the original lease to Jermyn, and a fact noted by those who objected to the preferential treatment that he had achieved.[29]

A map or chart drawn by Jonas Moore *c.*1662–3, although intended to show the river and the docks, also shows the start of the development by the Earl of St Albans (Fig. 2.1). The land around it is still open fields, but building along Pall Mall had begun. An Office of Works map dating from a little later shows the square sketched out in plan. The inhabitants were indeed the great and good of Restoration London, and St James's Square became, and remained, an aristocratic quarter for several centuries. In residence before 1675 were Lord Bellasis, sometime captain of the Band of Gentlemen Pensioners, the Earl of Arlington, who was Lord Chamberlain, Viscount Halifax, Thomas Jermyn (nephew of the Earl of St Albans) and the French ambassador, Honoré Courtin.[30]

The development of the Earl of St Albans' estate required a reconfiguration of royal interests in the bailiwick. The old highway from Charing Cross was obliterated and a new road, modern Pall Mall, was laid out on the site of the old pell mell. This had the effect of moving the houses built by Hugh Woodward in the 1650s (see p. 69) from being on the north side of the old highway to being on the south side of Pall Mall; it also created a long, narrow building plot between the park wall and the new road. This was quickly developed and the large mansions built there were occupied by the cream of Restoration society, including, famously, the King's mistress, Nell Gwyn (1650–87), who was presented with a house on the site of 79 Pall Mall. These houses had the great advantage of backing onto the royal gardens, and several of them built mounds or terraces so they could see over the high park wall and enjoy views of the park. The district also became the favourite retreat for the King's most tenacious mistress, Barbara Villiers, Duchess of Cleveland (*c.*1641–1709), for whom the King bought the freehold of Berkeley House opposite St James's.[31]

This fashionable new district lay at the gates of the house of St James's, and royal intervention ensured that its regal character was preserved. The streets round St James's Street were paved in a succession of campaigns between 1661 and 1678, and in 1665, Charles finally removed St James's fair from the environs of the house, relocating it to a new market built by the Earl of St Albans at the bottom of Haymarket. As a strong sense of local identity developed, the area's inhabitants began a petition to break away from the parish of St Martin's and form a new parish. Despite arguing for this from 1664, it was not until 1685 that a new parish was agreed and Sir Christopher Wren built St James's church on Piccadilly as its fashionable heart. The royal residence, however, remained in the parish of St Margaret's, Westminster, an important jurisdictional point that helped fuse St James's and Whitehall together.[32]

To make the development of St James's Square possible, the pell mell alley was relocated inside the park in February 1660; the new one, seen most clearly on Kip's perspective, begun in 1715 (see Fig. 2.28), had a brick drain beneath it to prevent it getting waterlogged. A keeper was appointed at the handsome rate of £100 a year. The alley was laid out to the south of a long, double tree-lined walk that had been planted before the Civil War, shown on Faithorne's survey (see Fig. 1.10). It lay in front of St James's, along the top of a gentle slope, giving views down into the park; it

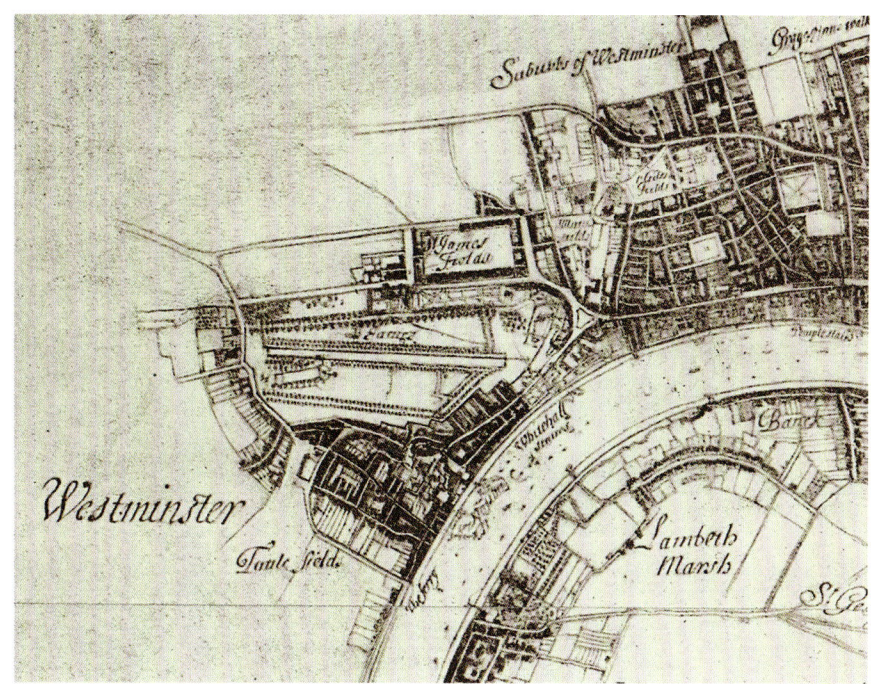

2.1

Jonas Moore, chart of London and the Thames commissioned by the Navy Office, *c.*1662–3. This is an important view, as it shows St James's just before it was laid out for housing. The old highway is still in position, soon to be replaced by Pall Mall; on its north are houses built in the 1650s. The map also shows that in 1662, part of the earthwork fort on the site of Mount Street, Mayfair, was still standing (BL, Maps, 188.h.1 (1))

2. THE RESTORATION TO QUEEN ANNE

2.2
Pen and ink drawing by an unknown artist of St James's house and park from The Mall, c.1710. The mature avenue predates the Civil War; the young trees were planted for the pell mell at the Restoration. The entrance to the Queen's Chapel can be seen in the park wall on the right (RCIN 923147)

also provided a private riding way from Charing Cross mews to Knightsbridge.[33]

In 1660, Charles II commissioned several new avenues for the park, another double one to the south of the pell mell, thus enclosing it between two double avenues, and two more double avenues of lime trees either side of a canal, 2,800 ft (853.4 m) long, that was dug running east to west and aligned on the Whitehall Stairs – the back door to the palace. At the west end of the canal, next to the palace, there was a half-semicircle of trees, with subsidiary avenues running out to the pell mell and Spring Garden (Fig. 2.2).

Adrian May, elder brother of the comptroller of works, Hugh May, was in charge of this ambitious remodelling. It was a unique undertaking in the history of gardening; nothing like it had ever been seen in England, and on the continent, such avenues were aligned on the entrance front of great palaces, not at their back door.[34] Charles II was reinforcing the character of the park that had been established by his father and grandfather:

it was a private enclosure for walking, riding and admiring nature – in short, for taking the air. In July 1666, walking in the new avenues, Hugh May told Samuel Pepys that 'our business here being ayre', the best form of garden was plain grass and gravel.[35] For Charles, James and other members of the royal family, the park was where they took their constitutionals, giving its name to Constitution Hill. The King, in particular, liked to take a stroll in the park before dinner, and he was surprisingly accessible there to any respectable and well-dressed person. People would walk there well into the night, making it a favoured place for illicit assignations.[36]

In 1661, Charles ordered the construction of an elaborate decoy in the south-east corner of the park. This was a grid of ornamental ponds contrived by the Dutch designer Shadrick Hilens, designed to trap ducks for food. The long canals were netted and ducks encouraged to swim into the waiting traps.[37] Soon, the exotic birds of the pre-Civil War period were returned to the watercourses, including

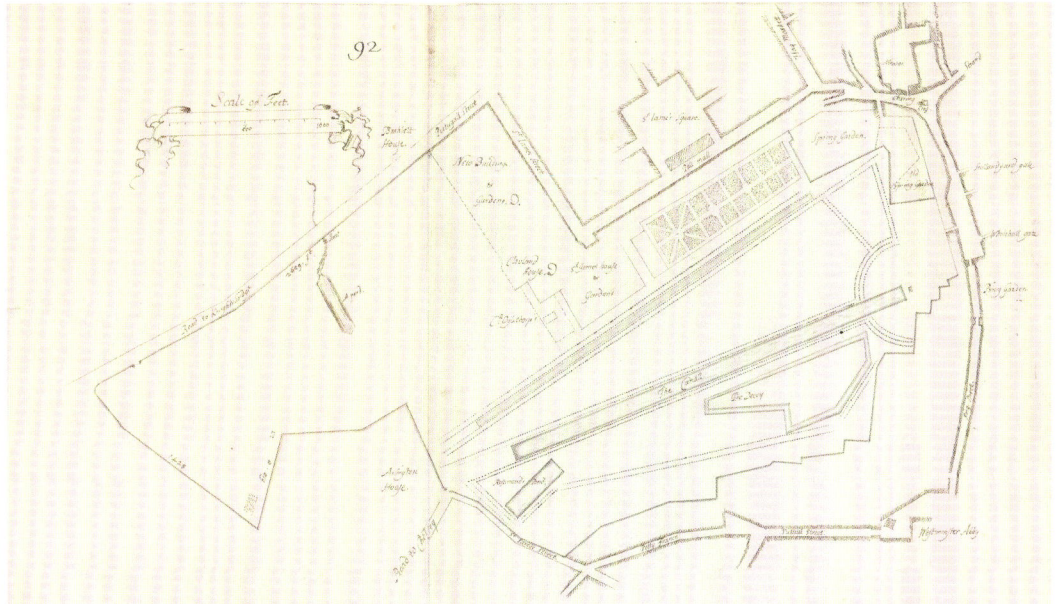

2.3
Survey of St James's Park by Nicholas Hawksmoor, *c*.1710. This valuable survey shows the park after its extension westwards by Charles II in 1668. The extension (now Green Park) is on the left. Also shown are Charles II's avenues and pell mell. St James's Square is shown north of Pall Mall, with the palace gardens to the south. The Royal Mews is at the top right. The house of Sir Theophilus Oglethorpe, later lived in by Lord Godolphin, is marked to the left of the palace building (AS, IV:92)

cormorants and cranes. Russian ambassadors presented pelicans to the menagerie, and the Moroccan ambassadors offered 30 ostriches. At least some of these were kept in cages or pens, giving its name to modern Birdcage Walk. Foreign visitors were deeply impressed by the exotic fowl, and a herd of unusual goats.[38]

In 1668, the King decided to enlarge the park. The area to the west of St James's Street had long been held on a Crown lease by the Pultney family. The land, which comprised 100 acres (40.5 hectares), was known as St James's farm and had provided hay for the royal stables at the Charing Cross mews. This land was taken into the royal park and enclosed with a brick wall built in 1668–70. It was a major project, involving massive earth-moving, brick-burning, bridge-building and water engineering; the total cost was more than £5,000.[39] A meticulously surveyed and drawn presentation plan by Nicholas Hawksmoor (?1662–1736) shows St James's Park at the completion of these works (Fig. 2.3).[40]

At the north-west corner of what is today known as Green Park, a small plantation and an ornamental pond were made. At the south-east corner, the King stopped up the western end of the old highway to Charing Cross. William Morgan's map of the area shows the road simply stopping at its western end (Fig. 2.4).

The eastern end left a convenient site for development, which was sold on a 60-year lease to Sir Philip Warwick, clerk of the signet. His petition to the King for the land encapsulates the ambition of courtiers to live in St James's; he complained that 'he had daily occasion to attend court, and is much inconvenienced by having no lodgings near'.[41]

Although all these improvements were executed in the vicinity of St James's, they were part of its context rather than its fabric. Under Charles II, St James's Park was regarded as part of Whitehall, a fact underlined by the restoration of the former royal orchard laid out by Charles I and Henrietta Maria in the 1630s (see pp. 46, 48). This garden had been denuded of its statues under the Commonwealth and its planting allowed to go to ruin. In 1661, André Mollet was recalled from retirement; with his nephew, Gabriel, he was given a house in St James's Park and (under Adrian May) was charged with laying out 'our Royal garden that is to be planted with fruit trees and flowers in St James Park between St James Park House and the Spring Garden wall'.[42]

The Spring Garden had been moved after the Restoration to the north-east corner of the park (see Fig. 2.4), and the former garden was allocated to Prince Rupert (1619–82), who built himself a mansion there (see Fig. 2.28).

2. THE RESTORATION TO QUEEN ANNE

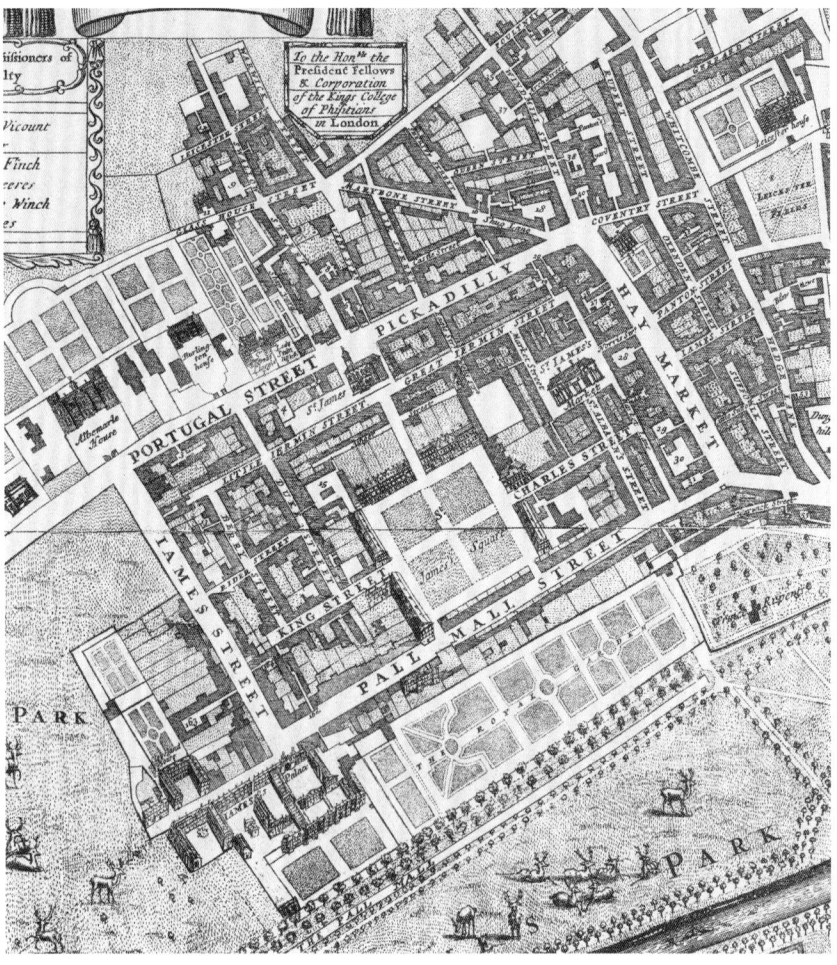

2.4
William Morgan, detail of map showing St James's and St James's Park, 1682. This is the first accurate mapping of St James's and its environs, although, since Morgan has shown important buildings in perspective, the plotting of the ground plan of the house is not very accurate; what it captures is its context (RCIN 1070350.e)

The garden laid out by the Mollets thus ran all the way along the northern boundary of the park to the new Spring Garden.[43] In 1670, five years after André Mollet was carried off by the plague, an English version of his *Garden of Pleasure* was published, dedicated to Charles II and including a layout of the St James's garden (Fig. 2.5). It was probably the garden that he had wished for rather than that which was built, because a survey carried out by the Office of Works, Jonas Moore's chart and William Morgan's map (see Figs 2.1, 2.3 and 2.4) all show a different layout. The garden was planted with dwarf fruit trees and flowers imported from André's nephew, Charles, in Paris. At its east end, it included some of the trees from the garden of the 1630s.[44]

In 1665, in succession to Mollet, the King's garden at St James's was placed in the care of John Rose (1619–77), who, as well as tending the ornamental parts, produced melons, soft fruits, herbs and salads for the King's table. In 1671, a new wall, 581 ft (177.1 m) long, was erected to enclose the southern part of the garden, work not readily identifiable on any map or plan.[45] Rose died in 1677 and was succeeded by Leonard Gurle (c.1621–85). The maintenance contract he was awarded that year, worth £320 annually, specified the complexities of growing melons, oranges and native fruits and herbs for the royal table at Whitehall. It does not seem as though there were many changes during his tenure, but in 1685, when he was succeeded by Antonio Verrio (c.1639–1707; better known as a painter), a fine new greenhouse was commissioned. Plants and seeds were sent from France to embellish the gardens, and he employed his co-religionists, the priests from the adjacent friary, as gardeners. In 1688, when Verrio relinquished his post, he left in store a considerable and valuable stock of plants and bulbs, valued at more than £140.[46]

The Queen's Chapel

The coming of the Restoration saw a balkanisation of the royal estate at St James's. Although it was the residence of the Duke and Duchess of York, Charles II took the largest part of the garden and annexed it to Whitehall. The library remained sovereign property and the King's librarian had his own entrance to come and go as he pleased, while the Queen's Chapel was a separate establishment, which at first was nominally Henrietta Maria's, but after Charles's marriage to Catherine of Braganza in 1662, was assigned to the Queen Consort.

Charles was diligent in making preparations for the arrival of his Roman Catholic bride. The English Catholic he trusted most was Father John Huddleston (1608–98), who had hidden him after his defeat at the Battle of Worcester. Huddleston had himself gone into exile and had taken Benedictine orders, but was recalled by Charles II in 1660 and installed at Somerset House. Huddleston was the most influential Catholic priest at court, and it was he who advised the King that it would be appropriate to establish a house of English Benedictines in

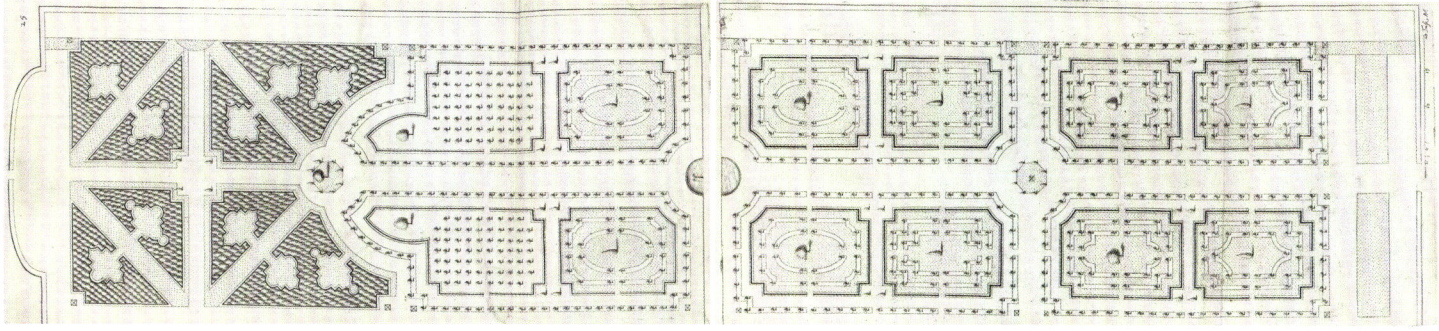

England for the Queen. There were to be six fathers and two lay brothers, selected from Benedictines in exile in France, and they were to be established at St James's, with a generous pension of £100 a year each. The men chosen came from old English families and could be relied upon to have the *savoir faire* necessary to be part of the Queen's court. Arriving before the Queen, and before any provision had been made for them at St James's, they were temporarily established at the old Savoy hospital on the Thames.[47]

Meanwhile, work was under way, bringing St James's chapel into full service. Royal glaziers removed the plain glass in the east window and installed a stained-glass crucifix, 3 ft wide and 4 ft high (0.9 by 1.2 m), flanked by two coats of arms, 3 ft 5 in. (1 m) high – presumably those of Braganza and Stuart. The altar was very plainly dressed, with six candlesticks and a silver tabernacle. The organ loft was rebuilt and an organ brought from Whitehall; nearby, a music room was appointed, approached by a flight of stairs; next to this was a withdrawing room that led to the privy closet, where a crimson damask cloth of estate and matching curtains were erected. A French visitor in 1663 saw the Queen sitting in the crimson enclosure and noted that in the same room were 24 velvet-covered chests, which contained textiles and plate for the chapel brought from Portugal. These included crimson hangings, embroidered with the arms of Portugal and England, which were hung in the chapel below.[48]

Catherine arrived at Whitehall in August 1662 with four priests, including Richard Russell (1630–93), the English bishop-elect of Portalegre (who had managed the diplomatic negotiations for her marriage treaty), a choir master, several musicians and some choir boys.[49] However, the two most important Catholic figures in her household were both aristocratic Englishmen: her grand almoner, Ludovic Stuart, 10th Seigneur d'Aubigny (1619–65), son of the Duke of Lennox, and his nephew, Philip Howard (1629–94), son of the Earl of Arundel and vicar general of the English Dominicans, who was her principal chaplain. D'Aubigny was responsible for supervising the preparations at St James's. In August, the chapel was not quite ready, so it was on 21 September that Catherine attended it for the first time. Pepys watched her arrive in her coach and followed her up to the closet, where he saw 'the fine altar, ornaments, and the fryers in their habits and the priests come in their fine copes … I heard their music too'.[50]

The energetic public revival of Roman Catholic worship at court so soon after the Restoration was extremely unpopular, and it was decided in the winter of 1663 that a more discreet entrance to the Queen's Chapel should be constructed. A section of garden wall was demolished in the park, and a paved causeway running north to south was laid between the new royal garden to the east and St James's privy garden in the west (see Figs 2.2 and 2.6). This gave the Queen, and court Catholics, a private way from Whitehall, across the park, to the chapel. The following year, for everyone else, a new porch, supported by seven columns, was made at the west end of the chapel.[51]

Catherine was extremely pious and her daily devotions were held in her privy closet in her own lodgings at Whitehall. It was only on feast days that she crossed the park to

2.5

Two plates from the English edition of Mollet's *Garden of Pleasure* (1670, pls 25–6), showing the royal garden at St James's. In the text, this garden is identified as 'of mine own invention and drawn with mine own hand'. While the shape and size of the garden is as laid out, maps contemporary with this print show a slightly different layout. All views agree that the west end was laid out as a wilderness, focusing on an ancient oak tree. The design shows clearly the flower beds cut out of the grass and the fruit trees, 5 ft (1.5 m) high, planted in them

2. THE RESTORATION TO QUEEN ANNE

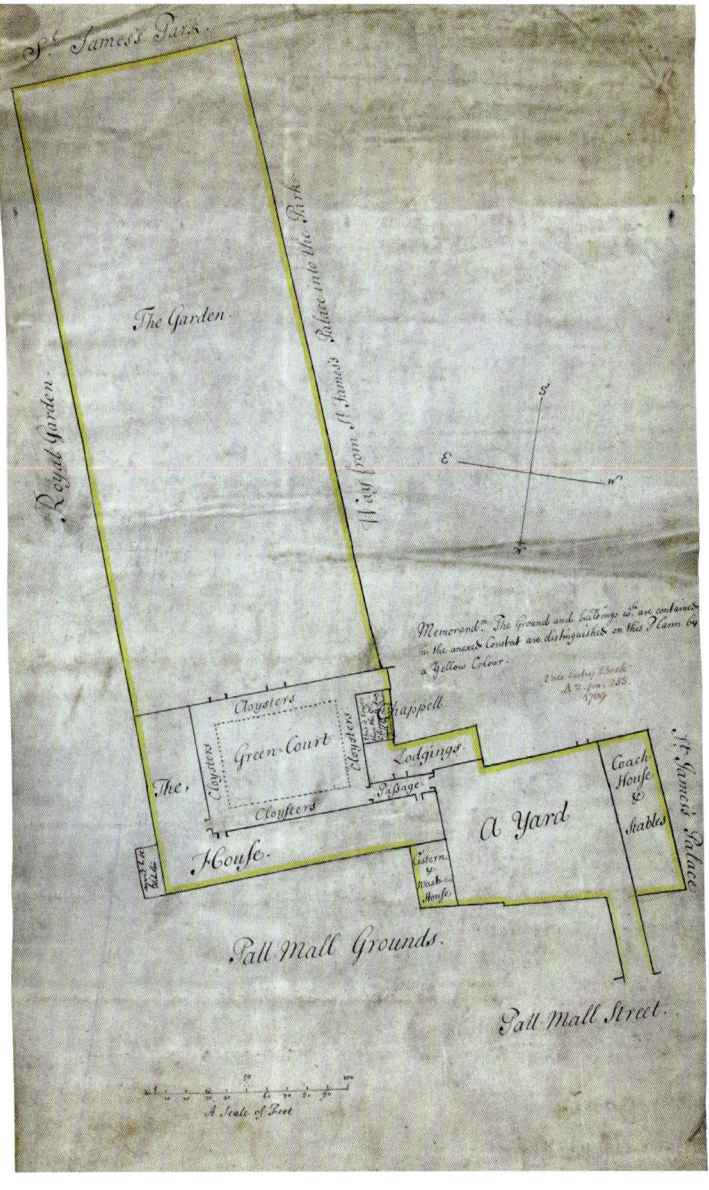

2.6
Survey of the former site of the Queen's friary, undertaken in 1709 in connection with Marlborough House and showing earlier property boundaries (TNA, MPE 1/485; north is at the bottom)

St James's. On these occasions, she could be seen by anyone who attended the chapel, and according to Pepys, the congregation was a complete cross-section of society, from duchesses to beggars. Soon after taking possession of the chapel, Catherine refitted the royal closet. Within it was constructed an elaborately carved and painted tribune, a sort of enclosed pew that looked down into the body of the chapel; adjacent compartments contained a large collection of relics.[52] A confessional was set up in the lower chapel, where there were also two side chapels. A new portable pulpit, reached by seven steps, was supplied.[53]

D'Aubigny died in 1665 and was replaced as the Queen's grand almoner by Philip Howard. Up to this point, the monastic geography of St James's is unclear, but under Howard's influence it was decided to build a friary, to accommodate a band of Franciscan friars to be brought from Portugal. These are commonly thought to have been Capuchins, like the Queen Mother's friars at Somerset House, but in fact they belonged to the Spanish order of St Peter of Alcantara, a reformed Franciscan order that enjoyed the patronage of European royalty. Twelve friars and a father guardian were invited to London; unlike the suave, aristocratic Benedictines, they were simple, severe and not well educated.[54]

The new friary had two aspects to it: a new residence for the Queen's Benedictines in the former tennis court, and a Franciscan friary to the east of the chapel. The latter was paid for from the Queen's privy purse, so there are no detailed accounts for it,[55] but work to convert the tennis court for the Benedictines is chronicled in the Office of Works accounts, even though it was paid for by the Queen. The tennis court was on the other side of Pall Mall from the chapel and connected to the rest of the house by a covered gallery (see p. 32). This gallery was retained, and the tennis court and keeper's house altered to provide new lodgings and a kitchen. A fence was erected in front of the new buildings to shield them from prying eyes.[56]

Because the friary on the other side of the road was swept away in 1709, and the chapel heavily remodelled on a series of subsequent occasions, its initial form has to be pieced together from the financial accounts of repairs by the Office of Works, the observations of visitors and later plans and drawings. A survey (Fig. 2.6) and a diagram provide the plan as it was in the reign of James II, and show the friary engulfing the existing chapel with conventual buildings. To the east was a full four-sided cloister, which had, on its north and east sides, the refectory, dormitory and cells of the friars; to the north of the chapel was the entrance to the friary and sacristy; and on the west, in front of the chapel, was another small cloister, the garth of which was used for burials. At the west end was the royal holyday closet, or tribune, as it was called; at the east end, on the first floor, was the friars' choir.[57]

Sir Christopher Wren, as Surveyor of Works, had ultimate responsibility for the design of the buildings, but he must have been following the lead of the Queen, who in 1669 was reported by the visiting Belgian abbot, Claudius Ageretti, to have a special interest in 'al decoro della Chiesa'. At first, Catherine seems to have been following Spanish rubrics in her chapel, as she purchased a 'Missa Sanctorum Hyspaneum' for it; sermons were preached in Portuguese and the music was in the Portuguese style – and painfully discordant to the ears of Englishmen.[58] These facts may suggest that the raised first-floor eastern choir was also of Iberian inspiration. First-floor choirs, such as that at the royal Jerónimos abbey of Santa Maria de Belém in Lisbon or in the royal basilica in the Escorial, however, had been placed at the west end of the church, providing a clear line of sight to the altar and a place for the display of relics to pilgrims outside, so they are unlikely to have provided the inspiration at St James's. Closer to the St James arrangement is the uniquely Spanish adoption of a camarín, an upper holy of holies, sited behind the high altar, that appeared first in Spanish churches in the fifteenth century. The basilica of the Escorial, for instance, had passages rising behind the high altar to a small upper communion chapel, and such arrangements may have been known to the Queen.[59]

Yet the chapel is, perhaps, unlikely to have had such a strong Iberian source, and Philip Howard, the Queen's English almoner, must have had a significant influence on the design. It was he who had founded the Dominican friary at Bornham (Bornem) in Flanders in 1658. At first, the church and house there were ruinous, and with the help of a lay brother skilled in architecture, one Sebastian Reynaerts, Howard had reconstructed them. He thus had experience of monastic architecture. He also had a cosmopolitan perspective, introducing Italian music into the Queen's new friary. Nothing is known of the eventual form of the house at Bornham, but there are French precedents for an eastern first-floor choir, which Howard may have known. The Capuchin church of Coulommiers in France, designed by Salomon de Brosse (1571–1626) in 1617–25, was, like St James's, a large, bare, barrel-vaulted vessel, with a two-storey eastern end; the lower floor contained a chapel, and the upper, the friar's choir.[60]

As well as the Queen and Father Philip Howard, Wren himself must have had significant input into the discussion about design. He probably had better first-hand experience of French Counter-Reformation church architecture than either the Queen or Howard. During his visit to Paris in 1665, he would have seen the Jesuit church of Saint-Paul-Saint-Louis, the Paris Oratory and the church of Val-de-Grâce, amongst others. These early seventeenth-century French churches had been the dominant influence on the Somerset House chapel under Henrietta Maria.[61] The Oratory had been founded in 1611 and was made the royal chapel of the Louvre by Louis XIII in 1623. François Mansart (1598–1666) had added an oval eastern choir as the Oratorians' private chapel. He also designed such a chapel behind the high altar at the abbey of Val-de-Grâce.[62]

In January 1667, Samuel Pepys was proudly shown round the new friary by Philip Howard himself, and wrote that he

> saw the Dortorie and the cells of the priests, and we went into one – very pretty little room, very clean, hung with pictures – set with books … A pretty library they have, and I was in the Refectory, where every man has his napkin – knife – cup of earth – and basin of the same – and a place for one to sit and read while the rest are at meals. And into the kitchen I went …Their windows looking all into a fine garden and the park. And mighty pretty rooms all.

A few months later, he visited again and was impressed by one of the Portuguese friars he heard preaching, and by the Italian music he heard there on Easter Sunday; on Christmas Eve, he thought 'all things very rich and beautiful'.[63]

Cosimo III of Tuscany (1642–1723) attended a service two years later and noted that under the tribune were two chapels, one of which was dedicated to the Virgin. As early as 1663, the chapel had been dedicated to the Immaculate Conception and a Confraternity of the Rosary was established there – the rosary being recited every day at 4pm. In 1669, Howard published the St James's Rosary for the benefit of English Roman Catholics. According to Cosimo of Tuscany, the friars observed the monastic hours in their upper choir and participated in monthly processions round both cloisters, carrying relics or a consecrated host. In these, the Queen herself participated.[64]

An important change came in 1669, when Henrietta Maria died and Catherine of Braganza inherited Somerset House. She had to make a choice as to which of the chapels was to be her primary place of worship, and she chose Somerset House, the community of Benedictines, relocating there in 1671. Her ownership of the St James's chapel was reasserted by a formal lease granted to her in July; soon afterwards it was handed over for the use of the Portuguese ambassador, and for the next five years it became the home of the London Portuguese community.[65]

Although the Queen did not use the chapel in this period, hostile public opinion was still drawn to St James's by the religion of the Duke and Duchess of York. The Duchess had always been extremely pious, and during the late 1660s, both she and the Duke began to move closer to Rome. The Duchess decided to convert in 1670, and she died in March 1671, a practising Roman Catholic. Soon after, the Duke also converted, a fact that became public after the Test Act, passed in 1673, caused his resignation as Lord High Admiral. For the heir to the throne to be acknowledged as a Roman Catholic was a significant threat to the Protestant status quo, and one that hugely intensified after the 'Popish Marriage' of the Duke to the 15-year-old Mary Beatrice d'Este of Modena in 1673. The prospect of a Catholic heir being born at St James's, and the consequences this would have for the Church in England, dominated English politics for the rest of Charles II's reign.

In the 1670s and 1680s, St James's, which had been a focus for anti-Catholic protest in the 1630s, once again became the target of suspicion and dislike of the royal family – especially the Duke and Duchess of York. Not only was the Portuguese community stationed at the Queen's Chapel, but the Duchess began to invite Catholics to her private chapel. The first of many measures to restrict Catholics from flocking to St James's was enacted by the King in December 1673, when he forbade them to enter the park or house, which he defined as being part and parcel of Whitehall.[66] In 1676, the Portuguese were expelled from the Queen's Chapel after being accused of distributing Roman Catholic literature in the Queen's household.[67] Also expelled were the Queen's Benedictines, after an order was passed in February 1675 banishing all English and Irish Catholic priests from England; an exception was made only for Father Huddleston.[68] This left the Queen's Portuguese friars at St James's as the only religious community at court.

In 1678, the Popish Plot was unveiled, and that winter, a wave of terror broke over London. People genuinely feared that Catholics would slit their throats at night and that England was on the eve of a popish rising. Charles reacted by energetically enforcing regulations against Catholics, and in November, under royal orders, Wren 'boarded and barred' seven doors of the chapel at St James's to prevent its use.[69] Parliament, meanwhile, pressed for new legislation, including, in 1680, a bill to forcibly transport disloyal papists out of London. In November, the bonfires blazed with effigies of the Pope, and the Queen's ladies trembled behind the locked gates of Somerset House. On the Strand, in the midst of a dense and hostile population, Somerset House was a major provocation, rebounding badly on the reputation of the royal family, so Charles ordered that the chapel there be shut and the Queen's 17 (Portuguese) priests (and Father Huddleston) be relocated to the much more secure and less inflammatory location of St James's. It was in this way that St James's once again became the centre of the Queen's religious life.[70]

After 1669, Queen Catherine had lavished attention on the chapel and friary at Somerset House, and its forcible closure, only a decade later, threatened to waste the considerable investment she had made. The friary was to be converted into lodgings for her treasurer and receiver general, and the Office of Works was commissioned to strip the building of its fixtures and fittings and remove them to St James's. Works at St James's to prepare for the arrival of the Queen's religious household and the fittings from Somerset House were very substantial, amounting to a complete remodelling of the chapel and friary in the winter of 1679–80, costing some £1,569.[71]

The remodelling drew heavily on the Counter-Reformation principle of enhancing the beauty and magnificence of the church, and in particular, the primary focus of the high altar. The presbytery was thus enlarged by moving the altar rails forward; a blue and gold tabernacle was added to the high altar, with a canopy above, and sanctuary lamps hung before it. An elegant, six-sided wine-glass pulpit was erected, with carved cherubs, swags of fruit and cockle shells. Two dozen prickets were nailed into the cornice to provide scope for more lighting. The whole interior was repainted and gilded. The antechapel was radically remodelled by forming two rooms beneath the privy closet with their own chimneys; one of them received an altarpiece dismantled from Somerset House. In anticipation of large congregations, collecting boxes were fixed to the walls.

The Queen's closet, and the withdrawing room to its south, were remodelled and repaired. A false floor was built to raise the Queen's chair, to give her a better view through the window that looked down onto the high altar – this was railed round and given two semicircular steps to reach it. It is likely that the privy chapel mentioned in the accounts was at first-floor level in this area. An especially beautiful key for the privy closet door was made for the Queen's personal use. A door on the north side of the closet, now blocked, led into the friary (see Plan C).

To the north of the friary was the sacristy, into which were moved chests of drawers and cupboards full of vestments and liturgical items from Somerset House. A red varnished shelf was built on one of these cupboards for candlesticks and a large cross. The room next door was set up as a lavatorium, with a sink and cistern. Nearby was the room for the choir children. Fourteen stalls removed from Somerset House were installed in the friars' choir, and four new ones were made to match.

The friary kitchen, pantry and larder were refurbished, and the refectory on the north side of the great cloister was furnished with 36 ft (11 m) of new benches. More accommodation had to be made for the friars, and a gallery that had been above the great cloister was divided up to make bedrooms. Chimneys were inserted, shelves and skirtings added and a clock erected in the passage outside. One room was converted into a library, fitted with 50 cupboards and supplied with folding library steps.

The great cloister was refurbished and improved; four niches in its walls and its 27 columns were redecorated. Purbeck slabs were laid in the walks and a balustrade added to the roof of the south walk to provide views over the friary garden (see Plan C). The Dean of the chapel was provided with lodgings near the coach house and stable in the outer yard.[72]

These improvements transformed the old friary. Henrietta Maria's friary at Somerset House had been much more modest in its architectural expression – at St James's, two cloisters, a full suite of conventual buildings and substantial ancillary accommodation were carefully planned and expensively executed. By 1684, the cost of running it was £3,590 a year in wages, plus a further £200 for the five singing boys of the chapel. The friary church was well attended; many Catholics married and baptised their children there in private; on Michaelmas October 1680, it was estimated that between 200 and 300 people attended the service.[73]

The friary was not to last long, however, for on the night of 18 March 1682, in what was seen by some as divine judgement, it was severely damaged by fire. With some glee, it was reported, 'The fire yesterday fell amongst the

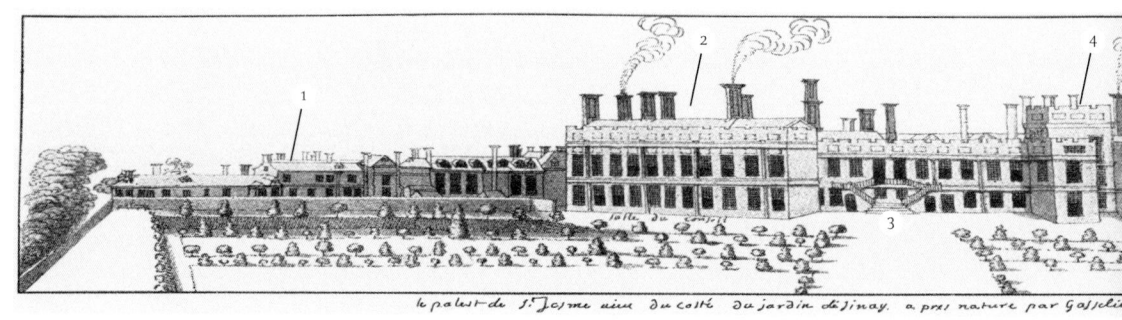

priests and fires at St James's burned down all the priory and the Queen's chapel. People condole not much seeing that it fell amongst them, and say that "the beads cract and ratled like anything"'. It must have been a serious blaze, as parts of the friary were blown up with gunpowder to stop the fire spreading to the main building, and looters infiltrated themselves amongst the firefighters. The lodgings of the Earl of Bath in the north-east corner of the house were damaged, showing how close the fire came to burning the outer court.[74]

The Queen immediately gave orders for the rebuilding of the Chapel, once more paid for from her own purse. Sir Christopher Wren was again the architect and he directed a campaign that lasted 14 months and cost, without fees, some £4,951 6s 8d. The detailed bills and enrolled accounts that survive for this amongst Catherine of Braganza's papers make it clear that this major reconstruction included 'new buildings' as well as repairs.[75]

Architecturally, the most significant part of the commission was the rebuilding of the friars' choir. This remained at first-floor level at the east end of the chapel, but was now centrally planned. It was fitted with 14 stalls, 6 ft (1.8 m) high, raised up on five steps, topped with a cornice and laid out in a semicircle beneath a dome. The kneelers were segmental, so followed the semicircle of stalls; two stalls were 'to open in the choir', and the Father Guardian's stall was larger and set against the door, with a pediment matching the doorcase; in front of this was a rotating lectern on a pedestal. There was an altar on two steps with a painted tabernacle on it, and a white marble chimneypiece. It is likely that the choir was circular – the accounts mention an 'angle room' containing shelves and a small altar.

In 1673–4, Wren had built a dome to bring light into the auditorium of the Theatre Royal

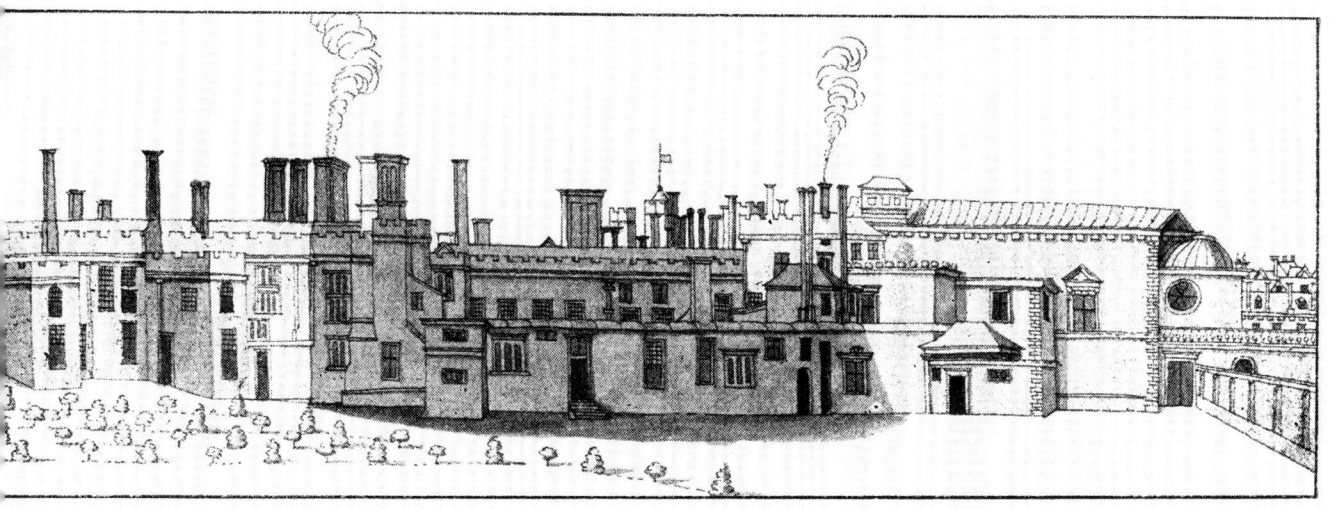

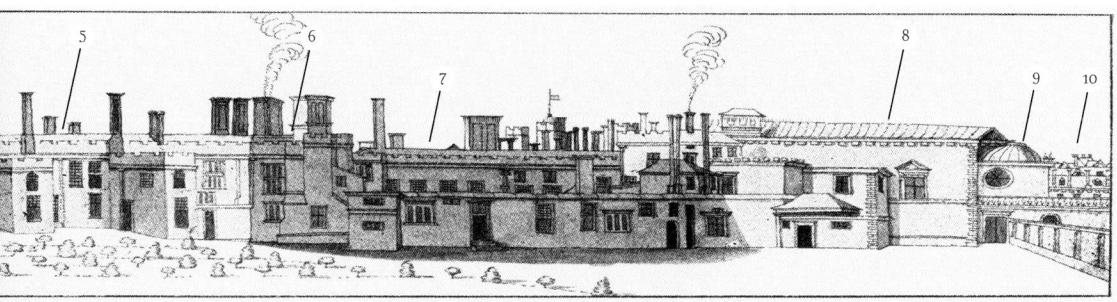

in Drury Lane; the year before that he had started work on St Stephen's Walbrook in the city, which was also lit centrally, with a dome, and was completed in 1677. Like St Stephen's, the St James's choir was lit by circular windows.[76] The dome was painted inside by Jacob Huysmans (c.1633–96), a Roman Catholic painter from Antwerp and self-styled painter to the Queen.[77] Mansard had been fascinated with circular and oval chapels, and at the royal chapel of the Louvre (the Paris Oratory) and Val-de-Grâce there were domed chapels behind the high altar. This must have been the inspiration for Wren's new upper choir, the outside of which can be seen on a drawing made in late 1703 (Fig. 2.7).[78]

The choir was integrated with the rest of the friary by a small stair that led down from it to the room behind the altar and a new passage made on the north side of the chapel that connected with the Queen's tribune.

2.7

St James's from the south by François Gasselin (d. 1703). Gasselin lived in England from 1693 to 1703. The appearance of Queen Anne's new building dates the view precisely to late 1703 (illustrated in Sheppard 1894, I, opp. p. 6)

1. The backs of courtier houses belonging to Viscount Fitzhardinge, the Earl of Roscommon and Sir Charles Hedges
2. Queen Anne's new Council Chamber and Drawing Room, built in 1703
3. Stairs from the Drawing Room to the garden, built in c.1697
4. Privy stairs rebuilt for James II in 1682, in Tudor style
5. Former privy gallery converted into lodgings for James II in the 1670s and 1680s
6. Royal library with privy kitchen below
7. Lodgings for Princess Anne
8. Queen's Chapel
9. Wren's dome over the friars' choir, built in 1682–3
10. Friary

2.8

Altarpiece at the Jesuit church of Saint-Paul-Saint-Louis, Paris, by Père François Derand, completed in 1641 and engraved and published by d'Edme Moreau in 1643. Such images of Counter-Reformation church interiors were widely available, and they provided models for Wren to follow in the Queen's Chapel (Musée Carnavalet, Paris, Topo GC XVII Bis E)

2.9

The Queen's Chapel, St James's, c.1685 (Magdalene College, Cambridge, PL 2972, p. 186)

The construction of this involved shaving off the deep architrave and pediment of two of the north windows.

The Queen took great interest in the refitting of the chapel interior, and Wren's design for a new altarpiece was made into a scale model by Grinling Gibbons (1648–1721). Wren looked to Counter-Reformation altarpieces in Paris for his inspiration, either on the instruction of the Queen or, more likely, as he had seen them himself. Also available were books and loose-leaf prints depicting altarpieces such as the extravagant creation at the Jesuit church of Saint-Paul-Saint-Louis in Paris by Père François Derand (1588/91–1644) (Fig. 2.8). This design, and several others for high altars, had been published by d'Edme Moreau in 1643, and again by Jean Marot c.1655.[79] Once erected, the new St James's altarpiece did not find favour with the Queen and required unspecified alteration; the finally executed piece is recorded in a contemporary engraving (Fig. 2.9). This shows a highly articulated structure, with a central painting of the Holy Family by Jacob Huysmans in an elaborate frame by Gibbons; either side of this were quadrants containing niches, and

2.10

The south-east corner of St James's, c.1690. The engraving shows the lodgings of the library keeper, and, to the right, the Queen's Chapel and friary in some detail. People can be seen arriving at the private door to the chapel by coach and sedan chair (Magdalene College, Cambridge, PL 2972, p.103b)

against the outer walls, portals leading to a passage behind the altarpiece and the room beneath the choir. On top of each of the portals was a large carved angel, and above the blocked east window were carved putti carrying the Queen's arms. Parry Walton, the King's 'mender and repairer' of paintings, was employed to work on 'five altar pieces' and 'three pieces put in each picture'. This seems to refer to the restoration of the huge canvasses set in the blocked east windows, which were presumably damaged by the fire.[80] The frames of these, and much of the carving, were subsequently gilded by the sergeant painter. Very much stripped-down and simplified, the carcass of this altarpiece remains, as do the Queen's arms supported by flying putti above the east window.

For the front of the organ balcony, Gibbons provided a new carved panel, and two large niches were cut out of the walls to take statues. These were filled with effigies of St Peter and St Paul by John Bushnell (1636–1701), which were taken down from the Somerset House chapel and erected on new pedestals. The engraving of the chapel shows St Augustine and St Benedict in these positions.[81] The presbytery was vastly enlarged and raised on a six-inch (15.2 cm) platform, with a new rail, 49 ft (14.9 m) long, with 59 balusters. Behind this were walnut stools and a form, as well as a large, turned Easter candlestick. This large platform, which markedly reduced the capacity of the chapel for worshippers, allowed a greater elaboration of liturgy.

All the fittings in the tribune were stripped away and a new rail installed with 72 balusters, with pedestals and an opening gate; meanwhile, a new screen was carved for the front of the balcony. There was a private chapel nearby for which a carved Madonna was gilded, and three small paintings and one large one were supplied. On the chapel roof, two little lanterns were erected; the south one can be seen on an engraving of c.1690 (Fig. 2.10).

Nothing like this chapel had been seen before in England (see Plans B and C); its richness and its uncompromising pursuit of the beauty of holiness made it the unquestioned centre of English Roman Catholicism. It also made it a target for those who regarded the Queen's religion with horror. As a result, the room next to the park was designated a guard room and was manned day and night, so as to admit only bona fide Catholics. Eighteen pass keys were cut to be distributed to the friars so they could gain access to the private parts of the friary. There was a large, secure chest containing

2. THE RESTORATION TO QUEEN ANNE   87

plate, in the care of the treasurer of the chapel, Emanuel Dias, and the sacristy, which contained more plate, had a guard who slept there each night. These precautions, along with the presence of iron bars on most of the windows, were not enough to prevent a serious theft in November 1687.[82]

The Duke and Duchess of York

St James's was the family home of the Duke and Duchess: here, the Duchess held Drawing Rooms and balls, and the Duke celebrated his birthday with plays performed in the guard chamber.[83] There were more formal events too. As the official seat of the heir to the throne, it was to St James's that ambassadors came to present themselves to the Duke and Duchess. In 1675, the Duke of Neuberg arrived at St James's, where the Duke, following the precedent set down by the King, received him in his bedchamber. After the formal audience, he took his guest out through his closets to the Duchess's bedchamber, then backwards through the Duchess's outer lodgings to the Great Stairs. Such privileged access was counted a very great honour.[84]

For the Duchess, St James's was also her lying-in house and nursery, and it was where she gave birth to eight children. The first was Charles, Duke of Cambridge (1660–61), with their second child, Mary, born two years later. A third, James, was born in 1663 and he also bore the title Duke of Cambridge. He was joined by another girl, Anne, in 1665. James died in 1667, as did another Charles, Duke of Kendal (1666–7). Edgar, Duke of Cambridge (1667–71), survived only a little longer. Anne herself died the day after giving birth to a baby girl, Catherine (b. and d. 1671), at the age of 34. St James's was home to all these children, but was also intermittently filled with harrowing scenes of grief, as their parents laid to rest six infant boys and a girl.

The children passed their summers in Richmond upon Thames, where part of the old Tudor palace had been converted into a house for them; St James's was their winter home.[85] Where the children's lodgings were to begin with is unclear, but in 1666, a nursery was created out of the old Tudor Council Chamber near the chapel for the Duke of Kendal.[86] As Mary turned 11 in 1673, she began to become part of court life, acting in plays and accompanying the King, her uncle, on state occasions. At the same time, work started on the construction of a small suite of rooms for her in the inner (bay garden) court. These rooms were back to back with the Duke's bedchamber and privy chamber, and were entered from his presence chamber. This meant that Mary could receive visitors who approached through the outer rooms of the King's lodgings. There was a bedchamber and two closets, including one lined with bookshelves; an independent stair led to service rooms below. This suite can be seen on William Dickinson's plan of c.1703–14 (see Fig. 1.4 and Plan B).[87]

After the death of Duchess Anne, and before the arrival of the Duke of York's new bride, Mary Beatrice of Modena, the consort's lodgings were given a lick of paint. She arrived at Whitehall on 26 November 1673 and was received by the Queen, before making her way across the park to her new home. We learn that 'they passed through the guard chamber, the guard, making a lane as they passed, into the bedchamber; where they reposed themselves for about ½ an hour, after that their regal highnesses came to dine in public seated under a state, the Duchess on the Duke's right hand'. The King came and visited Mary Beatrice in her new home, graciously sitting with her at table and conversing with her in public; soon, foreign ambassadors and English aristocrats followed, and she established her own Drawing Room (on a different day to the Queen's), to which courtiers came in large numbers. Also, of course, she was introduced to her stepdaughters, Mary and Anne.[88]

As a consequence of the Princesses growing up, and in anticipation of children being born to their youthful stepmother, it was decided to build more rooms into the Tudor galleries round the bay garden court. Mary's lodgings were joined to Anne's by a gallery, and Anne's rooms were close to the Roman Catholic chapel; this places them on the east side of the bay garden court.⁸⁹ In fact, it seems that in the 1670s, the cross gallery and north gallery were divided up, and two narrow communication galleries constructed on the inner side of the inner court to give access to the new rooms. It was probably these 'galleries on 2 sides of the bay garden' that were painted in 1675–6 and then reglazed in 1684 (see Plan C).⁹⁰ It is not clear which of the suites of rooms shown on William Dickinson's 1703 plan (see Fig. 2.24) belonged to Princess Anne, but the plasterer who was working on the 'passage and galleries and backstairs' belonging to 'lady mary and lady anne's lodgings' in 1676–7, was working round bay court, and Anne's new closet was approached by one of the passages.⁹¹

Just as the marriage treaties of Henrietta Maria and Catherine of Braganza had promised them freedom of worship and a Roman Catholic chapel, so Mary of Modena's treaty guaranteed her rights of religion. However, she had not been promised a private Roman Catholic chapel, and when she arrived at St James's, she was dismayed to find that the Catholic chapel was the Queen's, not hers, and that the Anglican chapel was not available either, as it was reserved for the Princesses Mary and Anne. A small private oratory had been established for her in her lodgings, and that was all; here, with her priests, she and the Duke of York (who was, at this date, a secret Catholic), could practise their devotions together. Despite this disappointment, she was very kindly treated by the Duke and the King, and introduced to the ways of the English court.⁹²

Her primary duty, however, was to bear James an heir, and much to her satisfaction, she gave birth to a daughter, Catherine, in January 1675. This child, who died in infancy, was one of four, delivered to the Duchess up to 1682, who were born alive; there were many miscarriages, and all the children, including a boy, Charles, born in 1677, died as children. Yet Mary Beatrice was still of child-bearing age, and in 1676, after the birth of Princess Isabella (1676–81), there was a reorganisation of accommodation at St James's. This was partly occasioned by the impending marriage of Princess Mary, who was by now 15.

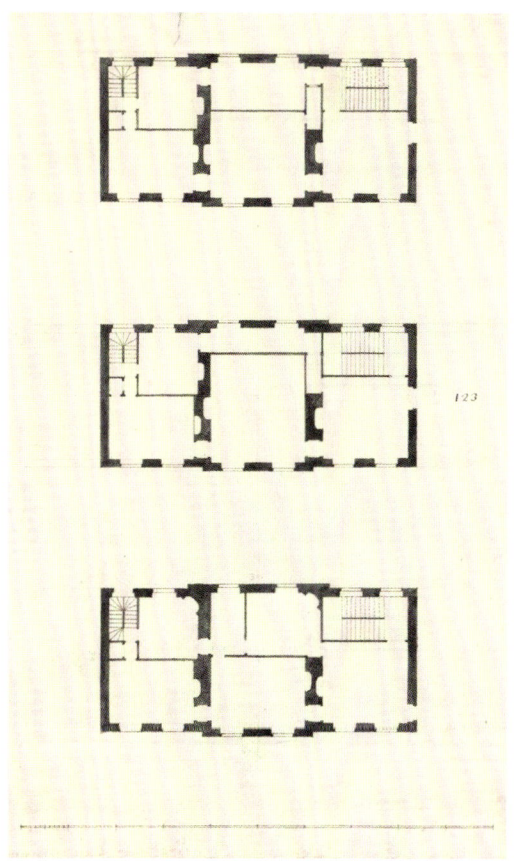

2.11
Edward Woodroofe, plans for the three storeys of the new nursery building on the south front of St James's, 1677. The ground floor is at the bottom, the first floor in the middle, with access to the Duchess's rooms through a door to the right of the plan. Three rooms followed: Presence Chamber, bedchamber and then closet with a WC and backstairs. On the top floor the block connected to the attics (AS, IV:124)

Although the Duke of York would have preferred a Catholic husband for his eldest daughter, there was no chance of that being agreed by the King, who had set his eye on William of Orange, with whom discussions started in earnest in 1677. Although the marriage was no *fait accompli*, the Office of Works was ordered to reconstruct both Mary and Anne's lodgings in the bay garden court. It is now not possible to correlate the changes detailed in the enrolled accounts with the survey by William Dickinson of c.1703–14 (see Fig. 1.4). This is partly because it is clear that Mary's and Anne's lodgings were on more than one floor, and the survey we have is of the first floor only. However, the sisters each had a presence chamber, bedchamber and closet with attached garderobe; Mary also had a dressing room and a wardrobe room. The rooms were given new panelling and fireplaces with marble hearths, while old stone casements were replaced with timber sashes.⁹³

It was in her closet, in October 1677, that the Duke of York told Mary that she was to marry

William of Orange. The Princess burst into tears and was not to be consoled for several days. The marriage followed fast and was celebrated privately by the Bishop of London in the Princess's bedchamber. After dinner, the newly-weds went to bed. This was probably in Mary's bedroom, recently refitted with a shallow step for the bed and boards around it, to prevent dogs from getting underneath. With Mary and William safely under the covers, Charles II pulled aside the bed curtains, exclaiming, 'Now, Nephew, to your work! Hey! St George for England!'. Not many weeks later, William and Mary left London for Holland, vacating her lodgings at St James's for good.[94]

Meanwhile, work had been under way on an entirely new building, designed to accommodate the royal children. This seems to have been agreed by the King in May, and the following October, he contributed £921 7s ½d to the cost. It was into these lodgings that Princess Anne and her half-sister, Isabella, now moved.[95] The new building was paid for out of the Duke and Duchess's own purse, and only a single contract survives in the Office of Works, for the panelling of the 'ladyes roomes'. This shows that the block was elegantly fitted out with panelling, incorporating overdoor and overmantel frames for paintings of the 'Corinthian order'.[96] Once completed, the Office of Works seems to have taken over maintenance and minor alterations; the accounts in 1677–8 mention the 'new building', the 'new nursery', 'the Duchess [sic] new nursery' and 'Lady Isabella's nursery in the new building'. The building was designed by Sir Christopher Wren, in whose hand a drawing survives; his draughtsman, Edward Woodroofe (c.1622–75), prepared what was perhaps a presentation version (Fig. 2.11), showing all three floors of the building (but not its basement, which was a cellar for the Duke's wine).[97]

As in the bay garden court, the Princesses were provided with a three-room suite of presence chamber, bedchamber and closet, with an attached garderobe. A formal staircase allowed the Princesses and their visitors to approach the rooms independently, and a backstairs was provided for servants. At ground-floor level, a door led into a passage through to the gardens, and on the first floor there was a doorway through to the Queen's withdrawing room. The building was of brick with stone dressings, and with large sash windows and a solid parapet, it contrasted strongly in style with the adjacent Tudor buildings. A similar block had been built at Hampton Court in 1670 for Charles II, also in the style of the day. There was no squeamishness about this conjunction, and the battlements on the little towers on the south front and elsewhere were carefully repaired, maintaining the predominantly Tudor air of the place.[98]

The construction of the new lodgings encouraged the Duke and Duchess to focus attention on their garden. The appropriation of the early Stuart gardens by the King and the Queen (for her friary) left St James's with the garden that more or less coincides with that enjoyed by the palace today. A wall was constructed in 1677, and earth terraces, approached by steps, built against it.[99] These elevated walks gave views over parterres planted in the flat levels of the garden below, and presumably also over the wall into the park. It is not known who designed and planted the parterres, but by 1685 the Duke had a gardener, who was 'keeper of the St James's House garden', called Mr Wright.[100] A painting dating from c.1690, after the completion of the new wing and laying out of the garden, shows the terraces and the new balcony, constructed at the same time, in front of the Queen's drawing room (Fig. 2.12).[101]

The lives of the Duke and Duchess at St James's were changed forever by the Popish Plot. The 'plot' itself was nonsense, but in the investigation that followed, papers were found in the house of Edward Colman, Mary Beatrice's former secretary, proving clandestine correspondence with various leading European Catholic figures, including Louis XIV's confessors. One letter appeared to implicate James in a plan to change monarch. Charles was forced to act to calm the ensuing uproar, and in March 1679, James and Mary were banished,

first to Brussels and then to Scotland, where James remained until March 1682.

Until her father's return, Princess Anne was the sole royal resident of St James's. The only significant work that took place on the building during this period was a remodelling of the Duchess's oratory next to her bedroom. This work was perhaps inspired by the major works then under way in the Queen's Chapel, and seems to have been paid for by the King. The room was enlarged and a closet made to it for the keeping of sacred vessels. A new altarpiece by Benedetto Gennari (1633–1715) (see pp. 94–5) was given a richly carved floral frame, and a window opened up above it.[102]

The return of the Duke and Duchess was celebrated by a series of receptions and balls at St James's, and was also accompanied by a reorganisation of their innermost rooms round the backstairs on the south front. This three-storey Tudor stair tower was dismantled and rebuilt, with the modern, regular stair seen on Dickinson's plan of c.1703–14 (see Fig. 1.4). At the same time, the Duchess's dressing room was reorganised and the oratory given a much larger window.[103]

In 1680, Princess Anne turned 15, and the question of whom she should marry became a topic of speculation and controversy in the highly charged atmosphere of the Exclusion Crisis. But it was not until after the Princess returned from a ten-month stay in Edinburgh with her father in 1682 that serious negotiations for her marriage began. Her husband was to be Prince George of Denmark (1653–1708), a distant cousin, who arrived in London in July 1683. George was a solid choice, a soldier of few words and, crucially, a devout Protestant, albeit a Lutheran. They met and wed at St James's soon after. As with her sister, Mary, the King gave encouraging words as they mounted their wedding bed. The Prince and Princess of Denmark did not make their home at St James's, but in 1684, they were granted an extensive suite in the Cockpit at Whitehall.[104]

2.12

The south front of St James's, painted in c.1690, after the completion of the nursery wing, terraces, garden and balcony. Previously thought to be by Hendrick Danckerts (c.1625–80), the attribution of this version of the painting is currently uncertain (RCIN 400009)

2. THE RESTORATION TO QUEEN ANNE

After the Commonwealth sales, the sole surviving royal contents of St James's were the royal library and medal cabinet that the Council of State had wanted to establish as a public resource. Even this had been plundered, and 279 books were returned to the King in 1660. Orders were given not to remove John Durie, the librarian, until he had made a full inventory of the books and manuscripts. The accounts of the royal wardrobe, which was working overtime to refurnish the King's houses, contain no bills for St James's other than for the rebinding of some 665 volumes.[105] The library was not destined to become part of the Duke's house; the King retained it under his own control and appointed his own librarian, Thomas Ross, who had a separate entrance and quarters, including his own kitchen (see Figs 2.10 and 2.18). In 1681, Charles even considered extending it to create a centre for the collection of rare manuscripts.[106]

In 1660, a series of measures were taken for the recovery of 'the King's Goods', and by the time Charles II set foot in Whitehall, large quantities of former royal paintings, tapestry and some furniture had been returned. As the recovered property arrived, the architect John Webb took responsibility for distributing it amongst the royal houses, including St James's. Recovery continued until 1672, but already by 1661, more than 1,000 pictures had been rehung on royal walls in and around London.[107] What is unknown is what was sent to St James's, and whether, when the royal family arrived, there was a redistribution of objects to suit everyone's tastes. The Duke and Duchess may not, in fact, have received much from the repossession committee, which was focused on retrieving sovereign property. At any rate, they were rich enough to commission new paintings, buy antiques and order new furniture and wall-hangings to their own taste. The substantial grants provided by Parliament (see p. 72) would have made a major contribution to this.

In June 1674, an inventory was made of the Duke of York's possessions.[108] The list divided objects between furniture in store and that which was disposed in 'rooms constantly up'. It was not systematically compiled, mixing rooms at Whitehall and St James's indiscriminately, but there is enough that is specific to St James's to paint a picture of what the palace looked like early in the Duke's second marriage. The outer rooms were hung with tapestry described as 'Arras'; these were most likely gold-woven sets of sixteenth-century tapestries, probably from Henry VIII's collection, and mainly depicting classical and biblical subjects, such as Samson, Abraham, Alexander and Marcus Aurelius. Most of these sets were 11 or 12 ft (3.4 or 3.7 m) high and gave a sense of great grandeur and tradition, setting off the damask canopies of state and seat furniture. In the more private rooms were more modern tapestries, including a set of Mortlake *Acts of the Apostles* (see p. 143). If the charming, whimsical set of Don Quixote tapestries listed in the inventory hung at St James's, as seems likely, they would have been in the privy lodgings; they were only 8 ft (2.4 m) high (Fig. 2.13).[109]

The presence chambers had canopies of state, beneath which were large Turkey carpets and two elbow chairs. Stools were ranged round the rooms. In the Duchess's drawing room was another canopy, under which there was an elbow chair of green and gold, and a matching set of six stools.

On the Duchess's side there were two bedchambers. We do not know which of the elaborate beds listed was the one normally used in the great, white-painted bedchamber, but when Duchess Anne lay in to give birth, a white calico bed, with white bone lace and four silvered lions, was placed in the alcove. The little bedchamber next door had a 'sad-coloured' silk bed, with pink satin lining and a gold and silver fringe. Two elbow chairs and four stools were upholstered to match. The white theme continued in the Duchess's closet, which was hung with white damask and contained low daybeds with white upholstered cushions. Nearby was her dressing room, hung with gilt leather and containing a bathing tub and green damask-covered seat furniture.

On the Duke's side, the little bedchamber was hung in yellow taffeta and silver lace, with matching bed and furniture. His library, the location of which has not been identified,

2.13

Don Quixote tilting at windmills, woven under the direction of Charles II's royal arras-maker, Francis Poyntz (d. 1685), 1660–84. This tapestry, commissioned by Catherine of Braganza for the Portuguese ambassador, measuring 10 ft 4 in. by 10 ft 11 in. (3.2 by 3.3 m), was once owned by James II. The comical and unconventional series shows that the Duke and Duchess of York did not lack a sense of humour (Metropolitan Museum of Art, New York, 2014.567)

contained elbow chairs, a couch and four stools; a neighbouring room hung in blue damask was the library closet, with white taffeta curtains hung over the books. A large closet, known as the white room, was hung with white sarsnet (a type of cotton) and blue mohair, and contained ten portraits of court ladies by Sir Peter Lely (1618–80), known as the 'Windsor Beauties'. These were not a set in the sense that they were the product of a single commission, but they were a gathering together of paintings of living court beauties, apparently commissioned by the Duchess of York and hung in the Duke's lodgings for his pleasure. According to the comte de Grammont, the Duke enjoyed admiring the paintings. The same room also contained six paintings by Andrea Schiavone (c.1510–63), purchased by the Duke (Fig. 2.14).[110]

The inventory also lists the contents of the two Princesses' closets and of the Anglican chapel ('lady Maryes chapel'); in here, there were two elbow chairs, two cushions and a carpet. Much more magnificent were the Duke and Duchess's private chapels. Rich, fringed altar cloths, cushions, pulpit and desk cloths, kneeling cushions and curtains give an impression of great splendour. The Duchess, like the Queen, had developed a liking for the work of the Bolognese painter, Benedetto Gennari, and owned several altarpieces and other devotional paintings by him. In 1682, on her return from Scotland, she commissioned two paintings from him for her remodelled

2. THE RESTORATION TO QUEEN ANNE

2.14

Andrea Schiavone, *The Meeting of Jacob and Rachel*, 1530–60. This is one of a group of paintings by Schiavone that presumably were hung above or below the 'Windsor Beauties' in the Duke of York's closet (RCIN 402890)

2.15

Benedetto Gennari, *The Holy Family*, dated 1682 and painted for the Duchess of York's private oratory at St James's. The painting, which depicts Joseph lifting the Christ Child to Mary's breast to feed, measures 7 ft by 5 ft 5 in. (213 by 167.6 cm), and, with its architectural frame, shows just how large the private chapel must have been (Birmingham Museum and Art Gallery, 1974P12)

oratory (Fig. 2.15), one depicting St François de Sales, Bishop of Geneva, to whom she was especially devoted.[111]

The Duke and Duchess owned a lavish collection of other items, including cabinets, tables, fire furniture, looking glasses, candlesticks, chandeliers and sconces. There were few paintings, but the Duke collected model ships, and visitors to his rooms were impressed by these. Together, all this confirms the impression gained by contemporaries that the house, and in particular the Duchess's rooms, were majestically furnished.[112]

James II and Mary Beatrice of Modena

When James came to the throne, he had abstained from publicly taking the Anglican sacrament for 13 years, and for nine of those, he had been a papist recusant. Now, as King, nothing was to hold him back, and on the first Sunday after his accession, he attended Mass in public at the St James's chapel. The chapel became the property of his Queen, Mary Beatrice, and the Dowager Queen's Alcantarine friars quickly moved out and re-established themselves at Somerset House, where Catherine was living. The grant of house and chapel to the new Queen was made official in December 1685.[113] For the King, a new, much larger Roman Catholic chapel was to be built at Whitehall. Orders for designing this must have been issued immediately, as Wren already had a design and estimate for the work in early May. The Whitehall privy gallery was emptied of furniture, which was piled up in the Banqueting House, and the court decamped to St James's. Building progressed at a tremendous rate, and in December 1687, the new apartments at Whitehall were being furnished.[114]

In a reign that lasted less than four years, James therefore spent two and a half of them in his old quarters at St James's. With the house now both James II's London home and the main residence of the sovereign, it was perhaps inevitable that the chapel would require further adaptation. Two chairs of state were ordered for the chapel tribune, allowing monarch and consort to sit side by side. Two small staircases were built, to allow James and Mary Beatrice to descend from the tribune to the body of the chapel at appropriate moments in the liturgy, and a side altar was built (or enlarged), with a rail and tabernacles supplied for it. In anticipation of a royal baptism, a large niche was cut out of the brickwork (probably below the organ loft) for a font.[115]

Benedetto Gennari, who had already supplied paintings for the private chapel at St James's, was commissioned to paint a huge Holy Family for the high altar in the Queen's Chapel. This was designed to be replaced over the Easter period by two other paintings of the same size: a Crucifixion on Good Friday, and a Resurrection for Easter Sunday. He was also commissioned to paint a smaller altarpiece for the new side chapel, an image of St James, presumably the chapel's designation.[116]

With the Queen's friary empty, James re-established it as a Benedictine monastery. Thirteen monks and two lay brothers were drawn from three English Benedictine houses and placed under the Augustinian Howard as superior.[117] The friary buildings were put in good repair and the King ordered a new library of sacred books for the well-educated monks. As the Whitehall chapel came closer to completion, it was decided in 1686 to take some of the best fittings from St James's to adorn it. These had been paid for initially by the Queen, and she was reimbursed some £1,298 13s 9d in compensation for their removal.[118]

James was not only interested in the welfare of his own soul, but also wanted to re-establish the Roman Catholic Church in England. Since the 1620s, English Roman Catholics had been under a series of vicars general, but in 1685, James invited John Leyburn (1620–1702), Bishop of Adrumetum, to England, and he was invested with the powers of a vicar apostolic. He took up residence in St James's. In 1688, three other vicars apostolic were consecrated, and each was given a quarter of England over which to preside – Leyburn taking the south. In this way, James, with the Pope's authority, re-established a Roman Catholic hierarchy in England, and its titular headquarters was at St James's.[119] This was reflected in a parade of high-profile services in the monastery: in May 1687, for instance, Ferdinand, count d'Adda (1649–1719), the papal nuncio, was consecrated Archbishop of Amasia by the Archbishop of Armagh, John Leyburn and another Irish bishop, in a ceremony of great magnificence.[120]

As a temporary resident at St James's, the King ordered some improvements for his own comfort in his inner lodgings, including an elaborate flushing privy, and a room built out into Bay Court as a dining room for the pages of his backstairs. A council chamber was also set up, with its own private stair and room for the clerks, as that at Whitehall was being rebuilt.[121]

James and Mary Beatrice moved into the newly completed apartments at Whitehall in January 1688. That month, James ordered a comprehensive inventory to be made of all 'Plate, Jewells, Hangings, Bedding, Furniture Pictures Statues and Household goods whatsoever' in all his houses and offices. This inventory drew on earlier inventories made during the emptying of the state rooms and the storage of the King's goods in the Banqueting House.[122] One version of it includes the details of some rooms at St James's and it is clear from this inventory that the paintings listed were the Duke and Duchess's personal collection, amassed since 1662. It confirms that the great outer rooms were still hung with tapestry, and it was the smaller inward rooms of the privy lodgings that contained paintings. In the King's drawing room there was a Magdalen over the chimney by Lely, and a sea-piece over a door; the remainder of the room was hung in tapestry. In store were paintings that were clearly of the Duke's taste – a series of ten half-length admirals and captains, and portraits of the Earl of Sandwich (1625–72), Prince Rupert and General Monck. In the Queen's great bedchamber, the overmantel was the same painting of St Agnes that Henrietta Maria had chosen before the Civil War – it may even have remained in this position through all the troubles.[123]

As James and Mary Beatrice re-established themselves at Whitehall, the atmosphere around them became increasingly tense: the Queen was four months pregnant and the Catholic priests were happy to tell anyone who listened that it would be a boy. It was assumed that she would give birth in her new bedchamber at Whitehall, but, feeling her time was near, she suddenly announced that she would have the child at St James's. The Queen's lying-in there, and the birth of a healthy son to her in June 1688, was destined to be a turning point in English history, and the source of one of the great conspiracy theories of the age.

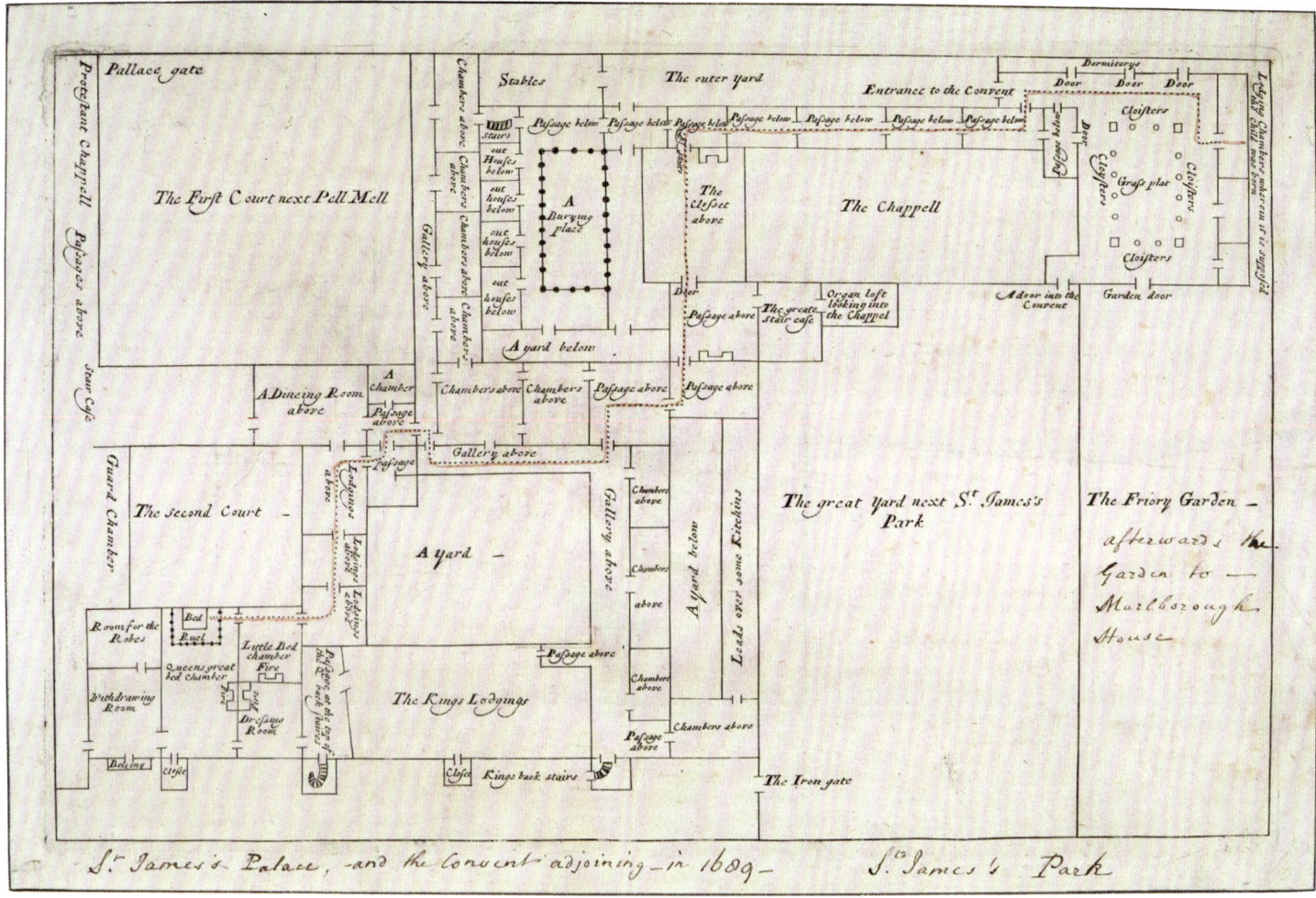

2.16

J.G. Crace, *St James's Palace and the convent adjoining*, 1689. This sketch plan that accompanied a long account of the supposed delivery of a baby to the Queen's bedchamber is the earliest plan of the first-floor royal rooms at St James's Palace (BL, Maps, Crace Port., 13.28)

The conspiracy theorists believed that the Queen's pregnancy was a fabrication, aided by blood- and milk-filled sponges applied, at appropriate moments, to her undergarments. They suspected that St James's was chosen for the birth as it was where there was

> a convent adjoining where a woman might be kept at the time of her bigness, or come in to it any evening and none perceive, as is evident from its situation; here a woman might cry out as loud as she would in labour, ... it being a large place within walls and cloisters, out of all hearing, or any intercourse of people to disturb them.

The writer of the full account of the alleged deception, published in late 1688, appealed to 'all persons that know the rooms stairs and passages, belonging to the convent and palace, whether there are not two several direct and commodious ways, whereby a child so born may be privately conveyed from the said convent (it not being above three rods), to the Queen's bedchamber.' These ways, we learn from the same source, 'are so plain, so direct, and without the least intricacies or windings, that the most hardened cannot deny ... but as if they had been made on purpose.' A plan was published, showing any not convinced, by 21 pages of detailed argument, the route by which a child born in the friary could be smuggled into the Queen's bedchamber in a warming pan (Fig. 2.16).[124]

Nobody today believes that James Francis Edward Stuart (1688–1766), the Old Pretender, was anyone other than the son of the King and Queen. When James heard that the Queen was in labour on the morning of the birth, he came from Whitehall with almost the whole Privy Council and others, and arrived in the Queen's great bedchamber. The men stood away from the bed alcove in which the Queen lay in a curtained state bed. They heard the Queen's shrieks as she gave birth, and soon after, saw the child itself. At one point, there was a warming pan full of coals that was placed into the Queen's bed, and it was this that became the vehicle of deception of popular rumour.[125]

There was enough public scepticism over the veracity of the birth that the King called an extraordinary meeting of the Privy Council, attended, amongst others, by the lord mayor of London and all the aldermen. At this, the large number of people present at the birth made sworn statements as to what they had seen. The published report makes fascinating, if repetitive, reading, and confirms in detail the layout of the Queen's lodgings shown in the conspiracy theorists' plan (see Fig. 2.16).[126]

A nursery was set up for the young Prince, with his own kitchen, and a building with a room 10 foot square (9 m^2) was built in Bay Court for his governess.[127] On 15 October, in a well-attended ceremony of great splendour and solemnity, the Prince of Wales was christened in St James's chapel, with Catherine of Braganza and the Pope (represented by count d'Adda, his nuncio) as godparents.[128] James's overt and extravagant use of the chapel ensured that, as his regime crumbled over the following months, it once again became a hated symbol of popery.

William of Orange landed in Torbay in Devon on 5 November 1688 and marched, via Exeter, for London. In early December, with a Protestant army on its way to the capital, London erupted in an explosion of anti-Catholicism. The provisional government was alerted to a mob who wanted to demolish the chapel, and a troop of 80 horse guards was sent to secure it; it arrived just as rioters broke in and started to destroy the organ.[129]

On 17 December, with James still in his lodgings at Whitehall, three battalions of William of Orange's foot guards and some cavalry occupied St James's house and park. The following day, William himself arrived in huge grandeur and splendour, establishing himself at St James's. There he remained for two days, hesitating as to what to do. Assemblies of peers met in the Queen's presence chamber to give their advice. It was not until it became clear that James had fled the country that William took up his role of regent, pending a political settlement.[130]

William and Mary

Mary joined William in London on 12 February 1689 and returned to her childhood home, where she spent the night for the first time since 1677. The following day, William and Mary were declared joint sovereigns, and the day after, the Privy Council met in James II's new council chamber at Whitehall. The general expectation was that William and Mary would now move into Whitehall, but it was not to be. William knew London well and had stayed at both Whitehall and St James's on his previous three visits. His reaction to neither house is recorded, but on becoming King he made it clear that he did not want to live at Whitehall. Despite James's reconstruction of the Queen's lodgings, it was big, dirty, confusing and very public – everything that his houses in the Dutch Republic had not been. The smoke of a hundred chimney stacks exacerbated his asthma, and only nine days into their reign they moved out to Hampton Court, where the air was clearer, there was more space and there were fewer people. Soon furnishings were being sent upriver from Whitehall, and on 12 March, orders were given for the court's general remove to Hampton Court.

The King was now physically divorced from the permanent machinery of government in Westminster and from the houses of his ministers in the West End. There was great pressure for him to move back to Westminster, and to please the English politicians, William and Mary decided to purchase a house on the western edge of Hyde Park from Lord Nottingham (1647–1730). Kensington House would become their London residence and Whitehall would be used only for official business. A new road was built across St James's

2.17
After Jacob Schnebbelie (1760–92), *Chapel Royal, St James's Palace*, 1816. This is the earliest view of the interior of the Chapel Royal, showing it before the substantial reconstruction of the windows and organ loft. The windows are in their Tudor positions. The lower part of the walls would have been hung with tapestries (RCIN 703059)

Park and along the edge of Hyde Park, allowing the King to travel between Westminster and Kensington in private.

Kensington was not to have any large assembly rooms, a public chapel or even large kitchens for banquets. It was a very domestic residence, far more so than St James's, for instance. It still needed alteration to be fit for royal residence, and work continued at high speed, being completed in time for William and Mary to move in on Christmas Eve 1689. At the same time, work was under way at Hampton Court to rebuild the state rooms, and, at Whitehall, to complete the improvements to the Queen's privy lodgings left unfinished by James II.[131]

William and Mary pushed through a revolution in the geography of royal life in their first year on the throne. Their personal lives revolved round Kensington and Hampton Court, official functions took place at Whitehall, and St James's was superfluous to requirements. Although, under the terms of her lease, the chapel was still Catherine of Braganza's, she had no use for it, and in 1688, it was granted to a congregation of French Protestants, and the following year the organ was granted to the church of St Anne, Soho.[132] The Anglican Chapel Royal, which remained in service, underwent some simplification in appearance: in 1691, the chapel was scaffolded and 'the knobs that hang from the ceiling' were taken down; the pediment of the reredos was removed to let more light into the east window, and the painting in it was substituted for a blank panel of timberwork (Fig. 2.17).[133] The house itself was granted out to William's leading courtiers; even the state rooms were assigned to individuals, and for them, alterations and improvements were made at Crown expense.[134]

The royal library continued to have a separate existence within St James's. In 1689, Henri Justel (1620–93), a bibliophile, librarian and manuscript expert, was appointed royal librarian, giving his friend, the diarist John Evelyn, hope that the library would now be restored and properly cared for. Various alterations and repairs were commissioned in the keeper's lodgings.[135]

Justel died in 1693 after only a short tenure, and it was the appointment of Richard Bentley (1662–1742) in his stead that put the library in the spotlight. Bentley was the most brilliant classical scholar of his generation and a noted bibliophile; he attracted to his lodgings at St James's a circle of dazzling intellectuals, including Sir Christopher Wren, John Evelyn, John Locke and Isaac Newton.[136] Amongst other things, they discussed the appalling neglect of the royal library. Bentley had, in fact, exacerbated the problems: after he realised that, under the 1662 Licencing Act, a copy of every book published in England was to be deposited with the Stationers' Company for the royal library, he obtained from the Company nearly 1,000 deposited volumes, which were delivered to St James's. They only added to the chaos, with books lying on the floor, suffering damage, and many not properly bound.

In April 1695, as the floors started to give way, all the books were removed and the floor reinforced; a new chimneypiece was installed, probably replacing the elaborate Jacobean one (see p. 34), and two adjacent rooms, the 'little room' and the study, were also repaired. On the ground floor, a new library room was made with 500 ft (152.4 m) of shelving.[137] This was a step forward, but not the friends' ultimate goal, for they wanted to obtain an Act of Parliament to convert the royal library into a public library, and had printed a pamphlet entitled *A Proposal for Building a Royal Library, and establishing it by Act of Parliament* (1697). In this, they wrongly claimed that the library had been established for public use, a notion that perhaps had its origin in the ambitions of the Council of State in the 1650s to create a public library at St James's (see p. 60). The pamphlet suggested that the King should make available a corner of St James's Park for a new library and keeper's house. It should be supplied with revenue by an annual parliamentary grant, and have the capacity for 200,000 volumes, as well as space for the meeting of learned societies. The inner walls of the library, it was suggested, should be lined with antique marbles.[138] This idea, like its earlier incarnation, was forward-looking and ambitious, but got nowhere. Indeed, in 1697, Bentley was complaining again that there were some 2,000 books on the floor. Wren was called in to look at the problem, but nothing was done.[139]

In 1701, an Act of Parliament had made possible the acquisition of Sir Robert Cotton's famous library in Cotton's house in the old Palace of Westminster. Like St James's library, Cotton House was completely unsuitable for its function, and in December 1706, serious consideration was given to the possibility of transferring the royal library from St James's to Cotton's house. Wren, who was requested to survey both buildings to ascertain the desirability of this, described the St James's

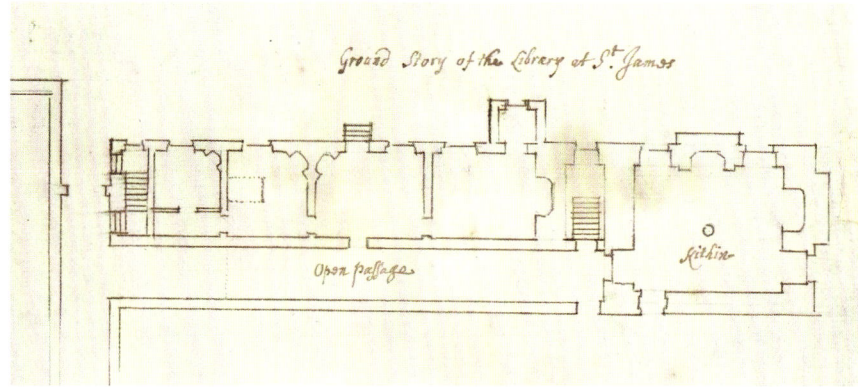

library as 'a lofty room and shelved as full as it can well be and yet a great number of books remain in heaps for want of room on the shelves'. His plan (see Fig. 1.13) shows not only the arrangement of the library, but the ground-floor rooms occupied by the library keeper on the north side of the house (Figs 2.18 and 2.19).[140] The St James's library was finally moved, some time around 1707, to Cotton House, Westminster, where it was put in locked cases awaiting a better solution.[141]

Since William and Mary's accession, Anne had been dividing her time between her lodgings in the Whitehall Cockpit and Burford House in the grounds of Windsor Castle. In 1692, Mary and Anne disagreed over the lodging of Anne's favourite, Sarah Churchill (later Duchess of Marlborough: 1660–1744), at Whitehall.

2.18

Sir Christopher Wren's 1706 ground-floor plan of the library keeper's lodgings at St James's. North is at the left. The main library was the room above the kitchen (see Fig. 1.13) (TNA, T/100, fol. 184)

2.19

Watercolour of the Queen's Chapel from the south, c.1800. On the left are the lodgings of the library keeper; in the middle of the drawing is the park entrance to the chapel (London Metropolitan Archives, SC/GL/PR/WR/JAM/PAL/P5407479)

2. THE RESTORATION TO QUEEN ANNE

2.20

This reconstruction shows St James's Palace in 1696. The streets of the area surrounding St James's to the top of the image are only indicative, but by this date enough information survives to make the reconstruction of the principal buildings fairly accurate. On the south front can be seen the nursery building of 1677, with the drawing room balcony to its east. North of the nursery is Princess Anne's dancing room, built the same year. The friary buildings remain, unused, to the east of the Queen's Chapel, and in the bottom left-hand corner stands Godolphin House

2.21

Hieronymus Janssens (1624–93), *Charles II dancing at a Ball at Court*, c.1660. On 22 May 1660, the eve of his departure for England, a banquet was held in Charles II's honour at the Mauritshuis, hosted by Prince Maurice of Nassau (1567–1625) and the States General of the Dutch Republic. Charles and his sister Mary, Princess of Orange and mother of William III, are depicted dancing the French *courante*, which was described by a dancing master in 1725 as a 'very solemn Dance' which 'gives a more grand and noble Air than other Dances' (RCIN 400525)

Anne abandoned the Cockpit lodgings, swapping them with Lord Berkeley of Stratton for his fine house in Piccadilly that lay to the west of Clarendon House. Mary vindictively ordered that no courtier should visit Anne at Berkeley House, on pain of exclusion from court. For three years, Anne and George lived at Berkeley House, suffering petty humiliations inflicted upon them by the Queen.[142]

On 28 December 1694, Mary died of smallpox at Kensington. William, and indeed, the political nation, were consumed with horror and grief. Work at Hampton Court came to an immediate halt and the court went into deep mourning; the state rooms at St James's were hung in black. The funeral did not take place until 5 March, and the Queen's body was to lie in state at Whitehall. It was decided that the Chapel Royal should be fitted up for the King's use during this time, and alterations were made to allow William to have a pew near the altar. Four long forms were upholstered in purple satin, and a purple-covered armchair and footstool beneath a canopy were provided for the use of a bishop. A pulpit cloth and carpet, also of purple, were delivered, as were special purple cushions for the King to kneel on when taking the sacrament.[143]

Princess Anne

While Mary had been alive, there was still some hope that she would bear a son and heir, but her death confirmed Princess Anne's position as heiress apparent, and her son, William, Duke of Gloucester (1689–1700), was now perceived, and treated, as England's future King. With the Jacobites looking over their shoulders, Anne and William were forced to forge an uneasy truce, aimed at securing the Duke of Gloucester's right to the throne. William offered Anne the Queen's lodgings at Whitehall as a London residence befitting her status, but Anne was in no hurry to move from Berkeley House, and remained there, holding court, with full recognition of her position. In October 1695, William, returning from the continent, visited Anne in Piccadilly, offering her St James's as a residence (Fig. 2.20); her son, William of Gloucester, was offered the Order of the Garter, a household

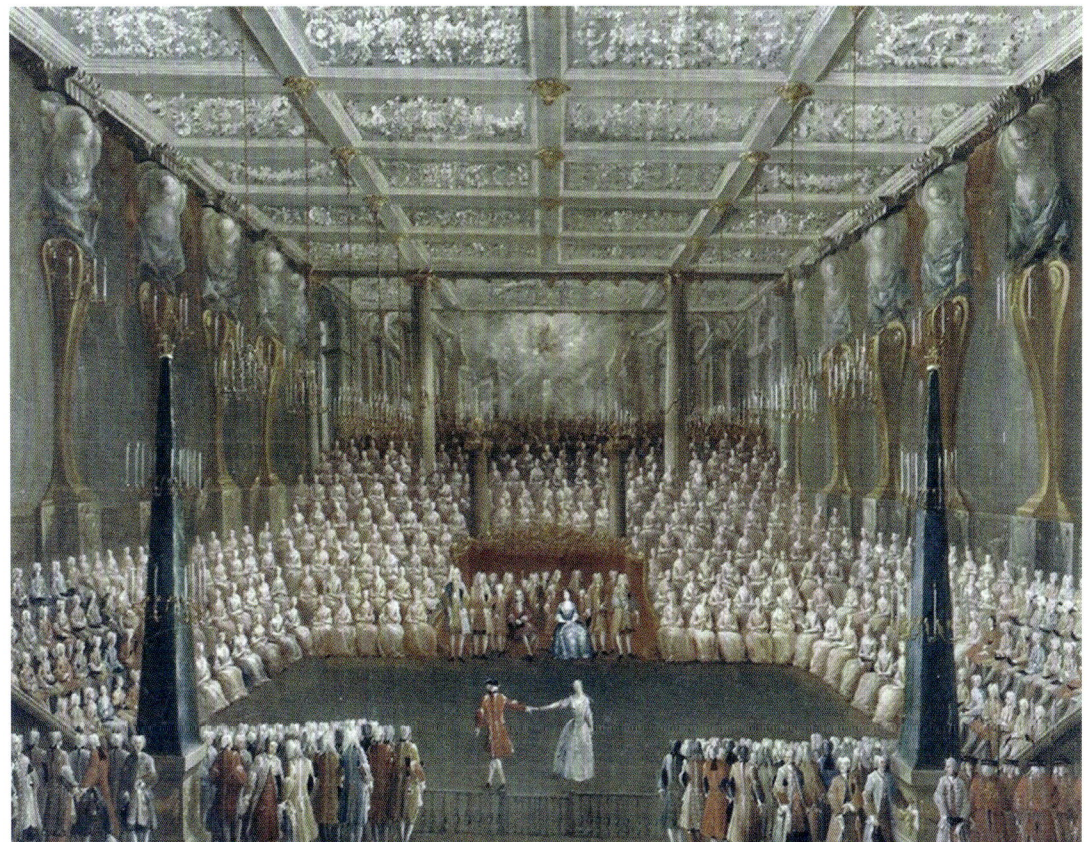

2.22

Painting by Willem van der Hagen (d. 1745), depicting a state ball held in St Patrick's Hall, Dublin Castle, 1731. Tiered seating, as shown here, was often added. At St James's, the banked seating depicted by Flitcroft in 1729 and in a plan and section by Soane in 1792 is likely to have been a permanent fixture (private collection)

and a residence of his own. All these Anne graciously accepted.[144]

St James's was still in use by a number of prominent courtiers and politicians, and in 1689, Thomas Osborne (1632–1712), Duke of Leeds and Lord President of the Council, had been assigned the principal royal lodgings as the highest-ranking minister of the Crown. Now, facing impeachment by Parliament, he was keen to curry favour with the Princess and vacated the rooms.[145] The house required work to make it suitable for Anne, as she was expected to keep court there, 'as if she were a crowned head'. William had made it clear that this was to be at her own expense, and in 1696–7, she spent some £2,200 preparing the house, including the construction of 'a large room to dance in'.[146]

The new room was christened the ballroom, the first instance of a room with this name being added to an English royal residence. Balls were new to England in 1660. Before the Civil War, the court masque – the complex and costly theatrical event that culminated in the audience dancing – took place in the largest outer rooms of the royal houses, often the great hall (where there was one) or the great chamber. The masque had fallen from fashion by 1660, and Charles II had acquired a taste for French court ballet that took place at a gathering called a *bal*. From 1660, the English court assembled *en fête* for balls, most often held in the great hall or in the great chamber at Whitehall and Somerset House, or sometimes in the Banqueting House, Whitehall. Although English country dances were enjoyed by the guests, Charles II was obsessed with French dances, especially the *courante*, an apparently simple dance, but one that, in reality, was extremely challenging to master, both mentally and physically (Fig. 2.21).[147]

Greatly to the disapproval of Puritan minds, the Princesses Mary and Anne spent much of their youth in the hands of dancing masters, and although Mary later said that she thought it a waste of time, Anne remained a lover of dancing until lameness and obesity prevented it. William III, although undeniably happier in the saddle than in his ballet shoes, also participated regularly in court balls. He had been taught French dances by the Duke of Monmouth at The Hague, and he and Mary held balls most years.[148]

Therefore, in 1696, when a ballroom was built at St James's, balls had been an integral part of court life for nearly 40 years. Anne, though, was past dancing, being carried upstairs in a sedan chair because her legs were so bad. The ballroom was not for her pleasure; it was built because she now assumed the role of consort and had to perform the social functions previously undertaken by Mary. Hosting balls was one of the most important of these, particularly the annual ball held for the Queen's birthday – a highlight of the court almanac.[149] In 1695, St James's did not have a large enough room in which to stage these.

The new ballroom was designed by Wren and sited on the west side of the palace, joined to the top of the principal stairs by a small length of Tudor gallery, now known as the Matted Hall. It occupied the site of the former gallery and stairs that linked the kitchens with the state rooms. Externally, the building was raised upon a rusticated Portland stone arcade and was lit by nine large sash windows on the north front, and probably two on the south front. Centrally placed on the south wall was the fireplace. On the south side was also a service stair and lobby, to allow food to be brought up from the kitchens. On the north front was a large external staircase, providing access from the courtyard. This enabled carriages to deposit people in the outer court, from where they would pass through the ground-floor passage at the south end of the Chapel Royal, and ascend to the ballroom separately from the State Apartments. This arrangement made it much more like the Banqueting House at Whitehall than a reception room integrated with the rest of the house. It may have also reflected the fact that Princess Anne regarded her role at court balls as a spectator rather than a participant.

The first time the room was used was for the balls to celebrate Princess Anne's birthday in February 1697, and for the next three years, the room played host to February court balls. These often involved the construction of staging to allow spectators a view of the dancing (Fig. 2.22).[150] The importance of the new ballroom was hugely increased in 1698, when a catastrophic fire on 4 January devastated Whitehall Palace. William, who had never loved the palace, ordered that the Banqueting House be saved at all costs; it was, but the remainder of the state rooms were utterly destroyed, leaving only the courtier lodgings at the Cockpit. St James's was now the only central London residence of the monarchy, and the ballroom the largest court space available in a working royal palace outside Hampton Court.[151]

In 1696, the royal closet in the Chapel Royal was redecorated for Anne's use. The walls were hung with crimson damask and a suite of matching furniture was delivered: four forms, and a chair of state with a cushion and stool.[152] Soon, however, the Princess had to share the chapel with the King, because the Whitehall fire not only deprived William of a place for court festivals, it also robbed him of the principal Chapel Royal. It was resolved to set up the Banqueting House as a chapel, so that the major Anglican royal liturgies, such as Maundy Thursday, could be celebrated in public. But this was not an everyday solution and it was decided that he should normally use the Chapel Royal at St James's. William had ceremoniously attended chapel at St James's before the fire, the great sword of state being carried before him and placed in a sword rest while he sat in the royal pew, but after the fire, he also attended Easter services at St James's and also the important annual service of commemoration of the execution (or martyrdom) of Charles I.[153]

As promised by the King, when the Duke of Gloucester was eight, in 1697, he was given his own household. Parliament made a grant for its funding, and William and the Princess argued over how it was to be staffed and organised. The boy had been brought up at Whitehall, and, after his lodgings there had been destroyed by fire, at Campden House, Kensington. With the destruction of Whitehall in 1698, it was agreed that he should have rooms at St James's, and he moved into the nursery block built by his grandfather for Anne and Mary (see pp. 88–90). At the same time, it is likely that Anne commissioned a set of stairs to provide access to the gardens directly from the drawing room. This replaced the former balcony and allowed Prince William to get to the gardens easily from his new quarters.[154]

If the death of Mary II had destabilised the political order, giving hopes to the Jacobites and anxiety to the Protestants, the death of the 11-year-old William, Duke of Gloucester, in July 1700, left huge uncertainty for the future of the nation. Not one child from Anne's numerous pregnancies had survived, William III was childless and unmarried, and at Saint-Germain-en-Laye lived the healthy 12-year-old Prince of Wales with his father, the deposed James II. For Anne, however, this was principally a terrible personal tragedy, sending her into almost complete seclusion for more than a year.[155]

The changes to the lives of William and Anne following the Whitehall fire were momentous for St James's. For the first time, the house now began regularly to be referred to as 'a palace', and there was a gradual shift in perceptions of its status.[156] The district of St James's began to change rapidly too. The relocation of major court ceremonial to St James's attracted polite society to the surrounding area. Before the fire, there were only two chocolate houses – White's (1663) and Ozinda's (1664) – but after 1698 half a dozen more opened, as people's social lives relocated from Whitehall. In 1704, Thomas Southern could complain of people 'coming in herds' to the coffee houses of St James's to gossip and talk about current affairs. This meant a shift in the character of the area from being a fashionable place in which to live to becoming the centre of fashionable shops and eating and drinking houses. Dudley Ryder records his visit to a Drawing Room at St James's in 1715; he was typical of many when he wrote: 'before we went in [to the palace] we went to St James's Coffee House … There were several noblemen there which we took no notice of, though the place looked more like a handsome parlour than a coffee house'.[157]

Queen Anne: St James's Becomes a Palace

When, in 1683, Anne married Prince George of Denmark, Sarah, Lady Churchill, was made lady of the bedchamber, and two years later, became Anne's groom of the stool. Their relationship was extremely close, Anne doting on Sarah, the vivacious, intelligent and worldly wise social climber, who was five years older than herself. It was a row over Sarah's association with a Jacobite plot that had led to Mary II's orders to expel her from Whitehall, and Anne's determination to leave the palace too (see p. 102). After the death of Mary, Sarah was reconciled with William III, and when Anne acceded to the throne in 1702, she became one of the most powerful subjects in the land. Her posts included groom of the stool, mistress of the robes, Keeper of the Privy Purse and ranger of Windsor Park, with a combined salary of some £6,000 a year. The Earl and Countess of Marlborough, as they had become in 1689, were granted extensive lodgings at St James's the following year, and in 1702, the Queen's great bedchamber and the rooms next to it were remodelled to allow Sarah and Anne to have adjoining bedrooms.[158]

Like her uncle, father and grandfather, Anne was a stickler for proper ceremony and form, her head full of 'ceremonies and customs of courts', and 'fashions and rules of precedence'. Unlike her uncle, Charles II, who had used court ceremonial to brilliant effect to enhance his majesty and to entertain his court, Anne, though articulate and fun-loving, never had the gift of showing people a good time – her conversation, thought Sarah Churchill, 'had nothing of brightness or wit'.[159] It is for these reasons that the court of Queen Anne has normally been regarded as dull and uninspiring.

This allegedly lacklustre court was headquartered at St James's, but, as with her predecessors, there was a seasonal pattern to Anne's movements. Apart from 1710 and 1714, the court removed to Windsor each summer, and in the winter, the Queen often preferred to reside at Kensington. In June 1702, recognising the rapid urban development that had taken place round St James's Palace, the Queen told

2.23

Nicholas Hawksmoor, sketch plan of proposed alterations to St James's Palace for Queen Anne in 1702 (north is to the right). This shows the proposal at ground floor to build an entrance colonnade, to create an apse in the Chapel Royal, a guard chamber and a new great stair. The plan also shows the first-floor arrangement of the state rooms as proposed. Presumably, the Council Chamber was to be located in the 1677 building erected for the royal Princesses, subsequently used by the Duke of Gloucester (AS, I:30)

2.24

William Dickinson, sketch plan of the parts of St James's under consideration for remodelling in 1703 (north is at the bottom). In pencil, at the top, can be seen the outline of the proposed new range, overlying the former Princesses' lodgings on the south front (Bodl., MS Gough misc. antiq. 17, fol. 89v)

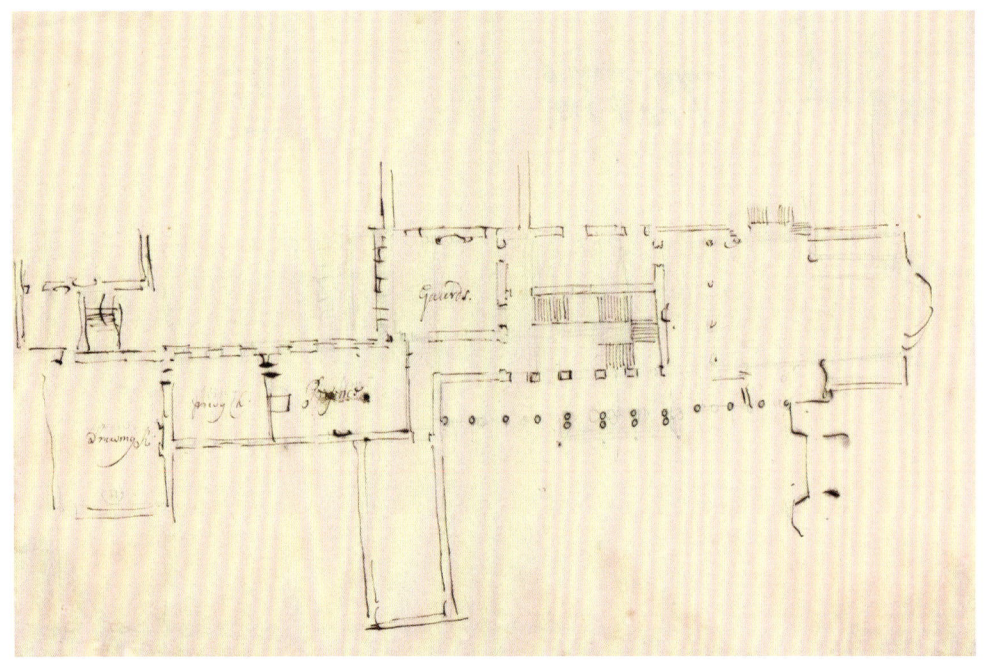

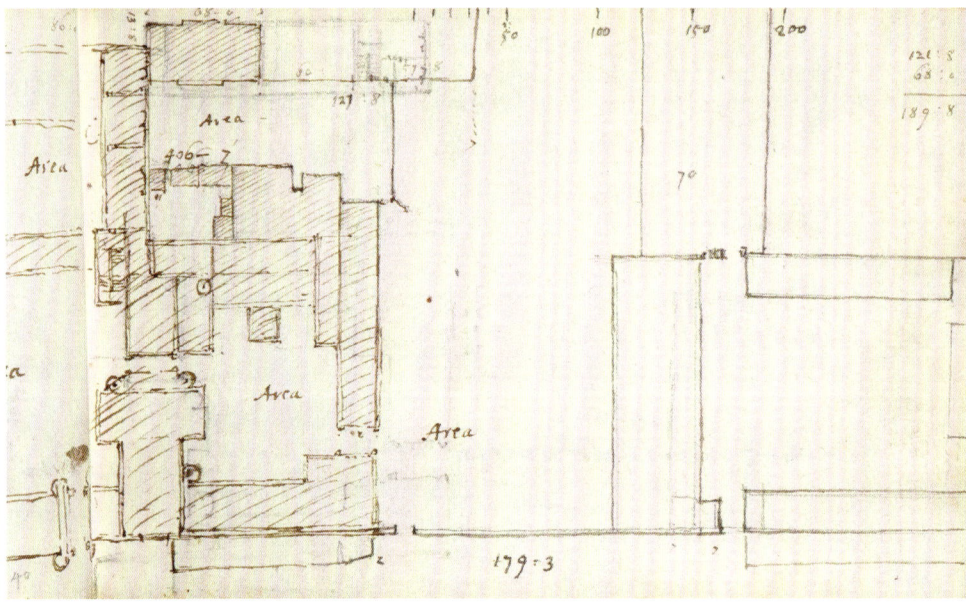

Lady Marlborough that 'though St James's is ye best part of London, it must be very stinking and close at this time of year, and cannot be wholesome'. Kensington was much more rural and had extensive gardens, which Anne liked; from 1706, she and George spent the winter there, and apart from a short break after the death of Prince George, Anne made Kensington her winter residence.[160]

St James's was thus used by Anne as her official seat – wearing the mantle lost by Whitehall in 1698, it was the centre of national government and ceremonial. When residing at Kensington, the Queen would make the short carriage ride to St James's to undertake her duties, before being driven back.[161] It is for this reason that one of the first changes ordered by the Queen was the setting up of a council chamber. Initially, a large table was erected in the presence chamber, but this was inconvenient, and the ballroom was appropriated for council meetings. When it was required for entertaining, the table and furniture were removed and returned the

following day.[162] Queen Anne attended the council, on average across her reign, once a week. It was thus crucially important that St James's had a permanent home for their meetings.

Anne also required access to a suitable chapel, as it was imperative that she demonstrate her Anglican piety publicly; and on all 12 collar days,[163] 14 saint days, and most Sundays, while the court was in London, the Queen attended chapel in public and in state. In 1702, a German visitor saw the winding procession to chapel proceeding down the main stairs and into its west end, the sword of state and four great maces carried before the Queen.[164]

In 1702, neither the Council Chamber nor the chapel was deemed suitable for the needs of a Queen regnant, and Anne ordered alterations to both; only three months into her reign, in June, the Office of Works presented a scheme showing how this might be done. A sketch in the hand of Nicholas Hawksmoor, Sir Christopher Wren's draughtsman at the Office of Works, together with the written estimate, illustrates what was originally proposed (Fig. 2.23).[165] It was a pragmatic series of alterations that created more space in the state rooms (principally, a larger drawing room and council chamber) and a larger chapel. Both were to be entered by an impressive colonnade, and the state rooms reached by a new staircase.

The design for the chapel is of particular interest, as Anne had already decided to restore the Banqueting House at Whitehall to secular use and move the Chapel Royal permanently to St James's. For this, the chapel was, according to one observer, to be converted 'into the form of a cathedral'. This was somewhat of an

2.25
View of the outer courtyard of St James's Palace, showing soldiers mounting guard, c.1790. In the background is the Doric colonnade erected by Queen Anne before it was shortened by six columns in 1865. This finally provided a formal entrance for people to descend from their carriages and approach the grand staircase. The idea was copied from the King's entrance at Hampton Court (BM, 1880,1113.2137)

2. THE RESTORATION TO QUEEN ANNE

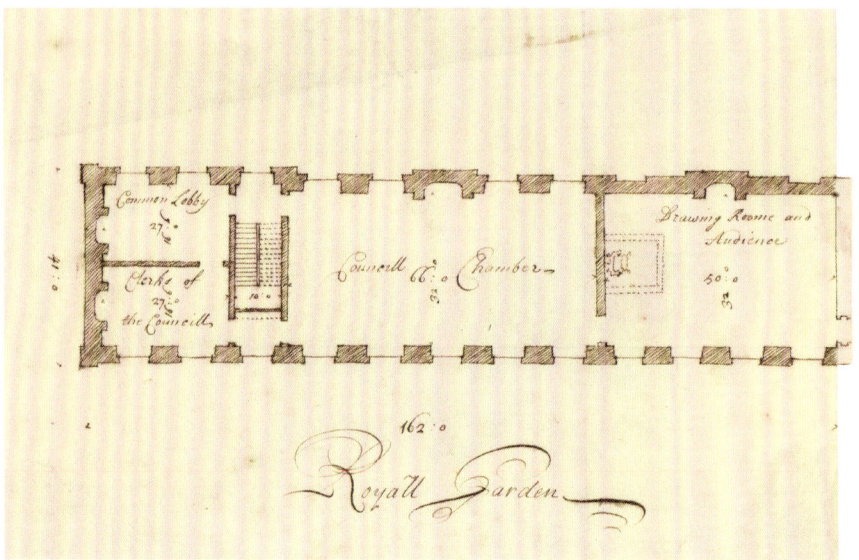

2.26
William Dickinson, first-floor plan, with dimensions, of the extension to the state rooms at St James's, 1703. This is almost as built, though in the final scheme, the Audience and Council Chambers were the same size, at four bays each. The position of the dais and canopy of state is marked (AS, I:32)

exaggeration, but Hawksmoor's drawing shows the chapel being given a structural chancel, reflecting Anne's ceremonialised tastes in Anglican worship.[166]

The estimate of costs, totalling £3,775, was accepted, but soon afterwards the Queen changed her mind and put a stop to work, asking for a more comprehensive remodelling.[167] For this, Wren used the services of another draughtsman in the Office of Works, William Dickinson. Dickinson had been in Wren's office since 1691 and was commissioned to survey the parts of St James's under discussion, in preparation for a detailed series of options. His site survey notebook survives in the Bodleian Library (Fig. 2.24), and based on this, under the direction of Wren, he drew a number of presentation plans for the Queen. One of these suggested the demolition of the former Princesses' lodgings and their replacement with a new block, containing an audience chamber and council chamber.

It was a version of this scheme that was agreed by the Queen in March 1703, costed at nearly £5,500. Anne was in a hurry and ordered that it be completed in six months, in time for the start of the winter court. Meanwhile, the Great Wardrobe was instructed to begin the preparation of tapestries and furniture. Eventually, the building works alone cost the Queen nearly £7,000, and furnishing, several thousand more.[168]

Although the idea of a new stair was dropped, a Doric colonnade was built to give a sense of arrival in the Tudor outer courtyard (Fig. 2.25). It screened the (mainly Tudor) west elevation, both providing shelter at the stair foot and linking the Great Stairs with the chapel. Such an expedient had been adopted at Hampton Court in 1691, executed in Portland stone in an Ionic order. The version of this design built at St James's was a cost-saving solution which reused the columns of the existing porch at the foot of the great stair.[169]

Work on the new apartments on the south front started immediately. Great care was taken to blend the new brick façade with the existing elevations, to present a single harmonious structure to the park.[170] The two new rooms completely changed the scale of St James's State Apartments; although smaller than the Ballroom, the Audience Chamber and Council Chamber were now the largest state rooms (Fig. 2.26). At 48 ft (14.6 m) long, the Council Chamber was the size of the (then unfinished) Queen's presence chamber at Hampton Court, itself a larger room than any of the King's rooms there.

The new rooms spoke of the identity and authority of the Queen in council. The Privy Council had an official membership of 55 in 1708, and although it was rare for everyone to attend, there were occasions when the whole council, plus other leading aristocrats, assembled. Indeed, when it met at Hampton Court, it gathered in the enormous Cartoon Gallery. But most council meetings were smaller, and by 1706, the new room at St James's was known as the 'great council chamber'; and when the Queen met with her smaller, 'cabinet committee', they met in a room known as the 'little council chamber' at the top of the Great Stairs, probably in the rooms occupied by the early Stuart council chamber next to the chapel gallery.[171]

The Council Chamber was both part of the machinery of government and a piece of court theatre. The stair at its west end provided a separate entry for people attending; they waited in the 'common lobby' to be called. The clerks had their own room next door.

Peter Wentworth, equerry to Prince George, described how he 'went to the backstairs to the waiting room before the council, where I knew I should see the Great men'. This was the arrangement that Charles II had built, but never used, at Winchester in the 1680s, but the splendid council chamber there was 18 ft (5.5 m) shorter than Queen Anne's.[172]

The room contained a huge council table, covered in a carpet, with 30 chairs, and at its head, a chair of state under a canopy for the Queen. A large screen covered the doors at the west end, and full-length curtains could be drawn across the windows. The walls were hung with tapestry and silver sconces; over the fireplace was St Catherine by Correggio (c.1489–1534), and over the doors to the waiting room and stairs were portraits of doges of Venice. Thomas Tompion (1639–1713) supplied a clock.[173] The effect of being summoned to the council at St James's must have been overawing and reflected the increased importance of the council in the government of the realm.

The new drawing room-cum-audience chamber was no less part of the theatre of the new political status quo established under Anne. Indeed, it was a new concept in royal accommodation. Since before the Civil War, the Queen's drawing room had been one of the most important rooms at court. Here, weekly social gatherings, or Drawing Rooms, were held; because they were in the Queen's lodgings, the King, when present, could circumnavigate the rules of protocol that governed behaviour in his own rooms and engage informally with ambassadors, ministers and courtiers. As a result, these gatherings became, under Charles II, the most important assemblies at court.[174] Under Anne, a Queen regnant, Drawing Rooms were held in the sovereign's apartments, conducted under the rules of etiquette pertaining to a monarch, so their informality was much reduced.

Anne's Drawing Rooms, held thrice weekly when her health allowed it, were thus more like audiences than the convivial gatherings of Catherine of Braganza's time. The immobile Queen, sitting on her chair of state beneath a canopy, rather than circulating round the room, and surrounded by her ladies-in-waiting, was difficult to approach, let alone to secure an introduction. Jonathan Swift claimed, in 1711, that he generally knew between 30 and 50 people at a Drawing Room; the gathering, he said, 'serves me as a coffee-house, once a week I meet acquaintance that I should not otherwise see in a quarter'; there could be found 'all her Ministers, Foreigners and Persons of Quality'.[175]

These subtle, but important, changes resulted in the new room being dubbed an audience chamber, a new term in the nomenclature of English courtly topography. Under the crimson canopy of state were two giltwood armchairs, upholstered in crimson damask; round the walls, to match, were 12 stools and four benches. The window curtains were crimson Genoa velvet with valances; tapestries covered the walls, and a full-length portrait of Catherine of Braganza was over the fireplace.[176] On 22 May 1707, the Venetian ambassadors were received at St James's. As they swept into the outer court, they were followed by dozens of coaches filled with the cream of English aristocracy. Met by the principal officials at court, the guests, followed by the English nobles, ascended to the guard and presence chambers, both containing canopies of state, and passed between lines of Yeomen of the Guard and Gentlemen Pensioners to the new audience room, where they had their audience with the Queen.[177]

The first full, dimensioned survey of the palace dates from Anne's reign and shows the royal apartments at first-floor level, including the new rooms (see Fig. 1.4). The Queen's apartments pivoted on her privy chamber: turning right (west) from this, the audience/drawing room and council chamber were reached, and to the left were the great and little bedchamber, the dressing room, various royal closets (yellow and green) and the waiting rooms at the backstairs. In the south-east range, overlooking the garden, were the rooms known as the private apartments.[178]

While the former consort's lodgings, which had been occupied by Mary of Modena, now became the Queen's apartments, James II's became those of Prince George. In 1703–4, extensive refurnishing took place in both,

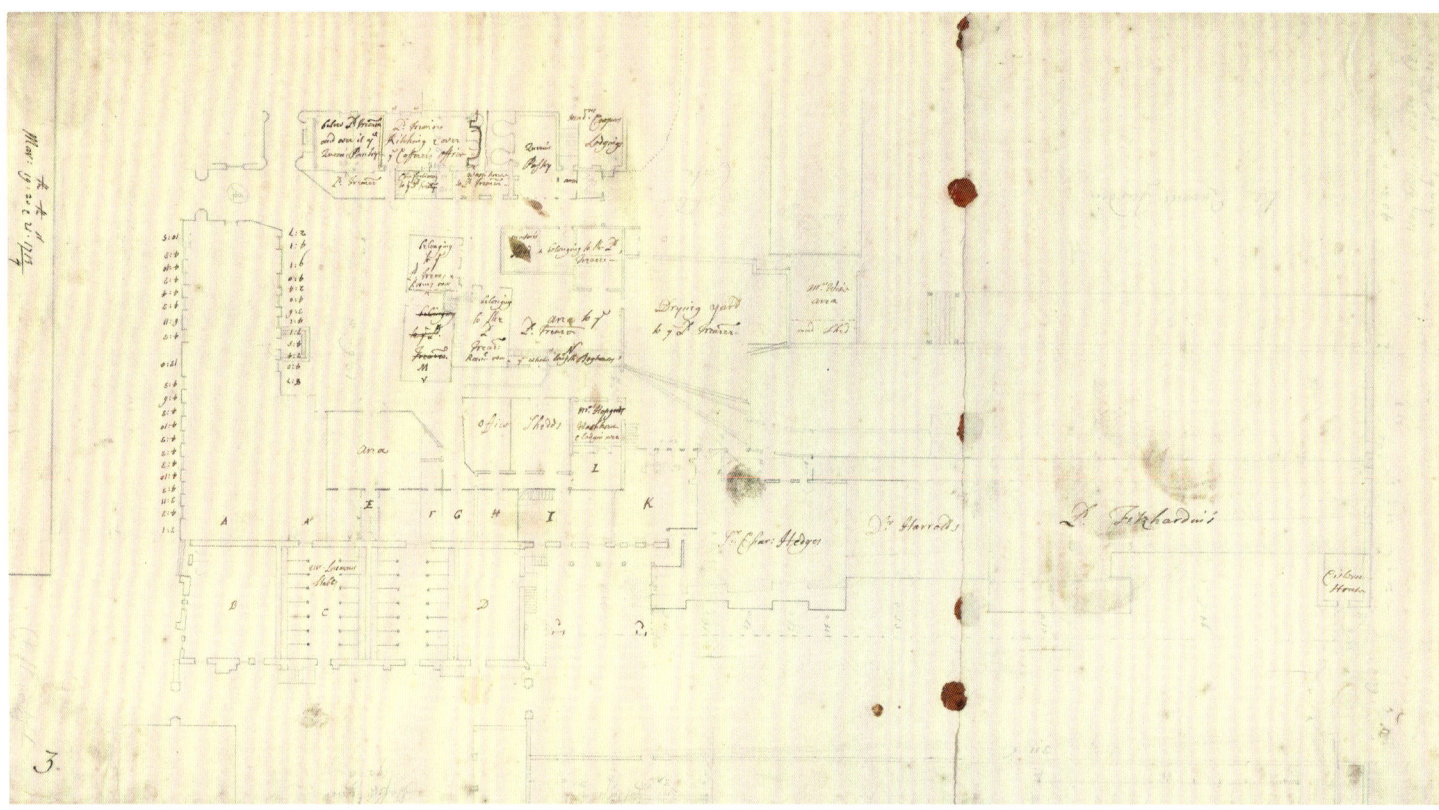

2.27
William Dickinson, survey of the outbuildings occupied by the Lord Treasurer, 1714. Along the bottom of the drawing runs Stable Yard Road, and the three houses above it, belonging to Sir Charles Hedges, Dr Harrold and Lord Fitzhardinge, are on the site of modern-day Clarence House and its garden. To the left is Prince Henry's riding house, and above that, a yard full of outhouses. At the top of the drawing is the western range of the outer service court, containing the pastry house and what may have been the bakehouse (AS, III:3)

but without altering the essential decorative formula of tapestried outer rooms, and inner chambers hung in silk and easel paintings. Huge quantities of new furniture, hangings and other decorative items were installed. The Queen herself was very engaged in the redecoration, visiting work while it was under way. Her closet, for instance, was rehung in green mohair (a watered silk), and supplied with a large couch with down-filled cushions and pillows, as well as an armchair, also with large cushions, all for the increasingly lame monarch to rest on. For the Queen's dogs, fat, feather-filled cushions were provided.[179]

Many of the paintings were rehung. In the great bedchamber was Guido Reni's (1575–1642) St Agnes over the fireplace, and a portrait of the Queen's eldest son, the Duke of Gloucester, over one of the doors. The Queen's oscillating affection for the Marlboroughs was represented by Sir Godfrey Kneller's (1646–1723) group portrait of Sarah Churchill's daughters. The Queen's dressing room next door was also filled with family paintings, including some of the children of the Duke and Duchess of York who had died in infancy. The Queen's little bedchamber had a portrait of Charles II as an overmantel. The Queen's closet contained some 24 pictures: there were family portraits by Van Dyck, William Dobson (1611–46) and Lely, religious subjects, including three madonnas, and a collection of historical portraits, amongst which were Mary, Queen of Scots (1542–87) and Henry VIII. Prince George had Paul van Somer's (c.1576–1621) portrait of Anne of Denmark over the chimney in his bedroom.[180]

In February 1703, the Queen held her first birthday ball as monarch, and it was reported that 'great preparations were made' and that 'there had not been such a magnificent appearance at court for twenty years past'. The floor of the ballroom was planed and rails were set up at the top of the stairs to control the crowds; the best damask-covered furniture was protected by serge case covers.[181] This was only the first of her court balls, when 'the court was extraordinarily numerous and magnificent'. In 1711, her birthday was celebrated 'in richer habits than has been known since 1660'. Other festivals marked by gatherings, music and sometimes dancing were New Year's Day, the Queen's accession and coronation days, Prince George's birthday and the feast of St George.[182] On occasion, a theatre was set up in the ballroom, with a green baize-covered stage, upholstered benches and a throne for the Queen.[183] All these public events were subject to the Queen's health, and that of her consort, and for several years, the Queen was either too ill to attend, being laid up with painful gout, or (in 1708) was in mourning for Prince George.

The last alteration to be carried out in Anne's time was the rebuilding of the gallery from the Great Stairs to the chapel. This was the inexplicably narrow passage, barely 5 ft (1.8 m) wide, which had forced processions to go downstairs and outside rather than directly into the royal closet. As part of the wider strategy of making the palace more suitable for full court ceremonial, the range to the south of the chapel was remodelled, with a gallery 10 ft (3 m) wide and a new door into the closet.[184]

The Fringes of St James's

When Henry VIII's architects planned St James's in the 1530s, they set out a western courtyard to contain the kitchens and service rooms. Over the following 185 years, there were continual improvements, alterations and additions to the original facilities, many of which are chronicled in the financial papers of the Office of Works. As there is no plan before 1703, and by that time much had changed, it is extremely difficult to be certain of their original layout. The papers after 1660, however, do make it clear that the kitchens were linked to the state rooms via a gallery that joined at the Great Stairs, and that the gallery itself was accessed by a flight of stairs at its west end.[185] This gallery, and the stairs, were partially obliterated in 1695, when the ballroom was built, although on its south side it had a service stair to allow refreshments to be brought up from the kitchen.

William Dickinson's plan (Fig. 2.27) shows what must have been the Tudor kitchen abutting the ballroom with a vast fireplace, and to the west of that, the ovens of the pastry house and what may have been the bakehouse.

The remainder of the service court must have contained the usual collection of larders, sculleries, pantries, working houses and store rooms. All these, in the early seventeenth century, were still within the high-security precinct of the house. Kip's perspective shows the dauntingly windowless western walls of the service courts, designed to keep people out (Fig. 2.28).

Kip's view also shows the gradual build-up of structures to the west of the original service court, between its western wall and Prince Henry's riding house. This contained humbler offices – there are several mentions in the accounts of the common house of easement, the communal latrines that most Tudor and early Stuart houses possessed. These are shown on one of Dickinson's plans as the common 'bogg houses'. As in most royal houses in the sixteenth and seventeenth centuries, there were also strategically placed outdoor urinals.[186]

Further west still was the stable court, or stable yard. This was entered by an archway on the site of the junction between modern Cleveland Row and Stable Yard Road. Like the kitchens, there were many alterations to the yard over a century and a half, but many of these are easier to identify, as the buildings were large and retained a single purpose. In the summer of 1675, a range of stables and coach houses were built and a pond dug in the middle of the yard. The stables, which backed onto Godolphin House, are shown on Flitcroft's survey of the palace of 1729 (see Fig. 3.14).[187]

With most household appointments came lodgings in a royal residence. These were either granted at pleasure or for life. The Earl of Bath, who was the keeper of St James's for life, succeeded in occupying the keeper's lodgings on the north-east corner of the outer court for an impressive 41 years. Grants for life were considered part of the valuable perks of office, and courtiers sometimes sold their interest on to other courtiers, although the Crown was normally careful to reserve its right to buy back a property, reimbursing the occupant for their outlay on it. In this way, private individuals gained possession of long leases of parts of royal residences.[188] St James's was not

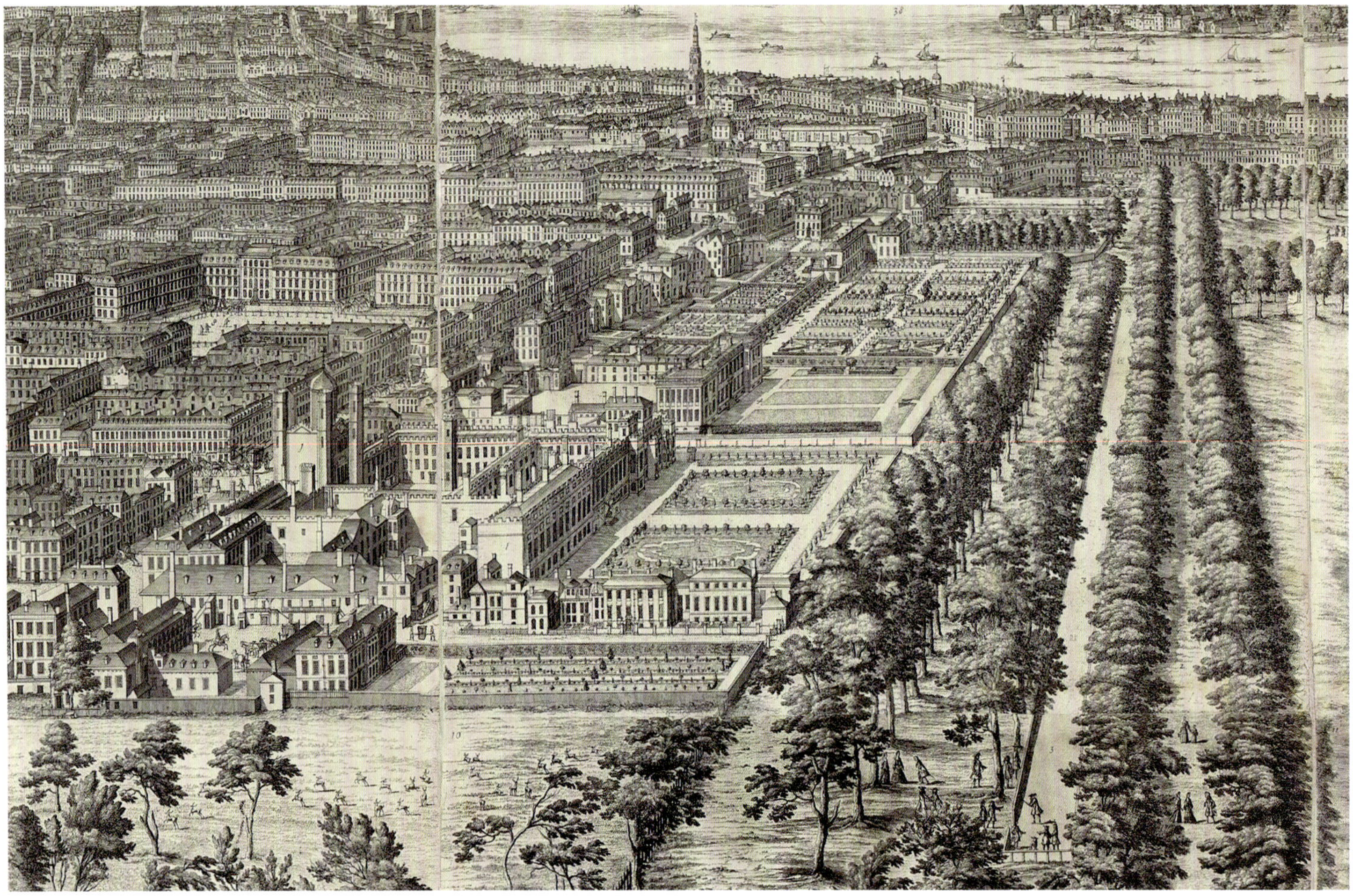

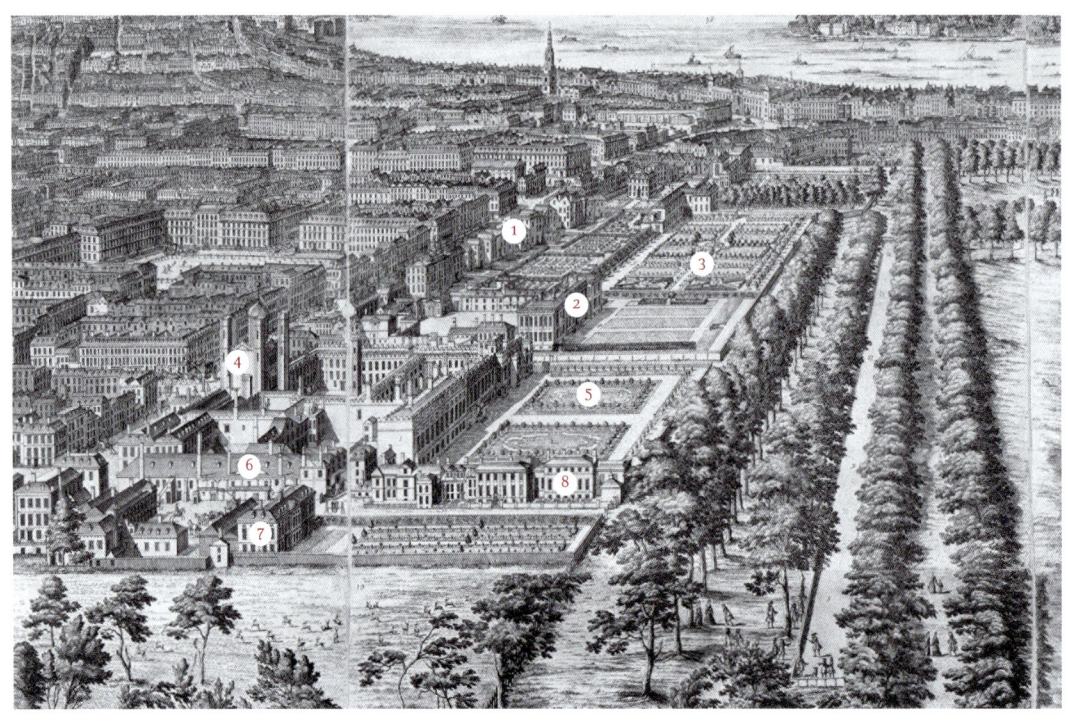

2.28

Johannes Kip (1652/3–1722), *View and Perspective of London, Westminster and St James's Park*, c.1727 (RCIN 702207)

1. Houses lining Pall Mall overlooking the park wall into the royal gardens
2. Marlborough House, designed by Christopher Wren for the Duchess of Marlborough, 1709–11
3. Former orchard and gardens, let in 1708 to Lord Carlton, and later the site of Carlton House
4. Great Gatehouse of St James's
5. Privy garden
6. Former riding house
7. Godolphin House
8. Houses belonging to Sir Charles Hedges (left) and Viscount Fitzhardinge (right)

immune to these practices, and from the reign of Charles II, several large houses in private occupation became attached to the palace, each of which had a significant bearing on its future.

It has already been mentioned that Berkeley House was granted to Barbara Villiers, Duchess of Cleveland (see p. 75).[189] Under Queen Anne, the palace became framed by two more extremely large mansions, Marlborough House and Godolphin House, given, respectively, to the greatest general and the greatest politician of the age (Figs 2.29 and 2.30).

Godolphin House was built on a sliver of St James's Park on the west side of the stable yard, on land granted, in November 1685, to the thuggish army officer and chief equerry to James II, Sir Theophilus Oglethorpe (1650–1702). Nicholas Hawksmoor's drawing of St James's Park identifies the land granted to Oglethorpe (see Fig. 2.3). His wife, Eleanor Wall (1662–1732), was Charles II's head laundress and seamstress, and had developed a private residence and garden next to her laundry on the west side of the stable yard. In 1685, high in favour with James II, this property, 200 ft long and 135 ft deep (61 by 41.1 m), was granted to the couple on a 32-year lease.[190] Due to Oglethorpe's Jacobite sympathies and the loss of his wife's position at court, the house passed from his ownership and was granted, in 1691, to Robert Sutton, Lord Lexington (1661–1723), gentleman of the bedchamber to William III and sometime gentleman of Prince George of Denmark's horse.[191]

In 1698, Lexington became ranger of Cranbourne Chase near Windsor, in succession to Sidney Godolphin (1645–1712), who became the 1st Earl of Godolphin in 1706. The rangership came with an official residence, Cranbourne Lodge, and under a private arrangement, Godolphin swapped this for Lexington's house at St James's.[192] Godolphin had an astonishing career, brilliantly managing the nation's finances and navigating the politics of the Act of Union; amidst this, he rebuilt the house as a power base next to the court. He created the substantial brick pile of 11 bays and three storeys with an extensive garden that fronted the park. It is not known who designed

2.29
Marlborough House, engraved by Sutton Nicholls (*fl.* 1680–1740), 1720–28. The house has since been extended and enlarged, but this print shows the original brick mansion with stone dressings. Commissioned by Sarah Churchill and designed by Sir Christopher Wren, it was completed in 1711 (BM, 1880,1113.2272)

2.30
Thomas Hosmer Shepherd (1793–1864), watercolour of Godolphin House, St James's, 1825. By 1748, two large bay windows had been added to its southern elevation. In 1825, the house was demolished and replaced by York House, subsequently renamed Stafford House, and now Lancaster House (see p. 188). The road between Godolphin House and Clarence House remains today as Stable Yard Road (BM, 1880,1113.2125)

2. THE RESTORATION TO QUEEN ANNE

2.31

Robert Dennis Chantrell (1793–1872), *St James's Palace and the back of the houses on Stable Yard Road*, 1813. On the left can be seen the range of courtier houses that grew up after the Restoration and which were eventually swept away for Clarence House (Sir John Soane's Museum, London, SM 76/5/1)

this, although Godolphin had sought the help of Robert Hooke for his lodgings at Whitehall. In this handsome mansion, as Lord Treasurer, Godolphin often presided over meetings of the Treasury.[193]

On the east side of the palace lay land granted to the Duke and Duchess of Marlborough, as they had become in 1702. The site had been acquired by Sarah Churchill on a 50-year lease in the summer of 1708, just as her relationship with the Queen was beginning to deteriorate and she felt she needed an independent base in London. The Duke was sceptical that the four and a half acres (1.8 hectares) of the old friary would be large enough for his wife's grandiose ideas, but in 1609, after obtaining an additional two acres (0.8 hectares) of former royal garden, Sarah commissioned Sir Christopher Wren to design a house, seemingly with the assistance of his son, Christopher (1675–1747). The old friary buildings were finally demolished, and the building that survives as Marlborough House was begun. Since then, it has been extensively altered, but the relatively plain, brick, two-storey mansion shown on early prints was completed in 1711, forming a pendant to Godolphin's house on the other side. The Duchess and Wren were careful to exploit its position close to St James's, in particular to ensure that it had views across the royal gardens. In 1711, Sarah was asked to move out of her lodgings at St James's into her new house, which she did with considerable bad grace. This became her main London residence, where she died, as an old lady, in 1744.[194] There now being a large house and garden between the palace and the former royal gardens in the east, these were let, in 1708, on a 31-year lease, to one of Godolphin's closest associates, the Secretary of State, Henry, Lord Carleton (1669–1725), who built Carleton (later Carlton) House there.[195]

In addition to these three substantial mansions, a row of lesser houses grew up against the west wall of the privy garden. Although shown on a number of maps and prints (see Figs 2.28 and 2.31), they were first accurately planned by the Office of Works draughtsman, William Dickinson, in 1714 (see Fig. 2.27). He shows that the southern house had been occupied by John Berkeley, 4th Viscount Fitzhardinge (1650–1712), Queen

Anne's treasurer of the chamber. This large mansion had originally been two separate dwellings: the northernmost had been granted, in 1677, to Wentworth Dillon, 4th Earl of Roscommon, who became Master of the Horse to the Duchess of York. He and his wife had extended and altered their lodging to become a house with an attached pavilion.[196] The southern portion had been granted to Fitzhardinge in 1689, whose lodgings at Whitehall had been destroyed in the fire. He had the distinction of being the keeper of the pell mell, while his wife was governess to the Duke of Gloucester. In 1695, Fitzhardinge bought out Roscommon's widow and united the buildings into a single residence.[197]

The northernmost house along the west side of the palace (Fig. 2.31) is shown, in Dickinson's survey of 1714, as being occupied by Sir Charles Hedges (1650–1714), an Admiralty judge and leading Tory politician under William III and Anne, and sometime Secretary of State. He was granted the house by Queen Anne while he was working closely with Godolphin, as a leading mouthpiece and business manager for the court in Parliament. Hedges convened meetings of leading politicians in an office in his house that was maintained at Crown expense.[198] Dickinson shows the plan of a regular house, with shallow projecting wings in the centre and on either side. Kip's view, made a decade later, shows the southernmost of these extended. This house was most probably built by Hedges, who made a considerable fortune through his legal practice and offices of state.[199]

During Anne's reign, St James's was reconfigured to make it into a true replacement for Whitehall. Not only was the Council Chamber recast as the hub of the palace, but the key political players had houses within minutes' walk of the chamber. This was a shift in status for the palace that was reflected in Leonard Knyff and Johannes Kip's *Britannia Illustrata, or Views of Several of the Queen's Palaces, as also of the Principal Seats of the Nobility and Gentry of Great Britain*, published in 1707 (Fig. 2.32). The first six plates of the book, which set out to depict the great royal and aristocratic seats of England, were of royal palaces. They were shown in order of precedence, with St James's Palace and Park being the first two (Fig. 2.33), and Somerset House the third. These were followed by the Tower of London, Hampton Court and Windsor Castle. Ten years previously, Whitehall would have taken precedence, but *Britannia Illustrata* proclaimed St James's as the principal seat of the English monarchy, recording it warts and all.[200]

For many, it was all warts. A German visitor in 1710 was

> amazed that it was such a straggling, low and irregular building. But when we saw the interior we found that the rooms were large and handsome … we had already seen the chapel several times; but it is very small and wretched, even the Queen's own chair. The garden adjacent to St James, and of the same length of the building but very narrow, was not of much account.[201]

This damning judgement on the palace was to set the scene for more than a century of criticism, of a building that had never sought primacy amongst British royal residences or parity with those abroad, but one that was constantly judged as if it had done so.

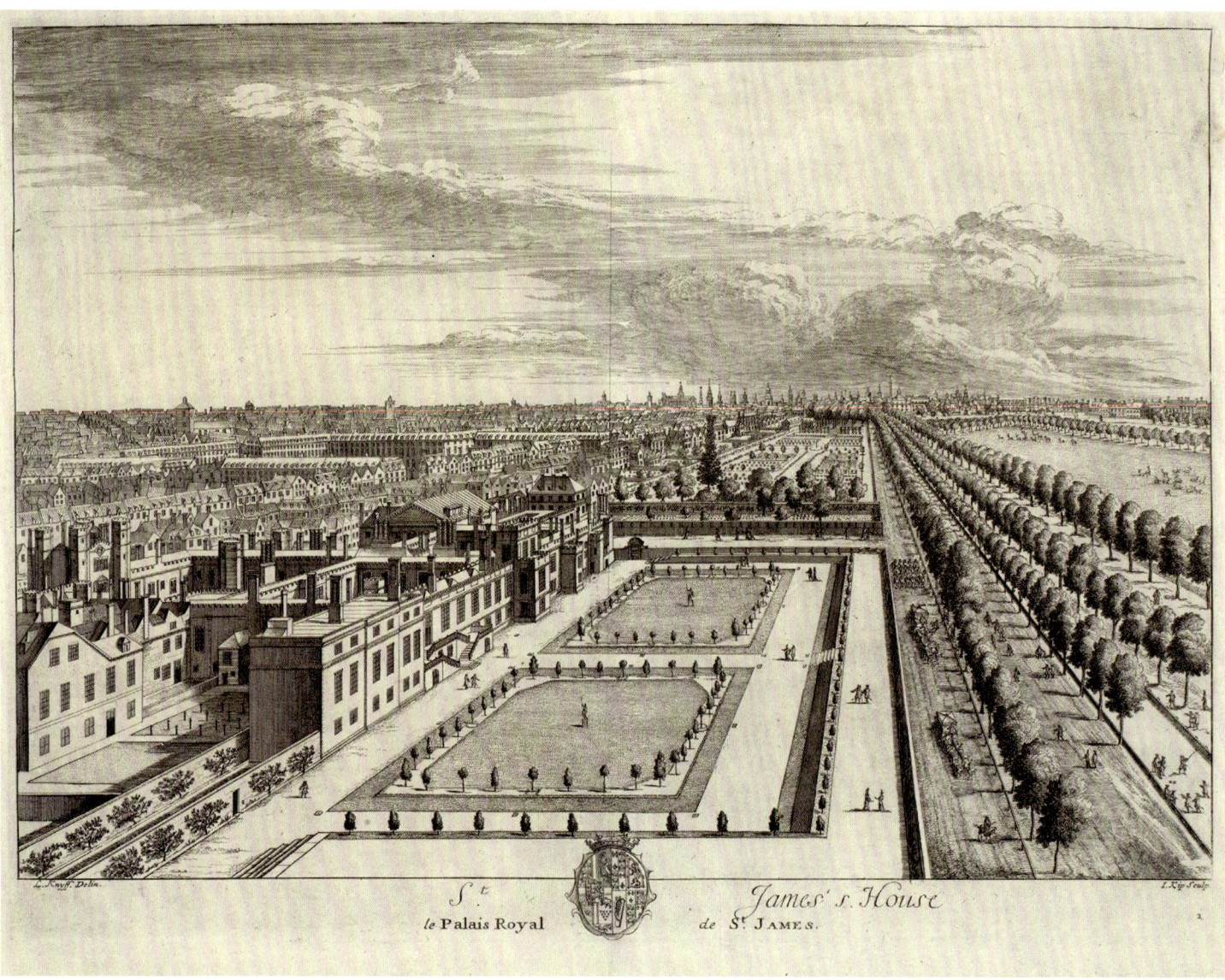

2.32

St James's Palace from the west, from Leonard Knyff (1650–1722) and Johannes Kip, *Britannia Illustrata, or Views of Several of the Queen's Palaces, as also of the Principal Seats of the Nobility and Gentry of Great Britain*, 1707. The Dutch landscape painter, Leonard Knyff, and his lesser-known brother, Jacob (1639–81), were pioneers of the bird's-eye view in England. In the late 1690s, Leonard conceived an idea for a great book of bird's-eye views, depicting the country houses of England. Subscribers were sought for this in mid-1701. Sixty of Knyff's drawings were engraved by Johannes Kip, and the book was published in 1707 as *Britannia Illustrata*, and sold by the publisher and bookseller, David Mortier (1673–1728) (RCIN 703040)

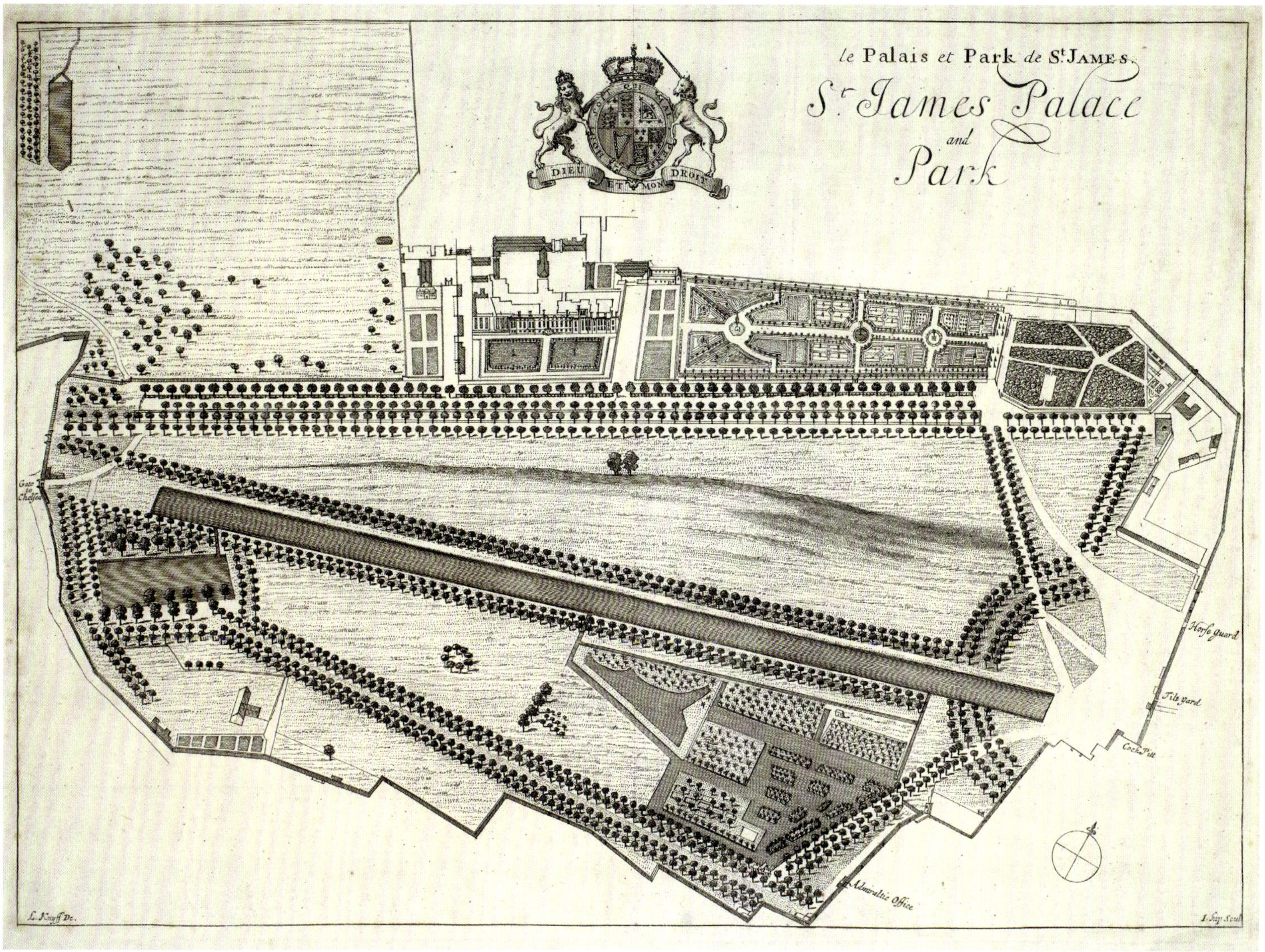

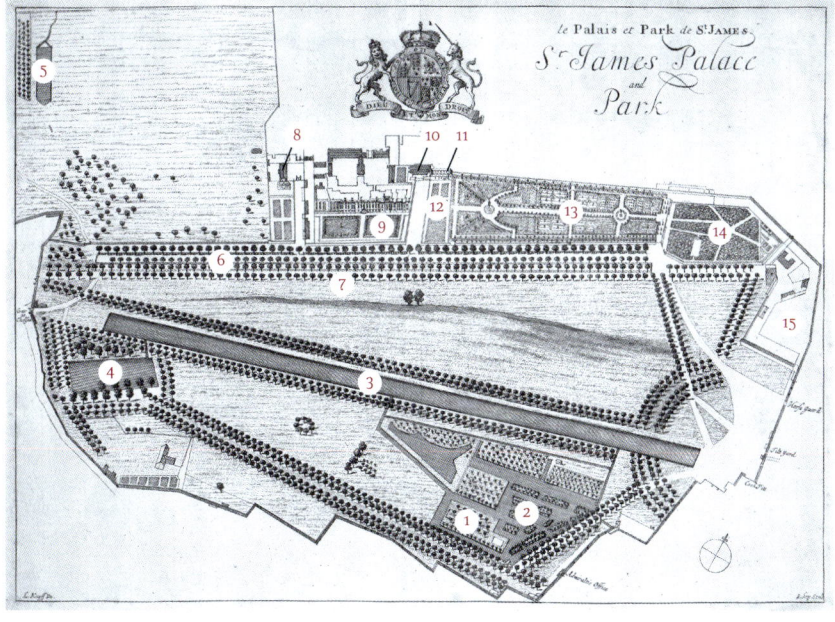

2.33

Johannes Kip after Leonard Knyff, *St James's Palace and Park*, as illustrated in *Britannia Illustrata* (RCIN 703032)

1. Aviary
2. Duck traps
3. Canal
4. 'Rosamunds Pond' (see p. 66)
5. Ornamental pond and plantation, laid out 1668–70
6. The pell mell, laid out 1660
7. Double avenue of lime trees, planted in the early 17th century
8. Lord Lexington's house (later Godolphin House)
9. Privy garden
10. The Queen's Chapel
11. Former Queen's friary
12. Friary garden
13. King's garden, attached to Whitehall Palace
14. The wilderness, or upper Spring Garden
15. Spring Garden

3. The Georgian Court

RUFUS BIRD

At St James's Palace, the century from the accession of George I in 1714 to the death of his great-grandson in 1820 was one of intense use and heavy occupation by members of the royal family. No fewer than three monarchs occupied the palace, the first two cramming their families, retinue and court into the building. It may seem remarkable that St James's was not rebuilt at some stage during the period to reflect the wealth and importance of Great Britain. There are perhaps several reasons for this. First, the new dynasty from Hanover was undoubtedly reluctant to impose in such a heavy-handed way on an unsympathetic nation. Moreover, the palace had been built by Henry VIII and it may have been the case that George I was content not only to live in an old building, as he did in Hanover, but that he also preferred to maintain a tangible, architectural link between his own Guelphic line and that of the Tudor dynasty. Second, the palace's role across the century evolved: from 1714 to 1762, it served as the seat of the head of state, as well as accommodation for the royal family and the court. After George III's purchase of Buckingham House, St James's role changed: it functioned almost entirely as the ceremonial headquarters of the monarchy, until, with the advancing illness of the King, it became, once again, the London base for the accommodation of the younger princes.

George I and the new dynasty's use of St James's Palace, 1714–27

George I succeeded to the British throne by virtue of the Act of Settlement of 1701, which decreed that henceforth all British monarchs must be of the Protestant faith and descended from the 'Electress' Sophia of Hanover (1630–1714), daughter of Elizabeth of Bohemia, 'the Winter Queen' sister of Charles I. This effectively ruled out over 50 claimants with closer and stronger claims, but who were confessed Roman Catholics.

At the accession of George I, there was a renewed expectation that Great Britain would finally build a great metropolitan palace as the seat of the monarchy. This anticipation may have arisen from Queen Anne's improvements at St James's in the first decade of the eighteenth century, or was possibly inspired by the precedent set in Hanover, where great palaces had been built to magnify the splendour of the Guelph dynasty. The most ambitious branch of the Guelph (or Welf) dynasty were the Hanoverian Dukes of Brunswick-Lüneburg: in 1692, the dynastically determined Duke Ernest Augustus (1629–98), father of George I, had (after years of lobbying) achieved elevation to the Imperial Electoral College, after which he was known as the Elector of Hanover. The honour of the electoral cap, giving the right to vote for the selection

OPPOSITE

St James's Palace from The Mall, c.1730 (detail of Fig. 3.11)

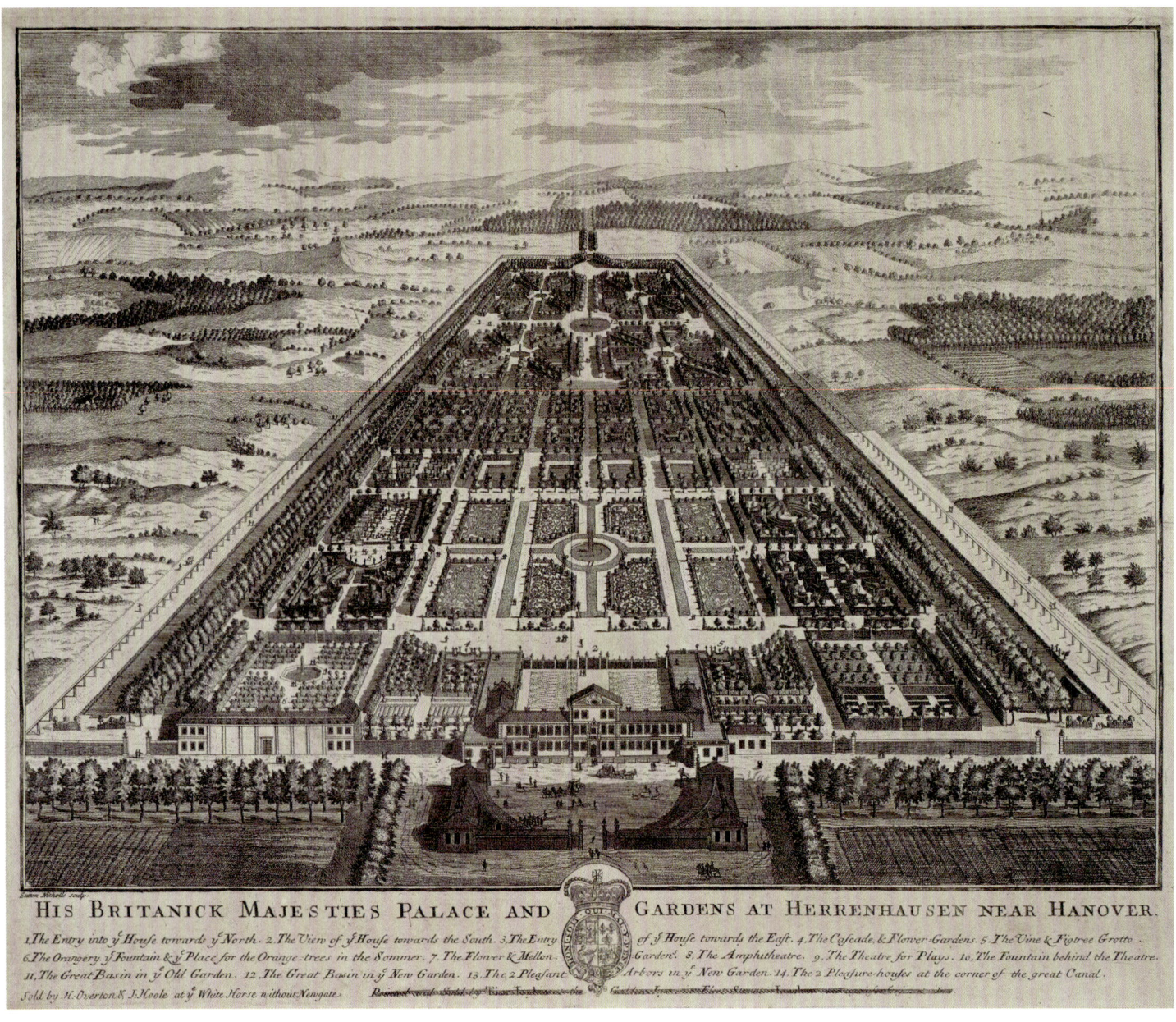

3.1

Sutton Nicholls, *His Britanick Majesties Palace and Gardens at Herrenhausen near Hanover*, c.1730 (RCIN 704536)

of the Holy Roman Emperor, had finally been bestowed on his ducal house.[1] In pursuit of these dynastic laurels, Duke Ernest Augustus made improvements to the Leineschloss, chosen as the ducal seat in 1636 by his father, George, Duke of Brunswick-Lüneburg, who built over the medieval Minorite monastery in the centre of Hanover. Ernest Augustus's improvements to what was a rather uninspiring building beside the River Leine included the addition of an enormous opera house – large enough to seat 1,300 spectators – and a great room of assembly, the Rittersaal. A few miles outside the city was Hanover's great glory, the summer palace of Schloss Herrenhausen (Fig. 3.1), with its extensive formal gardens, filled with fountains and gilded statuary. A notable addition to Herrenhausen, around the same time as the remodelling of the Leineschloss, was the *Galeriegebäude*, or 'gallery building', built by Ernest Augustus's wife, Sophia, which included 28 busts of Roman emperors acquired from Louis XIV.[2] These two buildings, the seventeenth-century metropolitan Leineschloss and the suburban Herrenhausen, might plausibly be paralleled in the British equivalents of the largely Tudor palaces of St James's and Hampton Court, the latter with its formal gardens and State Apartments added by Sir Christopher Wren.

At the very beginning of George I's reign, the architects of the Office of Works, under the surveyorship of Sir Christopher Wren, lost little time in providing the new King with several architectural schemes for improving the ancient Tudor palace of St James's. Three alternative schemes, dated 1712, are inscribed in French by John Vanbrugh for the benefit of the King, whose English was sketchy. The project may have been conceived by Vanbrugh while Anne was still alive, but there is no evidence that she considered them. The most ambitious of these (Fig. 3.2) would have razed the Tudor palace and rebuilt it to a size approximately twice that of Blenheim Palace, the enormous country house designed by Vanbrugh for the Duke of Marlborough. The new building was to be symmetrical and rectangular in plan, with eight courtyards around a large central court; at the east and west extremities, a theatre would balance a new Chapel Royal, and in the centre of the south front, a grand hexastyle portico would lead into a square colonnaded hall.[3]

A less ambitious plan – essentially a modified version of the grand scheme, retaining the most important parts of the Tudor building, and its later accretions by Jones, Wren and others – was also produced (Fig. 3.3). A new, and very grand, wing would replace the existing south wing (which contained the King's State Apartments), with a hexastyle portico as its focal point. Contained within this complex new structure were two State Apartments, one on either side of a central colonnaded hall.[4] The third scheme presented a modest reordering of the State Apartments along the south front, with a number of new buildings being added to the south-west corner.[5]

In the event, the King rejected all three schemes, perhaps considering it ill-judged to begin his reign in a new country with a costly and seemingly vainglorious building project. Furthermore, continuity in the appearance of the royal palaces may have been considered a valuable element in building up the new

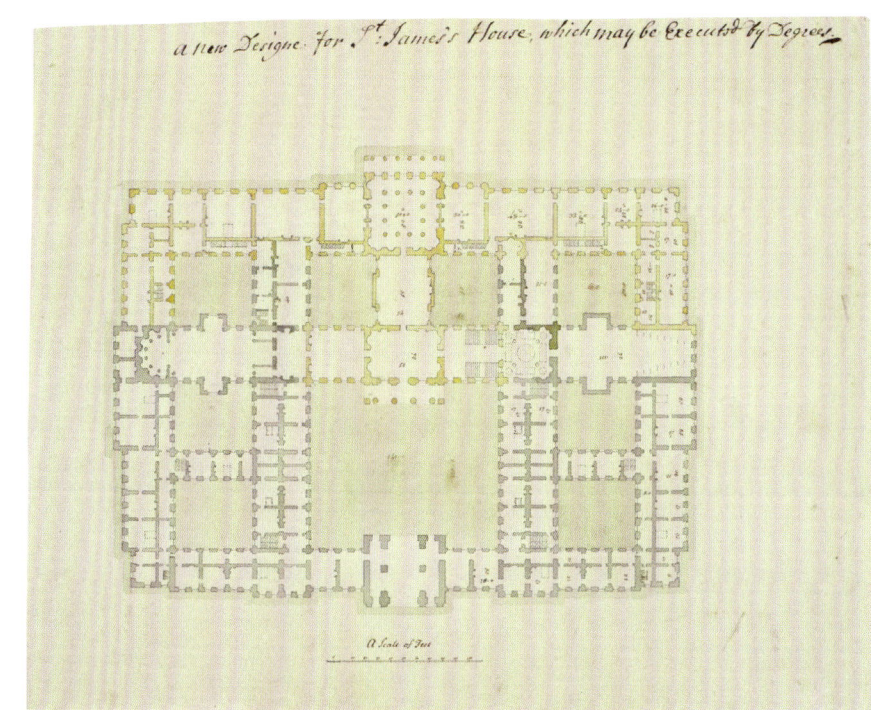

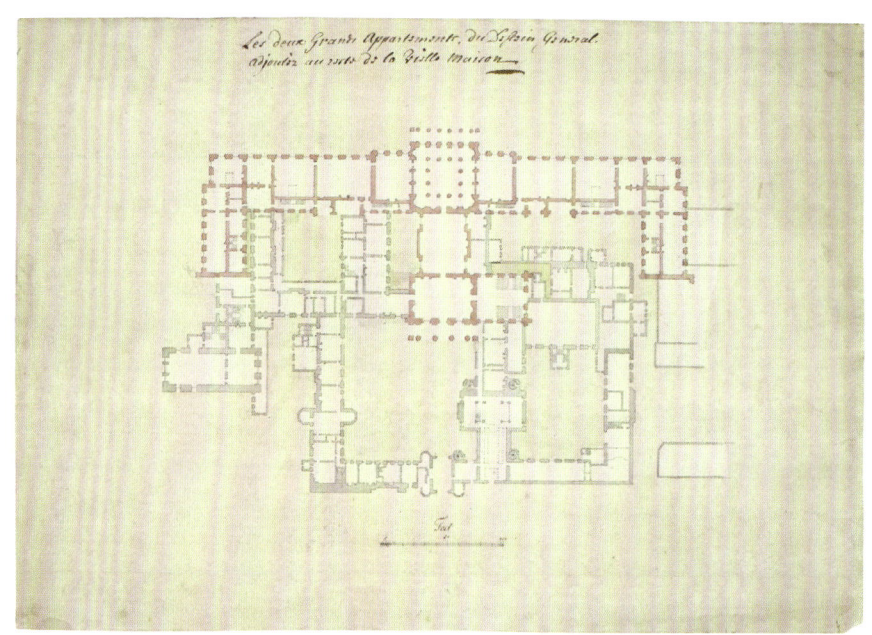

3.2
Sir John Vanbrugh, *A new design for St James's House*, possibly 1714, showing a scheme that would have extended the palace in phases (RCIN 926301; north is at the bottom)

3.3
Sir John Vanbrugh, 'The two State Apartments on the general layout, linked to the remains of the old house', possibly 1714 (north is at the bottom). Vanbrugh's ground plan includes the existing buildings to the north in black and the new wing planted over the south façade, here inscribed in pink (RCIN 926302)

3. THE GEORGIAN COURT

INTREDE van Z.K.M. GEORGE I, KONING van GROOT BRITANIE &c&c&c in LONDON. 1714

3.4

Abraham Allard (c.1676–1725), *State Entry of George I and the Prince of Wales into London, 1714*, coloured engraving, printed in Amsterdam. A strong contrast is made between the magnificence of the court, which occupies the whole foreground, and the relative modesty of the palace (RCIN 750365)

dynasty's popularity. George was to govern Britain in a very different way to his German electorate. Hanover, like almost all princely European states at the turn of the seventeenth century, was governed by a single absolute ruler. By contrast, Britain had evolved a constitutional monarchy in which the sovereign required the support of Parliament to raise money through taxation or by other means. It therefore behoved George to play a safe hand and opt for discretion – and financial prudence – rather than display.

Queen Anne had died on 1 August 1714, two months after her cousin, the Electress Sophia. The divorced George I, accompanied by his son George, Prince of Wales, landed in England, at Greenwich, on the evening of 18 September. Having stayed overnight at the Queen's House,[6] their journey the following day, from Greenwich to St James's Palace, passed through the City of London (Fig. 3.4) and was marked by numerous joyful acclamations – so many, in fact, that their retinue only arrived at the Great Gatehouse of St James's at night. The *Flying Post* recorded the cheerful scene: 'After his Majesty had pass'd thro' the Joyful Shouts of his Loving Subjects; and arriv'd at St James's the Guns of the Park were fir'd and the Evening concluded with Ringing of Bells, Bonfires, Illuminations, Fireworks and all other possible Demonstrations of Joy'.[7] The King's opinion of his new home and palace is not known, but judging by the tone of the accounts of foreign visitors (for example, César de Saussure's detailed account noted below), and by comparison with the surroundings with which he was familiar in the German Electorate, St James's may have come as something of a disappointment to him and his court.

Although George was accompanied by 100 or so ministers, courtiers and servants from Hanover, many of his retinue returned to Hanover and remained there following return visits made by the King in 1715 and 1716.[8] The King's immediate family, including his daughter-in-law and their children, all came to London in the autumn of 1714, with the exception of the seven-year-old Frederick (later Prince of Wales), eldest son of George Augustus, Prince of Wales, who, as heir in direct line of succession to his father, remained as the sole family representative in Hanover. It was not until December 1728 that Frederick finally set foot on English soil. George I brought with him his mistress, Ehrengard Melusine von der Schulenburg (1667–1743), and his half-sister, Countess Sophia Charlotte von Kielmansegg (1675–1725; formerly Sophia von Platen, and later created Countess of Darlington and Leinster). His estranged wife, Sophia Dorothea (1666–1726), remained at Schloss Ahlden, exiled from court life in Hanover as punishment for humiliating her husband in her affair with the German count, Philipp Christoph von Königsmarck. The Hanoverian courtiers and ministers who arrived with the new King in 1714 established a ministry in London – the Hanoverian, or German, Chancery, which, after 1716, seems to have numbered only about 25 staff.[9] In order for the King to maintain his role as Elector of Hanover, he returned to Hanover regularly throughout the course of his 13-year reign, always during the summer months. This familiar rhythm of returning to the Electorate would continue during the reign of George II, but ceased after 1760, even though George III was Elector, like his predecessors, and later also King of Hanover.[10] For the years when George I or George II remained in Britain, the court removed in the spring from St James's Palace to Kensington Palace – on four occasions, removing to Hampton Court Palace for the summer months, returning to St James's for the autumn and winter.[11] Windsor was visited by George I in 1724 for hunting in the Great Park, but was otherwise not used, other than for intermittent Garter installations and their accompanying feasts, until the reign of George III – and then only after 1776.[12]

In spite of this peripatetic circulation around suburban palaces, and periodic return visits to Hanover, the King's seat of authority remained the ancient Tudor palace of St James's, and it was here, in the Great Council Chamber, that he, like Queen Anne before him, met with his ministers, surrounded by tapestries and portraits of Venetian doges and a painting of St Catherine by Correggio (later destroyed).[13]

A little more than two years into his reign, George I found himself in a ministerial predicament, with Sir Robert Walpole and Viscount Townshend in opposition to one another, precipitating a political crisis. The political tensions within George I's cabinet, which had simmered through the spring of 1717, reached fever pitch in the autumn. The situation was made no easier by a fractious relationship between father and son: the Prince of Wales was incensed that during the King's absence in Hanover in 1716, he had only been named Guardian of the Realm – a position which came without responsibility: the ancient precedent for a Prince of Wales to be named thus was found in the Black Prince, made guardian at the age of eight during Edward III's absences on the continent. The Prince had expected to be named regent – de facto monarch – in his father's absence. Thus, the Prince withdrew from the Cabinet Council and began to establish his own interest within Parliament, at odds with his father's already fragmented and fragile ministry.[14]

Matters came to a head following the birth, on 20 October 1717, of Prince George William (who later died in infancy). According to precedent, the King insisted that the Lord Chamberlain, the Duke of Newcastle (1693–1768), be godparent; the Prince disagreed. After the baptism on 28 November 1717, the Prince of Wales spoke abusively to the Duke of Newcastle,

3.5

Stable Yard House, photographed in 2019. Designed in 1716 by Nicholas Hawksmoor, the stables were drastically rebuilt between 1979 and 1981, during conversion to offices

who thought he had been challenged to a duel. The King showed both his dissatisfaction toward his son's behaviour and his desire to impose his will on his son and subject, and expelled the Prince of Wales from the palace – and from the court – claiming guardianship of his children, who would remain in his care at St James's. The Princess of Wales, who had not been expelled, decided to follow her husband, and in early 1718, the Prince and Princess of Wales set up their own court at Leicester House, the town house built *c.*1631–5 by Robert Sidney, 2nd Earl of Leicester, situated on the north side of present-day Leicester Square, less than a mile from St James's. The house was rented to them for £500 per annum, and they remained here until the death of George I in 1727.[15] The King permitted the Princess to visit her children, but he made it clear that anyone received by the Prince and Princess of Wales would not be welcome at St James's.[16]

At the same time, the King found himself in a ministerial crisis and in need of bolstering his own faction. Thus, the naturally shy monarch, who detested court appearances and the rigid formality of such occasions, decided to reinstate the royal ritual of public dining and to hold evening Drawing Rooms at St James's three times a week. Between 21 November 1717 and 5 April 1718 – a parliamentary session – he also established a very popular weekly public dining table at court that attracted MPs, ambassadors and foreign ministers who had nowhere else to dine, known as the 'Green Cloth Table', presided over by the clerks of the Board of Green Cloth. The following winter, the King again held an evening assembly three times per week, re-established the public table at court and held a public ball (in the ballroom added to the palace in 1696) at least once a week. The balls were often raucous affairs: following one ball, the vice chamberlain informed the Board of Green Cloth that 'the room where the Side Board was kept' was 'so stained with claret [that] it was necessary to provide Sayl cloth against another Ball to prevent the like damage'.[17] On 8 December 1718, William Byrd of Westover, Virginia, 'went to Court, where there was a Ball and [he] got almost drunk and came home about 1 o'clock'.[18]

In 1720, there was a reconciliation between father and son, and the crisis of the ministry had passed. The Prince had an audience of the King in the King's Closet at St James's on St George's Day, 23 April, and the following day, both attended a service at the Chapel Royal. The Prince was welcomed back into the fold: although he was not resident at St James's, his guardsmen were returned to him.[19] The 'Green Cloth Table' was discontinued after 1721.

The first significant piece of building alteration at the palace came in early 1716, and was for the better accommodation of the grooms and coachmen in the stable yard, at the western end of the palace complex (Fig. 3.5).[20] An estimate for the scheme was soon followed by a commission for Nicholas Hawksmoor of the Office of Works to redevelop the stable block with an 'Arcade of Brick'.[21] Soon after, the Treasury gave approval 'for several extraordinary works to be performed in His Majesty's Stable Yard at St James's'.[22] The new block was originally intended to house 23 horses, at an estimated cost of £1,800. The works began immediately and the building was completed in 1717, at the slightly lower cost of £1,771.[23]

The greatly increased numbers at court, compared with the previous reign – members of three generations of the royal family, plus courtiers and staff within the households of the King and the Prince and Princess of Wales – led to greater use of the palace generally, thus placing extra strain on the royal kitchens, which were situated in the south-east corner of the palace, near to the King's private apartment. As a result, in 1716, a request came from the Prince of Wales's household for a new kitchen; the existing staff complained of having to cook quantities of provisions for the King and for the Prince's family in the same space. This new kitchen was to be located in the western half of the palace buildings, somewhat detached from the rest, in what later became known as Kitchen Court (the western part of today's Ambassadors Court). It was to contain cellars, sculleries, rooms and offices for cooks and staff, and a vault for German (Rhineland) wine.[24] By July 1717, work had still not started, and the Board of Green Cloth, the department of the Royal Household responsible for providing food and drink, implored the Lord Chamberlain, the Duke of Newcastle, to act, following which the Duke wrote to the Treasury on 12 July 1717, explaining the great inconvenience in preparing food for the two households.[25]

The following week, the Treasury commissioned an estimate for the building which was to rise on a site in 'the Back Court' of St James's.[26] The site was selected, no doubt, on account of its proximity to existing kitchen buildings (see Fig. 2.27).[27] The great kitchen was to rise the full height of the building, with a coved ceiling pierced with oculi, surmounted by a rectangular lantern (Fig. 3.6). The King's Kitchen, as it became known, was completed in 1719, at a total cost of £2,603 18s 7¼d (Fig. 3.7). Though no architect has been identified, it was most likely designed by Sir John Vanbrugh, at that time Comptroller of the Office of Works, possibly with assistance from Nicholas Hawksmoor (secretary to the board of the Office of Works, 1715–18). Another architect in the royal orbit around this time was Colen Campbell (1676–1729), whose *Vitruvius Britannicus* provided a printed source for Palladian architecture in Britain. Campbell was

3.6

St James's Palace: The New Kitchen, c.1819; watercolour by James Stephanoff (c.1786–1874), published in Pyne's *History of the Royal Residences* (1819) (RCIN 922167)

3. THE GEORGIAN COURT

3.7

The 'new' or King's Kitchen, photographed in 2019, built in 1719 and attributed to Sir John Vanbrugh. The first-floor link on the left was added when the ballroom was converted into a supper room (now known as the Banqueting Room) in 1824

responsible for designing another royal kitchen building, also with a plain, unadorned brick exterior – the 'German kitchen' at Hampton Court Palace – which was an early example of Palladian architecture, constructed in 1715.[28]

The building works in the 1720s were of minor consequence.[29] After the falling-out between father and son in 1717, the Prince and Princess of Wales had vacated their apartments; the young Princesses, Anne (1709–59), Amelia (1711–86) and Caroline (1713–57), continued to be cared for at the palace, and numerous minor works were undertaken for their benefit. Alterations to the King's library amounted to £331 11s.[30] Such a small sum suggests that rooms were to be fitted up for housing volumes, but that this library was not intended to supersede or replace the magnificent and historic royal collection of books and manuscripts lodged at Essex House on the Strand, where it was stored with the Cottonian Library. The King's books were either to be lodged in two rooms in the south-eastern corner of the palace, facing St James's Park, or a new building was to be constructed as an extension of the historic library rooms in the palace.[31] Perhaps to be included within the King's library was an armillary sphere, which was repaired and embellished in 1725 – at the considerable cost of £480.[32]

Such projects were very much the exception: energies were concentrated, on the whole, in below-stairs areas concerning various minor works, such as window cleaning and brickwork repairs. However, there are glimpses revealing the King's interests: in 1723, the pressing matter of cheese storage arose, with a 'frame in the King's Cellar, whereon the King's Chese is laid, to be hung with Irons instead of ropes'.[33] The King's wines were also a matter of concern: 'His Majesty's wines are much prejudiced for want of good vaults'.[34]

Something of the character of the palace interior is to be found in observations made by visitors, recorded in their correspondence and diaries. On the whole, these accounts reflect a degree of bafflement or bemusement that the seat of monarchy of a global power such as Great Britain lay within the creaking, cramped and old-fashioned building of St James's Palace. Probably the most detailed account of a visitor to the palace during George I's reign was made by the Swiss writer and traveller, César de Saussure, who recounted the spectacle of visiting a Drawing Room, accompanied by his (anonymous) English friend, on a Sunday at St James's Palace, just one week after his arrival in London in May 1725.[35] His account reflects the importance attached to the ceremonial court ritual of Sunday worship, perhaps of some fascination to the Calvinist de Saussure. Arriving at midday, he and his companion passed through various rooms where noblemen and courtiers were loitering, awaiting the opening of the King's apartments, and 'as soon as the signal was given all these people disappeared inside them, we being unable to follow on account of the crowd'. De Saussure and his friend found a vantage point from which to observe the great procession in the Chapel Royal: soon, six Yeomen of the Guard (whom de Saussure compared to the Swiss Guard at Versailles) appeared at the head of the procession, followed by court officers, the Lord Chamberlain (the Duke of Grafton) and the Master of the King's household (the Duke of Dorset). Behind them came two sergeants-at-arms carrying silver-gilt maces, followed by a courtier bearing the sword of state. Then came the King, accompanied by the three young Princesses, the children of the Prince and Princess of Wales. De Saussure did not attend chapel; instead, 'Whilst His Majesty was attending service in the chapel we visited the interior of the Palace'. Like others,[36] he was rather underwhelmed by its exterior appearance: 'This Palace does not give you the impression from outside of being the residence of a great King, but it is a large and roomy building'. The account continues with a description of the layout: 'In the first court, where a company of foot-guards mount guard, is a whale's carcase, twenty ft [6.1 m] long, fastened to the wall by iron cramps'. In fact, the so-called whale's carcass was a single rib of a whale, of enormous size. An earlier visitor had recorded its presence at St James's: 'In one of the Courts of St James's Palace, there is the Rib of a Whale twenty foot long'.[37] It was certainly still there in 1796.[38] De Saussure's account of his visit continues to describe the interior of the palace:

The King's chambers consist firstly of a big room which leads into the bedchamber, the bed being covered with crimson velvet, braided and embroidered in gold. The bed stands in a sort of alcove, shut off from the rest of the room by a balustrade of gilded wood. To the right of the grand ante-chamber is the drawing-room, where the King gives audiences and receives ambassadors. In these two chambers there are canopies of purple velvet, embroidered in gold and silver, surmounting two armchairs, also covered in crimson velvet.

Such an arrangement had existed in the King's bedchamber since the reign of Charles II. George I's bedchamber – symbolically the most important space within the palace – found direct parallels in its furnishing with the great European princely palaces of the late seventeenth and early eighteenth centuries, such as Versailles in France, the Hofburg in Vienna and the Munich Residenz, whose state bedchambers also featured a bed either within a recess or behind a rail running across the room – or both. 'All these rooms look onto the park gardens, and are hung with beautiful old tapestries. On the walls I saw paintings, mostly original; the chandeliers are of silver, and some of them silver-gilt'. He remarks on the beauty of the Queen's Chapel, finding it far superior to the Chapel Royal, which he describes as 'being in no manner remarkable'. De Saussure's aesthetic views may have been formed on account of being a member of the Swiss Reformed Church.

At two o'clock, the Drawing Room commenced and our visitor returned to that room, where the King appeared with the young Princesses, Anne, Amelia and Caroline. The King was presented with three (unidentified) ladies and he kissed them all affectionately on the lips, that the King 'seemed to take most pleasure in kissing the prettiest of the three'.[39] The Prince and Princess of Wales also joined the Drawing Room, and while the King greeted the Princess with affection, he made no attempt to speak to or acknowledge his son, the Prince of Wales. De Saussure tells us that three Drawing Rooms were held every week, on Sunday afternoons

3.8

Alessandro Tiarini (1577–1668), *St Cecilia*, c.1620. Hung in the Drawing Room by Queen Anne, George I returned this painting as part of the hang in the room renamed the second great antechamber (RCIN 402926)

(from 2pm until 3pm), and on Monday and Friday evenings (from 8pm until 10pm or 11pm).

When it came to the fitting-out of St James's Palace, the King's consideration of the palace interiors was consistent with his architectural ambitions. While a certain amount of refurnishing in the palace was no doubt essential, the overriding impression the new dynasty may have wanted to give was one of continuity and stability, not change. In the State Apartments of the King and the Prince of Wales, a limited amount of redecoration took place, with an emphasis on the reuse of existing furniture, lighting and tapestries, while the picture hang remained much the same. A notable change in paintings hanging in the King's bedchamber was the substitution of Kneller's portrait of the daughters of the Duke of Marlborough (which had no relevance for George I) for the artist's portrait of the Archduke of Austria, by this date the Holy Roman Emperor Charles VI (1685–1740).[40] At that time, Hanover, and by association, Britain, was allied to the Emperor: it may be significant that the Empress, Elisabeth Christine of Brunswick-Wolfenbüttel (1691–1750), was a Guelph relation of George's. The King had also played a glorious role in the imperial allies' defeat of the Ottomans at the Battle of Vienna in 1683.[41] Sometime afterwards, he was sent two Turks: Mehmet was brought to Hanover by an officer, and Mustafa was transferred to George after serving a Swedish officer. Such was their longevity of service and trustworthiness that a myth was allowed to circulate that one had reputedly saved George I's life in battle. In 1716, Mehmet was ennobled by George I, calling himself Ludwig Maximilian Mehmet von Königstreu.[42] Employing Turkish valets had been a Viennese symbol of status: that George eschewed the English custom of court officers attending the King as he dressed was a sign of both his distaste for court ritual and ceremony and his adherence to continental European court practice.[43]

Around 100 paintings were recorded hanging in the State Apartments in an inventory made before 1723, which may be usefully compared with the preceding inventory, made during the reign of Queen Anne in 1710.[44] Tapestries, which mostly covered the walls in the State Apartments, were inventoried in 1695, but after that are recorded in the Wardrobe accounts when undergoing repairs, and only infrequently noted with their location within the palace. In the King's second great antechamber, which had been the Great Drawing Room in 1710, Huysmans's portrait of Catherine of Braganza as a shepherdess (RCIN 405665) hung over the chimney; Tiarini's (1577–1668) *St Cecilia* (Fig. 3.8), thought to be by Caravaggio in the 1710 inventory, and Allori's (1577–1621) *Judith with the Head of Holofernes* (RCIN 404989) hung over the doors. The only change from the reign of Queen Anne was the substitution of a 'mans Picture' by Tintoretto for the Judith and Holofernes, which had hung in the Great Council Chamber during Anne's reign.[45] The walls were hung with an unidentified tapestry series, but almost certainly one woven in gold and silver thread, perhaps one of the *Abraham* series, which was noted as hanging at St James's in 1735. Two years later, nine tapestries woven with gold and silver thread were cleaned; they were noted as hanging in the Great Drawing Room and Great Council

Chamber. Of the tapestries inventoried at St James's in 1695, only the *Abraham* series was woven with gilt-metal-wrapped thread.[46]

The Presence Chamber was hung with nine pieces of the *Sciences* series of tapestries (untraced), and over the doors were portraits of Edward III and the Black Prince (RCINS 404044, 404037). Next door, the Privy Chamber (also called the King's First Antechamber) was hung with four tapestries from the *Planets* series (two sets of this series were recorded in the 1695 inventory). Over the chimney stood a marble bust, and over the doors were a portrait of Potruski, Russian envoy to Charles II, a portrait of Tintoretto, Ferrardo or Salviati, the Florentine ambassador, in a black doublet holding a palette, and a painting of the figure of *Temperance*, described in the George I inventory made before 1723 as 'A Woman Pouring a Drink for a Soldier' (RCIN 406089).[47] The little drawing room was hung with three pieces from the *Seasons*; over the doors, a *Shepherd Playing the Flute* and *Shepherdess*, both by the English copyist Henry Cooke (1642–1700; untraced); and over the chimney, a copy by Parry Walton of Giordano's (1634–1705) *Cyclopses Working in their Forges* (this arrangement persisted through to the early nineteenth century).[48] On the Prince's side in 1715, the only tapestries noted in the Wardrobe accounts (which required mending) were two from the *Apostles* series, made after Raphael's (1483–1520) cartoons.

The greatest expenditure on new furnishings was concentrated in the apartments of the royal women, where new furniture was required and the rooms decorated in up-to-the-minute fashions. As there was no consort to accommodate, the rooms which in the previous reign had been allocated to Prince George, Queen Anne's consort, were now given over to the Prince of Wales. Caroline, Princess of Wales, was given her own apartment at St James's: the first Princess of Wales for more than 200 years (the last Princess having been created in 1501, when Katherine of Aragon married Arthur, Prince of Wales), and the first to be accommodated at St James's Palace. A new staircase was inserted, in order to provide access to the Princess's new apartment and communication between her apartment and that of her young daughters, whose rooms were located nearby, most probably on the floor below.[49] The Princesses (in 1714, Anne was aged five, Amelia aged three and Caroline a baby of one year) were given an apartment, including an antechamber, a blue closet, a bedchamber, a waiting room and a dining room; furniture and fittings included a lacquer screen, green curtains, yellow curtains and beds covered in crimson mohair.[50] The Princess of Wales's apartment was extensively fitted out with new furniture supplied by Gerrit Jensen; the most expensive piece was a mirror for the bedchamber (£120), with a gilded table and gilded stands positioned below (£40). Her rooms were hung with crimson and yellow silk damask, in the newest fashion.[51]

The apartment of the King's mistress, Ehrengard Melusine von der Schulenburg, later created Duchess of Kendal and Munster, was also expensively fitted out – more than £4,000 was spent for her comfort during the reign of George I.[52] Other members of the court given accommodation at the state's pleasure included the Princesses Anne, Amelia and Caroline (Fig. 3.9);[53] the King's half-sister, Countess Sophia Charlotte von Kielmansegg; Johanna Sophie zu Schaumburg-Lippe, known as the Countess of Bückeburg; the King's Turkish grooms of the chamber, Mehmet and Mustafa; Mr Ulrick, 'the King's dwarf'; composer and organist, William Croft (1678–1727); and Henrietta Howard (c.1688–1767), lady of the bedchamber to the Princess of Wales and the Prince of Wales's mistress.[54] The two leading Hanoverian ministers, Johann Kaspar ('Hans') von Bothmer (Fig. 3.10) and Andreas Gottlieb Freiherr von Bernstorff (1649–1726), were also accommodated in rooms in the palace that were often refurnished.[55]

Other senior courtiers of the Hanoverian Chancery in London from 1714 included the heads of the Chancery, Johann Philipp von Hattorf, and his successor, Ernst Freiherr von Steinberg, the latter in charge of the Chancery in London from 1737 to 1748; he was succeeded by the brothers Gerlach and Philipp Adolf

3.9
Martin Maingaud (*fl.* 1692–*c*.1725), *Princesses Anne, Amelia and Caroline*, 1721. The Princesses were assigned lodgings at the palace in 1714 (RCIN 404985)

3.10
John Faber Sr (1660–1721), *Johann Kaspar ('Hans') von Bothmer*. Bothmer was one of the King's Hanoverian ministers allocated lodgings at the palace in 1714 (National Portrait Gallery, London, D32723)

Freiherrn von Münchhausen, both of whom were influential in the 1740s and 1750s. After political machinations to remove Bernstorff, the influence of the German Chancery in British affairs was reduced, though it continued in existence for the duration of the personal union between Great Britain and Hanover, until the accession of Queen Victoria in 1837.[56] Grand Marshal Hardenburg's rooms were lavishly hung with six tapestries, hired through Mr Lockmann.[57]

There was a constant stream of requests to replace or improve existing accommodation, such as fitting a new backstairs for the young Princesses.[58] Other work included the insertion of walls to divide up apartments, or the taking down of partitions to enlarge them; the repair of window sashes and shutters; the repairing of roofs, doors (quite frequently for the young Princesses), gutters and pavements, and, occasionally, making new furniture for functional areas such as the kitchen, including an elm dresser for the new 'king's kitchen', and a dining table for the Yeomen of the Guard, reusing old oak.[59]

Three chapels were in use at St James's throughout the eighteenth century: the principal space was the (Tudor) Chapel Royal, with its box pews facing across the central aisle, which was aligned north to south. The Dean and Sub-Dean of the Chapel Royal presided here; administratively, they were answerable to the Lord Chamberlain. The German or Lutheran chapel, which was situated in a room on the south side of the great court, on the ground floor, below the Prince of Wales's Guard Chamber and Presence Chamber, was led by Anthony Boehm, who was succeeded on 1 July 1722 by Frederick Michael Ziegenhagen. The German congregation was made up mostly of the Hanoverian Chancery. The French or Huguenot chapel held its services at the Queen's Chapel, whose preacher during George I's reign was the Revd Dr John Menard. The same space was shared by the Dutch chapel (thus occasionally referred to as the French and Dutch chapel), which was led by the preacher Revd John Peter Nucella, succeeded by Mr Phineas Pielat.[60] The Huguenot congregation was established in the wake of the Revocation of the Edict of Nantes by Louis XIV in 1685, precipitating waves of French Protestant emigration. The Dutch congregation was begun during the reign of William III.

The King and the Prince of Wales attended their first Sunday service in the Chapel Royal on 26 September 1714, when they took Holy Communion and heard music composed by George Frederick Handel (1685–1759). It is not known which piece was chosen, but it could have been the appropriately religious 'Utrecht' *Te Deum*, first performed in St Paul's Cathedral to celebrate the Peace of Utrecht in 1713, or newly composed church music.[61] Both also attended a subsequent service on Sunday 17 October, to give thanks for the safe passage to Great Britain of Caroline, Princess of Wales, and the young Princesses, at which the shorter 'Caroline' *Te Deum*, also composed by Handel, was performed.[62] In almost every subsequent year, the King attended a service at the Chapel Royal to give thanks for the safe return of the monarch, which usually coincided with other formal court rituals, such as dining in state (i.e. in public).[63] The chapel was very sumptuously furnished: for instance, the crimson Genoa velvet – the best kind – cost 40s per yard, as expensive as that used for the walls of the principal State Rooms. The gold and silver fringing used on the altar frontal and elsewhere was especially rich. Lavish expenditure on the chapel not only emphasised the importance of religion at court, but, with the King's regular attendance, showed how seriously he took his religious responsibilities.[64]

Throughout the eighteenth century, the Chapel Royal was one of several centres in London of musical creativity. The official composer to the Chapel Royal was the Englishman William Croft, whose appointment ahead of any one of the bevy of talented foreign composers may have been deliberate. However, Handel, one of the outstanding composers in London in the 1720s, familiar to George I from his court position at Hanover, was appointed, in 1723, Composer of Music for His Majesty's Chapel Royal. This was a court, not a Chapel Royal, appointment.[65] After the performances of Handel's *Te Deum* in the autumn of 1714, any new compositions thereafter were written by Croft, who held the official appointment of composer (as well as organist and choirmaster) of the Chapel Royal. Significantly, Croft provided music for the King in the winter of 1719, at the peak of the estrangement between King and Prince. At that time, court rituals increased in richness, in order to enhance the attractiveness of the King in contrast to his son.[66]

While St James's Palace thus remained George I's principal metropolitan palace and seat of the monarchy, it was left by him largely as it was found, with the exception of the addition of a new stable block and a second kitchen. By contrast, the King left a significant architectural mark at Kensington Palace, where his major rebuilding and redecorating works were completed only months after his death on 11/22 June 1727. This contrast is brought sharply into focus in the pages of the accounts of the Office of Works: while the architect, painter and designer, William Kent (1685–1748), was supplying pedestals and marble-topped tables for Kensington Palace, only mundane jobbing repairs, such as adding a new tin funnel to a chimney, were taking place at St James's.[67]

George II and Queen Caroline, 1727–60

Following the death of George I in June 1727 at Osnabrück, the English court was plunged into mourning: black cloth was hung in the State Apartments. Just over a month later, arrangements for the coronation of the new King were put in hand.[68] Preparations for the accommodation of the royal family were also enacted, and the new King and Queen moved back into the palace which they had left in 1717. Both were fond of public appearances and content to lead traditional royal rituals such as public dining. However, unlike contemporary European princes, George II's architectural patronage was limited – like his father's. He was perhaps more concerned with the well-being of his horses than his court – a spectacular new royal mews was constructed to the designs of William Kent at Charing Cross.[69] Kent was also responsible for the construction of a new library

3.11

Possibly English School, *The Mall and St James's Palace from the South-East, with Marlborough House*, c.1730 (Yale Center for British Art, B1981.25.555)

within the grounds of St James's Palace for Queen Caroline, whose interest in architectural patronage, as well as her intellectual proclivities, far outweighed those of her husband. Before her marriage to George, she had lived first at the court of Dresden and then at Berlin, where she was exposed to the sophisticated court cultures of Saxony and Brandenburg respectively. Her new library would be a short-lived monument to her intellectual tastes. Besides these commendable projects, the story at St James's under George II (Fig. 3.11) is again one of maintenance, renewal and repair, especially in the provision of apartments for newly married members of the family. And it is in the sphere of nuptial celebrations that the most interesting occasions in the early part of the reign can be found: while the actual ceremonies and entertainments, for the most part, passed off well enough, the unions provided the beginnings for internal family jealousies and divisions to be played out.

The palace played host to three royal weddings between 1734 and 1740. These public weddings were a departure from the English tradition of private royal nuptials. The first of the royal children to be married was Anne, Princess Royal, married in the Queen's Chapel (Figs 3.12 and 3.13). A British–Dutch alliance was considered to be advantageous to both nations, and it was agreed that Anne would marry William IV, Prince of Orange-Nassau (1711–51), Stadholder of Friesland, Groningen and Gelderland. However, the marriage – planned in great detail and sumptuousness for November 1733 – had to be postponed to March of the following year, as the Prince fell seriously ill the day before the wedding. William Kent (Master Carpenter in the Office of Works) designed decorations and the temporary structures required for the large number of guests and the elaborate celebrations. The cabinet-maker Benjamin Goodison (c.1700–67), delivered two mahogany kneeling desks to be put before

the altar, and two large armchairs with carved and gilded frames, presumably for the newly married couple to sit on. Matching these were eight square stools, two armchairs and six kneeling stools (all giltwood), supplied by the joiner to the Great Wardrobe, Henry Williams (1717–58).[70] Goodison and Williams were makers of high standing and their workshops were capable of supplying large amounts of furniture to the royal palaces: Goodison made mainly case furniture (chests, cabinets, bookcases) for the palaces from 1729, and Williams was a joiner, or maker of turned pieces (chairs, tables, beds), but sometimes also made case furniture. Goodison's workshop was at the sign of the 'Golden Spread Eagle' on Long Acre, and Williams's was on the same street.[71]

The Queen's Chapel was to be linked to the Privy Chamber by a specially constructed walkway, making a ceremonial path for the wedding procession. For this, the Wardrobe hired lights from Goodison, including '7 Christial Lusters for the Body of the Chappel' and '32 Brass rings to carry 12 candles Each with Gilt chain for the long Gallery leading from the privy chamber to the said Chappel', at a cost of £288.[72] The chandeliers in the chapel were supplemented by 408 single brass arms hung in the side chapel. The lighting as first estimated was considered inadequate, and by

3.12
Sketch of the marriage of Anne, Princess Royal, to William, Prince of Orange-Nassau, at the Queen's Chapel, St James's, 1734 (BM, 1927,0721.1). The stool visible in the foreground may be associated with the set of eight stools supplied by Henry Williams at a cost of £88 (TNA, LC 9/289, acct no. 28; for the stools see RCIN 1230)

3.13
Engraved by John Francis Rigaud (1742–1810) after William Kent, *Marriage of Princess Anne and William, Prince of Orange*, 1734. This print shows the Queen's Chapel fitted out with specially commissioned furniture and light fittings for the wedding (RCIN 750381)

3. THE GEORGIAN COURT

the time the Prince actually made it to the altar, Goodison had supplied an additional 90 pairs of wrought brass arms and a further 16 brass rings to carry 12 candles for the gallery. Lord Hervey, Vice Chamberlain in Queen Caroline's household, provides a detailed account of the nuptials: 'The chapel was fitted up with an extreme good taste, and as much finery as velvets, gold and silver tissue, galloons, fringes, tassels and gilt lustres, and sconces could give. The King spared no expense on this occasion'.[73] Four new tapestry borders were ordered to be attached onto two arches, while nine large tapestries were to be hung about the chapel.[74] An anthem was composed by Handel for the occasion: *This Is the Day*.

Perhaps the excitement of this first royal wedding at last introduced a more cheerful note to court proceedings, which probably contrasted with the sometimes vituperative atmosphere of the court during the reigns of George I and George II.[75]

Two years later, Frederick, Prince of Wales, married Augusta of Saxe-Gotha (1719–72) in the smaller space of the Chapel Royal. The 16-year-old Princess was received by the King and Queen in the great drawing room of the palace on 27 April.[76] The service was performed with some splendour and was presided over by Dr Edmund Gibson, Bishop of London and Dean of the Chapel Royal.[77] Perhaps on account of the compact venue, rather less furniture was required for this wedding than the large amount ordered for the nuptials of Princess Anne. Once again, Benjamin Goodison and Henry Williams supplied lighting, seating and other furniture. The staircase and colonnade were lit by 17 glass lanterns, provided by Goodison, who also supplied 13 side lanterns.[78] Henry Williams repaired four armchairs and eight stools, presumably the same chairs and stools used at Princess Anne's wedding. Williams was also paid for putting up and taking down the furniture, and also for his own time in attendance at the wedding itself. The Earl of Egmont was not impressed by the musical accompaniment: 'An anthem composed by Hendel [*sic*] for the occasion was wretchedly sung by Abbot, Gates, Lee, Bird and a boy.'[79] The ceremony was over by 9pm and was followed by a splendid banquet in the palace. Lord Hervey, somewhat drily, noted the banality: 'At supper nothing remarkable happened but the Prince's eating several glasses of jelly … When they [the Prince and Princess] were in bed everybody passed through their bedchamber to see them, where there was nothing remarkable but the Prince's night cap, which was some inches higher than any grenadiers cap in the whole army.'[80] It is not clear why the King lavished expenditure on the wedding of his eldest daughter, whereas his son and heir's marriage was a modest affair by comparison, though relations between father and son were already deteriorating. The Queen's Chapel may have been selected because of its larger size and greater attendance capacity. The magnificence of the marriage of Princess Elizabeth, only daughter of James I in 1613, and that of Princess Mary, elder daughter of Charles I in 1641, may have been historic examples followed by George II.[81] Furthermore, as the previous wedding celebration of a Prince of Wales had taken place in 1501, there were no obvious precedents.

On 8 May 1740, Princess Mary (1723–72) was married by proxy to Prince Frederick of Hesse-Cassel (1720–85) at the Chapel Royal, with Prince William Augustus, Duke of Cumberland (1721–65), standing in for her husband; the Archbishop of Canterbury officiated.[82] There was thus a renewed effort on the part of Goodison and Williams to ensure that the chapel was suitably fitted out – and that the furnishings already installed were cleaned and repaired. Again, Williams was paid for his men's time in putting up and taking down furniture, and for his own time in attendance.[83]

Goodison charged mainly for repairing, cleaning, lacquering and gilding, but he also charged for the removal of a large brass chandelier at Somerset House, and for putting it up in the Chapel Royal.[84] The ceremony was preceded by a Drawing Room at 6pm, and the wedding ceremony over by 9.15pm; at about 10.30pm, the King and members of the royal family went to the banqueting room and sat down for supper.[85] A month later, Princess Mary sailed for the Netherlands and on to Cassel, where she was married in person on 28 June.[86]

The Tudor Chapel Royal and the Stuart Queen's Chapel were much used as spectacular wedding venues during George II's reign. After weddings came births and baptisms, which usually took place in the Chapel Royal, with the long-standing Jonathan Higgate, confessor to His Majesty's household, leading many of the ceremonies. These marriages and baptisms are recorded in the register of the Chapel Royal, which shows the great range of people who obtained permission for baptisms, marriages and other religious ceremonies there. Those baptised and married at the chapel included members of the royal family, household staff and locals, some of whom, seemingly, were without clear connection to the household. If a licence could be obtained, then a marriage could be performed. For example, on 4 April 1727, Mr George Sale (of the Inner Temple and translator of the Koran, published in 1734) was married to Mrs Mary Ann d'Argent of St Bride's, a marriage licence having been obtained from the Bishop of London's office (the bishop also being Dean of the Chapel Royal).[87] Lord Hervey's son, William, was baptised on 2 June 1732 in his lodgings at St James's by Dr Hoadly, Bishop of Salisbury.

Besides the wedding ceremonies described above, services of thanksgiving for the safe return of the royal family from the continent continued to take place in the autumn of each year, as in the previous reign, though in parallel with George I's reign, it was principally Maurice Greene's music that was heard at the Chapel Royal, not Handel's. Although Handel had been appointed to the honorary position of Composer of Music for His Majesty's Chapel Royal in 1723, and was also music master to the young Princesses and had written music for George II's coronation in 1727, as a foreigner, he could not hold an official court post. Despite this largely bureaucratic hurdle, as the pre-eminent composer of his generation, his music was performed there.[88] Other occasions when the Chapel Royal was the focus of celebration included a special service of thanksgiving on 27 November 1743, for the King's victory over the French at the Battle of Dettingen earlier that year, when Handel's 'Dettingen' *Te Deum* and his Dettingen Anthem were first performed. Another service of thanksgiving was held on 24 April 1749, following the Peace of Aix-la-Chapelle. Once again, Handel composed a new *Te Deum* and anthem for the service; the members of the royal family who attended included the King, the Prince and Princess of Wales, Princess Amelia and the Duke of Cumberland. Through the reigns of both George I and George II, the Chapel Royal remained the religious focus of the household (Hervey remarked in 1736 on 'that Chapel to which the King constantly goes on a Sunday'[89]), and through its magnificent music-making it provided a musical high point in the history of the chapel, as well as being an important artistic centre of London.[90]

The Princesses and their brothers were expected, if married, to live with their spouses, or, if unmarried, to be accommodated in spacious apartments at St James's. Henry Flitcroft (1697–1769), clerk of works at Whitehall, Westminster and St James's Palace from 1726 to 1746, produced a ground plan of St James's in 1729 (Fig. 3.14). When compared with Dickinson's earlier plans made during Queen Anne's reign, and with Soane's 1792 ground plan, Flitcroft's plan shows how many more additions were made to the palace between 1729 and 1792, in particular the filling in of Paradise Court in the south east and additional buildings at the western extremities.

The Great Gatehouse (north) is at the bottom of the plan, with the State Apartments at the top (south). The King's private apartment is in the upper-left corner, and the King's State Apartment in the upper centre and upper-right corner. The Council Chamber is the large room in the upper-right corner, with four windows looking south, and with a staircase next door. The Queen's Chapel is at far left; the new kitchen building is at far right centre.

The accommodation of the King's two sons, Frederick, Prince of Wales, and William, Duke of Cumberland, required careful consideration. Although both George I and George II had considered that one son might inherit either

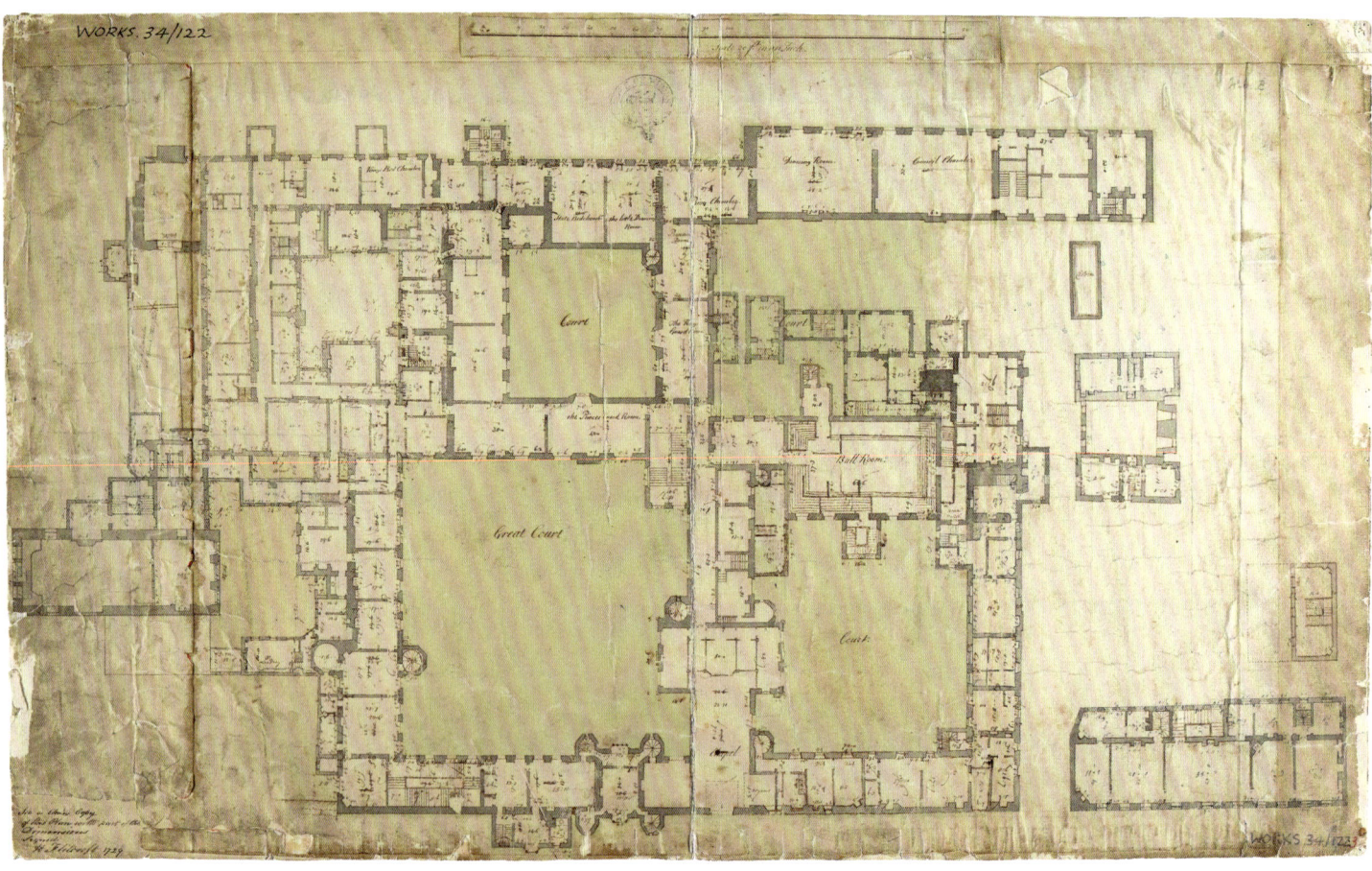

3.14
Henry Flitcroft, plan of the principal floor of St James's Palace, 1729 (TNA WORK 34/122; north at the bottom)

the Electorate of Hanover or the kingdom of Great Britain, such a plan may not ever have been formally agreed.[91] Whatever intentions George II and Queen Caroline held for their sons, William had been indulged at the expense of his elder brother, Frederick, who, in 1714, at the age of seven, had been left to fend for himself in Hanover. When Frederick arrived in London in 1728, both brothers were established with their own households and apartments. In 1736, orders were given to convert rooms above the stables (built a decade earlier by Hawksmoor) into offices for the Prince of Wales.[92] Goodison was employed to make new furniture for 'the Prince of Wales's new room', which may have been his staff's offices. This delivery comprised six 'Wainscott' (imported oak) dining tables and a total of 138 chairs, 66 in walnut, 60 in beech and 12 described only as 'wooden'.[93] The total cost of fitting up the offices for the Prince of Wales cost £463 4s 9d, and to convert the rooms above the stables,

£570 2s 7½d.[94] Augusta, Princess of Wales, was also provided for, and the furniture supplied by Goodison for her closet reveals her interest in porcelain, for two carved and gilded corner shelves were made to hold china (£52).[95] A later account, also from Goodison, for the closet and probably other, unspecified rooms at St James's, underlines this interest in displaying porcelain: four carved and gilt ornaments with branches, over the chimney, were designed to display Chinese porcelain.[96] The Princess's musical interest was demonstrated when she was sent a mahogany music desk with two brass arms (for candles) and castors to fit a frame of a harpsichord.[97]

Without doubt, the most significant architectural addition to the palace precincts and buildings during the eighteenth century was the compact, box-like building designed by William Kent to house Queen Caroline's library. By 1735, the Queen's collections of books, which reflected her own intellectual

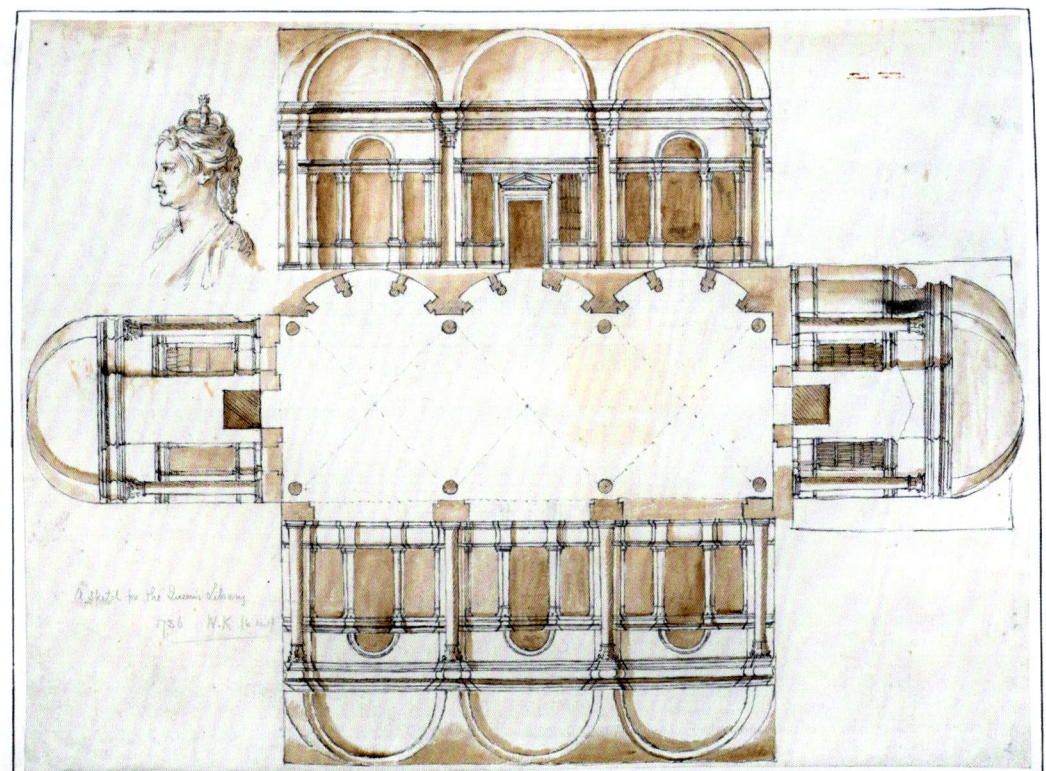

3.15
William Kent, *St James's Palace, Preliminary designs for Queen Caroline's Library*, 1736–7. Plan and laid-out wall elevations, and sketch portrait of Queen Caroline, all in Kent's hand (Sir John Soane's Museum, London, SM 147/197)

development, as well as universal European princely intellectual concepts, were held in various rooms across St James's Palace.[98] The Queen vacated some of these rooms in order to provide accommodation for her husband's latest mistress, Amalie Sophie Marianne von Wallmoden (1704–65), later Countess of Yarmouth, whom he had met during his sojourn in Hanover in 1735. It was Caroline herself who not only suggested the King return with his new mistress in tow, but was happy to arrange accommodation in the rooms occupied by his previous mistress, Henrietta Howard, Countess of Suffolk, who had fallen from the King's favour the year before: 'I will get Lady Suffolk's lodgings ready immediately, and enlarge them by adding the two rooms where my books now are which join to Lady Suffolk's lodgings'.[99] The Queen turned to William Kent, who in 1735 had become Deputy Surveyor at the Office of Works, for her new library building. The various stages of its development are documented in Kent's original design and a series of five presentation drawings, almost certainly drafted by Stephen Wright, Kent's personal draughtsman of the Office of Works.[100] A preparatory laid-out drawing in Kent's hand (Fig. 3.15), with a portrait of the Queen drawn in one corner, shows a double-cube building with three wide colonnaded bays on each long side, one side with curved recesses and the other flat – presumably for selection. Fireplace apertures are drawn in at each end, with door cases on either side. It is inscribed, 'A sketch for the Queen's Library / 1736 W. K. (To [?]…)'.

It seems that this scheme was rejected and an elevation with five window bays was adopted, as shown in the five highly finished presentation drawings (Figs 3.16–3.20). Three of these drawings show two schemes for the door arrangements on the end wall elevations: one scheme showed a large central door case, with half-columns and an open pediment; the other with a chimneypiece in the centre of the end wall, flanked by door cases – it was the latter scheme that was adopted. An engraving by Paul Fourdrinier (1698–1758) of the end wall – perhaps yet another proposed scheme or what was actually built – depicts a central chimneypiece surmounted by a mirror (or

3. THE GEORGIAN COURT

3.16

3.17

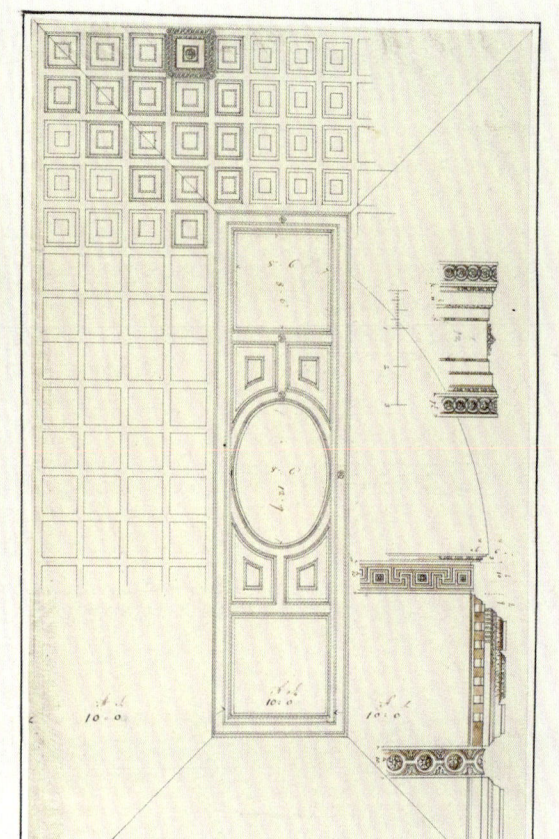

3.18

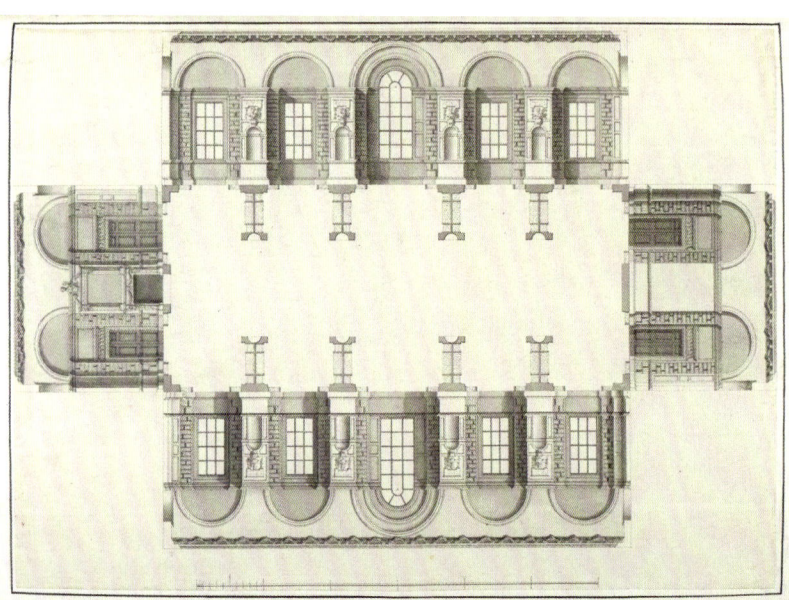

3.19

3.20

space for a painting) within a fluted columnar frame, and a scrolled open pediment with three marble busts. On either side of the door frame are arched recesses containing built-in bookcases. It is this engraving which shows one of the surviving marble chimneypieces (Fig. 3.21) and also the (unexecuted) ceiling decoration.

Had the decoration of the interior been completed (Fig. 3.4), the ceiling cove was to have been painted with a series of worthies within roundels encircled by acanthus foliage, and divided by vases, above pairs of putti holding laurel wreaths over the roundels.[101] Judging by Charles Wild's watercolour view (Fig. 3.23), made 80 years later, the Queen's library ceiling vault was left plain.

However, below the elaborately carved cornice and between the arches stood a series of terracotta busts, of English kings, queens and princes, raised on brackets. This important sculptural commission, which was almost certainly devised by the Queen herself, was given to the émigré Flemish sculptor, John Michael Rysbrack (1693–1770).[102] The precise iconographic programme which lay behind the scheme is obscure, and perhaps any explanation of it died with Queen Caroline. The 11 busts produced by Rysbrack portrayed the Black Prince (1330–76), Edward VI (r. 1547–53) and Elizabeth I (r. 1558–1603) (the three which survive; Figs 3.24 and 3.25 for the first two), King Alfred (r. 871–99), Edward III (r. 1327–77) and Queen Philippa of Hainault (c.1312–69), Henry V (r. 1413–22) and Catherine of Valois (1401–37), Henry VII (r. 1485–1509) and Elizabeth of York (1466–1503), and Henry, Prince of Wales (1594–1612). The uneven number of busts suggests that the commission may originally have been more extensive: for a classical, symmetrical library building, an even number of busts, perhaps in marble, may have been intended.[103] The Queen's sudden death at the end of 1737 brought any further expenditure on the building to an abrupt end, and no doubt curtailed the full extent of the commission.[104]

In total, the cost of the building amounted to £1,618 8¼d.[105] The library furniture was made

by Benjamin Goodison, including making 21 bookcases and supplying lighting in the form of eight pairs of brass wall candle branches and two mirrors, also fitted with brass candle branches.[106] Upholstery was supplied by Sarah Gilbert and by the laceman William Weekes: between them they provided couches (or 'forms' as they were known) covered in green mohair trimmed with silver lace,[107] and walnut tables and chairs.[108]

Had the new library come into regular use under Queen Caroline, it would no doubt have provided her, and the court, with an elegant and comfortable setting for intellectual activities. The Queen took a lively interest in scholarly subjects, and had corresponded over philosophical and mathematical matters involving Dr Samuel Clarke and Gottfried Leibniz. In fact, her books were organised along the same lines as those arranged by Leibniz, whom she had known as court librarian in

OPPOSITE
3.16–3.20
William Kent's design, drafted by Stephen Wright (d. 1780), *St James's Palace, Preliminary designs for Queen Caroline's Library*, 1736–7 (Sir John Soane's Museum, London, SM 147/193–196, 198)

3.16 Part-plan of ceiling and elevation of long side of room
3.17 Part-plan of elevation of long side of room and part-plan and elevation of end of room
3.18 Plan and details of ceiling
3.19 Plan and laid-out wall elevations of library
3.20 Plan of end bays and elevation of end wall

3.21
Paul Fourdrinier (1698–1758), engraving after William Kent, *Design for Queen Caroline's Library, St James's Palace*, 1737 (RCIN 703052)

3. THE GEORGIAN COURT 139

Hanover and Wolfenbüttel.[109] As her librarian, she employed Francis Say, who had been secretary to the Bishop of Ely, Thomas Green, and his predecessors, William Fleetwood and John Moore, and whom she may have encountered at the time of George I's purchase of Moore's library.[110]

The character of the Queen's book collection, most of which was in French, was universal and encyclopaedic, as may be judged by the 'Catalogue of the Royal Library of Her Late Majesty Queen Caroline Distributed into Faculties', completed in 1741 and comprising nearly 3,000 volumes (RCIN 1028932). It seems likely, therefore, that a collection such as this was intended more as a means of stimulating discussion and ideas than for the Queen's private use.

After 1741, the room gradually fell into disuse. By 1790, the building had become a storeroom: George III had built up his own extensive book collection, housed in a series of library rooms at Buckingham House.[111] In 1825, less than ten years after Charles Wild made his watercolour for inclusion in William Henry Pyne's (1769–1843) lavish three-volume publication, *History of the Royal Residences*, published in 1819 (see Fig. 3.23), the beautiful library building was pulled down to make way for a new townhouse for Frederick, Duke of York.[112]

The relationship between George II and Frederick, Prince of Wales, bore an unhappy resemblance to that of George II and his own father. During the years of estrangement in the reign of George I, neither father nor son had profited, and George II did not seek to reprise intergenerational conflict. However, Frederick had been left to fend for himself in Hanover, where he established his own independent interests, sought to put in place a favourable marriage alliance for himself, and emerged as the less-favoured child behind his younger brother, William, Duke of Cumberland. Rather than arriving on British soil at the accession of his father in 1727, his departure from Hanover was delayed; on 4 December 1728/9 he was abruptly summoned to Britain during a ball in Hanover. A month after his arrival on British soil, he was created Prince of Wales (8 January

1729) and lodged in the palace in his own suite of rooms, in a range on the north side of Kitchen Court, including a bedchamber hung with yellow silk damask, fitted up in 1728/9.[113] The Prince's rooms, whilst not anything like as grand as the State Apartments, included a library, for which Benjamin Goodison supplied two large mahogany bookcases in 1732.[114] Another injury to his status came when, during the King's visits to Hanover, he was passed over as regent in favour of his mother. The relationship foundered again following his union with Princess Augusta: Frederick sought parliamentary opposition support to achieve a financial settlement for himself of £100,000 per annum. In the end, the opposition was defeated, but in anticipation, Walpole had persuaded the King to settle £50,000 on the Prince of Wales and £50,000 on the Princess of Wales.

In 1734, the State Apartments were richly fitted out by Goodison, Williams, Sarah Gilbert and William Weekes.[115] The Prince of Wales's state bedchamber was furnished with a large pier glass and frame (£70), a carved and gilt table and frame with cover (£20) (Fig. 3.26),

OPPOSITE

3.22
Reconstruction of the interior of Queen Caroline's Library in 1737 (looking north), designed by William Kent. The ceiling decoration incorporates roundels of (left to right) Socrates, Homer, Galileo, Spenser, Shakespeare and Milton. The sculpted white busts depict kings, queens and princes of England by John Michael Rysbrack. The central writing table does not survive in the Royal Collection today: its design is inspired by the writing table seen in Fig. 3.23, and a library table in the Palace of Westminster (POW 15). The chimneypieces at each end were later removed to the Throne Room and the Entrée Room in the State Apartments (see Fig. 4.12)

3.23
Charles Wild's watercolour of *The Queen's Library, St James's Palace*, c.1816–19 (RCIN 922168)

3. THE GEORGIAN COURT

3.24 and 3.25

John Michael Rysbrack's terracotta busts of *Edward, Prince of Wales, the Black Prince*, c.1737, and *Edward VI*, signed and dated 1738. These are two of the three surviving busts from a series of eleven sculpted to adorn the Queen's library. The finished surface of the busts was originally white paint, perhaps to imitate marble, which has then been over-painted at a later date in brown wash, resembling the colour, if not the finish, of the terracotta underneath (RCINS 37067 and 53346)

a chimney glass (£40) and two walnut bedside tables on castors (£4 10s); other notable introductions included a lacquer cabinet on a giltwood stand and a six-leaf lacquer screen.[116] Henry Williams supplied the bed frame and tester, which was fitted with classical 'Vitruvian' vases with feathers, costing £60, supplied with a modestly priced walnut armchair: £2 5s. All of this was covered in crimson Genoa silk damask, 646 yards (590.7 m) of it, which cost £598 3d and was ordered from the mercer, Henry Cookes. The predominant crimson colour was relieved by an order from another mercer, John Bell, who provided the Prince with 284 yards (259.7 m) of green Genoa damask for a bed, chairs, stools and couch, which cost £234 6s.[117] In the mid-1730s, the King's apartments were also given some new furniture, all supplied by Benjamin Goodison: the King's presence chamber, privy chamber, little withdrawing room and state bedchamber received mainly giltwood furniture, including 'eight carved & gilt two-branch sconces £88', which were made for the presence chamber. In the Privy Chamber, some old sconces were retained, and in the little withdrawing room, a large pier glass in a gilt frame (£85) was installed. No doubt placed directly below the mirror was a marble tabletop on a carved and gilt frame (£22). Reflecting the importance of the space, the very richest furniture was reserved for the State Bedchamber, where a large pier glass in a carved and gilt frame (£105), and a carved and gilt table and stand with leather covers (£41), were supplied. The library was fitted up with a new walnut bookcase with glass doors (£36).[118] The design of this furniture is not known, as none survives, but it is likely that it followed the design of furniture supplied by Benjamin Goodison to contemporary clients: for instance, at Longford Castle, Wiltshire, where several pieces of furniture that were supplied to the 1st and 2nd Viscounts Folkestone have been attributed to Goodison on the strength of unspecified payments totalling £1,585 19s 6d.[119]

On the walls of the State Apartments, few changes, if any, were introduced, and the picture hang remained much as it did at the beginning of George I's reign. No picture inventory was taken during the reign of George II, so it is hard to be certain of picture moves. Tapestries certainly proliferated, and in 1731, in the presence chamber, ten tapestries from the *Sciences* series (one more than was noted hanging there in 1715) were cleaned.[120] Elsewhere in the Prince of Wales's apartments, six tapestries from the *Constantine* series and four tapestries from the *Elements* series were cleaned and mended (no specific location being given).¹²¹ In the following year, five tapestries from a set hanging in the King's apartments, referred to only as 'the cartoons', were cleaned. These may have been a set woven at Mortlake after Raphael's cartoons of the Acts of the Apostles, acquired by Charles I when Prince of Wales, in 1623. However, as two *Apostles* tapestries were referred to in the same account book, 'the cartoons' may be another series. The principal rooms of assembly and reception in the palace, namely the Presence and Privy Chambers, Great Council Chamber and Great Drawing Room, were, by 1746 (and probably since the Whitehall fire of 1698), hung with the best tapestries, and described as 'very fine pieces of tapestry hangings', which required gold- and silver-wrapped thread for restoring these tapestries.¹²² The only sets of tapestries woven with gold or silver threads in the royal collection in the eighteenth century were the *Abraham* series (see p. 128) and the *Hercules* series, which was at Hampton Court in the late seventeenth century, although five tapestries from the set appear to have been moved to St James's by 1738.¹²³

It was during the year 1737, leading up to the birth of the Princess's first child, Augusta (1737–1813), that the volatile relationship between father and son reached breaking point. Henry Williams was at work producing nursery furniture in the quarter leading up to Michaelmas 1737, when he made a richly carved and gilded state cradle. Besides this, a quantity of ordinary oak furniture (beds, chairs, night tables and pans) was provided, while Goodison supplied mahogany chests, tables, stands and airers.¹²⁴ Prince Frederick had insisted that his wife give birth at the principal seat of the British monarchy, St James's. The Princess of Wales went into labour on the night of 31 July, while the court was lodged at Hampton Court for the summer months; Frederick bundled Augusta into a carriage, which he ordered to be driven to St James's. Their daughter, Princess Augusta, was born at St James's a few hours later. Servants at the palace were completely unprepared for this surprise visit, so the Princess's unconventional birth took place without official witnesses. The King was furious: he wrote to the Prince of Wales on 10 September to inform him that 'it is my pleasure that you leave St James's with all your family when it can be done without prejudice or inconvenience to the Princess'.¹²⁵

The Prince and Princess of Wales left St James's on 12 September and removed to Carlton House (see p. 8), which had been acquired for the Prince from Lord Burlington in 1733. Towards the end of 1737, he rented Norfolk House, a more spacious and prestigious house in St James's Square, where his eldest son, George, later George III, was born on 24 May 1738. From the winter of 1742, Frederick moved again, to Leicester House – the same house rented by his father some years before, when he too had been expelled from St James's by his father, George I.¹²⁶

Two months after the Prince of Wales left St James's, the Queen complained of pains, and in early November 1737, it was discovered that the cause was a rupture in her stomach wall, sustained after the birth of Princess Louisa (1724–51) in 1724. After two weeks of

3.26

Attributed to Benjamin Goodison, a gilded gesso side table, c.1730. Owing to the imprecise descriptions of furniture recorded in the accounts, it is not possible to be certain whether this table was that supplied for St James's. However, similar tables were made for leading British patrons in the 1730s, and a table of this general design was likely to have been placed in the State Apartments (RCIN 35268)

3.27
Attributed to the school of Samuel Scott (1701/2–72), *St James's Palace*, c.1740. This view shows the various buildings attached to the principal façade of the palace by courtiers and office holders in the early eighteenth century
(RCIN 402435)

excruciating pain, she died at St James's at 11pm on 20 November 1737.[127] The court was plunged into mourning. The *Gentleman's Magazine* remembered her as 'ever dear to every Friend of our Religion and Liberties. For the World has not at any time produc'd an example of greater distinction in the several relations of life whether we consider Her Majesty as a Queen, a wife, a mistress or Friend'.[128] New mourning furniture was ordered specifically, much of which was painted or lacquered ('japan'd') purple or black: Benjamin Goodison provided appropriate furnishings, on the King's side, for the state bedchamber, presence, privy and great chambers, the great and little withdrawing rooms, and, on the late Queen's side, for the privy and presence chambers and bedchamber.[129]

If the years of George II's reign up to 1740 were characterised by alterations, new accommodation and refurnishing, the last 20 years were defined by comparative inactivity. After the Queen's death, little additional work was undertaken in the palace; besides regular replacement and general maintenance, expenditure was limited. Outside, on Crown land adjoining the palace, a number of houses sublet to a Mr Locke, including an alehouse with a particularly offensive 'necessary house', were to be pulled down.[130] The exterior walls of St James's (Fig. 3.27), over years, had become accreted with limpet-like small buildings, including alehouses and suttling houses (premises supplying provisions). Some years later, other such buildings, including the premises of Halsey, barber to the household (who petitioned against their demolition and instead received £41 'in consideration'), were also taken down.[131] In 1748, tenants of 'Old Houses lately taken down near St James's', perhaps inadvertently, had removed property belonging to the Crown, and on 15 November, 'Mr Seddon, Mr Smith and the person who kept the China Shop' were summoned to

3.28

George Vertue, *A Plan and Elevation of the Royal Fireworks in St James's Park*, 1749 (RCIN 750427)

explain themselves and to return any stolen property.[132]

By 1742, problems with water were again being discussed: 'there being an extream want of Water at His Majesty's Palace of St James's'.[133] The supply of water to the palace was to be a recurring theme throughout the century – perhaps exacerbated by the increased numbers living there after 1714. The pipes which supplied water to the palace were maintained by the Chelsea Water Company from a conduit in Hyde Park. By late 1738, the Office of Works had taken action: 'The reason of making an Arch in Hyde Park & St James's Park was occasioned by the water having at several times been cutt off from Coming to his Majestys Palace at St James's.'[134] In the same year, the Duke of Cumberland requested the relocation of 'an Elaboratory' (a laboratory for conducting scientific experiments) in St James's, which the Office of Works was reluctant to build for him for reasons of safety.[135] In the 1740s, the Duke's apartments on the south side of the Stable Yard were furnished, including a model ship-case and stand in mahogany, supplied by Benjamin Goodison.[136]

The tenor of activity at St James's remained subdued and the monthly amounts spent on the palace were comparatively small. In February 1749, the Duke of Cumberland requested that Mr Ford, clerk of the stables to the Duke, be allocated to rooms in the Stable Yard at St James's.[137] A set of *Horsemanship* tapestries (after Jacob Jordaens) was bought by Frederick, Prince of Wales, who thought he was buying back a set that had belonged to Charles I (who indeed did own a set, which was sold in the Commonwealth Sale of 1650). Seven panels can be seen in Charles Wild's watercolour views of the Queen's levee room and the old bedchamber, made in 1815–16 (see Figs 3.51 and 3.52), though it is not known if the panels were installed in those rooms by Frederick before his death in 1751, or moved there later.[138]

A more exciting occasion perhaps was on 27 April 1749, when fireworks celebrating the Peace of Aix-la-Chapelle of 1748 were set off in St James's Park (today's Green Park; Fig. 3.28),

3. THE GEORGIAN COURT

preceded by an orchestral suite composed by Handel, *The Music for the Royal Fireworks*.[139] The fireworks display was organised by the Board of Ordnance, and the Office of Works laid on the safety equipment, including making ready the fire engines.[140] The King and members of his family and senior courtiers watched the display from the late Queen's library, on the west side of the palace precincts, overlooking the park. Eyewitness accounts of the fireworks display varied considerably: The *Gentleman's Magazine* elaborated in great detail the order of release and type of firework.[141] Lady Jemima Grey wrote to Lady Mary Gregory the day after the display: 'For about an Hour they succeeded literally speaking A Merveille; for the Number, the Sizes & various Forms of the Rockets were quite surprising, one Explosion particularly which they say was of Six Thousand was beyond all Imagination.'[142] Horace Walpole (1717–97) was less impressed:

> The rockets and whatever was thrown up in the air succeeded mighty well, but the wheels and all that was to compose the principal part, were pitiful and ill-conducted, with no changes of coloured fires and shapes: the illumination was mean, and lighted so slowly that scarce anybody had patience to wait the finishing; and then what contributed to the awkwardness of the whole, was the right pavilion catching fire, and being burned down in the middle of the show.[143]

The press, on the whole, were also unimpressed by the event and the foreign peace it celebrated. One newspaper referred to the event as 'The Funeral-Pile of our departed Glory'.[144]

Walpole's report of the pictures and interiors of St James's at the end of George II's reign gives a vivid impression of the essentially unchanging nature of life there across the two decades since Queen Caroline's death. Walpole describes the pictures hanging in the most important rooms, including the King's Closet, where hung portraits of Henry VII, Mary, Princess of Orange, Henrietta, Duchess of Orléans, the Duke of Cambridge (son of James II and Anne Hyde) and Queen Caroline. The choice of Tudor and Stuart forebears is perhaps significant. One or two pictures hanging in other rooms are also noted. Queen Caroline's dressing room was hung with paintings by William Kent, depicting the history of Henry V. The bedchamber was hung with a portrait of the Princess Palatine, Elisabeth Charlotte, 'Liselotte' (1652–1722), with whom Queen Caroline corresponded. Both rooms were situated along the south side of the great court. The King's private rooms were now on the ground floor, looking south on to St James's Park, close to the apartment of his mistress, Amalie von Wallmoden. His simple taste was mocked by Walpole, who described George II's dining room and bedroom as 'wretched', although the bed was of green damask, accompanied by a bureau, two or three chairs and a green couch (perhaps upholstered in matching green damask). The room was not 'hung', suggesting no pictures. His description of the King's state apartments above concludes by noting that George II lay in a bed of crimson damask next to the King's Closet, in which room there hung a portrait of Charles II above the chimney. Next door, or enclosed within the series of rooms adjoining the King's bedchamber, was a room used during the reign of Queen Anne by the Duchess of Marlborough, and over the chimney therein hung an 'indecent picture of a Woman & Satyr'.[145]

During the final decade of George II's reign, extremely limited amounts of work took place at the palace. Only extraneous factors seem to have disturbed the cyclical nature of repair work. The building of nearby Spencer House occasioned a request to remove a wall in front of the house's façade, looking westward into Green Park, and to carry a sewer through the King's store yard nearby. Both were agreed to.[146]

George III and Queen Charlotte, 1760 to the 1790s

With the accession of George III, at last Britain could boast a monarch born on British soil – the first since Queen Anne. The King moved into his apartments in the palace in the autumn of 1760, and it seems that no preparatory building works or alterations were deemed necessary. George III had ascended the throne at a low ebb of public popularity for the royal family, and it was a result of the longevity of his reign, the regularity and frugality of his living circumstances, his many public appearances at Kew, Frogmore and Windsor, and the certitude of his patriotism, that at his death, some 59 years after his accession, he was mourned as a popular monarch. The court he presided over was still steeped in politics and factions, but owing to constitutional convention, the King, arguably perhaps, was able only to influence policy, not create it. Besides politics, St James's was once again a centre of fashionable society: the levees, Drawing Rooms, balls and receptions given by the King and Queen, and later, by their grown-up children allocated apartments within the palace walls, were a focus of social activity for the nobility of Britain and London 'society'. George III's act of balancing the monarch's requirements in public ceremonial life with private simplicity are contrasted with the respective uses of St James's Palace and Buckingham House: the stuffiness and pomp of the Drawing Room, levee or State Opening of Parliament is thrown into relief beside the abundance of royal offspring and the king's own paternalistic concern for his children's upbringing – the latter, in Hanoverian dynastic tradition, not always successful.[147] It is during the reign of George III that the character and use of St James's Palace alters slightly from the part it had been given to play since the fire at Whitehall in 1698. With the acquisition of Buckingham House in 1762, following his marriage the year before (it was soon after known as the Queen's House), the palace's role, at a stroke, became principally ceremonial, with royal accommodation concentrated, at least until the final years of the century, at the Queen's House. Indeed, it was thanks to his 'early associations' with the site of Buckingham House that George IV, in the 1820s, insisted on building his palace there, and not on a new site in Green Park, as favoured by his architect, John Nash.

On 8 September 1761, the King was married to Princess Charlotte of Mecklenburg-Strelitz in the Chapel Royal at St James's Palace (Fig. 3.29),

and two weeks later, on 22 September, with his Queen Consort, he was crowned at Westminster Abbey – perhaps the first truly public royal wedding.[148] Princess Charlotte arrived at St James's Palace on the day of her marriage; Horace Walpole wrote to Anne, Duchess of Grafton that 'when she first saw the Palace she turned pale'.[149] The marriage took place between 9pm and midnight. The service was conducted by the Archbishop of Canterbury and the Bishop of Winchester, Clerk of the Closet, and the chapel was hung with crimson velvet, laced and fringed with gold, and at each side, tapestries after the Raphael cartoons were hung as pictures, bordered with broad gold braid (known at the time as 'lace'). The King was dressed in a splendid new suit, embroidered with flowers in silver thread, and wore the Garter collar. Queen Charlotte wore a dress of silver tissue, with a purple cap on her head; she was covered with diamonds, wearing a diamond aigrette in the form of a crown, diamond earrings and diamond necklace, diamond sprigs of flowers on her sleeves, and her extraordinary diamond stomacher. At the moment the King placed the wedding ring on the Queen's finger, a rocket was let fly from the top of the Chapel Royal (in an echo of

3.29
Sir Joshua Reynolds (1723–92), *The Marriage of George III*, 1761. This oil sketch shows the interior of the Chapel Royal at St James's Palace, with (on the left) Thomas Secker, Archbishop of Canterbury, blessing the royal couple at the altar. Thomas Hayter, Bishop of London and Dean of the Chapel Royal, stands on the right. Behind the bride are ladies and bridesmaids, and behind the King, members of the royal family. A herald is in the left foreground. Galleries may have been constructed in front of the north (liturgical east) window (RCIN 404353)

3.30
George Bickham (c.1704–71), publisher, *The Three Cherokees who came over from the head of the River Savannah to London, 1762, and their interpreter that was poisoned*, c.1762
(BM, 1982,U.3745)

Charles II's baptism 131 years earlier), as a signal to fire the guns which were in Green Park and at the Tower of London.[150] After the ceremony, the King and Queen and guests enjoyed supper in the palace, which lasted until 3am. However, this sort of elaborate celebration was very much the exception, and the King and Queen rarely entertained or dined out – when they could, they went to bed by 11pm, and the King rose around 5am.[151]

After the great ceremonies of the wedding and coronation were over and Their Majesties were accommodated at St James's, familiar complaints about the palace's shortcomings resurfaced; and once again, expectations of a new palace on the site of St James's were rehearsed. Walpole wrote in July 1761: 'The great apartment at St James's is enlarging, and to be furnished with the pictures from Kensington: this does not portend a new palace.'[152] In spite of the purchase of a new royal home close to St James's, it was evident that the Tudor palace would remain the centre of court assembly and activity. Walpole's comment does not refer to any actual building work, rather that the number of rooms in the apartment may have increased in number. Indeed levees, Drawing Rooms and balls were just as cramped and crowded as they had been during previous reigns. The Hanoverian count, Frederick von Kielmansegge, during his visit to England in 1761–2, noted:

The Court at noon was remarkably crowded, and the crush, as usual on such occasions, very great. In the evening we went to look on at the ball from the benches prepared for the foreign ambassadors, placed below and on the right hand of the King. The room is poor, and looks more like the refectory of an old convent than the principal room of the palace of the King of England; but it is in entire keeping with the rest of the building … You cannot easily imagine a worse building than this, especially when seen from the outside.[153]

Throughout almost the whole reign, court events followed a regular weekly pattern when the court was in London through winter and spring. Levees (gatherings of courtiers who, by virtue of their court position, were entitled to attend the King's morning 'rising' or 'levee'), for men only, took place on Wednesday and Friday mornings; up to 1788 (the first year of the King's illness), a levee took place on a Monday when Parliament was sitting. Drawing Rooms took place on Thursdays and Sundays and were attended by both sexes, and by the King and Queen, and were convened in the King's drawing room.[154]

Although much of the King and Queen's domestic and family life transferred to the Queen's House after 1762, the seat of the court remained St James's Palace, and as the senior metropolitan palace, it played host to numerous visitors, some of whom wrote down their impressions.

On 8 August 1762, Native American Cherokees were granted an audience with the King at the palace (Fig. 3.30), and Elizabeth Percy, Duchess of Northumberland (1716–76), Lady of the Bedchamber to Queen Charlotte, recorded in her diary:

The Chief had the Tail of a Comet revers'd painted in Blue on his forehead, his Left Cheek black & his Left Eyelid Scarlet his Rt Eyelid Black & his Right Cheek Scarlet, all his [?teeth] were cut thro like Rings. He had a Blue Cloth Mantle laced with Gold & a silver Gorget. The second had nothing particular except his Eyelids which were painted Scarlet, the 3d had painted in Blue on his Cheeks a large pair of wings which had a very odd Effect as they look'd directly as if his Nose & Eyes were flying away. The two last were in Scarlet and Silver with Silver Gorgets. They had a private Audience of the King.[155]

On 21 April 1763, Their Excellencies Monsignori Querini and Morosini, ambassadors of the Republic of Venice, were presented to the King at St James's. *The London Gazette* recounted their reception: the ambassadors were brought from Somerset House to St James's by Henry Yelverton, 3rd Earl of Sussex, and Sir Charles Cottrell-Dormer, master of ceremonies; 'the Foot Guards upon duty were drawn up in the court, and their Officers saluted their Excellencies with Pike, Drum, and Colours, pulling off their hats as they passed by'. After resting a while in the Little Council Chamber, they were brought by senior courtiers to the Guard Chamber, and then greeted at the door of the Great Council Chamber by the Duke of Marlborough (1739–1817), the Master of the Household. Signor Morosini 'then made an Harangue to his Majesty in Italian, which His Majesty having answered in English, their Excellencies again retired to the Little Council Chamber'.[156]

Mirza Sheikh Itesamuddin, an envoy of the Mughal emperor Shah Alam II, visited England in 1765; he did not record his impressions of the court, but remarked that St James's was

> neither magnificent nor beautiful. The outer walls are not even plastered. It could easily be passed off as the multi-storeyed mansion of a merchant of Benares … but the Queen's palace is very handsome. I was told, however, that the interior of the King's palace is very elegant, and that the suites of rooms and the chambers of the harem are painted an attractive verdigris.[157]

In the summer of 1768, plans were put in place to receive the King of Denmark, husband of Princess Caroline Matilda (1751–75), the King's fourth sister. Her marriage by proxy had taken place on 1 October 1766 in the Drawing Room.[158] The Queen remained in Denmark, while her husband, Christian VII (1749–1808), completed an eight-month tour of England and France (Fig. 3.31). The King was to be accommodated in an apartment to the west of the Great Gatehouse, overlooking Cleveland Row. The apartment had been created for the Prince and Princess of Wales after their marriage in 1736, but had hardly been used since their flight from St James's to Leicester House the following year. Subsequently, it accommodated Duke Charles II of Brunswick-Wolfenbüttel (1735–1806), who had married Princess Augusta, eldest sister of George III, in 1764. Although he was certainly well looked after, the King of Denmark's visit was not an unqualified success. On the same day that the Office of Works put in hand preparations to receive His Danish Majesty, Lady Mary Coke noted in her journal that 'forty of his attendance are to be lodged there, & his apartment is to be well furnished'.[159] In common with other foreign visitors, he found the palace underwhelming and initially refused to stay in the apartments that had been put at his disposal. However, his indignation may have been more the result of his crazed condition, possibly schizophrenia, which contributed to the estrangement and eventual banishment from Denmark of his wife. Walpole was interested to see this king who had married a British princess, and wrote to George Montagu (1730–80): 'I came to town to see the Danish king. He is as diminutive as if he came out of a kernel in the fairy tales'.[160] He later recorded in his *Memoirs* that George III was very much against welcoming the Danish King, in spite of being his first cousin and brother-in-law, and denied him the usual royal welcome:

> Not a single nobleman – not a single equipage was sent on the road to receive, escort, or convey the Danish King … The only attention paid to him was, that an apartment was new furnished, gilt plate brought from the Tower, and an expensive table kept for him and his suite. Neither the King nor Queen were at St James's to receive him; and the King even arrived there to his levee an hour later than usual.[161]

The second half of the eighteenth century saw Britain's dominions grow in the east, in India, while contracting in the west, with the loss of

3.31
John Westwood Senior (1744–92), medal commemorating the visit of Christian VII of Denmark to England, 1768 (RCIN 443258)

3.32
George Noble (*fl.* 1795–1828), *View of the Court at St James's with the Ceremony of introducing a Lady to her Majesty*, 1778–80. This view of a Drawing Room is set at St James's but the room is not accurately portrayed (Museum of London, 2002.139/609)

America. The King was reluctant to capitulate to the American Revolutionaries and was saddened by the loss of the American colonies at the Treaty of Paris, which recognised the United States of America as an independent nation. One of the most vivid descriptions of the Court of St James's (Fig. 3.32) at this date was recorded by the first minister plenipotentiary of the United States of America, John Adams, later second President of the United States (Fig. 3.33). Adams had an audience of George III on 1 June 1785 at St James's Palace, and the following day, in a letter to John Jay, US Secretary of Foreign Affairs, he described the day's events:

> When We arrived in the Antichamber, the *Œil de Beuf* [*sic*] of St James's, the Master of the Ceremonies met me and Attended me, while the Secretary of State went to take the Commands of the King. While I Stood in this Place, where it Seems all Ministers Stand upon Such occasions, always attended by the Master of Ceremonies, the Room very full of Ministers of State, Bishops and all other Sorts of Courtiers, as well as the next Room which is the Kings Bedchamber, you may well Suppose that I was the Focus of all Eyes. I was relieved however from the Embarrassment of it, by the Swedish and Dutch Ministers, who came to me and entertain'd me, in a very agreable [*sic*] Conversation during the whole time. Some other Gentlemen whom I had Seen before came to make their Compliments too untill the Marquis of Carmarthen returned, and desired me, to go with him to his Majesty. I went with his Lordship, through the Levee Room into the Kings Closet, the Door was Shut, and I was left with his Majesty and the Secretary of State alone. I made the three Reverences, one at the Door, another about half Way and the third before the Presence, according to the Usage established at this and all the northern Courts of Europe, and then address'd myself to his Majesty.[162]

The King was evidently much moved by Adams's address, in spite of the rather formulaic procedure of presenting a letter of credence. The audience was a tense occasion: the King's well-known attachment to America, his reluctance to give up Britain's dominions there and the ensuing struggle for independence will have contributed to the atmosphere and significance of their meeting. According to Adams (who confessed he may not have recorded his words precisely), the King replied:

I will be very frank with you. I was the last to consent to the Seperation: but the Seperation [*sic*] having been made, and having become inevitable, I have always Said as I say now, that I would be the first to meet the Friendship of the United States as an independent Power. The moment I See Such Sentiments and Language as yours prevail, and a disposition to give to this Country the Preference, that moment I Shall Say let the Circumstances of Language, Religion and blood, have their natural and full Effect.[163]

A week later, he returned to St James's to be presented to Queen Charlotte. Again, Adams wrote to John Jay the following day, recounting in some detail his visit to court:

The Queen, then asked me, if I had provided myself with a House? I answered, I have agreed for one, Madam this Morning. She then made her Curtesy and I made my Reverence and retired, into the Drawing Room where the King, Queen, Princess Royal and the younger Princess her Sister, all spoke to me, very obligingly. I attended untill the Drawing Room was over, and then returned home.[164]

Few architectural changes of significance were undertaken at the palace during the first 30 years of George III's reign. The first piece of building work of any note was completed in 1768, with the introduction of a laundry for the Queen (Fig. 3.34). This was to be located in the north-eastern corner of the palace, in coach houses which belonged to the Duke of Marlborough.[165] In May of the same year, works were ordered to enlarge the apartment allocated to Lady Charlotte Finch (1725–1813), following the birth of George, Prince of Wales, on 12 August 1762. Lady Charlotte was appointed governess to the Prince, and subsequently also to his siblings, the younger Princes and Princesses.[166] Her apartment, which she occupied until her death, was located directly to the east of the Great Gatehouse, next to the Queen's new laundry, and the bow window visible on Cleveland Row was introduced at that time.[167] Her apartment was provided with furniture, some of it made by John Bradburn (1750–81), including a clothes press and a mahogany bookcase, which together cost £24.[168]

At the beginning of the reign the State Apartments were refreshed with new furniture and new silk damask. Katherine Naish (*fl.* 1759–72), joiner to the Wardrobe, supplied a new mahogany four-post bedstead, with a tester and carved cornices and a headboard. These carved

3.33
Engraving of John Adams, American Minister in London, 1785–8, and second President of the United States. Adams visited St James's Palace in 1785 (RCIN 618911)

3.34
Plan of the ground floor of the north-eastern corner of St James's Palace, after 1768. This is one of the earliest eighteenth-century plans specifying the use of rooms, including the Queen's laundry and rooms allocated to Lady Charlotte Finch and others (TNA, WORK 34/133; north is at the bottom)

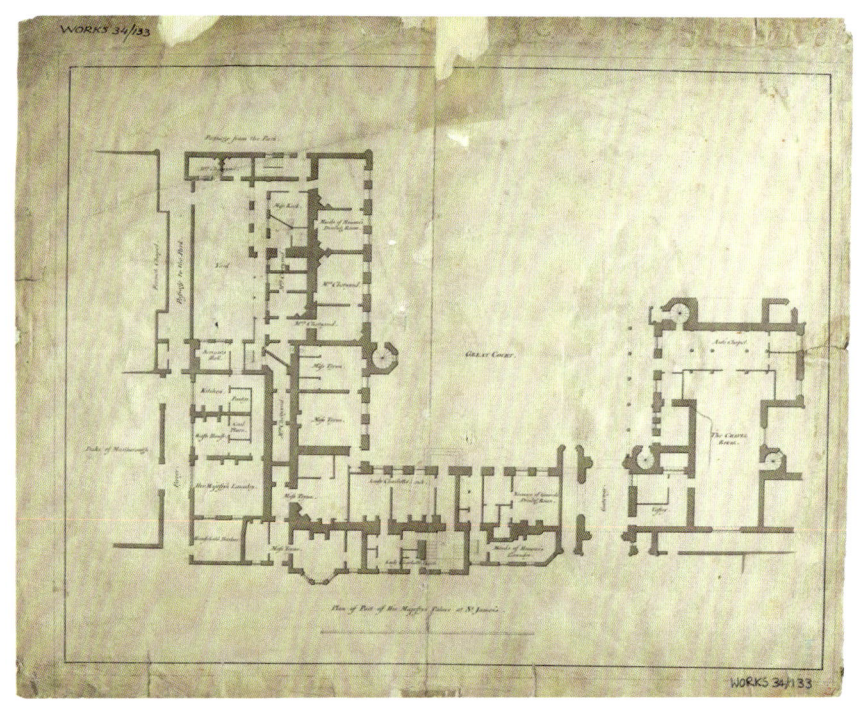

3. THE GEORGIAN COURT   151

3.35
William Vile, secretaire cabinet, c.1762–7. Supplied for the Queen in 1761, it was probably cleaned by John Bradburn in 1767 (RCIN 2571)

3.36
Queen Charlotte's jewel cabinet, made by William Vile and John Cobb at a cost of £138 10s. It was made to hold the Queen's spectacular jewellery (RCIN 35487)

wooden elements cost £75, and the upholstery was provided by Robert Carr, mercer, who supplied 412½ yards (377.2 m) of crimson silk damask for the new bed, as well as two 'draw up' curtains, fabric to cover two armchairs, four 'back stools' (i.e. chairs without arms) and two square stools, and for hangings of the room. The total cost of the damask amounted to £367 16s 3d.[169] In the King's dressing room, the cabinet-maker William Vile (c.1700–67) supplied a plain, but well-made mahogany clothes-press.[170] New textiles for the King's State Apartments were made up by William France (d. 1773), including a crimson flowered canopy, using crimson lace, velvet and satin supplied by the King. France also reupholstered a state chair, two high stools and the frame of a footstool. The new reign stimulated some removals too: in 1765, for example, William France charged to remove and clean the old crimson velvet canopy of state, and move it to the King's presence chamber, in order to make room for the new canopy to be installed in the King's privy chamber.[171] These were the rooms which were put to heavy use by the King and Queen, and later, by their family, for entertaining and for official court functions, including balls, levees, audiences and dinners.

After the King and Queen were married in September 1761, new furnishings for the Queen's State Apartment at St James's were required. Katherine Naish made a mahogany bed for the Queen, which was accompanied, according to traditional court custom, by two armchairs, six side chairs and two stools; the Queen's seat-furniture was carved and gilt.[172] Naish also provided 'a large state canopy frame', a chair and footstool and two high stools, all to match. Benjamin Goodison provided mostly lighting and mirrors, in particular rounded glass to be fitted to large wall lanterns.[173] William Vile is recorded as supplying 'a large mahogany clothes press' (£13), and a '2 flap'd table with gadroon edge for the Queen to breakfast off – £3 15s'.[174] One of the most elegant of pieces supplied to the Queen was undoubtedly the 'exceeding fine mohogany secretary with drawers & a writing drawer, a set of shelves at top with a crown carv'd at top & the Side & back all handsome cutt work – £71' (Fig. 3.35).[175]

Most magnificent of all was the jewel cabinet (Fig. 3.36) made to hold the Queen's remarkable jewellery. Its destination was not specified, yet it was the most expensive piece of furniture supplied to the Queen by the cabinet-makers Vile and Cobb, who were in partnership from around 1751 until 1763. It was perhaps considered appropriate for the Queen's dressing room. It was described in Vile's bill as

> a very handsome jewel cabinet made of many different kinds of fine Woods on a mohogany frame very richly carv'd all the Front Ends and top inlaid with Ivory in Compartments and neatly Engraved the top to lift up & 2 doors in front and 2 drawers under the doors all lined with fine black velvet with fine locks & the Brass work gilt – £138 10s.[176]

The Queen's jewellery was legendary: Horace Walpole noted its splendour at the marriage of George III and Princess Charlotte on 8 September 1761: 'Her tiara of diamonds was very pretty, her stomacher sumptuous'.[177] Both William Vile and John Cobb (c.1715–78) were cabinet-makers by trade: Vile was the elder partner and Cobb the ambitious younger half. Their business, as for many of the leading London cabinet-makers in the second half of the eighteenth century, was as an upholder, meaning that they furnished houses entirely, supplying not only furniture, but also upholstery and metalwork, although for the royal family, Vile and Cobb supplied carved mahogany and case furniture for St James's and the Queen's House between 1761 and 1763, at the same time as Benjamin Goodison and Katherine Naish.

A sky-blue colour scheme predominated in some of the Queen's apartments. This was a departure from the standard palette of silk damask colours used to furnish royal apartments, which were normally restricted to crimson, green or yellow. Thomas Hinchliff, mercer, supplied 110 yards (100.6 m) of 'sky blue rich lustring' to line a damask bed (£47 13s 4d), with 26 yards (23.8 m) of the same provided for curtains, and the same amount again for 16 side chairs, eight armchairs, two sofas and a curtain for an organ. A further 182 yards (166.4 m) was used for festoon curtains.[178] The following year, Hinchliff supplied 25 yards (22.9 m) of rich blue damask for a couch in the Queen's private apartments (£19 15s 10d), while crimson lustring was used for the curtains in the State Apartments.[179] Textiles were also supplied: for the Queen's bedchamber at St James's, for example, Vile and Cobb upholstered a bed and headboard in blue silk damask, although it is not clear if this was for the state or private apartments. Vile and Cobb were also employed to furnish the private apartments.[180]

Based on the evidence available, the Queen's rooms were furnished more richly than the King's. For the Queen, Vile supplied 'a grannate table with brass mouldings … £57', for the 'Musick Room'. In the 'Passage Room', which evidently was fitted up as the Queen's library, Vile made a bookcase for £100, a writing table for £22, and a carved and gilded oval mirror, surmounted by a crown, to go above the chimney, fitted with a candle branch at each side, for £58 10s. Greater expense was lavished on the 'Wardrobe' room: here, two large mahogany wardrobes, with sliding shelves

3.37

Cabinet made for Queen Charlotte's apartments at St James's Palace. Veneered in exotic padouk and rosewood, and inlaid with brass, it follows designs published in Thomas Chippendale's (1718–89) *Gentleman and Cabinet-Maker's Director* (1762). The overall design of the cabinet combined with the lavish use of brass inlay and gilded brass mounts may accurately reflect Queen Charlotte's personal taste in furniture, which was certainly richer than the King's. The cabinet may be associated with one supplied by William Vile in 1761 (RCIN 39228)

behind doors in the lower part, and the doors in the upper part with octagonal glazing, lined with green 'curtains', were charged together at the not insignificant amount of £135.[181] Two mahogany cabinets with brass handles, charged at £25 each, were also supplied, one for an unspecified location in the Queen's apartments, the other for the Wardrobe.[182]

Expensive textiles were not allowed to go to waste: the state canopy used at the wedding of the King and Queen was altered and remade by Katherine Naish, at a cost of £12, and installed in the Chapel Royal.[183] New furniture was supplied by Naish for the Queen's private apartments at St James's: in the bedchamber, a mahogany night chair, and in the dressing room, a mahogany square stool and 'a large mahogany couch … with a single head to fold down over the seat … £10 10s'. In the music room, the height of seven music stands was reduced, adding new 'Wainscot tops', and each with two new brass candlesticks.

The contrasting approaches – and interests – of King and Queen (Fig. 3.37) can be seen in two entries in an account provided by William Vile. For the Queen's 'bow closet' at St James's, Vile made 'large additions of carv'd bracket for China to the chimney glass – £20 18s', while for the King's apartment there, Vile made '23 mohogany shelves to the grand medal case full of holes lin'd with green cloth – £8 1s' (Fig. 3.38).[184]

Throughout the reign of George III, the Lord Chamberlain's accounts contain infrequent references to new furniture for the King's apartment; and when new furniture was ordered for the King, it was usually of a type conforming to his sphere of interest – for example, a mahogany library table (no doubt with the King's bibliographic interests in mind), with black leather top and 13 locks fitted to the King's key, cost £25 10s to make. This table was to be placed not in the library, as one might imagine, but in the King's new dressing room, formerly George II's state bedchamber.[185]

In 1784, the Office of Works received orders to put in hand refurbishments in the Queen's apartment at St James's: no explanation was given, but after more than 20 years' use, the rooms may have begun to look tired. The accounts record that just over £400 was spent on her private apartment. The Lord Chamberlain's office arranged the ordering and delivery of furnishings, and the upholders Samuel Beckwith (1774–1808) and William France were called upon to provide new furniture and some new textiles for the apartments.[186] The 'Bow Window Closet' was given new crimson tammy (wool, or wool and cotton fabric) to line three window curtains; the 'New Dressing Room' also received new crimson tammy curtains and was rehung with 164 yards (150 m) of elephant paper, 'hung compleat' (£1 14s 2d). There was to be a large sofa with 'Feet gilt in burnish'd gold' (£23 5s), four large chairs (£18 18s 4d), two large bergeres 'to match those in the late Bed Chamber' (£10 5s 2d), and two large 'scroll head' stools, 3 ft 11 in. (1.2 m) long, for the window, 'the Frames neatly carved & gilt with burnish'd gold' (£9 10s). The dining room was rehung with 'office crimson silk damask', and a large mahogany sofa was retained, but re-stuffed, re-upholstered and re-covered with the same 'office Damask' (£4 16s) as a pair of armchairs and a pair of window stools. One of the more expensive new items were two carved and gilded candelabra with ormolu branches; some regilding was also carried out, including for the frame of a portrait of Prince Frederick. More work of a similar nature was undertaken in the organ room.[187] Work carried on into the early part of 1785, when Beckwith & France supplied furnishings for the Presence Chamber, drawing room, new drawing room and dining room (again). The most spectacular objects were three gilded fire screens with flower-printed satin.[188] In the same year, the pictures at St James's were inventoried, and in the Presence Chamber, the portraits of Edward III and the Black Prince, which had hung there since at least the reign of Queen Anne, were exchanged for those of two French kings: a full-length portrait of Henry IV, attributed to Jacob Bunel (1558–1614; RCIN 406167), and a portrait of Louis XIII, after Philippe de Champaigne (1602–74; RCIN 406127); both had been at Somerset House in 1710. The former can be seen in the early nineteenth-century watercolour of the Presence Chamber prepared by Charles Wild for the engravings included in Pyne's *History of the Royal Residences* (see Fig. 3.50). Could these changes in the picture hang reflect a general shift towards French taste, or was it that these French kings of the seventeenth century no longer represented a threat to Britain and thus were deemed acceptable to

3.38
William Vile and John Cobb, mahogany medal cabinet, 1760–61. This shows one part of George III's medal cabinet, made for the King's apartments at St James's Palace, altered *c*.1820, after George III's collection of medals was presented to the British Museum by George IV (V&A, no. W:11.1 to 135-1963). The companion cabinet is at the Metropolitan Museum of Art, New York (acc. no. 64.79)

3. THE GEORGIAN COURT   155

3.39
Sir Peter Lely, *Portrait of a Lady*, c.1658–60. This is possibly the portrait of the duchesse de Mazarin that hung in the Privy Chamber during the reign of George I (RCIN 405363)

be hung in the State Apartments? The room is depicted lined with tapestry, though in the absence of documentation, it is not possible to be certain whether the *Sciences* set which hung here in the early part of the eighteenth century was still hanging at the time the watercolour was made. In the Privy Chamber, portraits of James, Duke of York, by William Dobson (RCIN 406985), the duchesse de Mazarin by Peter Lely (possibly Fig. 3.39), and the Duke of Monmouth by Adriaen Hanneman (1603/4–71), now titled *William III when Prince of Orange* (RCIN 404919), replaced the pictures recorded there in George I's reign. However, the three paintings in the Great Drawing Room and the five Italian paintings in the Council Chamber were unchanged. In the State Bedchamber, where George I had introduced Kneller's full-length portrait of Charles VI, Holy Roman Emperor, George III had the room hung with portraits by Hanneman of Mary, Princess of Orange (RCIN 404436), and Henrietta, Duchess of Orléans (RCIN 406079; now attributed to John Michael Wright) – both sisters of Charles II – and a painting of *The Genius of Poetry* (called 'St Cecilia') by Benedetto Gennari (RCIN 406791).

These improvements notwithstanding, the appearance of the palace to foreign visitors remained as dreary and unimpressive as it had been at the beginning of the century. The duc de la Rochefoucauld, on the whole an approving commentator on English life, could only muster the following: 'The palaces of the King and Queen look over the park and are two houses of tasteless brick, without ornament or architectural distinction. They are said to be very commodious inside, but from the outside they certainly do not appear to be worthy of the habitation of a King and Queen'.[189] Indeed, one has some sympathy with his views: in the same year, 1784, Sir William Chambers wrote with some indignation to Sir Francis Drake, a naval officer and a collateral descendant of the famous Elizabethan seafarer of the same name, complaining of 'the great Quantity of Dirt and filth lying before the front of the [Palace]' on St James's Street: 'It does not seem proper, to leave so necessary a Work as keeping a Street before a Royal Palace clean, to chance'.[190]

New courtiers' apartments were also furnished by the upholder John Trotter, laceman Edward Parker, cabinet-maker Benjamin Goodison and joiner Katherine Naish.[191] John, 3rd Earl of Bute (1713–92), the King's former tutor and principal adviser, and at that time Secretary of State for the Northern Department (a precursor of the Foreign Office), was provided with furniture and furnishings for his rooms by William Vile and John Cobb. His three festoon-blind curtains were made of 'Crimson Lustring', charged at 23s per yard, totalling £3 9s. A 'Good Large Wilton carpet … 75 yards', at 8s per yard, was charged at £30. He was also provided with a library table (£14) and 'a handsome Pier Glass … £18'.[192]

While regular maintenance continued throughout the apartments across the palace, refurbishment usually occurred upon the death or departure of an incumbent. Other work, below stairs, in the early part of the 1760s, was concerned with the reorganisation of the various larders and offices, part of the Lord Steward's responsibilities. A 'Herb Office, with a Chamber and Garret over it', was to be established in the Stable Yard; and in the 'three Arches next my Lord Godolphin's passage be fitted up for a Butter and Egg Office …

and also that the Laundry late the Duke of Cumberland's be converted into a Larder for His Majesty's Service'.[193] The old spicery was proposed to become a new silver vault, and a debenture office and the various larders to be moved to new locations.[194] Office moves and the relocation of larders were not the only issues to handle: the water supply was once again deemed deficient, and various attempts were made over the coming years to improve it, including 'proposed alteration of the Companys Pipes'.[195] Though a great deal was spent on improving the palace, much of the work was piecemeal in nature and often unspecified in the Office of Works accounts, falling under general maintenance.[196]

The King and Queen's first child, George, Prince of Wales, was born on 12 August 1762, and much nursery furniture, including an airing horse, a state canopy frame (perhaps to be used at the christening) and state cradle with canopy top (£52) with embroidered canopy (£70) was ordered.[197] The Prince of Wales was shown to the public from behind a gilded screen and railing, lying in this cradle described as having three ostrich feathers.[198] The Queen's state bedchamber (presumably where she was to give birth) was to be in the former Great Drawing Room. Katherine Naish was asked to provide a new state bed, with 'a large crown in each pediment £205', for the 'Queen to sit up in the Gt Drawing Room there', while the upholders William Vile and John Cobb charged £75 10s for the 'sitting up bed in the Great Council Chamber with crimson velvet and three rows of gold lace'. They also supplied three thick and two thin mattresses (one of the thicker mattresses was filled with horsehair, the others with wool).[199]

William Gwillim, feather dresser, provided the feather mattress for the bed and '4 fine large White Ostrich Plumes ... £134.8', and the mercer Hinchliff supplied 127½ yards (116.6 m) of crimson velvet (£180 12s 6d).[200] Richest of all, however, was the 'Suit of Superfine Flanders Point Lace to Cover all over a Crimson Sattin Counterpane', costing the large sum of £269 9s, supplied by Priscilla MacEune, laceman.[201] William Vile also made nursery furniture of a simpler variety: for the 'Pap Room', he supplied two mahogany chests of drawers and a bookcase. For the 'Fifth Room', he made '2 thick Mohogany Rockers to the Wicker Cradle with 4 carv'd Roses to each Rocker ... £1 15s'.[202] Besides the spectacular jewel cabinet (see Fig. 3.36) Vile and Cobb also supplied a work box, an 'India wood musick desk', four mahogany stands for birdcages, a mahogany desk to go on a clavichord and two mahogany houses for a 'Turkey Monkey', as well as other smaller objects, including a sliding screen.[203] Katherine Naish supplied more chairs, beds, sofas and other furniture for St James's, including a small mahogany tub chair for the Prince of Wales.[204] The long-serving cabinet-maker Benjamin Goodison was also called upon to supply mirrors and lighting, including fitting six new glasses in the bottom of lanterns in the King and Queen's apartments, and two new tops to mirrors in the nursery.[205]

In 1769, the eastern tower of the Great Gatehouse was considered to be in danger of toppling and was taken down (and rebuilt). The following year, the western tower was given the same treatment. These were merely repairs; the towers remained unchanged.[206] Through the 1770s there was almost no building work of any significance: there was only minor refurbishment, replacement or additions and alterations to the many apartments across the palace.[207] Queen Charlotte's brother, Duke Ernest of Mecklenburg-Strelitz (1742–1814), who had come to England with his sister, was accommodated at St James's, and his apartments were given new furnishings in 1771.[208] Furniture was periodically refreshed with new textiles, either as they faded or wore out, or as fashion dictated. In 1771, for example, the mercer Robert Carr supplied 9½ yards (8.7 m) of crimson damask 'to new cover the Seats of 2 Settee Fourms ... 16 / 6 per yard £7 16s 9d'.[209] In 1775, the offices of the Board of Green Cloth were refurbished; in the same year, the Board of Green Cloth noted that 'His Majesty's Larder is very much out of repair ... and that a Room may be fitted up at one End of it for the Larder Man'.[210]

By the end of the decade, a general survey of the palace was undertaken, presumably

3.40
The Yeomen of the Guard's headquarters at St James's Palace today, in a corner of Ambassadors Court

with a view to resolving at once as many as possible of the numerous minor defects.²¹¹ By the early 1780s, judging by the quantity of references to cleaning and repairs, the palace was once more in a dismal state. The ceilings of the State Apartments required cleaning, 'there being many disagreeable patches of dirt on the Cielings [sic] of the Great Apartment at St James's'. Sir William Chambers, Surveyor General of the Office of Works, was careful to ensure that pictures and works of art were to be given adequate protection during redecoration.²¹² Later in 1783, the reshuffling of office accommodation around the palace meant that the Yeomen of the Guard, who had been accommodated next door to the Great Gatehouse, would give way to the pay office of the paymaster, and were moved to 'two rooms under the Arcade in the Board of Greencloth Court, at His Majesty's Palace of St James's, late occupied by M. Wilson, for the use of the Yeomen of the Guard, to dine and keep their Cloths' (Fig. 3.40).²¹³

Throughout the reign of George III, the Chapel Royal continued in use for major royal ceremonial, underlining the palace's status as the official seat of monarchy. Following George III and Queen Charlotte's marriage in 1761, their 15 children were baptised there in turn.²¹⁴

Since 13 February 1752, the Chapel Royal had been under the watchful eye of William Lovegrove, serjeant of the vestry and clerk of the cheque, responsible for many entries in the 'New Cheque Book' – a historic register of the Chapel Royal's activities, as well as his own personal manuscript, recording advantages and perquisites of his post (the Cheque Book was begun in the 1580s). It was Lovegrove who recorded in writing the various conventions of the Chapel Royal, such as how staff were permitted to supplement their income. On the first page of his manuscript he writes, 'Take my word for it you cannot be to Cautios [sic] and Circumspect, nor too Tenacious of your own Advantages, Privileges, Fees and Perquisits; the less others know of your Affairs the better.' He notes there that in 1761 he disposed of old furniture, gold lace, velvet and feathers, having obtained a warrant from the Lord Chamberlain to sell the furniture, for a personal profit of £157 14s 6d.²¹⁵ While the serjeant of the vestry could claim proceeds from the sale of old furniture when new was supplied, the yeoman of the vestry could claim the residue of wax candles, and the groom of the vestry, the residue of tallow candles.

Since the late seventeenth century, the Queen's Chapel had been used, first by the French Huguenots, and later, during the reign of William and Mary, by the Dutch congregation, and was known as the French, or the French and Dutch chapel (see p. 130). Such an arrangement had prevailed since the sixteenth century, when French and Dutch nonconformists were granted a chapel on the site of a former Augustinian priory within the walls of the City of London.²¹⁶ The Huguenot and Dutch community in London had grown considerably in the previous century, following the Revocation of the Edict of Nantes in 1685, which made France an exclusively Catholic country. England had much to gain from welcoming persecuted French skilled labourers, soldiers and, in particular, craftsmen – some of whom found places at court. The French Huguenot community was centred on the French chapel in Threadneedle Street and a chapel in the Savoy. However, through the eighteenth century, as the Huguenot community evolved and assimilated into London society, dependency on these two centres waned. In 1781, the French and Dutch congregation exchanged chapels with their German counterpart. This chapel swap was perhaps effected by the growth of the German community at court, as well as marking a decline in the dependency of French and Dutch members of the household on the larger venue of the Queen's Chapel as a place of worship.[217] The German congregation had met within the chapel below the Queen's guard chamber, in a room beyond the colonnade on the south side of the Great Court. The French and Dutch moved to this space. New pews were installed in the Queen's Chapel, which was henceforth known as the German chapel (until the early twentieth century, when it reverted to the Queen's Chapel); new matting was ordered in 1785.[218]

Later in the reign, one of the more notorious royal marriages took place when George, Prince of Wales, was married to Princess Caroline of Brunswick (1768–1821) on 8 April 1795 in the Chapel Royal (Fig. 3.41).[219] The whole ceremony had a farcical aspect: the Prince had steeled himself by drinking all day and was drunk throughout the ceremony. Lord Malmesbury, the diplomat who had brought Princess Caroline from Brunswick a few days earlier, recorded:

> the marriage ceremony took place late on the evening of Wednesday, the 8th April, at St James's Chapel Royal. The Ceremony was performed by the Archbishop of Canterbury (Moore). The usual etiquette observed – we had assembled in the Queen's apartment; from thence to the usual drawing-rooms (very dark). The procession, preceded by the heralds and great officers of the Court, amongst which I was ordered to attend – walked to the chapel, very crowded – Prince of Wales gave his hat, with a rich diamond button and loop, to Lord Harcourt to hold, and made him

3.41
William Hamilton (1751–1801),
The Marriage of George, Prince of Wales, and Princess Caroline of Brunswick, c.1795–7
(RCIN 404486)

> a present of it. After the marriage we returned to the Queen's apartment … The Prince very civil and gracious, but I thought I could perceive he was not quite sincere, and certainly unhappy; and as proof of it, he had manifestly had recourse to wine or spirits.[220]

Indeed, on account of his inebriation, the Prince had to be supported throughout the proceedings by the Dukes of Bedford and Roxburghe. Nathaniel Wraxall recorded that Dr Moore, Archbishop of Canterbury, 'when reading the matrimonial service at the Chapel Royal, gave unequivocal proofs of his apprehension lest some engagement of a moral or religious nature antecedently contracted by the Prince might form a bar to the union he was about to celebrate'. When he came to speak the words, 'any person knowing of a lawful impediment',

> he laid down the book and looked earnestly for a second or two at the King as well as at the royal bridegroom. The latter was much affected and shed tears. Not content with this tacit allusion to the report [that the Prince of Wales had some years earlier married Maria Fitzherbert in secret], the Archbishop twice repeated the passage in

3. THE GEORGIAN COURT

which the Prince engages to live from that time in nuptial fidelity with his consort'.[221]

Hours later, at Carlton House, where the couple spent their first night together, Queen Caroline later recounted that the Prince 'passed the greatest part of his bridal-night under the grate, where he fell, and where I left him'.[222]

Outside these exceptional family events, the chapel continued as a place of formal worship, where George III and Queen Charlotte took communion through the year, usually on the main festivals of the religious year, as well as on lesser feast days, such as the feast of St John the Evangelist, Easter Tuesday and Whitsun Tuesday.[223]

The Princes and their Apartments, 1790s–1809

In the 1790s, court life at St James's continued much as it had done at the beginning of the reign, 30 years earlier. Queen Charlotte recorded in her diary for January 1794 that the King attended levees at St James's on Wednesdays, and both King and Queen attended a Drawing Room on Thursdays. Queen Charlotte also records that other members of the royal family were included in Drawing Rooms at St James's, often held on a Sunday afternoon.[224] The following year, another major diplomatic delegation, that of the Turkish ambassador, His Excellency Yusuf Agah Efendi, was received at the palace on 29 January 1795. The ceremonial followed the presentation to George III and Queen Charlotte of the Venetian ambassadors 30 years previously. The audience took place in the Great Council Chamber; the ambassador wore 'the Tarban, called "chorafsan" (which is only worn by the minister of the Sublime Porte)'.[225]

The majority of works undertaken at St James's in the two decades around the turn of the eighteenth century were to make ready apartments for the younger sons of George III. Their eldest son, George, Prince of Wales, had been given Carlton House at his coming of age in 1783.[226] Three years earlier, from the start of the year 1780, apartments at St James's began to be fitted up for the younger sons, Prince William and Prince Edward.[227] Benjamin Parran supplied a 'Large Mahogany Library table of very fine Mottled Jamaica wood … to direction from a Design of Gen; Bude's … £30'. General Jacob de Budé was a Swiss émigré soldier, appointed a Gentleman of the Bedchamber to George III in 1770, and aide-de-camp in 1779.[228] An intimate friend of the King's, around 1773, he was appointed sub-governor to the young Princes.[229]

Prince Edward, later Duke of Kent (1767–1820), was dispatched, in 1785, to Lüneburg in the Electorate of Hanover, where he was a cadet in the Hanoverian foot guards; at the same time he was allocated an apartment at St James's.[230] Only a handful of pieces of furniture were made for his apartment (mainly by the joiner John Russell, *fl.* 1773–1822), suggesting it was only partially fitted out for his use, probably owing to his posting abroad. By 1787, the cabinet-maker William Gates (*fl.* 1774–*c.*1800), and others, had provided furniture for an unnamed apartment in the same location as that planned originally for Prince Edward, 'at the west end of the Palace at St James'.[231]

During the latter part of 1792, the architect John Soane was asked to provide designs for a new guard room (Fig. 3.42) in a more convenient location. Soane had been appointed Surveyor to the Bank of England in 1788, and in October 1790 he was appointed Clerk of Works for St James's, Whitehall and Westminster, marking his entry into the royal sphere.[232] Surviving drawings show that he made a survey of the existing guard room. This was a two-storey apartment located on the north side of the palace, overlooking Cleveland Row, to the west of the Great Gatehouse. The old suttling house stood very near against the north wall, and indeed it is possible that the survey depicts the suttling house itself. The apartment (today, York House) had been fitted out in the 1730s for Frederick, Prince of Wales. It is therefore probable that the Prince had his eye on it as accommodation for himself, requiring the foot guards to be relocated.[233]

Soane made two alternative designs, both of which were simple and picturesque, for a

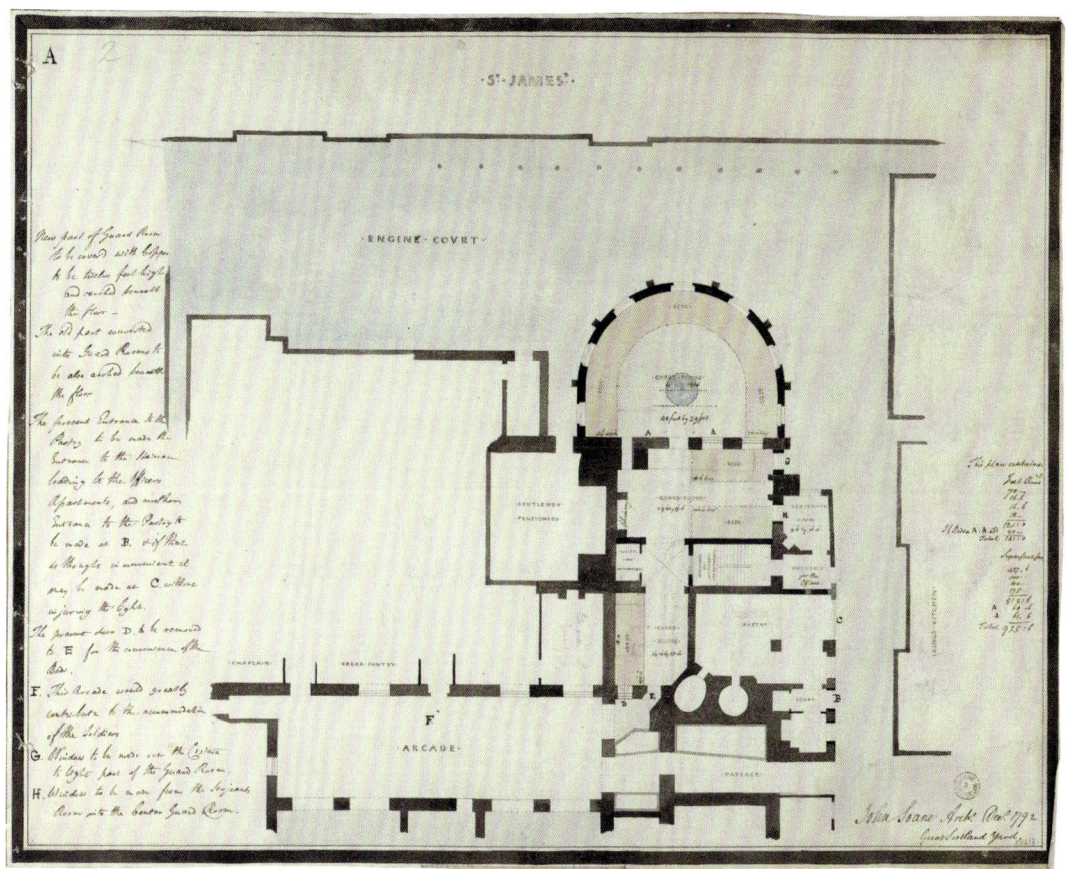

3.42
One of two designs prepared by Sir John Soane for a 'Sergeant and Guard Room at St James's'. This design, with its semicircular plan, signed and dated December 1792, was adopted for the new building (Sir John Soane's Museum, London, SM 37/2/3; north is at the bottom)

new guard room in Engine Court, projecting south from the pastry kitchen. One design is for a rectangular room, the other semicircular. The suggested copings were to be plain, or of imitation cannon balls, no doubt made from carved stone (or a composition such as Mrs Coade's stone). The drawings are dated between December 1792 and 4 October 1793. Indeed, Soane recorded in his diary for 23 January 1793, 'At the Office of Works about guard Room,' at which point he oversaw the creation of a new ground-floor plan of the palace (Fig. 3.43) – the first since Flitcroft's plan of the late 1720s (see Fig. 3.14).[234] The semicircular plan was selected, with plain copings. The dining room of the guard room on the first floor, for the use of the officers, was fitted out by Beckwith & France, with a new English 'Turkey' carpet, an oil-gilt mirror, a set of tables to join together, and a large mahogany sideboard, 7 ft (2.1 m) long, with a lead-lined cellaret at one end, partitioned for nine bottles, and a hot cupboard at the other end. There were also 18 mahogany dining chairs, one of which was an armchair, a pair of single brass wall lights, a double brass wall light, and a mahogany folding fire screen.[235]

Perhaps unsurprisingly, the juxtaposition of guard room with pastry kitchen caused the latter to be relocated. The King approved its move to a building on the west side of Engine Court, to the south of the King's kitchen.[236] Another alteration to the palace was the addition of a colonnade on the south side of the great court, to match the colonnade added almost a century earlier, which connected the Great Gatehouse to the Great Stairs. New windows were added above.[237]

A few years later, the younger sons of the monarch began to return to Britain from their naval and military duties. As the Princes returned, they were given their own accommodation in the capital (see Fig. 3.43). George, Prince of Wales, was already lodged (at great expense) at Carlton House, and before his brothers were given their own accommodation,

3. THE GEORGIAN COURT

they also often lodged there. Frederick, Duke of York, promoted to field marshal by his father in 1795, was put up in a house in Gloucester Place. The Duke of York was one of the commanders in the unsuccessful military campaign of the 1790s, fighting the French Republican troops in northern France and Flanders. Following the King's recovery from illness in 1788, Prince William, later William IV, was made Duke of Clarence and St Andrews and Earl of Munster, and with these honours his naval career was over: he had proved himself a competent naval officer, but unsuited to high command.[238]

From 1791, work began to make an apartment ready for his use: this was a series of rooms and buildings in St James's which, in the 1820s, mushroomed into Clarence House, and became a large and comfortable house within the palace's precincts.[239] Not unlike his eldest brother, George, Prince of Wales, Prince William habitually changed his mind about the work to be undertaken, incurring additional expense. Edward, Duke of Kent, was allocated an apartment at the palace, but was mostly absent abroad on military duty through the 1790s, principally in Canada, the United States and the Caribbean. He returned in November 1798 and was given an apartment at Kensington Palace. Augustus, Duke of Sussex (1773–1843), was also allocated an apartment at Kensington, to which he moved in 1805, the year after his return to Britain from Rome.[240]

APARTMENT FOR THE DUKES OF CLARENCE AND CUMBERLAND

From 1791, and for the next five years, the Duke of Clarence's spacious apartment,which was later to become Clarence House (see Fig. 2.31), located on the south side of the King's kitchen, next to Harrington House, was lavishly fitted out.[241] Once again, the upholders Beckwith & France and the joiner John Russell were employed. The dining room was hung with chintz pattern cotton and there were 18 mahogany chair frames (supplied by Russell for £27), which were covered in red morocco leather with two rows of burnished nails (£24), and a large shaped mahogany sideboard (with a plate warmer, cellaret for 12 bottles and water cistern lined with lead: £28); the dining table consisted of one square frame with two flaps and two round ends with a flap to each (£24), all supplied by Beckwith & France. The study was lined with 76 yards (69.5 m) of tulip-patterned glazed cotton chintz, and there were two oval giltwood pier glasses in carved frames (£24); carpet was charged by the yard, and 106 yards (96.9 m) of fine Brussels carpet and border was fitted to the floor of the dining room and the study; furnishings were supplied to the antechamber, print room and drawing room, and the breakfast room was hung with two pier glasses 'in exceeding rich carved frames with ornaments & the coronet at top of each gilt in burnish'd gold – £63'; in the same room, John Russell provided six bamboo armchairs.[242] Once the Duke was established in his apartment, the upholsterers and cabinet-makers were, at least for a short while, retained on a repairing brief, mending window pulleys, fixing blinds, repairing furniture and the like. The cabinet-makers Beckwith & France charged for varnishing and polishing satinwood card tables and a Pembroke table, and also for lining card-table folding tops with 'fine green cloth', while John Russell was asked to secure the joints of eight japanned chairs and touch up the decorated surface.[243]

In 1807, the Duke sought further enrichments, and an estimate for alterations to his apartments amounted to the not inconsiderable sum of £4,077.[244] His bed was hung with 'very rich grey silk cord French fringe colour'd silk', supplied by Winter & Hay (silk lacemen), with all sorts of elegant gimp, fringing and silk roses. Meanwhile, John Thomas Groves, clerk of the works at St James's, had fallen ill, and by April 1808, the Duke was clearly irritated that the works had not begun. He requested that the Office of Works find a suitable replacement for Groves: one who was 'properly qualified to undertake the superintendence thereof', and was also 'instructed to wait upon His Royal Highness on Thursday [14 April] at 11 o clock prepared with the plan and every explanation relative thereto that may be required'. Groves,

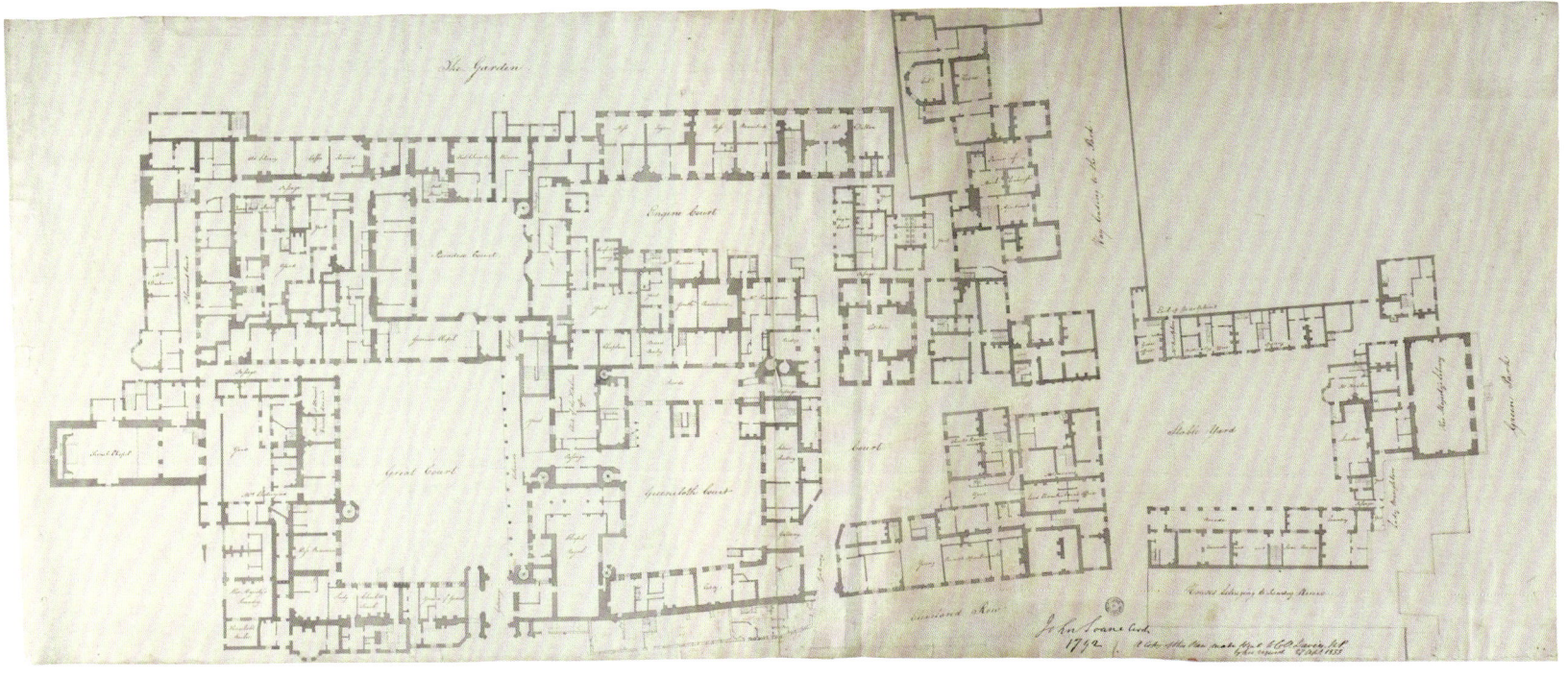

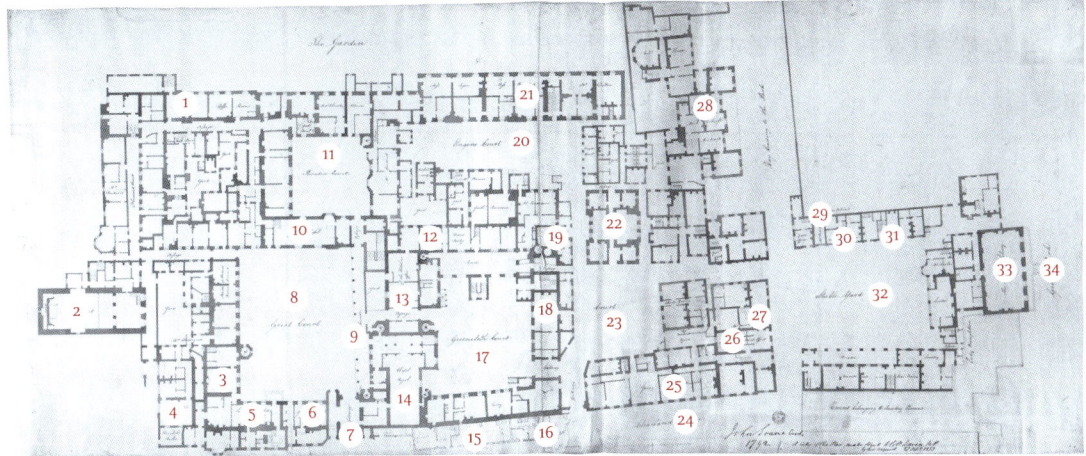

3.43

Detail of Sir John Soane's ground-floor plan of St James's Palace, 1792. Bar scale of 5/11 in. to 10 ft (Sir John Soane's Museum, London, SM 62/2/6; north is at the bottom)

1. Old library
2. French Chapel (later Queen's Chapel)
3. Miss Boscawen
4. Laundry for the Queen
5. Lady Charlotte Finch
6. Yeomen of Guard
7. Great Gatehouse
8. Great Court
9. Colonnade
10. German Chapel
11. Paradise Court
12. Chaplain (of the Chapel Royal)
13. Clerk of the Kitchen's office
14. Chapel Royal
15. Guard Room
16. Suttling house
17. Greencloth Court
18. Silver scullery
19. Pastry kitchen
20. Engine Court
21. Miss Beauclerk
22. Kitchen
23. Kitchen Court
24. Cleveland Row
25. Young Princes' apartments
26. Lord Chamberlain's office
27. Mr Barnard, the King's librarian
28. 'Prince of Mecklenburgh's' (possibly apartments for Duke Ernest of Mecklenburg-Strelitz)
29. Mr Godolphin
30. Butter and Egg Office
31. Spicery
32. Stable Yard
33. Queen Caroline's Library
34. Green Park

meanwhile, set off for the seaside, in hope of recovery.[245] By 1807, expenditure on the furnishing of the Princes' accommodation stood at: £5,865 17s 1d on the Duke of Clarence's apartment; £10,137 8½d on the Duke of Kent's apartment at Kensington Palace; £6,453 14s on the Duke of Cumberland's apartment; £4,111 9s 6d on the Duke of Sussex's apartment at Kensington Palace; and £4,346 6s on the Duke of Cambridge's apartment at St James's.[246]

After the fire of 1809 (see p. 167), which did not affect the Duke of Clarence's apartments (nor the Duke of Cumberland's), lavish redecoration of his apartments continued, with the Duke of Clarence giving instructions to the cabinet-maker Samuel Beckwith from his country residence at Bushy Park. Many rooms of his 'new apartments' followed a scarlet and black upholstery scheme. In the first waiting room, there were to be two sofas covered in red morocco leather with black tufting (£70). In the 'Anti Room', the cornice followed the elegant upholstery scheme, with a carved cornice covered with scarlet cloth and black velvet-covered ornamental ends (£1 7s). The chief glory of the dining room was probably two large sideboards, with open mahogany 'Sarcophagusses' (wine-coolers) to stand underneath (£31 18s).[247] The first-floor dressing room included a mahogany lady's dressing table (£20 10s). For the small library, Beckwith made two bookcases with pilasters and 'vestal heads and feet', with a dove-grey marble shelf (£46 18s). The drawing room (and its furnishings) was luxuriously upholstered in 130 yards (118.9 m) of 'fine Crimson & Gold Tissue', at 31s per yard, totalling £201 10s, and 150 yards (137.2 m) of 'fine Blue Sarsnet', at 7s 9d per yard, totalling £58 2s 6d. Beckwith charged £28 10s for hanging the extremely elaborate, hand-finished blue sarsnet (a fine, soft farbric) hangings, which were furnished with crimson tissue panels with crimson silk 'mantels', hung from ornamental pins with blue velvet trimmed with silk fringing.

By far the most expensive item of furniture was a large gilt frame with a large plate glass (£213). A marble-topped gilt and black painted pier table was made to go under the pier glass (£52). Beckwith's account for his work totalled the substantial sum of £4,370.[248] The upholsterers William France & Son supplied some of the fabric, including two pairs of scarlet 'Salisbury Flannel' window curtains with gilt cornices (£40 10s). They also provided a mahogany library table on pedestals, with a rising top with a double stand (known as a 'horse') (£46 15s).[249] John Russell, joiner, submitted his account for seat and bed furniture and other joinery at the same time, which totalled £704 18s.[250]

The apartments for both the Duke of Clarence and the Duke of Cumberland (Figs 3.44 and 3.45) were the subject of repeated improvement, alteration and aggrandisement over the course of the first decade of the nineteenth century. Indeed, one of the very first such improvements was ordered to be made in May 1799: 'to provide a Kitchen & it's appendages for the convenience of Prince Ernest', in 'Prince Edward's' apartment on the north side of Kitchen Court, overlooking Cleveland Row (today, York House). No doubt owing to Prince Edward's continuing military service overseas, the apartment considered for his use a decade earlier was allocated, in 1799, to his younger brother, Prince Ernest (1771–1851). He had returned to England in February 1796, following a military career commanding Hanoverian forces in Flanders. In April 1799, he was created Duke of Cumberland and Teviotdale.[251] In spite of work recently completed there, the Office of Works was asked by Charles Long, junior secretary to the Treasury and later friend and artistic adviser to the Prince of Wales, to 'put [Prince Edward's apartments] into a State of proper repair for the reception of one of the Princes'.[252] These were not rooms on a grand scale such as those at Duchess Street created by Thomas Hope (1769–1831), the great arbiter of Regency taste. Rather, they were closer in scale to rooms in a well-to-do eighteenth-century London terraced house. Astonishingly, the repair work now deemed necessary amounted to £1,092.[253] Charles Elliott was paid £157 10s for, amongst other jobs at St James's, 'pulling down the Old Tapestry at Prince Edward's'; new

wallpapers were hung by Messrs Isherwood; curtains were made by Winter & Hay; John Russell fixed the pulley laths in the windows and made window blinds, as well as supplying a dressing chair and other seat furniture.[254] Richard Taitt, cabinet-maker and upholsterer, supplied simple mahogany furniture and worked on the windows and curtains. While the Brussels carpets were generally the most costly item, the most expensive case furniture was in the drawing room, but this was easily exceeded by the expense of several mirrors supplied for the apartment by Taitt.[255]

The business of furnishing the Duke's apartments began in the latter part of 1798. The accounts covering the supply of furniture and furnishings are extensive and detailed, and convey a general impression of comfort and expense. The entrance hall was given ten mahogany hall chairs with oval backs (£20), each of which was painted with the arms and crest of the Duke on a rose ground encircled by the Garter. The Prince's bedroom was given a four-poster bed, made of an oak frame by John Russell at the modest cost of £6 5s, hung with yellow chintz. The curtains were of matching yellow chintz surmounted by gilded and 'French grey' decorated carved cornices; the most expensive item, as was usually the case, was the mirror: a giltwood overmantel mirror picked out in white, and fitted with a pair of single candle branches (£30). There were '2 indulgent Chairs' for the bedchamber, and textiles together with gilded cornices were supplied by Richard Taitt. In the dining room, John Russell supplied 12 armchairs, painted and japanned with a yellow ground (£20). The library was again to be hung with yellow chintz curtains, also made by Richard Taitt, and there was to be a 'very good' mahogany library

3.44
James Ward (1769–1859), *His Royal Highness the Duke of Clarence*, 1801 (RCIN 605514)

3.45
Sir William Beechey (1753–1839), *Ernest, Duke of Cumberland*, c.1797–1802 (RCIN 404564)

3. THE GEORGIAN COURT 165

table, which cost no less than £25. The dressing room was also hung with yellow chintz. The ballroom and breakfast room were provided with carved frames and carved panels from the specialist carver, William Adam. In the ballroom, he made two panels 'with trophies of musick, tied together with a knot of ribbons & sprigs of laurel leaves', to go on top of the mirrors, and carved a 'chimney frame with trophies of musick … to correspond with the frames'. John Russell provided ten painted and japanned armchair frames.[256] In 1802, the Duke of Cumberland sought further improvements to his own apartments, which was to be a recurring theme over the coming decade.[257]

The Duke of Cumberland laid on various parties and entertainments. One such occasion, on 11 May 1802, was deemed worthy of several paragraphs in *The Times* the following day. The paper recorded that the King and Queen, the Prince of Wales, the five Princesses, and the Dukes of York, Clarence and Cambridge were all in attendance; the ball began at 10pm, with the supper rooms 'thrown open' at midnight. In the centre of the supper table was an elaborately decorated parterre, with emblematic decorations in marble dust. At the top of the table was the emblem of Britannia, and at the bottom, Ceres – military trophies stood between them. Confectionary was served by the pâtissier Gunter, 'in a very superior style', and there were four other supper rooms, with two tables in each. The ballroom floor was painted in distemper with various figures, and the room splendidly illuminated.[258]

Two years later, in 1804, the Duke of Cumberland complained to the Board of the Office of Works about the nuisance caused by a sewer pump for the offices in his apartment, which were below the level of the sewer.[259] At the same time, yet more fashionable furniture flowed into the Duke's apartments: Richard Taitt supplied 'a Square Mahogany Egyptian Couch, carved heads, Stuffed Ends', costing £36.[260] However, soon after 1805, the Duke sought additional space. Officials were asked what space in the palace could be placed at the disposal of Their Royal Highnesses.[261] Meanwhile, the Duke of Cumberland continued to grumble about his own apartments, and the pressing need for alteration and improvement. The Lord Chamberlain wrote to the Office of Works on 29 June 1810, requesting that some action be taken in respect of the Duke's apartments, and on 19 October, an estimate was drawn up for the works to be done there, which amounted to £3,698. Other parts of the palace were not neglected: the housekeeper's apartment was deemed by James Wyatt, in a letter to Groves, as 'in great want of repair and extremely unsafe to inhabit'; and Mr Marsh was asked to explain his estimate of £807 to improve the state of the apartment in the great court, near to the Chapel Royal, for Claudius Francis Dupasquier, page to the Prince Regent.

Although largely on active service overseas, the youngest brother, Adolphus, Duke of Cambridge (1774–1850), was allocated apartments at St James's, in the south-eastern corner of the palace, overlooking The Mall and St James's Park. Works were approved in July 1801 and estimated to cost £3,350.[262] Some modest furnishings were supplied and a great many repairs carried out by Beckwith & France, William Adam and John Russell over the course of 1802 and 1803.[263] Again, when the Duke returned to England in 1805, further alterations and additions to his apartment at St James's were put in hand.[264] Three years later, a further 'plan of alteration' was produced by Mr Harrison and Mr Marsh, totalling some £6,300 – an estimate that was approved.[265] The Duke of Cambridge's apartment was to be in the south-eastern corner of Paradise Court, and was to be fitted up in the apartment of Mrs Tracey, enlarging the living room, converting it to a drawing room and creating an anteroom. Rooms for the Duke's private secretary, steward, housekeeper and porter were also created. The apartment was furnished by William France and an estimate was prepared, which amounted to £6,300. The apartments of Lady Charlotte Finch, Miss Boscawen, Miss Beauclerk and Miss Planta, all of which were located in the east wing of the palace, close to the outbreak of fire in the Duke of Cambridge's apartments, were also attended to by William France & Son.[266]

Fire and Dilapidation, 1809–20

Before the Duke of Cambridge's apartment was complete, disaster struck. In the early hours of the morning of 21 January 1809, a fire enveloped and destroyed much of the south-eastern corner of the palace (Fig. 3.46). That morning, Charles Craig of the Office of Works wrote to James Wyatt, surveyor of the Office of Works, at that time at Wilton House, Wiltshire:

I am just returned from St James's Palace where a most dreadful Fire has taken place this morning breaking out, about 2 oclo- It began in ye Court next St James's Street (and is supposed thro' a Servant of Miss Rice's, leaving a Candle in her sleeping room, whom I believe has perished in the flames) thence it continued its destructive course in the front next the Park – and totally consumed the whole of the Duke of Cambridge's, and part of the Queen's apartments – the Walls are standing, and great part of the Paintings and Furniture are saved.[267]

The *Morning Chronicle* reported that 'The cause, or by what accident the fire happened, remains a matter of doubt, but it is certain that it broke out on or near the King's back stairs'. The fire was identified by the Duke of Cambridge, who, having returned from Mrs Haggerston's, was told by his porter of a strong smell of fire, which could not be located. The Duke went up into the King's guard chamber in the State Apartments and saw the flames leaping. Unfortunately, there was not nearly enough water for the fire engines to prove effective, although, as Craig reported to Wyatt, many works of art were saved. The *Morning Chronicle* reported:

The soldiers on duty, as well as the firemen, when they arrived, were employed in saving the furniture in the Palace, and other property. The whole of the Duke of Cambridge's property, with the exception of some wine and liquors, were saved ... The whole of the Queen's private apartments, the Duke of Cambridge's, the apartments of two of his Majesty's pages, who have sustained very considerable loss; Miss B. Planta's and other apartments are entirely destroyed. The Dutch Chapel, nearly under the Armoury-room, has sustained considerable injury. The fire extended to the King's Closet, which is entirely consumed, as is the adjoining room where it ceased.[268]

The *Gentleman's Magazine* recorded that the Prince of Wales and his brothers, the Dukes of York, Kent, Cumberland, Sussex and Cambridge, all stayed until a late hour, encouraging the firemen.[269] On 21 January, the Prince of Wales wrote a letter to the Hon. Mrs Fielding, enquiring after the health of Lady Charlotte Finch, and 'how she has borne the terrible alarm' of the fire, acknowledging that he had been informed that Lady Charlotte was 'lodged in safety' in the Duke of Cumberland's apartment.[270]

Perhaps surprisingly, no steps were taken to rebuild or stabilise the destroyed fabric of the palace. No explanation is given in the papers

3.46

Drawing by an unknown hand, showing the corner of the palace badly damaged by fire in 1809 (Westminster City Archive, Gardner Box 36, No. 10b)

of the Office of Works: perhaps the palace was deemed beyond repair. It was not until more than a year later, on 26 May 1810, that the Lord Chamberlain requested a survey and an estimate for the 'Expense attending the rebuilding of such part as was destroyed, and making necessary Repairs to those places which may have received damage'.[271] In the end, little was done beyond making the adjoining rooms safe and water-tight.

The tragic fire was not the final act of misfortune: the following year, scandal engulfed the palace. Mystery surrounded the curious death of the Duke of Cumberland's Sardinian valet, Joseph Sellis, found on the night of 30 May 1810 with his throat slit ear-to-ear, in his room in the Duke's apartment. At the inquest (held by the coroner of the Royal Household), the Duke explained he had been asleep when he was struck several times, and when he rose from his bed, he discovered his assailant had fled. He claimed to have seen nothing, although a night-lamp burned in his bedchamber. Sellis was discovered moments later in his room, a razor lying on the floor next to his body. It may be significant that Sellis and another of the Duke's valets, Cornelius Neale, were bitter rivals, though Neale was never placed under suspicion. Public opinion considered that the Duke himself had committed the murder. Ultimately, the foreman of the jury, the tailor and radical freethinker Francis Place, returned a verdict of suicide.[272]

This notorious episode, involving a son of George III, seems likely to have drawn attention to the lavish expenditure on the Princes' apartments, a matter that was beginning to be a cause of some concern at the Treasury. The first clerk of the Lord Chamberlain's office, Thomas B. Marsh, was therefore required to provide accounts of expenditure on 'repairs alterations and improvements of apartments forming the habitual Residence of the younger branches of the Royal Family from the 5th April 1806 to the 10 October last' (i.e. 1811).[273] Enquiry was duly made, and the amount expended on the Duke of Cumberland's apartments up to 2 August 1811 was calculated to be £6,058 3s 6d.[274] Efforts to economise, including reusing old furniture, were suggested to the Duke of Clarence, to little avail.[275] It was probably the corollary of suspicious princely behaviour and lavish spending that caused an enquiry to be opened into expenditure at Kensington and St James's Palaces from 1800 to 1812. The total spent on St James's in that 12-year period was calculated at £30,170 2s 10¾d.[276]

By 1813, the future of the palace was becoming uncertain: the Lords Commissioners of the Treasury had considered the cost of alterations and repairs for offices for the Lord Steward and the Board of Green Cloth, but wrote to the Prince Regent and the Treasury, referring to the 'present uncertainty as to the future appropriation of this Palace'.[277] The Treasury was simply not willing to pay for repairs beyond what might be absolutely necessary for keeping the remaining buildings proof against wind and rain.

James Wyatt's death in 1813 led to the reorganisation of the Office of Works. John Nash, personal architect to the Prince Regent, was appointed acting Surveyor General for the royal palaces for 15 months. The dilapidated condition of St James's led Nash to state that to maintain the palace would be a poor use of public funds – the architects Thomas Leverton (1743–1824) and Thomas Chawner (1774–1851) were invited by the Office of Works and the Office of Woods, Forests and Land Revenues, to submit designs for redeveloping the entire site.[278] Was Great Britain at last to build its sovereign a new metropolitan palace? Such a patriotic gesture, in the wake of the victory over Napoleon, must surely have been considered appropriate. However, Chawner and Leverton's plans show several proposals for a series of luxury houses, not a splendid new palace. Six alternative watercolour plans show eight layouts, with varying concentrations of housing, revealing a bold, but solidly conventional classical building, with a central colonnade and archway (Fig. 3.47). Six of the proposals retain Marlborough House; all include a wide avenue, linking St James's Street, Pall Mall and St James's Park (Fig. 3.48).

In the summer of 1814, following Napoleon's abdication in April of that year, and his

3.47
Thomas Leverton and Thomas Chawner, *Design for building upon the site of St James's Palace; prepared by Order of The Commissioners of His Majesty's Woods, Forests and Land Revenues. Front towards Pall Mall and St James's Street.* 1815 (TNA, WORK 34/139)

3.48
Thomas Leverton and Thomas Chawner, *Sketch of a Design for building on the site of St James's Palace, Novr. 1815* (TNA, WORK 34/138 (4); north is at the bottom)

subsequent exile on the island of Elba, the Allied monarchs and generals assembled in London. Lord Londonderry recalled, in his account of the campaign:

the allied sovereigns except the Emperor of Austria, as it is well known, paid London a visit at the conclusion of the peace of Paris. Their brilliant reception, the enthusiasm which was demonstrated, especially in favour of the Silesian hero [Blücher], the sumptuous and splendid entertainments that were exhibited by a British sovereign and his city of London, which in one single fête to Alexander expended 25,000*l.* sterling … I constantly accompanied my friend Marshal Blucher to all the feasts and dinners given to him.[279]

3. THE GEORGIAN COURT

The King of Prussia was given accommodation in the apartments of the Duke of Clarence. Marshal Blücher (1742–1819) was also lodged in St James's, in Mr Gorton's (comptroller of His Majesty's kitchen) apartment in Kitchen Court: 'Prince Blucher becomes quite domesticated in London; he sits and smokes his pipe several hours in the day, shewing himself at intervals to the populace who constantly surround the entrance to "Wahlstadd Palace" … public curiosity has made the Kitchen Court at St James's the focus of London'.[280] Blücher's heroic reputation was such that at the time of his residency at the palace, it was referred to informally as 'Wahlstadd Palace', after Blücher's title, Fürst von Wahlstatt, given to him by Frederick William III (1770–1840), the Prussian King, when in Paris on 3 June 1814.[281]

An example of a characteristically mundane undertaking at St James's at the start of the Regency was the installation of 'two water closets in the most convenient places near to the Royal Closet in the Chapel Royal St James's for the accommodation of the attendants upon the Royal Family'.[282] Otherwise, the familiar cycle of maintenance and repair was followed; courtiers' and servants' apartments were altered and improved, and Miss Finch, daughter of Lady Charlotte Finch, was put into the rooms formerly occupied by the late Mrs Albert.[283] The silver scullery was to be put to use as an office for the Lord Steward, and the clerk of the kitchen's office would be turned into a silver scullery.[284] As Nash's position in the Office of Works was still unofficial, a letter was sent to the Office of Works which 'instructed [tradesmen] to obey the directions they may receive from Mr Nash', though the instruction applied only to the 'Palaces which are the Personal Residence of His Royal Highness the Prince Regent'.[285] As the Duke of Cumberland had been sent abroad earlier in the year, he left instructions for 'his residence to be repaired', resulting in an estimate which totalled £797.[286]

An act of Parliament in 1815 established new arrangements at the Office of Works. Nash was replaced as Surveyor General by Benjamin Stephenson, and responsibility for the Crown estate was divided amongst three architects: Nash, John Soane and Robert Smirke (1780–1867). Nash was responsible for Kensington Palace, Carlton House, St James's Park and Palace, Hyde Park and Windsor Great Park.

While the various private apartments across the palace had been redecorated time and again, the principal State Rooms had not been updated since the King's accession. Finally, in 1815, these rooms were considered worthy of attention – and a Treasury warrant was issued for 'doing repairs to the state apartments at St James's Palace to the amount of £751:0:0'. Evidently the Prince Regent got wind of the improvements and caused an instruction to be sent to the Office of Works that 'no alterations of the original plan of any rooms in the Royal Palaces, can be done without the permission of his Royal Highness the Prince Regent'.[287] Elsewhere in the palace, as rooms became available, they were considered for adaptation to modern living: Wyatt had commissioned an estimate to turn 'the four Rooms late the Princesses Dressing Rooms and the Apartments late Mrs Albert's at St James's into a habitable state of Repair'.[288]

In 1815, the victory at Waterloo brought much rejoicing in London, but the victory was not marked in any way at St James's. Instead, illuminations were erected at the Palace of Westminster and before Carlton House.[289] Six months later, a general survey of the palace was undertaken by Nash. The survey on the 'State and Condition' of the palace was delivered to the Office of Works on 13 April 1816. An occupation survey with comments on the condition of the fabric had also been completed at the same time.[290] Nash wrote to Benjamin Stephenson, surveyor general of the Office of Works, on 10 April 1816, explaining that the buildings of

> St James's Palace are in general so dilapidated (except the apartments occupied by His Royal Highness the Duke of Clarence, His Royal Highness the Duke of Cumberland and the German Chapel) that they are not susceptible of permanent repair … any sum laid out … would be money wasted … I recommend no repairs to be done to any other of the buildings beyond what shall be necessary to keep them from falling.[291]

Nash wrote again to Stephenson, on 26 January 1818, emphasising his opinion that 'any attempt to restore it would be attended with more expense than rebuilding it … and if any apartments become vacant not to reoccupy them if possible, so as, to entail the necessity of doing such repairs as occupation must always require and to facilitate the possession of the Palace whenever it shall be required to take the building down.'[292]

Presumably as a consequence of Nash's negative letters to the Commissioners, ensuing works across the palace were confined to maintenance and repair, mainly of the habitable and occupied parts. For example, on 15 July 1816, the chaplains of the German chapel wrote to the Office of Works, requesting 'some necessary Repairs'. Seemingly, nothing was done and the Bishop of London, Dean of the Chapel Royal, was thus impelled to write to the Lord Chamberlain (who directed the letter on to the Office of Works), 'representing that the Closets in the Chapel Royal Saint James's Palace are in a very dirty state, not having been painted for more than twenty years'.[293]

In 1817 Nash wrote suggesting at least partial demolition: he had inspected a roof above Mrs Boyle's apartments, 'and found them in so dangerous a state as to direct the whole of that part of the Building being pulled down'.[294] Many residents paid out of their own pocket for the repair of the premises they occupied. Mr Timothy Brent, secretary of the Board of Green Cloth, requested 'permission to repair a House in St James's Palace, at his own Expence', which probably included a new entrance door; approval for its installation was given by the Treasury, but only at Mr Brent's expense.[295]

Soon after Leverton and Chawner had produced their plans for redeveloping the palace, and after Nash's latest damning communication on the stability of the fabric of the building, the publisher William Henry Pyne commissioned Charles Wild to make seven watercolour views recording the interiors (and one exterior) of the palace (see also Stephanoff's watercolours, Figs. 3.6 and 3.23). These were intended to join other sets of

3.49
Charles Wild, *The Guard Chamber, St James's Palace*, c.1818 (RCIN 922162)

3.50
Charles Wild, *The King's Presence Chamber, St James's Palace*, c.1816 (RCIN 922163)

3. THE GEORGIAN COURT

3.51
Charles Wild, *The Queen's Levee Room, St James's Palace*, c.1816 (RCIN 922164). The giltwood table visible on the far wall of the room is still in the Royal Collection and was probably formerly a stand for a lacquer cabinet (RCIN 20580)

3.52
Charles Wild, *The Old Bedchamber, St James's Palace*, c.1819 (RCIN 922165)

watercolours of the royal residences of Windsor Castle, the Queen's House, Hampton Court Palace, Kensington Palace, Carlton House and Frogmore, which were made at the same time. The watercolours were engraved and eight interior views of St James's were included in Pyne's *History of the Royal Residences* (Figs 3.49–3.53), issued in parts, but as a three-volume set in 1819.

The interiors in Charles Wild's watercolours show no obvious sign of deterioration to the palace, and the State Apartments remained in use – as they had been for more than a century. The furnishings in the rooms, however, were decidedly old-fashioned: walls were hung with seventeenth-century tapestries and eighteenth-century mirrors, and lined with chairs and stools seemingly made in the mid-eighteenth century. In fact, some of the paintings depicted (and, no doubt, the tapestries too) had remained in the same place for more than half a century. In the King's presence chamber, the portrait of Henry IV of France (RCIN 406167), which can be seen over the door to the left of the canopy, was recorded in the same place in the 1785 inventory of pictures at St James's. The painting by Cristofano Allori of *Judith with the Head of Holofernes*, which hangs over the chimneypiece in the bedchamber view, was recorded nearby in 1785, in the Queen's drawing room (the levee room).[296]

A later inventory of pictures, taken in 1819, records fewer individual locations than in earlier inventories, but does include the King's dressing room and presence chamber. Thirty-three paintings are noted in the 'Gallery'. This is puzzling, as there had been no formal gallery space at the palace since the seventeenth century: the name may refer to an agglomeration of the principal rooms of the State Apartments which contained important paintings, or possibly a connecting gallery at principal-floor level, linking the Duke of Cumberland's apartment to the north with the ballroom on the south side of Green Cloth Court.[297] The 1819 inventory also notes some 50 paintings hanging in the Duke of Cumberland's apartments, many of which formed part of Consul Smith's collection, purchased by George

3.53
Charles Wild, *The German Chapel, St James's Palace*, c.1816 (RCIN 922166)

III in 1762 for Buckingham House. The selection mixes eighteenth-century Italian view paintings with seventeenth-century portraits, often of royal sitters, for example, Canaletto's (1697–1768) 'Palladian Rialto' (RCIN 404029) and Paul van Somer's full-length portrait of *Elizabeth, Queen of Bohemia* (RCIN 404015); and sixteenth- and seventeenth-century, mainly Italian and Italianate Old Master paintings, such as Domenico Fetti's (c.1588–1623) *Sacrifice of Elijah Before the Priests of Baal* (RCIN 405466) and *Salmacis sees Hermaphroditus Bathing* by a follower of Francesco Albani (RCIN 402770).

Minimal maintenance continued for the rest of the reign and the poor state of the building was clear: the Lord Chamberlain's office gave notice to Mrs Boyle to vacate her apartments 'with as little delay as possible', on account of danger to her person.[298] One of the few improvements involved the installation of modern exterior street lighting: the Gas Light and Coke Company provided an estimate amounting to £1,369 5s, for 'fitting up ready for lighting with Gas, 147 Lamps round St James's Park, Constitution Hill, St James's Palace, Buckingham House & Treasury Passage'.[299]

3. THE GEORGIAN COURT

4. George IV to the Second World War

MICHAEL TURNER

George IV, 1820–30

George IV was proclaimed King outside Carlton House, his principal London residence, on 31 January 1820, followed by further proclamations at the traditional locations of Charing Cross, Cheapside and the Royal Exchange.[1] The King, when Prince of Wales, had seen Carlton House and Brighton Pavilion transformed from modest eighteenth-century houses, by a succession of architects adopting an astonishing variety of exotic styles.[2]

Since 1818, George had been considering residing at Buckingham House, which would require enlarging, notwithstanding the considerable expenditure lavished on his Carlton House residence. The Prime Minister, Lord Liverpool (1770–1828), stressed this could only be achieved by selling St James's Palace, to help defray costs. In July 1821, the King appointed his compliant architect John Nash, then busy at Brighton Pavilion, to draw up plans for altering and enlarging Buckingham House to create Buckingham Palace at the west end of St James's Park. Projects between George IV and Nash generally resulted in a complex saga of design changes initiated by the King and financial mismanagement on Nash's part. Buckingham Palace was no exception, and was effectively uninhabitable until Queen Victoria took up residence 16 years later.[3]

St James's Palace, meanwhile, remained in a poor condition (Fig. 4.1), some of it a burnt-out shell – hence Liverpool's suggestion to sell the site. The palace had long ceased to be the secure enclave created by Henry VIII. The clock tower gates were never closed and lack of adequate policing was symptomatic of a general neglect, which led to 'lads, men and females of the most depraved character resorting there … many of the persons of this description, sleeping in corners and other parts of the Palace, remaining there all night'.[4] The Westminster constables had no power within the palace precincts. That resided with the Marshalmen under the Board of Green Cloth, who had a small lock-up in the south-east corner of the gatehouse for offenders.[5] Matters came to a head around 1821, when the Duke of York, in Godolphin House on the south side of Stable Yard (see Fig. 2.30), complained to the Board of Green Cloth that he and other residents could not pass from their residences without being annoyed or insulted. Consequently, the Marshalmen's attendance at the palace gates was increased, to ensure that one was on duty at all times.[6]

In March 1821, Edward Crocker, clerk of works at St James's, wrote concerning its continued dilapidated state.[7] The Office of Works sought Nash's opinion, who responded the following month: 'I beg to state that every

4.1

Thomas Shotter Boys (1803–74), *St James's Palace*, 1842 (Art Institute of Chicago, 1940.603.26)

part of the Building in St James's Palace is in so ruinous a state that to repair them will be an attempt almost impracticable'. After listing the numerous defects, he concluded, 'In short, I consider every shilling laid out on the Buildings as money thrown away – and any repairs short of rebuilding as most improvident.'[8] Nash recommended demolishing those parts likely to fall down, and enclosing the vacant site, to be used as the government saw fit.[9] But repeated calls for its demolition in the early nineteenth century were always countered by the response that St James's was the only London palace with rooms large enough for royal ceremonial occasions. In the interim, there was no option but to retain it as the official seat of the monarchy, and to embark on costly alterations to the State Apartments to facilitate court functions.[10] The decision to reprieve St James's was made soon after Nash's letter: in August 1821, it was reported that 'The gable of one of the guard chambers, which was open, is now closed up, with a wall and buttresses, in character with the old building', referring to the buttressed east end of the first-floor guard room.[11] By autumn 1821, the ruins of the former private royal apartments at the south-eastern corner of the palace destroyed by fire in 1809 were finally completely cleared and the site secured.[12]

Nash's French neo-classical style at Buckingham Palace reflected the King's more considered architectural taste, encouraged by Sir Charles Long, paymaster general in Lord Liverpool's Tory government.[13] Long was a confidant of the King. His prime passion was in the arts – cultivated during his grand tour in the 1780s. As an arbiter of taste, Long's opinion was frequently called upon regarding public patronage of the arts, and in early 1824 he developed the brief for the reconstruction of Windsor Castle, which reinforced the castle's Gothic origin.[14] One of the difficulties at St James's was that extensive rebuilding would be too costly. The King and Long therefore confined themselves to providing an additional reception room for the State Apartments by utilising the site of the destroyed private apartments, replanning the public circulation within the palace, and remodelling the Wren state rooms to include a new picture-hang, emphasising Britain's martial achievements. Nash was already overworked with Buckingham Palace and it is clear from William Jerdan, editor of the *Literary Gazette and Journal*, that the St James's labourer in trust, Thomas Frederick Hunt (c.1791–1831), was responsible for all the architectural detailing at St James's Palace. Hunt had trained under Soane and was an able architect, but lived beyond his means. He became bankrupt and at one time was forced to take refuge from his creditors at the top of the gatehouse tower, only emerging on Sundays. Nevertheless, Hunt was 'an acknowledged expert on medieval and especially Tudor architecture', and from 1825 to 1830, he published four books promoting the picturesque Tudor style for small domestic buildings, which ran into several editions.[15] In most of the State Apartments, however, Hunt's work is reminiscent of Nash, to whom the remodelling has previously been attributed.[16]

Expenditure on the palace gives an indication of progress. In 1820, the annual Civil List expenditure for St James's and Clarence House amounted to £1,800. In 1821, this rose to £9,500. From 1821 to 1826, the average annual expenditure was nearly £13,400 (the highest being £19,600, in 1824). The overall total expenditure by mid-1824 appears to have been in the order of £60,000.[17]

By September 1821, a new suite of rooms costing £10,000 was being built, including the new room at the east end of the south range.[18] In October, *The Times* reported: 'The alterations and improvements in St James's Palace will be on a much larger scale than was originally contemplated. They will embrace the suite of apartments occupied by the Duke of Cumberland [alongside Cleveland Row]. A grand portico will be opened into St James's Park, directly in front of St James's Street.'[19] But those ambitious proposals were abandoned, possibly on the grounds of cost, or perhaps because George IV had simply changed his mind. A 'new grand stone staircase' leading to the State Apartments

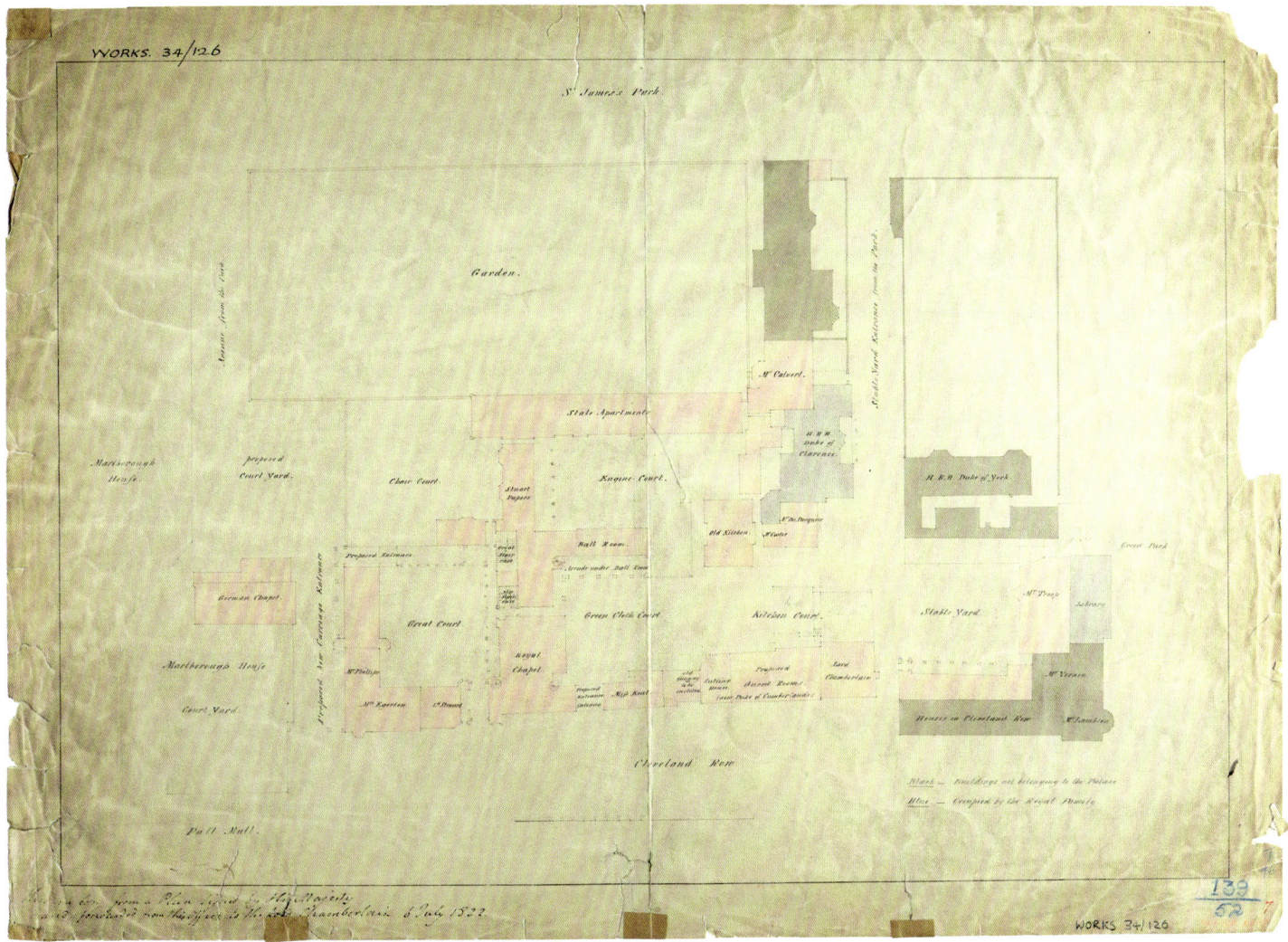

was nearly complete by 16 November 1821.[20] In January 1822, the Lord Chamberlain's office requested the Office of Works to remove the two chimneypieces from Queen Caroline's library (which was being dismantled prior to its complete demolition in 1825) and one from the drawing room at Kensington Palace, for reuse in the state rooms 'now repairing'.[21]

The works were subject to George IV's usual revisions. While they were in progress, Colonel Benjamin Stephenson, surveyor general, visited the King at the Brighton Pavilion on several occasions, to discuss a more radical replanning of the palace to improve access to the State Apartments for court functions. In July 1822, the King approved a block plan, outlining further alterations, and instructed their immediate execution (Fig. 4.2).[22]

St George's Day (23 April) 1824 was the deadline for completion, being the date appointed to celebrate the King's official 62nd birthday, because his actual birthday on 12 August occurred too late in the London season for it to be celebrated with a public holiday (see p. 186).[23] The furnishings and fittings were provided by some of the top London craftsmen, several of whom held royal or official appointments, trading from nearby premises in Westminster, and all located within the former bailiwick of St James's.[24]

In order to provide a more elegant and convenient approach for those entitled to entrée, in December 1823, the Lord Chamberlain's department instructed the Office of Works to remove the north–south range separating Green Cloth Court and

4.2

St James's Palace, block plan, 1822 (north is at the bottom). The plan is endorsed: 'This is a copy of a plan signed by His Majesty and forwarded from this Office to the Lord Chamberlain 6 July 1822' (TNA, WORK 34/126)

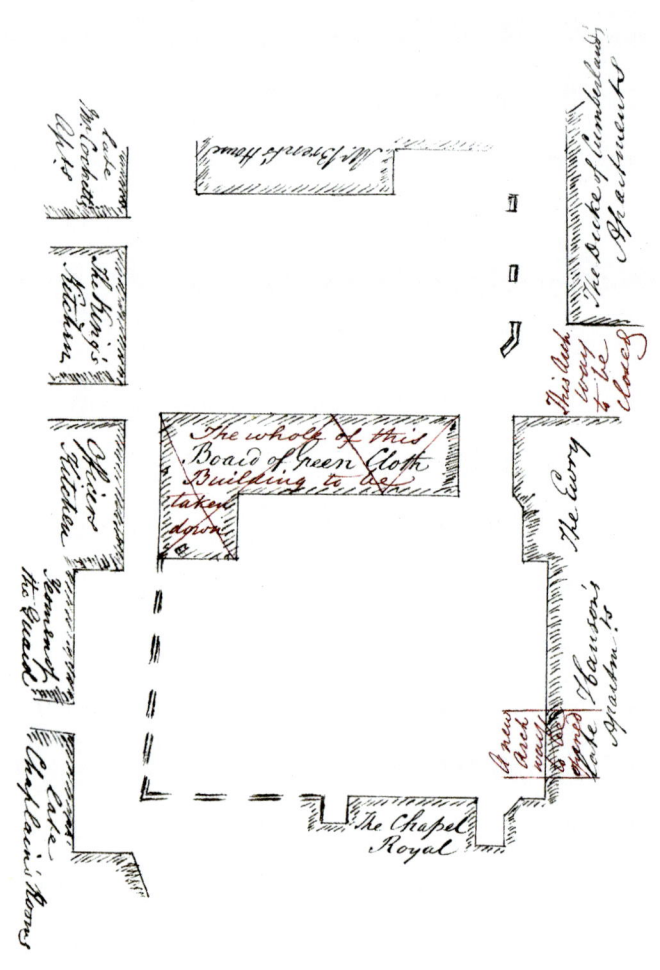

4.3

Plan accompanying the Lord Chamberlain's department letter of 15 December 1823, indicating demolitions and alterations (in red) to create the larger Ambassadors Court (north is to the right) (TNA, WORK 1/12, fol. 285)

Kitchen Court, thereby creating a larger courtyard for waiting carriages; to block the gateway from Cleveland Row; and to form a new arched entrance immediately to the west of the Chapel Royal (Figs 4.3 and 4.4).[25]

The King was unable to appropriate the Duke of Cumberland's apartments to relocate the suttling house. But the new gateway provided direct access to an entrance within a three-bay brick arcade with rusticated Portland stone dressings, in the south-east corner of an enlarged court, renamed Ambassadors Court, to accommodate the carriages of those entitled to entrée.[26] This matched the arcading under the former ballroom to create a coherent design. The arcade led to a second, separate Portland stone staircase, which was more spacious than the former narrow entrée staircase.[27] The 'ugly wainscoting' to the original south stairs was removed and replaced with stucco painted to imitate marble, and the low wall between the two stairs was topped with Ionic scagliola columns imitating grey granite, similar to those in Long's own house at Bromley Hill, Kent (see Fig. 4.50).[28]

This imposing neo-classical staircase hall was furnished with reduced bronze copies of the celebrated Barberini candelabra from Hadrian's Villa, standing on black marble plinths and supporting three-branch lamps, supplied by the glass lustre manufacturer William Perry: two in Hunt's shell-headed niches at either end of the stairs, with seven more arranged on the landing and within the open arches of the first-floor corridor.[29] Drawings and casts of the candelabra had been sent from Rome, by Charles Heathcote Tatham (1772–1842) to Henry Holland (1745–1806), in the 1790s, possibly for use in Carlton House, and Tatham published a further drawing in his influential *Etchings … of ancient ornamental architecture* of 1799.[30]

The general company approached the State Apartments via a new five-bay neo-Tudor arcade opposite Marlborough House and the German chapel. The arcade was completed by December 1823 and adjoined the truncated and buttressed east range, recorded in Buckler's watercolour of 1827 (Fig. 4.5).[31]

The enclosed colonnade on the south side of Colour Court led to the south set of stairs rising to the Armoury. Here, as throughout the state rooms, a new stove was supplied, with a suitable fender and fire irons.[32] Pyne's *Royal Residences* illustrates the 'ill-shaped clumsy fireplace which previously disgraced this approach to the grand rooms' (so-described by the correspondent in the *Literary Gazette* in April 1822) (see Fig. 3.49).[33]

Hunt drew on his expertise in Tudor design to replace it with a large neo-Tudor chimneypiece, modelled on a newly uncovered original in the adjacent Tapestry Room (see Fig. 1.1). The latter, carved in what Hunt calls 'Sussex stone' (probably Reigate), had been concealed behind a seventeenth-century bolection-moulded chimneypiece and panelling. It was preserved and repaired under the orders

4.4
J.C. Buckler, *View in the Kitchen Court of Saint James's Palace*, 1827, showing the new archway from Cleveland Row and the Ambassadors Court entrance arcade (BM, 1880,1113.2144)

4.5
J.C. Buckler, *South-West View of the German Chapel at St James's*, 1827. At this date, the new arcade terminated at the south end of the truncated and buttressed Tudor range. Marlborough House sits behind the German chapel, before the garden wall was moved forward with the creation of Marlborough Road in 1856 (BM, 1880,1113.2275)

4.6
J.C. Buckler, *South-East View of Saint James's Palace*, 1827. The new ballroom occupies the four windows on the right-hand side (BM, 1880,1113.2142)

4.7
The Queen Anne Room, photographed in 1889 by Henry Bedford Lemere (1865–1944). The stencilled cove was added by William Morris (1834–96) in 1881, when he also cleaned and rehung the mid-nineteenth-century yellow silk damask wall hanging. The barriers (referred to as 'the pen') were designed to funnel the general company attending levees and Drawing Rooms along the window wall, and to regulate the flow into the Entrée Room via the south door (Historic England Archive, BL09450)

of Colonel Stephenson, and subsequently drawn by Hunt and published in 1827 in a pattern book dedicated to Lord Farnborough (as Long had become on his elevation to the peerage in 1826).[34] Hunt also designed a similar chimneypiece in the Guard Room. The combination of the Tapestry Room's original chimneypiece and the Charles I tapestries (the only room in the State Apartments to retain them) may have encouraged Hunt to reinforce the Tudor origins of these three public rooms surviving from the original palace, perhaps to emphasise the historic antecedents of the British monarchy. Hunt's contextual use of neo-Tudor detailing met with contemporary approval, but George IV's response to these rooms is not recorded.[35] Weapons and armour were also decoratively arranged following the traditional devices for the decorative treatment of a Guard Chamber, which had been established at Windsor Castle and copied at Hampton Court. A complete set of armour was placed above the chimneypiece, supported on a bronze bracket supplied by Edward Wyatt (1757–1833), appointed carver and gilder to the Office of Works in 1798 (see Fig. 4.62).[36]

A six-spouted Roman lamp, 'designed after the Antique', with Argand burners, was supplied by Perry for both the Armoury and the east guard chamber.[37] Hunt bricked up the four centre-arched side windows to the Armoury, and in the Tapestry Room he rebuilt the large bay window, which is clearly visible in the change of brickwork in the open courtyard outside, called Friary Court since at least 1841, on account of the proximity of the former friary.[38] This room leads into Hunt's new great drawing room, partly occupying the site of the former privy chamber, and now misleadingly called the Queen Anne Room, on account of the portrait of Queen Anne initially hung above the chimneypiece.[39] Externally, the south (garden) elevation was aligned with and carefully copied the detailing of the Wren range, making it difficult to discern the join between the two builds (Fig. 4.6).

Hunt created a triple enfilade for the three principal state rooms on the south front by inserting central doors into the Entrée and Throne Room. All three rooms have embellished ceiling coves, created by sacrificing space on the attic floor above. The lavish use of gilding executed by Edward Wyatt reflects George IV's liking for the opulence of French late seventeenth- and eighteenth-century interiors.[40] The King's changes of mind during the alterations, and consequently exceeding the Treasury budgets, led to quarrels between Benjamin Stephenson and the Lord Steward's department.[41] One cause of friction was the frequent changes in specification to the gilding from one room to another, including gilding the glazing bars to the throne and supper rooms; these alterations were carefully detailed in letters submitted by Crocker as clerk of works.[42] Large pier glasses with gilded frames by Bailey & Sanders reflected the light from the candelabra, designed in imitation of the Louis XIV style.[43] As well as newly commissioned pieces, all three rooms incorporated the recycled chimneypieces: the early eighteenth-century chimneypiece from Kensington Palace was fixed to the east wall of the ballroom (Fig. 4.7), while both the Entrée Room and Throne Room retain the two relocated chimneypieces from Queen Caroline's library.[44] The oak joinery was partly gilded and additional doors and architraves were copied to match the existing ones.[45] Crimson

4.8
John Wootton, *The Siege of Lille*, 1742, commissioned by Frederick, Prince of Wales, in 1742, and hung in the ballroom by George IV (RCIN 407182)

4.9
J.M.W. Turner (1775–1851), *The Battle of Cape Trafalgar*, 1822–4 (National Maritime Museum, Greenwich, BHC0565)

silk damask lined the walls and was also used for the curtains, which hung from valances, with elaborate gilt cornices running the length of each room.[46]

A proposal to fresco the ceilings of the rooms on the south front, following a programme devised by Charles Long, never materialised, but Long was surely the author of the remarkable didactic arrangement of history paintings in these rooms, depicting British martial victories since the early eighteenth century.[47] State portraits of Queen Anne, George I and George II hung in the ballroom, accompanied by two large canvasses commissioned by Frederick, Prince of Wales, from John Wootton (c.1682–1764). Both are dated 1742 and depict *The Siege of Lille* (1708) (Fig. 4.8) and *The Siege of Tournay* (1709) – significant Allied victories in the War of the Spanish Succession.[48]

The Entrée Room (see Fig. 4.10) was 'a kind of anti-chamber, where the nobility are permitted to sit down, whilst their majesties are present in the further room, there being stools and sofas for that purpose'.[49] Here, the portrait of George III in his Garter robes by Sir Thomas Lawrence (1769–1830; George IV's official art adviser),[50] was flanked by de Loutherbourg's (1740–1812) *Glorious First of June*, depicting the

4. GEORGE IV TO THE SECOND WORLD WAR

4.10

The Entrée Room. The pier glass, pier table and lamp bracket were all supplied by Bailey & Sanders in 1824

4.11

The enriched plaster ceiling cove in the north-east corner of the Throne Room, depicting the collar of the Order of the Thistle, comprising alternate thistles and sprigs of rue (symbols of Picts and Scots), framing the star of the Order – a St Andrew's cross with a thistle in the centre – surrounded by the motto of the Order, *Nemo me impune lacessit* ('No one provokes me with impunity')

4.12

The Throne Room with the re-created 1824 picture-hang: George Jones, *The Battle of Vittoria*, 1822; Sir Thomas Lawrence, *George IV*, 1821; and George Jones, *The Battle of Waterloo*, 1822

ST JAMES'S PALACE

first battle in the French Revolutionary Wars under the command of Lord Howe in 1794, and by Turner's only royal commission – and his largest to mirror the size of de Loutherbourg's – *The Battle of Cape Trafalgar* (Fig. 4.9).

The elaborate frames for the Turner and de Loutherbourg paintings were designed en suite with that for George III by James Henderson of New Bond Street.[51] In 1829, the King presented both naval paintings to the National Gallery of Naval Art, established in December 1823 in the Painted Hall at Greenwich Hospital to commemorate the achievements of the Royal Navy.[52]

The Throne Room is the climax of the suite of State Apartments, and here the decoration is the most elaborate of all. The coved ceiling is richly embellished with block gilt plasterwork incorporating the stars and collars of the four major orders of chivalry in the corners: the Garter, the Thistle, St Patrick and the Bath (Fig. 4.11).

Lawrence's imposing 1821 coronation portrait of the King hangs above the chimneypiece (Fig. 4.12). The elaborate gilt picture frame surmounted by a crown on a cushion for the Lawrence portrait was supplied for the Throne Room by Bailey & Sanders in 1824, and it has remained there ever since.[53] This is flanked by Edward Wyatt's gilded rearrangement and augmentation of salvaged drops of Grinling Gibbons carving, of which, it was stated in 1822, 'many are preserved in the palace', and by two panoramic battle scenes commissioned by the King from George Jones (1786–1869) in 1822, and framed in 1824 by Bailey & Sanders: *The Battle of Vittoria* and *The Battle of Waterloo*, celebrating Wellington's victories. The subject of these paintings, and the prominence given to them, are an indication of George IV's pride in these victories, which the King recounted so frequently that in later years he came to believe he was personally responsible for these military and naval achievements.[54]

The St James's throne canopy survives, with its 'Cornice most superbly enriched with Composition Ornament Gilt in Burnish [*sic*] and Oil Gold',[55] although its giltwood coat of arms was removed after 1938 (Fig. 4.13).[56] The velvet

4.13

The Throne Room, *c.*1893, showing the coat of arms over the canopy and the copy of Winterhalter's portrait of Queen Victoria to the left of Lawrence's *George IV*. The elaborate stencilled ceiling and the picking-out to the cove were added by William Morris in 1882; both were removed in 1904 (RCIN 2950788)

cloth retains its embroidered Garter star on the soffit, and its elaborate valance and backcloth, both initially embroidered by George d'Almain Junior, but subsequently modified with the arms and monogram of Queen Victoria.[57] The original throne was described in Bailey & Sanders' account as 'a Superb State Chair … the frame covered in part and richly decorated with Composition Ornaments Gilt in Burnished and Oil Gold'.[58] It was reused for William IV's coronation and taken to Chatsworth House by the 6th Duke of Devonshire as a perquisite.[59] Edward Bailey submitted a supplementary invoice for a second 'large State Chair' for the St James's Throne Room, costing £178 10s, and £87 15s to cover, because Bailey also supplied the crimson silk velvet and deep crimson and gold fringe, broad gold lace, gimp and cord.[60] The current throne at St James's is likely to be this second state chair, which, in 1831, was reduced in height to suit its new position on the dais, with new ornaments and a new footstool added by Bailey.[61] Beyond the Throne Room was the King's Closet or Audience Room (later known as the Royal Closet, and now the Council Chamber). It was furnished for George IV with a rosewood 'Buhl' writing table and inkstand by Bailey & Sanders (Fig. 4.37).[62]

To exit a function, guests were directed to a door at the north-west corner of the new

4. GEORGE IV TO THE SECOND WORLD WAR   183

4.14

A grand banquet to celebrate the 200th anniversary of the enrolment of the Coldstream Guards was held on 22 May 1850 in the supper or Banqueting Room at St James's Palace, attended by the Duke of Cambridge as the regiment's Colonel. This was only the second time the room had been used for a banquet since the death of William IV (*Illustrated London News*, 1 June 1850, p. 380)

4.15

The Banqueting Room in 1847, when Winterhalter's portrait of the royal family (RCIN 405413) was temporarily displayed there. This shows the heavily enriched door architrave, with a garlanded overdoor incorporating a badge of one of the orders surmounted by a crown, and elaborately framed panels to the walls (*Illustrated London News*, 8 May 1847, p. 300)

ballroom and into a new corridor supported on an arcade, which replaced a number of buildings on the east side of Engine Court. Five royal portraits hung in this narrow gallery (Henry VIII, Mary I, Elizabeth I, James I and Charles I), which led into the Matted Hall, from where the requisite staircase could easily be reached.[63]

The external staircase to the old ballroom which had projected into the former Green Cloth Court was swept away to facilitate carriages turning, after those with the right of entrée had alighted.[64] The room was converted to a supper room by removing its gallery and banked seating, and lining the walls with canvas and paper. This was a room designed to be used at night: all the windows appear to have been covered over, creating a bold stone or pearl-coloured room, embellished with applied mouldings of giltwood and composition again suggestive of a late Louis XIV style.[65]

Much of the joinery, including carving six gilt shields, stars, mottoes and jewels, 'Carved in close Imitation of the Real Stars', was carried out by Robson and Hale of Piccadilly, who employed a much wider range of skills than simply paper hanging.[66] The inspiration for the chivalric devices was doubtless the four overdoors in the old Throne Room at Carlton House, comprising trophies of the orders of chivalry richly carved and gilded by Edward Wyatt in 1807.[67] The supper room was lit by five large ormolu lustres, and the ceiling was ventilated by 12 'perforated ornaments' (Figs 4.14 and 4.15).[68] In 1824, the *Literary Gazette* described the newly finished room:

> The walls are of a pearl colour, and divided into many panels, or compartments, by the most fanciful gold mouldings. Here, from roof to floor, runs a belt like scale armour; there, a cornice strikes you by its novelty and beauty, and around the middle is a frieze of curious workmanship and exquisite effect. Over the six doors are shields with the stars of the six chivalrous Orders, of which the Sovereign is the head and fountain; these are unique and truly fitting ornaments for this, in every respect, magnificent place, which a crimson floor-cloth serves to set off to the greatest advantage.[69]

Charles Long, who was also a director of Greenwich Hospital, was able to convince his fellow commissioners to exchange 35 paintings from the King, mostly of admirals, for an 'ornamented Chimney piece' lately removed from the Naval Asylum boardroom in the Queen's House, with the intention of relocating it in the supper room.[70] The marble chimneypiece, with its tightly bound swags of fruit (Fig. 4.16), appears by the quality of its carving to date from the time of William

Kent, although modelled on a design by Inigo Jones and published as such by Kent in 1727.[71] To service the new supper room, previous alterations were countermanded in order to create a direct first-floor bridge link to Vanbrugh's great kitchen (Fig. 4.17).[72]

In May 1826 George IV was still in Carlton House because Buckingham Palace was incomplete. Further alterations to enable him to reside temporarily in St James's were under way. The Board of Green Cloth gave directions to the Office of Works to make wine vaults in the cellars and to fit up rooms to receive His Majesty's china and plate from Carlton House.[73] The King left Carlton House before October 1826; the building must have been uninhabitable by then, as it was reported that most of the furniture and fixtures, including chimneypieces and cornices, had been removed and temporarily stored in the King's riding house (on the site of the later National Gallery) and St James's Palace.[74] The King's new suite of private apartments was appropriated from apartments formerly occupied by Queen Charlotte's maids of honour on the south side of the palace. These were conveniently sited beneath the Throne Room and closet, and on either side of the Sovereign's Stairs linking them. The surprisingly plain decoration of those modest rooms contrasted with the state rooms above: 'The decorations throughout are of a very humble description, sans glitter, sans gold, sans finery'.[75]

Before the year was out, the refurbished palace was again threatened by the King's mercurial temperament, when he pronounced that in future courts should be held in Buckingham Palace. He considered St James's could be demolished for housing, but this was vetoed by Lord Liverpool on account of the potential for criticism in view of the public money already expended, and reiterating the fact that the state rooms at St James's remained the only suitable location in which to hold courts.[76] In 1827, 'a shower bath, douche & warm bath' were installed for the King, and double sashes to keep out the cold.[77] Further works at the palace in 1827 and 1828 included installing a new roasting stove in the King's

4.16

The chimneypiece in the Banqueting Room was relocated to St James's from the Queen's House in Greenwich. This photograph of 26 July 1907 shows it against the background of William Morris's 'St James's' wallpaper and dado panelling, the latter painted cinnamon red and the mouldings gilded (London Metropolitan Archives, SC/PHL/01/522/5026)

4.17

The first-floor link in Engine Court, between the Vanbrugh kitchen and the supper room, constructed in 1824–5

4. GEORGE IV TO THE SECOND WORLD WAR

4.18
J.C. Buckler, view of Colour Court, 1827 (BM, 1880,1113.2143)

4.19
One of Paul Storr's silver-gilt ice pails, which were copies of the Warwick Vase, a colossal antique marble discovered at Hadrian's Villa near Rome in 1770. The body is cast with masks of Bacchus and Hercules between two satyrs (RCIN 50811.1)

coffee room, alterations in the rooms housing the King's medals, additional double sashes in the Entrée Room, with crown glass in the upper lights and plate glass in the lower, and three dormers over the supper room for additional ventilation.[78] Work continued throughout George IV's reign, although on a reduced scale: from 1826 to 1830, annual expenditure fell progressively from £9,100 to £5,700.[79]

In the early years of his reign, George IV continued to hold levees and Drawing Rooms in Carlton House, as he had done as Prince Regent, while St James's Palace was undergoing alterations. His first birthday Drawing Room at St James's following the completion of the State Apartments was held on 20 May 1824 (see p. 177); it was the first court held in the palace 'for upwards of ten years'.[80] The general company passed through the new cast-iron gates at the north end of what is now Marlborough Road, the gates incorporating George IV's monogram, the Garter star and the date 1823.[81] They began entering the palace via the arcade from 1pm until 3.30pm, by which time the new drawing room, Tapestry Room, Armoury and staircase were completely full. Members of the royal family, including the Duchess of Kent (1786–1861) and Prince Leopold (1790–1865), arrived via the Colour Court gates, passed under the colonnade (Fig. 4.18), and assembled with the King in his closet. At 2.25pm, the King entered the Throne Room and received those with the right of entrée, including foreign ambassadors, cabinet ministers and officers of state. Charles Long was among more than 1,000 attendees, of whom more than 273 were presented in a ceremony which lasted until 4.45pm. At the end of the Drawing Room, the company left via the corridor leading to the Matted Hall, where both staircases could be accessed, as required.[82]

Notwithstanding the cost of altering the palace, George IV thereafter made infrequent use of it for state ceremonial. His next two birthday Drawing Rooms took place on 23 April 1828 and 1829, but in 1830 it was postponed on account of his ultimately fatal illness.[83] His first levee was on 9 June 1824, but others were held only sporadically, which resulted in large attendances.[84]

State balls, however, were a regular feature of the reigns of both George IV and William IV. On the evening of 26 May 1828, George IV hosted a grand ball in the State Apartments to which were invited members of the royal family, foreign ambassadors and ministers and their ladies, and members of the nobility and gentry.[85] Dancing took place in the new grand ballroom (the Queen Anne Room) and the adjoining Entrée Room, which allowed four sets of quadrilles, as well as waltzing. The elaborate preparations included installing external Italian Canaletti blinds to the windows, which angled out at the base, with fine gauze internal blinds on which the foremost heraldic artist, Thomas Willement (1786–1871), had painted the King's armorial badges, to allow the sash windows to remain open at night for ventilation. 'Representations of foliage and wreaths in various devices' were executed in distemper on the wooden floor.[86]

The guests numbered about 250, excluding members of the royal family. Dancing commenced once the King and his relatives had taken their seats in the ballroom at 10.30pm. Supper was served at 1am in the Banqueting Room, where an impressive array of gold plate was displayed on a sideboard. The table was sited along the middle of the room, arranged around the Neptune centrepiece of 1741/2, attributed to Nicholas Sprimont (1716–71).[87] Many of the items formed part of George IV's Grand Service, including ice pails by Paul Storr (1771–1844), modelled on the Warwick Vase (Fig. 4.19).[88] Dancing resumed after supper, until the King retired at 3am.[89] (The format was largely the same for other state balls, such as the first state ball hosted by Queen Adelaide on 25 April 1831, in honour of the 55th birthday of Princess Mary, Duchess of Gloucester.[90])

The debilitating and visible effects of gout doubtless contributed to George IV's increasing reclusiveness from the general public, and in 1828, the open-railed St James's garden gate was replaced by a close-boarded one, to prevent the public from seeing him being carried to and from his carriage.[91]

In 1824, a mains water supply was established within the palace by the hydraulic engineer James Simpson (1799–1869), which made redundant the palace's principal reservoir in Green Park, as well as the smaller, brick-built reservoir managed by the Chelsea Water Works at The Mall entrance to Stable Yard (see p. 195).[92] In 1829, gas was supplied to the palace precincts by the Westminster Gas Light and Coke Company. A combination of light fittings was used: wrought-iron wall-mounted lanterns and cast-iron standards and columns to the 'heavy chisel' office pattern which have

4.20
Cast-iron gas lamp outside the Great Gatehouse, showing George IV's monogram and the manufacturer's name, 'T Edge'

battered and fluted bases, embossed with George IV's monogram and the name of the London brass-founder and gas apparatus manufacturer, Thomas Edge (Fig. 4.20).[93]

Princess Augusta (1768–1840), George IV's eldest unmarried sister, had a residence in the palace, between Clarence House to the north and Harrington House to the south. She frequently acted as hostess at court functions, initially on account of the King's estrangement from Caroline of Brunswick. Relatively little work appears to have been done to her apartments, although in 1824 she had three cast-iron balconies installed by Thomas Tapster of Regent Street, to a Gothic pattern.[94]

Three of the King's brothers also lived within or on the periphery of the palace: Frederick, William and Ernest. Frederick, Duke of York, became next in line to the throne after the tragic death in childbirth of George IV's daughter Princess Charlotte (1796–1817). He lived in Godolphin House at the south end of Stable Yard, and in 1821 decided to build an imposing York stone palazzo on the site, and initially employed Robert Smirke to design

4.21

The Great Chamber at St James's Palace, with the remains of ... the Duke of York lying in state ... / drawn on stone by J.D. Harding from a sketch taken ... 18th. Jan (Wellcome Collection)

it, and subsequently Benjamin Dean Wyatt (1775–1855). Work commenced in 1825, and required the demolition of Queen Caroline's library.[95] The Duke achieved immense popularity in 1825, with his opposition to a Tory bill for Catholic emancipation.[96] But he was virtually penniless, and the site was so heavily mortgaged that when the mortgagees threatened to foreclose, the government advanced money on the site in order to prevent speculators obtaining the ground and filling it with dwellings.[97] The Duke died on 7 January 1827, before the building was finished. The government sold it to the 2nd Marquis of Stafford in 1828, who renamed it Stafford House and employed Sir Charles Barry (1795–1860) to complete it. In 1913, Stafford House was sold to Sir William Lever, and the following year it was presented to the nation and renamed Lancaster House.[98]

Due to the remodelling of Windsor Castle, it was decided that the Duke's body would lie in state, on 18 and 19 January 1827, in the 'Great Chamber' (the Queen Anne Room), prior to the funeral procession to St George's Chapel, Windsor (Fig. 4.21). This was the last lying-in-state within the State Apartments. Queen Anne's Ballroom was entirely lined in flowing folds of drapery, imitating a campaign tent – an allusion to the Duke's military character. The room was lit by 15 wall sconces and a central gold chandelier. The Duke's embalmed body lay in a mahogany coffin, covered with a black velvet pall, on which lay his field marshal's baton, sword, coronet and orders. The coffin sat under a state canopy, draped with black cloth and topped by a plume of black ostrich feathers. It was guarded by Grenadier Guards with muskets reversed, Gentlemen Pensioners bearing standards, heralds and gentlemen ushers. Behind the coffin, in full mourning dress, sat Sir Herbert Taylor, General Sir George Cooke and Colonel Benjamin Stephenson.[99]

The Lord Chamberlain's office was unprepared for the huge numbers attending – 20,000 people on the first day and 60,000–80,000 the next – and *The Times* detailed the catalogue of accidents and distress caused by the crush.[100] A reporter took three hours to get through the palace on the second day and witnessed 'at least a dozen females borne senseless from the crowd; most of them without shoes or bonnets, and some of them with their gowns actually torn from their backs'. The account continued:

> The pickpockets were most industrious on this occasion, and we saw a fellow in the crowd a few yards off, cut a gentleman's pocket with a pair of scissors, and very leisurely put its contents into his hat. The gentleman, however, having been apprised of the robbery, seized the fellow, and gave him a terrible thrashing with a good stick with which he was provided.[101]

William, Duke of Clarence, had lived in apartments opposite his brother Frederick in Stable Yard, at the west end of the palace, since 1798. They were refurnished by his mistress, Mrs Jordan (1761–1816), between 1708 and 1709, and by 1816 were generally known as Clarence House.[102] The Duke married Princess Adelaide (1792–1849) in 1818, as part of the scramble for the royal dukes to produce legitimate heirs.[103] For reasons of economy, the Clarences lived abroad until 1822, when they returned to reside in Bushy Park.[104] But by 1824, they were spending more time in Clarence House, whose size and condition were inadequate, and Nash obtained the King's approval to provide a new house which incorporated parts of the older buildings.[105] In 1826, the spectacle of George IV constructing Buckingham Palace, and two royal dukes in a building frenzy at St James's, led the radical Whig politician, Thomas Creevy, to write:

> To think of these two men [George IV and the Duke of York] … both turned sixty, and terrible bad lives, having new palaces building for them! The Duke of York's is 150 ft by 130 [45.7 by 39.6 m] outside, with forty compleat [*sic*] sleeping apartments, and all this for a single man … Billy Clarence, too, is rigging up in a small way in the Stable Yard, but that is doing by the Government.[106]

Clarence House was entered on the west side through a two-storey Doric cast-iron portico. It abutted a range of earlier buildings behind, including Princess Augusta's apartments at the south-east corner.[107] Nash's three-storey stuccoed and painted astylar front contrasted with the adjoining brick façade of the State Apartments. The contractors included Bernasconi & Sons (plasterers) and Matthew Wyatt (painter; 1777–1862).[108] Hunt clashed with Nash over the latter's mismanagement; and unexpected complex underpinning and changes of design raised the cost from Nash's initial estimate of £9,000–£10,000 to more than £22,000 by 1829.[109]

For most of George IV's reign, the Duke of Cumberland's apartments, fronting Cleveland Row, remained vacant, while the Duke lived abroad with his wife, Frederica of Solms-Braunfels (1778–1841). Nevertheless, he requested alterations in his absence. In 1825, Nash produced a scheme costing £12,000.[110] But the Duke required additional accommodation, and Nash was at his wits' end to know how to provide it, so he persevered with piecemeal works.[111] In October 1828, the Treasury gave authority for additional repairs costing £5,700, to repair brick parapets and chimney stacks, replace the roof, reinstate rooms lost at the east end when the range dividing the former kitchen court and Green Cloth Court was demolished, and make further alterations to provide accommodation at the west end for the Duchess and her son, Prince George (1819–78).[112] All this was in response to the Duke's decision to return to England in February 1829, to galvanise Tory opposition to their government's bill promoting Roman Catholic emancipation. In 1829, the Duke decided to live permanently in England once more, and to bring his family over from Germany.[113]

With the death of George IV in June 1830, Nash lost his patron and ally. At the insistence of the Treasury, Nash was dismissed in October as architect to the Office of Works by Colonel Stephenson.[114] Further alterations to appropriate three additional rooms at the east end of the Cumberland apartments were overseen in early 1832 by Sydney Smirke (1798–1877), younger brother to Robert, towards the end of his brief tenure as clerk of works at St James's.[115]

4.22

Block plan of St James's, 2 July 1830, showing the extent of the palace and its occupiers at the onset of William IV's reign. The King's residence (Clarence House) is grey, Princess Augusta's apartment, orange; and Harrington House, black. The lease to the Earl of Harrington expired in 1831 and the house was demolished in 1838 (Sheppard 1894, pp. 49–50; TNA, WORK 1/23, fols 171–172). The plan is derived from the 1822 block plan proposals (see Fig. 4.2); it was partially updated, showing the new Clarence House. The Engine Court guard room is also shown because its proposed removal did not take place in 1822. But other areas were not corrected on this plan: the additional entrée staircase was built larger than shown, and the suttling house projecting into Cleveland Row is omitted, although its removal did not take place until 1840 (TNA, WORK 34/134; north is at the bottom)

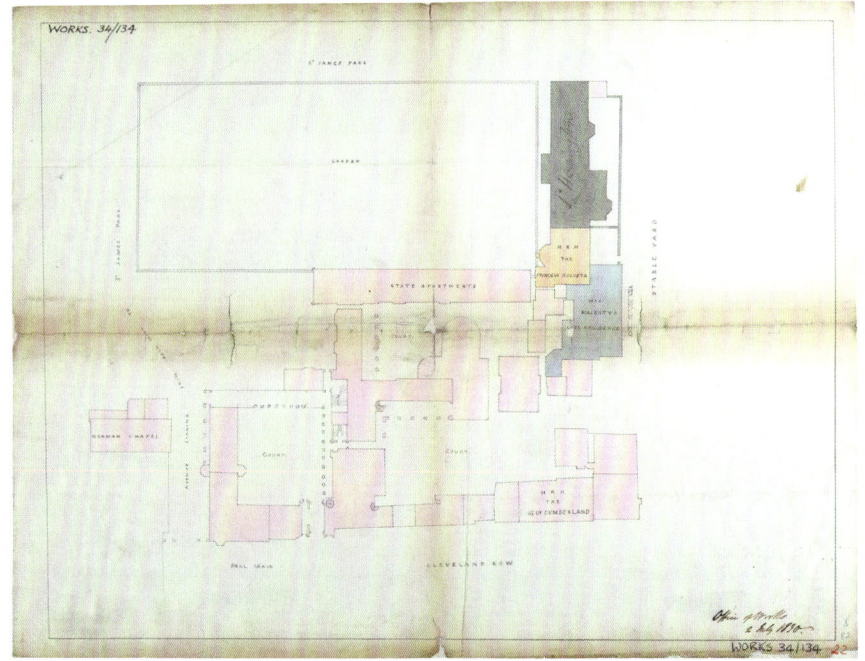

4.23

Sketch scheme for two southern wings and a corridor north (top) of the State Apartments, linking Marlborough House to the proposed Queen's apartments, partly drawn by William IV and annotated by Sir Jeffry Wyatville, 1 November 1834 (RCIN 929718)

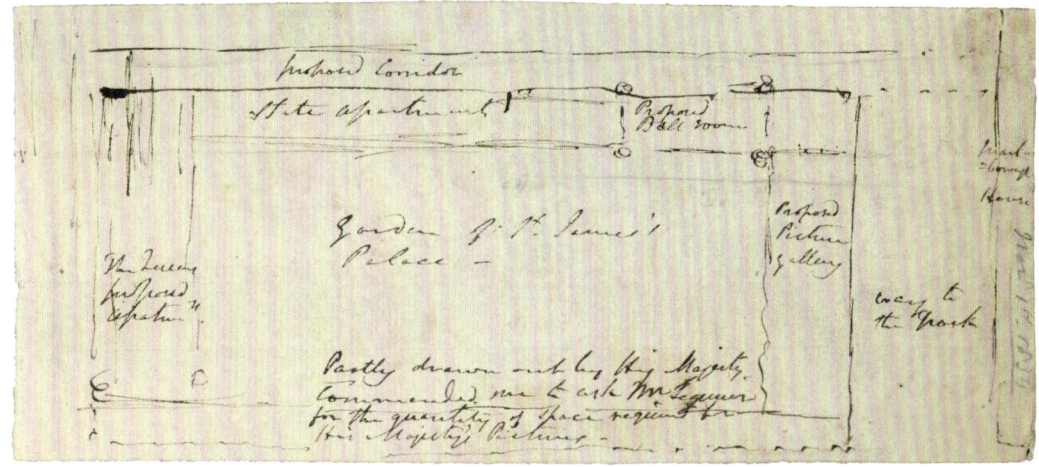

William IV, 1830–37

On 28 June 1830, William IV appeared at the window of the Presence Chamber (today's Tapestry Room), while in Friary Court below, Sir George Nayler (1764–1831), Garter King of Arms, proclaimed him King in front of the assembled crowd. This was the first time the accession had been proclaimed there, and the practice has continued ever since.[116] Buckingham Palace was incomplete and the work suspended.[117] Consequently, William IV remained at Clarence House when in London (Fig. 4.22), although he preferred to live at Windsor Castle. In order to improve internal circulation for the King, Sydney Smirke designed a modest first-floor link in 1830 between Clarence House and the State Apartments, which over-sailed the carpenter's shop (such was the jumble of buildings in this corner of the palace), and a hexagonal turret for the backstairs.[118]

In March 1831, William expressed little enthusiasm to move into Buckingham Palace, which, if completed, he hoped would be devoid of gilding.[119] Nevertheless, in August 1831, he approved the recommendation of a parliamentary select committee that work on Buckingham Palace should recommence under the direction of the architect Edward Blore (1787–1879; who had a reputation as 'the cheap architect').[120] At the same time, the majority of the committee members considered that there should be no further outlay on St James's Palace once Buckingham Palace was completed.[121]

In 1817, part of the Duke of Marlborough's lease on Marlborough House at the east side of the palace expired, and the building became the London home of George IV's daughter, Princess Charlotte, and her husband, Prince Leopold of Saxe-Coburg-Saalfeld. The Prince retained Marlborough House after Charlotte's death, but in July 1831, he accepted the kingship of the newly created state of Belgium.[122] The full lease on Marlborough House did not revert to the Crown until 1835; nevertheless, William IV considered that the vacant property could provide him and Queen Adelaide with spacious private apartments, directly linked to the St James's State Apartments by a new first-floor corridor.[123] In November 1831, William commissioned Sir Jeffry Wyatville (1766–1840), the architect then directing the extensive remodelling of Windsor Castle, to draw up proposals for an additional large ballroom east of the Queen Anne Room.[124] Further instructions were issued in April 1832, but that scheme was put on hold temporarily, although William continued to maintain that St James's should be 'the royal Residence of the King of England'.[125] Meanwhile, there was further public interest in improving the external appearance of the palace. In May 1834, Charles Gossett wrote to the Office of Works, commending the effect of Nash's brick Regent Street terraces, which were rendered with stone-coloured cement, and lobbying (unsuccessfully) for St James's Palace to be given the same

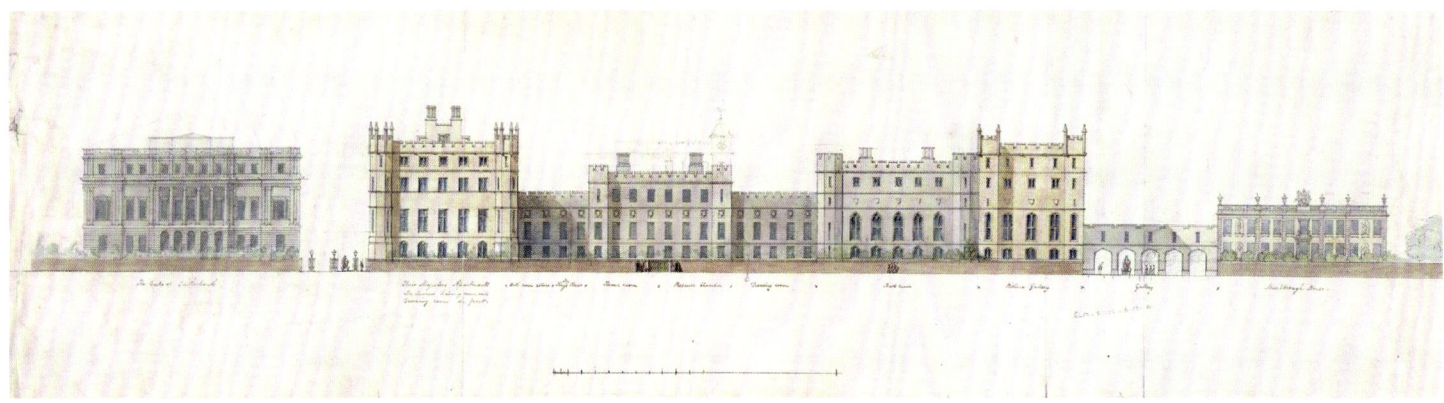

treatment or, preferably, to be faced with stone.¹²⁶ Wyatville initially worked on designs for a temporary corridor to link St James's with Marlborough House, at a cost of £1,200, but in July he forwarded drawings to the Office of Works for a permanent corridor at double the cost, on the basis of the King's wish to avoid needless expense on temporary works.¹²⁷

Following the destruction of the Palace of Westminster by fire in October 1834, St James's Palace was mooted as a temporary home for Parliament. But William IV wanted to make St James's work as a palace. He was also determined to avoid moving into Buckingham Palace, which he immediately offered as an alternative location for Parliament.¹²⁸ In November, the King instructed Wyatville to devise a much more ambitious scheme for St James's, apparently based on his own sketch for an additional southern range at the east end of Wyatville's proposed ballroom, to extend the full depth of the garden to form a picture gallery (Fig. 4.23). The intention was to balance the gallery with a larger wing on the west side, south of Clarence House, to contain the Queen's private apartments, with all the buildings encased with castellated Gothic detailing, creating the unifying effect Gossett had advocated (Fig. 4.24).¹²⁹ Wyatville's thorough reworking and heightening of the south range of the palace and the inclusion of a picture gallery builds on Sir Thomas Baring's suggestion to build a new St James's Palace, 'and unite with it a gallery for the reception of specimens of the fine arts at a small additional expense', aired during a House of Commons debate on Westminster public buildings on 1 March 1824.¹³⁰ That debate included the remark of Colonel Thomas Davies that 'St James's palace looked more like an almshouse than a kingly residence, and was a disgrace to the country'.¹³¹

Wyatville proposed a broad corridor immediately north of the State Apartments, to link the palace, via a gallery over an arcade, with the south-west corner of Marlborough House, where the King would reside.¹³² Wyatville considered it necessary to demolish part of the guard house in Engine Court, and drawings to convert the former Stable Yard stables into accommodation for the guard are related to the proposed demolitions.¹³³ In retrospect, given the problems the government had over Nash's financial mismanagement of Buckingham Palace, and the continued expense of Wyatville's work at Windsor Castle, it is hardly surprising that this grand vision for enlarging St James's never materialised, and the King continued to live more modestly in Clarence House throughout his reign. Wyatville only succeeded in achieving trifling internal alterations at St James's: a simple marble chimneypiece in the ground-floor Entrée Gallery on the south side of Colour Court and a rearrangement of the arms and armour in the Armoury.¹³⁴

A portion of the Chapel Royal ceiling, 'about a yard in diameter' (0.9 m), had fallen into an empty pew during the April 1817 Good Friday service, and the chapel was closed for repairs from August 1817 to February 1818.¹³⁵ When the 'highly decorated' chapel reopened, there

4.24
Sir Jeffry Wyatville, southern elevation of his proposed remodelling of St James's Palace to create a more dignified exterior, 1834. Labelled from left to right: The Earl of Sutherland, Their Majesties' Apartments, Ante Rooms, The King's Closet, Throne Room, Presence Chamber, Drawing Room, Ball Room, Picture Gallery, [first floor] Gallery, Marlborough House (RIBA, SB98/4)

4. GEORGE IV TO THE SECOND WORLD WAR   191

was criticism of the continued practice of charging strangers for admission, 'as if it were one of the public Theatres, with *half price* for *standing room*'.[136] The only service at which the public was admitted free was the annual feast of Epiphany on 6 January. Here, the sovereign was formerly conducted from the royal pew to make an offering of gold, frankincense and myrrh before the altar, but since the late eighteenth century this had been performed by gentlemen ushers.[137]

No works of any substance were carried out in the chapel during George IV's reign. In June 1824, the Lord Chamberlain's office sought an enlargement of the organ gallery above the sanctuary, but nothing was done.[138] But in June 1836, William IV met Benjamin Stephenson and Robert Smirke to discuss structural changes and an increase in accommodation.[139] The ground floor was refaced with brick by Smirke, the north elevation given a render coat of brown Roman cement (see Fig. 4.1, which suggests it may have also received a light wash of colour), and the roof entirely replaced, owing to the poor condition of the timbers.[140] Smirke was presumably concerned about the fragile Tudor ceiling hanging from his new beams, so he covered the new roof with copper instead of lead. The 1819 Thomas Elliott organ was removed, the wall blocked, and the organ loft relocated two bays further south to its current position, removing a Tudor window of two tiers and three lights. A new organ by Hill & Davidson was installed in 1838.[141] Smirke created additional west and east galleries, with a smaller choristers' gallery opposite the organ loft, formed by removing a considerable portion of the former Tudor walls. The Tudor ceiling was restored by the architect Charles James Richardson (1806–71), who reinstated the blue ground which had latterly been painted white (see Fig. 1.7), while for the ceiling over the new royal pew at the south, he imitated the pattern and ribs of the original ceiling, with panels painted incorporating similar grotesques, but dated 1837 and displaying devices and arms of William IV and Queen Adelaide.[142] Smirke marked the division between the two ceilings by a flat arch supported on angel corbels. The very top of the north window behind the altar was partly obscured by Smirke's new cornice, a solecism criticised at the time. Within the main body of the chapel, he lined the walls with tall oak panelling and added an enriched cornice at the original sill level of the former upper windows. He replaced the *c.*1700 box pews with lateral benches and oak fronts with Gothic detailing.[143] On 28 April 1837, William IV, the Archbishop of Canterbury and the Bishop of London (Dean of the Chapel Royal) visited the refurbished chapel and were received by the Lord Chamberlain, Benjamin Stephenson, Smirke and Joseph Morris, clerk of works since 1832. The first service was held on 21 May in the presence of Princess Augusta.[144]

William IV and Queen Adelaide made considerably more use of the State Apartments than had George IV. This was partly because the Queen hosted her own Drawing Rooms.[145] William's first levee after his accession was on Wednesday 21 July 1830.[146] The King held regular levees throughout his reign. In his first year, levees continued to 15 December. In 1831, from 23 February to 19 October, William generally travelled from Windsor to hold a punishing 33 levees over 35 weeks, a feat which must have reinforced his popularity. Thereafter, they were generally held from late February until late August or early September, totalling between 19 and 25 levees each year. His last levee was held on 17 May 1837, five weeks before he died.[147] From 1831 to 1836, William IV's birthday was celebrated on 28 May each year with a Drawing Room in the palace, held on his behalf by the Queen. But in 1837, the King was at Windsor and too ill to attend the Drawing Room, which this time was held on his behalf by his sister, Princess Augusta.[148]

On 24 May 1831, William IV and Queen Adelaide gave the first of an annual series of 'juvenile balls' in honour of the birthday of Princess Victoria, who was next in line to the throne, with a supper table in the banquet room laid for 260 guests, mostly junior members of the nobility.[149] The general arrangements mirrored those of state balls. The Court Circular's description for the 1832 ball is typical: Weippert's band played in the

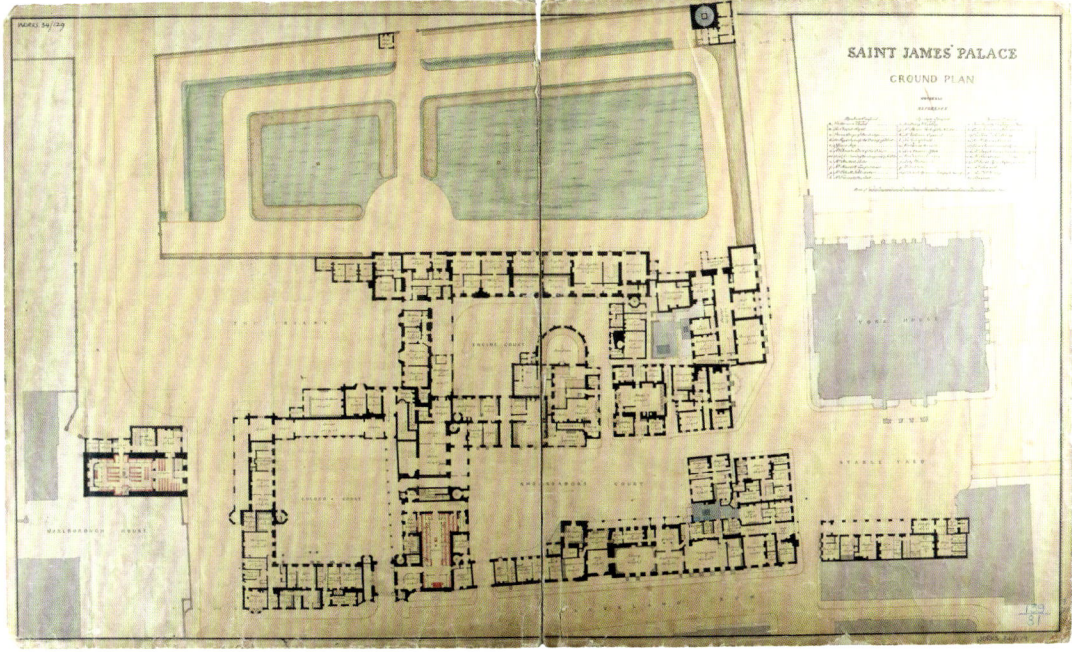

4.25
Ground-floor plan of St James's Palace, 1841. From this date, the Office of Works produced an intermittent series of detailed floor plans of the palace at a scale of 20 ft to 1 in. (1:240). The plan shows the extent of the palace, occupiers and room functions before the major changes that took place in Queen Victoria's reign (but after Harrington House at the west end of the garden and the suttling house in Cleveland Row had been demolished). A narrow enclosed colonnade ran along the south side of Colour Court, and circulation through the State Apartments remained as created for George IV; Soane's guards' building dominated Engine Court, and Clarence House was still as Nash had left it. Carriages accessing Stable Yard had to negotiate the narrow opening at the end of Cleveland Row. All this was to change during the Queen's long reign (TNA, WORK 34/129: north is at the bottom)

throne room, and that of Collinet and Musard in the ball rooms.[150] The floors were chalked, and raised seats were placed along the sides of the ballrooms. Refreshments were served in the portrait gallery, and a supper of fruit, pastry and confectionary commenced in the banquet room at 11pm. Galops were introduced 'and dancing was kept up with great spirit'. The Duchess of Kent and Princess Victoria left at midnight and the company dispersed.[151] The juvenile balls in May 1833 and June 1834 were similarly arranged, but with different music, including new Viennese waltzes, at both of which the young Princess 'was _very much_ amused'.[152] At the 1834 juvenile ball, a new quadrille was composed especially in honour of Princess Victoria, called the *Alexandrina* after her actual first name.[153]

Princess Victoria's 18th birthday on 20 May 1837 cemented her claim to the throne without the need for a regency. The ball given in her honour on 24 May was hosted by Princess Augusta, as the King was ill and unable to attend, and he and Queen Adelaide remained at Windsor.[154] A levee scheduled for 27 May 1837 was cancelled; the King's birthday Drawing Room on 29 May went ahead, but without him.[155] On 10 June 1837, the first in a series of sombre bulletins on the King's deteriorating health was posted in the Queen Anne Room. The Lord and Groom in Waiting were in attendance, and the Yeomen of the Guard lined the guard chamber and the portrait gallery. The public was admitted to the palace to read the bulletin and present their cards at the table.[156] The King died on 20 June, and preparations were immediately set in train to proclaim Victoria as the new Queen.

Queen Victoria, 1837–1901

Queen Victoria left Kensington Palace for Buckingham Palace on her succession, but the inadequacies of the palace became apparent following her marriage to Prince Albert in 1840, and the subsequent increase of her family. In January 1845, Edward Blore drew up plans for a new east wing to close the quadrangle.[157] In June, the aspiration for a new National Gallery to replace William Wilkins's inadequate building in Trafalgar Square was raised in Parliament.[158] A few days later, the Prime Minister, Robert Peel, in a memo to colleagues, suggested further enlarging Buckingham Palace to accommodate the Queen and court, and demolishing St James's (Fig. 4.25), which he

4.26

St James's Palace, proposed bow window to Ambassadors Court, 1890 (TNA, WORK 34/864)

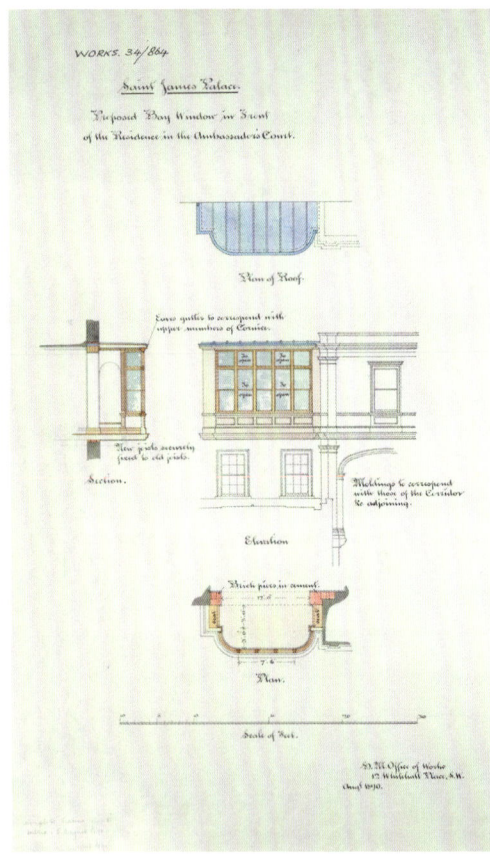

considered a 'blemish', to erect the proposed new gallery on its site.[159] Peel also argued:

> In times of public Excitement it would be much better that the Sovereign should hold the Levees &c at the Palace where she resides than that she should have to pass through an immense Concourse of People and to return on every occasion at which a Levee or Drawing room is held.[160]

But the plan was dropped following adverse comments from colleagues, particularly Henry Gouldburn, Chancellor of the Exchequer. The enlargement of Buckingham Palace was eventually authorised by John Russell's Whig administration in September 1846, and work dragged on until 1852.[161]

After William IV's death, Ernest, Duke of Cumberland, became King of Hanover, and his apartments formed the residence now known as York House on the north side of Ambassadors Court. The Queen expected her mother, the Duchess of Kent, to occupy them, but the Duke refused to give them up. Victoria, in consultation with Lord Melbourne (1779–1848), acknowledged it would be diplomatic not to turn him out; consequently, the apartment generally remained empty, and the Duchess initially rented a house in Belgrave Square.[162] The King of Hanover returned to St James's for three months in the summer of 1843, to attend the marriage of his niece, Princess Augusta of Cambridge (1822–1916), to the Grand Duke of Mecklenburg-Strelitz (1819–1904), in the Chapel Royal on 28 June. Relations with the Queen were strained, and seeking to assert his precedence over Prince Albert, he took the pen from her after she had signed the register and there was a tussle with the Prince, who managed to sign next.[163] Following the Duke's death in 1851, the Queen gained possession of his apartments. They were occupied the following year by the widowed Duchess of Cambridge (1797–1889), who remained there until her death in April 1889.[164]

Extensive alterations to the residence were then immediately undertaken by the Office of Works architect John Taylor: in addition to modernisation of services, an attic floor was added for servants' bedrooms; the ground floor was reclaimed from the robes office (which moved eastwards to the rooms within the blocked-up archway); a bow window was added overlooking Ambassadors Court (Fig. 4.26); and the north front to Cleveland Row was considerably altered.[165] The apartment was offered to Prince Eddy, Duke of Clarence and Avondale (1864–92; eldest son of Edward, Prince of Wales), and his fiancée, Princess Mary (May) of Teck (1867–1953). The couple began to plan its redecoration in December 1891, but Eddy died unexpectedly in January 1892.[166] May became engaged to his younger brother, Prince George, Duke of York, in May 1893, and the couple married in the Chapel Royal two months later.[167] The Duke and Duchess of York used the apartment as their London home (Figs 4.27 and 4.28). Now named York House, following the Duke's wishes, the house was always dark and the Duke did not like it: 'this is a beastly house and I think very unhealthy'.[168]

Clarence House was taken over by the Queen's unmarried aunt, Princess Augusta, in 1837. Her former house immediately to the south was demolished, along with the adjoining Harrington House (p. 162), and the ground was levelled to provide the south elevation with a garden.[169] The lodge on the west side of the road to Stable Yard was also demolished, and in 1838, Robert Smirke designed a new gate lodge (Fig. 4.29) on the east side, enveloping the remains of the redundant reservoir managed by the Chelsea Water Company, which had served the palace before mains water was laid on in 1824 (see p. 187).[170]

Following Augusta's death in 1840, the Queen's mother, the Duchess of Kent, moved into Clarence House. The Duchess undertook a number of alterations, totalling £1,400, including gilding by the younger Edward Wyatt (1787–1860), and a conservatory and entrance into the garden.[171] The Duchess continued to occupy Clarence House when in London, until her death at Frogmore in 1861. Alfred, Duke of Edinburgh (1844–1900), Queen Victoria's second son, was given Clarence House in 1866. He married the Grand Duchess Marie Alexandrovna (1853–1920), daughter of Tsar Alexander II, in 1874, and enlarged Clarence House at his own expense. The building firm Waller & Sons undertook the work, and the designs were produced in-house by Charles Bullen Waller.[172] The choice of a builder instead of an architect provoked some criticism, but Queen Victoria doubtless saw the firm as a safe pair of hands: Thomas Waller was confidential clerk to Thomas Cubitt (1788–1855), the trusted builder of Osborne House, who had worked closely with the Prince Consort; his son, Robert John (father of Charles), took over the Cubitt firm in 1856.[173] The former entrance portico on the west side was removed and the principal entrance repositioned on the south elevation, which was brought forward to line up with Nash's breakfast room, and widened to link with the State Apartments. This was essentially an enlargement, including an extra storey, and the principal details of the Nash elevations were retained, although Waller designed larger windows for the centre of the new south

4.27
Ambassadors Court, 1900, showing the recently refronted York House on the right (Birmingham Reference Library, Benjamin Stone Collection Box 144, Print 4)

4.28
The Danish court photographer Mary Steen (1856–1939) took this informal photograph of the Duke and Duchess of York with Prince Edward and Heather the collie in the first-floor sitting room of York House around 1895 (RCIN 2928619)

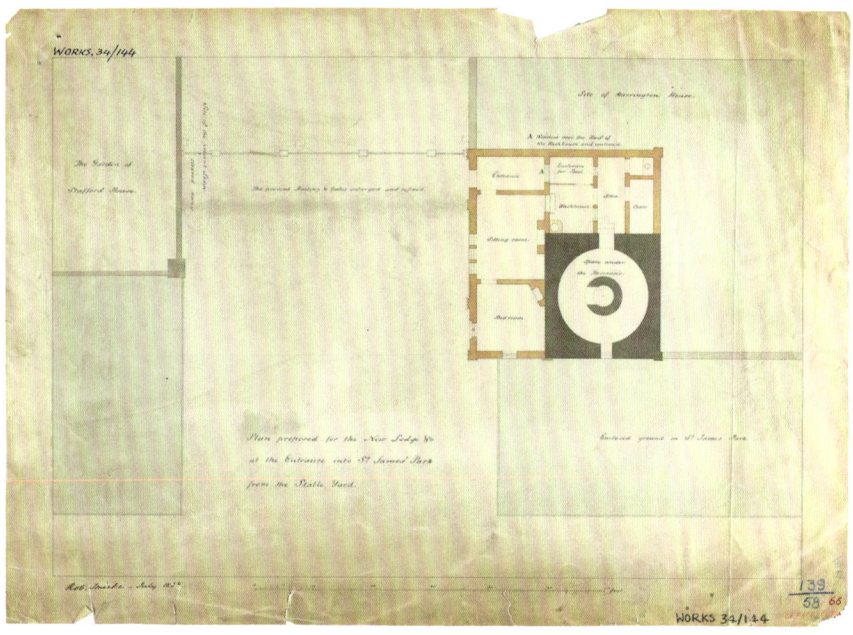

4.29
Stable Yard Lodge, built by Robert Smirke, 1838, embracing the redundant reservoir. The circular brick footings survive beneath the floor (TNA, WORK 34/144)

4.30
Clarence House, a painted and gilded niche within the former Russian Orthodox chapel. The stencilled decoration was preserved because the niche was converted into a cupboard after the Duke of Connaught was given the property in 1900 (Historic England Archive, BB88/05/99)

front.[174] The Duke was in command of HMS *Galatea* on two world cruises between 1867 and 1871, which may have influenced his eclectic choice of interior design.[175] Parts, including the dining room, were unchanged, but elsewhere, Alfred adopted an astonishing array of styles, including Old English, Japanese and 'Moorish', as well as a modest Russian Orthodox chapel for the Duchess on the first floor, where a priest and chanter officiated daily (Fig. 4.30).[176] The first-floor conservatory incorporated a salvaged black and white Roman mosaic of unknown provenance depicting a Triton, while the house was richly furnished with works of art garnered during the Duke's travels.[177] The couple moved to Germany in 1893, when Alfred's uncle, Duke Ernest of Saxe-Coburg and Gotha, died without an heir and Alfred inherited the dukedom. Alfred retained Clarence House, but rarely occupied it, and died almost bankrupt in Coburg in 1900.[178] The Duchess did not require Clarence House, which was then occupied by Alfred's younger brother, Arthur, Duke of Connaught (1850–1942; see p. 214).[179]

Dowager Queen Adelaide used Marlborough House as her London residence from 1838, following improvements, until her death in 1849.[180] In 1850, Marlborough House was settled on Edward, Prince of Wales, for when he reached 18. Meanwhile, the building was temporarily used to display several collections of works of art, including pictures presented to the nation by Robert Vernon, before their removal in 1856 to the newly built 'Brompton Boilers' in South Kensington – the predecessor of the Victoria and Albert Museum. Marlborough House was also temporarily the headquarters of the Government School of Design, with Professor Lyon Playfair, Henry Cole and Richard Redgrave.[181] A major attraction was the Duke of Wellington's bronze funeral carriage, which was displayed in the courtyard from 1852 until 1860, when it was removed to St Paul's Cathedral.[182]

Extensive internal and external alterations were carried out for the Prince of Wales by the Office of Works architect, James Pennethorne (1801–71), including a porte cochère and additional storeys. Pennethorne also fitted a new stable block on the constrained urban site, with a ramped access to first-floor stables, enabling carriages to be housed on the ground floor.[183] The Prince and Alexandra, Princess of Wales (1844–1925), took up residence in April 1863.[184] Their growing family necessitated extensions and additional storeys in 1870, 1874–5 and 1885, by Pennethorne's successor in the Office of Works, John Taylor.[185] The building gave its name to the Prince's high-living coterie, collectively known at the time as the 'Marlborough House set'.[186]

The Queen's Chapel had served the resident German congregation since 1700, and was known as the German chapel.[187] Dowager Queen Adelaide attended it in the 1830s and 1840s, preferring the simplicity of its Lutheran service to the Chapel Royal.[188] But in 1856, the chapel was very nearly demolished to make way for a new road. A parliamentary select committee was appointed to determine the best routes for connecting the growing development of Belgravia, south west of Buckingham Palace, with the rest of London.[189] Amongst the proposals was a link from Pall Mall to Buckingham Palace, in place of the narrow passage through Stable Yard. The committee eventually recommended a new north–south road, necessitating the demolition of the German chapel, at an estimated cost of £25,000.[190] In May, Pennethorne was instructed to make detailed measurements of the chapel to assist with its rebuilding.[191]

Funding for the new road was debated in the Commons on 6 June 1856. William Tite, MP for Bath, an architect and vice-president of the Royal Institute of British Architects, put up a spirited defence of the German chapel, 'which inside was one of the prettiest pieces of architecture in the kingdom [and] was built by Inigo Jones'.[192] Tite was something of an authority on Jones, and he had included the chapel among the 57 buildings in his 1854 composite bird's-eye watercolour *Composition of the Works of Inigo Jones*.[193] Tite suggested losing a strip of the palace garden, 40 ft (12.2 m) wide, which would push the road to the west, thereby saving the chapel. Moving the road further from Marlborough House,

4.31
J. Findlay (*fl.* 1825–57), view of St James's garden wall and the German chapel, *c.*1823–56. Like Fig. 4.32, this shows the gates and arcade added by George IV in 1823, but before the creation of Marlborough Road in 1856 (RCIN 926142)

4.32
J. Findlay, view of Marlborough Road depicting the alterations to the garden walls of Marlborough House and St James's Palace to accommodate the new road. The road surface was dressed with broken Aberdeen granite, giving it a red tinge. The scheme also included six cast-iron lamp posts and lanterns painted oil bronze-green, gates with dark bronze-green lead paint, and lead-coloured railings. A second storey on the north side of Friary Court housing the Yeomen of the Guard's apartments masks part of the gatehouse. John Phipps's arcade extension on the north side of Friary Court is not shown, which dates this view to 1856–63 (RCIN 926140)

4. GEORGE IV TO THE SECOND WORLD WAR

4.33

Henry Pether (1828–65), *Changing of the Guard at St James's Palace, London*. This painting captures the informality of the changing of the guard in the mid-nineteenth century. The guards' standard (the colour) from which the courtyard got its name ceased to be placed here after the daily changing of the guard was permanently moved to Friary Court in 1862, but the timber socket remains (Sheppard 1894, pp. 396–7, 429). Col. Charles Phipps, Keeper of the Privy Purse, lived in the far right-hand apartment, hidden by the projecting stair turret (Christie's, London, 13 Nov. 2019, lot 233)

already earmarked as the future residence of the Prince of Wales, was a further benefit. After a fierce debate, the funding was rejected by an overwhelming majority.[194] The Queen immediately offered to sacrifice part of the gardens of St James's Palace, to create a straight road and retain the German chapel (Figs 4.31 and 4.32).[195] Any extra cost was more than offset by the saving on dismantling and re-erecting the chapel. Pennethorne produced the specification for the new road, which was laid out by James Chadwick, and the walls were built by H. & R. Holland.[196] Pennethorne was also responsible for a new gatekeeper's lodge, wall and gates within the front court of Marlborough House, also by Holland.[197] The road was opened to the public in November 1856, and the following month, Benjamin Hall wrote confidentially to Charles Phipps (1801–66; Keeper of the Privy Purse and Prince Albert's private secretary, resident in St James's apartment 29, on the north-east corner of Colour Court; Fig. 4.33) of his misgivings over retaining the chapel: 'Everyone seems satisfied with the new roadway from Pall Mall and Equally dissatisfied with the "Gem of Art" which hides the view & causes various right angles'.[198]

With the chapel safeguarded, various works were carried out in the 1860s, including alterations to the pews and additional sleeping accommodation for Frederick Weber, organist and chapel keeper, achieved by inserting a mezzanine floor above the royal pew, which disfigured the Inigo Jones overmantel.[199] In the 1860s, a swell organ was placed on top of the Snetzler chamber organ from Buckingham Palace (given by William IV c.1830), and large pipes stacked against the side walls (Fig. 4.34).[200] This had the unfortunate effect of blocking off the light from the centre east window, as well as interfering with the original arrangement of the sanctuary.[201] From 1880, following the private intervention of the Princess of Wales, permission was given by the Bishop of London for Danish Lutheran services also to be held here.[202]

The Chapel Royal came to public prominence in 1840, with the marriage of Queen Victoria to Prince Albert before the Archbishop of Canterbury on 10 February (Fig. 4.35).[203] The extensive preparations within the chapel included enlarging the north window to increase the amount of light, by adding two two-light windows on either side of the

Tudor five-light window. All the pews were removed and banquettes substituted, with additional temporary galleries. Banked seating was constructed for spectators to watch the procession from the State Apartments and Colour Court.[204]

The Queen's huge procession numbered approximately 120, all of whom processed from the royal closet behind the Throne Room, through the State Apartments and into the chapel. A contemporary souvenir, *Spooner's Panoramic View of the Procession of Queen Victoria*, published in 1840, although inaccurate in detail, gives a good indication of the scale of the event: when unfolded, it measures 319 cm long.[205] It was a conscious decision of Queen Victoria not to wear robes, so as not to emphasise the difference in rank between her and Prince Albert. Instead, she wore a simple white satin court dress, entirely composed of materials of British manufacture, including Spitalfields silk satin trimmed with Honiton lace.[206]

In 1857, similar temporary alterations took place in and around the Chapel Royal, for the

4.34
The German chapel in 1920 (Historic England Archive, AL2481/017/01)

4.35
Sir George Hayter (1792–1871), *The Marriage of Queen Victoria, 10 February 1840*, 1840–42. Queen Victoria later thought the chapel 'too small'. Hayter has exaggerated its scale for effect (RCIN 407165)

4. GEORGE IV TO THE SECOND WORLD WAR

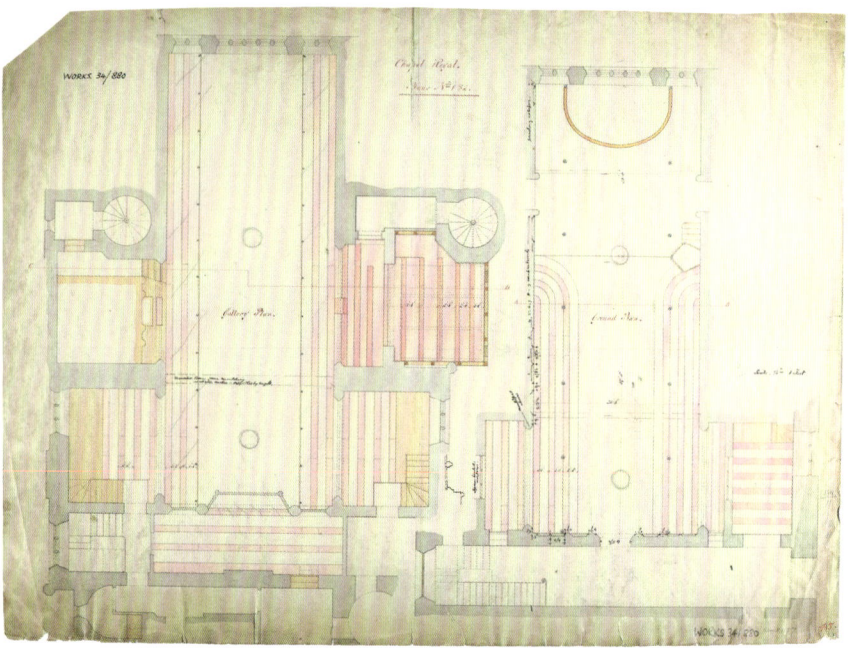

4.36

Plan of the Chapel Royal, St James's Palace, prepared for the wedding of the Princess Royal and Prince Frederick of Prussia (TNA, WORK 34/880)

marriage of Queen Victoria's eldest daughter, Victoria (1840–1901), to Prince Frederick of Prussia (1831–88) (Fig. 4.36).[207] The east window was further enlarged by adding a row of nine lights across the bottom of the existing ones.[208] The wedding took place on 25 January 1858.[209] *The Times* disparagingly described the palace as 'That dingy mausoleum of departed grandeur'.[210] On the wedding day, it stated that St James's compared unfavourably with 'the spacious courts and lofty ceilings of Continental palaces', but conceded, 'St James's is not so much a residence as a tradition'.[211]

In 1867–8, a new organ was installed and gas ceiling-mounted sunburner lanterns substituted for wax tapers.[212] Lateral wainscot pews and new oak seats were added in 1876.[213] The organ was augmented in 1890, and in 1891, the Queen returned to the Chapel Royal to act as sponsor at the christening of her great-granddaughter, Princess Alexandra (1891–1959), daughter of Princess Louise of Wales (1867–1931) and Alexander, Duke of Fife (1849–1912). Past associations with Prince Albert influenced Queen Victoria's thoughts and habits throughout her later life, and she noted in her Journal: 'I had not been in the ugly old Chapel, since Vicky's wedding 33 years ago!'[214] The Queen returned to the chapel for the last time for the wedding of the Duke of York to Princess Victoria Mary (known as May) of Teck in July 1893.[215] On both occasions, the Queen eschewed the royal pew where traditionally the monarch would have sat, instead sitting within the body of the chapel, close to the altar.[216] In 1893, she considered the chapel 'small and very ugly'.[217] As usual, the pews were removed and replaced with banquettes.[218] An innovation was the addition of two Flemish tapestries from the *Abraham* series, originally commissioned by Henry VIII for Hampton Court, which were mounted high on the wall either side of the chancel, where they remained until 1921.[219]

Queen Victoria discontinued juvenile balls at St James's Palace when her children were young and Buckingham Palace was more convenient for family celebrations.[220] St James's was increasingly eclipsed by Buckingham Palace as a venue, a trait which continued into the twentieth century (see p. 212). There were no other balls at St James's during Victoria's lifetime, although the formality of the birthday Drawing Room was generally held at the palace for the Queen around 24 May each year, up to 1860 (Fig. 4.37).[221] That ceremony was preceded by a reception of archbishops and bishops in the royal closet, where the Archbishop of Canterbury presented their loyal address, and the Queen responded. The birthday Drawing Room which followed was always one of the most well attended of the season, and often lasted two hours or more.[222]

Levees could also be long and tiring. Queen Victoria's first levee, a month after her accession, was exceptionally full, and she recorded it lasting two and a quarter hours and having her hand kissed nearly 3,000 times.[223] At the levee on 20 June 1838, there were 700 presentations in 1 hour 15 minutes, and 400 presentations on 1 July 1840, when the Queen sat on the throne for much of the time, although Prince Albert stood throughout. Between 200 and 250 presentations was more usual.[224] Particularly challenging were the levees in 1855, attended by officers returning from the Crimea, some severely wounded, but determined to be presented.[225]

4.37
Sir John Gilbert (1817–97), *The Queen receiving a birthday address from the Archbishops and Bishops, in the Royal Closet, St James's Palace, 25 May 1840* (RCIN 917241). Prior to Queen Victoria's reign this room was known as the King's Closet. David Morier's equestrian portrait of George II hangs behind the Queen and Prince Albert; the 'Buhl' writing table and inkstand were supplied for this room by Bailey & Sanders in 1824 (TNA, LC 10/16, fol. 43)

The State Apartments in St James's were redecorated for the first time since George IV's reign, in readiness for the Queen's Drawing Room on 25 March 1844. This mostly comprised regilding, and new soft furnishings, such as crimson silk damask curtains trimmed with gold fringe in the south front enfilade. As usual, the most elaborate work was in the Throne Room: as well as re-covering the state chair in crimson velvet, the walls were lined with rich crimson brocade. The sumptuous curtains and valances comprised an under-drapery of crimson silk velvet, overlain with the recently invented and highly prized *tissu de verre*, comprising gold-coloured glass fibre and silk interwoven with a repeating pattern of flowers, giving the effect in candlelight of lustrous embroidery on a light crimson ground.[226]

At Drawing Rooms, the ladies were ushered into successive rooms on the approach to the Throne Room, their passage controlled by barriers and gates (some of which remain) forming a series of pens, of which the arrangement in the Queen Anne Room was the most elaborate (see Fig. 4.7). All ladies kissed the Queen's hand, which was answered by a bow. The Queen also maintained the custom of kissing some ladies on the cheek. That practice seems to have fallen in abeyance when the Princess of Wales (who was not entitled to sit on the throne) began to hold Drawing Rooms on the Queen's behalf from 1863.[227]

Those attending Drawing Rooms and levees were required to leave their card three days before with the Lord Chamberlain's office. On the day, a second card was given to the page in the Tapestry Room, as described in 1835 and pictured in the *Illustrated London News* in 1847, or as Arthur Coxe recorded in 1856, 'depositing my card in the basket', from which the list of attendees was compiled for the Court Circular.[228] A third card was taken into the Throne Room, enabling the Lord Chamberlain to announce those being presented.

Between 8 March 1854 and 12 March 1857, the average attendance at St James's at each levee or Drawing Room was about 500.[229] Prince Albert held two levees on behalf of the Queen in February and March 1857, prior to the birth of Princess Beatrice (on 14 April). The first Drawing Room held by the Queen that year was 6 June, when the total attendance was 926, including 256 presentations. This was late: at this time, the London season normally lasted until the end of July, and the typically four or five levees and three or four Drawing

4. GEORGE IV TO THE SECOND WORLD WAR

4.38
Elevation of the proposed new staircase adjoining the Banqueting Room, *c*.1858 (TNA, WORK 34/142)

OPPOSITE

4.39
After Jeremiah Barrett (1814–1906), *A Drawing Room at St James's Palace* (engraving published in 1869 after an original painting of 1864). Barrett's painting may have been based on the Drawing Room of 19 June 1861, although the Prince of Wales's attendance was not recorded in the Court Circular (reported in *The Times*, 20 June 1861, p. 9); nor did Barrett choose to depict the Queen's black dress. Nevertheless, he includes the interesting detail of the Lord Chamberlain announcing those being presented before carelessly tossing their calling cards at a basket by his feet (RCIN 813910.1)

4.40
Part of the ground-floor plan of St James's Palace, 1869, showing the 1863 access improvements: the corridor on the south side of Colour Court doubled in width and the external arcade was extended around the south-east corner (TNA, WORK 34/1505; north is at the bottom)

4.41
The 1823 five-bay arcade opposite the German chapel, with John Phipps's 1863 extension running around the south end of the Tudor range into Friary Court. Photographed in 1896 (London Metropolitan Archives, SC/PHL/01/522/78/4557)

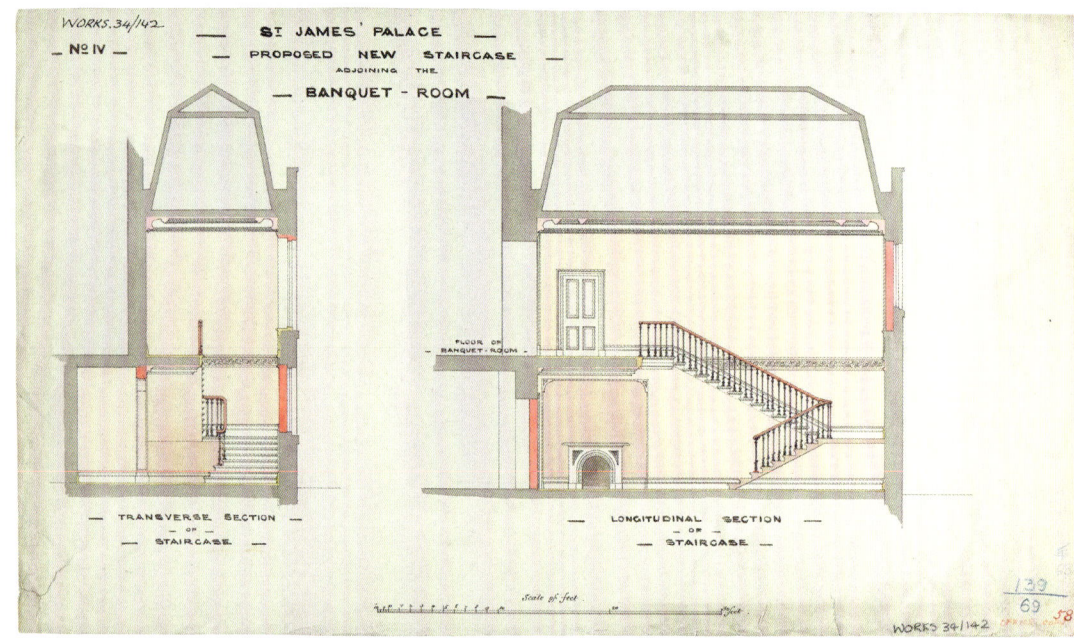

Rooms per year were over in the fourth week of June.[230] At the first levee held by the Queen, on 18 June, a total of 1,654 attended, with 625 presentations, which was the Queen's most highly attended levee apart from that on her accession.[231] A new arrangement was in place, abandoning the custom of issuing spectators with tickets in order to make space for those arriving, and a total of 500 seats were placed throughout the various rooms, and admittance restricted at any one time according to the number of seats available.

But when numbers were large, confusion arose when the general company were entering and leaving the Tapestry Room at the same time.[232] On 3 June 1856, the Chancellor of the Exchequer, George Cornewall Lewis, wrote to Colonel Phipps, suggesting improvements. Sir Benjamin Hall, the First Commissioner of Works, favoured 'a very large room in which possibly commoners & those not having the Entrée might congregate with a staircase up and a staircase down', and Prince Albert approved the initiative.[233] No funds were available, and the proposal was dropped the following year when Hall wrote to Phipps, stating, 'The announcement [in the Commons] that further accommodation would be provided for drawing rooms was ill received'.[234] But a partial solution was achieved by the removal of a furniture store at the west end of the Banqueting Room, to insert a new entrée staircase from Ambassadors Court (Fig. 4.38). This was opened for the first time on 23 February 1859.[235]

The new entrée staircase enabled each of the two grand stairs to be linked and used for one-way traffic for the general company, but this still left a bottleneck in the lower corridor. To alleviate this, an enlarged or double corridor was required, and the Office of Works architect, John Phipps, prepared an estimate in November 1861 to extend the Marlborough Road arcade by one bay further south, in order to access the ground-floor Yeomen of the Guard's room. The work was authorised by the Treasury, but deferred owing to the Prince Consort's death in December 1861.[236]

The Queen's final levee of 1861 was held on 14 March. Her mother, the Duchess of Kent, died two days later. The court was in full mourning from 16 March to 2 May, and there was no birthday Drawing Room that year.[237] The Prince Consort held two levees on behalf of the Queen, on 4 and 15 May.[238] The Queen did, however, hold two Drawing Rooms in June (Fig. 4.39). At the first, on 19 June, the requirement for all ladies to appear in

mourning dress was strictly enforced.²³⁹ The Queen wrote on that day: 'Lunched early, & dressed afterwards, of course in deep black. Alice & Bertie went with us to St James's Palace. He had never been to a Drawingroom before … All my ladies & those of the Corps Diplomatique, in mourning. It was stiflingly hot & the Drawingroom lasted full 2 hours. There were 215 presentations.'²⁴⁰

The death of the Prince Consort on 14 December 1861 effectively plunged Queen Victoria into mourning for the rest of her life. Her reclusiveness put an end for the time being to public engagements, and her Journal suggests that her occasional visits to the palace were private affairs to see family and friends.²⁴¹

The Queen did not attend any further Drawing Rooms or levees at St James's. None were held in 1862, but the following year, the Prince and Princess of Wales began holding them on the Queen's behalf. On 25 February 1863, there were more than 1,000 presentations at the Prince of Wales's first levee. About 2,000 attended, and such was the crush that the barriers were broken.²⁴² So great was the attendance that 'extreme discomfort' was experienced by visitors, and Spencer Ponsonby, Comptroller in the Lord Chamberlain's office wrote on 7 April, cautioning that an even

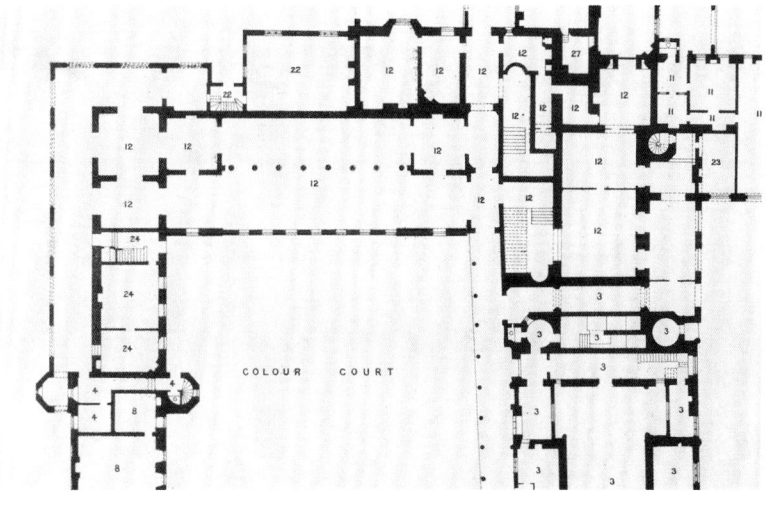

4. GEORGE IV TO THE SECOND WORLD WAR   203

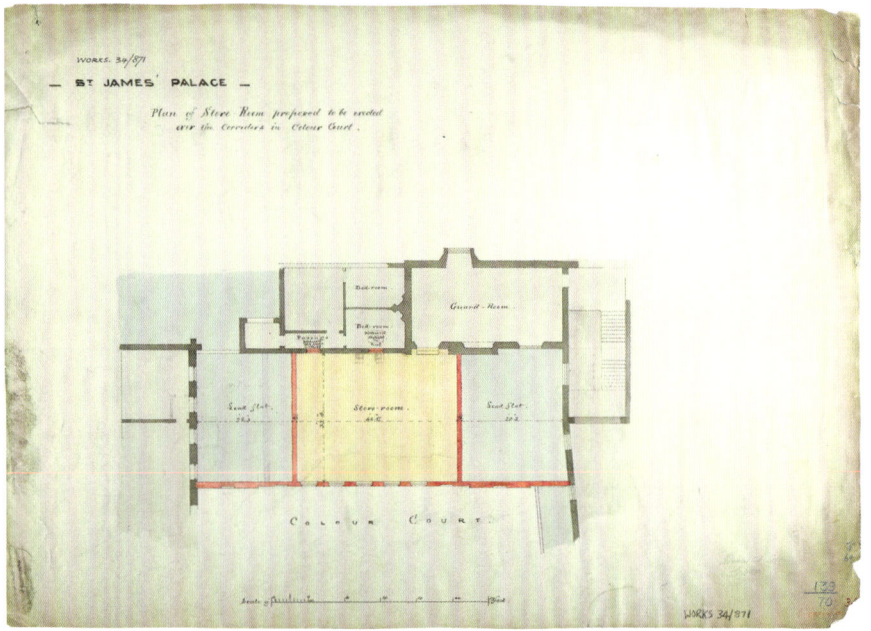

4.42
Plan of the first-floor addition for a storeroom above the entrée corridor, 1865–6 (TNA, WORK 34/871; north is at the bottom)

greater crush was expected for the newly married Princess of Wales's Drawing Room in May, when 'serious inconveniences' must be suffered by the ladies attending, occasioned chiefly by inadequate circulation space in the corridor south of Colour Court, where visitors arrived and departed.[243] Ponsonby emphasised the urgency of implementing Phipps's previously proposed corridor.[244] The Marlborough Road arcade was duly extended to wrap around the south end of the Tudor range (Figs 4.40 and 4.41); the 1795 colonnade on the south side of Colour Court was widened to form a new exit corridor, and an opening made at the foot of the former entrée stairs to access it.[245] Two years later, the corridor was topped by an additional storeroom (Fig. 4.42).[246]

The works were complete in time for the Princess of Wales's Drawing Room, held on 16 May 1863, which turned out to be as full as expected: some 2,200 visitors were recorded, excluding the court.[247] In 1864, Phipps enlarged the first-floor entrée passage between the Matted Hall and the ballroom, to help those with the right of entrée exiting the State Apartments. He took down the wall fronting Engine Court and rebuilt the outer wall on an arcade in Engine Court, doubling its width to about 33 ft (10.1 m), economically refixing the existing 1820s sash windows in the new wall.[248] The larger wall surface provided the opportunity to create a picture gallery with 16 paintings, mostly of successive monarchs associated with the palace from Henry VIII onwards, and also Henry, Prince of Wales. Paintings already in the palace were augmented by Richard Redgrave with copies, or others retrieved from Hampton Court.[249]

In December 1863, redecoration was proposed, but excluding the Tapestry Room, Armoury, Guard Room, Garden Entrance Hall, staircases and sundry waiting rooms. Tenders were approved from T. Tapling & Co. of Cheapside for 1,500 yards (1,372 m) of crimson Wilton carpet; Johnstone & Jeanes, New Bond Street, for 300 yards (274 m) of wide width brocatelle silk; and Holland & Sons, Mount Street off Berkeley Square, for 1,100 yards (1,006 m) of wide width damask silk.[250] Tapling was instructed to lay the carpets from 2 March 1864, in time for the first levee on 7 May.[251] In August 1864, William Cowper, First Commissioner of Works, in response to Queen Victoria's preference for amber, blue and red silk for the State Apartments, proposed to line the walls of the Throne Room with crimson silk, and the royal closet with blue, and to paper the other rooms on the south front on account of the recent increase in the cost of silk. Sir Thomas Biddulph reported that the Queen suggested the blue silk in the Drawing Room at Buckingham Palace was a very good colour, and that she hoped silk might be used for the remaining rooms another year. A request from the Queen to insert a lantern over the throne to provide more light proved impracticable due to the roof structure, and the matter was abandoned.[252]

Battle pictures were no longer considered appropriate for Drawing Rooms, and it was decided to relocate them to the Banqueting Room. This required removing the applied gilded mouldings on the walls.[253] It was last decorated in 1844, presumably in a colour similar to George IV's pearl, because when Richard Redgrave's opinion was sought regarding an appropriate colour, he suggested it should be darker, proposing a neutral green or purplish crimson, broken with citrine green.[254] John G. Crace, the leading interior decorating firm in the country, carried out the work in January 1865, incorporating green flock and gold wallpaper, gilt mouldings and a deep ornamental frieze, with the 'VR' motif in relief and a painted Garter motto, fixing gilt scrolls around the newly installed gas sunlight burners.[255] Presumably, Crace also reopened the upper tier of sash windows. Redgrave transferred eight large battle paintings to the Banqueting Room as part of a comprehensive rehang of the State Apartments: both Jones's paintings from the Throne Room and his *Battle of Waterloo with the Death of the Duke of Brunswick*; both Woottons from the ballroom, plus Armitage's *Battle of Meeanee* (which had been purchased by the Queen in 1847 and had been in store in Buckingham Palace); and Huggins's *Battle of Trafalgar*; as well as portraits of Charles II and William, Prince of Orange, by Kneller and Wissing respectively.[256] The Prince Consort had apparently been critical of the lack of pictures when he first saw the Banqueting Room, and it is entirely consistent with the Queen's lifelong desire to seek to implement what she thought the Prince would have wished.[257] The vacant spaces in the other state rooms were filled with portraits: 13 in the Queen Anne Room; retaining a naval theme in the Entrée Room with a copy of Shee's *William IV* (the 'sailor king') over the chimneypiece, accompanied by portraits of *Lord Nelson* and *Lord St Vincent* (both Hoppner), and *Admiral Barrington* and *Admiral Rodney* (both Reynolds); in the Throne Room, Lawrence's *George IV* was retained, flanked by copies of Winterhalter's *Queen Victoria* and *Prince Albert* (see Fig. 4.13).[258]

In 1865, the job of decorating the Guard Room was given not to Crace, but to the firm that would eventually eclipse Crace's pre-eminence: Morris, Marshall, Faulkner & Co.[259] The firm, founded in 1861, included William Morris, Philip Webb (1831–1915), Edward Burne Jones (1833–98), Ford Madox Brown (1821–93), and Dante Gabriel Rossetti (1828–82).[260] In Rossetti's words: 'We are not intending to compete with Crace's costly rubbish or anything of that sort, but to give real good taste at the price, if possible, of ordinary furniture'.[261] The establishment of the firm was a key event at the dawn of the Aesthetic Movement and brought about a revolution in interior decoration.[262] The St James's commission apparently came via Rossetti, who had been introduced to William Cowper, the First Commissioner of Works, by John Ruskin (1819–1900) in 1865, and who persuaded Cowper of the qualities of the firm.[263] The Guard Room was treated traditionally, with the ceiling and cornices partly gilt.[264] In 1866, the firm was commissioned to redecorate the Armoury and the Tapestry Room.[265] The architect Philip Webb was responsible for the design, and his notebook entries for August 1866 to January 1867 detail several visits to the palace for measuring and preparing patterns.[266] George Warrington Taylor, the company's forthright but short-lived business manager, remarked to Webb in 1866: 'Just remember we are embezzling public money now – what business has any palace to be decorated at all?'[267] Later, Taylor wrote to Rossetti:

> The large profit you had put before you was not made on stained glass, but on the Palace decorations. The whole of that work was done by Webb; if Webb had been busy with architecture, it could not have been done. You could never depend upon such work again. Moreover, Webb was miserably paid for his designs.[268]

Webb's approach in both rooms was to combine theories of medieval and early Renaissance polychromatic design, in covering surfaces with colour and pattern to create two intricate and sophisticated schemes; in the words of Morris's biographer, Fiona MacCarthy: 'almost overpoweringly Gothic and tenebrous, rich, dense and highly patterned'.[269] In the Armoury, Webb devised a tight, reticulated stencil pattern of gold and green on a very dark green ground – influenced, perhaps, by sixteenth- or seventeenth-century Italian silks brocaded with gold (Figs 4.43, 4.45 and 4.46). The cornice was similarly treated and the ceiling was covered with a stencil pattern. The chimneypiece

4.43
The Armoury in 1887 (Historic England Archive, BL08325)

4.44
The Tapestry Room, *c*.1900 (Birmingham Reference Library, Benjamin Stone Collection, Box 44, Print 32). A photograph taken in 1907 shows the stencilling painted out

was completely painted in a robust Tudor polychromatic manner. When the work was complete, in 1868, the Tower armouries installed a new arrangement of arms and armour.[270]

In the Tapestry Room (Figs 4.44, 4.47 and 4.48; see Fig. 1.1), Webb used a similar colour scheme for the dado and chimneypiece, but to a more open pattern, suggesting motifs found in the tapestry borders, and with a different stencilled design for the ceiling and cornice. In 1894, the palace's historian and Sub-Dean, Edgar Sheppard, who misdated the decorations, suggested a Portuguese source for this room: 'copied from designs in the Palace of Mafra, near Cintra'.[271] In undertaking this work, it is unlikely Webb adhered to any particular source. As Sir Nikolaus Pevsner wrote, in the context of Webb's Red House of 1858: 'Webb uses elements and motifs of the past, as they strike him suitable'.[272]

The only major addition to St James's at this time was the replacement of Soane's guards' accommodation in Engine Court, with a new

LEFT: ABOVE AND BELOW
4.45 and 4.46
The Armoury, details of Philip Webb's painted dado panelling, including dog-roses within a net-like pattern (top)

RIGHT: ABOVE AND BELOW
4.47 and 4.48
Webb's stencilled dado panels in the Tapestry Room (top), and a design incorporating stylised daisies which was used for the doors to the Tapestry Room and the Armoury (bottom)

building designed in 1876 by the architect John Taylor (Fig. 4.49). Nothing further of any substance was carried out in the remaining State Apartments until 1877, by which time they were looking tired and dirty.[273] In December 1877, and again in October 1878, the Lord Chamberlain's office requested £10,000 to redecorate; both times the Treasury refused.[274] The Queen wished the Princess of Wales to hold Drawing Rooms at St James's in March 1879 on her behalf, and in February, her private secretary, Henry Ponsonby (1825–95),

4.49
Plan for John Taylor's half-octagonal stock-brick Guard Room to retain the existing limited circulation space existing in Engine Court (TNA, WORK 34/899; north is at the bottom)

4.50
The Grand Staircase photographed by Bedford Lemere in 1889, decorated with the 'St James's' wallpaper printed by Morris & Co. in 1881 (Historic England Archive, BL09442)

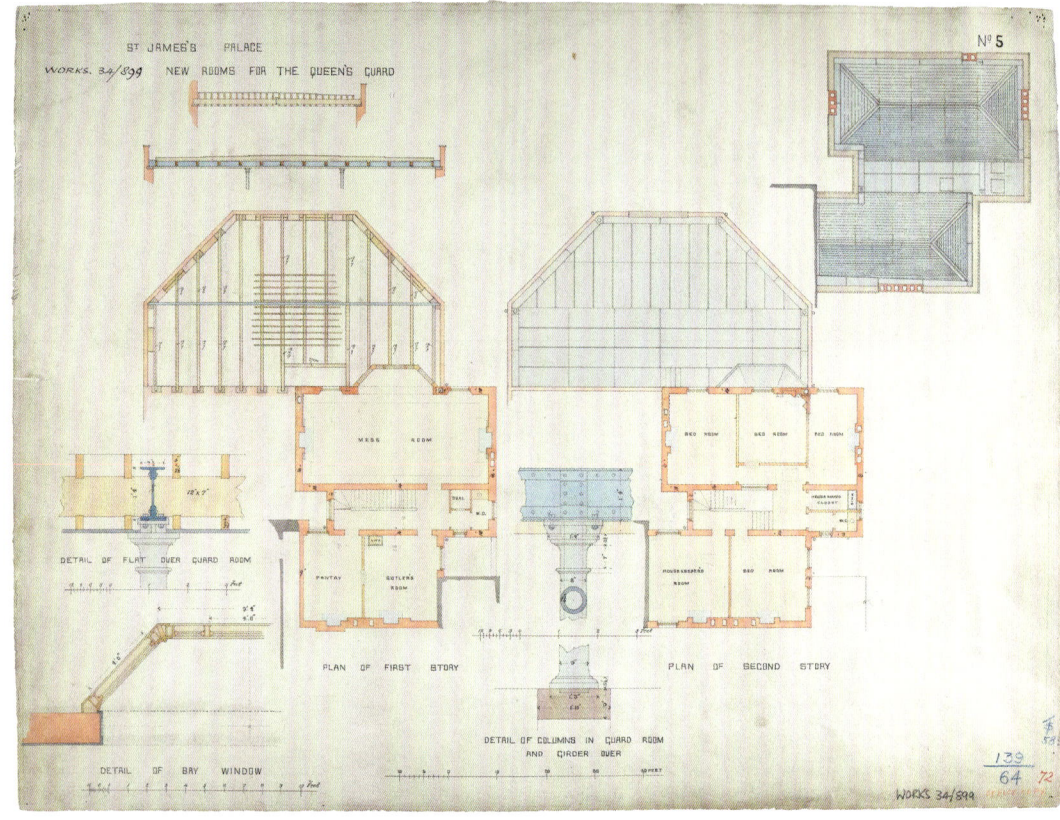

complained to the Lord Chamberlain, the Marquess of Hertford (1812–84), that the palace was unfit for court purposes.[275] Hertford concurred, but there was no time to work before the March Drawing Rooms. On 22 March, the Office of Works accordingly requested the Treasury to agree to a staged programme of repairs: £1,800 for new carpets for the next year, £5,000 for 1880–81, for repairs to approaches to state rooms and the Queen's robing room (the Council Room), and £5,000 for 1881–2, for the Throne Room and other state rooms; £3,600 was also required for curtains.[276]

New carpets were required for the Armoury and Tapestry Room, and Morris & Co. (in Morris's sole ownership since 1875) was consulted regarding the pattern, on the basis of the firm's previous involvement.[277] Morris advised a bespoke handwoven Axminster, but the Office of Works insisted on machine-woven on the grounds of economy, and Morris's popular 1875 design, incorporating acanthus leaves and peonies, with a poppy and chrysanthemum border, was used for the carpets and rugs in both rooms. They were laid in March 1880 and survived in the State Apartments for more than a hundred years.[278]

Morris was also responsible for the succeeding phased repairs and redecoration. This time, Webb was not involved. Morris was by now the pre-eminent flat-pattern designer, and his approach to redecoration was very different from Webb's painted work, although throughout, Morris introduced sophisticated colouring – especially with wall and ceiling papers, most of which he designed.[279] In 1880–81, work was carried out on the approaches to the State Apartments: the visitors' entrance (lower corridor), Grand Staircase, Garden Entrance and Ambassadors' Stairs. In the visitors' and Ambassadors' Entrances, Morris altered the large sheet glass in the windows and doors into smaller panes with mouldings, to conform with older details found elsewhere in the palace, and in the visitors' entrance, new gas brackets were supplied to the firm's design, a new dado rail added, the joinery painted a 'dark colour', and the walls decorated with a boldly designed paper.[280] The Grand Staircase

ABOVE

4.51

The Queen's, or Sovereign's Stairs, decorated by Morris & Co. in 1881, and photographed in 1900 (Birmingham Reference Library, Benjamin Stone Collection, Box 144, Print 36)

LEFT

4.52

Sample of William Morris's 'St James's' paper, 1881 (V&A, E.2862-1980)

RIGHT

4.53

Sample of William Morris's 'St James's' ceiling paper, 1881, printed in a single colourway as used in the Grand Staircase and the Banqueting Room (V&A, E.594-1919)

4. GEORGE IV TO THE SECOND WORLD WAR

On the upper parts of the Grand Staircase walls and on the Queen's stairs, Morris used his 'St James's' wallpaper and its companion ceiling paper (Figs 4.51–4.53), both specially designed for this commission. This was the largest and most ostentatious design produced by the firm: a repeat of 47 by 44 in. (119.4 by 111.8 cm), covering two widths to make one repeat and requiring 70 wood blocks.[283] The Grand Staircase scheme was complemented by a series of mostly seventeenth- and eighteenth-century royal portraits, transferred from Hampton Court in July 1881 and hung in the upper corridor.[284]

In 1881, it was proposed to adapt the existing turret clock facing St James's Street (Fig. 4.54) to illuminate the dial. But the clock was found to be beyond repair; the following year it was replaced with a new mechanism, and a cast-iron dial, 7 ft 9 in. (236.2 cm) diameter, with blue figures and glazed with opal glass, which could be illuminated at night by gas.[285]

In 1881, William Morris turned to the internal decoration of the south range of State Apartments. Stencilled patterns were painted on the ceiling coves – part of the floral design in green, red and amber survives behind the cornice in the Queen Anne Room – and the woodwork painted flat white and regilded.[286] In the Queen Anne Room, Morris took down, cleaned and rehung the existing yellow silk damask as an economy measure (see Fig. 4.7).[287] In the Entrée and Throne Rooms, he devised alternative designs for a jacquard loom crimson silk damask: 'St James's' (the chosen design) and 'Oak'.[288] The Throne Room was the most elaborately decorated of the state rooms. The flat of the ceiling incorporated a repeating stencilled pattern (see Fig. 4.13). Morris also removed the velvet background to the panels over the chimneypiece attributed to Gibbons, and replaced it with canvas gilded and tinted with a tessellated pattern.[289] The Council Chamber similarly had new silk, but the joinery was painted blue and gilded, reflecting its alternative name: the Blue Room. The Boudoir beyond was not part of the public State Apartments, and was papered with the Morris 1877 'Chrysanthemum' design,

4.54
St James's Palace from St James's Street in 1896. The lowest set of windows in the Chapel Royal (to the right) were added for the wedding of the Princess Royal in 1858 (London Metropolitan Archives, SC/PHL/01/522/70/10417)

4.55
The Guard Room, photographed in 1900 and showing Morris's simple decoration (Birmingham Reference Library, Benjamin Stone Collection, Box 144, Print 39)

(Fig. 4.50) was recast 'in the Holbein style': a new dado rail was introduced, below which Morris hung an embossed and gilded paper, printed by Jeffrey & Co., featuring the 'Peacock and Armorini' design by Walter Crane (1845–1915) which had won a gold medal at the Paris exhibition of 1878.[281] Morris combined this with stencilled decoration within the arches, which was carried out by the decorative artist, David Parr (1854/5–1927), who was employed by F.R. Leach & Sons of Cambridge.[282]

210   ST JAMES'S PALACE

elaborately embossed, gilt and lacquered to give the appearance of stamped and gilt Spanish leather.[290] The Guard Room was plainly painted by Morris in 1881, with olive green panelling and dark red canvas wall lining (Fig. 4.55).[291]

The Waterloo, or Banqueting Room, was the largest room in the palace, and the 'St James's' wall and ceiling paper was again used there.[292] The ceiling retained the elaborate 1820s ceiling vents and the gas sunburners with their Crace borders. Here, the room's scale, and the large military paintings hung on the walls, inspired Morris to paint the joinery cinnamon red, highlighted with gilding (Fig. 4.56; see also Fig. 4.16).[293]

The woodwork in the Matted Hall was painted flat white and gilt, with the walls papered with Morris & Co. 'Mallow', designed by Kate Faulkner, expensively printed gilt on a cream ground instead of the usual blue (Fig. 4.57).[294] Some of the original paper also survives elsewhere beneath later paint.[295] The scheme in the Picture Gallery, or Ambassadors' Room, was less inspired: a new chimneypiece and mirrored overmantel were added, together with a dado 5 ft (1.5 m) high. The flock paper was removed, and silk from the Throne and Entrée Rooms was dyed red and rehung, with the joins concealed by the picture-hang. Curtains from the Throne and Entrée Rooms were also reused for this room.[296]

The final works carried out by Morris comprised new silk curtains and linings with elaborate valances in the Throne, Entrée and Council Rooms.[297] But budgetary constraints imposed by the Office of Works forced Morris to compromise on materials by reducing the amount of silk passmanterie and modifying the valances, and also substituting merino wool linings for satin, except at the inner edges (which, Morris noted, had been done previously).[298] The final total cost for the project on completion in 1882 was around £12,500, and was nevertheless highly profitable for the firm.[299]

On 20 July 1897, the Prince of Wales hosted a dinner in the Banqueting Room to celebrate his appointment as Grand Master of the Order of the Bath. The Court Circular recorded:

4.56

The Banqueting Room, photographed in 1907 (London Metropolitan Archives, SC/PHL/01/522/81/8822)

4.57

Kate Faulkner's (1841–98) blue 'Mallow' wallpaper (1879) was used in secondary circulation areas, for example between the Council Room and the Boudoir (V&A, E.811-1915)

4. GEORGE IV TO THE SECOND WORLD WAR

4.58

Messrs Dickinson, *A Levée at St James's Palace*, c.1905. The interior of the Throne Room is crowded with guests and royal officials; the King stands in the foreground, with the Prince of Wales (later King George V) to the left, and Prince Charles of Denmark (later King Haakon VII of Norway) to his left. His Majesty's Body Guard of The Honourable Corps of Gentlemen at Arms stands in the centre of the room and also guards the doors into the Throne Room (RCIN 407149)

'Afterwards a special exhibition of the American Biograph was given by Mr Koopman'.[300] This was a notable event in the history of British cinematography: a showing before members of the royal family by Elias Koopman, one of the founders of the American Mutoscope and Biograph Company, of its 68-mm format film of Queen Victoria's Diamond Jubilee procession the previous month, along with footage of the review of the fleet at Spithead on 26 June before the Prince of Wales, and the military Jubilee Review at Aldershot on 1 July.[301] A private viewing of all three films had been held on the lawn at Clarence House on 8 July, in front of the Duke and Duchess of Saxe-Coburg and Gotha and other members of the royal family.[302] That same month, the company recorded *Afternoon Tea in the Garden of Clarence House*, informally capturing three generations of the royal family, including the Prince of Wales and the future King George V (r. 1910–36).[303] The company's initiative at St James's appears to have been a deliberate and successful attempt to court royalty, and they filmed many events during King Edward VII's reign.

Edward VII, 1901–10

The King held his Accession Council in the palace on 23 January 1901, when ministers formally surrendered their office and were then reappointed. The ceremony was very much like a levee, and all present went through the ceremony of kissing hands.[304] Edward was proclaimed King in Friary Court the following day.[305] The court was in mourning for a whole year, so no levees were held in 1901.[306] At the commencement of King Edward VII's reign, the Lord Chamberlain's Office was connected to the government telephone system, but the palace was still lit by gas, for in 1902 little more than the State Apartments had electric lighting.[307] In March 1902, the King and Queen Alexandra finally moved from Marlborough House to Buckingham Palace.[308] Five levees took place in St James's Palace that year, and generally, three or four took place per year. But the King signalled the further marginalisation of St James's by the court in the twentieth century by replacing the St James's Drawing Rooms with evening courts in Buckingham Palace, attended by Their Majesties.[309]

Between 1902 and 1904, C.H. Bessant of Bertram & Son redecorated a number of state rooms and corridors in Buckingham Palace. As part of a general shift in taste away from Victorian polychromatic schemes, ceilings and walls were painted white, the latter often embellished with carved and gilded woodwork, reflecting the King's French taste.[310] The state rooms in St James's Palace had not been comprehensively redecorated since Morris in the 1880s, and in May 1904, J.B. Wescott, architect in the Office of Works, issued a specification for a white and gold colour scheme (apart from the three rooms surviving from the Tudor palace).[311] Bertram & Son failed to secure this commission; the lowest tenderer was White Allom & Co., a well-established firm of upholsterers, cabinet-makers and decorators, founded in Mayfair *c*.1894 by George White, Charles Carrick Allom (1865–1947) and Sydney Herbert Donaldson.[312] Allom described himself as a 'decorative artist', and criticised the St James's staircase columns and 'clumsy bases'. In the Banqueting Room, he recognised similarities with Wren doorcases in the Cartoon Gallery at Hampton Court, and suggested introducing similar panelling as there.[313] Allom ended by apologising for his criticisms, stating 'it is much more important to save the fine work in such Palaces, than the securing of contracts such as this, which it is always an honor [*sic*] to carry out, and from which I have not the slightest desire to make any money'. In a 'P.S.', he enclosed Henry Tanner's 1902 *English Interior Woodwork of the XVI, XVII & XVIIIth Centuries*, illustrating mouldings in the King's Gallery at Hampton Court.[314]

Allom considered that the paintings unnecessarily dominated the Banqueting Room and proposed high panelling to raise them, but his scheme was not adopted and the room was omitted from White Allom's final estimate, possibly because of cost and because the continued dominance of the paintings was precisely the effect required by Lionel Cust (1859–1929), Surveyor of the King's Pictures.[315] In the main rooms, Allom was instructed to retain the existing silk wall coverings and curtains, refresh the Morris scheme of white and gold woodwork, but to overpaint the stencilled ceilings while retaining gilding. The result is shown in the Dickinson painting of *c*.1905 (Fig. 4.58).

Allom's major architectural interventions focused on the two staircases. He completely transformed the Grand Staircase (Fig. 4.59), removing Hunt's 1820s columns and bases and Morris's flamboyant paper and stencilling. He introduced double-fluted Ionic columns on the half-landing, a new arch and cornice, and extensive fibrous plaster enrichments and trophies to the ceiling in the style of Louis XVI, retaining the 1820s dentilled cornice, but adding a new plaster pulvinated frieze below, new architraves to the windows and Armoury door, and enriching the four corridor arches with iron handrails, and adopting the white and gold used in the other state rooms.

The Sovereign's Stairs were similarly transformed, with the Morris paper removed and enriched mouldings added to the ceiling, walls and skirting. The mahogany handrail was retained, but the timber balustrade was replaced with wrought-iron in the style of

4.59
The Grand Staircase looking south, as altered by White Allom

4. GEORGE IV TO THE SECOND WORLD WAR 213

4.60
Sovereign's Stairs, as altered by White Allom. The Office of Works' specification for decorating the new balustrade included 'gilding all the usual parts' (TNA, WORK 19/132)

William Kent, and the walls and ceiling painted white and gold (Fig. 4.60). All the redecoration was completed before the first levee of 1905 on 9 March.[316]

The Picture Gallery was the least successful of Morris's 1880s decorations (Fig. 4.61). Here, White Allom's work was limited to washing and touching up the woodwork, and distempering the ceiling and cornice.[317] In November 1908, proposals were in hand to replace the Morris chimneypiece in the Picture Gallery with a new chimneypiece 'in the Tudor style', in spite of the fact that the room was entirely a creation of the nineteenth century. Cust drew attention to the 'fine Elizabethan Chimney-Piece' of 1565–7, originally from the first-floor Court of Equity, known as Queen Elizabeth's Chamber in the old Palace of Westminster (only the right-hand half is original), but which had recently been inserted as a dummy in the Queen's Closet, Kensington Palace. The Office of Works adopted Cust's suggestion that this genuine chimneypiece would be preferable to the expense of making an imitation, to which they added a new, and somewhat overbearing, timber Jacobethan overmantel.[318]

The arms and armour were rearranged between 1900 and 1907 (Fig. 4.62), with the arms above the chimneypiece altered to make Wyatt's 1820s bronzed bracket more visible. Guy Francis Laking was presumably responsible for the new scheme. Laking, a leading expert in the decorative arts and 'art adviser' at Christie's, was appointed Honorary Inspector of the Armouries at the Wallace Collection in 1900, and in January 1902, Edward VII created for him the post of Keeper of the King's Armoury at Windsor.[319] The nineteenth-century Gothic revival brass chandelier also appeared at this time, hung from the central ceiling rose (Fig. 4.63). It is modelled on German or Netherlandish chandeliers of *c*.1480, such as that formerly at Temple Church, Bristol, which has a Virgin and Child with St George beneath. Appropriately for the Armoury, the chandelier incorporates an armoured St George and slain dragon, but without the Virgin and Child.[320]

The Duke and Duchess of Connaught moved to Clarence House from their apartments in Buckingham Palace in 1902, while the Duke and Duchess of York (created Prince and Princess of Wales in November 1901) moved into Marlborough House in April 1903.[321] The weekly German Lutheran service was discontinued in the 'German chapel' after 21 July 1901, although Danish Lutheran services continued. Thereafter, it was known as the Marlborough House chapel, and the adjoining apartments in the south wing, formerly occupied by the organist and keeper Frederick Weber, became the official residence of the Sub-Dean of the Chapel Royal, the Revd Edgar Sheppard.[322] York House was not permanently occupied, but served as additional accommodation for the King when required, for example, by the French presidents Loubet and Fallières during their visits, in 1903 and 1908 respectively.[323]

George V, 1910–36

York House remained available as guest accommodation at the beginning of King George V's reign, and in 1911 it was prepared for the Crown Prince and Crown Princess of Romania, who attended the King's coronation.[324] The complete installation of electric lighting throughout the palace was agreed after the fall of a gas chandelier, which fortunately did not catch fire. Even so, the installation was not fully achieved until after 1913.[325] Proximity to Whitehall meant St James's was a convenient venue for international conferences. In 1912–13, the State Apartments hosted the first Balkan Peace Conference, attended by delegates from the warring parties, whose arrangements were

TOP

4.61

The Picture Gallery in 1938. The tall dado panelling was installed by Morris & Co. in the 1880s, but the chimneypiece and overmantel were inserted by the Office of Works in 1908. By 1938, picture lighting had also been installed (Historic England Archive, P/G04399/010)

ABOVE

4.62

The Armoury, 1907 (London Metropolitan Archives, SC/PHL/01/522/5011)

LEFT

4.63

The St George chandelier in the Armoury, installed under the supervision of Guy Francis Laking in c.1907

4. GEORGE IV TO THE SECOND WORLD WAR

4.64
The King's proclamation of peace following the signing of the Treaty of Versailles, read in Friary Court, St James's Palace, before an enthusiastic crowd on 2 July 1919

overseen by Percy Armytage, a gentleman usher in the Lord Chamberlain's office at St James's. The resultant Treaty of London was signed there on 30 May 1913.[326]

On the outbreak of the First World War in 1914, valuable works of art were removed to the safety of the cellars, and in 1915 a number were transferred to the National Gallery.[327] York House was appropriated in 1915 as a London residence for Lord Kitchener, Secretary of State for War, until his death in June 1916.[328] Two charities headed by Queen Mary and the Prince of Wales, relating to the war, were based in the palace.[329]

The Treaty of Versailles was signed on 28 June 1919,[330] and at 11.30am on 2 July, the Garter King of Arms (Sir Henry Burke, 1859–1930) read the King's proclamation of peace, accompanied by the Welsh Guards, in Friary Court (Fig. 4.64).[331]

With the return of peace, the King resumed holding levees at St James's in 1919. In 1920, the Ambassadors' Stairs was improved with panelling, plus an impressive giltwood and gesso chandelier designed by the Office of Works.[332] But circulation at state functions had still not been fully resolved after more than a hundred years of alterations. Congestion at the end of a levee prompted a request in May 1929 to enlarge the lobby at the foot of the Ambassadors' Stairs, including the conversion of two windows facing Ambassadors Court into doors (Fig. 4.65). It was completed by June 1931.[333]

INTERNATIONAL DIPLOMACY

In March 1921, St James's and Lancaster House formed the joint venue for the London Conference, which aimed to address Germany's default against the terms of the Treaty of Versailles.[334] Armytage was again responsible for the domestic arrangements.[335] On 30 August 1924, the London Agreement was signed at St James's Palace, which committed the French to evacuate the Ruhr.[336] Other significant inter-war conferences in the State Apartments included the London Naval Conference, held in April 1930, and two Indian Round Table Conferences in 1930 and 1931 (Fig. 4.66).[337] Mahatma Gandhi refused to attend the first conference, although he did attend the second (Fig. 4.67). His visit to the impoverished East End of London was celebrated in the media at the time, but the conference was a failure, as it proved impossible to reach an understanding between the various parties.[338]

By this time, a tried and tested arrangement of accommodation had been devised, with minor variations, to suit the circumstances of individual conferences. A plan produced for the 1936 League of Nations Council Meeting (Fig. 4.68) shows the Queen Anne Room set aside for the Public Council Room, and taking advantage of the hierarchical plan of the State Apartments to create a suite of increasingly secure rooms moving westwards: Public Council Room (Drawing or Entrée), Secret Council Room (Throne Room) and Secretaries' Room (Council Chamber), culminating at the extreme east end in the Secretary General's Room (Boudoir). Translators were housed in the adjacent Picture Gallery, and typists producing conference material in the Banqueting Room. The press occupied the

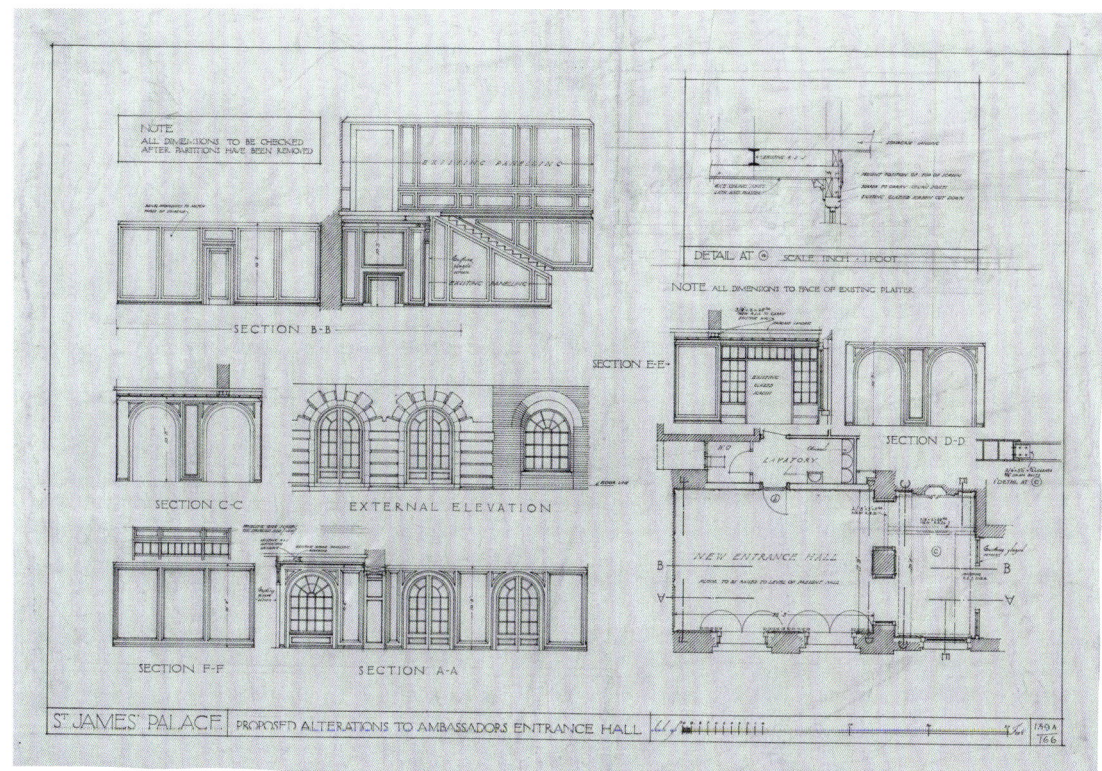

4.65
Proposed alterations to the Ambassadors' Entrance Hall, c.1930 (Historic England Archive, MA/JPL0004)

4.66
Albani Roy, *St James's Palace, Indian Round Table Conference, November 1930*. Roy was given permission to illustrate the conference on the recommendation of H.S. Ede at the Tate Gallery. The engraving captures Prime Minister Ramsay Macdonald addressing the assembly in the Queen Anne Room. Roy helpfully provided a key to identify the 86 delegates he portrayed in deep chiaroscuro (RCIN 751077.a)

Tapestry Room and Armoury, listening to the debates relayed via loudspeakers, with the Guard Room converted into a telegraph cable room, with newspaper direct-line telephones beyond. The press was supplied with a further cable room and telephones in the lower corridor.[339]

The palace was also used intermittently as a venue for a variety of committee meetings, such as that of the Mint Advisory Committee, which met in the Tapestry Room in 1936 to determine the design of King Edward VIII's proposed (but unissued) coinage.[340]

In 1926, King George V commissioned the 72-year-old Alfred Gilbert (1854–1934) to create a memorial to Queen Alexandra, which became a deeply personal tribute to the artist's former patron and friend. It is imbued with Christian imagery depicting Faith, Hope and Charity, and executed with Gilbert's timeless *fin-de-siècle* handling (Fig. 4.69). It was unveiled by the King on 9 June 1932, and was Gilbert's last public sculpture.[341] At the time of the commission, Gilbert was working in the St James's garden

4. GEORGE IV TO THE SECOND WORLD WAR

4.67
Gandhi leaving the recently enlarged Ambassadors' Entrance Hall, St James's Palace, during the second Indian Round Table Conference, held in the autumn of 1931

4.68
Plan of temporary room allocations in the State Apartments for the League of Nations Council Meeting, held on 14 March 1936 (TNA, WORK 19/248; north is at the bottom left)

studio belonging to Lady Feodora Gleichen (1861–1922), to complete figures for the Duke of Clarence's memorial in the Albert Memorial Chapel, Windsor Castle.[342]

From 1863 to 1910, King Edward VII and King George V successively occupied Marlborough House as Princes of Wales. Clarence House was unoccupied during the Duke of Connaught's governorship of Canada, 1911–16, and soon after his return, the Duchess died. The Duke thereafter tended to use Clarence House only during the summer months, when he undertook the annual June inspection of the Yeomen of Guard, which took place in the garden.[343] From 1923, the ceremony was often featured in cinema newsreels.[344]

In February 1902, excavations in Colour Court revealed a lead coffin containing a mature male,

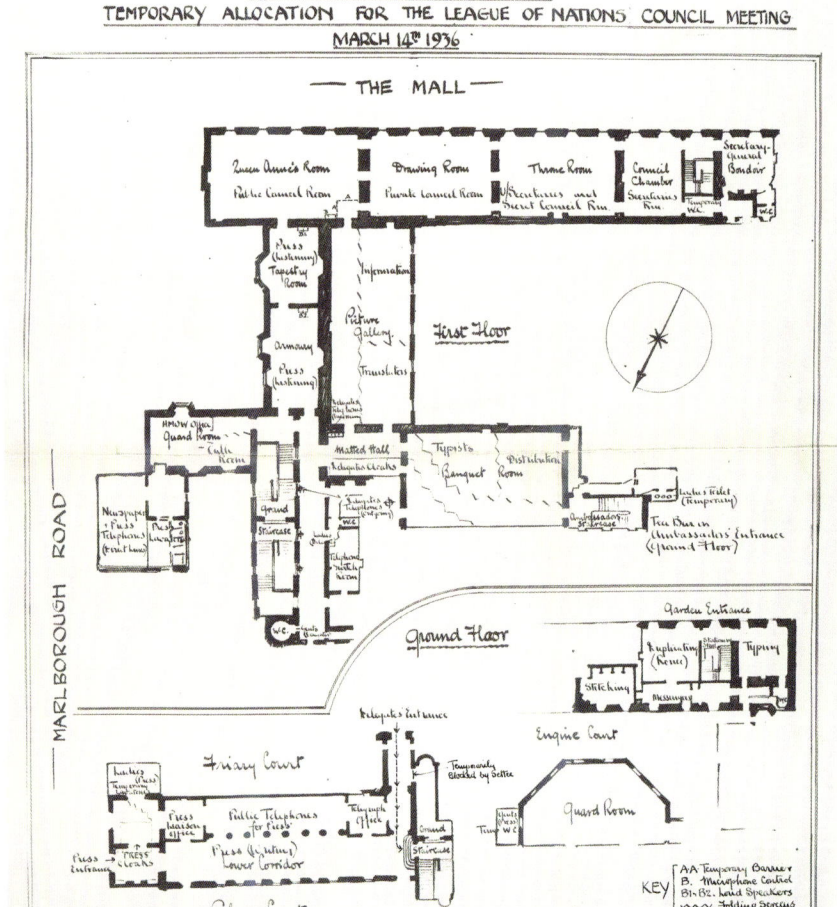

4.69
Memorial to Queen Alexandra by Alfred Gilbert, Marlborough Gate, 1927–32

decorated with a cable-pattern cross, about 1 m below the surface. Charles Read, Keeper at the Department of British and Medieval Antiquities and Ethnography in the British Museum, concluded he may have been one of the brethren who ministered in the leper hospital, and dated the coffin to the thirteenth century, on the basis of similar coffins excavated at the Temple Church in the City of London in the 1840s. The remains were photographed and reburied close to their original location.[345]
In August 1925, excavations for a drain in Colour Court exposed more human remains, at depths varying between 1.1 m and 1.7 m, together with 25 thirteenth-century encaustic tiles, measuring 11.4 cm in diameter and 2.5 cm thick, which were assumed to be part of the hospital chapel. A record made by R.S.O. Harman triangulated the remains of a complete female skeleton towards the south-east corner of the courtyard. They were again reburied in boxes in their original position, but lower down and covered with concrete, to enable the drain to pass over them, at the suggestion of Jocelyn Bushe-Fox, Inspector of Ancient Monuments for England. Charles Peers, Chief Inspector of Ancient Monuments, had some of the tiles framed and mounted in the corridor of the Chapel Royal in 1927, where they remain (see Fig. 1.3).[346]

In August 1929, excavations on the south and east sides of Friary Court for a new gas main exposed structural remains of the Tudor palace, including three culverts running west to east, substantial brick footings, and three steps tentatively identified as Bristol pennant stone (Fig. 4.70).[347]

None of these three excavations prompted more extensive investigation, but it is noteworthy that the detail and quantity of recording improved each time. This suggests an increasing interest by the Office of Works in understanding and preserving the historic remains of the palace (Figs 4.71 and 4.72), exemplified by the 1930s restoration of the Queen's Chapel (see p. 223).[348]

Edward VIII, 1936

As Prince of Wales, King Edward VIII had lived in York House since 1919. He became King on 20 January 1936. He had an office in Buckingham Palace, and only intended to remain in York House temporarily, but because

4.70

Foundations of the Tudor palace exposed in Friary Court during excavations, 18 August 1929 (Historic England Archive, OWS01/02/S01298)

4.71

The west door of the Great Gatehouse during masonry repairs, 23 October 1933, showing the carved spandrels retained and the remaining loose stone cut away prior to applying a mortar repair (Historic England Archive, AL2480/024/02)

4.72

The west door of the Great Gatehouse after repairs to its masonry (Historic England Archive, AL2480/026/02)

of the Abdication in December, he never moved out. For the first time in nearly a hundred years, the royal standard flew above St James's Palace clock tower when he was in residence.[349] During the King's short reign, he only held one levee at St James's.[350] His primary contribution to the development of the palace lies with his extensive redecoration of York House between 1928 and early 1936. In the spring of 1928, he employed the society 'art decorator', E.G. Lehmann of Wigmore Street, London, to redecorate and furnish a number of rooms. Lehmann became a royal warrant holder for the Prince, as 'decorator and house furnisher' from 1931 to 1936. Some of the work included panelling and fittings in a late eighteenth-century style, such as the sitting room, but also employing plenty of chintz, replacing the 1890s mosaic floor of the staircase hall with stone flags, and graining the panelling to simulate pine.[351] While the style did not appeal to the Prince's Equerry, Major John Aird, it did meet with Queen Mary's approval.[352] In 1933, Lehmann submitted invoices for more than £3,000 for unspecified work in York House, nearly £1,000 in 1934, and more than £240 in early 1935.[353] Lehmann also submitted separate invoices for redecorating Fort Belvedere (the Prince's weekend retreat in Windsor Great Park since 1929), and in 1932, he supplied the Prince with furniture worth £2,000 for unspecified locations.[354]

By 1935, the Prince was increasingly undertaking duties on behalf of his father, which required more formal entertaining than hitherto. From mid-1935, he carried out a further round of decoration to the main reception rooms in York House.[355] Payments to Lehmann do not feature in the Prince's private accounts after May 1935. There are no separate entries for York House, suggesting invoices for work there may have been grouped together under the Prince's Fort Belvedere account. The interior decorator and society hostess, Sibyl Colefax (1874–1950), carried out a small amount of work recorded under the Fort account in October 1935, and Syrie Maugham (1879–1955) was also involved, but the majority of the work under that account (totalling more than £1,500 in invoices submitted between 2 July 1935 and 26 May 1936) was undertaken by the Mayfair firm, Elden Ltd, owned by the flamboyant, Dutch-born interior decorator, Herman Schrijver (1904–72).[356] Schrijver had recently redecorated Wallis Simpson's (1896–1986) London flat in Bryanston Court and it is likely that she introduced him to the Prince.[357] Richard Fisher corresponded with Schrijver while writing his biography of Syrie Maugham, and states, presumably on Schrijver's authority: 'Herman Schrijver, who had helped to decorate York House for the Prince, claims to have done the work at the Belvedere as well'.[358] Schrijver had a penchant for heavily trimmed and fringed curtains, and mirrors to give the illusion of more space, but he also endeavoured to express his client's personality within the schemes he created.[359]

The primary visual evidence for this royal patronage at York House and Fort Belvedere is a set of photographs taken before work began and again in 1936, 'showing the rooms as decorated by The King'. But the photographs are not specifically dated, so it is not always possible to determine whether Lehmann or Schrijver was responsible for any particular room.[360] On the ground floor, the waiting room off the hall was hung with a specially commissioned, hand-painted English chinoiserie wallpaper by an unknown studio, but rumoured to have been carried out by otherwise unidentified 'ladies of Pimlico' (Fig. 4.73).[361] It is not known who oversaw the wallpaper commission, but the doors on the end walls probably date from mid-1935, as they were lined with mirrored plate glass to enhance the sense of space, a typical Schrijver touch (Fig. 4.74).[362] The adjoining dining room to the west previously sported thin Adam-style ceiling decoration, with heavy Victorian furniture, including a dining table and deeply buttoned balloon-backed chairs, a sideboard with a dominant backboard, stout pedestals supporting vases sprouting electric lamps either side of the chimneypiece, and a silk damask-covered screen. A series of Winterhalter's circular portraits of Queen Victoria's children, painted between 1849 and 1859, were hung above the panelling.[363] In 1935, these portraits were removed and a fussy, 1890s, Adam-style overmantel mirror with a broken pediment was replaced with a reeded frame, to echo the marble chimneypiece (Fig. 4.75). The walls and panelling were repainted. Greater refinement and reference to the Prince was largely achieved through the judicious choice and arrangement of furniture, including a more elegantly proportioned sideboard, symmetrically arranged urn-shaped

4.73
Hand-painted chinoiserie wallpaper, 1930s, in the Chinese Room at York House

4.74
The Chinese Drawing Room, York House, looking west, past a mirrored door into the Drawing Room, 1936

4.75
The Dining Room, York House, looking west, 1936

OPPOSITE

4.76
The Drawing Room, York House, looking west, before 1936

4.77
The Drawing Room, York House, looking east, 1936

4.78
The Library, York House, looking west, 1936

wine coolers, an imposing Coromandel lacquer screen, and a set of Sheraton-style shield-back chairs with the Prince of Wales's feathers on the splats (confirming that the ensemble pre-dates 20 January 1936). The walls of the drawing room to the east of the Chinese Room had curved ends, lined with silk-moiré paper, and late nineteenth-century plaster ceiling decoration around the central light. The ceiling mouldings were removed, and the walls were remodelled with illuminated neo-classical shell-headed niches to display porcelain (a practice advocated by Schrijver); the proportions of the new wall panelling was designed to fit three portraits on the chimney wall. Two-leafed doors were similarly lined with mirrored glass, while heavily buttoned Victorian furniture was replaced with modern easy chairs (Figs 4.76 and 4.77). On the principal floor, the former Boudoir was transformed into an imposing library (Fig. 4.78), with built-in shelves either side of a timber chimneypiece with a baroque overmantel, within which the King hung a reduced copy of Sir William Llewellyn's (1858–1941) 1914 portrait of Queen Mary.[364] Schrijver was presumably responsible, as this room was not completed until 1936. The King was anxious about his mother's opinion. A huge coloured and framed map of the world filled the end wall, dominating the room. This was somewhat reminiscent of the boardroom of a major shipping company, which may have prompted Queen Mary's crushing verdict on first seeing it: 'What a funny sort of room to find in a palace, David'.[365] Nevertheless, the York House interiors followed mainstream inter-war interior decoration in their use of historical styles, and were hardly avant-garde. Edward's embrace of contemporary design and fashion was reflected in his wardrobe, and more ephemeral everyday objects, such as his art deco monograms: 'EP' (when Prince of Wales) on bathroom towels, and 'ERI VIII' on stationery, or a York House tea set in the celebrated Clarice Cliff (1899–1972) 'Bizarre' pattern.[366]

Some of the work, including the library map and much of the panelling, was short-lived; in November 1936, the Duke and Duchess of Gloucester requested alterations, and commissioned Campbell, Smith & Co. to redecorate some of the rooms before they took up residence following the Abdication.[367]

George VI, 1936–52

Edward was succeeded as King by his brother, George VI, on 11 December 1936. George was crowned on 12 May 1937. The King held three levees at St James's in 1937, and three in 1938. His only levee at St James's in 1939 was on 18 July; they were discontinued thereafter for the duration of the war.[368]

Notwithstanding the uncertainty of the international situation, the first stage of a detailed and scholarly restoration of the Queen's Chapel was completed in 1938. In 1922, it was suggested by the director of works, A.W. Heasman, that the royal pew could be restored, but nothing was done. In 1927, the residence that had been occupied by Sheppard's widow was granted to his successor, the Revd Prebendary L.J. Percival. He required further alterations to the royal pew to convert it into a bedroom.[369] In 1937, the High Church architect W.H. Randoll Blacking (1889–1958) produced a scheme for reordering the chapel on behalf of Queen Mary. It was referred to the Office of Works, who advised caution until their expert, architect and Inspector of Ancient Monuments, George Chettle (1886–1960), could examine the building.[370] Chettle had just finished restoring Inigo Jones's Queen's House, Greenwich. He was keenly interested in the history of the palace, and during his career often gave lectures on the subject.[371] Chettle's contribution to this remarkable restoration of the chapel's interior was published in 2001.[372] The project was unique in that it involved Queen Mary's formidable taste and guidance, coupled with the Office of Works' commitment to re-create the Inigo Jones interior. Chettle confirmed Jones's authorship through identifying a drawing in Oxford with the surviving chimneypiece in the royal pew, which had been disfigured by an inserted mezzanine floor, and by his examination of the original building accounts.[373] Blacking's proposals for the reredos were modified, and the Office

4. GEORGE IV TO THE SECOND WORLD WAR

4.79
Prime Minister Winston Churchill addresses the conference of Allied and Imperial statesmen on 12 June 1941 in the Picture Gallery at St James's Palace, which retained its pre-war picture hang of royal portraits

4.80
Damage to St James's Palace and a crater in Pall Mall, caused by a high explosive bomb (Westminster City air raid incident 1710) during a night-time raid, 23 February 1944 (Westminster City Archives, CD133/13)

succeeded in removing the 1860s swell organ, which towered over the *c*.1760 Snetzler organ, itself positioned above the reredos. Part of the current dark brown paint and earlier layers were removed by the chief artist craftsman at the Office of Works, J.F.S. Jack, to reveal Jones's original colour scheme of green, buff and warm white, with gilding on the vault to demarcate the sanctuary. A proposal to re-create the original decorative scheme was modified by Queen Mary.[374]

A dedicatory service was held in the redecorated chapel in October 1938.[375] In 1939, the old name, Queen's Chapel, was adopted once more,[376] but major elements of Chettle's proposals were postponed, due to lack of funds and Queen Mary's preference to retain the restored Snetzler organ in its present position, although it still obscured almost half of the central light behind the reredos. The war then intervened and the complete repair and restoration was delayed until 1949–51, including relocating the organ to its original gallery on the south side, and reopening the royal closet.[377]

On 3 September 1939, the Prime Minister, Neville Chamberlain, broadcast via the BBC from the Cabinet Room in 10 Downing Street that Britain was at war with Germany. There was no formal declaration at St James's Palace, nor was there a peace proclamation in 1945. Kenneth Clark, Surveyor of the King's Pictures, implemented a prearranged plan to remove the best paintings from the Royal Collection to the safety of Wales. But the chronological hang of royal portraits in the Picture Gallery, for example, remained in place during the war, presiding over the international conferences held there.[378] At the beginning of the war, staff in St James's numbered about 170, including 30 members of the King's Guard, 65 Office of Works employees, 20 in the Lord Chamberlain's department and 30 Museum of London staff based in Lancaster House. Gas-proof air-raid precautions shelters, capable of accommodating 214 persons, were created by reinforcing the wine cellars beneath the south range of the State Apartments, accessed from Engine Court. They were considered adequate for everything but a direct hit.[379] Most of the Lord Chamberlain's office was relocated to Frogmore House, Windsor, and its offices in Stable Yard were given over to the Joint War Organisation of the Red Cross and the Order of St John. Much of the charity's work was focused on the relief of prisoners of war, and in time, more than 300 people worked for the joint organisation, taking over 'every nook and cranny of the Palace', including Clarence House, following the death of the Duke of Connaught in 1942.[380] In the summer of 1944, the Joint War Organisation staged an exhibition in Clarence House and the palace gardens, illustrating the daily life and living conditions of prisoners of war, complete with a full-scale mock-up of part of a German Stalag.[381] The following year, another exhibition, titled *Out from the Battle*, showcased the care of the wounded on the battlefield, including a mobile X-ray unit, operating tent, blood transfusion and penicillin.[382]

The palace and adjoining buildings were affected by blast damage during hostilities. On 15 October 1940, a landmine in St James's Park damaged windows to the State Apartments, Clarence House and apartments in Ambassadors, Engine and Friary Courts.[383] Marlborough House lost most of its windows, much to Queen Mary's dismay at Badminton House, Gloucester, where she had been evacuated.[384] On 10 November 1940, a bomb fell in Cleveland Row, causing damage to York House and the palace generally.[385] But on 10–11 May 1941, some 300 German bombers took part in the last of the big night raids on London.[386] The southern part of Friary Court suffered a direct hit from a 250 kg high explosive bomb, which largely demolished the two-storey Apartment 21, containing Ministry of Works offices, as well as servants' rooms belonging to Lady Helena Gleichen (1873–1947) in Apartment 25, although there were no casualties.[387]

The palace assumed a prominent international role after the Blitz. On 12 June 1941, nine exiled governments attended the Inter-Allied Meeting at St James's (Fig. 4.79), in Winston Churchill's words, 'itself not unscarred by the fire of the enemy'.[388] Great Britain, Canada, Australia, New Zealand and the Union of South Africa, and the exiled governments of Belgium, Czechoslovakia, Greece, Luxembourg, the Netherlands, Norway, Poland, Yugoslavia and of General de Gaulle of France vowed to continue the struggle against German and Italian oppression. They signed the Declaration of St James's Palace, proclaiming:

> the only true basis of enduring peace is the willing co-operation of free peoples in a world in which, relieved of the menace of aggression, all may enjoy economic and social security; and that it is their intention to work together, and with other free peoples, both in war and peace to this end.[389]

This declaration formed the basis of the United Nations Pact of 1 January 1942.[390]

As early as 1942, the Allied governments in exile convened a conference to discuss post-war punishment for war crimes, and Anthony Eden, Foreign Minister, praised the decision to hold it at St James's: 'This historic building has become in a very real sense a centre for resistance of the oppressed nations of Europe to German aggression. Never has it had a more inspiring role to play.'[391]

Air attacks were renewed in 1944. On 23 February, a high explosive bomb landed in Pall Mall opposite the main gate to Marlborough House, killing eight people and injuring 48 others (Fig. 4.80).[392] The north elevation of St James's received the full blast and suffered structural damage which severed the eighteenth-century brick façade from the cross walls. Most of the windows were blown out on the north-east corner of the palace, including the Tapestry Room and Guard Room. There was also structural damage and loss to the roof and parapet of Apartment 29, where many of the upper ceilings had fallen.[393] The gatehouse was damaged, but Lord Claud Hamilton, Queen Mary's comptroller, observed, 'The clock in St James's Palace is still going and striking, but the hands and face have gone'. The damaged state of the palace's striking clock could almost be symbolic of Britain's wartime resilience, epitomised in the phrase, 'keep calm and carry on'.[394] The north window of the Chapel Royal had also been blown out, the altar destroyed, and the panelling pitted with shards of glass. On 31 March, the window remained without glass, but arrangements to purchase a new altar and undertake repairs were made by the Sub-Dean Wallace Elliott, facilitated by the generosity of the Queen, who took a particular interest in ensuring the chapel remained open.[395] The Queen's Chapel also suffered internal and external damage, including to the windows, panelling and ceiling.[396] Further blast damage to the State Apartments and residences occurred on 18 June 1944.[397] Emergency structural repairs were carried out to avoid collapse, but shortage of materials and labour delayed the completion of the work until August 1945.[398]

5. The Palace Today

SIMON THURLEY

Post-war reconstruction

At the end of the war, the government was faced with the enormous task of reconstruction. National infrastructure was in tatters, more than 3 million people were homeless, building materials were scarce and rationing of these was to continue until 1954. King George VI found himself in a difficult position. All the royal residences in central London had suffered bomb damage and required repair, and several were in urgent need of modernisation, but the King realised that it was impossible for the Royal Household to be treated as a special case. This reticence was also to be felt by Princess Elizabeth, who had married Lieutenant Philip Mountbatten (1921–2021) in 1947. The cost of their wedding was kept to a minimum, and discussions about their future home were dominated by issues of expense.

At St James's there was an urgent need to rebuild and repair the parts of the palace that had been damaged by the war. The old Ministry of Works offices and one of the apartments facing Friary Court required complete rebuilding, and the roof of the Picture Gallery needed strengthening, but most work was required in the two chapels. The bomb in Cleveland Row had seriously damaged the north end of the Chapel Royal. Make-do-and-mend repairs were immediately effected, but it quickly became clear that the whole structure was parlous. Repairs were ordered to the roof, but these could not be undertaken until services could be relocated to the Queen's Chapel.[1]

The Queen's Chapel had also been damaged by bombing, and in 1948, it was decided not only to repair the damage, but also to complete the restoration started before the war (Figs 5.1 and 5.2). Queen Elizabeth made it clear that

5.1 and 5.2

The Queen's Chapel before and after the reconstruction of 1948–50, showing the effect of the removal of the Sub-Dean's residence and the re-creation of the royal pew (TNA, WORK 19/1068)

5.3
The interior of the Chapel Royal, photographed in 1988, facing north, after the restoration of 1970 (Historic England Archive, BB88/05357)

OPPOSITE
5.4
The Chapel Royal in 2018, shown after the further restoration undertaken to commemorate the Golden Jubilee

the work should not be accelerated on her account, but George Chettle, Chief Inspector of Ancient Monuments, was keen to continue where he had left off (see pp. 223–4) and remove the residence of the Sub-Dean that had been built into and under the royal pew, restoring the chapel to its seventeenth-century arrangement. The work, undertaken with scholarly exactitude, was complete by the summer of 1950. As services moved into the newly completed Queen's Chapel, work began on strengthening the roof of the Chapel Royal and reordering the interior, to make it suitable for modern worship. The present arrangement of the stalls and the royal pew date from this restoration.[2]

Whilst post-war work saved the Chapel Royal from collapse, by the late 1960s the dark Victorian varnish on the woodwork and the lack of any light on the ceiling created an oppressive atmosphere. A committee of taste, led by the Ancient Monuments department and advised by the historian Sir John Summerson, and the Honorary Surveyor of The Queen's Works of Art, Francis Watson, came up with proposals to redecorate the chapel; these were approved by The Queen in November 1969. In 1970, the panelling was lightened and highlighted with gilding, the walls repainted and hung with tapestry, and red upholstery textiles replaced the previous blue. The north window was reduced to its Tudor size, by blocking the lower and upper side lights (Figs 5.3 and 5.4).[3]

From the accession of King Edward VII, the ceremonial life of the monarchy had become increasingly complex, and the bureaucracy to manage it proportionately larger. The Lord Chamberlain's office and its sub-departments grew and, after 1972, occupied much of York House, which was refurbished for them in 1984–7.[4] Many senior staff were granted apartments nearby; the Lord Chamberlain, for instance, was quartered in the north range of Colour Court, east of the gatehouse.[5] In 1986, the Lord Chamberlain, the Earl of Airlie, a former chairman of Schroders, commissioned financial consultants Peat Marwick McLintock to review the efficiency of the Royal Household – the resulting changes had important implications for St James's.

The most significant, perhaps, was the establishment of a new Department in the Royal Household to oversee the Royal Collection. Previously, the monarch's art collection had been managed by the Lord Chamberlain through the Royal Librarian, the Surveyor of Pictures and the Surveyor of Works of Art. The new Royal Collection Department, soon to be placed under Sir Geoffrey de Bellaigue (1931–2013), brought curatorial discipline and museum standards to the world's greatest private art collection. In 1993, when The Queen decided to pay income tax, a trust was formed to receive the revenues from the public opening of the occupied royal palaces, for the benefit of the Collection and to help pay for the restoration of Windsor Castle after the disastrous fire of 1992. In 1986, the new Department made its headquarters in Stable Yard House at St James's.

In a parallel process, the Royal Household took control of the maintenance and repair of the occupied royal palaces. The Office of Works had long before morphed into the

5.5
The dining room in the Officers' Mess, Engine Court, photographed in 2018

Ministry of Works, and then the Department of the Environment, and responsibility for maintaining public buildings, and the occupied royal estate, had passed to the Property Services Agency (PSA). In 1991 the Royal Household established its own property section and thereby control over priorities, in terms of maintenance, conservation and redecoration.

The Airlie review also recommended that the Lord Chamberlain's offices should be moved from York House to Buckingham Palace, where they could be closer to The Queen. Only the Central Chancery of the Orders of Knighthood and the Marshal of the Diplomatic Corps remained behind. Soon after, the private offices of The Prince and Princess of Wales moved from Buckingham Palace to St James's.

Still based at St James's are The Queen's Guards, both historic and contemporary. The Gentlemen at Arms and the Yeomen of the Guard, who provide a ceremonial guard for The Queen on various occasions, both have their headquarters in the palace (see p. 158). The modern military guard are still housed in Engine Court, in the purpose-built quarters of 1876, while the Officers' Mess (Fig. 5.5) retains an impressive collection of memorabilia.

Most of these changes in responsibility and accommodation required little intervention in the fabric of the palace, but the conversion of Stable Yard House was an exception. During and immediately after the war, the State Apartments had been used for international conferences, but in 1950, Lancaster House, which had been occupied by the London Museum, was handed back to the government and it was decided to use this building for conferences, and Marlborough House as the headquarters of the Commonwealth Secretariat.[6] Stable Yard House, Nicholas Hawksmoor's elegant stable of 1716, had been vacated by the Lord Chamberlain's department before the war and was in a poor state of repair. In 1971, the government decided to take on the building and convert it into four apartments, which would complement its use of Lancaster House. Permission was sought from The Queen, who agreed that the building could be borrowed by the government. The conversion of 1979–81 was insensitive, undertaken for the government by the PSA using Crown exemption; it erased not only the fabric of the historic building, but also its character. The harsh pointing and new dormer windows still today disfigure one of the palace's most interesting eighteenth-century buildings (see Fig. 3.5).[7] In 1983, the PSA gave up Stable Yard House, and the Royal Household converted it into offices for the Royal Collection.

THE STATE APARTMENTS

In 1902, when King Edward VII and Queen Alexandra left Marlborough House for Buckingham Palace, the Drawing Rooms, dinners and balls that had been held at St James's went with them, and St James's now only hosted levees. The last of these was held in 1939, so by 1952, St James's had already lost its role as London's social centre. In the first decade of The Queen's reign, as the monarchy became more democratic, the role of St James's as a royal palace became increasingly unclear. Most ceremonial events, including the new garden parties, which replaced the old court presentations, now took place at Buckingham Palace.[8]

Consequently, the state rooms, which had been used for official functions since the reign of George IV, have been much less used by The Queen. In the past, some state visits included a formal presentation in the Throne Room – a legacy of the palace's senior role – but in more recent times, this has been rare. The state rooms are now principally used by members of the Royal Family to host charitable events. The Queen, like all British monarchs for a century or more, is the national head of philanthropy and, with individual members of the Royal Family, is the patron of thousands of charities.[9] Since the 1970s, St James's has been the venue for many thousands of receptions and events in aid of these good causes. Perhaps pre-eminent amongst them has been the Duke of Edinburgh's Award scheme, launched in 1956, which annually hosts a number of Gold Awards in the State Apartments (fig. 5.6). This use of the state rooms is emblematic of the change that has taken place in the duties of the monarchy during The Queen's reign: rooms formerly used for the exclusive reception of members of the upper classes in formalised and restrictive levees and Drawing Rooms now welcome huge numbers of the public engaged in charitable activities. To facilitate these large events, kitchens were built to the west of the Banqueting Room in 1968, lavatories have been created and durable carpets installed.

Changes to the state rooms have been minimal since the Second World War. In 1946, the part of the royal art collection that had been evacuated to slate mines deep in the Welsh hills, was returned and rehung by Anthony Blunt, then Surveyor of The Queen's Pictures.[10] Much of this picture-hang is intact, as the enormous size of the canvasses at St James's makes them difficult to rearrange. New silk wall hangings were made for the Queen Anne Room, the Throne Room and the Drawing Room in 1951, and for the Banqueting Room in 1961.[11] In 1973, to improve the wall space for pictures, the fireplace was removed from the Queen Anne Room (Fig. 5.6). Between 1976 and 1991, furnishing and redecoration of the state rooms (and other parts of the palace) was undertaken, at the request of the Lord Chamberlain, by a division of PSA, The Crown Suppliers. The Inspectorate of Ancient Monuments advised on historical accuracy; latterly, the Surveyors of the Royal Collection have been consulted on furnishing.

A little-known aspect of St James's in the early twentieth century was its use as an

5.6
Harold Yexley's drawing of 1973 shows how the Queen Anne Room would look without the William Kent fireplace installed in the 1820s (Historic England, MA/JPL0005). It was returned to Kensington, from whence it had come, in 1974

artists' studio. On the south side of Friary Court was the studio of sculptor and grace-and-favour resident, Victor Hohenlohe, Count Gleichen (1833–91), and then of his daughter, also a sculptor, Lady Feodora Gleichen. This had been subsequently used temporarily by Sir Alfred Gilbert (see p. 217).[12] The Queen had sat for the sculptor, Oscar Nemon (1906–85), at Buckingham Palace in 1958, and his work was so admired that he was invited to use the former Gleichen studio too; here, he sculpted Queen Elizabeth, Prince Philip, Earl Mountbatten (1900–79) and, perhaps his most famous work, a series of monumental effigies of Sir Winston Churchill.[13]

In 1981, the Lord Chamberlain, Lord Maclean, ordered the conversion of the sculpture studio into a workshop for the conservation of Royal Collection paintings, under the conservator, Viola Pemberton-Piggott. Between 2000 and 2001, when it became clear that sitting at his own studio would attract too much attention, Lucian Freud (1922–2011) painted The Queen in a series of sittings in the Friary Court studio. The studio remains in use today for conservation.

CLARENCE HOUSE

Queen Victoria had a large family, and with the extended families of King Edward VII and King George V, there were numerous close royal relations who needed accommodation; in this, St James's fulfilled an important role. Other than the future Edward VIII, when he was Prince of Wales, the most senior royal resident had been the Duke of Connaught, Queen Victoria's third son, who used Clarence House until 1942. Princess Mary, The Princess Royal, made use of an apartment in Engine Court until her death in 1965; the Duke and Duchess of Gloucester used York House until 1974; the Duke and Duchess of Kent resided in part of York House before they moved to Kensington Palace. More recently, Princess Alexandra, Princesses Beatrice and Eugenie of York, and The Princess Royal and her husband, Sir Tim Laurence, have had apartments at the palace. For them, over the years, new bathrooms and kitchens have been installed and lifts added. These have all been minor changes, but the most significant alterations of the present reign have been at Clarence House.

In November 1947, it was announced that Princess Elizabeth and Prince Philip would make their home at Clarence House. In William IV's time, it had been fully integrated with the State Apartments and, due to the improvements of Alfred, Duke of Edinburgh, in the 1870s, was the largest and most elegant of the apartments at St James's. During the war, it had been used by the Red Cross, and in 1945, it had few bathrooms, only skeleton central heating, limited electricity and Victorian kitchens.[14] In this unmodernised state, the house was inspected by Princess Elizabeth, Prince Philip and Princess Margaret (1930–2002) in October 1947, and the Ministry of Works noted Princess Elizabeth's intense interest in plans for refurbishment and, in particular, her concern that staff accommodation should be of good quality.[15]

Although the Ministry of Works oversaw the restoration, the couple were extremely closely involved, specifying work and supervising progress. Both the Ministry and the Royal Household kept a close eye on the budget, with all works being categorised as either war damage, backlog maintenance or improvement. The Duke and Princess Elizabeth paid for the latter category themselves, partly funded by money given as wedding presents. Work complete, they took up residence in June 1949.

In the same year, Christopher Hussey, former editor of *Country Life* and its leading architectural writer, requested permission to cover the finished house in the magazine. He also secured permission to write a book about it, with photographs of the private quarters (including the nursery of the royal children). They show the modern, elegant taste of the royal couple, and how the Victorian heaviness of the house had been scrubbed away and replaced by the minimalising aesthetic of a naval officer and the more domestic influence of the Princess (Fig. 5.7).[16]

Two bedroom suites were created and a nursery laid out; the house was rewired and

5.7
Princess Elizabeth and The Duke of Edinburgh, with their children Prince Charles and Princess Anne, in the grounds of Clarence House, their London residence, in 1951

central heating installed; there were new kitchens and a lift. Prince Philip requested a cinema in the basement, and was prepared to bear the cost himself if the Treasury would not pay – he was saved from this by the cinema industry, which offered to present a screen, seats and projectors as a wedding gift. Red tape nearly throttled the idea, as the Ministry of Works believed that Westminster City would not grant a licence, but in the event, the objections were over-ruled, and a 25-seat cinema was installed in 1951.

There were other gifts: the Canadian Pacific Railway gave white Canadian maple to panel the Duke's sitting room. Here, he devised an ingenious drawing table, constructed by Morris of Glasgow, which folded up into the window pier. The royal couple's 'quiet room', a small private sitting room, was panelled with jarrah wood, presented to re-create the feel of the Australian premier's office; and there was a long debate over the precise use of two gifts of mahogany from the Gold Coast and from St Vincent. The county of Lancashire presented an eighteenth-century fireplace.

Prince Philip took the advice of his uncle, Earl Mountbatten, who had recommended a friend of the Countess's, Isley Duncan, to design carpets, curtains and decorative effects. Photographs of the Mountbattens' remarkable flat in Brook Street, Mayfair, taken in 1939, show that the Duke and Princess shared, or perhaps imitated, the taste of the Mountbattens.[17] But the finished interiors were theirs: Princess Elizabeth bought an antique fireplace of Irish wood for £250 for her bedroom, and a cocktail

5. THE PALACE TODAY

bar was made to the Duke's specification, costing £270. At one point, when the decorators could not get the right aquamarine green for the Princess's sitting room, she mixed the colour herself. The paintings were chosen, and sparsely hung, by the Duke; most were modern British, including works by Paul Nash (1889–1946), Edward Seago (1910–74), Wilson Steer (1860–1942) and Charles Cundall (1890–1971); there were also portraits by Philip de László (1869–1937) and Edward Irvine Halliday (1902–84).

The interiors were fashionable for their day; a revival of interest in Georgian interiors in the 1930s had blended modernist minimalism with the clean lines of furniture by Chippendale and Hepplewhite, unfussy mouldings, light colours and a sparse picture-hang. Comfortable sofas were disposed next to televisions and radiograms in mahogany and walnut cases; like the new Elizabethan age itself, it was a delicate blend of the new and old orders.[18]

Having taken such care in decorating their new house, the royal couple had every expectation of a long residence, but the early death of King George VI in 1952 changed everything. After The Queen's accession, the couple expressed a wish to remain in the domestic comfort of Clarence House, and leave Buckingham Palace as an office and ceremonial headquarters. This suggestion was firmly rejected by the Prime Minister, Sir Winston Churchill. Due to the war, Buckingham Palace had become an architectural icon of the monarchy, the nation and what was left of the Empire. There was no question of it not becoming the home of the new royal family.[19]

Queen Elizabeth The Queen Mother, who was only 52, now needed to vacate Buckingham Palace; she would have liked to take Marlborough House, where the ailing Queen Mary was living – it would have been an independent residence with plenty of space, including a garage and fine private gardens – but it was not to be. Even though Queen Mary died in March 1953, the Queen Mother and Princess Margaret were assigned Clarence House, a building the Queen Mother thought 'loathsome'.[20] The Queen left Clarence House for Buckingham Palace the following month.

There was great sensitivity about the potential cost of the Queen Mother's move from Buckingham Palace to Clarence House, as so much had recently been spent preparing it for Princess Elizabeth. Yet it was acknowledged that a single widow did not need the same arrangements as a married couple with a young, growing family. The Treasury thus agreed expenditure in September 1952 to make adjustments.[21]

The twin bedroom suites were repurposed and the nurseries converted into rooms for Princess Margaret. The Queen Mother elected to use the Duke's former bedroom suite for herself, but had the shower removed from the bathroom; she also removed the Duke's Canadian and Australian panelling. Her tastes were more traditional than her daughter's, and the fireplace that The Queen had put into her sitting room was replaced with a Georgian one, the mouldings on the walls removed and the room tightly hung with Warner's silk to dado level.

It was agreed that, to provide more staff accommodation, the seventeenth- and eighteenth-century house to the north of Clarence House, formally occupied by Lord Clarendon, the Lord Chamberlain, should be amalgamated with Clarence House. There was some argument with the Treasury about this, with Arthur Penn, Treasurer to Queen Elizabeth The Queen Mother, complaining about the lack of comfort in staff accommodation. Money was found from the maintenance budget to carry out the changes, permanently enlarging Clarence House. On her marriage in 1960, Princess Margaret moved out of Clarence House to Kensington Palace.

Despite her early dislike of the house, it became the Queen Mother's much-loved home, furnished with a growing collection of works of art, many of which were bought in the country-house sales of the 1950s and 1960s. In 1965, Oliver Ford, doyenne of the eighteenth-century revival interior, became the Queen Mother's decorator, and over the following 27 years, until his death in 1992, he redecorated much of the house, with the Queen Mother's close involvement. Ford brought vivid colours to the walls and floors, and beautiful silks for curtains and upholstery. The Queen Mother praised him for his help and advice, 'in the battle to keep these old houses alive and beautiful'.[22]

In 1996, mirroring the book written to record The Queen and Prince Philip's alterations to Clarence House, John Cornforth, also a distinguished architectural editor of *Country Life*, was asked to write about the Queen Mother's collections there.[23] The photographs specially commissioned for the volume show the understated elegance that Ford helped to bring to the house (Figs 5.8 and 5.9). The Queen Mother lived at Clarence House with what has been described as an Edwardian lifestyle, entertaining grandly and being served by a large household staff; her annual appearances there on her birthday brought the house widespread public recognition.

After the separation of The Prince and Princess of Wales in 1995, the Prince moved from Kensington Palace into the former Lord Chamberlain's apartment to the east of the clock tower at St James's; he then occupied part of York House, but following the death of the Queen Mother in 2002, it was decided that the Prince should take up residence in Clarence House.

During the Queen Mother's long residence, little had been done to the infrastructure of the house, and in 2002, a major project was begun to remove asbestos, install automatic fire detection and rewire the building.

The Prince of Wales had employed the antique dealer and decorator, Robert Kime, at his country estate at Highgrove in Gloucestershire and to decorate previous apartments at St James's, and Kime was commissioned to prepare Clarence House once the builders had finished. His brief was to retain the Queen Mother's furniture and paintings, mixing them with objects from store at Windsor Castle and some of the Prince's own possessions. The house was to look like a much-loved family home (Figs 5.10–5.12). The Prince himself remarked that 'if my grandmother

5.8
The Drawing Room, Clarence House, from the south in 1949, painted in ivory and grey, with neo-Georgian ceiling mouldings added by HRH The Duke of Edinburgh

5.9
The same room at Clarence House photographed in 1996, when it was in use by Queen Elizabeth The Queen Mother as her drawing room. The colours are warmer and richer and the room more densely furnished

5.10
Clarence House, view from the Library into the Dining Room, as arranged for The Prince of Wales by Robert Kime

5.11
The Garden Room at Clarence House

came back she would recognise it at once'.[24] On completion of the works the Prince moved in on 4 August 2003, the Queen Mother's birthday. At the same time it was announced that the house would be open to visitors each summer.[25]

THE CHAPEL ROYAL

The only part of St James's Palace to retain a ceremonial function into the present reign has been the Chapel Royal, as the headquarters of The Queen's religious household. In celebration of The Queen's Golden Jubilee, money was raised from the 12 great livery companies in the City of London to make a stained-glass window for the north window (see Fig. 5.4). The work undertaken in 1970 was undone, and the upper lights and side lights reopened. Based on a watercolour by John Napper (1916–2001), the new window depicts a tree bearing the names of the Commonwealth countries, accredited to the Court of St James's. The east wall was repanelled with blank tracery in oak, to a design by Martin Ashley, to complete Smirke's work of 1836. The walls were painted ochre, to match a colour used in the 1830s, revealed by scientific research. At the same time, two new panels were added to the ceiling, replacing former ventilation grills and containing the badges of The Queen, The Duke of Edinburgh and The Prince of Wales. The pews were re-covered in wool velvet of the same purple as the royal pew in Crathie Kirk at Balmoral.[26] The chapel remains in regular use, most recently for the christening of Prince Louis (b. 2018), youngest son of the Duke and Duchess of Cambridge (both b. 1982) (Fig. 5.13).

LEFT

5.12

The Prince of Wales and The Duchess of Cornwall with King Willem-Alexander and Queen Maxima of the Netherlands at Clarence House, during their State visit to the UK in October 2018

BELOW

5.13

The Duke and Duchess of Cambridge arrive with Princess Charlotte and Prince George for the christening of Prince Louis at the Chapel Royal in 2018. After the service the official photographs to commemorate the christening were taken at Clarence House

Afterword

It is remarkable that 488 years after St James's Palace was begun by Henry VIII as a home for the heir to the throne, HRH The Prince of Wales retains it today as his official residence. Few now, perhaps, understand the circuitous route that has led to this happy coincidence. For St James's is the accidental palace – a secondary residence that was forced to become the seat of the most powerful monarchy in the world. As St James's lost its role to Buckingham Palace in the twentieth century, it became a residence in search of a purpose. In the last two decades it has found one. Now home to TRH The Prince of Wales and The Duchess of Cornwall (b. 1947), St James's has become the headquarters of the Prince's charitable activities and his official duties in a way that his distant ancestor, Henry VIII, could never have imagined, but would, it is to be hoped, have approved.

5. THE PALACE TODAY

NOTES

References in notes given out of chronological order refer to the sequence of statements in the text.

Introduction

1. Thurley 1997.
2. *The Times*, 5 Aug. 1825.
3. Somerset House was known thus prior to 1603 and after 1775, and as Denmark House in the intervening period.
4. The suggestion was made by Alasdair Hawkyard to David Starkey (pers. comm.).
5. Baron Bielfeld (1710–70) was a German writer and statesman for the Prussian court.
6. See p. 191.
7. Banks 1740, I, p. 30.
8. Hooper 1768–70, IV, pp. 57–60.
9. HMC 1904–8, III, p. 193.
10. Hutton 1978, p. 156.
11. Sedgwick 1931, I, p. 66.
12. Defoe 1761, II, p. 138.
13. Brindle 2018, pp. 262–9; Thurley 2003, p. 282.
14. H. Smith 2006, p. 205.
15. Toynbee 1903–5, III, pp. 434–5.
16. Clifford Smith 1931, with introductory chapters on the building and site by Christopher Hussey, pp. 30–3; Thurley 2009b, pp. 75–6.
17. *HKW* 1976, pp. 133–8.
18. Ibid., p. 204.
19. *Survey of London* 1940, pp. 69–76; *Carlton House* 1991, pp. 9–12.
20. Yorke 2001, pp. 15–24.
21. Corp 2000, p. 243; Mörke 2007, pp. 227–36; Black 2004, pp. 21–37, 191–3.
22. *HKW* 1973, pp. 151–5.
23. Ibid., pp. 263–77.
24. See p. 190.
25. Port 1976, p. 20; Quinault 1992, p. 80.
26. See p. 199.
27. Beavan 1896, pp. 105–8.
28. Cannadine 1989, pp. 157–8.
29. Golby and Purdue 1988, pp. 81–5; Cannadine 1983, pp. 133–8; J. Parry 2007, pp. 54–8.

1. From the Hospital of St James to the Civil War

1. Rawcliffe 2006, pp. 145–7; Honeybourne 1967, pp. 20–1.
2. *Rot. Chart. John*, p. 117, col. b; *CChR 1226–57*, p. 269.
3. TNA, C 66/304, m. 31.
4. Sullivan 1994, pp. 41–2; Thomas *et al.* 2006, pp. 9–12.
5. WAM 17122.
6. Rosser 1989, p. 305.
7. Tout 1967, III, pp. 368–9.
8. TNA, C 66/304, m. 31.
9. R.G. Davies, 'Clifford, Richard (d. 1421)', *ODNB*, online edn, 2004 <www.oxforddnb.com/view/article/5657> (accessed 11 July 2019).
10. Talbot and Hammond 1965, pp. 204–5.
11. Allmand 1992, pp. 356–7.
12. R.C.E. Hayes, 'Alnwick, William (d. 1449)', *ODNB*, online edn, 2004 <www.oxforddnb.com/view/article/421> (accessed 11 July 2019).
13. TNA, C 66/322, m. 28.
14. ECR 61 RR A 66, rot. 3.
15. Rosser 1989, pp. 308–9, 192; ECR 16 J 002.
16. Rosser 1989, p. 310.
17. Roffey 2012, pp. 219, 223.
18. TNA, C 66/322, m. 28.
19. The two most illuminating documents are grants in 1496/7 and 1505: see ECR 60 03 01, fols 132v–133r and 141v–142v.
20. RCHME 1925, p. 130; Betts 2002: the tile types are W5, W62, W77, W112, W137.
21. Everett 2015, pp. 73–81; Rosser and Thurley 1990, pp. 58–75; Thurley 1997, pp. 98–101.
22. Thurley 2017, p. 294.
23. *HKW* 1963, I, pp. 537–8.
24. *CSP Spain 1553*, p. 214; von Bülow 1895, p. 256; *CSP Ven. 1632–6*, no. 285.
25. Sheppard 1894, I, p. 3.
26. AS, Wren I:2; Geraghty 2007, p. 166, no. 250.
27. BL, Royal MS 14 B IV A.
28. Green and Thurley 1987, pp. 76–7.
29. String 1996, pp. 139–51.
30. Thurley 1993, p. 102.
31. Wells-Cole 1997, pp. 11–12.
32. Croft-Murray 1962, p. 20; Frommel 2003, pp. 65–6, 72–3; Forster and Tuttle 1971, pp. 288–90; Thurley 1993, pp. 107–10.
33. Thurley 1993, pp. 113–20; Thurley 2017, pp. 204–10.
34. AS, Wren III:3; Geraghty 2007, p. 167, no. 252.
35. Starkey and Ward 1998, p. 384; TNA, E 351/3234.
36. *L&P Hen. VIII*, XIII (2), no. 855; *L&P Hen. VIII*, XII (2), App. 44; *L&P Hen. VIII*, X, no. 1231 (TNA, SP 1/103, fol. 220v); *L&P Hen. VIII*, XIV (2), pp. 321, 333, 334, 335, 342. Letters signed there include *L&P Hen. VIII*, XIII (1), nos 507 (pp. 189–90), 581 (p. 214), 760 (p. 287), 1059 (p. 389). See also MacCulloch 2018, pp. 439, 498, 503, 512.
37. *L&P Hen. VIII*, XII (2), no. 20 (pp. 8–9). See also *L&P Hen. VIII*, XIII (1), no. 659 (p. 240).
38. Thurley 2003, pp. 66–9.
39. Nichols 1855, pp. 1–21; Douglas Hamilton 1875–7, I, pp. 53–4.
40. TNA, SP 1/129, fols 234–234v; BL, Lansdowne Roll 14; Bodl., MS Vet. E.1b.6; Bodl., MS Eng. Hist. b. 192/1, fols 32v, 33v, 75. Buckler's drawing of the fireplace is in BL, Add. MS 36370, fol. 120.
41. TNA, OBS 1/1419. For the Privy Council, see, for instance, *L&P Hen. VIII*, XVII, nos 1215 (p. 259), 1219 (p. 430), 1222–3 (pp. 430–1), 1228 (p. 432); *L&P Hen. VIII*, XVIII (1), no. 275 (p. 157).
42. Thurley 1999, p. 52; Starkey and Ward 1998, pp. 383–5.
43. TNA, E 351/3238.
44. TNA, E 351/3223.
45. Thurley 2003, pp. 24–6.
46. TNA, E 351/3257.
47. TNA, E 351/3238.
48. TNA, E 351/3232.
49. Thurley 2003, pp. 56–7.
50. TNA, E 351/3215.
51. TNA, E 351/3214, E 351/3210. For other examples, see Thurley 1993, figs 46 and 54 and plans 7 and 15. For the staircase, see also TNA, WORK 5/1, fol. 275v.
52. TNA, E 351/3238.
53. Bodl., MS Eng. Hist. b. 192/1, fol. 33b.
54. TNA, E 351/3218, E 351/3241.
55. TNA, E 351/3257.
56. *CSP Dom. 1547–80*, nos 39, 234; Nichols 1857, I, pp. xcvi–xcvii, cx, 53, 59; Alford 2002, p. 76 n. 52.
57. *CSP Spain 1547–9*, p. 332; H. Robinson 1846–7, II, p. 648; Haynes 1740, p. 108; Jordan 1966, p. 19; Brigden 1990, pp. 107–8.
58. Jordan 1966, p. 100; Thurley 2017, p. 287.
59. TNA, E 351/3225, E 351/3230; Thurley 2017, pp. 289–92; Jordan 1970, pp. 165–6.
60. Thurley 2017, pp. 303–4.
61. Nichols 1848, p. 44; *CSP Spain 1553*, pp. 214, 238, 252.
62. Two contemporary descriptions of Wyatt at St James's are printed in Pollard 1902, pp. 188–90, 250–1; Nichols 1849, pp. 42, 44, 47.
63. Manning 1855, p. 167; Nichols 1848, pp. 64, 110, 122; Douglas Hamilton 1875–7, II, p. 131.
64. BL, Add. MS 6113, fols 133, 142v; Nichols 1848, p. 158.
65. Nichols 1848, p. 60.
66. Whitelock 2009, pp. 302–5; Starkey 2001, pp. 252–8.
67. Strangford 1853, pp. 3, 38; Nichols 1848, p. 16.
68. Von Bülow 1895, p. 237.
69. Guy 2016, pp. 104–11, 312–13.
70. Harrison 1928, p. 222; Ashbee and Harley 2000, I, pp. 54–5.
71. TNA, E 351/3216.
72. TNA, E 351/3228.
73. TNA, E 351/3227, E 351/3229; S. Adams 1995, pp. 194, 196–8, 208.
74. TNA, E 351/3205, E 351/3234.
75. TNA, E 351/3223.
76. TNA, E 351/3228.
77. HMC 1883–1940, XV, pp. 347–8.
78. *CSP Dom. 1603–10*, p. 132.
79. TNA, E 351/3239; BL, Add. MS 12498, fol. 3v.
80. BL, Add. MS 12498, fols 3, 3v, 4.
81. TNA, E 351/3239, E 351/3241; Strong 1986, pp. 42–4; Goodman 1839, I, pp. 16–18.
82. TNA, E 351/3239, E 351/3241.
83. TNA, LR 1/56 fol. 226; TNA, E 317/Middx/42.

84 TNA, E 317/Middx/71, and see also TNA, E 317/Middx/72.
85 Craigie 1944–50, I, pp. 120–1. The 'pell mell' is first mentioned in the royal accounts in 1630: LC 5/132, p. 192; *CSP Dom. 1660–61*, p. 292; *Survey of London* 1960, XXX, pp. 24–5.
86 TNA, E 351/3242.
87 G. Worsley 2004, pp. 52–68.
88 TNA, E 351/3241, E 351/3243; *HKW* 1982 (part 1), pp. 162–4.
89 Girouard 1962, pp. 33, 76 (RIBA, Smythson SC229/I/14).
90 Birch 1760, p. 97; Wrighte 1796, pp. 85–6; Bray 1806, pp. 22–6.
91 Birch 1760, pp. 128–9; Sears and Johnson 1956, pp. 14–17.
92 A. White 1999, pp. 29–31.
93 TNA, E 351/3244. TNA, SP 14/63, no. 55: the account mentions 38 term 'cases' (i.e. bases) and 43 term 'cases' plus 83 term heads, that is 81 heads for the bases and two heads for the fireplace.
94 Gapper *et al.* 2002, pp. 77–8.
95 TNA, T 1/100, fols 174, 184v.
96 TNA, E 351/3244.
97 TNA, E 351/3241, E 351/3243. TNA, WORK 5/1, fols 232v, 261v: this is corroborated in the accounts for 1660–1.
98 A rough calculation suggests that this is the case: the three galleries measured 550 linear feet of wall space without windows or doors, that is to say, 183 yards (167.3 m). Allowing for 16 windows at 4 ft (1.2 m), one opening of 9 ft (2.7 m) on the south, four doors of 3 ft (0.9 m), and four chimneys of 9 ft (2.7 m) – 40 yards (36.6 m) of gaps – that is, 143 yards (130.8 m) of wall at 6 yards (5.5 m) high, giving 858 square yards (717.4 m²). The 18 ft (5.5 m) height of the rooms is given in TNA, WORK 5/2, fol. 213.
99 There is detailed analysis of the monthly payments in Wilks 1987, p. 283. I am grateful to Dr Timothy Wilks for providing me with a copy of this.
100 Birch 1760, pp. 184–6; McClure 1939, I, p. 293; HMC 1924–40, III, p. 216.
101 Hatfield House, CP 134/163.
102 BL, Harley MSS 252/3 and 642/241.
103 *CSP Ven. 1610–13*, no. 159.
104 Bray 1806, p. 17; *HKW* 1975, pp. 121–7.
105 Strong 1986, pp. 184–200; Wilks 2005, pp. 149–72.
106 *CSP Ven. 1610–13*, no. 159.
107 Strong 1986, pp. 190–1.
108 C. White 1982, nos 148–149, pp. xiv–xvi; Van Gelder 1963, pp. 541–4. See also the list of paintings at St James's from 1613 printed in Rye 1865, p. 161.
109 Wilks 2005, pp. 149–54.
110 TNA, E 351/3245; Strong 1986, pp. 197–9.
111 TNA, E 351/3244; TNA, SP 14/63, no. 55, is 'the charges of st james howse for the new lybrary, gallery and altering of officers lodgings' (June 1610 to end April 1611), totalling £1,025 13s 1d.
112 Birch 1760, pp. 272–5; *CSP Ven. 1610–13*, no. 727.
113 *CSP Dom. 1611–18*, p. 361; *CSP Ven. 1610–13*, no. 698.
114 Turnor 1806, pp. 1–12.
115 Birch 1848, I, pp. 252, 256–7; HMC 1891–1931, IX, p. 14; Heylyn 1658, p. 13.
116 *HKW* 1982, pp. 246–7; Girouard 1962, pp. 54, 144 (RIBA, Smythson SC237/III/8(1)). For the housekeeper, see TNA, E 351/3252.
117 TNA, E 351/3256, E 351/3257.
118 Finet 1656, pp. 73, 103, 137.
119 TNA, SP 14/139, no. 63; SP 14/140, no. 21; *CSP Dom. 1611–8*, pp. 516, 536, 563.
120 McClure 1939, II, p. 494.
121 Rawson Gardiner 1869, pp. 120, 299–300; *CSP Ven. 1621–3*, no. 771.
122 Birch 1848, II, p. 400; TNA, SP 14/144, no. 42; HMC 1879, appendix, p. 258; McClure 1939, II, p. 494; *CSP Ven. 1623–5*, nos 55, 65. The houses were ordered to be vacated: Acts of the Privy Council, James I, VI (1621–3), p. 493.
123 TNA, E 351/3241, E 351/3243. TNA, E 351/3250: a new bird house was built there in 1615–16.
124 J. Harris 1972, nos 27, 28 and figs 23, 24; Harris and Higgott 1989, pp. 182–5. In addition there is a sketch of one of the ground-floor windows by John Webb: Harris and Tait 1979, fig. 121.
125 TNA, E 351/3260; Palladio 1570, IV, pl. XXIII.
126 G. Worsley 2007, pp. 105–11.
127 Beltramini 2001, pp. 96–9; Bertotti Scamozzi 1776–83, I, pls 37–39.
128 Harris and Higgott 1989, pp. 103–5.
129 Thurley 2009b, pp. 49–55.
130 Hart 2011, pp. 153–83.
131 TNA, E 351/3257.
132 *CSP Ven. 1625–6*, p. 3; ibid., p. 11; Birch 1848, I, pp. 3–4; Lyle 1934, p. 3.
133 *CSP Ven. 1625–6*, nos 34, 52; Birch 1848, I, p. 33.
134 BL, Kings MS 136, fol. 414. A letter of 1623 apparently corroborates that there were four altars: Griffey 2015, p. 309 n. 133.
135 TNA, E 404/153/Pt I, fol. 10.eo.
136 BL, Kings MS 136, fol. 415; *CSP Ven. 1625–6*, p. 398; HMC 1887, p. 94.
137 HMC 1888–1905, I, p. 473; HMC 1887, p. 57.
138 Thurley 2009b, pp. 49–55; Hibbard 2009, pp. 317–37; Thurley 2009c, pp. 299–302.
139 TNA, LC 5/132, fol. 188.
140 *CSP Ven. 1623–5*, p. 146; *CSP Ven. 1636–9*, p. 143.
141 Griffey 2015, pp. 109–15.
142 TNA, SP 16/168, no. 64; Bodl., MS Eng. Hist. e. 28, fol. 8v. Eyewitness accounts are in Loomie 1987, pp. 88–90; BL, Egerton MS 2553, fol. 34; BL, Egerton MS 1818, fols 78r–v; BL, Harley MS 791, fol. 40. See also *CSP Dom. 1629–31*, pp. 269, 282; TNA, LC 5/132, pp. 196, 201; TNA, AO 1/2426/60, fol. 8v.
143 TNA, E 351/3263.
144 Strong 1998, pp. 87–103.
145 TNA, SP 40/1 fol. 44; Chew 2004, p. 91 n. 25. I am grateful to Dr Timothy Wilks for this reference.
146 TNA, E 351/3245; Thurley 2003, pp. 89–95; Jacques 2017, pp. 54–5, 95.
147 Puget de la Serre 1639; the translation used here is in 'The Entry of Mary de Medicis to England in 1638 by the Sieur de la Serre', Grose 1775, I, p. 267; De Mandelslo 1719, p. 749.
148 BL, Royal MS 14 B IV A.
149 TNA, E 351/3215; *Survey of London* 1940, p. 58.
150 TNA, E 351/3246; *CSP Dom. 1603–10*, p. 359; *CSP Dom. 1603–10*, p. 153; *CSP Dom. 1611–18*, p. 57.
151 TNA, E 351/3251; Nichols 1828, III, p. 590; McClure 1939, II, p. 294; Young 1987, pp. 95–6, 208. For Prince Henry running at the ring at St James's, see Rye 1865, p. 62.
152 TNA, E 351/3255.
153 *CSP Dom. 1629–31*, p. 165.
154 In the late 1630s, Parkinson was granted a walled garden of 100 ft by 180 ft (30.5 by 54.9 m), next to the tennis court, for his specimen plants. He was also granted a house from which he supervised a nursery. Parkinson 1629; Burnby 1994, pp. 3–4; J. Burnby, 'Parkinson, John (1566/7–1650)', *ODNB*, online edn, 2004 <www.oxforddnb.com/view/article/21372> (accessed 11 July 2019); *CSP Dom. 1660–61*, p. 290; TNA, E 317/Middx/71.
155 Everett Green 1857, pp. 19–20.
156 National Library of Wales, Wynnstay MS 173, 19v; TNA, SC 6/chasI/1705; Wynnstay MS 176.
157 Puget de la Serre 1639; the translation used here is in 'The Entry of Mary de Medicis to England in 1638 by the Sieur de la Serre', Grose 1775, I, p. 267; De Mandelslo 1719, p. 749.
158 Webb 1665, p. 99.
159 Palladio 1570, I, p. 17, II, pl. 40, J. Harris 1972, cat. 30, fig. 26.
160 TNA, AO 1/2427/63.
161 Peacham 1906, p. 108.
162 TNA, AO 1/2429/73, AO 1/2428/69.
163 TNA, E 351/3263; Howarth 1989, pp. 75–109; Avery 1980–82, pp. 148–51.
164 Millar 1970–72, pp. 139–50; *CSP Dom. 1651*, p. 47; TNA, E 351/3266.
165 TNA, LC 5/132, pp. 116, 192, 252; see also repair in 1640: TNA, LC 5/134, p. 425; De Mandelslo 1719, p. 749.
166 *Survey of London* 1960, XXIX, pp. 21–8.
167 There are many references to this in the Lord Chamberlain's warrant books, for example, TNA, LC 5/134, pp. 83, 89.
168 TNA, AO 1/2427/63, AO 1/2429/72, LC 5/134, p. 93.
169 TNA, E 351/3265, E 351/3271.
170 TNA, LC 5/134, pp. 50, 185, 242; TNA, E 351/3269.
171 TNA, LC 5/51, p. 320.
172 TNA, AO 1/2429/73; *CSP Dom. 1629–31*, p. 313; Loomie 1987, pp. 195, 246; MacGregor 1989, pp. 360–1.
173 Eades Bentley 1941, I, pp. 230, 236–8, 324–5; TNA, AO 1/2428/69.
174 Loomie 1987, p. 244; Keay 2008, pp. 21–7.
175 C. Marsden, 'Doort, Abraham van der (1575/85–1640)', *ODNB*, online edn, 2004 <www.oxforddnb.com/view/article/28069> (accessed 11 July 2019); Millar 1958–60, pp. xiii–xvi.
176 Wilks 2005, pp. 162–5.
177 Millar 1963, no. 143, pp. 93–5; S.J. Barnes *et al.* 2004, no. IV.47, pp. 462–4.
178 TNA, E 351/3265; Millar 1970–72, p. 37. I am grateful to Desmond Shawe-Taylor for his views on this.
179 TNA, E 351/3265, AO 1/2427/65–67, E 351/3266.

180 Millar 1958-60, pp. 76–156, with references to the fittings at St James's on pp. 139-40.
181 Osborne 2011, pp. 30-6; *CSP Ven. 1636-9*, p. 519; TNA, LC 5/134, pp. 272, 274, 296, 306.
182 Puget de la Serre 1639; the translation used here is in 'The Entry of Mary de Medicis to England in 1638 by the Sieur de la Serre', Grose 1775, I, p. 267.
183 TNA, PRO 31/3/72, fols 155-161: Montereuil to Chavigny, 31 May 1640; *CSP Dom. 1640*, p. 172.
184 TNA, PRO 31/3/72, fol. 177: Montereuil to Chavigny, 5 July 1640, and fols 197-199: Montereuil to Chavigny, 26 July 1640; *CSP Ven. 1640-42*, p. 114; *Journal of the House of Lords*, IV, p. 244; *Journal of the House of Commons*, II, p. 419.
185 *Journal of the House of Commons*, II, pp. 199, 226; Pardoe 1890, III, pp. 401-10.
186 HMC 1876, Appendix, p. 60; TNA, LC 5/136A, p. 58.
187 *Journal of the House of Commons*, II, p. 903; *Journal of the House of Lords*, V, 504, m. 581-3; *Journal of the House of Commons*, II, p. 847.
188 Firth and Rait 1911, I, pp. 265-6; Spraggon 2003, pp. 83-97.
189 Vicars 1644, p. 294; *Journal of the House of Lords*, VI, p. 215.
190 *Journal of the House of Commons*, III, p. 146; J.T. Peacey, 'Holland, Cornelius (1600–1671?)', *ODNB*, online edn, 2004 <www.oxforddnb.com/view/article/13517> (accessed 11 July 2019).
191 *Journal of the House of Lords*, VI, 393; *Journal of the House of Commons*, III, p. 516; *Journal of the House of Lords*, VI, 475-6, 513; TNA, LC 5/135, unpaginated.
192 Strickland 1872, pp. 158-62; J. Eales, 'Vere, Mary, Lady Vere (1581–1671)', *ODNB*, online edn, 2004 <www.oxforddnb.com/view/article/40534> (accessed 11 July 2019); D.L. Smith, 'Sackville, Mary, countess of Dorset (bap. 1586, d. 1645)', *ODNB*, online edn, 2004 <www.oxforddnb.com/view/article/92426> (accessed 11 July 2019).
193 *Journal of the House of Commons*, III, p. 148; *Mercurius Aulicus*, 21-27 April 1644, pp. 952-3; *The Spie, Communicating Intelligence from Oxford*, 1–8 May 1644, issue 15; *Journal of the House of Commons*, II, p. 847.
194 *Mercurius Britanicus*, 6–13 May 1644, issue 35, pp. 272-3.
195 Thurley 2002, p. 242.
196 *Journal of the House of Commons*, IV, p. 270; Peck 1736, II, pp. 1-2; G.A. Drake, 'Percy, Algernon, tenth earl of Northumberland (1602–1668)', *ODNB*, online edn, 2004 <www.oxforddnb.com/view/article/21923> (accessed 11 July 2019).
197 *Journal of the House of Commons*, IV, p. 611; ibid., V, p. 500; West Sussex Record Office, PHA 617. See also HMC 1872, p. 86.
198 *HKW* 1975, pp. 154-63.
199 TNA, AO 1/2429/72, AO 1/2429/73, AO 1/2430/76, AO 1/2431/79, AO 1/2432/82.
200 TNA, AO 1/2429/72.
201 E. Clarendon 1888, I, p. 327.
202 F.C. Turner 1948, pp. 16–19; Callow 2000, pp. 46–50.
203 *Journal of the House of Lords*, X, p. 219.
204 Herbert 1813, pp. 173-95; E. Clarendon 1888, IV, p. 483; Whitelocke 1853, II, p. 522.
205 *CSP Dom. 1644*, p. 243; *A Perfect Diurnall of some passages in Parliament*, 10 June 1644.
206 *Journal of the House of Commons*, V, p. 436, Jan. 1648; Whitelocke 1853, II, p. 262; BL, Harley MS 6988, fol. 216; J.M. Blatchly, 'D'Ewes, Sir Simonds, first baronet (1602–1650)', *ODNB*, online edn, 2004 <www.oxforddnb.com/view/article/7577> (accessed 11 July 2019).
207 Whitelocke 1853, III, pp. 74-5; *Journal of the House of Commons*, VI, p. 272; Spalding 1990, p. 243; J.T. Young, 'Durie, John (1596–1680)', *ODNB*, online edn, 2004 <www.oxforddnb.com/view/article/8323> (accessed 11 July 2019); Warner and Gilson 1921, I, pp. xxii, xxiii, xxiv; Ashmole 1658, I, pp. x–xi.
208 *CSP Dom. 1649-50*, p. 285; *CSP Dom. 1650*, p. 418.
209 *CSP Dom. 1649-50*, pp. 248, 581.
210 Kelsey 1997, pp. 29–45.
211 Bachrach and Collmer 1982, pp. 42-3.
212 *CSP Dom. 1649-50*, p. 155; *Journal of the House of Commons*, VI, p. 246; Madge 1938, pp. 102-3.
213 Sears and Johnson 1956, pp. 20–1, 293; *Journal of the House of Commons*, VI, p. 148; Millar 1970-72, pp. 139-57, 256-74, 298-321.
214 *CSP Dom. 1651*, pp. 47, 78, 218, 252, 257; Sachse 1961, pp. 10-11.
215 Millar 1970-72, pp. 139-57, 256-74, 298-321.
216 *CSP Dom. 1653-4*, pp. 152, 211, 234, 238, 273, 291.
217 *CSP Dom. 1654*, pp. 353-4; *Journal of the House of Commons*, VII, p. 404; Whitelocke 1853, IV, p. 155; *CSP Dom. 1655*, p. 148; *CSP Dom. 1656-7*, pp. 97, 140-1; *CSP Dom. 1657-8*, p. 127.
218 *HKW* 1975, pp. 165-8: 25 Oct., John Embree, £1,235 for repairs at 'St Jas mews, som Ho, Whitehall and parliament', p. 589; 29 Mar., £400 for 'embree for st jas' and 'guards there', p. 595.
219 *CSP Dom. 1658-9*, pp. 130, 142, 200, 222, 354.
220 Firth 1894, II, p. 69.
221 *CSP Dom. 1659-60*, p. 577; *CSP Ven. 1659-61*, pp. 121, 148; *CSP Dom. 1659-60*, p. 595; R. Hutton, 'Monck, George, first duke of Albemarle (1608–1670)', *ODNB*, online edn, 2004 <www.oxforddnb.com/view/article/18939> (accessed 11 July 2019).
222 Act of Parliament, 27 Eliz. 1 c.31.
223 Powys Marks 1964.
224 Barber 2012, pp. 36-7.
225 Nurse 2017, pp. 22-5.
226 'Notes on London and Westminster by John Norden, 1592', printed in Rye 1865, p. 100.
227 *Survey of London* 1960, XXX, p. 431.
228 Ibid., pp. 21-4, 215.
229 TNA, LC 5/132, fol. 192.
230 TNA, E 317/Middx/71.
231 Kingsford 1925, p. 1.
232 *CSP Dom. 1628-9*, pp. 198, 513.
233 TNA, E 317/Middx/39. The survey is of 'houses neere adjoining to St James'; *Survey of London* 1960, XXX, pp. 431-71.
234 The original map is in BL, Add. MS 38104. It was reproduced by the London Topographical Society in 1915, and it was redrawn with extensive analysis and explanation in Gatty 1921, II, pl. 31.
235 Sullivan 2006, pp. 49-50, 335-9, 400-4.
236 TNA, E 351/3244, E 317/Middx/41; *CSP Dom. 1603-10*, pp. 562, 574; *CSP Dom. 1611-18*, p. 29; *CSP Dom. 1628-9*, p. 192; Levy Peck 2000, pp. 225-7.
237 *L&P Hen. VIII*, XI, no. 202 (p. 84 (4)).
238 *HKW* 1982, pp. 157-60.
239 *CSP Dom. 1603-10*, p. 410; *CSP Dom. 1611-18*, p. 19; MacGregor 1989, pp. 154, 407.
240 Ellis 1824, II, p. 148; *CSP Dom. 1623-5*, p. 13; Coryat 1611.
241 *Survey of London* 1960, XXIX, p. 25.
242 *HKW* 1975, pp. 140-4; McIlwain 1918, p. 343.
243 Duggan 2000, pp. 140-61.
244 Smuts 1991, pp. 121-3.
245 TNA, E 317/Middx/39; Thrush and Ferris 2010, <www.historyofparliamentonline.org/volume/1604-1629/member/howard-sir-thomas-1587-1669> (accessed 27 Jan. 2020; *Survey of London* 1960, XXX, pp. 490-1.
246 TNA, E 317/Middx/27; Gatty 1921, I, pp. 99-109; Clifford Smith 1931, pp. 14-19.
247 Duggan 2003, pp. 54-64; BL, Maps, Crace Port., 11.61.
248 *Survey of London* 1966, XXXIV, pp. 416-18, 441-2; I. Atherton, 'Sidney, Robert, second earl of Leicester (1595–1677)', *ODNB*, online edn, 2004 <www.oxforddnb.com/view/article/25525> (accessed 11 July 2019).
249 *Survey of London* 1966, XXXIV, pp. 360-3.
250 Ibid., pp. 380-3; Wilks 2007, pp. 198-201.
251 On this subject, see Brett-James 1935, pp. 268-91; Brett-James 1928, pp. 1-35; V. Smith and Kelsey 1996, pp. 117-18.
252 Lithgow 1643, reprinted in W. Scott 1809-15, IV, pp. 540-1; *CSP Ven. 1642-3*, p. 192.
253 *CSP Dom. 1653-4*, p. 366; *CSP Dom. 1654*, pp. 39, 311; *CSP Dom. 1656-7*, p. 71.

2. The Restoration to Queen Anne

1 *CSP Ven. 1659-61*, p. 148.
2 TNA, WORK 5/1, fols 231v, 259v, 260v, 263.
3 Ibid., fols 231v, 261, 272.
4 Ibid., fols 196, 200, 206.
5 *HKW* 1976, pp. 6-7, 476; Dobrée and Webb 1928, IV, p. 12.
6 TNA, WORK 5/1, fols 232v, 233, 234, 243v, 261v.
7 Ibid., fols 213v, 215.
8 *CTP 1556-1696*, p. 156; TNA, WORK 5/1, fol. 266v, WORK 5/2, fol. 185.
9 Airy 1897, p. 298.
10 De Beer 1955, III, pp. 340-1. The royal grant for the site of Clarendon House is printed in Wheatley 1870, pp. 83-4.
11 F.C. Turner 1948, p. 69 n. 2.
12 De Monconys 1695, p. 38.
13 TNA, WORK 5/2, fols 195, 209, 210, 214, 217v; Thurley 1999, p. 106.
14 TNA, WORK 5/3, fol. 254; WORK 5/4, fol. 192.
15 TNA, WORK 5/1, fols 213, 214, 214v.
16 TNA, WORK 5/3, fol. 251; WORK 5/4, fol. 167; TNA, WORK 5/4, fol. 168; WORK 5/5, fol. 146.

17 TNA, WORK 5/2, fols 209, 210, 213; WORK 5/9, fol. 216; WORK 5/5, fol. 162.
18 TNA, WORK 5/3, fol. 248: two partitions came out: one, 20 ft wide (6.1 m), was the dividing wall between the rooms; the location of the other, 14 ft wide (4.3 m), is unclear.
19 Ibid., fols 248, 248v. TNA, WORK 5/4, fols 167, 170.
20 TNA, WORK 5/3, fol. 254; WORK 5/5, fol. 146.
21 TNA, WORK 5/3, fol. 167v; WORK 5/1, fol. 271; WORK 5/4, fol. 167v; WORK 5/5, fol. 158; WORK 5/9, fol. 213.
22 TNA, WORK 5/1, fols 171, 178, 282, 295r–v; WORK 5/2, fols 178, 364; WORK 5/9, fol. 210.
23 *CSP Dom. 1661-2*, p. 451.
24 *CSP Ven. 1661-4*, pp. 132–3; Latham and Matthews 1970–83, VII, p. 145, IX, p. 206; Magalotti 1821, pp. 345–6.
25 TNA, WORK 5/9, fols 428–432: extraordinary account, Feb. 1666 to May 1667. Other rooms identified in TNA, WORK 5/10, fol. 175; WORK 5/13, fol. 165; WORK 5/21, fol. 121; WORK 5/25, fol. 135.
26 TNA, WORK 5/17, fol. 129; WORK 5/11, fols 196v, 167v.
27 TNA, SP 44/13, p. 340.
28 TNA, SP 29/75, no. 27; Thoms 1914.
29 The lease of 1662 is TNA, C 66/3005, and specifies that buildings shall be erected 'According to such designs and plots as by his said majesties his heirs or successors under their privy signet privy seal or great seal and his or their surveyor general of the works for the time being shall be directed or approved'. *Survey of London* 1960, XXX, pp. 56, 61.
30 Dasent 1895, pp. 19–22, using BL, Add. MS 22063.
31 *Survey of London* 1960, XXX, pp. 322–4, 377–8, 491.
32 Ibid., XXX, pp. 323, 431; TNA, WORK 5/19, fol. 347; *CTB 1676-9*, p. 1152; De Beer 1955, III, p. 328.
33 TNA, WORK 5/1, fol. 296; *CSP Dom. 1660-61*, pp. 240, 521; De Monconys 1695, p. 24.
34 *CSP Dom. 1663-4*, p. 57; Jacques 2017, pp. 84–5.
35 Latham and Matthews 1970–83, VII, p. 213.
36 Browning *et al.* 1991, pp. 145, 234, 238; Westergaard 1947, p. 451; Gilbert 1913, pp. 15–16.
37 TNA, AO 1/2481/292. The decoy was extended in the 1680s: Yonge Akerman 1851, p. 82.
38 Gilbert 1913, p. 19; Browning *et al.* 1991, p. 245; Luttrell 1857, I, p. 156; *CSP Ven. 1661-4*, p. 250; Yonge Akerman 1851, pp. 178, 198–9, 206; De Beer 1955, III, pp. 398–400; TNA, WORK 5/15, fols 194r–v; De Monconys 1695, p. 38.
39 TNA, WORK 5/15, fols 425–440; WORK 5/45, pp. 24, 39; Yonge Akerman 1851, p. 65; *Survey of London* 1960, XXIX, p. 27.
40 Geraghty 2007, cat. 412, p. 266; Bolton and Hendry 1924–43, VII, pl. XXX. The drawing names Cleveland House, so must be after 1668.
41 *CSP Dom. 1670*, p. 678.
42 *CTB 1660-67*, p. 280.
43 *Survey of London* 1940, pp. 58–9.
44 Jakobson *et al.* 2006–7; Pattacini 1998, pp. 3–18.
45 *CSP Dom. 1660-61*, p. 369; TNA, WORK 5/29, fols 467–468, WORK 5/17, fols 362–363v. Rose already had the maintenance contract for Mollet's garden: *CSP Dom. 1660-61*, p. 369; *CTB 1660-67*, p. 294.
46 Munby 1996, pp. 57–64; Yonge Akerman 1851, p. 122.
47 Lunn 1980, pp. 135–8; A.S. Barnes 1900.
48 TNA, WORK 5/3, fols 168, 207, 208, 211, 211v, 217, 221, 223v, 226, 227; TNA, LC 5/137, p. 172; Ashbee 1986, I, pp. 32, 43; De Monconys 1695, pp. 36–7.
49 Leech 2001, p. 575.
50 Latham and Matthews 1970–83, III, p. 202.
51 TNA, WORK 5/4, fols 193, 202–203, 212, WORK 5/13, fol. 168v, WORK 5/5, fols 149, 153–154, 157v.
52 Latham and Matthews 1970–83, V, p. 63, VIII, pp. 588–9; *HKW* 1976, pp. 245–6. For the Queen's devotions, see TNA, WORK 5/4, fol. 167v; TNA, LS 13/170, fol. 177v.
53 TNA, WORK 5/4, fol. 180, WORK 5/3, fol. 249v.
54 A.S. Barnes 1900; Anstruther 1958, pp. 315–61; Maziere Brady 1971, III, pp. 113–14, 125.
55 Work to supply the friary with water and build a sewer, and to make new openings in the park wall, was paid for by the Office of Works: TNA, WORK 5/7, fols 339–342, WORK 5/8, fols 343–345, WORK 5/9, fol. 206, WORK 5/6, fol. 97.
56 TNA, WORK 5/9, fols 440–444, 446–450, WORK 5/5, fol. 157, WORK 5/9, fol. 175. A survey of the court and house in 1650 is in TNA, E 317/Middx/42, which suggests that it had at least six fine 'chambers', in addition to parlours, a 'lodging room', closets and garrets. TNA, WORK 5/13, fol. 180: the building accounts mention the room of one of the Benedictine lay brothers, Benedict Hankinson, being in the new building, and a visitation of the chapel in 1669 suggests that he and the brothers were lodged in the house; Maziere Brady 1971, III, p. 113.
57 TNA, WORK 5/13, fol. 182, WORK 5/11, fol. 156, WORK 5/10, fol. 190v, WORK 5/15, fols 165, 169, 169v, WORK 5/5, fol. 138, WORK 5/15, fol. 179.
58 Maziere Brady 1971, III, p. 117; TNA, SP 29/55; Latham and Matthews 1970–83, III, p. 202.
59 Kubler and Soria 1959, pp. 23–4; Pereira 2002; Kubler 1982, p. 86, fig. 2.
60 Evans 1964, pp. 119–20; Leech 2001, pp. 570–87.
61 Thurley 2002, pp. 258–61.
62 Babelon and Mignot 1998, pp. 183–7; Pérouse de Montclos 1994, pp. 370–2, 475–8; Evans 1964, pp. 24–6.
63 Latham and Matthews 1970–83, VIII, pp. 25–7, 116, 154, 588.
64 Anstruther 1958, pp. 320–1; Magalotti 1821, pp. 345–6; Maziere Brady 1971, III, p. 112.
65 *CTB 1669-72*, p. 916; HMC 1890, p. 67; *CSP Ven. 1671-2*, p. 76; Weale 1941, pp. xxix–xxxii.
66 *CSP Ven. 1673-5*, p. 193.
67 *CSP Ven. 1673-5*, p. 357; *CSP Dom. 1676-7*, p. 201; Pike 1913, p. 65.
68 Raymund Palmer 1867.
69 TNA, LC 5/143, p. 191; TNA, WORK 5/30, fol. 156.
70 *True Domestic Intelligence*, no. 51 (Tues., 30 Dec. 1680), no. 52 (Fri., 2 Jan. 1680); J. Miller 1973, pp. 21–2, 154–88. After their relocation from Somerset House to St James's, the Office of Works accounts mention (in contemporary spelling) lodgings for Fathers Jasent, Atanasisio, Lsidence, Deonisio, Michell, Garden, Deogo, Verissimus, Emanuell, Frerero, Jacenthe, Atanasisos, Sankestree, Bandelemuss, Poldolmedos, Ferdinandas, Aggesteen, President, Christopher and Huddlestone: 20 in all, plus lay brothers Mr Pereros, Mr Anthony, Mr Roche and Mr Timothy and Mr Ffrararos.
71 Thurley 2009b, pp. 70–2; Thurley 2002, pp. 258–63. The extraordinary account for this work is in TNA, WORK 5/32, fols 343–393.
72 TNA, WORK 5/32, fols 343–393.
73 TNA, LR 5/76 (unpaginated); the chapel establishment is in BL, Add. MS 15897, dated 1678; *CSP Dom. 1680-81*, p. 47.
74 HMC 1890, p. 185; Yonge Akerman 1851, p. 50; Luttrell 1857, I, p. 172; *London Gazette*, no. 1706 (27 Mar. 1682); TNA, WORK 5/37, fol. 143.
75 TNA, LR 5/76: the bills for work in 1682–3 are in the papers of Catherine of Braganza's receiver general. They include authorisations signed by Wren to pay the workmen and one enrolled account of 16 pages. There are no folio or piece numbers. The contract for a joiner, John Turnor, is in TNA, WORK 5/145, fol. 145, and a brickwork contract is in ibid., p. 92. TNA, E 101/675/17: a bill from another joiner, William Cleer, clearly states that his work is for new building.
76 Thurley 2004, pp. 84–8; TNA, WORK 5/145, fol. 145.
77 TNA, E 101/674/31.
78 Croft-Murray and Hulton 1960, p. 327.
79 Carnavalet 1985, pp. 34–5.
80 For Walton, see Martin 2005, I, pp. 111–12.
81 *CTB 1685-9*, pp. 1299–1300.
82 *London Gazette*, no. 2292 (5 Nov. 1687).
83 HMC 1890, p. 59; Westergaard 1947, p. 28.
84 Latham and Matthews 1970–83, IX, p. 284; TNA, LC 5/2, p. 78.
85 Strickland 1846, X, pp. 242–5; Cloake 1996, II, pp. 2–3.
86 TNA, WORK 5/5, fols 146, 147, 157, WORK 5/13, fol. 168. Work for the Duke of Kendal is in TNA, WORK 5/9, fols 197, 434.
87 TNA, WORK 5/11, fols 170, 172, WORK 5/21, fols 133, 139, 161, WORK 5/25, fol. 155, WORK 5/23, fols 143, 151, WORK 5/26, fol. 179; Strickland 1846, X, pp. 250–3.
88 TNA, WORK 5/21, fol. 150v; TNA, LC 5/2, p. 50; Strickland 1846, IX, p. 61; Browning *et al.* 1991, p. 114.
89 TNA, WORK 5/28, fol. 429.
90 TNA, WORK 5/25, fol. 131. See also TNA, WORK 5/38, fol. 145v.
91 TNA, WORK 5/28, fol. 137, WORK 5/21, fol. 136. See also TNA, WORK 5/21, fols 129v, 133, 136, 143, WORK 5/28, fol. 140v.
92 Strickland 1846, IX, pp. 61–3; TNA, WORK 5/25, fol. 124, WORK 5/28, fol. 114v.
93 Two extraordinary accounts in TNA, WORK 5/28, fols 428–441.
94 G.P. Elliott 1847, pp. 5–6, 9; E.M. Thompson 1878, p. 154; TNA, WORK 5/28, fol. 439, WORK 5/30, fol. 144.

95 *CTB 1676–9*, pp. 437, 1152; TNA, WORK 5/30, fol. 148; *CTB 1669–72*, p. 897.
96 TNA, WORK 5/145, fol. 59v.
97 TNA, WORK 5/27, fol. 146, WORK 5/28, fols 117v, 144, 146, 141. A later survey of the plan of the building by William Dickinson is Bodl., MS Gough misc. antiq. 17, fol. 9v; Geraghty 2007, cats 242–243, p. 161; Bolton and Hendry 1924–43, XII, pl. X.
98 Thurley 2003, pp. 137–9; TNA, WORK 5/1, fols 251r–v, 252v.
99 TNA, WORK 5/28, fol. 366, WORK 5/29, fols 462, 464; *CTB 1676–9*, p. 1152.
100 *CSP Dom. 1684–5*, p. 349; TNA, WORK 5/42, fol. 124.
101 There are at least three versions of this painting: one in the Royal Collection (RCIN 400009), one in the possession of Lord Sackville at Knole House, and a third that was sold by Richard Green in 2002. Oliver Millar identified a fourth version sold at Bonhams in 1962: Millar 1963, no. 443.
102 *CTB 1681–5*, p. 217; TNA, WORK 5/32, fols 390–393.
103 *London Gazette*, no. 1711 (10 Apr. 1682); *Loyal Protestant*, no. 194 (12 Aug. 1682), no. 212 (26 Sept. 1682); TNA, WORK 5/37, fols 116v, 120, 132, 139v, 140, WORK 5/145, fol. 84v.
104 TNA, WORK 5/37, fol. 139; TNA, LC 5/2; *London Gazette*, no. 1846 (28 July 1683); De Beer 1955, IV, p. 357.
105 I am grateful to Olivia Fryman for this reference. BL, Add. MS 17916, fol. 120; TNA, LC 5/39, p. 259, LC 5/40, p. 79; *CSP Dom. 1660–1*, item 90.
106 TNA, WORK 5/13, fol. 181v, WORK 5/19, fol. 145, WORK 5/17, fol. 143; Durrant Cooper 1858, p. 219.
107 Barclay 2015, pp. 629–49; Gleissner 1994, pp. 102–15.
108 Bodl., MS Bodl. 891. I am extremely grateful to Olivia Fryman for providing me with her transcript.
109 I am very grateful to Dr Thomas P. Campbell for these observations.
110 Millar 1963, I, pp. 124–7; MacLeod and Marciari Alexander 2001, pp. 53–4; Wenzel 2002, pp. 205–13; Hamilton [1794], p. 198.
111 Gennari's own list of the paintings that he produced in London identifies the two for St James's: Bagni 1986, p. 155, no. 82, p. 156, no. 96; Barclay 2002, pp. 81–2, 85; D.C. Miller 1983, pp. 24–9; Birmingham Museum and Art Gallery 1990, pp. 139–40.
112 Magalotti 1821, p. 346; De Monconys 1695, p. 38.
113 *CTB 1685–9*, p. 498.
114 Bodl., MS Clarendon 6, fol. 301; De Beer 1955, IV, pp. 480, 493, 537; Luttrell 1857, I, p. 338; HMC 1889, II, p. 98; Thurley 1999, pp. 127–33.
115 *CTB 1685–9*, pp. 275, 695; TNA, WORK 5/39, fols 140, 302–396; Yonge Akerman 1851, p. 111. One of the stairs can be seen in TNA, WORK 34/121.
116 Bagni 1986, p. 97, no. 60, p. 150, no. 28, p. 155, nos 81–2.
117 Bennet Weldon 1881, p. xxvi; Gilbert Dolan 1899.
118 TNA, WORK 5/40, fol. 130; Yonge Akerman 1851, pp. 156, 185, 138; Bodl., MS Rawl. C. 987, p. 31; BL, Add. MS 32095, fol. 241.
119 Gibson 2009, p. 74; Thoms 1852, pp. 298–9; Thoms 1853, pp. 242–3.
120 Cartwright 1843, p. 52.
121 TNA, WORK 5/40, fols 104v, 105v, 106v, 110v, 113v, 117v, WORK 5/42, fols 108, 110, WORK 5/40, fol. 127.
122 TNA, T 27/11, fol. 122; Barclay 2010, pp. 1–13.
123 BL, Harley MS 1890, fols 85v–86v; GUL, MS Hunter 238, fols 87–91.
124 Anon. 1689, p. 8.
125 Burnet 1815, pp. 448–51; H. Clarendon 1765, II, pp. 202–3. See also Weil 1992; Schwoerer 1992, pp. 65–70.
126 Anon. 1688.
127 TNA, WORK 5/42, fols 118, 131, 123, 126.
128 *London Gazette*, no. 2391 (15 Oct. 1688); H. Clarendon 1765, II, p. 229.
129 *London Courant*, no. 2 (12–15 Dec. 1688).
130 *London Gazette*, no. 14 (11 Feb. 1689); De Beer 1955, IV, pp. 610–11, 623–4; Beddard 1988, pp. 59, 63, 180.
131 Thurley 2003, pp. 151–2, 168, 184; Thurley 1999, pp. 137, 140–3; Thurley 2009a, pp. 6–7; TNA, MPE 1/482.
132 *London Gazette*, no. 2414 (31 Dec. 1688); *CTB 1685–9*, p. 365.
133 TNA, WORK 5/45, fols 137–138. TNA, WORK 5/45, fol. 145: a vestry with a six-light window was also made in the gatehouse.
134 There is a full lodgings list of the occupants of St James's in 1692 in TNA, LC 5/201, pp. 76–7, and another of 1695 in LC 5/201, pp. 171–4.
135 TNA, C 66/3329; TNA, LC 3/31, p. 59 (I owe these references to Jane Roberts); HMC 1888–1905, II, p. 148; De Beer 1955, III, p. 441; TNA, WORK 5/43, fol. 138.
136 Wordsworth 1842, I, p. 152.
137 TNA, WORK 5/48, fols 124v, 128v, 130v, 132v, 134v; Wordsworth 1842, I, pp. 113–14, 155; De Beer 1955, V, pp. 224, 280.
138 The pamphlet is conveniently printed in E. Edwards 1859, I, pp. 423–6.
139 *CTB 1697–8*, p. 131; Wordsworth 1842, I, p. 152. On Bentley, see also McDayter 2003.
140 TNA, T 1/100, fols 174, 184v.
141 Warner and Gilson 1921, I, pp. xxviii–xxix; Quarrell and Mare 1934, p. 122; Sears and Johnson 1956, pp. 21–2.
142 Thurley 2018, pp. 243–4; Luttrell 1857, III, pp. 420, 422; Gregg 1980, pp. 94–5, 102–4.
143 TNA, WORK 5/47, fols 144v, 290; TNA, LC 5/43, fols 158v–159.
144 *Post Man*, no. 92 (Tues., 10 Dec. 1695), no. 92/3 (Thurs., 12 Dec. 1695); *Post Boy*, no. 95 (Tues., 17 Dec. 1695); Luttrell 1857, III, pp. 531–2, 551.
145 Foxcroft 1898, II, p. 112 n. 5; Luttrell 1857, III, pp. 475, 510; TNA, WORK 5/44, fol. 145, WORK 5/45, fol. 147, WORK 5/46, fols 132, 141, 143, 151, 152, WORK 5/47, fol. 124, WORK 5/48, fol. 132.
146 Luttrell 1857, III, p. 426; *CTP 1697–1702*, p. 556; *CSP Dom. 1697*, p. 293.
147 Hilton 1977, pp. 160–72; Goff 1995, pp. 202–31; Latham and Matthews 1970–83, III, pp. 300–1, VII, pp. 371–3; HMC 1891–1931, III, p. 294.
148 De Beer 1955, IV, pp. 650–1, V, p. 362; Anderson Winn 2014, pp. 1–3; Barclay 2007, pp. 255–7.
149 TNA, WORK 5/53, fol. 130: the earliest references to the room call it the 'dancing room'. For examples of the Queen's birthday ball, see, for instance, G.P. Elliott 1847, p. 9; Latham and Matthews 1970–83, VII, pp. 371–3; HMC 1888–1905, II, p. 32.
150 *Post Boy*, nos 273, 279, 430, 434, 438, 599, 605, 737. See also Anderson Winn 2014, pp. 224–6. For details of the banked seating in the ballroom, see TNA, WORK 34/122 and Sir John Soane's Museum, London, SM 62/2/1–3.
151 *CSP Dom. 1698*, pp. 36, 69. TNA, WORK 5/50, fol. 120: The ballroom was pressed into use for purposes other than dancing; in 1699, it is referred to as 'the great dining room'.
152 TNA, LC 5/43, fol. 194r–v.
153 *Post Man*, no. 99; *Post Boy*, nos 610, 614, 625, 632, 643, 747, 760, 774, 783, 909, 916, 921; *Post Boy*, nos 428, 595, 890.
154 Gregg 1980, pp. 114–16; Luttrell 1857, IV, p. 328. The stairs are shown on a plan by William Dickinson: Bodl., MS Gough misc. antiq. 17, fol. 92.
155 Gregg 1980, pp. 120–4.
156 The first time St James's was called a palace, as far as can be ascertained, was in the Commonwealth (TNA, AO 1/2429/72), but this was a random usage and it was still known as St James's house at the Restoration. Only after 1689 does the term 'palace' become regularly used.
157 *Survey of London* 1960, XXX, p. 432; *CSP Dom. 1703–4*, p. 551; Matthews 1939, p. 77.
158 TNA, WORK 5/50, fol. 113, WORK 5/53, fols 427, 431.
159 King 1930, p. 230.
160 *CTB 1708*, p. 348; Gregg 1980, p. 136; Impey 2003, p. 47.
161 For instance, *Post Boy*, no. 2833 (4 July 1713).
162 TNA, WORK 5/52, fol. 147, WORK 5/53, fols 138–139.
163 The collars were the chains of 'S's that the principal aristocrats wore on the most important festivals.
164 Quarrell and Mare 1934, pp. 115–16.
165 AS, Wren I:30; Geraghty 2007, cat. 244, pp. 162–3; TNA, WORK 6/2, fols 72–73, printed in Bolton and Hendry 1924–43, VII, pp. 210–12.
166 Luttrell 1857, V, pp. 159, 350.
167 *Post Boy*, no. 1117 (11 July 1702); *CTB 1703*, pp. 20, 26, 167; *CTP 1702–7*, p. 37; *CTB 1702*, pp. 60–1, 479.
168 TNA, WORK 6/14, fol. 21; *CTB 1703*, pp. 20, 26, 73, 167, 272, 378, 473; *CTB 1704–5*, p. 339. The various schemes are discussed in Geraghty 2007, pp. 162–5.
169 TNA, WORK 5/53, fols 426, 431; Thurley 2003, pp. 183–4. An unexecuted design for this portico is amongst the drawings at All Souls, Oxford: Geraghty 2007, p. 245 (Bolton and Hendry 1924–43, VII, pl. xxix). Geraghty rightly makes the point that, stylistically, this looks later than 1703; the design may, in fact, be related to Vanbrugh's proposals of a decade later.
170 TNA, WORK 5/145, fol. 231; for details of the construction, see *HKW* 1976, p. 238.

171 Gregg 1980, pp. 140–1; *London Gazette*, no. 4240 (27 June 1706), no. 4242 (23 July 1706); *Daily Courant*, no. 1378 (13 Sept. 1706); *London Gazette*, no. 4840 (23 Apr. 1711).
172 Bucholz 1993, pp. 187–8; Thurley 2000, p. 230.
173 TNA, LC 5/45, pp. 93, 96, 102–3, LC 9/283 (year ending Michaelmas 1710); RCIN 1112574, fol. 71; *CTB 1708*, p. 398.
174 Thurley 2014; Keay 2008, pp. 126–30.
175 Williams 1948, II, pp. 322–3, 328, 363, 421, 490, 522, 595–6, 603, 629, 645, 659.
176 TNA, LC 5/44, fols 203, 210, 215v; RCIN 1112574, fol. 71.
177 *London Gazette*, no. 4334 (22 May 1707), no. 4840 (23 Apr. 1711), no. 5233 (8 June 1714).
178 TNA, LC 5/45, p. 91.
179 HMC 1888–1905, II, p. 176; TNA, LC 9/282, fol. 28r–v, LC 5/44, fols 210v, 215v, 219v.
180 RCIN 1112574, fol. 72.
181 *English Post*, no. 363 (3–5 Feb. 1702); Luttrell 1857, V, p. 266; Boyer 1703–13, I, p. 215; TNA, WORK 5/53, fol. 143; TNA, LC 5/45, p. 179.
182 Bucholz 1993, pp. 213–19, 222.
183 TNA, LC 9/282, fol. 28v, LC 5/44, fol. 215v.
184 *CTP 1708–14*, p. 555.
185 TNA, WORK 5/8, fol. 126, WORK 5/9, fol. 434.
186 For instance, TNA, WORK 5/9, fol. 185.
187 TNA, WORK 5/26, fols 432–438, WORK 5/27, fol. 429.
188 Thurley 1998, pp. 20–4.
189 See also Thurley 1993, pp. 140–1.
190 Aschbach Ettinger 1936, pp. 18, 27–9; *CTB 1685–9*, pp. 326, 443. Plans of all three storeys of the house and its outbuildings are held at NRO, F(M)G/722–4, F(M)G/728–30.
191 *CTB 1689–92*, p. 1124.
192 J. Roberts 1997, pp. 284–5.
193 Hayton et al. 2002, <www.historyofparliamentonline.org/volume/1660-1690/member/godolphin-sidney-i-1645-1712> (accessed 27 Jan. 2020); F. Harris 2002, pp. 259–63.
194 Green 1967, p. 145; F. Harris 1991, p. 154; Searle 1982; Field 2002, pp. 213, 300; Bolton and Hendry 1924–43, VII, pp. 225–9.
195 *CTB 1708*, p. 427.
196 *CTB 1676–9*, pp. 109–10.
197 *CTB 1698–9*, pp. 198, 206; *CTB 1693–6*, p. 1008.
198 TNA, T 1/91, fol. 343.
199 Hayton et al. 2002, <www.historyofparliamentonline.org/volume/1690-1715/member/hedges-sir-charles-1650-1714> (accessed 27 Jan. 2020).
200 Harris and Jackson Stops 1984; B. Adams 1983.
201 Quarrell and Mare 1934, p. 104.

3. The Georgian Court

1 Before 1692, the other electors comprised the dukes of Bavaria, Saxony, Brandenburg and the Palatine, and the Archbishops of Mainz, Trier and Cologne. After 1692, the electorate of Hanover was disputed, but was officially confirmed by the Imperial Diet in 1708.
2 Burchard 2014, pp. 58–60. Sophia was Electress of Hanover until Ernest Augustus's death in 1698, when the honour passed to their son, George.
3 Downes 1966, fig. 19a; see also Geraghty 2007, p. 160, no. 241, 'Design for a new Palace', *c.*1718, probably in Vanbrugh's hand (the St James's Palace designs and (?) Kensington Palace proposal sheets share identical watermarks).
4 Rather in the manner of Enrico Zuccalli (1642–1724) and Joseph Effner's (1687–1745) New Palace at Schleissheim, begun in 1700–01, the main building completed by 1726.
5 Burchard 2014, pp. 70–1, nos 22–23.
6 G.C. Gibbs, 'George I (1660–1727)', *ODNB*, online edn, 2004 <www.oxforddnb.com/view/article/10538> (accessed 11 July 2019).
7 *Flying Post*, 18–21 Sept. 1714.
8 Beattie 1967, p. 220.
9 Ibid., p. 258.
10 George I returned to Hanover during the summer months of 1716, 1719, 1720, 1723, 1725 (staying until Jan. 1726) and 1727 (he died at Osnabrück en route to Hanover); George II returned to Hanover during the summer months of 1729, 1732, 1735, 1736, 1740, 1741, 1743, 1745, 1748, 1752 and 1755; George III never visited Hanover; George IV visited Hanover in 1821 (as King of Hanover). The Electorate was elevated to a kingdom in 1801, occasioning a change in the Royal Arms of Great Britain.
11 Hatton 1978, p. 134.
12 The court removed to Kensington Palace during the summers of 1718, 1721, 1722, 1724 and 1726, alternating with the king's return to Hanover (see S. Edwards 2018, p. 110), and to Hampton Court Palace during the summers of 1717, 1718 (from 13 Aug. until 25 Oct., after a sojourn at Kensington) and 1728, and again in 1731 and 1737 (Thurley 2003, pp. 261, 269, 272, 279). See J. Roberts 2018, pp. 262, 266–8.
13 BL, Stowe 567, fols 67v–68.
14 A more recent precedent was found in Henrietta Maria's appointment as Guardian during the reign of Charles I.
15 'Leicester Square, North Side, and Lisle Street Area: Leicester Estate, Leicester House and Leicester Square North Side (Nos 1–16)', in *Survey of London* 1966, XXX, pp. 441–72.
16 'George I', *ODNB*, op. cit.: see above, ch. 3, n. 6.
17 TNA, LS 13/115, fol. 97; Beattie 1967, pp. 267–76.
18 Wright and Tinling 1958, p. 204.
19 Burrows 2005, pp. 167–8.
20 TNA, WORK 4/1, fol. 95.
21 Ibid., fol. 104, 29 Feb. 1715 (i.e. 1716).
22 Ibid., 2 Aug. 1716.
23 *HKW* 1976, p. 240.
24 TNA, WORK 6/6, fols 196–198, WORK 5/141, accounts for the year Dec. 1718–Dec. 1719: 'The new Kitchen at St James's £2076.14.3 / ditto £527.4.4¼'.
25 TNA, WORK 6/7, fol. 12.
26 Ibid., fols 12–13, 47, 52–55.
27 BL, Maps, Crace Port., 13.29; Edgar 2017, p. 3; Geraghty 2007, p. 167, nos 252, 253.
28 TNA, WORK 5/141; Edgar 2017, pp. 4–5. The German kitchen building at Hampton Court was built in 1715, probably to the designs of William Benson (1682–1754) and Colen Campbell: Thurley 2003, pp. 261–2.
29 TNA, WORK 4/3 (21 July 1725) gives a good indication of the tenor of works at the palace towards the end of the reign of George I.
30 TNA, WORK 4/2, fol. 87, approved 13 Dec. 1722: ibid., fol. 87v.
31 *HKW* 1976, p. 242. I am grateful to Jane Roberts for drawing my attention to this and other details regarding libraries at St James's.
32 TNA, WORK 4/3 (6 Apr. 1725). Mr Rowley was 'taxed in Whitehall for the Office of Engine Keeper to His Majesty at Windsor at 40£[?] p ann.': ibid. (28 Apr. 1725).
33 TNA, WORK 4/2, fol. 104v (24 Apr. 1723).
34 TNA, WORK 4/3 (4 Nov. 1724): 'Received from the Board of Greencloth a Letter setting forth that His Maj.ty Wines are much prejudiced for want of good Vaults, and that the Stables in St James's Mewse are speedily to be rebuilt, the Board of Greencloth Conceive that place very proper (if agreeable to the Board of Works Sentiments) for making the said Vaults'.
35 Van Muyden 1902, pp. 38–49.
36 Viz. Defoe 1761, II, p. 138, who writes: 'The Palace of *St James's*, tho' the Winter Receptacle of all the Pomp and Glory of this Kingdom, is really mean, in Comparison of the glorious Court of *Great Britain*'.
37 Ozell 1719 [originally written *c.*1698], p. 359. I am grateful to Michael Turner for this reference. See also Ward 1703, pp. 169–70: 'We pass'd thro' a Lofty Porch into the first Court, where a parcel of Hob-Nail'd Loobies were gazing at the Whales Rib with great Amazement'.
38 TNA, WORK 5/83, account for Martha Palmer (Smith): '2 Standards to go round the whale bone'.
39 Van Muyden 1902, p. 43.
40 BL, Stowe 567.
41 Hatton 1978, p. 43.
42 Ibid., pp. 99–100.
43 H. Smith 2006, p. 97 n. 168.
44 RCIN 1112550; BL, Stowe 567, fols 65–78 (transcript in the Royal Collection, RCIN 1112573).
45 RCIN 1112550, fol. 71; BL, Stowe 567, fol. 67.
46 RA GEO/MAIN/82030, 82117.
47 RA GEO/MAIN/81155; BL, Stowe 567, fol. 66r–v.
48 BL, Stowe 567, fol. 68.
49 TNA, LC 5/156, fols 116, 125.
50 Bird 2014, pp. 164–5.
51 TNA, LC 5/156, fols 72–73, 144, 175, 232, 286, 347; Bird 2014, pp. 162–3.
52 Paymaster's accounts for 1717, 1718, 1721, 1723; *HKW* 1976, p. 239.
53 TNA, LC 5/156, fols 70, 125, 127, 143, 216, 223, 248–249, 286. See also TNA, WORK 4/1, fols 27, 29, 30, 31, 53, for Hawksmoor creating a new room behind the Princesses' dressing room, July 1715. I am grateful to Michael Turner for the latter reference.
54 Bird 2014, pp. 147–203; the stories of the lives of some of the members of the early Hanoverian court are told in L. Worsley 2010; TNA, WORK 4/3 (21 July 1725): 'remove & replace wainscot in Mahomett's bedchamber,

54 ...point up with plaster and glass to keep out the rats'.
55 G. Schnath, 'Bothmer, Johann Kaspar Graf von', *NDB*, S. 488 f., online version <www.deutsche-biographie.de/pnd11865943X.html#ndbcontent>, and H. Kellenbenz, 'Bernstorff, Andreas Gottlieb Freiherr von', *NDB*, S. 137–138, online version <www.deutsche-biographie.de/pnd118656554.html#ndbcontent> (accessed 11 July 2019).
56 Black 2005, pp. 306–11.
57 RA GEO/MAIN/81235v.
58 TNA, WORK 4/1, fol. 10: '31 May 1715 / A Staircase at St James's to be made for the Young Princesses not to Exceed 30~ [£ pounds]'.
59 TNA, WORK 4/1 (10 Feb. 1720).
60 RA LC/CHAPELR.
61 Somewhat ironically, it was Handel's composition of a new *Te Deum* for the service of Thanksgiving at St Paul's on 7 July 1713, to mark the Peace of Utrecht, which led to his dismissal from his post in Hanover: the peace treaty between France and Britain did not favour Hanover's interests: Burrows 2005, pp. 75–7.
62 Ibid., p. 117.
63 Ibid., pp. 115, 117, 172.
64 RA GEO/MAIN/81182; Bird 2014, p. 161.
65 Burrows 2005, p. 177; TNA, LC 3/63, p. 282.
66 Burrows 2005, p. 173.
67 TNA, WORK 4/3 (25 Aug. 1726). The pedestals cost £26 12s 9d each; the four marble tables cost £24 each.
68 TNA, WORK 4/3 (22 June 1727, 15 Aug. 1727).
69 Weber 2013, pp. 277–80.
70 TNA, LC 9/289, acct no. 28: Goodison supplied 'For The French Chappel at St James's to be made use of at the Marriage of her Royal Highness the Princess Royal with his most Serene Highness the Prince of Orange For 2 Large Arm Chairs Frames richly carved & gilt – £45 / for 8 Square Stool Frames suitable – £88 / for 2 Arm Chair Frames gilt – £6 10s / for 6 Kneeling Stool Frames Do. – £6'.
71 British and Irish Furniture Makers Online, <https://bifmo.history.ac.uk> (accessed 11 July 2019).
72 TNA, LC 9/289, fol. 28v.
73 Sedgwick 1931, I, pp. 264–71.
74 RA GEO/MAIN/81925.
75 Ibid.
76 Sedgwick 1931, III, p. 116.
77 Sheppard 1894, II, p. 72.
78 TNA, LC 9/289, no. 43, fol. 113.
79 Egmont, *Diary*, 27 Apr. 1736, quoted in Burrows 2005, p. 342. The anthem composed by Handel for the occasion was *Sing unto God*.
80 Sedgwick 1931, III, p. 119.
81 Burrows 2005, p. 342.
82 *London Gazette*, no. 7980, 6 May 1740.
83 TNA, LC 9/289, no. 46, fol. 237.
84 Ibid., no. 47, fol. 238. Goodison charged £5 5s for taking down the chandelier and putting it up in the Chapel Royal, and £3 3s for its return to Somerset House.
85 John Perceval, later Earl of Egmont: R. Roberts 1923, p. 138.
86 D. Williamson, 'Mary, Princess (1723–1772)', *ODNB*, online edn, 2004 <www.oxforddnb.com/view/article/18253> (accessed 11 July 2019).
87 A. Vrolijk, 'Sale, George (b. in or after 1696?, d. 1736), Orientalist', *ODNB*, online edn, 2004 <www.oxforddnb.com/view/article/24529> (accessed 11 July 2019).
88 Burrows 2005, p. 281.
89 Sedgwick 1931, III, p. 119.
90 Burrows 2005, p. 434.
91 RA GEO/MAIN/52795–52803, 53039–53061; Hatton 1978, pp. 168–9; A. Thompson 2010, p. 77.
92 TNA, WORK 4/7 (21 June 1736).
93 TNA, LC 9/289, fol. 123, acct no. 79: 'for 66 Wallnuttree Chairs wth. Matted Seats … at [?]23 – £75 18s / For 60 beech Chairs wth. India Backs & Matted Seats – £39 / For 12 wooden chairs – £7 16s'. For 'wainscot', see Bowett 2012, pp. 242 ff.
94 TNA, WORK 4/6 (20 July 1736).
95 TNA, LC 9/289, fol. 124, acct no. 80.
96 Ibid., fol. 135, acct no. 20.
97 Ibid.
98 Jay 2006.
99 Croker 1855, II, pp. 182–4: 'In this letter too, the king having desired the Queen to prepare Lady Suffolk's lodgings for Madame Walmoden […] "If you can but once get this favourite to St James's she will in three months be everything Lady Suffolk was, but deaf; and it is really, Madam, the true state of the case, and your only option is whether you will fear her at a distance or despise her near." "Well," said the Queen, "we shall soon see, for I have this very day wrote the King word that I will get Lady Suffolk's lodgings ready immediately, and enlarge them by adding the two rooms where my books now are which join to Lady Suffolk's lodgings, and I will hire some rooms for my books in the mean time till my library that is building in the Park shall be fit to receive them".' See also Sheppard 1894, II, p. 386; Burchard 2011, p. 186.
100 Sir John Soane's Museum, London, SM 147/193-198; Weber 2013, p. 296 n. 128.
101 Steven Brindle has drawn comparisons with Kent's ceiling for the North Hall at Stowe House, 1728-31: Brindle 2013, p. 135.
102 Marschner 2014, pp. 86–91.
103 Ibid., p. 87.
104 TNA, WORK 4/7 (11 Jan. 1737/8): 'past Mr Risbrack's Bill for the Busto's in the Queen's Library at St James's and Order'd that he be Writ too, to send to the Office (there to be kept) the Models of the faces he made for Working after'.
105 TNA, WORK 5/59 (July 1736–Sept. 1737).
106 TNA, LC 9/289, fol. 160, acct no. 84: 'for the Queen's Library at St James's / For fine brass wire for 42 book case doors & fixing do. – £95 / For 2 Glass sconces in carved and gilt Frames with 2 wro.t Arms to Each – £14 / For 8 pair of wro.t Brass Arms – £3 12s'.
107 TNA, LC 9/167, fol. 15.
108 TNA, LC 5/73, fol. 165v.
109 Marschner 2014, p. 140; Jay 2006, p. 45.
110 Marschner 2007, p. 267; Say was paid £100 annually, and his deputy, John Hamilton, £40 annually (*Gentleman's Magazine*, 7, Nov. 1737, p. 189). John Moore's library was bought by George I and given to Cambridge University in Sept. 1715.
111 Pennant 1790, p. 111; Jay 2006, p. 46.
112 *HKW* 1976, p. 243.
113 TNA, LC 9/288, fol. 40v: 'No. 111 Henry Shelley, Mercer / For the Prince of Wales's Bed Chamber at St James's/ For 220 Yds of Yellow Genoa Damask for a Bed, Window, Curtains, Chairs & Stools at 16s 6d – £181.10.0 / 16 Yds of yellow Florence Taffeta to line the counterpain of the Bed at 7s 6d £6.-'; fol. 42: 'No. 123 – Sarah Gilbert, Upholsterer / For Prince of Wales's Bedchamber at st James's / Yellow Damask bed &c. £20.-.5.'
114 Ibid., fol. 159: 'No. 35 Benjamin Goodison / For the Prince of Wales's Library & Next Room at St James's / 2 Large Mahogany Bookcases with Glass Doors, Brass Pilaster mouldings & Large Brass handles £64'.
115 TNA, LC 9/289, year ending Mich. 1734, fol. 22, acct no. 16, fols 56v–59v, acct nos 89, 90; year ending Mich. 1735, acct nos 15–17, 25–27, 39–41, 65, 67–69 *et seq*.
116 Ibid., fol. 103, acct no. 27: 'an India cabinet (right old japan) with a carved & gilt frame – £71', and a six-leaf lacquer screen (£60).
117 TNA, LC 9/289, year ending Mich. 1736, fols 98, 97v, acct nos 11, 14, fol. 102, acct no. 26: new furniture was also supplied for the Prince of Wales at St James's for the state dressing room, closet, withdrawing room, private bedchamber, dressing room and dining room.
118 TNA, LC 9/289, year ending Mich. 1735, fol. 87, acct no. 69.
119 British and Irish Furniture Makers Online, <https://bifmo.history.ac.uk> (accessed 11 July 2019).
120 RA GEO/MAIN/81811v.
121 RA GEO/MAIN/81818.
122 RA GEO/MAIN/82451.
123 RA GEO/MAIN/82155v.
124 TNA, LC 9/289, fol. 159, acct no. 83, fol. 160, acct no. 84.
125 Sedgwick 1931, III, p. 223.
126 M. Kilburn, 'Leicester House (act. 1743–1760)', *ODNB*, online edn, 2004 <www.oxforddnb.com/view/article/96922> (accessed 11 July 2019); 'Leicester Square, North Side, and Lisle Street Area: Leicester Estate, Leicester House and Leicester Square North Side (Nos 1–16)', in *Survey of London* 1966, XXXIV, pp. 441–72.
127 Dennison 2017, pp. 328–30.
128 *Gentleman's Magazine*, 7, Nov. 1737, p. 700.
129 TNA, LC 9/289, fol. 175, acct no. 24: 'For taking down & removing all ye [silver?] wth. The carv'd & gilt Glasses, chandeliers branches tables & in order to prepare ye rooms for putting up the [mourning?] & afterwards fixing up & placing all the above purple and black chandeliers, sconces &ca. – £27 4s'.
130 TNA, WORK 6/16, fol. 45 (1 July 1736): 'We humbly beg leave to inform your Lordships that an Alehouse adjoining to the Palace at St James's did greatly annoy their Majesty's

last Winter, Insomuch that they were several times from the Stench of a Necessary house belonging to it oblig'd to remove out of their Apartment. For which reason we have treated with Mr Locke (the Owner of the said Alehouse and of Another Tenement behind it), who demanded for the purchase of both (the particulars of which we have inclosed), the sum of Eight hundred, forty six pounds Tenn shillings & seven pence, clear of all deductions.' Other references to this include ibid., fol. 51; TNA, WORK 6/17, fols 40, 45, 48v, WORK 4/9 (26 May 1747, 26 Jan. 1747/8, 2 Feb. 1747/8, 9 Feb. 1747/8, 16 Feb. 1747/8). I am grateful to Michael Turner for the latter references.

131 TNA, WORK 4/10 (24 May, 21 June, 13 Sept. 1748). Excavations in the 1990s by the Museum of London beneath Apartment 29 uncovered quantities of 18th-century ceramic wig curlers between the palace wall and the Tudor elevation shown in Scott's painting (see Fig. 3.27). See also TNA, WORK 6/17, fols 48, 49, 50 (9 Aug.–8 Nov. 1748). I am grateful to Michael Turner for this information.

132 TNA, WORK 6/17 (15 Nov. 1748). The interview took place on 22 Nov. 1748, and the accused produced vouchers to show that it was in fact Mr Carne (who had purchased the houses and contents by auction before they were taken down: see entry for 7 June 1748) who no doubt removed the said property.

133 TNA, WORK 6/16, fol. 144v (19 Aug. 1742): 'we humbly beg leave to acquaint your Lordships, that there being an extream want of Water at His Majesty's Palace of St James's; the Chelsea Company at present not serving any, and but very little coming from the Conduits in Hyde Park: We have caused the Pipe from the main Conduit to the receiver to be examined and find it is so eaten in holes & decay'd by length of time that no water at all came through it to the Receiver'.

134 Ibid., fol. 83 (5 Oct. 1738).

135 TNA, LC 9/290, fol. 156, acct no. 26; the cost was estimated at £320. TNA, WORK 5/141, year ending 31 Dec. 1738, under Extra Works: 'Building an Elaboratory at St James's for His Royal Highness the Duke of Cumberland, 17 Oct 1738 £371.17.6¾'.

136 TNA, LC 9/290, fol. 156, acct no. 26: 'for a Mohogony stand for ship case – £2 16s / For a Mohogony case for a large model of a ship with very large plate glass sides & ends and a frame to do. – £101'.

137 Ibid. (28 Feb. 1748/9).

138 Hefford 2003, pp. 126–8.

139 The Peace of Aix-la-Chapelle (or Aachen) marked the conclusion of the War of the Austrian Succession and ended hostilities between Britain and France. British troops had fought alongside Hanoverian, Hessian and Dutch troops, in support of the Austrian cause and the Pragmatic Sanction of 1713 issued by Emperor Charles VI (in favour of the future Empress Maria Theresa): J. Cannon, 'George II (1683–1760)', *ODNB*, online edn, 2004 <www.oxforddnb.com/view/article/10539> (accessed 11 July 2019). See also A. Thompson 2010, pp. 187–91; *Whitehall Evening Post or London Intelligencer*, 27–29 Apr. 1749, issue 498, p. 1 Handel's *Music for the Royal Fireworks*.

140 TNA, WORK 4/10 (27 Apr. 1749).

141 *Gentleman's Magazine*, 19, Apr. 1749, pp. 186–7.

142 Bedfordshire Archives and Records Service, L30/9a/2.

143 Lewis 1937–83, XX, pp. 47–8, Walpole to Horace Mann, 3 May 1749.

144 *The Remembrancer*, 29 Apr. 1749.

145 Toynbee 1927–8, pp. 15–17. The picture referred to in the Duchess of Marlborough's former room might be RCIN 403005: *A Woman Listening to a Satyr Piping, c.*1650–80, in the style of Francesco Albani (1578–1660).

146 TNA, WORK 4/12 (2 May 1758): 'Mr Vardy from Mr Spencer signified to the Board that Mr Spencer desired he might have leave to take down part of the Old Wall which is before the West Front of his new building in St James's Palace [?Place] that belongs to His Majesty's Store Yard which wall he will rebuild on the same spot of ground with stone at his own expense and further desires leave to carry his sewer through the said store yard, near the said wall … The Board taking the same into consideration and finding it no ways inconvenient to his Majesty's Store Yard'.

147 Lloyd 2004.

148 'St James's, Tuesday 8 September 1761. This Evening the Solemnity of His Majesty's Marriage, with Her Serene Highness Princess Charlotte of Mecklenburg was performed in the Chapel Royal, by the Archbishop of Canterbury': *London Gazette*, no. 10138, 8 Sept. 1761, p. 1. 'St James's, September 22. This day the Ceremony of their Majesties coronation as performed in the Abbey Church at Westminster': *London Gazette*, no. 10141, p. 1. See also Ashbee and Harley 2000, II, p. 107 (p. 126 of William Lovegrove's MS).

149 Lewis 1937–83, XXXII, p. 3, Walpole to Duchess of Grafton, 12 Sept. 1761.

150 Greig 1926, pp. 31–2.

151 Ibid., pp. 231–2; M. Winterbottom 2004, p. 231.

152 Lewis 1937–83, IX, pp. 376–7, Walpole to Montagu, 10 July 1761.

153 Von Kielmansegge 1902, p. 198.

154 J. Roberts 2004, p. 113.

155 Greig 1926, p. 47.

156 *London Gazette*, 30 Apr. 1763; Pegge 1791, I, pp. 73–4. Boswell (1950, p. 242) observed the landing of the ambassadors at the Tower of London: 'it was very elegant to see the fine barges and then the procession of their coaches, music and attendants was exceedingly splendid'.

157 Haq 2002, p. 59. I am grateful to Emily Hannam for this reference.

158 Home 1889–96, I, p. 65: 'at seven O'clock many of Us went into the Drawing [room], where the ceremony was to be perform'd'.

159 TNA, LC 9/319, acct no. 28 (22 July 1768): 'Rece'd by Sir Robert Wilmot Lord Chamberlains directions to this Board to put in proper order as soon as possible the Prince of Wales's apartment at St James's (lately made use of by the Prince and Princess of Brunswick) for the reception of the King of Denmark and his suite'; Home 1889–96, II, p. 318, 22 July 1768. I am grateful to Sir Hugh Roberts for this reference.

160 Lewis 1937–83, X, p. 264, Walpole to George Montagu, 13 Aug. 1768.

161 Le Marchant 1845, III, p. 236.

162 Adams refers to the antechamber at St James's as the 'Salon de l'Oeil de Boeuf', the name for the equivalent chamber in the king's state apartment at Versailles, where Adams was previously ambassador. The room in Versailles was named for its bull's-eye-shaped window.

163 John Adams to John Jay, 2 June 1785, *Founders Online,* National Archives (USA), <http://founders.archives.gov/documents/Adams/06-17-02-0078> (accessed 11 July 2019). Original source: Lint *et al.* 2014, pp. 134–45.

164 *Founders Online, op. cit.*, 10 June 1785. Original source: Lint *et al.* 2014, pp. 175–8.

165 TNA, WORK 5/105, qtr ending 31 Dec. 1767: 'An Accompt of the Extraordinary [Treasury Warrant dated 23 Oct. 1767] New Washhouse & Laundry for the Queen at St James's – £469.11.1½'; TNA, WORK 4/14 (22 Jan. 1768): 'D. for building a new Laundry for the Queen at St James's on a piece of ground [?] of the Duke of Marlborough'; ibid. (18 July 1771). The sum of £469 11s ½d was approved for the works: ibid. (5 Feb. 1768).

166 J. Shefrin, 'Finch, Lady Charlotte (1725–1813)', *ODNB*, online edn, 2004 <www.oxforddnb.com/view/article/75524> (accessed 11 July 2019).

167 TNA, WORK 4/14 (6 May 1768): 'Sign'd a memorial to the Treasury for enlarging the apartment belonging to Lady Charlotte Finch at St James's amo. to £496'; TNA, WORK 5/105, qtr ending 30 Sept. 1768: 'An Accompt of the Extraordinary [Treasury Warrant dated 18 May 1768] Building additional Apartments for Lady Charlotte Finch at St James's £616.12.1¼'. See also TNA, WORK 6/18, fols 175, 179. I am grateful to Michael Turner for the latter reference.

168 TNA, LC 9/319, acct no. 28.

169 TNA, LC 9/306, acct no. 7 (25 Oct.–17 Nov. 1760); ibid., qtr ending Christmas 1760.

170 TNA, LC 9/292, fol. 157, acct no. 54.

171 TNA, LC 9/311, qtr to Midsummer 1765, acct no. 51. In Jan. 1762, John Barnard, who had been appointed page of the backstairs on 26 Dec. 1760, was paid £37 16s for '9 Musicians playing at 2 balls at St James's': RA GEO/MAIN/17108, 17112; Bucholz 2006, pp. 29–30.

172 TNA, LC 9/306, qtr to Mich. 1761, acct no. 73.

173 TNA, LC 9/307, acct nos 6, 55.

174 Ibid., acct nos 7, 21.

175 Ibid., acct no. 21.

176 TNA, LC 9/308, no. 8, qtr to Christmas 1762.

177 Lewis 1937–83, XXXVIII, p. 116, Walpole to Conway, 9 Sept. 1761.

178 TNA, LC 9/307, qtr to Mich. 1761, acct no. 70.

179 Ibid., qtr to Midsummer 1762, acct no. 51.

180 TNA, LC 9/292, fol. 169, acct no. 71 (5 July–10 Oct. 1761).

181 Ibid., fol. 179, acct no. 75.

182 Ibid., fols 179, 180: both described as 'a fine mohogany comode [*sic*] chest of drawers with large brass handles on the drawers & ends and near wrot brass feet and ornaments up the corners finished with gold lacquer and fine locks fitted to the Queens master key of the drawer – £25'.
183 TNA, LC 9/307, acct nos 5, 54.
184 TNA, LC 9/307, acct no. 56.
185 Ibid., acct no. 84, for the King's Dressing Room.
186 TNA, WORK 4/16 (16 July 1784): 'Rec. from the Treasury a Warrant for doing the Works at the Queens Apartment at St James's'; TNA, WORK 5/106: '¼ ending 5 January 1785, by warrant 9 June 1784, St James's Queen's private Apartments £428.0.3'; for furnishings, see TNA, LC 5/197, pp. 26–31 (13 Sept. 1784), p. 42 (1 Dec. 1784).
187 TNA, LC 11/1, qtr ending 5 Jan. 1785, acct no. 73.
188 Ibid., qtr ending 5 Apr. 1785, acct no. 5.
189 Marchand 1995, p. 18.
190 TNA, WORK 6/20, fol. 264 (14 May 1784).
191 TNA, LC 9/292, fols 129–134v, acct nos 15–18 (7 Nov. 1760–10 Oct. 1761).
192 Ibid., acct no. 50, fol. 151v, acct no. 54, fol. 154.
193 TNA, WORK 6/17, fol. 212 (27 July 1761). See also TNA, WORK 4/3 (31 Mar. 1725) for putting 28 ft (8.5 m) of rail and spikes on top of pails fronting His Majesty's herb office, 'to prevent His Majesty's herbs being stole'. I am grateful to Michael Turner for the latter reference.
194 TNA, WORK 4/13 (3 Feb. 1762).
195 Ibid. (20 Jan. 1761): 'Mr Pelham acquainted the Board that there is a great want of Water at His Majesty's Palace at St James's from neglect of the Chelsea Company not serving the palace conformable to their Contract'; ibid. (19 May 1762).
196 TNA, WORK 5/105, qtr ending 30 Sept. 1761: 'An Accompt of the Ordinary / St James's … £3042.4.6½.' Compared with other palaces and royal buildings, this sum was comfortably the highest amount paid out by the Office that quarter; for four out of the five following quarters, St James's received the greatest expenditure of any royal building in the care of the Office of Works.
197 TNA, LC 9/307, acct nos 82, 88. Richard Harrison, embroiderer, also provided 'Embroidery for Prince of Wales's Cradle &c. £86' (acct no. 89).
198 Thackeray 1861, p. 171.
199 TNA, LC 9/293, fol. 30r-v, acct no. 80, fol. 37, acct no. 82 (5 Apr.–5 July 1762).
200 TNA, LC 9/307, qtr to Mich. 1762, acct nos 82, 96. Gwillim also supplied '4 Pasteboard Cases with turned Pedistals for the said Four Plumes £1.15.0'; ibid., acct no. 79.
201 Ibid., acct no. 91. At the same time, Priscilla MacEune charged for a 'Suit of Like Lace to cover a Toilet Table Compleat £1079 14s', for Queen Charlotte's dressing table, shown in the painting by Johan Joseph Zoffany (1733–1810; RCIN 400146).
202 Ibid., acct no. 84.
203 TNA, LC 9/308, acct no. 8.
204 Ibid., acct no. 20.
205 Ibid., acct no. 24; in the following quarter, to Lady Day 1763, payments to Vile and Cobb totalled £1,117 13s 6d; Katherine Naish was paid £342 18s, and Goodison £98 15s 6d.
206 TNA, WORK 4/13 (8 Sept. 1769): 'Sign'd to the Treasury a Memorial acquainting their Lordships that the Tower on the East side of the Entrance gateway of St James's Palace is decayed & to prevent accidents, is taking down'; ibid., 20 July 1770: 'Rece'd their Lordships fiat for Rebuilding the East Tower of the Entrance to St James's Palace amounting by Estimate to £455'. See also TNA, WORK 6/18, fols 222, 246.
207 TNA, WORK 4/15. Examples of the usual level of activity include requests for the repair of roofing (16 and 30 July 1773), and a general charge (£420) to enlarge an apartment in the Stable Yard for one of the Queen's pages, Mr Nicholay, 1 July 1774 and 27 Jan. 1775.
208 TNA, LC 9/318, acct nos 4, 5, 55, 58, 74. Benjamin Parran, cabinet-maker, made a clothes press, shaving stand and breakfast table.
209 TNA, LC 9/319, acct no. 3.
210 TNA, WORK 6/19, fol. 71 (14 July 1775), fol. 77 (18 July 1775).
211 TNA, WORK 4/16 (18 June 1779).
212 TNA, WORK 6/20 (4 July 1783), fol. 140: 'the Clerk of the Works at St James's will attend at the Lord Chamberlain's Office to point out the proper places first to be covered to prevent damage to the furniture and pictures'.
213 Ibid., p. 212 (28 Nov. 1783). The Yeomen of the Guard are today accommodated in the same rooms.
214 Sheppard 1894, II, pp. 52–60, 78–95. Sheppard notes the following royal marriages at St James's during the reign of George III: 8 Sept. 1761, George III and Queen Charlotte (Chapel Royal); 16 Jan. 1764, Princess Augusta and Prince Charles William Ferdinand of Brunswick-Wolfenbüttel (Council Chamber); 8 Dec. 1766, Princess Caroline Matilda and Christian VII of Denmark (Council Chamber); 8 Apr. 1795, George, Prince of Wales, and Princess Caroline of Brunswick (Chapel Royal); 18 May 1797, Princess Charlotte and Prince Frederick William of Württemberg (Chapel Royal); and royal baptisms at the Chapel Royal during the reign of George III: 8 Sept. 1762, George, Prince of Wales; 14 Sept. 1763, Frederick, Duke of York; 18 Sept. 1765, William, Duke of Clarence; 27 Oct. 1766, Princess Charlotte; 30 Nov. 1767, Edward, Duke of Kent; 6 Dec. 1768, Princess Augusta; 17 June 1770, Princess Elizabeth; 1 July 1771, Ernest, Duke of Cumberland; 25 Feb. 1773, Augustus, Duke of Sussex; 24 Mar. 1774, Adolphus, Duke of Cambridge; 19 Mar. 1776, Princess Mary; 1 Dec. 1777, Princess Sophia; 23 Mar. 1779, Prince Octavius; 21 Oct. 1780, Prince Alfred; 18 Sept. 1783, Princess Amelia; 11 Feb. 1796, Princess Charlotte of Wales.
215 Ashbee and Harley 2000, I, p. 204, II, pp. 6–7, 106–7.
216 Noorthouck 1773.
217 TNA, WORK 6/19, fol. 354 (17 May 1781): 'We the underwritten Chaplains of His Majesty's German Chapel in St James's beg leave to represent, that at the ensuing exchange of this Chapel with that of the french and dutch in the Friary, granted by His Majesty and agreed to by both Congregations, it will be necessary to have the first, the German Chapel; repaired so far as to be white-washed, painted, and a few alterations made with regard to the Pews … We therefore most respectfully beg that Your Lordship will be pleased to cause the proper direction to be given for that purpose to the Board of Works, and we have the honor to be / Your Lordships / most obedient and most humble servants / H. V. Schrader J. F. [?] Mithoff'. See also Randall 2013, pp. 16, 25, 33.
218 TNA, WORK 5/106, qtr ending 30 Sept. 1781: 'An Accompt of the Extraordinary [warrant of 30 Aug. 1780] St James's / In repairs at the French Chapel £812.7.5'; ibid., qtr ending 31 Dec. 1781: 'An Accompt of the Extraordinary [warrant of June 23rd 1781] St James's / New Pews at German Chapel £51.10.4'; and four years later, TNA, WORK 4/17 (18 Nov. 1785): 'A Reference and Order for new Matting the German Chapel at St James's'.
219 TNA, WORK 4/18, fol. 103 (2 Jan. 1795), fol. 214 (16 Dec. 1796).
220 J.H. Harris 1844, III, p. 220.
221 Wheatley 1884, V, p. 391.
222 Campbell Bury 1838, I, pp. 36–7, quoted in Fraser 2012, p. 62.
223 Ashbee and Harley 2000, p. 203.
224 RA GEO/ADD/43/3. The rhythm of family life centred around Friday to Monday at Windsor (with the odd exception) and Monday to Friday in London. I am grateful to Jane Roberts for this information.
225 TNA, LC 5/5, pp. 15–20.
226 *Carlton House* 1991, p. 9.
227 TNA, LC 9/328, qtr ending 5 Jan. 1781, acct nos 2, 4, 5, 6, 7, 8. The accounts for furnishing the apartments of Prince William and Prince Edward continue through this volume (1781).
228 RA GEO/ADD/15/0754; RA GEO/ADD/150/760.
229 RA GEO/ADD/4/204/12: letter from General Budé to Prince William, informing him of the birth of his brother, Prince Alfred.
230 E. Longford, 'Edward, Prince, Duke of Kent and Strathearn (1767–1820)', *ODNB*, online edn, 2004 <www.oxforddnb.com/view/article/8526> (accessed 11 July 2019).
231 TNA, LC 5/197 (23 Aug. 1787): 'a wainscot dining table for the Pages' rooms'; ibid. (4 Oct. 1787); ibid. (14 Nov. 1787): '12 Strong brass Hat Hooks'; ibid. (24 Nov. 1787): '2 Cotton Curtains & Vallances'. For the apartment at the west end: TNA, LC 9/328, acct nos 5, 7, 9; TNA, WORK 4/18, fol. 42 (8 Nov. 1793).
232 D. Watkin, 'Soane, Sir John', *Grove Art Online* <https://doi.org/10.1093/gao/9781884446054.article.T079428> (accessed 11 July 2019); TNA, WORK 4/17 (5 Nov. 1790).
233 TNA, WORK 4/18, fol. 133 (24 July 1795).
234 TNA, WORK 5/106, qtr ending 5 July 1793, warrant dated 21 Feb. 1793: 'St James's New Guard Room £1294.10.10¼'; Dean 2006, p. 226; TNA, WORK 6/22, fol. 82.

235 TNA, LC 11/3, qtr ending 5 Jan. 1794, acct no. 72.
236 TNA, WORK 5/106, qtr ending 5 Jan. 1794: 'warrant 13 August 1793. St James's New Pastry Kitchen £1337.8.8½'; TNA, WORK 6/22, fol. 103v, letter from Charles Long (1760–1838) to the Office of Works, 11 June 1793: 'that the present pastry at St James's Palace should be converted into a kitchen for the use of the Officers of the Foot Guards when on Duty and that a new Pastry and Scullery should be built in a situation shown in a plan laid before His Majesty'. *Schedule of Occupiers of Apartments in St James's Palace*, drawn up in June 1816 by Thomas Leverton and Thomas Chawner, notes on p. 33: 'The King's Pastry' in a 'Building at the West End of the Engine Court … The Pastry to the King's Kitchen … The Pastry occupies the height of two stories' [*sic*]. The King's kitchen (i.e. Vanbrugh's kitchen) was situated next door.
237 TNA, WORK 5/83: the mason Matthew Jenkinson was paid to erect the colonnade, and Mr Clarke, joiner, made the sashes and window frames to go above.
238 M. Brock, 'William IV (1765–1837), king of the United Kingdom of Great Britain and Ireland, and king of Hanover', *ODNB*, online edn, 2004 <www.oxforddnb.com/view/article/29451> (accessed 11 July 2019).
239 TNA, WORK 4/17 (29 July 1791): 'Sir William wrote to Mr. Long Secretary to the Treasury and Enclosed an Estimate of Repairs and alterations at His Royal Highness the Duke of Clarences apartments at St James's amounting to the sum of 900.15.6'; TNA, WORK 5/106, qtr ending 5 Jan. 1792: 'warrant dated 11. August 1791 St James's Repairs and Alterations to His Royal Highness the Duke of Clarence's Apartments £900.15.6'.
240 Fryman 2018, pp. 191–200.
241 TNA, WORK 6/22, fol. 74, letter to Charles Long from W. Chambers, 24 Nov. 1792: 'The works done at His Royal Highness the Duke of Clarence's Apartments have exceeded the estimate given in by three hundred twenty-nine pounds, two shillings and two pence. The reasons given for this Excess are the various alterations made from time to time at the express desire of His Royal Highness, the various reparations done, though not intended when the Estimate was given in, both in the upper and lower apartments'.
242 TNA, LC 11/3, qtr ending 5 Apr. 1791, acct nos 3, 28.
243 TNA, LC 11/7, qtr ending 5 Jan. 1801.
244 TNA, WORK 4/20 (11 Dec. 1807): 138 yards (126.2 m) of crimson flock paper was supplied by Isherwood & Co., paperhangers; 47 yards (43 m) of 'Swiss glazed' crimson damask cotton (at £15 8s 9d) and 42 yards (38.4 m) of 'printed blue' cotton at (£6 16s 6d) was charged by Samuel Beckwith, who also supplied 108 yards (98.8 m) of blue silk ferret (a type of tape) costing £1 16s; ibid. (4 Nov. 1808).
245 TNA, WORK 4/20 (8 and 22 Apr. 1808). Groves is recorded again as clerk of the works at St James's and in work at the Secretary of State's office: ibid. (13 Jan. 1809). He remained in post until his death in 1811.
246 TNA, LC 1/3, letter dated 23 Dec. 1807 from Harrison to Treasury Chambers, refusing to authorise certain articles for the Duke of Kent.
247 TNA, LC 11/11, qtr ending 5 July 1809, pp. 7–9: '2 Large Maho.y Sideboards 7ft 9 by 1ft 10 [2.4 by 0.6 m] … banded with coromandel wood blk mouldings … railing elegantly wrought with Honeysuckles and other ornaments 2 do. 5ft 10 by 1ft 10 [1.8 by 0.6 m] to match £140 12s'.
248 Ibid., pp. 7–31: 'Men Hanging the whole of Drawing room with blue Sarsnet fluted by hand with pannels of crimson Tissue also making rich crimson silk mantles to hang on the above tied up to ornament pins lined bound & pannell'd with Blue Velvet & trim'd with the Office Silk fringe compleat'.
249 Ibid., pp. 48–9.
250 Ibid., pp. 88–95.
251 A. Palmer, 'Ernest Augustus (1771–1851)', *ODNB*, online edn, 2004 <www.oxforddnb.com/view/article/8840> (accessed 11 July 2019).
252 TNA, WORK 6/22, fol. 128, Charles Long to the Board of Works, 25 Sept. 1793: 'The apartments at St James's called Prince Edward's should be put into a State of proper repair for the reception of one of the Princes'.
253 Ibid., fol. 127, Office of Works to secretary of Lord Chamberlain, 6 Sept. 1793: 'Estimate to be made of Repair necessary to be done in the Apartment at St James's called Prince Edward's for the reception of One of His Majesty's Sons … amount to the sum of one thousand and ninety two pounds'.
254 TNA, LC 11/4 qtr ending 5 July 1794, acct no. 51: 'eight mock bamboo elbow chairs with cane seats painted and japan'd' (£8) for the breakfast room or study. TNA, LC 11/4, qtr ending 5 Apr. 1795, acct no. 28: the dining room on the ground floor was given '12 mahogany 3 Splatt [?bell] Seated Chair frames for stuffing over the Rails Moulded backs and pannelled Splatts turned front legs and cross Stretching Rails varnished – £16 4s For 2 Do. with elbows to match – £4 2s'.
255 In the drawing room there were: '2 sattin wood pier tables with astragal corners on thin legs, the tops & [?rails] cross banded, a border of [?Jasmine] painted all round the tops, a tablet in the centre of the rail ornamented, the whole very highly varnished and polish'd – £20'; TNA, LC 11/4, qtr ending 5 July 1794, acct no. 51, qtr ending 5 Apr. 1795, acct no. 28: 'for 2 large plates of French glass with top plates in strong blind frames and moulding frames richly carved and gilt in burnish'd gold with pannel'd tops with white grounds & ornaments carv'd in Do. for Drawing Room – £144'.
256 TNA, LC 11/7 *passim*, including: 'maho. Library table with [?]hole in middle, and drawers down to the floor, good locks, key, and brass handles, top lined with black leather on Castors – £25'.
257 TNA, WORK 4/19 (22 Oct. 1802).
258 *The Times*, 12 May 1802. The floor decoration was known as 'chalking': drawing patterns in distemper on the wooden dance floor was a short-lived, ephemeral and expensive art, which was both highly decorative and practical (providing grip for the smooth leather soles of the dancers' shoes). For the practice of chalking, see Kane 2012. The Prince of Wales attended a private masked ball in Stanhope Street, London, in 1800, which featured chalking 'in various devices': *The Times*, 28 May 1800, p. 3. The fashion was taken up by the Prince at Carlton House.
259 TNA, WORK 4/19 (6 July 1804).
260 TNA, LC 11/9, qtr ending 1805.
261 TNA, WORK 4/20 (10 July 1807).
262 TNA, WORK 4/19 (31 July 1801).
263 TNA, LC 11/8, qtr ending 5 Apr. 1803: 'taking down all the furniture in the various apartments preparatory for workmen making alterations [?]doing it carefully by and again cleaning & fixing 2 Glasses in Peirs and 1 over chimney in drawing room a chimney glass in Dining Parlour a Ditto in Library moving cleaning perfecting and arranging all the other furniture – £7 15s'.
264 TNA, WORK 4/19 (5 Sept. 1806).
265 TNA, WORK 4/20 (4 Nov. 1808); the Treasury accepted the estimate on 25 Nov. 1808.
266 TNA, LC 11/11, qtr ending 5 July 1809, pp. 45–7; TNA, WORK 4/20 (25 Nov. 1808), WORK 6/24, fol. 223.
267 TNA, WORK 6/24, fol. 245.
268 *Morning Chronicle*, 23 Jan. 1809.
269 *Gentlemen's Magazine*, 79, Jan. 1809, pp. i, 82–3, quoted in *HKW* 1976, p. 366.
270 RA GEO/ADD/15/449.
271 TNA, WORK 19/19, letter 15, WORK 6/25, fol. 59v, WORK 4/20 (1 June 1810); TNA, LC 1/4 (25 May 1810).
272 Wardroper 2002, pp. 50–7; Stockdale 1810; W. Thomas, 'Place, Francis (1771–1854)', *ODNB*, online edn, 2004 <www.oxforddnb.com/view/article/22349> (accessed 11 July 2019).
273 TNA, WORK 4/20 (8 Nov. 1811). On Marsh, see TNA, WORK 19/19, fol. 35, and also n. 292 below. I am grateful to Michael Turner for the latter information.
274 TNA, WORK 4/20 (10 Jan. 1812).
275 TNA, LC 1/4, Treasury minute, 31 Aug. 1811: 'new Furniture as might be necessary should be provided with as little expense as possible'.
276 TNA, WORK 4/20 (24 July 1812).
277 TNA, LC 1/6 (8 Nov. 1813).
278 In 1810, Leverton and Chawner were joint surveyors to the Office of Woods, Forests and Land Revenues. I am grateful to Sir Hugh Roberts for this information.
279 Vane 1830, p. 331.
280 Hamilton Roche 1815, pp. 53–4.
281 H. Haussherr, 'Blücher von Wahlstatt, *Gebhard Leberecht* Fürst', in *NDB*, S. 317–319, online version <www.deutsche-biographie.de/pnd118511882.html#ndbcontent> (accessed 11 July 2019).
282 TNA, WORK 4/20 (3 Apr. 1812).
283 TNA, WORK 4/21 (26 Feb. 1813, 12 Mar.

1813, 19 Mar. 1813), WORK 6/26, fol. 63v (24 June 1813, 27 May 1814) – for the repair of the apartment of the king's librarian, Mr F.A. Barnard. TNA, WORK 19/19, fols 23, 39: Miss Finch was seamstress to the King and occupied an apartment on the south-east corner of Colour Court, where the southern extremity had been damaged by the fire, close to rooms occupied by her mother, Lady Charlotte Finch.
284 TNA, WORK 4/21 (3 Sept. 1813, 24 Sept. 1813). The estimate to fit up the silver scullery for the use of the Lord Steward amounted to £326 14s, and that to fit up the clerk of the kitchen's office as a silver scullery totalled £280 10s.
285 Ibid. (4 Oct. 1813).
286 Ibid. (14 May 1813).
287 Ibid. (20 Jan. and 17 Feb. 1815).
288 TNA, WORK 6/26, fol. 46 (16 Feb. 1813).
289 TNA, WORK 4/21 (23 June 1815).
290 Ibid. (8 Feb. and 1 Mar. 1816).
291 TNA, WORK 19/19, letter 42.
292 Ibid., letter 49.
293 TNA, WORK 4/22 (15 July 1816, 28 July 1817, 11 Sept. 1817).
294 TNA, WORK 19/19, fol. 32: Mrs Boyle was one of the four bedchamber women in rotation on the ground floor, south front. These apartments lay immediately to the west of fire-damaged rooms, hence the reference to the roof. Fol. 32 says that over these apartments are two of the State Rooms, one part-dismantled by the fire, the other used every last Sunday in the month to display the bulletin of the King's health.
295 TNA, WORK 4/24 (11 Dec. 1819, 13 Jan. 1820). See also the master's apartments, TNA, WORK 4/24 (8 Sept. 1820): 'Expence of this Alteration should not be charged in the Office Accounts'. TNA, WORK 19/19, fol. 27 (1816 schedule of occupiers): Timothy Brent, secretary to the Board of Green Cloth.
296 RCIN 1112546, p. 27.
297 RCIN 1112572; 49 paintings in the Duke of Cumberland's apartment are recorded in this inventory.
298 TNA, WORK 4/23 (14 June 1819).
299 Ibid. (23 July 1819).

4. George IV to the Second World War

1 Ordinarily, the proclamation would have been made on 30 Jan., but it was deferred owing to that day being the anniversary of Charles I's execution, which was observed in the Church of England as a solemn fast day: *The Times*, 1 Feb. 1820, p. 2.
2 For Carlton House, see *HKW* 1973, and for the Royal Pavilion, see Dinkel 1983.
3 These works to Buckingham Palace are summarised in *HKW* 1973, pp. 263–86.
4 *The Times*, 6 Apr. 1822, p. 2. Palace historian Edgar Sheppard suggests the only time the clock tower gates were shut was during the Chartist disturbances in 1848: Sheppard 1894, I, p. 350.
5 The Marshalmen reported nuisances to the Court of Marshalsea, which was presided over by the Lord Steward as judge until its abolition in 1849. Tomsett Judge 1848, p. 100; Sheppard 1894, I, p. 397.
6 *The Times*, 6 Apr. 1822, p. 2. Godolphin House as it appeared in 1825 is illustrated in Sheppard 1894, I, p. 51.
7 TNA, WORK 4/24, fol. 459, WORK 1/10, fols 369–370. For Crocker, see *HKW* 1973, pp. 115, 116, 676.
8 TNA, WORK 19/19, fol. 56.
9 Ibid.
10 *HKW* 1973, p. 367.
11 *Morning Post*, 22 Aug. 1821, p. 3.
12 BL, Add. MS 43794, fol. 25, Mich. qtr 1821 (this is a fragment of a ledger containing particulars of carpenters' and joiners' work at St James's Palace, 1816–21); Sheppard 1894, I, p. 406. The *Morning Post* suggests the remains were not fully cleared before 22 Aug. 1821: *Morning Post*, 22 Aug. 1821, p. 3.
13 D.R. Fisher 2009a.
14 H. Colvin, 'Long, Charles, Baron Farnborough (1760–1838)', *ODNB*, online edn, 2004 <www.oxforddnb.com/view/article/16962> (accessed 11 July 2019). Sir Jeffry Wyatville faithfully followed Long's brief at Windsor: see Brindle 2018, pp. 320–3.
15 Colvin 2008, pp. 547–8; *HKW* 1973, p. 119; Jerdan 1853, pp. 52–4. TNA, WORK 1/20, fols 2–3; *The Times*, 26 Dec. 1825, p. 2: in the 1832 reforms of the Office of Works, labourers in trust were redesignated clerks of works.
16 Bradley and Pevsner 2003, pp. 594–601.
17 Even if the roughly £19,000 cost of works to Clarence House from 1825 to 1826 is excluded (see p. 189), the annual average for the palace was still in excess of £13,000; *HKW* 1973, pp. 367–8 (quoting TNA, WORK 5/108), 664–5.
18 *New Monthly Magazine and Literary Journal* (1821) 3, p. 475.
19 *The Times*, 12 Oct. 1821, p. 2.
20 *Morning Post*, 16 Nov. 1821, p. 3.
21 TNA, WORK 4/25, fol. 181, WORK 4/27, fol. 249 (18 July 1825). The works even extended to cleaning the carved spandrels to doorways flanking the main gatehouse arch: *Literary Gazette and Journal … for the year 1822*, 1823, p. 233. Hunt illustrated the spandrels in Hunt 1830, pl. XXV.
22 TNA, WORK 4/25, fols 225, 227, 247, 250, 320, 322. See TNA, WORK 34/126 for a copy of the plan. For Stephenson, see *HKW* 1973, pp. 101–22.
23 TNA, WORK 4/26, fols 248–249; *The Times*, 1 May 1829, p. 2.
24 The tradesmen's bills for the State Apartments are in TNA, LC 10/16. The following are listed in H. Kent 1823: Bailey & Sanders, cabinet-makers, 13 Mount Street, Grosvenor Square (p. 18) (see also Beard and Gilbert 1986, pp. 29–30); Cutler & Sons, furnishing ironmonger and iron founder, 16 Great Queen Street (p. 89); Hancock, Shepherd & Rixon, cut-glass manufacturers, Spring Gardens (p. 152); James Henderson, carver and gilder to George IV, 80 New Bond Street (p. 162; see also Beard and Gilbert 1986, p. 420); William Perry & Co., glass manufacturer to George IV, 72 New Bond Street (p. 260); Robson & Hale, paperhangers, 218 Piccadilly (p. 285); Benjamin Vulliamy, clockmaker to George IV, 68 Pall Mall (p. 344; see also Vulliamy 2002); and Edward Wyatt, carver and gilder to the Office of Works, 360 Oxford Street (p. 375; see also J.M. Robinson 1979, pp. 157–60).
25 TNA, WORK 1/12, fols 284–285: T.B. Mash to Col. Stephenson, no. 2874, 15 Dec. 1823.
26 TNA, WORK 34/136. This sketch elevation is signed with the initials of Henry Hake Seward, appointed assistant surveyor in the Office of Works in 1823: Colvin 2008, pp. 913–14.
27 For the former narrow stairs, see the comment in *The Times*, 21 May 1824, p. 2. For a description of the alterations, see the *Literary Gazette and Journal … for the year 1824*, 1824 (22 May), pp. 331–2. The editor of the *Literary Gazette* was William Jerdan, a friend of the architect T.F. Hunt, who doubtless supplied Jerdan with information on the progress of the works.
28 TNA, WORK 4/26, fols 347–348 (22 Mar. 1824). A report on a visit made to the palace before 13 Apr. 1822, while the works were in progress, is published in the *Literary Gazette and Journal … for the year 1822*, 1823, pp. 233–5. For a view of Long's Bromley Hill drawing room by John Buckler, see BL, Add. MS 36367, fol. 186: *Drawing Room at Bromley Hill, Kent: The seat of the Right Honble Charles Long. December 15th 1816*.
29 TNA, LC 10/16, fol. 52; *The Times*, 21 May 1824, p. 2.
30 Jacob 1970; Udy 1971. Full-size bronze copies of the Barberini candelabrum on the portico at Basildon Park, Berkshire, apparently arrived c.1840: National Trust 1986, p. 11.
31 Buckler's 1827 watercolours were based on his pencil sketches made on 29 Aug. 1827: BL, Add. MS 36370, fols 115–119; *Morning Post*, 2 Dec. 1823, p. 3.
32 *The Times*, 21 May 1824, p. 2. 'Stove' is used in the sense of the metal structure of a more or less open fireplace; TNA, LC 10/16, fols 71–72.
33 Pyne 1819, III, Carlton House, illus. facing p. 10; *Literary Gazette and Journal … for the year 1822*, 1823, p. 233 (the correspondent refers to the Armoury as the Guard Chamber); also quoted in *Morning Post*, 15 Apr. 1822, p. 3.
34 Hunt 1827, pp. 11–12, and pl. VIII. The chimneypiece was sketched by J.C. Buckler and inscribed 'Chimney piece lately discovered in the Guard Room at St James's Palace. May 24th 1822': BL, Add. MS 36370, fol. 120 (see Fig. 1.8). It was also sketched by Anthony Salvin, who correctly located it in the Presence Chamber: RIBA, V&A, SC97/17.
35 *Literary Gazette and Journal … for the year 1822*, 1823, p. 233.
36 TNA, LC 10/16, fol. 75.
37 Ibid., fol. 52; *The Times*, 21 May 1824, p. 2.
38 The northern blocked armoury window was recorded during repairs in Mar. 1992: Historic

England Archive, Swindon, STJ 7/1; *Literary Gazette and Journal … for the year 1822*, 1823, p. 234. Friary Court is labelled 'The Friary' on the Office of Works ground-floor plan, 1841: TNA, WORK 34/129.
39 TNA, LC 10/16, James Henderson, Suppl. acct, fol. 6.
40 TNA, WORK 4/26, fol. 331.
41 TNA, WORK 1/12, fol. 350: Stephenson wrote to the Treasury on 23 Jan. 1824, expressing his frustration with the changes of specification and consequent inability to provide an accurate estimate of the expenditure required.
42 For gilding, see TNA, WORK 4/26, fols 259, 284, 331, 333, 347–348, 350, 363, 369, 374, 390, 398; and Crocker's estimate for further gilding: TNA, T 1/2273, paper 6992 (12 Apr. 1824).
43 TNA, LC 10/16, fols 38v, 39v, 41v, 52v–53, 56.
44 TNA, WORK 4/25, fol. 181. In Fig. 4.7 the chimneypiece, pier table, candelabrum and two large gilt and burnished brackets (part of the 24 supplied by Bailey & Sanders) are all part of the 1824 scheme (TNA, LC 10/16, fols 38v, 39v, 41v, 42, 45v). The Queen Anne Room chimneypiece was returned to Kensington Palace in 1973: Historic England Archive, DoE 73045 AB1/2. The only new marble chimneypiece in the south range was supplied by Richard Westmacott (1775–1856), in 1824, for the King's Closet: TNA, WORK 4/26, fol. 270.
45 *Morning Post*, 2 Dec. 1823, p. 3, refers to 'handsome oak doorways', suggesting they were neither fully gilded nor painted.
46 TNA, LC 10/16, fols 38, 39, 41.
47 The proposed picture-hang was described in the *Literary Gazette and Journal … for the year 1822*, 1823 (20 Apr. 1822), p. 234.
48 *The Times*, 21 May 1824, p. 2; RCINS 407182, 407184.
49 Shepherd 1829, pp. 44–5.
50 RCIN 404932.
51 TNA, LC 10/16, fol. 73.
52 *Literary Gazette and Journal … for the year 1824*, 1824, p. 332. Both paintings, including their frames, measure approximately 309 by 418 cm: National Maritime Museum, BHC0470, BHC0565. For the Greenwich Hospital collection, see Van der Merwe 2006, and Greenwich Hospital General Court Minutes, 24 Dec. 1823: TNA, ADM 67/17, fol. 52. The Turner was unfairly criticised on account of its supposed inaccuracies, and Ruskin subsequently praised Turner's masterpiece above everything else at Greenwich: Lloyd 1992, p. 204.
53 TNA, LC 10/16, fol. 41.
54 RCINS 405918, 407186; *Literary Gazette and Journal … for the year 1822*, 1823, p. 234; TNA, LC 10/16, fols 75, 41v, 48. For a discussion of the arrangement of paintings at St James's, see Lloyd 1992, pp. 198–204. For George IV, see Reeve 1874, I, p. 241; Griffiths 1898, p. 227; Hibbert 1973, pp. 78, 309.
55 TNA, LC 10/16, fols 39v–40.
56 The canopy is *in situ* in photographs taken 15 Aug. 1938, neg. refs S3687, S3689, Ministry of Works Photographic Album 20, St James's Palace, fol. 5, Historic England Archive.
57 Sheppard 1894, I, pp. 131–2; TNA, LC 10/16, fol. 83. The canopy and dais were re-covered in 1913. TNA, WORK 19/132 (5 Nov. 1912): the 'V' on the canopy is from 1912, but the 'R' is 19th-century.
58 TNA, LC 10/16, fol. 40; *The Times*, 21 May 1824, p. 2. For the significance of the throne, see Riding 2000.
59 H. Roberts 1989, pp. 70–1 and fig. 17; H. Roberts 2007, pp. 45–6.
60 TNA, LC 10/16, Suppl. acct, fol. 19.
61 H. Roberts 2007, pp. 45–6.
62 *The Times*, 21 May 1824, p. 2; TNA, LC 10/16, fol. 43. Bailey & Sanders' 'elegant' table was subsequently displayed in the Queen's Presence Chamber at Windsor Castle, where it remained until 2020. It has since been returned to the Council Chamber at St James's Palace. I am grateful to Sir Hugh Roberts for his help in identifying this table.
63 *The Times*, 21 May 1824, p. 2; *Literary Gazette and Journal … for the year 1824*, 1824, p. 332; TNA, LC 10/16, fol. 45v.
64 TNA, WORK 4/26, fol. 250.
65 TNA, WORK 1/12, fol. 283, T.B. Mash to Col. Stephenson, no. 2874, 15 Dec. 1823, states the gallery was to be preserved, but presumably it proved impracticable.
66 TNA, LC 10/16, fols 84–87v. For an overview of the wallpaper trade in London at this time, see Rosoman 2009.
67 RA GEO/MAIN/25234: E. Wyatt, '1807. Carving and gilding done at Carlton House', 'To Richly Carving and Gilding in Four Pannels Over Doors in the Throne Room, the Orders of St George, the Bath St Patrick and St Andrew in Burnish Gold. £300'; Pyne 1819, III, pp. 28–9.
68 *The Times*, 21 May 1824, p. 2. TNA, WORK 19/19, fol. 105: to further aid ventilation, three dormers to be set into the roof were approved in May 1828. The general features of this style were employed on a smaller scale by Robert Smirke, who was familiar with the supper room, in the nearby 1830s ivory and gold state drawing room at Stafford (now Lancaster) House; see Yorke 2001, p. 35.
69 *Literary Gazette and Journal … for the year 1824*, 1824, p. 332; *The Times*, 21 May 1824, p. 2. TNA, WORK 19/20, fol. 474: in 1864 it was proposed to remove the gold mouldings and strip the canvas and paper.
70 TNA, ADM 67/17, 60–1; Van der Merwe 2006, pp. 19–38. I am grateful to Pieter van der Merwe for these references.
71 W. Kent 1727, I, pl. 62. This specifically credits Jones with the design, which is closely related to a chimneypiece by Serlio (1537, bk 4, ch. 8, fol. 57 [incorrectly numbered 52]). Kent used the same design in the 1730s for the drawing room in Devonshire House, Piccadilly: Bolton 1914, p. 263.
72 TNA, WORK 1/12, fol. 283: T.B. Mash to Col. Stephenson, no. 2874, 15 Dec. 1823; TNA, WORK 4/26, fol. 401 (21 May 1824).
73 TNA, WORK 4/27, fols 492 (15 May 1826), 498 (26 May 1826), 500 (27 May 1826), 512 (7 June 1826).
74 *The Times*, 31 Oct. 1826, p. 2; *Carlton House* 1991, pp. 33–4.
75 *Literary Gazette and Journal … for the year 1827*, 1827 (27 Jan.), pp. 57–8.
76 *HKW* 1973, pp. 267–8, 369. For Nash's recollections of conversations with George IV regarding the conversion of Buckingham House into a state palace, see W.A.R. 1836, pp. 26–9.
77 *HKW* 1973, p. 369.
78 TNA, WORK 4/28, fols 180 (2 Mar. 1827), 191 (19 Mar. 1827), 192 (20 Mar. 1827), 193 (22 Mar. 1827), 207 (31 Mar. 1827), 226 (28 Apr. 1827), 233 (8 May 1827), 519 (14 Mar. 1828), WORK 19/19, fols 101–102, 104–105.
79 Tabulated in *HKW* 1973, pp. 664–5.
80 TNA, WORK 4/26, fol. 399; *The Times*, 21 May 1824, p. 2.
81 TNA, WORK 4/26, fol. 304; TNA, WORK 34/894.
82 *The Times*, 21 May 1824, p. 2.
83 *The Times*, 24 Apr. 1828, p. 6, 1 May 1829, p. 2, 16 Apr. 1830, p. 2.
84 *The Times*, 10 June 1824, p. 2. A month's notice was given of the first levee of 1829, to be held on 29 Apr., and an estimated 1,300–1,400 attended: *The Times*, 30 Apr. 1829, p. 4.
85 *The Times*, 28 May 1828, p. 2.
86 The fashion was taken up by the King when Prince Regent in Carlton House: see above, ch. 3, n. 258. In July 1823, G. Glover submitted an invoice for five guineas for chalking the floor for the juvenile ball: TNA, LC 11/41, invoice 202. The report of the juvenile ball held on 26 May 1828 refers to floors 'chalked with fanciful and appropriate devices': *The Times*, 28 May 1828, p. 2. The last reference to chalking in the Court Circular was for the court ball at St James's on 15 June 1832: *The Times*, 18 June 1832, p. 2.
87 *The Times*, 29 May 1829, p. 2.
88 RCIN 51467.
89 *The Times*, 28 May 1828, p. 2.
90 *The Times*, 27 Apr. 1831, p. 2.
91 Hibbert 1973, pp. 280–1, quoting Jennings 1885, I, p. 408.
92 TNA, WORK 4/26, fol. 248, WORK 19/19, fol. 121.
93 TNA, WORK 19/19, fols 115–118, WORK 4/29, fols 275, 278–279, 283, 288, 290–291, 297, 313, 345. For reference to the 'heavy chisel' pattern, see TNA, WORK 16/298, Huxley & Heriot & Co. tender, 11 Oct. 1856. Edge had supplied external gas lighting for the King at Brighton Pavilion in 1821: Temple Newsam 1992, p. 31.
94 TNA, WORK 19/19, fols 63–64.
95 Sheppard 1894, I, pp. 50–3; TNA, WORK 4/27, fols 249, 404.
96 D. Winterbottom 2016, pp. 149–51.
97 Fulford 1973, pp. 92–3.
98 Lancaster House initially housed the Museum of London: Yorke 2001.
99 *The Times*, 10 Jan. 1827, p. 3, 22 Jan. 1827, p. 2. The paper described the decorations of the chamber in some detail: *The Times*, 13 Jan. 1827, p. 2, 18 Jan. 1827, p. 3, 19 Jan. 1827, p. 2.
100 *The Times*, 9 Jan. 1827, p. 3, 10 Jan. 1827, p. 3, 18 Jan. 1827, p. 3, 19 Jan. 1827, p. 2, 20 Jan. 1827, p. 3.
101 *The Times*, 20 Jan. 1827, p. 3.
102 Hussey 1949, pp. 50–1.

103 Their stories are told in Fulford 1973.
104 Ibid., pp. 131–9.
105 Knighton 1838, I, pp. 223–4; TNA, WORK 4/27, fols 167–168 (31 Mar. 1825).
106 Maxwell 1904, II, p. 99.
107 TNA, WORK 34/127 and WORK 34/134: compare the 1816 and 1830 block plans.
108 TNA, WORK 4/27, fols 264 (1 Aug. 1825), 280 (18 Aug. 1825).
109 HKW 1973, pp. 323–6. For a general history of Clarence House, see Marsden 2004.
110 TNA, WORK 19/19, fol. 81.
111 Knighton 1838, II, p. 54.
112 TNA, WORK 19/19, fols 108–109.
113 Fulford 1973, pp. 223–32.
114 Summerson 1980, pp. 178–9.
115 TNA, WORK 19/19, fols 137–139; HKW 1973, p. 369. Smirke was clerk of works at St James's Palace from Jan. 1830 to Apr. 1832, when that post was abolished: HKW 1973, p. 676. See also Crook 1976, pp. 50–65.
116 Sheppard 1894, I, pp. 190–7; *The Times*, 29 June 1830, p. 2.
117 HKW 1973, p. 274.
118 HKW 1973, p. 325; TNA, WORK 4/30, fols 241 (30 June 1830), 252 (7 July 1830). For the carpenter's shop, see the 1841 ground- and first-floor surveys of the palace: TNA, WORK 34/129 and 34/130. Smirke's 1830 plan for the backstairs was approved by William IV: TNA, WORK 19/19, fol. 140.
119 Maxwell 1904, II, p. 224. It is probable that in being reluctant to move into Buckingham Palace, the new King sought to distance himself from the extravagance of his late brother: Graves 1963, pp. 194–5.
120 Colvin 2008, p. 129; HKW 1973, p. 277.
121 Hansard, 9 *Parl. Deb.* 3rd ser., 6 Dec. 1831–6 Feb. 1832, pp. 144–6.
122 Beavan 1896, pp. 276–9.
123 HKW 1973, pp. 349, 369.
124 For Wyatville, see Colvin 2008, pp. 1197–1203.
125 RCINS 929710, 929716, 929717; RA GEO ADD/15/2187: 'G' to Sir Hector Taylor, 19 Mar. 1833.
126 TNA, WORK 19/19, fols 163–164. Gossett had previously written to the Office of Works regarding other public improvements. TNA, RG 9/30, fol. 75, p. 30: he wrote from the Junior United Services Club, and is possibly the Charles Gossett, Royal Navy Lieutenant, born *c.*1798, who is recorded in the 1861 census as living in Paultons Square, Chelsea.
127 TNA, WORK 19/19, fols 167–175.
128 *The Observer*, 20 Oct. 1834, p. 2.
129 Wyatville's coloured elevation of the proposed south front (see Fig. 4.24) is dated 1834 in Wyatville's list of 24 drawings titled 'St James's Palace. General alterations Etc': no. 21, 'Color'd elevation South ft including Sutherland & Marlborough Houses' (RCIN 929706.b).
130 Hansard 10 *HC Deb.* 2nd ser. 629, 1 Mar. 1824: Baring was MP for Chipping Wycombe; see D.R. Fisher 2009b.
131 Hansard 10 *HC Deb.* 2nd ser. 628, 1 Mar. 1824: Davies was MP for Worcester; see D.R. Fisher 2009c.
132 RCINS 929718, 918970, 929711, 929712. TNA, WORK 19/19, fols 165–175. Wyatville's proposed south elevation is illustrated and discussed in Colvin 1968, pp. 52–3.
133 TNA, WORK 19/19, fol. 174; RCINS 929722–929739.
134 Wyatville tracing, 'Alterations to a Chimney piece in the Entré [*sic*] Gallery at St James's Palace, Dec. 12th 1832' (RCIN 29720); and Wyatville's list of drawings, titled 'St James's Palace. General alterations Etc', dated 1831 and 1832, no. 11: 'Drawing for Altering Chimney piece in Entrée Gallery (executed)', and nos 13–17: elevations of the Armoury (called Guard Chamber by Wyatville) 'with a new arrangement of the Arms … Carried into Execution' (RCIN 929706.b). A more extensive list by Wyatville follows the same numbering, but totals 102 drawings for St James's (RCIN 929706.c).
135 *Morning Chronicle*, 8 Apr. 1817, p. 3, 11 Aug. 1817, p. 3; *The Times*, 2 Feb. 1818, p. 3.
136 *Morning Chronicle*, 13 Feb. 1818, p. 3.
137 Sheppard 1894, II, pp. 271–6. The restriction of free admission only at Epiphany continued until at least 1870: *The Times*, 7 Jan. 1870, p. 9.
138 TNA, WORK 4/26, fols 429–430 (17 June 1824).
139 *The Times*, 10 June 1836, p. 6; Colvin 2008, pp. 931–7.
140 Traces of Roman cement were found on the north elevation during repairs in 1992. For Smirke's brick skin, see English Heritage, STJ 8/1, dated June 1992, Historic England Archive. For the appearance before Smirke's work, see C. Wild's watercolour, RCIN 922161.
141 D. Baldwin 1990, p. 394.
142 Richardson 1837, pp. 3, 32. Richardson subsequently published his drawing of the original Tudor ceiling in Richardson 1840, p. 7 and Appendix, Ceilings, pl. 1. Sheppard 1894, II, pp. 205–8; C. Dodgson, rev. R. Thorne, 'Richardson, Charles James (1806–71)', *ODNB*, online edn, 2004 <www.oxforddnb.com/view/article/23547> (accessed 11 July 2019).
143 HKW 1973, p. 370.
144 *The Times*, 29 Apr. 1837, p. 2, 22 May 1837, p. 5.
145 E.g. for 1831, see *The Times*, 25 Feb., p. 2, 11 Mar., p. 3, 25 Mar., p. 3, 29 Apr., p. 2, 25 June, p. 4.
146 *The Times*, 22 July 1830, p. 2.
147 *The Times*, 18 May 1837, p. 3 *et passim*. A levee scheduled for 27 May 1837 was postponed indefinitely: *The Times*, 27 May 1837, p. 5.
148 *The Times*, 30 May 1831, p. 2, 29 May 1832, p. 2, 29 May 1833, p. 2, 29 May 1834, p. 2, 29 May 1835, p. 3, 30 May 1836, p. 5, 29 May 1837, p. 5.
149 *The Times*, 26 May 1831, p. 2.
150 Weippert described himself as 'harpist to their Majesties, all the royal Family, director of Band at Court' in *The Garland*: 'John Weippert's favourite set of waltzes, entitled The Garland, Composed by Miss Pocock, and performed by his band at the Court of St James's, Almack's &c &c … dedicated to Mrs Merry and the Ladies of the Berkshire Archery Society', <http://levysheetmusic.mse.jhu.edu/collection/026/032> (accessed 11 July 2019). Collinet and Phillipe Napoleon Musard performed together in London at Almack's Club in the 1820s: <https://archive.org/details/Musards1stSetOfNewQuadrilles> (accessed 17 Jan. 2020)
151 *The Times*, 26 May 1832, p. 6.
152 RA VIC/MAIN/QVJ, 24 May 1833, 30 May 1834 (Queen Victoria's handwriting).
153 *The Times*, 26 May 1836, p. 5.
154 *The Times*, 24 May 1837, p. 5, 26 May 1837, p. 5; RA VIC/MAIN/QVJ, 24 May 1837 (Lord Esher's typescripts).
155 *The Times*, 29 May 1837, p. 5, 30 May 1837, p. 5.
156 *The Times*, 12 June 1837, p. 5, 13 June 1837, p. 5, 14 June 1837, p. 4, 15 June 1837, p. 5, 19 June 1837, p. 5.
157 HKW 1973, pp. 286–9.
158 Hansard, 81 *Parl. Deb.* 3rd ser., 4 June–3 July 1845, pp. *1336[*sic*]–1338.
159 BL, Add. MS 40570, fol. 40, Peel memo, 1 July [1845]. In 1841, the author of the entry on St James's Palace in *London Interiors* wrote: 'No one can have looked upon St. James's for the first time, without feelings of disappointment. Its plainness, almost approaching to ugliness, its prevailing sombre heaviness, and its total want of pretension, either to architectural grandeur, or to consideration as the residence of so powerful a sovereign as the one seated on the British throne, have been the subject of frequent comment from the time of Anne downward' (Shepherd 1841, I, p. 78).
160 BL, Add. MS 40570, fol. 41, Peel memo, 1 July [1845].
161 HKW 1973, pp. 289–93.
162 RA VIC/MAIN/QVJ, 18 Dec. 1839 (Princess Beatrice's copies); ibid., 8 Jan. 1840 (Esher); Fulford 1973, pp. 247–8.
163 Fulford 1973, pp. 245–9.
164 RA VIC/MAIN/QVJ, 11 May 1852, 6 Apr. 1889 (Beatrice).
165 TNA, WORK 34/861–870, WORK 34/889. For Taylor, see Brodie *et al.* 2001, II, pp. 770–1.
166 Pope-Hennessy 1959, pp. 214–15, 220–33.
167 Ibid., pp. 261–71; Nicolson 1952, pp. 49–50.
168 RA VIC/MAIN/Z/476/23, 5 Nov. 1892; RA VIC/MAIN/Z/476/24, 14 Nov. 1892; Graves 1963, pp. 210–11. For York House at this time, see Pope-Hennessy 1959, pp. 290–8.
169 TNA, WORK 1/22, fol. 314 (16 Aug. 1837), WORK 1/23, fols 171–172 (14 Aug. 1838), WORK 2/2, fol. 162.
170 Historic England Archive, Birdsman's Lodge, St James's Palace, section and plan below floor level showing remains of reservoir in south-east corner of lodge, Jan. 2003; TNA, WORK 1/23, fols 178 (14 Aug. 1838), 192 (17 Sept. 1838), WORK 34/144.
171 Hussey 1949, pp. 79–81; Marsden 2004, p. 13.
172 For an album containing Waller's Clarence House drawings, see V&A, E.552-1975.
173 For the Wallers, see Hobhouse 1995, pp. 279–80; Marsden 2004, p. 14.
174 Hussey 1949, pp. 80–5.
175 Van der Kiste and Jordaan 1984, pp. 54–76.
176 Marsden 2004, pp. 13–19. Queen Victoria inspected the alterations in May 1875. She recognised the dining room, which had 'remained entirely as it was in dear Mama's time': RA VIC/MAIN/QVJ, 7 May 1875 (Beatrice).

For the Russian Orthodox chapel, see D. Baldwin 1990, p. 409.

177 The mosaic was covered by screed in the 20th century and was rediscovered and re-exposed in 2018. *The Cruise of His Royal Highness the Duke of Edinburgh, K.G., Round the World in H.M.S. 'Galatea', in the Years 1867, 1868, 1869, 1870, 1871 …* (South Kensington Museum, 1872); see also Anon. c.1875. A copy in the British Library, shelf mark 7804.pp.23, contains manuscript additions recording the prices fetched when much of the collection was auctioned in 1901: Van der Kiste and Jordaan 1984, pp. 98–9, 176–9.

178 Ridley 2012, p. 340.

179 Hussey 1949, pp. 86–7.

180 Beavan 1896, pp. 50–1, 240, 290–7; TNA, WORK 19/18/1, WORK 19/117.

181 Beavan 1896, pp. 253–8; TNA, WORK 19/117, WORK 17/13/9, WORK 17/26/11, WORK 17/24/4; Burton 1999, pp. 26–56.

182 Beavan 1896, pp. 247–53. The carriage is now displayed at the Wellington family estate at Stratfield Saye, Hampshire.

183 TNA, WORK 19/18/1. For the stables contract drawing, see TNA, WORK 34/848; Tyack 1992, pp. 232–9.

184 Magnus 1964, p. 68.

185 TNA, WORK 19/18/1. For a brief overview of the architectural development of the house, see Bradley and Pevsner 2003, pp. 591–4.

186 For an account of the building and its occupants in 1896, see Beavan 1896, pp. 1–104, 110–40. The 15th Earl of Derby refers to the 'Marlborough House set' in his diary on 14 Jan. 1885, quoted in Ridley 2012, p. 198.

187 Sheppard 1894, II, p. 245.

188 Thornbury and Walford 1887, IV, p. 106.

189 *Report from the Select Committee on St James's Park; with the Minutes of Evidence* (7 Mar. 1856), p. iii.

190 RA VIC/ADDQ/00/0284: B. Hall, Office of Works to C. Phipps, 4 Mar. 1856. The constricted corner at the west end of Cleveland Row, between the Lord Chamberlain's office and Stable Yard, was rounded off in 1866 to provide a more private royal route from Buckingham Palace through Stable Yard: Sheppard 1894, I, pp. 410–11; *Report from the Select Committee on St James's Park; with the Minutes of Evidence* (7 Mar. 1856), p. iv.

191 TNA, WORK 1/50, fols 8 (2 May 1856), 48 (7 May 1856).

192 *The Times*, 7 June 1856, p. 7; Hansard, 142 *HC Deb.* 3rd ser. 1138, 6 June 1856. For Tite, see Colvin 2008, pp. 1043–1044.

193 RIBA FRA/TITE/1. Modern scholarship has disproved many of Tite's other attributions to Jones: Lever 1984, p. 44. The chapel features on the left-hand side of Tite's picture, but that section is missing from the truncated photograph available online: <www.architecture.com/image-library/ribapix/image-information/poster/composition-of-the-works-of-inigo-jones/posterid/RIBA13252.html> (accessed 11 July 2019).

194 *The Times*, 7 June 1856, pp. 7, 9.

195 Ibid., 14 June 1856, pp. 6, 9. For a summary of the debate and a map of the routes, see *Illustrated London News*, 21 June 1856, p. 690.

196 TNA, WORK 1/51, fols 59 (4 July 1856), 95–7 (9 July 1856), 233–236 (24 July 1856), WORK 1/52, fol. 170 (16 Oct. 1856). For the 7 July 1856 contracts for the walls, road, gates, railings and lamp posts, see TNA, WORK 34/825.

197 TNA, WORK 1/52, fol. 324 (12 Nov. 1856).

198 Ibid., fol. 338 (14 Nov. 1856); RA VIC/ADDQ/00/0371: B. Hall to C. Phipps, 4 Dec. 1856. The description of the German chapel as a 'gem of art' by an unnamed MP (presumably Tite) is referred to in *The Times*, 29 Sept. 1856, p. 12. Phipps was resident in the palace from 1852 until his death: RA LC/LCO/AR/1852, Apartments in the Palaces, 11–12; RA LC/LCO/AR/1866, Apartments in the Palaces, 36–37.

199 TNA, WORK 19/945.

200 TNA, WORK 19/1047.

201 TNA, WORK 1/74, fol. 304 (13 Aug. 1863), WORK 1/79, fol. 368 (22 July 1865).

202 RA LC/LCO/AR/1880, General Remarks, 114.

203 Sheppard 1894, II, pp. 97–112; RA VIC/MAIN/QVJ, 10 Feb. 1840 (Beatrice).

204 TNA, WORK 21/12/1; Tyack 1992, pp. 80–3.

205 RCIN 813076. A copy is framed in the vestibule of the Chapel Royal.

206 Arch and Marschner 1990, pp. 53–6.

207 TNA, WORK 1/57, fol. 58 (29 Dec. 1857), WORK 34/880. A view of the alterations was published in *Illustrated London News*, 23 Jan. 1858, reproduced in D. Baldwin 1990, p. 396. TNA, WORK 34/878, WORK 1/56, fol. 416 (15 Dec. 1857). A temporary gallery on the grand staircase was retained for spectators viewing levees and Drawing Rooms, and was not removed until 1864: RA LC/LCO/AR/1864 General Remarks, 89.

208 TNA, WORK 21/12/2; RA VIC/ADDQ/00/0461: B. Hall to C. Grey, 10 Dec. 1857; RA VIC/ADDQ/00/0466: B. Hall to C. Grey, 14 Dec. 1857; Sheppard 1894, II, p. 208.

209 *The Times*, 26 Jan. 1858, p. 7; Sheppard 1894, II, pp. 113–25.

210 *The Times*, 31 Dec. 1857, p. 6, 1 Jan. 1858, p. 9.

211 Ibid., 26 Jan. 1858, p. 7.

212 RA LC/LCO/AR/1868, General remarks, no pag.; Sheppard 1894, II, p. 219.

213 Sheppard 1894, II, p. 224.

214 RA VIC/MAIN/QVJ, 29 June 1891 (Beatrice).

215 Sheppard 1894, II, pp. 125–30; Arch and Marschner 1990, pp. 71–6.

216 *The Times*, 30 June 1891, p. 9, 7 July 1893, p. 5.

217 Quoted in Pope-Hennessy 1959, p. 261. St George's, Windsor, was deemed unsuitable by the Queen because of Prince Eddy's funeral there the previous year. For the wedding, see RA VIC/MAIN/QVJ, 6 July 1893 (Beatrice); Pope-Hennessy 1959, pp. 266–71.

218 The arrangements are illustrated in Sheppard 1894, II, facing p. 126.

219 Sheppard 1894, II, pp. 130–3. The tapestries were taken from Princess Louise's apartments at Kensington Palace: RA LC/LCO/AR/1893, General Remarks, no pag.; RA LC/LCO/AR/1894, General Remarks, no pag. They were removed from the chapel in 1921 and were returned to the Great Hall at Hampton Court: RA LC/LCO/AR/1921, Chapels, St James's Palace, no pag.

220 E.g. in honour of Princess Alice's fourth birthday: *The Times*, 27 Apr. 1847, p. 6, and Prince Arthur's fifth: *The Times*, 2 May 1855, p. 12. Juvenile balls were also occasionally given at Buckingham Palace, e.g. *The Times*, 26 Apr. 1856, p. 8.

221 Victoria was at Osborne for her birthday in 1861.

222 E.g. RA VIC/MAIN/QVJ, 17 May 1838, 27 May 1848, 18 May 1860 (Beatrice). The event did not take place in 1846, 1850 or 1853, due to the recent births of Helen, Arthur and Leopold. Shepherd 1841, I, pp. 185–8.

223 RA VIC/MAIN/QVJ, 19 July 1837 (Esher).

224 Ibid., 20 June 1838, 1 July 1840 (Beatrice).

225 Ibid., 14 Mar., 11 May, 27 June 1855, 20 and 27 Feb., 12 Mar., 15 Apr., 7 May, 25 June 1856 (Beatrice).

226 The redecorated State Apartments are described in *Illustrated London News*, 30 Mar. 1844, p. 204. The patent for 'texture of glass entered with silk' by the Oxford Street silk mercers, Messrs Williams and Sowerby, was reported in *Art-Union*, 1 July 1844, 6, p. 195. The partnership was dissolved in 1851: *London Gazette*, 10 June 1851, p. 1528. At the 1851 Great Exhibition, silk tissued with glass was manufactured under Williams and Sowerby's patent and exhibited by Sanderson & Reid: *Great Exhibition* 1851, II, p. 503.

227 Armytage 1927, pp. 122–3.

228 *The Court and Country Companion* (London, 1835), p. 136; *Illustrated London News*, 8 May 1847, p. 300; Coxe 1856, p. 168. At the time, Coxe was the Episcopalian rector of Grace Church, Baltimore.

229 The Lord Chamberlain's Annual Reports commence in 1852: RA LC/LCO/AR/1852-6. Attendance numbers fluctuated between 252 and 997. The totals for three functions in 1855 are not recorded.

230 RA LC/LCO/AR/1857, General Remarks, fols 24–25v. For the London season, see Armytage 1927, pp. 46–9.

231 RA LC/LCO/AR/1857, Ceremonials and Court Proceedings, fols 15v–16, 24.

232 RA LC/LCO/AR/1857, General Remarks, fol. 25.

233 RA VIC/ADDQ/00/0326, 2 June 1856; RA PPTO/PP/QV/ADDX/A/171, 3 June 1856; RA VIC/ADDQ/00/0334, 14 June 1856; RA VIC/ADDQ/00/0337, 19 June 1856; RA VIC/ADDQ/00/0338, 20 June [1856].

234 RA VIC/ADDQ/00/0408, 13 June 1857.

235 RA LC/LCO/AR/1859, Ceremonials and Court Proceedings, p. 55; TNA, WORK 1/60, fol. 395 (16 Dec. 1858); TNA, WORK 34/142.

236 TNA, WORK 19/20, fols 448–450.

237 *The Times*, 26 Apr. 1861, p. 9; Sheppard 1894, I, p. 213.

238 *The Times*, 6 May 1861, p. 5, 15 May 1861, p. 5.

239 RA LC/LCO/AR/1861, 115.

240 RA VIC/MAIN/QVJ, 19 June 1861 (Beatrice).

241 For example, from 1877, the Queen tended to visit St James's around five times a year, mostly to see her aged Aunt Cambridge, until her death in Apr. 1889: RA VIC/MAIN/QVJ, 13 Jan. 1877, 25 Feb. and 6 Apr. 1889 (Beatrice).

242 Sheppard 1894, I, p. 215.
243 TNA, WORK 19/20, fols 482–483. For the problems created by a single corridor for entrance and exit, see *The Times*, 22 May 1855, p. 12, 23 May 1855, p. 7.
244 TNA, WORK 19/20, fols 482–483.
245 TNA, WORK 19/20, fols 484–489; RA PPTO/PP/QV/ADD/1815, 7 Apr. 1863. For the changes, compare the 1841 and 1861 plans: TNA, WORK 34/129 and 34/1505.
246 TNA, WORK 34/871–874.
247 TNA, WORK 19/20, fols 488–490; RA LC/LCO/AR/1863, 89.
248 TNA, WORK 19/20, fols 460–468, WORK 1/75, fol. 233 (10 Dec. 1863).
249 RA LC/LCO/AR/1864, General Remarks, 92–93, RA LC/LCO/AR/1865, General Remarks, 96. A list of pictures is provided in Sheppard 1894, I, pp. 363–4.
250 TNA, WORK 1/75, fols 209–210 (4 Dec. 1863), 216–217 (5 Dec. 1863), 230 (9 Dec. 1863), 261 (19 Dec. 1863), 274 (23 Dec. 1863), 294 (29 Dec. 1863), WORK 6/274 (4 Dec. 1863).
251 TNA, WORK 1/75, fols 333 (8 Jan. 1864), 394 (26 Jan. 1864), WORK 1/76, fol. 70 (25 Feb. 1864); *The Times*, 9 May 1864, p. 7.
252 TNA, LC 1/139, letter 251: W. Cowper, Office of Works to S. Ponsonby, Lord Chamberlain's office, 18 Aug. 1864; ibid., letter 250: T. Biddulph to S. Ponsonby, Lord Chamberlain's office, 21 Aug. 1864; TNA, LC 1/140, letter 153: Lord Sydney, Lord Chamberlain to William Cowper, Office of Works, 13 Aug. 1864; RA PPTO/PP/QV/ADD/2128, 14 Sept. 1864.
253 TNA, WORK 19/20, fol. 466.
254 Ibid., fol. 474.
255 Ibid., fols 476–481; TNA, WORK 1/78, fols 216 (13 Jan. 1865), 222 (16 Jan. 1865), 247 (23 Jan. 1865), WORK 1/80, fol. 59 (8 Sept. 1865).
256 Sheppard 1894, I, p. 365; TNA, LC 1/140, letter 31, 16 Feb. 1864.
257 *The Times*, 16 Feb. 1863, p. 5.
258 TNA, LC 1/140, letter 109: S. Ponsonby to T. Biddulph, 8 June 1864; RA PPTO/PP/QV/ADD/2167, 1 Dec. 1864; Sheppard 1894, I, pp. 361–5.
259 TNA, WORK 1/80, fol. 65.
260 MacCarthy 1994, pp. 166–85.
261 Quoted in MacCarthy 2012, p. 130.
262 Lambourne 1996, p. 18.
263 Le Bourgeois 1974. Cowper employed the firm to decorate the stairwell of his Curzon Street house, at the same time as giving them the St James's commission: Rodgers 1998, p. iv.
264 RA LC/LCO/AR/1865, General Remarks, 96.
265 TNA, WORK 1/81, fols 215, 297, WORK 1/82, fols 144, 178. The best overview of the Morris firm's work at the palace is Mitchell 1947. See also Kirk 2005, pp. 44–6.
266 Lethaby 1979, p. 43.
267 Henderson 1967, p. 82.
268 Ibid., p. 84.
269 MacCarthy 1994, p. 211.
270 TNA, WORK 19/20, fols 498, 501, 503–505, 516, WORK 1/82, fols 258–259, WORK 1/85, fol. 35. For a description of the armour in the State Apartments in 1894, see Sheppard 1894, I, pp. 369–70.
271 Mafra is a baroque palace, and Sheppard presumably meant either the palace of Sintra (*Palácio Nacional de Sintra*) or the Pena Palace (*Palácio da Pena*), which have intricate painted ceilings and decorative tiled walls from the 16th century and the 1840s to 1850s respectively. See Sheppard 1894, I, p. 129.
272 Pevsner 1972, p. 273.
273 RA VIC/MAIN/L/14/34: Lord Hertford to H. Ponsonby, 17 Feb. 1879.
274 TNA, WORK 19/20, fols 580, 581, 584, 587.
275 Ibid., fol. 589.
276 Ibid., fols 590, 596–599; RA LC/LCO/AR/1879, General Remarks, fol. 53.
277 TNA, WORK 19/20, fol. 606.
278 Ibid., fols 610–612, 617; L. Parry 2013, p. 91. The current replicas were laid in the 1990s. One of the original carpets was subsequently loaned to the National Trust for display in the Saloon at Chirk Castle, Wrexham. I am grateful to Sir Hugh Roberts for this information.
279 All the Morris papers were printed by Jeffrey & Co., Islington: M. Parry 2011, p. 40.
280 TNA, WORK 19/20, fol. 622: Morris & Co. to Office of Works, 20 Aug. 1880.
281 Ibid., fol. 627; Sugden and Edmondson 1926, p. 163.
282 Day 1899, pp. 7, 27. Morris subcontracted the painted work to F.R. Leach & Sons. The David Parr House, Cambridge, contains archive material citing the firm's work for Morris at St James's, as well as DDP Drawing Book 2, which includes alternative coloured patterns for cornice designs in the yellow room (the Queen Anne Room) and the Throne Room. I am grateful to Tamsin Wimhurst, Chair of the Trustees for David Parr House for this information. See <www.davidparrhouse.org> (accessed 11 July 2019).
283 TNA, WORK 19/20, fol. 622. For the 'St James's' wall and ceiling papers, see Clark 1974, p. 15 and figs 28, 29; Sugden and Edmondson 1926, p. 162.
284 RA VIC/MAIN/L/5/32: J. Ponsonby-Fane to H. Ponsonby, 14 July 1881. TNA, WORK 19/20, fols 635–636. Some of the pictures from this hang remained in 1894: RCIN 1048431, p. 5.
285 TNA, WORK 19/127: Gillett Bland & Co., Steam Clock Factory Croydon, to H. Wilson, Office of Works, 5 Mar. 1881, H. Wilson memo, 7 Mar. 1881; Sheppard 1894, I, pp. 12–14.
286 TNA, WORK 19/20, fol. 637: Morris & Co. to Office of Works, 20 July 1881.
287 Ibid.
288 Fairclough and Leary 1981, p. 41.
289 TNA, WORK 19/20, fol. 637: Morris & Co. to Office of Works, 20 July 1881.
290 Ibid., fols 637–638. For 'Chrysanthemum', see Clark 1974, p. 14 and fig. 22.
291 TNA, WORK 19/20, fol. 639: Morris & Co. to Office of Works, 20 July 1881.
292 Ibid., fol. 639v.
293 Ibid.
294 Ibid., fol. 639. The wallpaper pattern was not specified for this room, but a fragment was found on the walls during works in 1988. For 'Mallow', see V&A, E.811-1915: <http://collections.vam.ac.uk/item/O249047/mallow-wallpaper-faulkner-kate/> (accessed 11 July 2019).
295 E.g. in the passageway west of the Banqueting Room. TNA, WORK 19/20, fol. 650: Morris & Co. to Office of Works, 20 July 1881, fol. 652r-v: 17 Jan. 1881 [*sic*: this should read 1882].
296 Ibid., fols 639, 650, 20 July 1881.
297 Ibid., fol. 662r–v, 13 Mar. 1882. See 'First sketch design for valance St James's Palace', William Morris Gallery, Walthamstow, A41.
298 Ibid., fol. 656r–v, 20 Mar. 1882, and fol. 663, n.d. [but registered 29 Mar. 1882].
299 In Feb. 1881, Morris wrote to his wife, Jane, 'Work at St James all finished & happily, with good profit: so don't spare to ask for cash if you want it': Kelvin 1987, II, pp. 19–21.
300 *The Times*, 21 July 1897, p. 10.
301 Ibid., 28 June 1897, p. 7, 2 July 1897, p. 10.
302 Ibid., 10 July 1897, p. 14.
303 Christie 2016; Spehr 2008, pp. 474–8. Another early example of filming at the palace is footage of the changing of the guard at St James's, dating from 1896 or 1907, which was re-edited by British Pathé in the 1930s: <www.britishpathe.com/video/changing-the-guard-at-st-james/query/32+years+ago+guard> (accessed 27 Jan. 2020)
304 *The Times*, 24 Jan. 1901, p. 5; Armytage 1927, p. 127. King Edward VII abandoned the practice of kissing hands at levees and courts in 1902: RA LC/LCO/AR/1902, General Remarks, Palaces, 57.
305 *The Times*, 25 Jan. 1901, p. 7.
306 *London Gazette*, no. 2723, 25 Jan. 1901, pp. 556–7; RA LC/LCO/AR/1901, Court Proceedings, 62.
307 RA LC/LCO/AR/1901, General Remarks, Palaces, 37; RA LC/LCO/AR/1902, General Remarks, Palaces, 28.
308 Pope-Hennessy 1959, p. 375.
309 Armytage 1927, pp. 127–33; RA LC/LCO/AR/1902, Court Proceedings, Courts (no pag.), General Remarks, Palaces, 54.
310 The rooms included the Grand Hall, Grand Staircase, Ballroom, Ball Supper Room and the Marble Hall: Clifford Smith 1931, pp. 130, 133, 176, 177, 195. For contemporary domestic examples in the style of Louis XVI, see Cooper 1977, pp. 14–15.
311 TNA, WORK 19/132.
312 The firm was located at 8 Mount Street, off Berkeley Square, next door to the royal upholsterers, Holland & Sons: *Post Office London Directory for 1895* (London, 1895), p. 533. In Feb. 1895, White left the firm, as did Donaldson in Apr. 1901, but Allom continued to trade as White Allom & Co.: *London Gazette*, 18 Feb. 1895, p. 1024, 27 Apr. 1900, p. 2710. For Allom's obituary, see *The Times*, 5 June 1947, p. 7.
313 TNA, RG 13/1224, fol. 81, p. 55; TNA, WORK 19/132: C.C. Allom to J.B. Westcott, 4 June 1904.
314 Tanner 1902, pl. 46; see also pls 44, 45.
315 TNA, WORK 19/132: White Allom & Co., St James's Palace estimate, 9 July 1904; L. Binyon, rev. C. Lloyd, 'Cust, Sir Lionel Henry

(1859–1929)', *ODNB*, online edn, 2004 <www.oxforddnb.com/view/article/32684> (accessed 11 July 2019). The Morris scheme was replaced in 1923: TNA, WORK 19/956.

316 RA LC/LCO/AR/1904, General Remarks, Palaces, 20.

317 TNA, WORK 19/132: White Allom & Co., St James's Palace estimate, 9 July 1904. A photograph of the Picture Gallery, dated 26 July 1907, shows both ceiling and cornice distempered (Architectural Red Box Collection, City of Westminster, St James's Palace Interior, image 3823/100, Historic England Archive).

318 TNA, WORK 19/132: L. Cust to Col. Sir D. Dawson, Lord Chamberlain's office, 20 Nov. 1908, S.K. McDonnell to Col. Sir D. Dawson, 24 Nov. 1908, Sir John Donelly, Science and Art Department, South Kensington, to the Office of Works, 29 Sept. 1896; TNA, WORK 34/1737–1740; *HKW* 1982, p. 293.

319 In 1911, Laking also became the first keeper and secretary of the London Museum (the predecessor of the Museum of London), which was in temporary accommodation in Kensington Palace, before moving to Lancaster House, adjacent to St James's Palace, in Mar. 1914. See Yorke 2001, p. 161; C. Blair, 'Laking, Sir Guy Francis, second baronet (1875–1919)', *ODNB*, online edn 2004 <www.oxforddnb.com/view/article/53494> (accessed 11 July 2019).

320 The chandelier is not shown hanging in a 1900 Benjamin Stone photograph of the Armoury (Birmingham Reference Library, Benjamin Stone Collection, 10968), but is in this position in 1907 (Fig. 4.62). The Temple Church chandelier now hangs in the Berkeley Chapel, Bristol Cathedral.

321 RA LC/LCO/AR/1901, General Remarks, Palaces, 33; RA LC/LCO/AR/1902, Warrants for Apartments, no pag.; Nicolson 1952, p. 75; Pope-Hennessy 1959, pp. 355–6, 377–9; Windsor 1953, pp. 36–7.

322 RA LC/LCO/AR/1901, Chapels, 42; RA LC/LCO/AR/1901, General Remarks, Palaces, 37; TNA, WORK 19/945; D. Baldwin 1990, p. 373.

323 Armytage 1927, p. 246; *The Times*, 7 July 1903, p. 10.

324 Armytage 1927, p. 172.

325 RA LC/LCO/AR/1910, Palaces, St James's Palace, 21; RA LC/LCO/AR/1913, Palaces, St James's Palace, no pag.

326 Armytage 1927, pp. 240–5, 248; RA LC/LCO/AR/1912, General Remarks, Palaces, no pag.; *The Times*, 31 May 1913, p. 8. The St James's Conference, Feb.–Mar. 1939, to determine the future of Palestine, was also fraught with difficulties, because the Jewish and Arab delegates refused to sit together in the same room: *Illustrated London News*, 11 Feb. 1939, p. 214.

327 RA LC/LCO/AR/1914, General Remarks, Palaces, no pag.; RA LC/LCO/AR/1915, General Remarks, Palaces, no pag. This is in contrast to the Second World War, when the inevitability of aerial bombardment resulted in the entire National Gallery being emptied by the Director, Kenneth Clark, and sent to Wales for safe storage: Stourton 2016, pp. 156–60.

328 RA LC/LCO/AR/1915, General Remarks, Palaces, no pag. Following Kitchener's death, part of York House was used as offices for Lady Edward Carson's Ulster Division Committee: RA LC/LCO/AR/1915, General Remarks, Palaces, no pag.

329 These were Queen Mary's Needlework Guild, which was established in the palace on 10 Aug. 1914, to collect and distribute parcels of clothing to military hospitals: RA LC/LCO/AR/1914, General Remarks, Palaces, no pag.; *The Times*, 11 Aug. 1914, p. 9; and the Prince of Wales's National Relief Fund, to assist those in financial distress, which was based in York House: *The Times*, 7 Aug. 1914, p. 6, 10 Aug. 1914, p. 6. See also Pope-Hennessy 1959, pp. 490–1.

330 *The Treaty of Peace between the Allied and Associated Powers and Germany* (London, 1919).

331 *The Times*, 3 July 1919, p. 13.

332 TNA, WORK 34/1513–1519.

333 TNA, WORK 19/716.

334 George 1921.

335 Armytage 1927, pp. 245–6.

336 Nicolson 1952, p. 394.

337 *Documents of the London Naval Conference 1930* (London, 1930); Nicolson 1952, pp. 438–9; *Indian Round Table Conference* (London, 1931); TNA, WORK 19/248.

338 Nicolson 1952, pp. 502–9.

339 TNA, WORK 19/248.

340 Stourton 2016, p. 136. Coins were designed by Percy Metcalfe (1895–1970) to meet Edward VIII's suggestion for 'modern coinage', but because of the abdication, no coins were issued: <www.royalmintmuseum.org.uk/Blog/percy-metcalfe> (accessed 11 July 2019).

341 Dorment 1986, pp. 195–6.

342 Lady Gleichen's former studio now houses the Royal Collection Picture Conservation Studio. For the Duke of Clarence's tomb, see Brindle 2018, pp. 320–3, 410–11.

343 The annual inspection was cancelled in 1914, owing to fears of suffragettes entering the palace among the large crowd of friends of the Yeomen, who were normally allowed to visit the State Apartments after the ceremony: RA LC/LCO/AR/1914, General Remarks, Palaces, no pag.; Marsden 2004, p. 37.

344 RA LC/LCO/AR/1923, Court proceedings, no pag.; RA LC/LCO/AR/1926, General Remarks, Palaces. The 1931 Pathé News archive includes the inspection of the Yeomen of the Guard, and the changing of the guard with the Grenadier Guards: 'The Yeoman of the Guard 1931', British Pathé, <www.britishpathe.com/video/the-yeoman-of-the-guard/query/James+Palace> (accessed 11 July 2019); 'On parade! 1931', British Pathé, <www.britishpathe.com/video/on-parade/query/James+Palace> (accessed 11 July 2019).

345 TNA, WORK 19/243: C.H. Read, 'The leaden coffin found at St James's Palace', 11 Mar. 1902; RA LC/LCO/AR/1902, 27; D.M. Wilson, 'Read, Sir (Charles) Hercules (1857–1929)', *ODNB*, online edn, 2004, <www.oxforddnb.com/view/article/35693> (accessed 11 July 2019).

346 TNA, WORK 19/247.

347 Historic England Archive, MA/JPL0002; MA/JPL0003; ibid., WS01/02/S01295–8, four photographs taken 18 Aug. 1929. For excavations in Friary Court and Marlborough Road in 2018 and 2019, see S. Harris 2020.

348 For the Office of Works' attitude to investigation and repairs in the inter-war period see Thurley 2013, pp. 84–98, 131–47.

349 *Illustrated London News*, 8 Feb. 1936, p. 241. The strain on the flagpole proved too much and it was replaced with a stronger one in Mar. 1936: ibid., 21 Mar. 1936, p. 507.

350 *The Times*, 26 May 1936, p. 19. Other levees were held at Buckingham Palace and Holyroodhouse.

351 TNA, WORK 19/954, York House, 1919–39: Lionel Halsey [the Prince's comptroller] to the Secretary, Office of Works, 14 May 1928, stating the sitting room at York House had been redecorated at the Prince's own cost; RA EVIIIPWH/PS/0737: E.G. Lehmann, 116 Wigmore St, Portman Sq, London W., Oct. 1928, York House invoice to HRH Prince of Wales. Edward Lehmann was trading from 116 Wigmore Street until at least 1935: *Kelly's Directory of Marylebone and St John's Wood* (1935), p. 520. For E.G. Lehmann as warrant holder, see *London Gazette*, 3 Jan. 1931, p. 51, 3 Jan. 1936, p. 44.

352 Aird mischievously likened the upstairs equerry's room to 'a French brothel only there are no ladies': Ziegler 2001, p. 166; the graining was so accomplished that Aird thought the hall panelling was stripped, but in a 1953 article it was correctly recognised as 'grained pine panelling': Anon. 1953. Queen Mary favoured the look of exposed pine: she stripped the varnish off the pine panelling at Balmoral House; see Pope-Hennessy 2018, p. 219.

353 York House is covered in the Prince of Wales's private account: RA EVIIIPWH/TREAS/EVIIIPWACC/JNL [covering the period 1931–6], Account G7, House Sundries, 3–7, 3 May 1933–10 May 1935.

354 For the Prince of Wales's expenditure on Fort Belvedere: RA EVIIIPWH/TREAS/EVIIIPWACC/JNL [covering the period 1931–6], Account F, 'The Fort', 1–16, 4 May 1931–10 May 1935; and for furniture: Account G3, 'Furniture &c', 1, 26 Aug. 1932.

355 Windsor 1953, p. 224.

356 RA EVIIIPWH/TREAS/EVIIIPWACC/JNL [covering the period 1931–6], Account F, 'The Fort', 16–20, 2 July 1935–26 May 1936; Windsor 1953, pp. 221–3.

357 Schrijver purchased the Mayfair firm Elden Ltd in 1932. He made his name from working for Mrs Simpson and the Prince: *The Tatler*, 31 July 1935, p. 202; Burkhardt 1977, pp. 32–42; Spurling 1984, p. 124; Inchbald 1965, p. 131.

358 R.B. Fisher 1978, pp. 34–5.

359 For Schrijver's comments on 1930s domestic decoration, see Schrijver 1939, pp. 9–12.

360 A similar set of photographs was sold at Sotheby's in 1997: Sotheby's, New York, 11-19 Sept. 1997, lot 457. An accompanying card states: 'These old pictures of York House to be repeated showing the rooms as decorated by The King'. This is interpreted as an instruction to a photographer to repeat views shown in a series of pre-existing photographs with new views showing their redecoration, either literally as carried out by the King (i.e. Jan.–Dec. 1936) or, more likely, as initiated by the King when Prince of Wales c.1935, but continuing into 1936. The photographs depict Fort Belvedere, as well as 15 of York House, five of which show rooms prior to redecoration, and ten after. I am grateful to James Edgar for a discussion of the available evidence.

361 Allyson McDermott kindly told me she had encountered this suggestion. See Anon. 1953, pp. 47–8.

362 It may be significant that in Jan. 1939, when repairs were required to some of the Chinese wallpaper, the Office of Works turned to Lehmann: TNA, WORK 19/954: York House, 1919–39, memo J.T.L. Kendle, Office of Works, to A.W. Heasman, 1 Jan. 1936.

363 The three portraits illustrated in the pre-1936 photograph depict the Princess Royal, 1851, Princess Alice, 1851, and Prince Alfred, 1852.

364 Cf. photographs: RCIN 2102158 from 1901, and RCIN 2301756 from 1903.

365 As recounted by Alan Lascelles, Edward VIII's assistant private secretary since Jan. 1936: Pope-Hennessy 2018, p. 18. I am grateful to Andrew Barclay for drawing my attention to this reference. The original Llewellyn portrait (RCIN 404471) was commissioned in 1914 by Queen Mary and David (Edward) when Prince of Wales, as a Christmas present for George V.

366 The 'Bizarre' pattern was first produced by Wilkinson's Burslem factory in 1927. In Nov. 1936, the Office of Works found a stray 'tea pot, cup, saucer and plate' in York House, which they noted was to be 'packed with remainder of "Bizarre" set': TNA, WORK 19/954, York House, 1919–39, 'Decisions and comments made by Their Royal Highnesses the Duke and Duchess of Gloucester. (Visits of 7th, 8th & 9th November [1936])'.

367 Ibid.

368 *The Times*, 10 Feb. 1937, pp. 14, 19, 29 May 1937, pp. 14, 19, 23 June 1937, p. 10, 4 Mar. 1938, p. 8, 18 Mar. 1938, p. 9, 1 June 1938, p. 20, 19 July 1939, p. 20. The Duke of Gloucester also held a levee at St James's on behalf of the king on 23 May 1939: *The Times*, 24 May 1939, pp. 16, 22.

369 RA LC/LCO/AR/1926, Chapels, no pag.

370 For G.H. Chettle's obituary, see *The Times*, 27 Sept. 1960, p. 16.

371 Historic England Archive, Swindon, St James's Palace, folder of Chettle lecture notes, GHEU, file CB 057/000/A/00 PC1.

372 Bradley 2001. The primary archival source is TNA, WORK 19/945.

373 TNA, WORK 19/960, fols 225–226.

374 TNA, WORK 19/945.

375 *The Times*, 31 Oct. 1938, p. 19. Sir Philip Sassoon, First Commissioner of Works, wrote an article in *The Times* on the chapel's history and restoration: *The Times*, 28 Oct. 1938, p. 15.

376 *The Times*, 10 Jan. 1939, p. 12.

377 Bradley 2001.

378 Stourton 2016, pp. 171–2.

379 TNA, WORK 19/1298, including HMOW plan, 'St James's Palace – Refuge Scheme', reference 19c, 18-4-39.

380 K. Scott 2010, pp. 136–7. See also *Picture Post*, 30 Mar. 1940, pp. 35–9.

381 The exhibition was sponsored by the *Daily Telegraph*. *Prisoner of War*, 2, no. 24, Apr. 1944, p. 2.

382 TNA, WORK 19/242.

383 Graves 1963, p. 222.

384 Pope-Hennessy 1959, pp. 596–610. For personal portraits of Queen Mary at Badminton from Osbert Sitwell (1892–1969), see Sitwell 1974, pp. 21–61; and from the 10th Duke and Duchess of Beaufort, see Pope-Hennessy 2018, pp. 298–307.

385 City of Westminster Archives Centre, Incident Report CD3/974; Graves 1963, p. 222.

386 Sansom 1947, p. 82.

387 City of Westminster Archives Centre, Incident Report CD3/1540. The wartime functions of the Office of Works were expanded to create a new central building department, which was named the Ministry of Works and Buildings on 24 Oct. 1940: Kohan 1952, pp. 69–81. Lady Gleichen was the originator of the Home Guard: Graves 1963, p. 222, and a photograph of the damaged Friary Court building facing p. 206.

388 Command 6285, *Inter-allied meeting held in London at St James's Palace on June 12, 1941 Report of proceedings* (London 1941), p. 3.

389 Ibid., p. 15.

390 *Allied Peace Aims Treaties and Agreements National Peace Council* (London, n.d. [1942]), p. 13. A previous meeting took place at St James's in Sept. 1941: Command 6315, *Inter-allied meeting held in London at St James's Palace on September 24, 1941 Report of proceedings* (London, 1941).

391 Inter-Allied Information Committee London, *Punishment for War Crimes: The Inter-Allied Declaration signed at St James's Palace London on 13th January 1942* (London, 1942), p. 5.

392 City of Westminster Archives Centre, Incident Report CD3/1710; the statement in Graves 1963, p. 222, that those killed included two guardsmen on sentry duty is untrue. Lord Claud Hamilton wrote to Queen Mary on 29 Feb. 1944: 'As I suspected at the time – no member of the St James's Palace Guard suffered a scratch, far less than two being killed' (RA QM/PRIV/CC47/2044).

393 TNA, WORK 19/1299: T. Small to C.E. Clouting, 26 Feb. 1944, G.A. Gardner to C.E. Clouting, 4 Mar. 1944.

394 RA QM/PRIV/CC47/2045: Lord Claud Hamilton to Queen Mary, 1 Mar. 1944.

395 D. Baldwin 1990, pp. 387–9; TNA, WORK 19/1073, fol. 273. See also W.H. Elliott 1951, pp. 222–6.

396 TNA, WORK 19/1073, fol. 273, WORK 19/1299: T. Small to C.E. Clouting, 26 Feb. 1944; RA QM/PRIV/CC47/2044: Lord Claud Hamilton to Queen Mary, 29 Feb. 1944. For further information on this raid, see the West End at War website <www.westendatwar.org.uk/page_id__223.aspx?path=0p28p> (accessed 11 July 2019).

397 TNA, WORK 19/1299: C.A. Wand to C.E. Clouting, 18 June 1944.

398 TNA, WORK 19/1299: M. Trickett, memo to Deputy Secretary, 27 Apr. 1944; ibid., A.E. Clouting memo, 20 Aug. 1945.

5. The Palace Today

1 D. Baldwin 1990, pp. 387–90. Until 1901, the chapel was known as the German chapel; that year, King Edward VII renamed it the Marlborough House chapel. In 1939, it was announced that the chapel would revert to 'its original name', the Queen's Chapel.

2 TNA, WORK 19/1297, WORK 19/1068; drawings also in the Historic England Archive, Swindon. See also Bradley 2001, p. 299.

3 TNA, WORK 19/1073 (1942–51), WORK 19/1238 (1955–71).

4 TNA, CM 8/95. The drawings for this work are held in the Historic England Archive.

5 Cannadine 1983, pp. 139–60.

6 Yorke 2001, pp. 165–73.

7 TNA, WORK 99/279. The drawings for this work are held in the Historic England Archive.

8 Armytage 1927, pp. 127–36; Sandbrook 2005, pp. 514–22; Ziegler 1979, pp. 131–2; E.S. Turner 1959, pp. 365–8.

9 Prochaska 1995, pp. 248–58.

10 Millar 1977, pp. 212–17; Carter 2001, pp. 304–10.

11 TNA, WORK 19/1105 (1940–66).

12 Dorment 1980, pp. 47–54.

13 'Nemon, Oscar (1906-85)', *ODNB*, online edn, 2004 <www.oxforddnb.com/view/article/31492> (accessed 11 July 2019).

14 TNA, WORK 19/1074.

15 Unless otherwise noted, details of work from 1947 to 1953 are from TNA, WORK 19/1175.

16 Hussey 1949.

17 Ziegler 1985, pp. 457–8; Hussey 1939.

18 Higham and Moseley 1991, p. 151; Judd 1980, p. 139.

19 Lacey 2002, p. 189.

20 *News Chronicle*, 10 Apr. 1952, p. 3; Shawcross 2009, pp. 676–7.

21 Details of the refurbishment of 1952–5 come from TNA, WORK 19/1237.

22 Vickers 2005, pp. 398–401.

23 Shawcross 2009, pp. 778–9; Cornforth 1996.

24 Goodall 2018, p. 140.

25 Langlands 2015, pp. 136–51.

26 H.Baldwin 2002.

ABBREVIATIONS AND BIBLIOGRAPHY

Abbreviations
AS   All Souls College, Oxford
BL   British Library, London
Bodl.   Bodleian Library, Oxford
CCR   *Calendar of Close Rolls*
CChR   *Calendar of Charter Rolls*
CPR   *Calendar of Patent Rolls*
CSP Dom.   *Calendar of State Papers, Domestic*
CSP Spain   *Calendar of State Papers, Spain*
CSP Ven.   *Calendar of State Papers, Venice*
CTB   *Calendar of Treasury Books*
CTP   *Calendar of Treasury Papers*
ECR   Eton College Archives
GUL   Glasgow University Library
HMC   Historical Manuscripts Commission
Mich.   Michaelmas
NDB   *Neue Deutsche Biographie* 2 (1955)
NRO   Northamptonshire County Record Office
ODNB   *Oxford Dictionary of National Biography*
RA   Royal Archives, Windsor Castle
RCIN   Royal Collection Inventory Number
RIBA   Royal Institute of British Architects
TNA   The National Archives, Kew
V&A   Victoria and Albert Museum, London
WAM   Westminster Abbey Muniments

PRIMARY SOURCES

All Souls College, Oxford
AS, I:2, 30, 32; Wren III:3
Plan by William Dickinson of the first floor of St James's Palace, *c*.1703–14; by Nicholas Hawksmoor for a proposed architectural scheme at St James's Palace, 1702; by William Dickinson for a first-floor extension to the state rooms at St James's Palace, 1703; and by William Dickinson for Kitchen Court

Bedfordshire Archives and Records Service
L30/9a
Wrest Park, Lucas Collection, transcripts and extracts of correspondence sent from Jemima Yorke, 9 volumes, 1737–75

Bodleian Library, Oxford
Bodl., Gough Maps London 5
Map of Westminster, London, *c*.1650

Bodl., MS Bodl. 891
An inventory of household goods and pictures of James, Duke of York, 1 June 1674

Bodl., MS Clarendon 6
Clarendon State Papers, 16th–19th century

Bodl., MS Eng. Hist. b. 192/1
Accounts relating to the King's works in the time of Henry VIII, 16th century

Bodl., MS Eng. Hist. e. 28
Tracts and papers, in various hands, 17th century

Bodl., MS Gough misc. antiq. 17
William Dickinson, Sketch plan of the parts of St James's under consideration for remodelling in 1703

Bodl., MS Rawl. C. 987
Household papers of Mary of Modena

Bodl., MS Vet. E.1b.6
Accounts relating to the King's works, 16th century

British Library, London
BL, Add. MS 6113, fols 133, 142v
Notes of the creation of William, Lord Howarde, Baron Howarde of Effingham, March 1554; and William Clarenceaux, King of Arms, Nov. 1557

BL, Add. MS 12498
'James I of England: Notes and accompts of the charges for works, etc., at the various royal houses and residences', 1605–14

BL, Add. MS 15897
Establishment of the household of Catherine, the Queen Dowager, for one year, ending Mich. 1678

BL, Add. MS 17916
'A booke conteining severall of his Maties goods … by the order of a Committe of Lords, in April 1660'

BL, Add. MS 22063
Rent roll for the property of Henry Jermyn, Earl of St Albans, in the bailiwick of St James, 18 Dec. 1676

BL, Add. MS 32095, fol. 241
Warrant of James II to Henry Frederic Thynne, Keeper of the Royal Library at St James's, to allow the Royal Chaplains (Benedictine monks) at St James's the use of books out of the library there, Windsor, 14 Aug. 1687

BL, Add. MS 36367
Bromley, Kent: Drawings of church, etc., 1815–35

BL, Add. MS 36370
London Views and Drawings, 19th century

BL, Add. MS 38104
A plan of the Manor of Ebury, *c*.1663–70

BL, Add. MS 40570
London, National Gallery: Papers relating to proposed demolition of St James's Palace, 1845

BL, Add. MS 43794
Fragment of a ledger-book containing particulars, with the cost, of carpenters' and joiners' work carried out at St James's Palace, 1816–21

BL, Egerton MS 1818, fols 78r–v
'Relation of the Prince [Charles II], his birth and baptism at St James's, 29 May and 27 June 1630'

BL, Egerton MS 2553, fol. 34
Orders for the christening of Prince Charles [Charles II], 1630

BL, Harley MS 252
Various state tracts and papers, early 17th century

BL, Harley MS 642
'Basilica Oeconomica: or several Ordinances Rules & Orders for the government of the Household of the Kings & Queenes', 1610–50

BL, Harley MS 791, fol. 40
Relation of the christening of Charles II, 27 June 1630

BL, Harley MS 1890
'An inventory of pictures, sculpture and furniture belonging to James II at Whitehall Palace, Windsor Castle, Hampton Court, Newmarket and Ludlow, and the plate belonging to the Jewel House'; fair copy compiled *c*.1688

BL, Harley MS 6988
A volume of letters of the royal family in the reign of Charles I, 1625–48

BL, Kings MS 136
'Recueil de Lettres, de Memoires, d'Actes d'instructions et de Contracts, faits pour parvenir all Traité de Mariage d'entre Madame Honriette Marie soeur du Roy, et Charles Premier Roy de la Grande Bretagne', 1624–5

BL, Lansdowne Roll 14
Inventory of Whitehall Palace, 1542

BL, Maps, Crace Port., 11.61
A plan and description of Tart Hall House with the gardens; a 19th-century copy of an original dated 1633

BL, Maps, Crace Port., 13.28
J.G. Crace, Plan of St James's Palace and the convent adjoining, 1689

BL, Maps, Crace Port., 13.29
Christopher Wren, Plan of St James's Palace with the intended addition in the reign of William III, 1694

BL, Maps, Roll 17.a.3
Richard Newcourt and William Faithorne, 'An Exact Delineation of the Cities of London and Westminster and the Suburbs Thereof', 1658

BL, Royal MS 14 B IV A
'Accompts of payments to builders, gardeners, &c., for works at various palaces of Henry VIII', *c*.1532–3

BL, Stowe 567
'Royal Household, Wardrobe accompts, inventories, etc.', 1732

Eton College Archives, Windsor
ECR 60 03 01
Lease Book Register, 1445–1531

ECR 16 J 002
Hospital of St James, London: Account of repairs, 1454–6

ECR 61 RR A 66
Bursary accounts: Receivers' rent roll, 1451

Glasgow University Library, Glasgow
GUL, MS Hunter 238
'An inventory of pictures, sculpture and furniture belonging to James II at Whitehall Palace, Windsor Castle, Hampton Court, Newmarket and Ludlow, and the plate belonging to the Jewel House'; fair copy compiled c.1687

Hatfield House, Hertfordshire
CP 134/163
Letter from Henry, Prince of Wales, to Robert Cecil, 1611

Historic England Archive, Swindon
DoE 73045 AB1/2
H. Yexley, 'St James's Palace Queen Anne's Room Proposed Removal of Fireplace', 24 Oct. 1973

MA/JPL0002
HM Office of Works, St James's Palace Excavations, August 1929

MA/JPL0003
HM Office of Works, St James's Palace Excavations, August 1929

STJ 7/1
'St James's Palace Friary Court. Record of bricked-up window', March 1992

STJ 8/1
S. Sorley, St James's Palace drawing, Crown Buildings and Monuments Advisory Group, English Heritage, June 1992

London Metropolitan Archives
SC/PHL/01/522/5011
Photograph of the Armoury, St James's Palace, 1907

SC/PHL/01/522/70/10417
Photograph of St James's Palace, from St James's Street, 1896

SC/PHL/01/522/78/4557
Photograph of St James's Palace opposite the German chapel, 1896

SC/PHL/01/522/5026
Photograph of the chimneypiece in the Banqueting Room, 26 July 1907

SC/GL/PR/W2/JAM/PAL/p5407479
Watercolour of the Queen's Chapel from the south, c.1800

SC/PZ/WE/01/3048
St James's Palace and the Queen's Chapel from the park, c.1630

National Library of Wales
Wynnstay MS 173
Book of warrants, 1640–43

Wynnstay MSS 174–186
Account rolls of Sir Richard Wynn, treasurer and receiver general of the revenues of Queen Henrietta Maria, 1628–41

Northamptonshire County Record Office, Northampton
NRO, F(M)G/722-4
Plans of the ground, 'chamber' and garret floors of Lord Godolphin's house in Stable Yard, St James's Palace, May 1766

NRO, F(M)G/728-30
Rough plans of wash house, kitchen, porter's lodge and outbuildings at Stable Yard, St James's Palace

Royal Archives, Windsor Castle
RA EVIIIPWH/TREAS/EVIIIPWACC/JNL
The Prince of Wales's ledgers, 1911–36

RA EVIIIPWH/PS/0737
Correspondence of the Private Secretary of Edward, Prince of Wales, relating to York House, 1911–36

RA GEO/ADD/4/204/12
Letter from General Jacob de Budé to Prince William, 22 September 1780

RA GEO/ADD/15/449
Letter from George, Prince of Wales, to the Hon. Mrs Fielding, 21 Jan. 1809

RA GEO/ADD /15/0754–0843
Personal papers of General Jacob de Budé, 1770–1818

RA GEO/ADD/15/2187
The Howick Papers: letters from William IV, Sir Herbert Taylor, etc., to Lord Grey, 1806–37

RA GEO/ADD/43/3
Queen Charlotte's diary for the year 1794

RA GEO/MAIN/16795-17297
Privy Purse papers, George III, 1760–93

RA GEO/MAIN/25234
Privy Purse accounts, George IV, 1783–1830

RA GEO/MAIN/52697-53074A
Miscellaneous papers of and concerning George I and George II, 1716–69

RA GEO/MAIN/52795-52803
Report on a conference on the succession to Great Britain and the German Dominions, c.1737

RA GEO/MAIN/79070-82519
Great Wardrobe Accounts, bills, 1672–84, 1688–1748

RA LC/CHAPELR
New Cheque Book, 1721–1867

RA LC/LCO/AR
Lord Chamberlain's Annual Reports

RA PPTO/PP/QV/ADD
Privy Purse correspondence, c.1838–1900

RA PPTO/PP/QV/ADDX/A
Privy Purse correspondence, miscellaneous, 1843–1900

RA QM/PRIV/CC47
Queen Mary's letters, 1883–1953

RA VIC/ADDQ/00/0207–0956
Privy Purse correspondence with the Office of Works, concerning various property matters, 1855–76

RA VIC/MAIN/L/5
Royal household correspondence, residences, 1862–1900

RA VIC/MAIN/L/14
Royal household correspondence, political matters, 1876–82

RA VIC/MAIN/QVJ
Queen Victoria's Journal

RA VIC/MAIN/Z/476
Royal household correspondence, residences, 1862–1900

Royal Collection
RCIN 1028932
'Catalogue of the Royal Library of Her Late Majesty Queen Caroline Distributed into Faculties', completed in 1741

RCIN 1048431
'Catalogue of pictures in state rooms, St James's Palace, February 1894'

RCIN 1112546
'Catalogue of the pictures in His Majesty's Palace at Windsor', 1776

RCIN 1112550
'A list of pictures at Windsor Castle, 1710'

RCIN 1112572
'Catalogue of the pictures at the late Queen's house, Saint James's Park. With: Catalogue of the pictures at Saint James's Palace', 1819

RCIN 1112573
'Royal pictures at Kensington, Hampton Court, Windsor & St. James's', c.1720

RCIN 1112574
'A List of Her Majesties pictures in Kensington, Hampton Court and Windsor Castle', 1705–10

Royal Institute of British Architects, Drawings & Archives Collections, London
FRA/TITE/1
William Tite, Composition of the works of Inigo Jones, 1854, <www.architecture.com/image-library/ribapix/image-information/poster/composition-of-the-works-of-inigo-jones/posterid/RIBA13252.html> (accessed 11 July 2019)

SB98/4
J. Wyatville, St James's Palace, unexecuted design for additions, 1834

SC198/Jol&WeJ[29]
H. Flitcroft, Long section of the Queen's chapel, St James's Palace, c.1720

SC198/Jol&WeJ[30]
I. Jones, Design for a gateway for St James's, 1627

SC200/Jol&WeJ[61]2
I. Jones, Design for Prince Charles's lodgings at Newmarket, 1619

Smythson SC229/I/14
Robert Smythson, Prince Henry's Riding School, St James's Palace, London: survey elevation and plan, with a detail of a window shutter and a section of the roof, c.1609

Smythson SC237/III/8(1)
John Smythson, St James's Palace, London: survey drawing showing a two-storeyed building, the lower storey forming an arcade or gateway, c.1619

V&A, SC97/17
A. Salvin, Sketch elevation of chimneypiece in St James's Palace

Sir John Soane's Museum, London
SM 37/2/3
J. Soane, Plan proposal for a 'Sergeant and Guard Room at St James's', Dec. 1792

SM 62/2/1-3
St James's Palace, Plans and sections of the Ball Room, 1792

SM 62/2/6
J. Soane, Ground plan of St James's Palace, 1792

SM 147/193-198
W. Kent, St James's Palace, Preliminary designs for Queen Caroline's Library, drafted by S. Wright, 1736-7

The National Archives, Kew

ADM (Admiralty)
TNA, ADM 67/17
Royal Greenwich Hospital, General Court, various minutes, 1822-9

AO (Audit Office)
TNA, AO 1/2425/57
Account of H. Wickes, 1 Oct. 1626-30 Sept. 1627

TNA, AO 1/2426/60
Account of H. Wickes, 1 Oct. 1629-30 Sept. 1630

TNA, AO 1/2427/63
Account of H. Wickes, 1 Oct. 1633-30 Sept. 1634

TNA, AO 1/2427/65-67
Account of H. Wickes, 1 Oct. 1635-30 Sept. 1636

TNA, AO 1/2428/69
Account of H. Wickes, 1 Oct. 1637-30 Sept. 1638

TNA, AO 1/2429/72
Account of E. Carter, 1 June 1644-31 Mar. 1645

TNA, AO 1/2429/73
Account of E. Carter, 1 Apr. 1645-31 Mar. 1646

TNA, AO 1/2430/76
Account of E. Carter, 1 Apr. 1646-31 Mar. 1647

TNA, AO 1/2431/79
Account of E. Carter, 1 Apr. 1647-31 Mar. 1648

TNA, AO 1/2432/82
Account of E. Carter, 1 Apr. 1648-31 Mar. 1649

TNA, AO 1/2481/292
A. May, Accounts for plantations at Hampton Court, Greenwich, and St James's Parks, and of the New River, 1663-71

C (Chancery)
TNA, C 66/304
Patent Rolls, 22 June 1378-21 June 1379

TNA, C 66/322
Patent Rolls, 22 June 1386-21 June 1387

TNA, C 66/3005
Patent Rolls, 30 Jan. 1662-29 Jan. 1663

TNA, C 66/3329
Patent Rolls, William and Mary, 13 Feb. 1689-12 Feb. 1690

CM (Construction and Maintenance)
TNA, CM 8/95
St James's Palace, refurbishment of York House, 15 Aug. 1984-10 Apr. 1987

E (Exchequer)
TNA, E 101/674/31
Certificate by Christopher Wren as to value of paintings by John [Jacob] Huysmans in the Queen's Chapel of St James's, 1683

TNA, E 101/675/17
Warrant for payment of joiner's work on the Queen's new buildings at the Friary, St James's, 1682

TNA, E 317/Middx/27
St Martin in the Fields, St Margaret, Westminster: survey of lands near Goring House, Mar. 1651

TNA, E 317/Middx/39
St James in the Fields: survey of lands and tenements, July 1650

TNA, E 317/Middx/41
St Martin in the Fields: survey of a messuage and parcel of ground called 'the Mulberry Garden' near St James, July 1651

TNA, E 317/Middx/42
St Martin in the Fields: survey of Tennis Court House, St James's, July 1650

TNA, E 317/Middx/71
St Martin in the Fields: survey of Pall Mall Field, June 1650

TNA, E 317/Middx/72
St Martin in the Fields: additional survey, July 1650

TNA, E 351/3205
Works and Buildings, Declared Accounts, L. Stocket, 29 Sept. 1570-29 Sept. 1571

TNA, E 351/3210
Works and Buildings, Declared Accounts, L. Stocket, 29 Sept. 1574-29 Sept. 1575

TNA, E 351/3214
Works and Buildings, Declared Accounts, T. Fowler, 31 Mar. 1579-31 Mar. 1580

TNA, E 351/3215
Works and Buildings, Declared Accounts, T. Fowler, 31 Mar. 1580-31 Mar. 1581

TNA, E 351/3216
Works and Buildings, Declared Accounts, T. Fowler, 31 Mar. 1581-31 Mar. 1582

TNA, E 351/3218
Works and Buildings, Declared Accounts, T. Fowler, 31 Mar. 1583-31 Mar. 1584

TNA, E 351/3223
Works and Buildings, Declared Accounts, T. Fowler, 31 Mar. 1588-31 Mar. 1589

TNA, E 351/3225
Works and Buildings, Declared Accounts, T. Fowler, 31 Mar. 1590-31 Mar. 1591

TNA, E 351/3227-3229
Works and Buildings, Declared Accounts, T. Fowler, 31 Mar. 1592-31 May 1595

TNA, E 351/3230
Works and Buildings, Declared Accounts, H. Fadys, 1 June 1595-31 Mar. 1596

TNA, E 351/3232
Works and Buildings, Declared Accounts, H. Fadys, 1 Apr.-30 Sept. 1597

TNA, E 351/3234
Works and Buildings, Declared Accounts, W. Spicer, 1 Oct. 1598-30 Sept. 1599

TNA, E 351/3238-3239
Works and Buildings, Declared Accounts, A. Kerwyn, 1 Oct.-30 Sept. 1604

TNA, E 351/3241-3246
Works and Buildings, Declared Accounts, A. Kerwyn, 1 Oct. 1605-30 Sept. 1612

TNA, E 351/3250
Works and Buildings, Declared Accounts, A. Kerwyn, 1 Oct. 1615-30 Sept. 1616

TNA, E 351/3251-3252
Works and Buildings, Declared Accounts, H. Wickes, 1 Oct. 1616-30 Sept. 1618

TNA, E 351/3255-3257
Works and Buildings, Declared Accounts, H. Wickes, 1 Oct. 1616-30 Sept. 1624

TNA, E 351/3260
Works and Buildings, Declared Accounts, H. Wickes, 1 Oct. 1626-30 Sept. 1627

TNA, E 351/3263
Works and Buildings, Declared Accounts, H. Wickes, 1 Oct. 1629-30 Sept. 1630

TNA, E 351/3265-3266
Works and Buildings, Declared Accounts,
H. Wickes, 1 Oct. 1631–30 Sept. 1633

TNA, E 351/3269
Works and Buildings, Declared Accounts,
H. Wickes, 1 Oct. 1635–30 Sept. 1636

TNA, E 351/3271
Works and Buildings, Declared Accounts,
H. Wickes, 1 Oct. 1637–30 Sept. 1638

TNA, E 404/153
Warrants for Issues, 27 Mar. 1630–26 Mar. 1632

LC (Lord Chamberlain's Department)
TNA, LC 1/3
General In-letters, 1804–9

TNA, LC 1/4
Correspondence, 1809–12

TNA, LC 1/6
Correspondence, 1713–16

TNA, LC 1/139
Letters received, palaces, 1864

TNA, LC 1/140
Letters sent, palaces, 1864

TNA, LC 3/31
Establishments, 1626–97

TNA, LC 3/63
Appointment books, 1714–24

TNA, LC 5/2
Extracts from the notebooks of Sir John Cottrell, senior and junior, Masters of Ceremonies, 1660–1710

TNA, LC 5/5
Notes and memoranda of Sir Stephen Cottrell, Master of the Ceremonies, 1782–1812

TNA, LC 5/39-40
Great Wardrobe, copies of warrants, 1660–67

TNA, LC 5/43-45
Great Wardrobe, copies of warrants, 1692–1717

TNA, LC 5/51
Great Wardrobe, copies of warrants, 1625–35

TNA, LC 5/73
Great Wardrobe, warrants, 1727–40

TNA, LC 5/132
Warrant book, general, 1628–34

TNA, LC 5/134
Warrant book, general, 1 Apr. 1634–30 Apr. 1641

TNA, LC 5/135
Warrant book, general, 1 July 1641–31 Jan. 1644

TNA, LC 5/136A
Warrant book, general, July 1641–Jan. 1643

TNA, LC 5/137
Warrant book, general, 1660–63

TNA, LC 5/143
Warrant book, general, 1677–80

TNA, LC 5/156
Warrant books, 1714–17

TNA, LC 5/197
Orders to tradesmen, 1783–8

TNA, LC 5/201
Precedent book, 1660–89

TNA, LC 9/167
Great Wardrobe, accounts, 1736–7

TNA, LC 9/282-283
Tradesmen's bills, 1703–9

TNA, LC 9/288-289
Tradesmen's bills, 1729–40

TNA, LC 9/290
Tradesmen's bills, 1740–49

TNA, LC 9/292
Tradesmen's bills, 1756–61

TNA, LC 9/293
Tradesmen's bills, 1761–6

TNA, LC 9/306
Tradesmen's bills, 10 Oct. 1771–10 Oct. 1772

TNA, LC 9/307
Tradesmen's bills, 10 Oct. 1761–10 Oct. 1762

TNA, LC 9/308
Tradesmen's bills, 10 Oct. 1762–5 Apr. 1763

TNA, LC 9/311
Tradesmen's bills, 10 Oct. 1764–10 Oct. 1765

TNA, LC 9/318
Great Wardrobe, tradesmen's bills, 10 Oct. 1770–10 Oct. 1771

TNA, LC 9/319
Great Wardrobe, accounts, 10 Oct. 1771–10 Oct. 1772

TNA, LC 9/328
Tradesmen's bills, 10 Oct. 1780–10 Oct. 1781

TNA, LC 10/16
Bill books: State Apartments, St James's; New Royal Mews, Pimlico; Scottish heralds and pursuivants, 1824–9

TNA, LC 11/1
Tradesmen's bills, 1 Oct. 1783–5 Oct. 1786

TNA, LC 11/3
Tradesmen's bills, 5 Jan. 1791–5 Jan. 1794

TNA, LC 11/4
Tradesmen's bills, 5 Jan. 1794–10 Oct. 1796

TNA, LC 11/7
Tradesmen's bills, 10 Oct. 1797–5 Jan. 1801

TNA, LC 11/8
Tradesmen's bills, 1 Oct. 1802–1 Jan. 1805

TNA, LC 11/9
Tradesmen's bills, 1 Oct. 1805–5 Jan. 1806

TNA, LC 11/11
Tradesmen's bills, 1 Apr. 1809–5 Jan. 1811

TNA, LC 11/41
Tradesmen's bills, 1 July–31 Oct. 1823

LR (Land Revenue)
TNA, LR 1/56
Enrolment books, 24 Mar. 1603–27 Mar. 1625

TNA, LR 5/76
Warrants for payments to craftsmen for work at St James's Palace, 1672–85

LS (Lord Steward's Department)
TNA, LS 13/115
Board of Green Cloth, minutes, 1 Jan. 1714/15–30 June 1725

TNA, LS 13/170
Entry book of records, Nov. 1660–Dec. 1665

M (Maps and Plans)
TNA, MPE 1/482
Map showing the King's Road from Buckingham House to Fulham Gate, c.1715

TNA, MPE 1/485
Plan of Marlborough House and gardens, 1709

OBS (Obsolete lists and miscellanea)
TNA, OBS 1/1419
Itinerary of Henry VIII

CRO (Public Record Office)
TNA, PRO 31/3/72
Transcripts from French Archives relating to the affairs of Great Britain and Ireland, 1640–41

RG (General Register Office)
TNA, RG 9/30
1861 Census of England and Wales

TNA, RG 13/1224
1901 Census of England and Wales

SC (Special Collections)
TNA, SC 6/chasI/1705
Account of the treasurer of Queen Henrietta Maria, 27 Mar. 1641–31 Dec. 1649

SP (State Papers)
TNA, SP 1/103
State Papers, Henry VIII, 23 Mar.–19 May 1536

TNA, SP 1/129
State Papers, Henry VIII, 5 Feb.–9 Mar. 1538

TNA, SP 14/63
State Papers, James I, 1 Apr.–31 May 1611

TNA, SP 14/139
State Papers, Domestic, 1–18 Mar. 1623

TNA, SP 14/140
State Papers, Domestic, 19–31 Mar. 1632

TNA, SP 14/144
State Papers, Domestic, 1–14 May 1623

TNA, SP 16/168
State Papers, Domestic, 1–16 June 1630

TNA, SP 29/55
State Papers, Domestic, 28–31 May 1662

TNA, SP 29/75
State Papers, Domestic, letters and papers, June 1663

TNA, SP 40/1
State Papers, Domestic, precedent book, c.1554–1620

TNA, SP 44/13
State Papers, Petitions: Nicholas and Bennet, 1661–3

T (Treasury)
TNA, T 1/91
Calendar of Treasury Books, 16 June–19 Oct. 1704

TNA, T 1/100
Calendar of Treasury Papers, 1 Nov.–31 Dec. 1706

TNA, T 1/2273
Treasury Board Papers and In-letters, bundle 6992, 1824

TNA, T 27/11
Treasury, General Out-letter Books, 1687–9

WORK (Office of Works, later Ministry of Works)
TNA, WORK 1/10
General Letter Books, In- and Out-letters, 1 Jan. 1820–31 Aug. 1821

TNA, WORK 1/12
General Letter Books, In- and Out-letters, 1 May 1823–31 July 1824

TNA, WORK 1/20
General Letter Books, Out-letters, 1 Mar. 1832–31 Jan. 1834

TNA, WORK 1/22
General Letter Books, Out-letters, 1 Mar. 1836–31 Dec. 1837

TNA, WORK 1/23
General Letter Books, Out-letters, 1 Jan. 1838–30 Nov. 1839

TNA, WORK 1/50–51
General Letter Books, Out-letters, 1 May–31 Aug. 1856

TNA, WORK 1/52
General Letter Books, Out-letters, 1 Aug.–31 Dec. 1856

TNA, WORK 1/56
General Letter Books, Out-letters, 1 Sept.–31 Dec. 1857

TNA, WORK 1/57
General Letter Books, Out-letters, 1 Dec. 1857–31 Mar. 1858

TNA, WORK 1/60
General Letter Books, Out-letters, 1 Sept.–31 Dec. 1858

TNA, WORK 1/74
General Letter Books, Out-letters, 1 May–30 Sept. 1863

TNA, WORK 1/75
General Letter Books, Out-letters, 1 Sept. 1863–28 Feb. 1864

TNA, WORK 1/76
General Letter Books, Out-letters, 1 Feb.–30 June 1864

TNA, WORK 1/78
General Letter Books, Out-letters, 1 Nov. 1864–31 Mar. 1865

TNA, WORK 1/79
General Letter Books, Out-letters, 1 Mar.–31 Aug. 1865

TNA, WORK 1/80
General Letter Books, Out-letters, 1 Aug. 1865–31 Jan. 1866

TNA, WORK 1/81
General Letter Books, Out-letters, 1 Jan.–30 June 1866

TNA, WORK 1/82
General Letter Books, Out-letters, 1 June–30 Nov. 1866

TNA, WORK 1/85
General Letter Books, Out-letters, 1 Aug. 1867–28 Feb. 1868

TNA, WORK 2/2
Treasury Letter Books, In- and Out-letters, 1 Oct. 1835–31 Dec. 1840

TNA, WORK 4/1
Minutes, 1 May 1715–28 Feb. 1720

TNA, WORK 4/2
Minutes, 1 Feb. 1720–31 Aug. 1724

TNA, WORK 4/3
Accounts, 1689–90

TNA, WORK 4/6
Minutes, 1 Aug. 1733–30 Apr. 1736

TNA, WORK 4/7
Minutes, 1 Apr. 1736–31 Aug. 1739

TNA, WORK 4/9
Minutes, 1 Jan. 1744–31 May 1748

TNA, WORK 4/10
Minutes, 1 May 1748–30 Sept. 1752

TNA, WORK 4/12
Minutes, 1 Apr. 1757–30 Sept. 1761

TNA, WORK 4/13
Minutes, 1 Oct. 1761–31 Oct. 1766

TNA, WORK 4/14
Minutes, 1 Jan. 1767–31 Oct. 1772

TNA, WORK 4/15
Minutes, 1 Oct. 1772–30 Apr. 1778

TNA, WORK 4/16
Minutes, 1 May 1778–30 June 1785

TNA, WORK 4/17
Minutes, 1 July 1785–31 Dec. 1792

TNA, WORK 4/18
Minutes, 1793–9

TNA, WORK 4/19
Minutes, 1800–1806

TNA, WORK 4/20
Minutes, 1 Jan. 1807–30 Sept. 1812

TNA, WORK 4/21
Minutes, 1 Sept. 1812–31 May 1816

TNA, WORK 4/22
Minutes, 1 June 1816–31 Oct. 1817

TNA, WORK 4/23
Minutes, 1 Oct. 1817–31 Aug. 1819

TNA, WORK 4/24
Minutes, 1 Aug. 1819–31 May 1821

TNA, WORK 4/25
Minutes, 1 May 1821–28 Feb. 1823

TNA, WORK 4/26
Minutes, 1 Mar. 1823–31 Aug. 1824

TNA, WORK 4/27
Minutes, 1 Aug. 1824–30 June 1826

TNA, WORK 4/28
Minutes, 1 July 1826–31 Mar. 1828

TNA, WORK 4/29
Minutes, 1 Mar. 1828–30 Sept. 1829

TNA, WORK 4/30
Minutes, 1 Oct. 1829–30 Apr. 1831

TNA, WORK 5/1–11
Accounts, 1660–69

TNA, WORK 5/13
Accounts, 1669–70

TNA, WORK 5/15
Accounts, 1670–71

TNA, WORK 5/17
Accounts, 1671–2

TNA, WORK 5/19
Accounts, 1672–3

TNA, WORK 5/21
Accounts, 1673–4

TNA, WORK 5/23
Accounts, 1674–5

TNA, WORK 5/25–30
Accounts, 1675–9

TNA, WORK 5/32
Accounts, 1679–80

TNA, WORK 5/37–40
Accounts, 1683–7

TNA, WORK 5/42–48
Accounts, 1688–96

TNA, WORK 5/50
Accounts, 1699–1700

TNA, WORK 5/52–53
Accounts, 1701–3

TNA, WORK 5/59
Accounts, 1734–9

TNA, WORK 5/83
Accounts of works, 1798

TNA, WORK 5/105
Accounts, debt book, 1733–68

TNA, WORK 5/106
Debt Book, 1769–1806

TNA, WORK 5/108
Accounts, 1820–24

TNA, WORK 5/141
Accounts, 1706–52

TNA, WORK 5/145
Contracts, 1668–1724

TNA, WORK 6/2
Warrants and correspondence, 1685–1702

TNA, WORK 6/6
Warrants and correspondence, 1714–17

TNA, WORK 6/7
Correspondence, 1717–23

TNA, WORK 6/14
Memorials, 1702–9

TNA, WORK 6/16–19
Memorials, 1733–81

TNA, WORK 6/20
Memorials, 1781–4

TNA, WORK 6/22
Memorials, 1790–96

TNA, WORK 6/24–26
Memorials, 1805–15

TNA, WORK 6/274
Furniture correspondence: St James's Palace, Hampton Court, Kensington, Kew Gardens, Houses of Parliament, Dept of Science and Art, 1 Apr. 1863–31 Mar. 1864

TNA, WORK 16/298
Marlborough Gate entrance, St James's Park, 1856–1907

TNA, WORK 17/13/9
Accommodation for pictures at Marlborough House, 1856–9

TNA, WORK 17/24/4
Removal of pictures from Marlborough House. Erection of temporary building at South Kensington for National Gallery pictures, removed from Marlborough House, 1856–9

TNA, WORK 17/26/11
Art and Science Buildings, general, 1848–54

TNA, WORK 19/18/1
Marlborough House, miscellaneous works of repair and maintenance, 1753–1902

TNA, WORK 19/19–20
St James's Palace, miscellaneous records, 1783–1902

TNA, WORK 19/117
Marlborough House, walls and ceilings: paintings, 1837–1910

TNA, WORK 19/127
St James's Palace, Turret Clock, 1832–1903

TNA, WORK 19/132
State Apartments, works, 1896–1913

TNA, WORK 19/242
'Out of Battle' exhibition, St James's Palace, 1945

TNA, WORK 19/243
Discovery of human remains at St James's Palace, 1902

TNA, WORK 19/247
Discovery of human remains at St James's Palace, 1925–7

TNA, WORK 19/248
Indian, Burma, League of Nations and Imperial Conferences, 1930–37

TNA, WORK 19/716
St James's Palace, State Apartments: alteration to the Entrée Entrance, 1929–31

TNA, WORK 19/945
Marlborough House, Queen's Chapel: works, 1922–38

TNA, WORK 19/954
Grace and Favour Apartment Number 13, York House, St James's Palace, 1919–39

TNA, WORK 19/956
St James's Palace, State Apartments (including Lord Chamberlain's office accommodation): works, 1919–39

TNA, WORK 19/960
St James's Palace, Chapel Royal, works, 1921–39

TNA, WORK 19/1047
Installation of a new organ in the Chapel Royal, 1924–5

TNA, WORK 19/1068
Marlborough House, Queen's Chapel: works, 1939–53

TNA, WORK 19/1073
St James's Palace, Chapel Royal, works, 1942–51

TNA, WORK 19/1074
Clarence House: works and occupation by British Red Cross, etc., 1942–53

TNA, WORK 19/1105
St James's Palace, State Apartments: works, 1940–66

TNA, WORK 19/1175
Clarence House, occupation by Princess Elizabeth, 1947–53

TNA, WORK 19/1237
Clarence House, works, 1952–5

TNA, WORK 19/1238
St James's Palace, Chapel Royal, works, 1955–71

TNA, WORK 19/1297
Marlborough House, The Queen's Chapel, works, 1956–67

TNA, WORK 19/1298
St James's Palace, Air-raid shelter accommodation, 1938–44

TNA, WORK 19/1299
St James's Palace, Air-raid damage, 1944–7

TNA, WORK 21/12/1
Marriage of HM Queen Victoria 1840, general arrangements, 1839–41

TNA, WORK 21/12/2
Marriage of HRH The Princess Royal with HRH Prince Frederick William of Prussia at St James's Palace, general arrangements, 1857–8

TNA, WORK 34/121
H. Flitcroft, St James's Palace, ground-floor plan before east floor was destroyed by fire, 1729

TNA, WORK 34/122
H. Flitcroft, St James's Palace, first-floor plan, 1729

TNA, WORK 34/126
St James's Palace, block plan showing buildings occupied by the royal family

TNA, WORK 34/127
St James's Palace, block plan showing allocation of apartments, 1816

TNA, WORK 34/129
St James's Palace, block plan showing allocation of apartments, 1841

TNA, WORK 34/130
St James's Palace, principal floor plan, showing allocation of apartments, 1841

TNA, WORK 34/133
St James's Palace, plan of ground floor, showing Chapel Royal, Great Court and allocation of rooms, after 1768

TNA, WORK 34/134
St James's Palace, block plan showing portions occupied by His Majesty, HRH The Princess Augusta, HRH The Duke of Kent, and Lord Harrington, 1830

TNA, WORK 34/136
St James's Palace, Green Cloth Court, elevation of east side, 1823

TNA, WORK 34/142
St James's Palace, sections of proposed new staircase adjoining Banquet Room, early 19th century

TNA, WORK 34/144
R. Smirke, plan of proposed new entrance from Stable Yard, St James's Palace, 1838

TNA, WORK 34/825
J. Pennethorne, plan and specification of proposed new road from Pall Mall to St James's Park, between Marlborough House and St James's Palace, 1856

TNA, WORK 34/848
J. Pennethorne, elevation of the south front of the stables, Marlborough House, 1862

TNA, WORK 34/861–870
St James's Palace, Ambassadors Court, residences, various plans and elevations for works, 1889–90

TNA, WORK 34/871
Plan of proposed new store room over the corridors, Colour Court, St James's Palace, 1866

TNA, WORK 34/872
St James's Palace, Colour Court, sections of proposed new store room over the corridors, 1866

TNA, WORK 34/873
St James's Palace, Colour Court, elevation of proposed new store room over the corridors, 1866

TNA, WORK 34/874
St James's Palace, Colour Court, plan and section of iron column for new store room, 1866

TNA, WORK 34/878
Plan and section of gallery for spectators and floral decorations, Flag Court, St James's Palace, 1857

TNA, WORK 34/880
St James's Palace, Chapel Royal, ground-floor and gallery plans, showing seating, 1857

TNA, WORK 34/888
St James's Palace, block plan showing portion proposed to be used as National Gallery for painting and sculpture, late 19th century

TNA, WORK 34/889
Plan, elevations and detail of wrought-iron balconies, Cleveland Row, St James's Palace, (?) late nineteenth century

TNA, WORK 34/894
Plan and elevation of iron gates from Marlborough Road, St James's Palace, 1823

TNA, WORK 34/1505
St James's Palace, plan of ground floor with list of occupants, 1869

TNA, WORK 34/1513–1519
St James's Palace, Ambassador's Staircase, various schemes of decoration in wood panelling, 1919–20

TNA, WORK 34/1737–1740
St James's Palace, Picture Gallery, various elevations and sketches for oak panelling and proposed fireplace, 1908

TNA, WORK 99/279
St James's Palace, Stable Yard House, conversion to offices, 1 Jan. 1975–31 Dec. 1983

Victoria and Albert Museum, London
E. 552-1975
Designs for furniture and room settings by Messrs Waller & Sons, c.1895

Westminster Abbey Muniments
WAM 17122
Account of Fr John de Sydenham, Master of St James's Hospital near Westminster, 31 Mar. 1351–31 Mar. 1336

West Sussex Record Office
PHA 617
Record book of expenses for the royal children, 1646–9

PUBLISHED SOURCES

B. Adams 1983
B. Adams, *London Illustrated 1604–1851. A Survey and Index of Topographical Books and their Plates*, London

S. Adams 1995
S. Adams (ed.), *Household Accounts and Disbursement Books of Robert Dudley, Earl of Leicester, 1558–1561, 1584–1586*, London

Airy 1897
O. Airy (ed.), *Burnet's History of My Own Time*, 1, Oxford

Alford 2002
S. Alford, *Kingship and Politics in the Reign of Edward VI*, Cambridge

Allmand 1992
C. Allmand, *Henry V*, New Haven and London

Anderson Winn 2014
J. Anderson Winn, *Queen Anne: Patroness of Arts*, Oxford

Anon. 1688
Anon., *The Several Declarations Together with the Several Depositions made in Council Monday the 22, of October, 1688 Concerning the Birth of the Prince of Wales*, London

Anon. 1689
Anon., *A full Answer to the Depositions and to all other the Pretences and Arguments whatsoever Concerning the Birth of the Prince of Wales*, London

Anon. c.1875
Anon., *Catalogue of the Porcelain, Bronzes, Arms, Japanese Lacquer and Other Specimens of Oriental Art, Formed by H.R.H. The Duke of Edinburgh, K.G., During his Cruise in H.M.S. 'Galatea'. Also, the Collection of European China, Marbles, Bronzes, Pictures, Water-colour Drawings, and other Objects of Art and Vertu, at Clarence House, St James's*, London

Anon. 1953
Anon. 'York House, St James's Palace. The London Residence of TRH The Duke and Duchess of Gloucester', *Antique Collector*, **24**, pp. 45–53

Anstruther 1958
G. Anstruther, 'Cardinal Howard and the English court, 1658–94', *Archivum Fratrum Praedicatorum*, **28**, pp. 315–61

Arch and Marschner 1990
N. Arch and J. Marschner, *The Royal Wedding Dresses*, London

Armytage 1927
P. Armytage, *By the Clock of St James's*, London

Art-Union 1844
'"Tissu de Verre", Varieties', *Art-Union*, **6**, 1 July 1844, p. 195

Aschbach Ettinger 1936
A. Aschbach Ettinger, *James Edward Oglethorpe: Imperial Idealist*, Oxford

Ashbee 1986
A. Ashbee, *Records of English Court Music*, 10 vols, Aldershot

Ashbee and Harley 2000
A. Ashbee and J. Harley, *The Cheque Books of the Chapel Royal*, 2 vols, Aldershot

Ashmole 1658
E. Ashmole, *The Antiquities of Berkshire*, London

Avery 1980–82
C. Avery, 'Hubert Le Sueur: the "Unworthy Praxiteles" of King Charles I', *Walpole Society*, **48**, pp. 135–209

Babelon and Mignot 1998
J.-P. Babelon and C. Mignot (eds), *François Mansart: le Génie de L'Architecture*, Paris

Bachrach and Collmer 1982
A.G.H. Bachrach and R.G. Collmer (eds and trans.), *Lodewijck Huygens: The English Journal 1651–1652*, Leiden

Bagni 1986
P. Bagni, *Benedetto Gennari e la Bottega del Guercino*, Bologna

D. Baldwin 1990
D. Baldwin, *The Chapel Royal: Ancient and Modern*, London

H. Baldwin 2002
H. Baldwin, *H.M. Chapel Royal Sanctificetur Hoc Templum. Works to Mark Her Majesty's Golden Jubilee*, 2002

Banks 1740
J. Banks, *Matthew Prior's History of his Own Time*, 2 vols, 2nd edn, London

Barber 2012
P. Barber, *London: A History in Maps*, London

Barclay 2002
A. Barclay, 'Mary Beatrice of Modena: the "Second Bless'd of Woman-Kind"?', in C. Campbell Orr (ed.), *Queenship in Britain 1660–1837: Royal Patronage, Court Culture, and Dynastic Politics*, Manchester, pp. 74–93

Barclay 2007
A. Barclay, 'William's court as king', in Mijers and Onnekink 2007, pp. 241–62

Barclay 2010
A. Barclay, 'The inventories of the English Royal Collection, temp. James II', *Journal of the History of Collections*, **22**, pp. 1–13

Barclay 2015
A. Barclay, 'Recovering Charles I's art collection: some implications of the 1660 Act of Indemnity and Oblivion', *Bulletin of the Institute of Historical Research*, **88**, pp. 629–49

A.S. Barnes 1900
A.S. Barnes, 'Catholic Chapels Royal under the Stuart kings', *Downside Review*, **19**, pp. 246–52

S.J. Barnes et al. 2004
S.J. Barnes, N. De Poorter, O. Millar and H. Vey, *Van Dyck: A Complete Catalogue of the Paintings*, London

Barroll 2000
L. Barroll (ed.), *Shakespeare Studies*, **28**, Vancouver

Beard and Gilbert 1986
G. Beard and C. Gilbert (eds), *Dictionary of English Furniture Makers, 1660–1840*, Leeds <https://bifmo.history.ac.uk/> (accessed 11 July 2019)

Beattie 1967
J.M. Beattie, *The English Court in the Reign of George I*, Cambridge

Beavan 1896
A.H. Beavan, *Marlborough House and its Occupants Present and Past*, London

Beddard 1988
R. Beddard, *A Kingdom Without a King: The Journal of the Provisional Government in the Revolution of 1688*, Oxford

Beier et al. 1989
A.L. Beier, D. Cannadine and J.M. Rosenheim (eds), *The First Modern Society Essays in English History in Honour of Lawrence Stone*, Cambridge

Beltramini 2001
G. Beltramini (ed.), *Andrea Palladio: The Complete Illustrated Works*, New York

Bennet Weldon 1881
D. Bennet Weldon (ed.), *Chronological notes, containing the Rise, Growth and Present State of the English Congregation of the Order of St Benedict*, London

Bertotti Scamozzi 1776–83
O. Bertotti Scamozzi, *Le Fabbriche e i Disegni di Andrea Palladio*, 4 vols, Vicenza

Betts 2002
I.M. Betts, *Medieval 'Westminster' Floor Tiles*, London

Birch 1760
T. Birch, *The Life of Henry, Prince of Wales: Eldest Son of King James I*, London

Birch 1848
T. Birch, *The Court and Times of James the First*, 2 vols, London

Bird 2014
R. Bird, 'The furniture and furnishing of St James's Palace', *Furniture History*, **50**, pp. 147–203

Birmingham Museum and Art Gallery 1990
Foreign Paintings in Birmingham Museum and Art Gallery, London

Black 2004
J. Black, *The Hanoverians: The History of a Dynasty*, London

Black 2005
J. Black, 'Hanover and British foreign policy, 1714–60', *English Historical Review*, **120** (no. 486), pp. 306–11

Bolton 1914
A.T. Bolton, 'Devonshire House, London', *Country Life*, **36**, 22 Aug. 1914, pp. 262–7

Bolton and Hendry 1924–43
A.T. Bolton and H.D. Hendry (eds) *The Wren Society*, I–XX

Boswell 1950
J. Boswell, *Boswell's London Journal, 1762–1763*, New York

Bowett 2012
A. Bowett, *Woods in British Furniture-Making, 1400–1900*, London

Boyer 1703–13
A. Boyer, *A History of the Reign of Queen Anne, Digested into Annals*, 11 vols, London

Bradley 2001
S. Bradley, 'The Queen's Chapel in the twentieth century', *Architectural History*, **44**, pp. 293–302

Bradley and Pevsner 2003
S. Bradley and N. Pevsner, *The Buildings of England. London 6: Westminster*, London

Bray 1806
W. Bray, 'An Account of the Revenue, the Expenses, the Jewels etc. of Prince Henry', *Archaeologia*, **15**, pp. 13–26

Brett-James 1928
N.G. Brett-James, 'The fortification of London in 1642/3', *London Topographical Record*, **14**, pp. 1–35

Brett-James 1935
N.G. Brett-James, *The Growth of Stuart London*, London

Brigden 1990
S. Brigden (ed.), 'The letters of Richard Scudamore to Sir Philip Hoby, September 1549–March 1555', *Camden Miscellany*, **30** (Camden Fourth Series, **39**), pp. 67–148

Brindle 2013
S. Brindle, 'Kent the painter', in Weber 2013, pp. 111–49

Brindle 2018
S. Brindle (ed.), *Windsor Castle: A Thousand Years of a Royal Palace*, London

Brodie et al. 2001
A. Brodie, A. Felstead and J. Franklin (eds), *Directory of British Architects 1834–1914*, 2 vols, London and New York

Browning et al. 1991
A. Browning, M.K. Geiter and W.A. Speck (eds), *The Memoirs of Sir John Reresby*, 2nd edn, London

Bucholz 1993
R.O. Bucholz, *The Augustan Court: Queen Anne and the Decline of Court Culture*, Stanford

Bucholz 2006
R.O. Bucholz (ed.), 'The Bedchamber: Pages of the Backstairs 1760–1837', in *Office-Holders in Modern Britain: Volume 11 (Revised), Court Officers, 1660–1837*, London, *British History Online* <www.british-history.ac.uk/office-holders/vol11> (accessed 11 July 2019)

Burchard 2011
W. Burchard, 'St James's Palace: George II's and Queen Caroline's principal London residence', *The Court Historian*, **16** (no. 2), pp. 177–203

Burchard 2014
W. Burchard, 'Houses, palaces and gardens: the first Georgians and architectures', in D. Shawe-Taylor (ed.), *The First Georgians: Art and Monarchy, 1714–1760*, London, pp. 52–87

Burkhardt 1977
C. Burkhardt, *Herman and Nancy and Ivy: Three Lives in Art*, London

Burnby 1994
J. Burnby, 'Some early London physic gardens', *Pharmaceutical Historian*, **24** (no. 4), pp. 2–8

Burnet 1815
T. Burnet, *Burnet's History of My Own Time*, II, London

Burrows 2005
D. Burrows, *Handel and the English Chapel Royal*, Oxford

Burton 1999
A. Burton, *Vision and Accident: The Story of the Victoria and Albert Museum*, London

Callow 2000
J. Callow, *The Making of James II: The Formative Years of a Fallen King*, Stroud

Campbell 1771
C. Campbell, *Vitruvius Britannicus*, London

Campbell Bury 1838
C. Campbell Bury, *Diary illustrative of the times of George the Fourth, interspersed with original letters from the late Queen Caroline, and from various other distinguished perons*, 2 vols, London

Cannadine 1983
D. Cannadine, 'The context, performance and meaning of ritual: the British monarchy and the "invention of tradition", c.1820–1977', in Hobsbawm and Ranger 1983, pp. 101–64

Cannadine 1989
D. Cannadine, 'The last Hanoverian sovereign? The Victorian monarchy in its historical perspective, 1688–1988', in Beier et al. 1989, pp. 127–67

Carlton House 1991
Carlton House: The Past Glories of George IV's Palace, London, <www.rct.uk/collection/themes/publications/carlton-house> (accessed 11 July 2019)

Carnavalet 1985
Saint-Paul-Saint-Louis. Les Jésuites à Paris, Musée Carnavalet, Paris

Carter 2001
M. Carter, *Anthony Blunt: His Lives*, London

Cartwright 1843
T. Cartwright, *The Diary of Dr Thomas Cartwright, Bishop of Chester*, Camden Society, Old Series, **15**, London

Chew 2004
E.V. Chew, 'A mockery of the surveyor's style? Alternatives to Inigo Jones in seventeenth-century elite architecture', in B. Arciszewska and E. McKellar (eds), *Articulating British Classicism*, Aldershot, pp. 57–95

Christie 2016
I. Christie, '"A very wonderful process": Queen Victoria, photography and film at the fin de siècle', in Merck 2016, pp. 31–6

E. Clarendon 1888
E. Hyde, Earl of Clarendon, *The history of the rebellion and civil wars in England begun in the year 1641*, W.D. Macray (ed.), 6 vols, Oxford

H. Clarendon 1765
H. Hyde, Earl of Clarendon, *The State Letters of Henry, Earl of Clarendon during the Reign of King James the Second*, 2 vols, Oxford

Clark 1974
F. Clark, *William Morris: Wallpapers and Chintzes*, 2nd edn, London and New York

Clifford Smith 1931
H. Clifford Smith, with introductory chapters by C. Hussey, *Buckingham Palace: Its Furniture, Decoration and History*, London and New York

Cloake 1996
J. Cloake, *Palaces and Parks of Richmond and Kew*, 2 vols, Chichester

Colvin 1968
H.M. Colvin, *Royal Buildings*, London

Colvin 2008
H.M. Colvin, *A Biographical Dictionary of British Architects 1600–1840*, 4th edn, New Haven and London

Cooper 1977
N. Cooper, *The Opulent Eye*, London

Cornforth 1996
J. Cornforth, *Queen Elizabeth The Queen Mother at Clarence House*, London

Corp 2000
E. Corp, 'The Jacobite court at Saint-Germain-en-Laye: etiquette and the use of the royal apartments', in Cruickshanks 2000, pp. 240–55

Coryat 1611
T. Coryat, with a preface by H. Peacham, *Crudities*, London

Coxe 1856
A.C. Coxe, *Impressions of England or Sketches of English Scenery and Society*, New York and London

Craigie 1944–50
J. Craigie (ed.), *The Basilicon Doron of King James VI*, 2 vols, Edinburgh

Croft-Murray 1962
E. Croft-Murray, *Decorative Painting in England. I: Early Tudor to Sir James Thornhill*, London

Croft-Murray and Hulton 1960
E. Croft-Murray and P. Hulton, *Catalogue of British Drawings. Vol. 1: Sixteenth and Seventeenth Centuries*, London

Croker 1855
J. (Lord) Hervey, *Memoirs of the reign of George the Second, from his accession to the death of Queen Caroline*, J.W. Croker (ed.), 2 vols, London

Crook 1976
J.M. Crook, 'Sydney Smirke: the architecture of compromise', in J. Fawcett (ed.), *Seven Victorian Architects*, London, pp. 50–65

Cruickshanks 2000
E. Cruickshanks (ed.), *The Stuart Courts*, Stroud

CSP Dom. 1547–80
Calendar of State Papers Domestic: Edward VI, Mary and Elizabeth, 1547–80, London (ed. R. Lemon, published 1856), *British History Online* <www.british-history.ac.uk/cal-state-papers/domestic/edw-eliz/1547-80/p5a> (accessed 11 July 2019)

CSP Dom. 1603–10
Calendar of State Papers Domestic: James I, 1603–10, London (ed. M.A. Everett Green, published 1857), *British History Online* <www.british-history.ac.uk/cal-state-papers/domestic/jas1/1603-10> (accessed 11 July 2019)

CSP Dom. 1611–18
Calendar of State Papers Domestic: James I, 1611–18, London (ed. M.A. Everett Green, published 1858), *British History Online* <www.british-history.ac.uk/cal-state-papers/domestic/jas1/1611-18> (accessed 11 July 2019)

CSP Dom. 1623–5
Calendar of State Papers Domestic: James I, 1623–5, London (ed. M.A. Everett Green, published 1859), *British History Online* <www.british-history.ac.uk/cal-state-papers/domestic/jas1/1623-5> (accessed 11 July 2019)

CSP Dom. 1628–9
Calendar of State Papers Domestic: Charles I, 1628–9, London (ed. J. Bruce, published 1859), *British History Online* <www.british-history.ac.uk/cal-state-papers/domestic/chas1/1628-9> (accessed 11 July 2019)

CSP Dom. 1629–31
Calendar of State Papers Domestic: Charles I, 1629–31, London (ed. J. Bruce, published 1860), *British History Online* <www.british-history.ac.uk/cal-state-papers/domestic/chas1/1629-31> (accessed 11 July 2019)

CSP Dom. 1640
Calendar of State Papers Domestic: Charles I, 1640, London (ed. W.D. Hamilton, published 1880), *British History Online* <www.british-history.ac.uk/cal-state-papers/domestic/chas1/1640> (accessed 11 July 2019)

CSP Dom. 1644
Calendar of State Papers Domestic: Charles I, 1644, London (ed. W.D. Hamilton, published 1888), *British History Online* <www.british-history.ac.uk/cal-state-papers/domestic/chas1/1644> (accessed 11 July 2019)

CSP Dom. 1649–50
Calendar of State Papers Domestic: Interregnum, 1649-50, London (ed. M.A. Everett Green, published 1875), *British History Online* <www.british-history.ac.uk/cal-state-papers/domestic/interregnum/1649-50> (accessed 11 July 2019)

CSP Dom. 1650
Calendar of State Papers Domestic: Interregnum, 1650, London (ed. M.A. Everett Green, published 1876), *British History Online* <www.british-history.ac.uk/cal-state-papers/domestic/interregnum/1650> (accessed 11 July 2019)

CSP Dom. 1651
Calendar of State Papers Domestic: Interregnum, 1651, London (ed. M.A. Everett Green, published 1877), *British History Online* <www.british-history.ac.uk/cal-state-papers/domestic/interregnum/1651> (accessed 11 July 2019)

CSP Dom. 1653–4
Calendar of State Papers Domestic: Interregnum, 1653-4, London (ed. M.A. Everett Green, published 1879), *British History Online* <www.british-history.ac.uk/cal-state-papers/domestic/interregnum/1653-4> (accessed 11 July 2019)

CSP Dom. 1654
Calendar of State Papers Domestic: Interregnum, 1654, London (ed. M.A. Everett Green, published 1880), *British History Online* <www.british-history.ac.uk/cal-state-papers/domestic/interregnum/1654> (accessed 11 July 2019)

CSP Dom. 1655
Calendar of State Papers Domestic: Interregnum, 1655, London (ed. M.A. Everett Green, published 1881), *British History Online* <www.british-history.ac.uk/cal-state-papers/domestic/interregnum/1655> (accessed 11 July 2019)

CSP Dom. 1656–7
Calendar of State Papers Domestic: Interregnum, 1656-7, London (ed. M.A. Everett Green, published 1883), *British History Online* <www.british-history.ac.uk/cal-state-papers/domestic/interregnum/1656-7> (accessed 11 July 2019)

CSP Dom. 1657–8
Calendar of State Papers Domestic: Interregnum, 1657-8, London (ed. M.A. Everett Green, published 1884), *British History Online* <www.british-history.ac.uk/cal-state-papers/domestic/interregnum/1657-8> (accessed 11 July 2019)

CSP Dom. 1658–9
Calendar of State Papers Domestic: Interregnum, 1658-9, London (ed. M.A. Everett Green, published 1885), *British History Online* <www.british-history.ac.uk/cal-state-papers/domestic/interregnum/1658-9> (accessed 11 July 2019)

CSP Dom. 1659–60
Calendar of State Papers Domestic: Interregnum, 1659-60, London (ed. M.A. Everett Green, published 1886), *British History Online* <www.british-history.ac.uk/cal-state-papers/domestic/interregnum/1659-60> (accessed 11 July 2019)

CSP Dom. 1660-61
Calendar of State Papers Domestic: Charles II, 1660-61, London (ed. M.A. Everett Green, published 1860), *British History Online* <www.british-history.ac.uk/cal-state-papers/domestic/chas2/1660-1> (accessed 11 July 2019)

CSP Dom. 1661-2
Calendar of State Papers Domestic: Charles II, 1661-2, London (ed. M.A. Everett Green, published 1861), *British History Online* <www.british-history.ac.uk/cal-state-papers/domestic/chas2/1661-2> (accessed 11 July 2019)

CSP Dom. 1663-4
Calendar of State Papers Domestic: Charles II, 1663-4, London (ed. M.A. Everett Green, published 1862), *British History Online* <www.british-history.ac.uk/cal-state-papers/domestic/chas2/1663-4> (accessed 11 July 2019)

CSP Dom. 1670
Calendar of State Papers Domestic: Charles II, 1670, London (ed. M.A. Everett Green, published 1895), *British History Online* <www.british-history.ac.uk/cal-state-papers/domestic/chas2/addenda/1660-70> (accessed 11 July 2019)

CSP Dom. 1676-7
Calendar of State Papers Domestic: Charles II, 1676-7, London (ed. F.H. Blackburne Daniell, published 1909), *British History Online* <www.british-history.ac.uk/cal-state-papers/domestic/chas2/1676-7> (accessed 11 July 2019)

CSP Dom. 1680-81
Calendar of State Papers Domestic: Charles II, 1680-81, London (ed. F.H. Blackburne Daniell, published 1921), *British History Online* <www.british-history.ac.uk/cal-state-papers/domestic/chas2/1680-1> (accessed 11 July 2019)

CSP Dom. 1684-5
Calendar of State Papers Domestic: Charles II, 1684-5, London (ed. F.H. Blackburne Daniell and F. Bickley, published 1938), *British History Online* <www.british-history.ac.uk/cal-state-papers/domestic/chas2/1684-5> (accessed 11 July 2019)

CSP Dom. 1697
Calendar of State Papers Domestic: William III, 1697, London (ed. W.J. Hardy, published 1927), *British History Online* <www.british-history.ac.uk/cal-state-papers/domestic/will-mary/1697> (accessed 11 July 2019)

CSP Dom. 1698
Calendar of State Papers Domestic: William III, 1698, London (ed. E. Bateson, published 1933), *British History Online* <www.british-history.ac.uk/cal-state-papers/domestic/will-mary/1698> (accessed 11 July 2019)

CSP Dom. 1703-4
Calendar of State Papers Domestic: Anne, 1703-4, London (ed. R.P. Mahaffy, published 1924), *British History Online* <www.british-history.ac.uk/cal-state-papers/domestic/anne/1703-4> (accessed 11 July 2019)

CSP Spain 1547-9
Calendar of State Papers, Spain. Vol. 9: 1547-9, London (ed. M.A.S. Hume and R. Tyler, published 1912), *British History Online* <www.british-history.ac.uk/cal-state-papers/spain/vol9> (accessed 11 July 2019)

CSP Spain 1553
Calendar of State Papers, Spain. Vol. 11: 1553, London (ed. R. Tyler, published 1916), *British History Online* <www.british-history.ac.uk/cal-state-papers/spain/vol11> (accessed 11 July 2019)

CSP Ven. 1610-13
Calendar of State Papers Relating To English Affairs in the Archives of Venice. Vol. 12: 1610-13, London (ed. H.F. Brown, published 1905), *British History Online* <www.british-history.ac.uk/cal-state-papers/venice/vol12> (accessed 11 July 2019)

CSP Ven. 1621-3
Calendar of State Papers Relating To English Affairs in the Archives of Venice. Vol. 17: 1621-3, London (ed. A.B. Hinds, published 1911), *British History Online* <www.british-history.ac.uk/cal-state-papers/venice/vol17> (accessed 11 July 2019)

CSP Ven. 1623-5
Calendar of State Papers Relating To English Affairs in the Archives of Venice. Vol. 18: 1623-5, London (ed. A.B. Hinds, published 1912), *British History Online* <www.british-history.ac.uk/cal-state-papers/venice/vol18> (accessed 11 July 2019)

CSP Ven. 1625-6
Calendar of State Papers Relating To English Affairs in the Archives of Venice. Vol. 19: 1625-6, London (ed. A.B. Hinds, published 1913), *British History Online* <www.british-history.ac.uk/cal-state-papers/venice/vol19> (accessed 11 July 2019)

CSP Ven. 1632-6
Calendar of State Papers Relating To English Affairs in the Archives of Venice. Vol. 23: 1632-6, London (ed. A.B Hinds, published 1921), *British History Online* <www.british-history.ac.uk/cal-state-papers/venice/vol23> (accessed 11 July 2019)

CSP Ven. 1636-9
Calendar of State Papers Relating To English Affairs in the Archives of Venice. Vol. 24: 1636-9, London (ed. A.B. Hinds, published 1923), *British History Online* <www.british-history.ac.uk/cal-state-papers/venice/vol24> (accessed 11 July 2019)

CSP Ven. 1640-42
Calendar of State Papers Relating To English Affairs in the Archives of Venice. Vol. 25: 1640-42, London (ed. A.B. Hinds, published 1924), *British History Online* <www.british-history.ac.uk/cal-state-papers/venice/vol25> (accessed 11 July 2019)

CSP Ven. 1642-3
Calendar of State Papers Relating To English Affairs in the Archives of Venice. Vol. 26: 1642-3, London (ed. A.B. Hinds, published 1925), *British History Online* <www.british-history.ac.uk/cal-state-papers/venice/vol26> (accessed 11 July 2019)

CSP Ven. 1659-61
Calendar of State Papers Relating To English Affairs in the Archives of Venice. Vol. 32: 1659-61, London (ed. A.B. Hinds, published 1931), *British History Online* <www.british-history.ac.uk/cal-state-papers/venice/vol32> (accessed 11 July 2019)

CSP Ven. 1661-4
Calendar of State Papers Relating To English Affairs in the Archives of Venice. Vol. 33: 1661-4, London (ed. A.B. Hinds, published 1932), *British History Online* <www.british-history.ac.uk/cal-state-papers/venice/vol33> (accessed 11 July 2019)

CSP Ven. 1671-2
Calendar of State Papers Relating To English Affairs in the Archives of Venice. Vol. 37: 1671-2, London (ed. A.B. Hinds, published 1939), *British History Online* <www.british-history.ac.uk/cal-state-papers/venice/vol37> (accessed 11 July 2019)

CSP Ven. 1673-5
Calendar of State Papers Relating To English Affairs in the Archives of Venice. Vol. 38: 1673-5, London (ed. A.B. Hinds, published 1947), *British History Online* <www.british-history.ac.uk/cal-state-papers/venice/vol38> (accessed 11 July 2019)

CTB 1660-67
Calendar of Treasury Books. Vol. 1: 1660-67, London (ed. W.A. Shaw, published 1904), *British History Online* <www.british-history.ac.uk/cal-treasury-books/vol1> (accessed 11 July 2019)

CTB 1669-72
Calendar of Treasury Books. Vol. 3: 1669-72, London (ed. W.A. Shaw, published 1908), *British History Online* <www.british-history.ac.uk/cal-treasury-books/vol3> (accessed 11 July 2019)

CTB 1676-9
Calendar of Treasury Books. Vol. 5: 1676-9, London (ed. W.A. Shaw, published 1911), *British History Online* <www.british-history.ac.uk/cal-treasury-books/vol5> (accessed 11 July 2019)

CTB 1681-5
Calendar of Treasury Books. Vol. 7: 1681-5, London (ed. W.A. Shaw, published 1916), *British History Online* <www.british-history.ac.uk/cal-treasury-books/vol7> (accessed 11 July 2019)

CTB 1685-9
Calendar of Treasury Books. Vol. 8: 1685-9, London (ed. W.A. Shaw, published 1923), *British History Online* <www.british-history.ac.uk/cal-treasury-books/vol8> (accessed 11 July 2019)

CTB 1689-92
Calendar of Treasury Books. Vol. 9: 1689-92, London (ed. W.A. Shaw, published 1931), *British History Online* <www.british-history.ac.uk/cal-treasury-books/vol9> (accessed 11 July 2019)

CTB 1693-6
Calendar of Treasury Books. Vol. 10: 1693-6, London (ed. W.A. Shaw, published 1935), *British History Online* <www.british-history.ac.uk/cal-treasury-books/vol10> (accessed 11 July 2019)

CTB 1697–8
Calendar of Treasury Books. Vol. 13: 1697–8, London (ed. W.A. Shaw, published 1933), *British History Online* <www.british-history.ac.uk/cal-treasury-books/vol13/> (accessed 8 Nov. 2019)

CTB 1698–9
Calendar of Treasury Books. Vol. 14: 1698–9, London (ed. W.A. Shaw, published 1934), *British History Online* <www.british-history.ac.uk/cal-treasury-books/vol14> (accessed 11 July 2019)

CTB 1702
Calendar of Treasury Books. Vol. 17: 1702, London (ed. W.A. Shaw, published 1939), *British History Online* <www.british-history.ac.uk/cal-treasury-books/vol17> (accessed 11 July 2019)

CTB 1703
Calendar of Treasury Books. Vol. 18: 1703, London (ed. W.A. Shaw, published 1936), *British History Online* <www.british-history.ac.uk/cal-treasury-books/vol18> (accessed 11 July 2019)

CTB 1704–5
Calendar of Treasury Books. Vol. 19: 1704–5, London (ed. W.A. Shaw, published 1938), *British History Online* <www.british-history.ac.uk/cal-treasury-books/vol19> (accessed 11 July 2019)

CTB 1708
Calendar of Treasury Books. Vol. 22: 1708, London (ed. W.A. Shaw, published 1952), *British History Online* <www.british-history.ac.uk/cal-treasury-books/vol22> (accessed 11 July 2019)

CTP 1556–1696
Calendar of Treasury Papers. Vol. 1: 1556–1696, London (ed. J. Redington, published 1868), *British History Online* <www.british-history.ac.uk/cal-treasury-papers/vol1> (accessed 11 July 2019)

CTP 1697–1702
Calendar of Treasury Papers. Vol. 2: 1697–1702, London (ed. J. Redington, published 1871), *British History Online* <www.british-history.ac.uk/cal-treasury-papers/vol2> (accessed 11 July 2019)

CTP 1702–7
Calendar of Treasury Papers. Vol. 3: 1702–7, London (ed. J. Redington, published 1874), *British History Online* <www.british-history.ac.uk/cal-treasury-papers/vol3> (accessed 11 July 2019)

CTP 1708–14
Calendar of Treasury Papers. Vol. 4: 1708–14, London (ed. J. Redington, published 1879), *British History Online* <www.british-history.ac.uk/cal-treasury-papers/vol4> (accessed 11 July 2019)

Dasent 1895
A.I. Dasent, *The History of St James's Square*, London

Day 1899
L.F. Day, 'The decorative art of William Morris and his work', *Easter Art Annual: Art Journal Extra Number*, London

De Beer 1955
E.S. de Beer (ed.), *The Diary of John Evelyn*, 6 vols, Oxford

De Mandelslo 1719
A. de Mandelslo, *Les Voyages de Sieur Albert de Mandelslo*, Leiden

De Monconys 1695
B. de Monconys, *Les Voyages de Monsieur de Monconys en Angleterre et aux Pays-Bas*, Paris

Dean 2006
P. Dean, *Sir John Soane and London*, Aldershot

Defoe 1761
D. Defoe, *A tour thro' the whole island of Great Britain*, 3 vols, London

Dennison 2017
M. Dennison, *The First Iron Lady: A Life of Caroline of Ansbach*, London

Dinkel 1983
J. Dinkel, *The Royal Pavilion, Brighton*, London

Dobrée and Webb 1928
B. Dobrée and G. Webb (eds), *The Complete Works of Sir John Vanbrugh*, 4 vols, London

Dorment 1980
R. Dorment, 'Alfred Gilbert's memorial to Queen Alexandra', *Burlington Magazine*, **122** (no. 922), pp. 47–54

Dorment 1986
R. Dorment, *Alfred Gilbert: Sculptor and Goldsmith*, London

Douglas Hamilton 1875–7
W. Douglas Hamilton (ed.), *A Chronicle of England During the Reign of the Tudors from 1485 to 1559 by Charles Wriothesley*, 2 vols, London

Downes 1966
K. Downes, *English Baroque Architecture*, London

Duggan 2000
D. Duggan, '"London the ring, Covent Garden the jewell of the ring": new light on Covent Garden', *Architectural History*, **43**, pp. 140–61

Duggan 2003
D. Duggan, '"A rather fascinating hybrid", Tart Hall: Lady Arundel's casino at Whitehall', *British Art Journal*, **4**, pp. 54–64

Dupérac 1575
E. Dupérac, *I vestigi dell'antichità di Roma*, Rome

Durie 1650
J. Durie, *The Reformed Library Keeper*, London

Durrant Cooper 1858
W. Durrant Cooper (ed.), *Savile Correspondence: Letters to and from Henry Savile Esq.*, Camden Society, Old Series, **71**, London

Eades Bentley 1941
G. Eades Bentley, *The Jacobean and Caroline Stage: Dramatic Companies and Players*, 2 vols, Oxford

Edgar 2017
J. Edgar, 'Royal Household Buildings Gazetteer, St James's Palace, the King's Kitchen', unpublished report, Nov. 2017

E. Edwards 1859
E. Edwards, *Memoirs of Libraries Including a Handbook of Library Economy*, 2 vols, London

S. Edwards 2018
S. Edwards, 'George I at Kensington', in Fryman 2018, pp. 109–29

G.P. Elliott 1847
G.P. Elliott (ed.), 'The Diary of Edward Lake, Archdeacon and Prebendary of Exeter, Chaplain and Tutor to the Princesses Mary and Anne, daughters of the Duke of York, afterwards James II, in the years 1677–8', *Camden Miscellany*, **1** (Camden Old Series, **39**), London

W.H. Elliott 1951
W.H. Elliott, *Undiscovered Ends*, London

Ellis 1824
H. Ellis, *Original Letters Illustrative of English History*, 3 vols, London

Evans 1964
J. Evans, *Monastic Architecture in France from the Renaissance to the Revolution*, Cambridge

Everett 2015
M. Everett, *The Rise of Thomas Cromwell: Power and Politics in the Reign of Henry VIII*, New Haven and London

Everett Green 1857
M.A. Everett Green (ed.), *Letters of Henrietta Maria*, London

Fairclough and Leary 1981
O. Fairclough and E. Leary, *Textiles by William Morris and Morris & Co., 1861-1940*, London

Fantoni *et al.* 2009
M. Fantoni, G. Gorse and R.M. Smuts (eds), *The Politics of Space: European Courts c.1500-1750*, Rome

Field 2002
O. Field, *The Favourite: Sarah, Duchess of Marlborough*, London

Finet 1656
J. Finet, *Finetti Philoxenis: Some Choice Observations of Sir John Finet Knight and Master of Ceremonies to the two last Kings*, London

Firth 1894
C.H. Firth (ed.), *The Memoirs of Edmund Ludlow*, 2 vols, Oxford

Firth and Rait 1911
C.H. Firth and R.S. Rait (eds), *Acts and Ordinances of the Interregnum, 1642-1660*, 3 vols, London

D.R. Fisher 2009a
D.R. Fisher, 'Long, Charles (1760–1838), of Bromley Hill Place, Kent', *The History of Parliament: The House of Commons 1820-1832* (ed. D.R. Fisher), <www.historyofparliamentonline.org/volume/1820-1832/member/long-charles-1760-1838> (accessed 11 July 2019)

D.R. Fisher 2009b
D.R. Fisher, 'Baring, Sir Thomas, 2nd bt. (1772–1848), of Stratton Park, nr. Winchester, Hants and 21 Devonshire Place, Mdx.', *The History of Parliament: The House of Commons 1820-1832* (ed. D.R. Fisher), <www.historyofparliamentonline.org/volume/1820-1832/member/baring-sir-thomas-1772-1848> (accessed 11 July 2019)

D.R. Fisher 2009c
D.R. Fisher, 'Davies, Thomas Henry Hastings (1789–1846), of Elmley Castle, Worcs.', *The History of Parliament: The House of Commons 1820-1832* (ed. D.R. Fisher), <www.historyofparliamentonline.org/volume/1820-1832/member/davies-thomas-1789-1846> (accessed 11 July 2019)

R.B. Fisher 1978
R.B. Fisher, *Syrie Maugham*, London

Forster and Tuttle 1971
K.W. Forster and R.J. Tuttle, 'The Palazzo del Te', *Journal of the Society of Architectural Historians*, **30**, pp. 267–93

Foxcroft 1898
H.C. Foxcroft (ed.), *The Life and Letters of Sir George Savile, Bart., First Marquis of Halifax*, 2 vols, London

Fraser 2012
F. Fraser, *The Unruly Queen: The Life of Queen Caroline*, London

Frommel 2003
S. Frommel, *Sebastiano Serlio: Architect*, Milan

Fryman 2018
O. Fryman (ed.), *Kensington Palace: Art, Architecture and Society*, New Haven and London

Fulford 1973
R. Fulford, *Royal Dukes: The Father and Uncles of Queen Victoria*, 2nd edn, London

Gaimster and Stamper 1997
D. Gaimster and P. Stamper (eds), *The Age of Transition: The Archaeology of English Culture, 1400-1600*, Oxford

Gapper et al. 2002
C. Gapper, J. Newman and A. Ricketts, 'Hatfield: a house for a Lord Treasurer', in P. Croft (ed.), *Patronage, Culture and Power: The Early Cecils*, New Haven and London, pp. 88–93

Gatty 1921
C.T. Gatty, *Mary Davies and the Manor of Ebury*, 2 vols, London

George 1921
D.L. George, *Matters of Moment for the Million*, London

Geraghty 2007
A. Geraghty, *The Architectural Drawings of Sir Christopher Wren at All Souls College, Oxford: A Complete Catalogue*, Aldershot

Gibson 2009
W. Gibson, *James II and the Trial of the Seven Bishops*, Basingstoke

Gilbert 1913
G.D. Gilbert (ed.), *Memoirs of the Court of England in 1675 by Marie Catherine Baronne D'Aulnoy*, London

Gilbert Dolan 1899
D. Gilbert Dolan, 'Chapters in the history of the English Benedictine missions. Chapter VII: James II and the Benedictines in London', *Downside Review*, **18**, pp. 94–103

Girouard 1962
M. Girouard, 'The Smythson Collection of the Royal Institute of British Architects', *Architectural History*, **5**, pp. 21, 23–184

Gleissner 1994
S. Gleissner, 'Reassembling a royal art collection for the restored king of Great Britain', *Journal of the History of Collections*, **6** (no. 1), pp. 102–15

Goff 1995
M. Goff, '"The art of dancing, demonstrated by characters and figures": French and English sources for court and theatre dance, 1700–1750', *British Library Journal*, **21**, pp. 202–31

Golby and Purdue 1988
J.M. Golby and A.W. Purdue, *The Monarchy and the British People: 1760 to the Present*, London

Goodall 2018
J. Goodall, 'Fit for modern royalty', *Country Life*, **212** (no. 46), 14 Nov. 2018, pp. 134–43

Goodman 1839
G. Goodman, *The Court of King James the First*, 2 vols, London

Graeme 1929
B. Graeme, *The Story of St James's Palace*, London

Graves 1963
C. Graves, *Palace Extraordinary: The Story of St James's*, London

Great Exhibition 1851
Official Catalogue of the Great Exhibition of the Works and Industry of Nations, 3 vols, London

Green 1967
D.B. Green, *Sarah, Duchess of Marlborough*, London

Green and Thurley 1987
H.J.M. Green and S. Thurley, 'Excavations on the west side of Whitehall, 1960–62', *Transactions of the London and Middlesex Archaeological Society*, **38**, pp. 59–130

Gregg 1980
E. Gregg, *Queen Anne*, London

Greig 1926
J. Greig (ed.), *The Diaries of a Duchess: Extracts from the Diaries of the First Duchess of Northumberland, 1716-1776*, London

Griffey 2015
E. Griffey, *On Display: Henrietta Maria and the Materials of Magnificence at the Stuart Court*, New Haven and London

Griffiths 1898
A. Griffiths, *Wellington and Waterloo*, London

Grose 1775
F. Grose, *The Antiquarian Repertory*, 4 vols, London

Guy 2016
J.A. Guy, *Elizabeth: The Forgotten Years*, London

Hamilton [1794]
A. Hamilton, *Memoirs of Count Grammont: a new translation with notes and illustrations*, London

Hamilton Roche 1815
J. Hamilton Roche, *Wahlstadt Palace; or, Secrets from the Kitchen Court at St James's, during the Residence of Prince Marshal Blucher in London*, London

Hansard 1803–
Hansard: the official report of all parliamentary debates, <https://hansard.parliament.uk/> (accessed 11 July 2019)

Haq 2002
M. Sheikh I'tesamuddin, *The Wonders of Vilayet: Being the Memoir, Originally in Persian, of a Visit to France and Britain*, K. Haq (trans.), Leeds

F. Harris 1991
F. Harris, *A Passion for Government: The Life of Sarah, Duchess of Marlborough*, Oxford

F. Harris 2002
F. Harris, *Transformations of Love: The Friendship of John Evelyn and Margaret Godolphin*, Oxford

J. Harris 1972
J. Harris, *Catalogue of the Drawings Collection of the Royal Institute of British Architects: Inigo Jones and John Webb*, Farnborough

J.H. Harris 1844
J.H. Harris (ed.), *Diaries and correspondence of James Harris, first Earl of Malmesbury*, 4 vols, 2nd edn, London

S. Harris 2020
S. Harris, 'St James's Palace: rediscovering the lost Eastern Wing', *London Archaeologist*, **16** (no. 3), pp. 80–3

Harris and Higgott 1989
J. Harris and G. Higgott, *Inigo Jones: Complete Architectural Drawings*, London

Harris and Jackson Stops 1984
J. Harris and G. Jackson Stops (eds), *Britannia Illustrata*, Bungay

Harris and Tait 1979
J. Harris and A.A. Tait, *Catalogue of the Drawings by Inigo Jones, John Webb and Isaac de Caus at Worcester College, Oxford*, Oxford

Harrison 1928
G.B. Harrison, *An Elizabethan Journal: being a record of those things most talked of during the years 1591-1594*, London

Hart 2011
V. Hart, *Inigo Jones: The Architect of Kings*, New Haven and London

Hatton 1978
R.M. Hatton, *George I: Elector and King*, London

Haynes 1740
S. Haynes (ed.), *A Collection of State Papers relating to Affairs in the Reigns of King Henry VIII, King Edward VI, Queen Mary and Queen Elizabeth, from the Year 1542 to 1570*, London

Hayton et al. 2002
D. Hayton, E. Cruickshanks and S. Handley, *The History of Parliament: The House of Commons 1690–1715*, 5 vols, Cambridge, <www.historyofparliamentonline.org/research/members> (accessed 27 Jan. 2020)

Hefford 2003
W. Hefford, 'Brussells horsemanship tapestries owned by Charles I and Frederick Prince of Wales', in K. Brosens (ed.), *Flemish Tapestry in European and American Collections. Studies in Honour of Guy Delmarcel*, Turnhout, pp. 117–31

Henderson 1967
P. Henderson, *William Morris: His Life, Work and Friends*, London

Herbert 1813
T. Herbert, *Memoirs of the Last Years of the Reign of King Charles I*, London

Heylyn 1658
P. Heylyn, *A Short View of the Life and Reign of King Charles*, London

Hibbard 2009
C.M. Hibbard, 'The Somerset House chapel and the topography of London Catholicism', in Fantoni et al. 2009, pp. 317–37

Hibbert 1973
C. Hibbert, *George IV, Regent and King 1811–1830*, London

Higham and Moseley 1991
C. Higham and R. Moseley, *Elizabeth and Philip: The Untold Story*, London

Hilton 1977
W. Hilton, 'A dance for kings: the 17th-century French *courante*, its character, step-patterns, metric and proportional foundations', *Early Music*, **5** (no. 2), Oxford, pp. 160–72

HKW 1963
R.A. Brown, H.M. Colvin and A.J. Taylor (eds), *The History of the King's Works. Vols I and II: The Middle Ages*, London

HKW 1973
H.M. Colvin, J. Mordaunt Crook and M.H. Port (eds), *The History of the King's Works. Vol. VI: 1782–1851*, London

HKW 1975
H.M. Colvin, D.R. Ransome and J. Summerson (eds), *The History of the King's Works. Vol. III: 1485–1660*, London

HKW 1976
H.M. Colvin, J. Mordaunt Crook, K. Downes and J. Newman (eds), *The History of the King's Works. Vol. V: 1660–1782*, London

HKW 1982
H.M. Colvin et al. (eds), *The History of the King's Works. Vol. IV: 1485–1660*, London

HMC 1872
Third Report of the Royal Commission on Historical Manuscripts, London

HMC 1876
Fifth Report of the Royal Commission on Historical Manuscripts, London

HMC 1879
Seventh Report of the Royal Commission of Historical Manuscripts, London

HMC 1887
Manuscripts of Henry Duncan Skrine (Historical Manuscripts Commission. Eleventh report; appendix, part I), London

HMC 1883–1940
Calendar of the Manuscripts of the Most Hon. the Marquis of Salisbury, 24 vols, HMC IX, London

HMC 1888–1905
The Manuscripts of His Grace the Duke of Rutland, 4 vols, HMC XXIV, London

HMC 1889
The Manuscripts of His Grace the Duke of Rutland, G.C.B., preserved at Belvoir Castle; v. 2 (Historical Manuscripts Commission. Twelfth report; appendix, part V), London

HMC 1890
The Manuscripts of S.H. le Fleming, HMC XXV (appendix, pt VII), London

HMC 1891–1931
The Manuscripts of His Grace the Duke of Portland, 9 vols, HMC XXIX, London

HMC 1904–8
Calendar of the Manuscripts of the Marquis of Bath, 5 vols, HMC LXIII, London

HMC 1924–40
Report on the Manuscripts of the Marquess of Downshire, 6 vols, HMC LXXV, London

Hobhouse 1995
H. Hobhouse, *Thomas Cubitt, Master Builder*, 2nd edn, London

Hobsbawm and Ranger 1983
E. Hobsbawm and T. Ranger (eds), *The Invention of Tradition*, Cambridge

Home 1889–96
A. Home (ed.), *The Letters and Journals of Lady Mary Coke, 1756–1774*, 4 vols, Edinburgh

Honeybourne 1967
M.B. Honeybourne, 'The leper hospitals of the London area, with an appendix on some other mediaeval hospitals of Middlesex', *Transactions of the London and Middlesex Archaeological Society*, **21**, London, pp. 1–61

Hooper 1768–70
W. Hooper (ed. and trans.), *Letters of Baron Bielfeld*, 4 vols, London

Howarth 1989
D. Howarth, 'Charles I, sculpture and sculptors', in MacGregor 1989, pp. 73–113

Hunt 1827
T.F. Hunt, *Designs for Parsonage Houses, Almshouses, Etc.*, London

Hunt 1830
T.F. Hunt, *Exemplars of Tudor Architecture*, London

Hussey 1939
C. Hussey, 'Brook House, Brook Street', *Country Life*, **150** (no. 85), 24 June 1939, pp. 682–6

Hussey 1949
C. Hussey, *Clarence House: The Home of H.R.H. The Princess Elizabeth, Duchess of Edinburgh, and H.R.H. The Duke of Edinburgh, K.G.*, London

Hutton 1978
R. Hutton, *George I: Elector and King*, London

Impey 2003
E. Impey, *Kensington Palace: The Official Illustrated History*, London

Inchbald 1965
J. Inchbald (ed.), *ID&D '66: Interior Design and Decoration*, London

Jacob 1970
J. Jacob, 'A candelabrum to a design by C.H. Tatum', *The Connoisseur*, **174**, pp. 116–19

Jacques 2017
D. Jacques, *Gardens of Court and Country: English Design 1630–1730*, New Haven

Jakobson et al. 2006–7
A. Mollet, *Le jardin de plaisir / Der Lust Gartten / Lustgård / The Garden of Pleasure*, Å. Jakobson, G. Lindhal, K. Lundquist and Å. Nisbeth (eds), 2 vols, Uppsala

Jay 2006
E. Jay, 'Queen Caroline's library and its European contexts', *Book History*, **9**, pp. 31–55

Jennings 1885
L.J. Jennings, *The Croker Papers: The Correspondence and Diaries of the Late Right Honourable John Wilson Croker*, 3 vols, London

Jerdan 1853
W. Jerdan, *The Autobiography of William Jerdan*, IV, London

Jordan 1966
W.K. Jordan (ed.), *The Chronicle and Political Papers of King Edward VI*, London

Jordan 1970
W.K. Jordan, *Edward VI: The Threshold of Power*, Cambridge, MA

Journal of the House of Commons
Journal of the House of Commons. Vols 1–12: 1547–1699, London (published 1802–3), British History Online <www.british-history.ac.uk/commons-jrnl> (accessed 11 July 2019)

Journal of the House of Lords
Journal of the House of Lords. Vols 1–39: 1509–1793; Vols 62–4: 1830–32, London (published 1767–1830), British History Online <www.british-history.ac.uk/search/series/lords-jrnl> (accessed 11 July 2019)

Judd 1980
D. Judd, *Prince Philip: A Biography*, London

Kane 2012
K. Kane, 'The now-vanished ephemeral art: chalking the Regency ballroom floor', *The Beau Monde*, <http://thebeaumonde.com/the-now-vanished-ephemeral-art-chalking-the-regency-ballroom-floor/> (accessed 11 July 2019)

Keay 2008
A. Keay, *The Magnificent Monarch: Charles II and the Ceremonies of Power*, London

Kelly and Cornick 2013
D. Kelly and M. Cornick (eds), *A History of the French in London*, London

Kelsey 1997
S. Kelsey, *Inventing a Republic: The Political Culture of the Commonwealth 1649–1653*, Manchester

Kelvin 1987
W. Morris, *The Collected Letters of William Morris*, N. Kelvin (ed.), 2 vols, Princeton

H. Kent 1823
H. Kent, *Original London Directory 1823*, London

W. Kent 1727
W. Kent, *The Designs of Inigo Jones, Consisting of Plans and Elevations for Publick and Private Buildings*, 2 vols, London

King 1930
W. King (ed.), *Memoirs of Sarah, Duchess of Marlborough, together with her Characters of her Contemporaries and her Opinions*, London

Kingsford 1925
C.L. Kingsford, *The Early History of Piccadilly, Leicester Square, Soho and their Neighbourhood*, Cambridge

Kirk 2005
S. Kirk, *Philip Webb: Pioneer of Arts & Crafts Architecture*, London

Knighton 1838
Lady Knighton, *Memoirs of Sir William Knighton Bart*, 2 vols, London

Kohan 1952
C.M. Kohan, *Works and Buildings*, London

Kubler 1982
G. Kubler, *Building the Escorial*, Princeton

Kubler and Soria 1959
G. Kubler and M. Soria, *Art and Architecture in Spain and Portugal and their American Dominions, 1500 to 1800*, Baltimore

L&P Hen. VIII, X
Letters and Papers, Foreign and Domestic, Henry VIII, Volume 10, Jan.–June 1536, London (ed. J. Gairdner, published 1887), British History Online <www.british-history.ac.uk/letters-papers-hen8/vol10> (accessed 11 July 2019)

L&P Hen. VIII, XI
Letters and Papers, Foreign and Domestic, Henry VIII, Volume 11, July–Dec. 1536, London (ed. J. Gairdner, published 1888), British History Online <www.british-history.ac.uk/letters-papers-hen8/vol11> (accessed 11 July 2019)

L&P Hen. VIII, XII (2)
Letters and Papers, Foreign and Domestic, Henry VIII, Volume 12 Part 2, June–Dec. 1537, London (ed. J. Gairdner, published 1891), British History Online <www.british-history.ac.uk/letters-papers-hen8/vol12/no2> (accessed 11 July 2019)

L&P Hen. VIII, XIII (1)
Letters and Papers, Foreign and Domestic, Henry VIII, Volume 13 Part 1, Jan.–July 1538, London (ed. J. Gairdner, published 1892), British History Online <www.british-history.ac.uk/letters-papers-hen8/vol13/no1> (accessed 11 July 2019)

L&P Hen. VIII, XIII (2)
Letters and Papers, Foreign and Domestic, Henry VIII, Volume 13 Part 2, Aug.–Dec. 1538, London (ed. J. Gairdner, published 1893), British History Online <www.british-history.ac.uk/letters-papers-hen8/vol13/no2> (accessed 27 January 2020)

L&P Hen. VIII, XIV (2)
Letters and Papers, Foreign and Domestic, Henry VIII, Volume 14 Part 2, Aug.–Dec. 1539, London (ed. J. Gairdner and R.H. Brodie, published 1895), British History Online <www.british-history.ac.uk/letters-papers-hen8/vol14/no2> (accessed 11 July 2019)

L&P Hen. VIII, XVII
Letters and Papers, Foreign and Domestic, Henry VIII, Volume 17, 1542, London (ed. J. Gairdner and R.H. Brodie, published 1900), British History Online <www.british-history.ac.uk/letters-papers-hen8/vol17> (accessed 11 July 2019)

L&P Hen. VIII, XVIII (1)
Letters and Papers, Foreign and Domestic, Henry VIII, Volume 18 Part 1, Jan.–July 1543, London (ed. J. Gairdner and R.H. Brodie, published 1901), British History Online <www.british-history.ac.uk/letters-papers-hen8/vol18/no1> (accessed 11 July 2019)

Lacey 2002
R. Lacey, *Royal: Her Majesty Queen Elizabeth II*, London

Lambourne 1996
L. Lambourne, *The Aesthetic Movement*, London

Langlands 2015
A. Langlands, *Robert Kime*, London

Latham and Matthews 1970–83
R. Latham and W. Matthews (eds), *The Diary of Samuel Pepys*, 11 vols, London

Le Bourgeois 1974
J.V. le Bourgeois, 'William Morris at St James's Palace: a sequel', *Journal of the William Morris Society*, **3**, pp. 7–9

Le Marchant 1845
Horace Walpole, *Memoirs of the Reign of King George III*, 4 vols, D. le Marchant (ed.), London

Leech 2001
P. Leech, 'Musicians in the Catholic chapel of Catherine of Braganza, 1662–92', *Early Music*, **29** (no. 4), pp. 570–87

Lethaby 1979
W.R. Lethaby, *Philip Webb and His Work*, London

Lever 1984
J. Lever (ed.), *Catalogue of the Drawings Collection of the Royal Institute of British Architects, T–Z*, Amersham

Levy Peck 2000
L. Levy Peck, 'Creating a silk industry in seventeenth-century England', in Barroll 2000, pp. 225–7

Lewis 1937–83
W.S. Lewis (ed.), *The Yale Edition of Horace Walpole's Correspondence*, 48 vols, New Haven and London

Lint et al. 2014
G.L. Lint *et al.* (eds), *The Adams Papers*, XVII, Cambridge, MA

Lithgow 1643
W. Lithgow, *The Present Surveigh of London and England's State*, London

Lloyd 1992
C. Lloyd, *The Paintings in the Royal Collection*, London

Lloyd 2004
C. Lloyd, 'King, queen and family', in J. Roberts 2004, pp. 13–21

Loomie 1987
A.J. Loomie, *Ceremonies of Charles I: The Note Books of John Finet, 1628–1641*, Fordham

Lunn 1980
D. Lunn, *The English Benedictines, 1540–1688*, London

Luttrell 1857
N. Luttrell, *A Brief Relation of State Affairs from September 1678 to April 1714*, 6 vols, Oxford

Lyle 1934
Acts of the Privy Council of England. Vol. 40: 1625–6, London (ed. J.V. Lyle), British History Online <www.british-history.ac.uk/acts-privy-council/vol40> (accessed 11 July 2019)

MacCarthy 1994
F. MacCarthy, *William Morris: A Life for Our Time*, London

MacCarthy 2012
F. MacCarthy, *The Last Pre-Raphaelite: Edward Burne-Jones and the Victorian Imagination*, Cambridge, MA

MacCulloch 2018
D. MacCulloch, *Thomas Cromwell: A Life*, London

MacGregor 1989
A. MacGregor (ed.), *The Late King's Goods: Collections, Possessions and Patronage of Charles I in the Light of the Commonwealth Sale Inventories*, Oxford

MacLeod and Marciari Alexander 2001
C. MacLeod and J. Marciari Alexander (eds), *Painted Ladies: Women at the Court of Charles II*, London

Madge 1938
S.J. Madge, *The Domesday of Crown Lands: A Study of the Legislation, Surveys and Sales of Royal Estates under the Commonwealth*, London

Magalotti 1821
L. Magalotti, *Travels of Cosmo the Third, Grand Duke of Tuscany*, London

Magnus 1964
P. Magnus, *King Edward the Seventh*, London

Manning 1855
C.R. Manning (ed.), 'State papers relating to the custody of the Princess Elizabeth at Woodstock in 1554', *Norfolk Archaeology*, **4**, pp. 133–231

Marchand 1995
J. Marchand (ed.), *A Frenchman in England 1784: Being the Mélanges sur l'Angleterre of François de la Rochefoucauld*, London

Marschner 2007
J. Marschner, *Caroline of Ansbach: The Queen, Collections and Connoisseurship at the Early Georgian Court*, London

Marschner 2014
J. Marschner, *Queen Caroline: Cultural Politics at the Early Eighteenth-Century Court*, London

Marsden 2004
J. Marsden, *Clarence House: Official Souvenir Guide*, London

Martin 2005
G. Martin, *Corpus Rubenianum. Vol. XV: The Ceiling Decoration of the Banqueting Hall*, 2 vols, London

Matthews 1939
W. Matthews (ed. and trans.), *The Diary of Dudley Ryder, 1715–16*, London

Maxwell 1904
H. Maxwell (ed.), *The Creevy Papers*, 2 vols, London

Maziere Brady 1971
W. Maziere Brady, *The Episcopal Succession in England, Scotland and Ireland*, 3 vols, Rome

McClure 1939
N.E. McClure (ed.), *The Letters of John Chamberlain*, 2 vols, Philadelphia

McDayter 2003
M. McDayter, 'The haunting of St James's library: librarians, literature and the *Battle of the Books*', *Huntingdon Library Quarterly*, **66**, pp. 4–14

McIlwain 1918
C. McIlwain (ed.), *The Political Works of James I*, Cambridge, MA

Merck 2016
M. Merck (ed.), *The British Monarchy on Screen*, Manchester

Mijers and Onnekink 2007
E. Mijers and D. Onnekink (eds), *Redefining William III: The Impact of the King-Stadtholder in International Context*, Aldershot; ebook 2nd edn published 2016

Millar 1958–60
O. Millar (ed.), 'Abraham van der Doort's catalogue of the collections of Charles I', *Walpole Society*, **37**, London

Millar 1963
O. Millar, *The Tudor, Stuart and Early Georgian Pictures in the Collection of Her Majesty The Queen*, 2 vols, London

Millar 1970–72
O. Millar, 'The inventories and valuations of the king's goods, 1649–51', *Walpole Society*, **43**, pp. 139–50

Millar 1977
O. Millar, *The Queen's Pictures*, London

D.C. Miller 1983
D.C. Miller, 'Benedetto Gennari's career at the courts of Charles II and James II and a newly discovered portrait of James II', *Apollo*, **117** (no. 251), Jan., pp. 24–9

J. Miller 1973
J. Miller, *Popery and Politics in England, 1660–1688*, Cambridge

Mitchell 1947
C. Mitchell, 'William Morris at St James's Palace', *Architectural Review*, **101**, pp. 37–9

Mollet 1670
A. Mollet, *The Garden of Pleasure*, London

Mörke 2007
O. Mörke, 'William III Statholderly court in the Dutch Republic', in Mijers and Onnekink 2007, pp. 227–36

Munby 1996
J. Munby, 'Signor Verrio and Monsieur Beaumont, gardeners to King James II', *Journal of the British Archaeological Association*, **149**, pp. 55–71

National Trust 1986
National Trust, *Basildon Park, Berkshire*, London

Nichols 1828
J.G. Nichols, *The Progresses, Processions and Magnificent Festivities of King James the First*, 4 vols, London

Nichols 1848
J.G. Nichols, *The Diary of Henry Machyn: Citizen and Merchant-Taylor of London*, Camden Society, Old Series, **42**, London

Nichols 1849
J.G. Nichols, *The Chronicle of Queen Jane and of Two Years of Queen Mary*, Camden Society, Old Series, **48**, London

Nichols 1855
J.G. Nichols, 'Inventories of the Wardrobes, Plate, Chapel Stuff, etc. of Henry Fitzroy, Duke of Richmond, and of the Wardrobe Stuff at Baynard's Castle of Katharine, Princess Dowager', *Camden Miscellany*, **3** (Camden Old Series, **61**), London

Nichols 1857
J.G. Nichols, *Literary remains of King Edward the Sixth*, 2 vols, London

Nicolson 1952
H. Nicolson, *King George the Fifth: His Life and Reign*, London

Noorthouck 1773
J. Noorthouck, 'Book 2, Ch. 12: Broad Street Ward', in *A New History of London Including Westminster and Southwark*, (London, published 1773), *British History Online* <www.british-history.ac.uk/no-series/new-history-london/pp566-576> (accessed 11 July 2019)

Nurse 2017
B. Nurse, *London: Prints and Drawings before 1800*, Oxford

Olechnowicz 2007
A. Olechnowicz (ed.), *The Monarchy and the British Nation, 1780 to the Present*, Cambridge

Osborne 2011
T. Osborne, 'A queen mother in exile: Marie de Médicis in the Spanish Netherlands and England, 1631–41', in P. Mansel and T. Riotte (eds), *Monarchy and Exile: The Politics of Legitimacy from Marie de Médicis to Wilhelm II*, London, pp. 17–43

Ozell 1719
J. Ozell (trans.), *H. de Valourg Misson's Memoirs of Observations in his Travels over England*, London

Palladio 1570
A. Palladio, *I Quattro Libri dell'Architecttura*, 4 vols, Venice

Pardoe 1890
J. Pardoe, *The Life of Marie de Medicis, Queen of France*, 3 vols, London

Parkinson 1629
J. Parkinson, *Paradisi in sole Paradisus Terrestris. Or, A Garden of all sorts of pleasant flowers*, London

J. Parry 2007
J. Parry, 'Whig monarchy, Whig nation: Crown, politics and representiveness 1800–2000', in Olechnowicz 2007, pp. 47–75

L. Parry 2013
L. Parry, *William Morris Textiles*, 2nd edn, London

M. Parry 2011
M. Parry, *Morris & Co.: A Revolution in Decoration*, Denham

Pattacini 1998
L. Pattacini, 'André Mollet, royal gardener in St James's Park, London', *Garden History*, **26** (no. 1), pp. 3–18

Peacham 1906
H. Peacham, *Compleat Gentleman, 1634*, Oxford

Peck 1736
F. Peck, *Desiderata Curiosa*, 2 vols, London

Pegge 1791
S. Pegge, *Curialia: Or, An Historical Account of Some Branches of the Royal Household*, 5 vols, London

Pennant 1790
T. Pennant, *Of London*, London

Pereira 2002
P. Pereira, *Jerónimos Abbey of Santa Maria*, London

Pérouse de Montclos 1994
J.-M. Pérouse de Montclos, *La Guide du Patrimoin: Paris*, Paris

Pevsner 1972
N. Pevsner, *Some Architectural Writers of the Nineteenth Century*, Oxford

Pike 1913
C.E. Pike, *Selections from the Correspondence of Arthur Capel, Earl of Essex*, Camden Society, Third Series, **24**, London

Pollard 1902
A.F. Pollard, *Tudor Tracts, 1532–1588*, London

Pope-Hennessy 1959
J. Pope-Hennessy, *Queen Mary, 1867–1953*, London

Pope-Hennessy 2018
J. Pope-Hennessy, *The Quest for Queen Mary*, H. Vickers (ed.), London

Port 1976
M.H. Port (ed.), *The Houses of Parliament*, New Haven and London

Powys Marks 1964
S. Powys Marks, *The Map of Mid-Sixteenth Century London*, London

Prochaska 1995
F. Prochaska, *Royal Bounty: The Making of a Welfare Monarchy*, New Haven and London

Puget de la Serre 1639
J. Puget de la Serre, *Histoire de l'entree de la reyne mere du roy tres-chrestien dans la Grande-Bretagne*, London

Pyne 1819
W.H. Pyne, *The History of the Royal Residences*, 3 vols, London

Quarrell and Mare 1934
W.H. Quarrell and M. Mare (eds and trans.), *London in 1700 from the Travels of Zacharies Conrad von Uffenbach*, London

Quilley 2006
G. Quilley (ed.), *Art for the Nation: The Oil Paintings Collections of the National Maritime Museum*, London

Quinault 1992
R. Quinault, 'Westminster and the Victorian Constitution', *Transactions of the Royal Historical Society*, 6th ser., **2**, pp. 79–104

Rabe 2016
J. Rabe, 'Mediating between art and nature: the Countess of Arundel at Tart Hall', in S. Burghartz, L. Burkat and C. Göttler (eds), *Sites of Meditation: Connected Histories of Places, Processes and Objects in Europe and Beyond, 1450–1650*, Intersections: Interdisciplinary Studies in Early Modern Culture, **47**, Leiden, pp. 183–210

Randall 2013
E. Randall, 'A special case? London's French Protestants', in Kelly and Cornick 2013, pp. 13–42

Rawcliffe 2006
C. Rawcliffe, *Leprosy in Medieval England*, Woodbridge

Rawson Gardiner 1869
S. Rawson Gardiner (ed. and trans.), *El hecho de los tratados del matrimonio pretendido por el Príncipe de Gales con la seren*íssima *Infante de España María*, Camden Society, Old Series, **51**, London

Raymund Palmer 1867
C.F. Raymund Palmer, *The life of Philip Thomas Howard, O.P., Cardinal of Norfolk*, London

RCHME 1925
An Inventory of the Historical Monuments in London. Vol. 2: West London (Royal Commission on Historical Monuments of England survey), British History Online <www.british-history.ac.uk/rchme/london/vol2> (accessed 11 July 2019)

Reeve 1874
H. Reeve (ed.), *The Greville Memoirs*, 3 vols, 2nd edn, London

Richardson 1837
C.J. Richardson, *Observations on the Architecture of England*, London

Richardson 1840
C.J. Richardson, *Architectural Remains of the Reigns of Elizabeth and James I*, London

Riding 2000
C. Riding, 'The aura of sacred majesty: thrones in the new Palace of Westminster', in Riding and Riding 2000, pp. 179–93

Riding and Riding 2000
C. Riding and J. Riding, *The Houses of Parliament: History, Art and Architecture*, London

Ridley 2012
J. Ridley, *Bertie: A Life of Edward VII*, London

H. Roberts 1989
H. Roberts, 'Royal thrones, 1760–1840', *Furniture History*, **25**, pp. 61–85

H. Roberts 2007
H. Roberts, 'Thrones revisited', *Furniture History*, **43**, pp. 43–54

J. Roberts 1997
J. Roberts, *Royal Landscape: The Gardens and Parks of Windsor*, New Haven and London

J. Roberts 2004
J. Roberts (ed.), *George III and Queen Charlotte: Patronage, Collection and Court Taste*, London

J. Roberts 2018
J. Roberts, 'The long sleep, 1714–1776', in Brindle 2018, pp. 262–79

R. Roberts 1923
J. Perceval, *Manuscripts of the Earl of Egmont. Diary of the first Earl of Egmont*, III, R. Roberts (ed.), London

H. Robinson 1846–7
H. Robinson (ed.), *Original Letters Relative to the English Reformation*, 2 vols, Cambridge

J.M. Robinson 1979
J.M. Robinson, *The Wyatts: An Architectural Dynasty*, Oxford

Rodgers 1998
D. Rodgers, 'A catalogue of the original designs by Morris and Company in the collection of the William Morris Society', *Journal of the William Morris Society*, **13**

Roffey 2012
S. Roffey, 'Medieval leper hospitals in England: an archaeological perspective', *Medieval Archaeology*, **56** (no. 1), pp. 203–33

Rosoman 2009
T. Rosoman, *London Wallpapers: Their Manufacture and Use, 1690–1840*, London

Rosser 1989
G. Rosser, *Medieval Westminster, 1200–1540*, Oxford

Rosser and Thurley 1990
G. Rosser and S. Thurley, 'Whitehall Palace and King Street, Westminster: the urban cost of princely magnificence', *London Topographical Record*, **26**, pp. 57–77

Rye 1865
W.B. Rye, *England as seen by Foreigners in the Days of Elizabeth and James I*, London

Sachse 1961
W.L. Sachse (ed.), *The Diurnall of Thomas Rugg 1659-61*, Camden Society, Third Series, **91**, London

Sandbrook 2005
D. Sandbrook, *Never Had It So Good: A History of Britain from Suez to the Beatles*, London

Sansom 1947
W. Sansom, *Westminster in War*, London

Schrijver 1939
H. Schrijver, *Decoration for the Home*, Leigh-on-Sea

Schwoerer 1992
L.G. Schwoerer (ed.), *The Revolution of 1688–1689: Changing Perspectives*, Cambridge

K. Scott 2010
K. Scott, *St James's Palace: A History*, London

W. Scott 1809-15
W. Scott (ed.), *A collection of scarce and valuable tracts, on the most interesting and entertaining subjects: but chiefly such as relate to the history and constitution of these kingdoms*, 13 vols, 2nd edn, London

Searle 1982
A. Searle, 'A pleasing example of skill in old age: Sir Christopher Wren and Marlborough House', *British Library Journal*, **8**, pp. 37–45

Sears and Johnson 1956
J. Sears and F.R. Johnson (eds), *The Lumley Library: The Catalogue of 1609*, London

Sedgwick 1931
J. (Lord) Hervey, *Some materials towards memoirs of the reign of George II*, R. Sedgwick (ed.), 3 vols, London

Serlio 1537
S. Serlio, *The Fourth Book of Architecture: Rules for Masonry*, London

Shawcross 2009
W. Shawcross, *Queen Elizabeth The Queen Mother*, London

Shepherd 1829
T.H. Shepherd, *London and its Environs in the Nineteenth Century*, London

Shepherd 1841
T.H. Shepherd, *London Interiors: A Grand National Exhibition*, 2 vols, London

Sheppard 1894
E. Sheppard, *Memorials of St James's Palace*, 2 vols, London

Shotter Boys 1842
T. Shotter Boys, *Original Views of London*, London

Sitwell 1974
O. Sitwell, *Queen Mary and Others*, London

H. Smith 2006
H. Smith, *Georgian Monarchy: Politics and Culture, 1714–1760*, Cambridge

V. Smith and Kelsey 1996
V. Smith and P. Kelsey, 'The lines of communication: the Civil War defences of London', in S. Porter (ed.), *London and the Civil War*, London, pp. 117–48

Smuts 1991
R.M. Smuts, 'The court and its neighbourhood: royal policy and urban growth in the early Stuart West End', *Journal of British Studies*, **30** (no. 2), pp. 117–49

Spalding 1990
R. Spalding (ed.), *The Diary of Bulstrode Whitelocke*, Oxford

Spehr 2008
P. Spehr, *The Man Who Made Movies: W.K.L. Dickson*, New Barnet

Spraggon 2003
J. Spraggon, *Puritan Iconoclasm during the English Civil War*, Woodbridge

Spurling 1984
H. Spurling, *Secrets of a Woman's Heart: The Later Life of Ivy Compton-Burnett (1920–1969)*, London

Starkey 2001
D. Starkey, *Elizabeth: Apprenticeship*, Leicester

Starkey and Ward 1998
D. Starkey and P. Ward (eds), *The Inventory of King Henry VIII. Vol. I: The Transcript*, London

Stockdale 1810
J.J. Stockdale, *A minute detail of the attempt to assassinate His Royal Highness The Duke of Cumberland*, London

Stourton 2016
J. Stourton, *Kenneth Clark: Life, Art and Civilisation*, London

Strangford 1853
Viscount Strangford (ed.), 'Household Expenses of Princess Elizabeth during her Residence at Hatfield, October 1551 to September 1552', *Camden Miscellany*, **2** (Camden Old Series, **55**), London, pp. 1–48

Strickland 1846
A. Strickland, *Lives of the Queens of England*, 12 vols, London

Strickland 1872
A. Strickland, *Lives of the Last Four Princesses of the Royal House of Stuart*, London

String 1996
T.C. String, 'A neglected Henrician decorative ceiling', *Antiquaries Journal*, **76**, pp. 139–51

Strong 1986
R. Strong, *Henry Prince of Wales and England's Lost Renaissance*, London

Strong 1998
R. Strong, *The Renaissance Garden in England*, London

Sugden and Edmondson 1926
A.V. Sugden and J.L. Edmondson, *A History of English Wallpaper, 1509–1914*, London

Sullivan 1994
D. Sullivan, *The Westminster Corridor: An Exploration of the Anglo-Saxon History of Westminster Abbey and its People*, London

Sullivan 2006
D. Sullivan, *The Westminster Circle: The People Who Lived and Worked in the Early Town of Westminster, 1066–1307*, London

Summerson 1980
J. Summerson, *The Life and Work of John Nash, Architect*, London

Survey of London 1940
Survey of London. Vol. 20: St Martin-in-The-Fields, Pt III: Trafalgar Square and Neighbourhood (eds G.H. Gater and F.R. Hiorns), British History Online <www.british-history.ac.uk/survey-london/vol20/pt3> (accessed 11 July 2019)

Survey of London 1960
Survey of London. Vols 29 and 30: St James, Westminster, Pt 1 (ed. F.H.W. Sheppard), British History Online <www.british-history.ac.uk/survey-london/vols29-30/pt1> (accessed 11 July 2019)

Survey of London 1966
Survey of London. Vols 33 and 34: St Anne Soho (ed. F.H.W. Sheppard), British History Online <www.british-history.ac.uk/survey-london/vols31-2/pt2> (accessed 11 July 2019)

Talbot and Hammond 1965
C.H. Talbot and E.A. Hammond, *The Medical Practitioners in Medieval England: A Biographical Register*, London

Tanner 1902
H. Tanner, *English Interior Woodwork of the XVI, XVII and XVIIIth Centuries*, London

Temple Newsam 1992
Country House Lighting, 1660–1890: Temple Newsam Country House Studies, **4**, Leeds

Thackeray 1861
W.M. Thackeray, *The Four Georges*, London

Thomas et al. 2006
C. Thomas, R. Cowie and J. Sidell, 'The royal palace, abbey and town of Westminster on Thorney Island: archaeological excavations for the London Underground Jubilee Line extension project', *Museum of London Archaeology Service Monograph*, **22**, London

A. Thompson 2010
A. Thompson, *George II: King and Elector*, New Haven and London

E.M. Thompson 1878
E.M. Thompson (ed.), *Correspondence to the Family of Hatton*, 1, Camden Society, New Series, **22**, London

Thoms 1852
W.J. Thoms (ed.), 'English Catholic Vicars Apostolic, 1625–1689', *Notes and Queries*, 1st ser., **6** (no. 145), 7 Aug. 1852, p. 125

Thoms 1853
W.J. Thoms (ed.), 'Vicars Apostolic', *Notes and Queries*, 1st ser., **7** (no. 175), 5 Mar. 1853, pp. 242–3

Thoms 1914
W.J. Thoms (ed.), 'St James's Square, "Place Royall"', *Notes and Queries*, 11th ser., **9** (no. 216), 14 Feb. 1914, p. 126

Thornbury and Walford 1887
W. Thornbury and E. Walford (eds), *Old and New London*, 6 vols, London

Thrush and Ferris 2010
A. Thrush and J. Ferris (eds), *The History of Parliament: The House of Commons, 1604–1629*, Cambridge

Thurley 1993
S. Thurley, *The Royal Palaces of Tudor England*, New Haven and London

Thurley 1997
S. Thurley, 'Whitehall Palace and Westminster, 1400–1600: a royal seat in transition', in Gaimster and Stamper 1997, pp. 98–101

Thurley 1998
S. Thurley, *The Whitehall Palace Plan of 1670*, London

Thurley 1999
S. Thurley, *Whitehall Palace: An Architectural History of the Royal Apartments, 1240–1698*, New Haven and London

Thurley 2000
S. Thurley, 'A country seat fit for a king: Charles II, Greenwich and Winchester', in Cruickshanks 2000, pp. 214–39

Thurley 2002
S. Thurley, 'The Stuart kings, Oliver Cromwell and the Chapel Royal, 1618–1685', *Architectural History*, **45**, pp. 238–74

Thurley 2003
S. Thurley, *Hampton Court: A Social and Architectural History*, New Haven and London

Thurley 2004
S. Thurley, *Lost Buildings of Britain*, London

Thurley 2009a
S. Thurley, 'Kensington Palace: an incident in Anglo-Dutch architectural collaboration?', *Georgian Group Journal*, **17**, pp. 1–18

Thurley 2009b
S. Thurley, *Somerset House: The Palace of England's Queens, 1551–1692*, London

Thurley 2009c
S. Thurley, 'The politics of court space in early Stuart London', in Fantoni *et al.* 2009, pp. 293–316

Thurley 2013
S. Thurley, *Men from the Ministry: How Britain Saved its Heritage*, New Haven and London

Thurley 2014
S. Thurley, 'The king in the queen's lodgings: the rise of the drawing room in the English court', in M. Chatenet and K. de Jonge, *Le prince, la princesse et leurs logis*, Paris, pp. 67–74

Thurley 2017
S. Thurley, *Houses of Power: The Places that Shaped the Tudor World*, London

Thurley 2018
S. Thurley, 'The later Stuarts, 1685–1714', in Brindle 2018, pp. 240–9

Tomsett Judge 1848
J. Tomsett Judge, *Sketches of Her Majesties Household*, London

Tout 1967
T.F. Tout, *Chapters in the Administrative History of Medieval England*, 6 vols, 2nd edn, Manchester

Toynbee 1903–5
P. Toynbee (ed.), *The Letters of Horace Walpole, Fourth Earl of Orford*, 16 vols, Oxford

Toynbee 1927–8
P. Toynbee, 'Horace Walpole's Journals of Visits to Country Seats &c', *Walpole Society*, **16**, pp. 9–80

E.S. Turner 1959
E.S. Turner, *The Court of St James's*, London

F.C. Turner 1948
F.C. Turner, *James II*, London

Turnor 1806
E. Turnor, 'A declaration of the diet and particular fare of K. Charles the First when Duke of York', *Archaeologia*, **15**, pp. 1–12

Tyack 1992
G. Tyack, *Sir James Pennethorne and the Making of Victorian London*, Cambridge

Udy 1971
D. Udy, 'The neo-classicism of Charles Heathcote Tatham', *The Connoisseur*, **177**, pp. 269–76

Van der Kiste and Jordaan 1984
J. van der Kiste and B. Jordaan, *Dearest Affie*, Gloucester

Van der Merwe 2006
P. van der Merwe, '"A proud moment of the glory of England": the Greenwich Hospital collection', in Quilley 2006, pp. 19–38

Van Gelder 1963
J.G. van Gelder, 'Notes on the Royal Collection – IV: the "Dutch gift" of 1610 to Henry Prince of "Whalis", and some other presents', *Burlington Magazine*, **105** (no. 729), pp. 541–5

Van Muyden 1902
Madame van Muyden (ed. and trans.), *A foreign view of England in the reigns of George I and George II: the letters of Monsieur César de Saussure to his family*, London

Vane 1830
C.W. Vane, *Narrative of the War in Germany and France, in 1813 and 1814*, 2nd edn, London

Vicars 1644
J. Vicars, *Jehovah-Jireh. God in the mount. Or, Englands parliamentarie-chronicle. Containing a most exact narration of all the most materiall proceedings of this renowned and unparalleled Parliament …*, London

Vicars 1648
J. Vicars, *True information of the beginning and cause of all our troubles: how they have been hatched and how prevented*, London

Vickers 2005
H. Vickers, *Elizabeth: The Queen Mother*, London

Von Bülow 1895
G. von Bülow, 'Journey through England and Scotland made by Lupold von Wedel in the years 1584 and 1585', *Transactions of the Royal Historical Society*, new ser., **9**, pp. 223–70

Von Kielmansegge 1902
F. von Kielmansegge, *Diary of a journey to England in the years 1761-1762*, Countess Kielmansegge (trans.), London

Vulliamy 2002
D.G. Vulliamy, *The Vulliamy Clockmakers*, Ticehurst

W.A.R. 1836
W.A.R., 'Autobiographical passages in the life of Mr Nash', *The Mechanics' Magazine, Museum Register, Journal and Gazette*, **24**, pp. 26–9

Ward 1703
E. Ward, *The London Spy Compleat*, London

Wardroper 2002
J. Wardroper, *Wicked Ernest: The Truth about the Man Who Was Almost Britain's King*, London

Warner and Gilson 1921
G.F. Warner and J.P. Gilson (eds), *Catalogue of Western Manuscripts in the Old Royal and King's Collections*, 4 vols, London

Weale 1941
J.C.M. Weale (ed.), 'Registers of the Catholic Chapels Royal and of the Portuguese Embassy Chapel, 1662–1829', *Catholic Record Society*, **38**, London

Webb 1665
J. Webb, *A Vindication of Stone-Heng Restored*, London

Weber 2013
S. Weber (ed.), *William Kent: Designing Georgian Britain*, New Haven and London

Weil 1992
R.J. Weil, 'The politics of legitimacy: women and the warming-pan scandal', in Schwoerer 1992, pp. 65–82

Wells-Cole 1997
A. Wells-Cole, *Art and Decoration in Elizabethan and Jacobean England: The Influence of Continental Prints, 1558–1625*, New Haven and London

Wenzel 2002
M. Wenzel, 'The Windsor Beauties by Sir Peter Lely and the collection of paintings at St James's Palace, 1674', *Journal of the History of Collections*, **14** (no. 2), pp. 205–13

Westergaard 1947
W. Westergaard (ed.), *The First Triple Alliance: Letters of Christopher Lindenov, Danish Envoy to London 1668–72*, New Haven and London

Wheatley 1870
H.B. Wheatley, *Round About Piccadilly and Pall Mall*, London

Wheatley 1884
H.B. Wheatley (ed.), *The historical and the posthumous memoirs of Sir Nathaniel William Wraxall, 1772–1784*, 5 vols, London

A. White 1999
A. White, 'A biographical dictionary of London tomb sculptors, c.1560–1660', *Walpole Society*, **61**, pp. 1–162

C. White 1982
C. White, *The Dutch Pictures in the Collection of Her Majesty The Queen*, Cambridge

Whitelock 2009
A. Whitelock, *Mary Tudor: England's First Queen*, London

Whitelocke 1853
B. Whitelocke, *Memorial of English Affairs from the Beginning of the Reign of Charles the First to the Happy Restoration of King Charles II*, 4 vols, Oxford

Wilks 1987
T. Wilks, 'The court culture of Prince Henry and his circle, 1603–13', unpublished D.Phil. thesis, University of Oxford

Wilks 2005
T. Wilks, '"Paying special attention to the adorning of a most beautiful gallery": the pictures in St James's Palace, 1609–49', *The Court Historian*, **10**, pp. 149–72

Wilks 2007
T. Wilks, 'The pike charged: Henry as militant prince', in T. Wilks (ed.), *Prince Henry Revived: Image and Exemplarity in Early Modern England*, Southampton, pp. 180–211

Williams 1948
J. Swift, *Journal to Stella*, H. Williams (ed.), 2 vols, Oxford

Windsor 1953
The Duke of Windsor, *A King's Story: The Memoirs of HRH The Duke of Windsor, KG*, 2nd edn, London

D. Winterbottom 2016
D. Winterbottom, *The Grand Old Duke of York: A Life of Prince Frederick, Duke of York and Albany, 1763-1827*, Barnsley

M. Winterbottom 2004
M. Winterbottom, 'Dining with George III and Queen Charlotte', in Marsden 2004, pp. 231–42

Wordsworth 1842
C. Wordsworth (ed.), *The Correspondence of Richard Bentley, DD, Master of Trinity College, Cambridge*, 2 vols, London

G. Worsley 2004
G. Worsley, *The British Stable*, New Haven and London

G. Worsley 2007
G. Worsley, *Inigo Jones and the European Classicist Tradition*, New Haven and London

L. Worsley 2010
L. Worsley, *Courtiers: The Secret History of Kensington Palace*, London

Wright and Tinling 1958
L.B. Wright and M. Tinling (eds), *William Byrd: The London Diary, 1717-1721*, Oxford

Wrighte 1796
T. Wrighte, 'Particulars of the Expence of the Royal Household in the Reigns of Henry VII, Henry VIII, Queen Elizabeth, etc.', *Archaeologia*, **12**, pp. 80–8

Yonge Akerman 1851
J. Yonge Akerman, 'Moneys received and paid for secret services of Charles II and James II', Camden Society, Old Series, **52**, London

Yorke 2001
J. Yorke, *Lancaster House: London's Greatest Town House*, London

Young 1987
A. Young, *Tudor and Jacobean Tournaments*, London

Ziegler 1979
P. Ziegler, *Crown and People*, Newton Abbot

Ziegler 1985
P. Ziegler, *Mountbatten: The Official Biography*, London

Ziegler 2001
P. Ziegler, *King Edward VIII*, Stroud

INDEX

Page numbers in *italic* refer to illustrations; captions may be on a different page.

Act of Settlement (1701) 119
Adam, William 166
Adams, John (President) 150–1, *151*
Adelaide, Queen (wife of William IV) 188, 196, 197
Adolphus, Duke of Cambridge (son of George III) 164, 166–7
Ageretti, Claudius 81
Agnes, St 62, 95, 110
air-raid shelters 224
Albani, Francesco 173
Albert, Prince Consort 194, 198, *199*, 200, 201, 202, 205
Albert Victor (Eddy), Prince, Duke of Clarence 194
Alexandra, Queen (wife of Edward VII) 197, 203–4, 207, 217, *219*
Alfred, Duke of Edinburgh 195–6
Allom, Charles Carrick 213–14, *213–14*
Allori, Cristofano 128, 172
Alnwick, William 15–16
altarpieces 43, 83, 86–7, *86*, 91, 95
altars 43, 71, 79, 83, 84, 225
ambassadors 35, 36, 38, 44, 53, 77, 88, 109, 149, 160
Ambassadors Court 1, 178, *178–9*, 194, *194–5*, Plan D
Ambassadors' Entrance 209, 216, *218*
Ambassadors' Room *see* Picture Gallery
Ambassadors' Stairs 178, 209, 216
Anne, Princess Royal (dau. of George II) 132–4, *133*
Anne, Queen 105–11
    balls 104, 110–11
    Chapel Royal 107–8
    exclusion of 99, 102
    lodgings when Princess 84–5, 88–9, 90, Plan C
    marriage 91
    offered St James's 100–1, 102–3
    private apartments 109–10
    State Apartments 108–9, *108*
Anne Boleyn, Queen (wife of Henry VIII) 17, 18, 19, 22, 24
Anne of Cleves, Queen (wife of Henry VIII) 22, 23
Anne of Denmark, Queen (wife of James I) 46
Anne Hyde, Duchess of York (wife of James II) 72–3, 82, 88
anti-Catholicism 53–4, *55*, 79, 82, 97; *see also* Popish Plot
apartments
    of George IV 185–6
    of Georgian princes 160–6
    of Georgian queens 129, *152*, 153–5, *154*
    housekeeper's 166
    of Princesses 84–5, 88, 90, 129
    of Queen Anne 109–10
    of William IV 162, 164, 188
    see also lodgings; State Apartments
arcades 104, *124*, 125, 178, *179*, *203*, 204, Plan D

archaeological research 17, 218–19, *220*, 245 n. 131
Armoury 51, 62, *171*, 178, 180, 191, 205, *206–7*, 214, 215, Plan D
Armytage, Percy 215–16
Arthur, Prince, Duke of Connaught 196, 214, 218
Arundel House, London 48
Ashley, Martin 236
Aston, Sir Roger 31–2
Audience Chamber 20, 108, *108*, 109; *see also* King's Closet; Royal Closet
Augusta, Princess (of Cambridge) 194
Augusta, Princess of Wales 134, 136, 143
Augusta of Hesse-Kassel, Duchess of Cambridge 194
Augusta Sophia, Princess, (dau. of George III) 187, *189*, 192, 193, 195
Augustus, Duke of Sussex (son of George III) 162, 164
aviary 46, *117*

Bailey, Edward 183
Bailey & Sanders 180, *182*, 183, *201*
bailiwick of St James's 31, 45, 63–9, 74–8
bakehouse 110, *111*
balconies 3, *3*, 45, 90, *91*, 100–1, 187
ballrooms 20, 100–1, 103–4, 106–7, 110, *179*, 180, 181, 184
balls 102–3, 104, 110, 124, 166, 186–7, 192–3
Banqueting Room 184–5, *184–5*, 187, 204, 211, *211*, 213, Plan D
Banqueting Room stairs 202, *202*, Plan D
baptisms 135, 200, 236, *237*
barracks 60–1, 71
Barry, Sir Charles 188
Bay Court 20, 73, 74, 95, Plans B, C; *see also* Privy Court
Beaufort, Henry, Bishop of Winchester 16
Beckwith, Samuel 155, 161, 162, 164, 166
Beckwith & France 155, 161, 162, 166
bedchambers 20, Plans A, C
    lying-in preparations 44–5, 92, 95–7, *96*, 143
    Princess Mary 90
    Restoration period 72–3
    tapestries 145, *172*
    Tudor period 20, 26, 53
    see also State Bedchamber
Bell, John 142
Benedictine order 78–9, 80, 82, 95
Bentley, Richard 98–9
Berkeley, John, 4th Viscount Fitzhardinge 110, 112, 114–15
Berkeley House, London 75, 102
Berkshire House, London 31, *58–9*, 67, 69
Bernasconi & Sons 189
Bernstorff, Andreas Gottlieb Freiherr von 129, 130
Bertram & Son 212–13
Bessant, C.H. 212
Biddulph, Sir Thomas 204
Bielfeld, Jakob Friedrich 6
Birdcage Walk, London 77

Blacking, W.H. Randoll 223
Blake, Sir William 67
Blore, Edward 190, 193
Blücher, Marshall G.L. von 169–70
Blue Room *see* Council Chambers
Blunt, Anthony 231
Board of Green Cloth 124, 125, 157, 175, 185
bookcases 31, 34, 139, *139*, 142, 164
Bothmer, Johann Kaspar ('Hans') von 129, *130*
Boudoir 210–11, Plan D
Boyle, Henry, 1st Baron Carleton 114
Bradburn, John 151
Brent, Timothy 171
Brosse, Salomon de 81
Buckingham Palace (formerly House), London
    Edward VII and 212
    George IV and 9–10, 175
    organ from 198
    Queen Victoria and 193, 194
    as the Queen's House 7, 8, *8*, 147, 148
    role of *2*, 4
    William IV and 190
Budé, Jacob de 160
Bunel, Jacob 155, *171*
Burnet, Gilbert, Bishop of Salisbury 72
Bushe-Fox, Jocelyn 219
Bushnell, John 87
buttery 37–8, *37*, *58–9*
Byrd, William 124

cabinet room 36, 52–3, 60
Calvert, George, 1st Baron Baltimore 38, 39
Cambridge, Duke and Duchess of *see* Adolphus; Augusta of Hesse-Kassel
Campbell, Colen 125–6
Campbell, Smith & Co. 222–3
Canaletto, Antonio 173
canopies 92, 108, 109, 127, 152, 153, 154, 157, 183, *183*
Carlton House, London 8, 9, *9*, 114, 143, 160, 161–2, 184, 185
Caroline of Ansbach, Queen (wife of George II)
    apartments 129
    death of 143–4
    library 5, 6, 131–2, 137, *137–42*, 139, 141, 188, Plan C
    Somerset House, use of 7
Caroline of Brunswick, Queen (wife of George IV) 159–60, *159*
carpets *see* floor coverings
Carr, Robert 152, 157
Carter, Edward 57, 62
Carter, Francis 35
Catherine of Braganza, Queen (wife of Charles II) 5, 74, 79–80, 81, 82, 83, 84, *93*, 98, 128
Catholicism, Roman 38, 53–4, *55*, 95; *see also* anti-Catholicism; Popish Plot
Cavendish, William, 1st Duke of Newcastle 33
Cavendish, William, 6th Duke of Devonshire 183
Cecil, Robert, 1st Earl of Salisbury 30–1, 34, 36

Cecil, William, Lord Cranborne 32, 33
Cecilia, St 128, *128*, 156
ceilings
    Banqueting Room 184, *184*
    Chapel Royal *vi*, 22–3, *23*, 27, *98*, 191, 192
    coves 139, 180, *182*, 183, *183*
    papers 209, *209*, 210, 211
Chadwick, James 198
Chaloner, Sir Thomas 31, 36
Chambers, Sir William 156, 158
Champaigne, Philippe de 155
chandeliers 134, 214, *215*, 216
Chapel Royal *Plans A, B, C, D*
    baptisms 135, 200, 236, *237*, 246 n. 214
    bomb damage 225, 227
    Catholic images 56
    ceilings *vi*, 22–3, *23*, 27, *98*, 191, 192
    charges for 191–2
    closet 71, 104, 171
    galleries 192
    Georgian period 130, 131, 158, *163*
    organs 30, 192, 200
    Queen Anne and *106*, 107–8
    Restoration period 71, 93
    role of 5
    services of thanksgiving 131, 135
    Stuart period 50
    Tudor period 20, 21–3, *23*, 27, 30, *98*
    20th- and 21st-century restoration 228, *228–9*, 236
    weddings 134, 135, *147*, 194, 198–200, *199–200*, *210*, 246 n. 214
    William and Mary and *98*, 98, 102, 104
    William IV and *174*, 192
chapels 4–5
    Denmark House 38, 42, 44, 54
    Dutch chapel 130–1, 158–9, 167
    French chapel 130, 158–9, *163*
    German or Lutheran chapel 130, *163*
    at Greenwich Palace 21–2
    Huguenot chapel 130–1, 158–9
    at Marlborough House 214
    Russian Orthodox chapel, Clarence House 196, *196*
    at Somerset House 81, 82
    at Whitehall Palace 94, 95
    see also Chapel Royal; Queen's Chapel
Chapman, Clement 34
Charing Cross, London 66
Charles, Prince of Wales 233, 235–6, *236–7*
Charles I, King 43–60
    art collection 5, 51–2, *51*
    childhood 31, 32, 33, 66
    Civil War 54, 57
    Commonwealth sales 61
    gardens 45–50, *45*, *47–9*
    growth of Westminster 67
    land granted to 64–5
    marriage negotiations 38, 42, 43
    nursery 50–1

portrait *51*, 52
as Prince of Wales 37, 38
redecoration of St James's 43
trial and execution 57, 60
war with Scotland 53
Charles II, King 71–2, 78–88
    birth 45
    Catholics, expulsion of 82
    childhood 44, 50–1, *50*
    Civil War 54
    dancing *102*, 103
    garden 78, *79*
    household 51
    marriage 74
    marriages of nieces 89–90, *91*
    Queen's Chapel 78–88, *80*, *84–7*
    St James's Park 76–7, *76–8*
Charles VI, Holy Roman Emperor 128
Charlotte, Princess of Wales (dau. of George IV) 190
Charlotte of Mecklenburg-Strelitz, Queen (wife of George III) 7, 147–8, *147*, 152, 153–5, *154*, 160
Chatsworth House (Derbyshire) 183
Chawner, Thomas 168, *169*
Chettle, George 223–4, 228
childbirth 44–5, 92, 95–7, *96*, 143
children, royal
    of Charles I 44, *44*, 50–1, 54–5, *55*, 56, 57, *58–9*
    of Frederick, Prince of Wales 143
    of George II 123, 126, 129, *130*
    heirs to the throne 4, 7, 11, 19
    of Henry VIII 19
    of James I 30–2
    of James II 88, 89, 95–7, *96*
chimneypieces
    Armoury *171*, 178, 205–6
    ballroom 180, *180*
    Banqueting Room 184–5, *185*
    closet 73
    Entrée Gallery 191
    Guard Room 180
    Picture Gallery 211, 214
    Presence Chamber 73
    Queen Caroline's library 137, 139, *139*, 177, 180
    Queen's Chapel *39*, 40, 84
    see also fireplaces
Christian VII, King of Denmark 149, *149*
Churchill, Sarah, 1st Duchess of Marlborough 99, 105, *112–13*, 114
Churchill, Sir Winston 225, 234
Civil War defences *55*, 68–9, *68*
Clarence, Dukes of *see* Albert Victor (Eddy); William IV
Clarence House
    Arthur, Duke of Connaught, use by 214, 218
    charitable events 224–5
    cinema 233
    creation of 114, 162, 188–9
    film screening at 212
    Queen Victoria, alterations of 195–6, *196*

    20th-century refurbishment 232–6, *233*, *235–7*, Plan D
    use of 1, 4, 11
    William IV, use by *189*, 190
Clarendon House, London 72, *78*
Clark, Kenneth 224
Cleer, William 241 n. 75
Cleyn, Francis 43
Clifford, Richard 15
clocks 109, 210, *210*, 225
coach houses 33, 73, 83, 111, 151
Cobb, John *152*, 153, *155*, 156, 157
coffee houses 105
coffee room 185–6
Coke, Mary, Viscountess 149
Colefax, Sibyl 220
collections 5
    books and manuscripts 33, 34, 99
    coins and medals 36, 60
    during Commonwealth 61
    of Consul Joseph Smith 172–3
    curiosities 36
    of Gonzaga dukes of Mantua 49, 52
    inventories 25, 52, 61, 93, 95, 128, 129, 155, 172–3
    Marlborough House, displayed in 196
    sculptures 49, 61
    during wars 60, 216, 224
    see also paintings; portraits
Collinet, Hubert 192–3
Coloma, Don Carlos 38
colonnades 48, *48*, *107*, 108, 161, *163*, 186, *186*, 193, 204, Plan B
Colour Court 1
    colonnade *107*, 108, 186, *186*, 193, 204, Plan B
    corridor 203–4, *204*
    excavations 17, *17*, 218–19
    external arcade 203, *204*, Plan D
    keeper's lodgings 111, Plan C
    Tudor period 21, 22, 25, Plan A
    Tyburn river 13
Colt, Maximilian 34
Colvin, Sir Howard 2
Commonwealth sales 61
conduit house 21, 30, 66
Connaught, Duke of *see* Arthur, Duke of Connaught
Constitution Hill, London 76
Conway, Edward, 1st Viscount 38
Cooke, Henry 129
Cookes, Henry 142
Cornforth, John 235
Correggio, Antonio da 109
Correr, Marc Antonio 36
corridors 202, *203*, 204
Cosimo III, Grand Duke of Tuscany 82
Cotton, Sir Robert Bruce 34, 99, 126
Cotton, Sir Thomas 57
Cotton House, London 99
Coulommiers, France, Capuchin church of 81
Council Chambers

INDEX   275

Blue Room 210
furniture 157
nursery, used as 88
paintings in 128
plays in 35, 38
Queen Anne 20, *84-5*, 106-7, 108-9, *108*, Plan D
Restoration period 95
Tudor 27, 28, Plans A, C
weddings 246 n. 214
William Morris decoration 210, *211*
Court of St James's 4, 8-9, 150, 236
courtiers at St James's 30, 31, 77, 98, 103, 111, *112-14*, 113-15, 129, *130*, 156
Covent Garden, London 67
Cowper, William 204, 205
Crace, John G. 205
Craig, Charles 167
Crane, Walter 210
Creevy, Thomas 189
Crocker, Edward 175, 180
Croft, William 131
Cromwell, Oliver 62
Cromwell, Thomas 18, 22, 23-4
Cumberland, Dukes of *see* Ernest, King of Hanover; William, Duke of Cumberland
Curia, Rome *40*, 41
Cust, Sir Lionel 213, 214

D'Almain, George, jnr 183
dancing *102-3*, 103-4, 186, 193
Danvers, Henry, 1st Earl of Danby 46-7, 69
Davies estate 65, *65*
debts, royal 61, 74
Defoe, Daniel 6-7
Denham, Sir John 71, 72
Denmark House, London 38, 42, 43-4, 46, 49, 54; *see also* Somerset House
Denny, Sir Anthony 18
Derand, Père François 86, *86*
Devereux, Robert, 3rd Earl of Essex 32, 33
D'Ewes, Sir Simonds 60
Dickinson, William 19, *20*, 23, *106*, 108, *108*, 110, 114
Dillon, Wentworth, 4th Earl of Roscommon 115
dining rooms 23, 155, 161, 162, 164, 165, 221, *222*, 230
Dobson, William 156
Doort, Abraham van der 51, 52
Drawing Rooms 88, 109, 124, 127-8, 148, *150*, 160, 180, *180*, 186, 192, 200-2, *201*, 203-4, *203*, 207-8
Dudley, Robert, 1st Earl of Leicester 30
Duncan, Isley 233
Durie, John 60, 92

Eden, Anthony 225
Edge, Thomas 187, *187*
Edinburgh, Dukes of *see* Alfred; Philip
Edward, Duke of Kent (son of George III) 160, 162, 164
Edward VI, King 28, 33
Edward VII, King 11, 196-7, 203, 212, *212-15*, *212-14*
Edward VIII, King 11, *195*, 217, 219-23, *221-3*
Efendi, Yusuf Agah 160
Elden Ltd 220-1
Elizabeth, Queen of Bohemia (dau. of James I) 31, 37
Elizabeth, Queen, The Queen Mother (wife of George VI) 11, 225, 234-5

Elizabeth I, Queen 29-30, 33
Elizabeth II, Queen
    accession of *3*, 3
    chapel restorations *226-9*, 227-9
    Clarence House, residence at 11, 232-6, *233*, 235-7
    State Apartments 231-2
Elliott, Charles 164
Elliott, Thomas 192
Elliott, Wallace 225
Embree, John 62
Engine Court *x*, 1, 160, 161, *161*, 163, 204, 206-7, *208*, Plan D
entrances 25; *see also* gates; gateways; Great Gatehouse
Entrée Gallery 191
Entrée Room 180-1, *182*, 183, 186, 205, 210, 211, Plan D
Ernest, Duke of Mecklenburg-Strelitz 157, *163*
Ernest, King of Hanover, Duke of Cumberland (son of George III) 164, *164-5*, *165*, 166, 168, 189, 194
Ernest Augustus, Duke of Brunswick-Lüneburg 119-20
Eton College (Berkshire) 16, 18
Evelyn, John 72, 98
Eye, Manor of, London 65, *65*

Faithorne, William *31*, 32, 46, 63, 64
Faulkner, Kate 211, *211*
Ferdinand, count d'Adda 95
Fetti, Domenico 173
Finch, Lady Charlotte 151, *151*, *163*, 167
fireplaces
    Clarence House 234
    library 34, *34*, 99
    Queen Anne Room 231, *231*
    Tapestry Room *12*, 24, *24*, 178, 180, 206
    see also chimneypieces
fires 83-4, 167, *167*
fireworks 145-6, *145*
First World War 216
Fisher, Richard 221
Fitzalan, Henry, 12th Earl of Arundel 28
Fitzroy, Henry, Duke of Richmond 23
Flitcroft, Henry 135, *136*
floor coverings 27, 156, 162, 204, 208-9
Ford, Oliver 234-5
Fort Belvedere, Windsor 220, 221
Fowle, Alphonsus 46
Fowler, John 28
France, William 152, 155, 161, 162, 164, 166
Frederick, Duke of York (son of George III) 8, 162, 175, 187-8
Frederick, Prince of Wales (son of George II) 7, 8, 123, 134, 135-6, 141, 143, 145, 181, *181*
Freud, Lucian 232
friars 44, 54, 80, 87-8
friary 80-2, *80*, 83-4, *84-5*, *87*, 95, 100-1, 114, Plans B, C
Friary Court 1, *3*, 3, 4, 190, 216, *216*, 219, 220, 225
furniture
    bedchamber 141-2
    chapel 132-3, *133*, 134, 192
    Clarence House 233-4
    library 139, *139*
    mourning 144
    nursery 143, 157
    office 136

porcelain, display of 136
princes' apartments 160, 161, 162, 164, *165*, 165-6
State Apartments 151-5, *152*, *154-5*
tables *143*
York House 221-2, *223*
see also bookcases; tables

galleries
    chapel 111, Plan C
    Chapel Royal 192
    Entrée Gallery 191
    Stuart 34-5
    Tudor 24, 26-7, 28, 52, 72, 73, 89, Plans A, C
Gammon, Leonard 71
Gandhi, Mahatma 216, *218*
gardeners 47, 77, 78
gardens 1, 45-50, *90*, *91*
    annexed to Whitehall 77, *117*
    food, grown in 78
    garden walls *197*
    Mollet, designed by 75, 77, *77-9*, *78*
    mulberry 31, 65, *65*, 69
    orchard 46, 48, 49, 64, 77, 78, *84-5*, 112
    parterres 47, *47*, *90*, *91*
    physic 58-9, 64, 239 n. 154
    ponds *76*, *117*
    privy garden 45-6, *45*, 47-8, *47*, 49, *49*, 112, *117*
    sculpture gallery 48-9, *48-9*
    Spring Garden 22, 46, 49-50, 77-8, *78*, *117*
    tiltyard 46, 48
garderobes 89, 90
garrison 60-1, 71
gate lodges 195, *196*
gatehouse *see* Great Gatehouse
gates 48, *48*, 178, *178-9*, 186, *197*, Plan D
Gates, William 160
Gennari, Benedetto *91*, 93-4, *94-5*, *94*, 156
George of Denmark, Prince (husband of Queen Anne) 91, 102, 106, 109-10
George I, King 119-31
    alterations and furnishings 125-6, *125-6*, 128-9, *130*
    arrival in London 122-3, *122*
    background 119-21
    Hanover, returns to 123, 243 n. 10
    improvement schemes 6, 121, *121*
    palaces, use of 123
    and Prince of Wales 7, 123-4, 125
    public appearances 124
    visitors to St James's 126-7
George II, King 7, 131-46
    arrival in London 122, *122*
    courtly glory of 6-7
    expulsion of 7, 123-4
    exterior works 144-5, *144*
    fireworks 145-6, *145*
    Hanover, returns to 243 n. 10
    at Leicester House 7
    library of Queen Caroline 131-2, 137, *137-42*, 139, 141
    mistresses 129, 137
    music 135
    portrait *201*
    Queen Caroline, death of 143-4
    return of 125
    Royal Mews 131
    royal weddings 132-5

276 ST JAMES'S PALACE

State Apartments 141-3, 146
George III, King 146-61
 baptisms 246 n. 214
 birth 143
 and Buckingham House 7
 building work 151
 and Carlton House 8
 chapels 158
 court events and visitors 148-51, *148-51*
 courtiers 156
 Gatehouse 157
 larders and offices 156-7
 library 141
 marriage 147-8, *147*
 nursery 157
 portrait 181
 redecoration 158
 reign 146-7
 State Apartment 151-5, *152, 155*, 170
 weddings 246 n. 214
George IV, King 175-89
 birth 157
 and Buckingham House 9-10, 175
 Drawing Rooms and balls 186-7
 Grand Service *186*, 187
 Hanover, visit to 243 n. 10
 marriage 159-60, *159*
 Nash, work with 175, 176
 neo-Tudor work 178, *179*, 180
 opulence, liking for 180
 portrait *182-3*, 183
 private apartments 185-6
 proclamation of 175
 reclusiveness of 187
 State Apartments 176-84, *177-85*
George V, King 194, *195*, 200, 214, 215-19, *216-19*
George VI, King 223-5, 227
Gibbons, Grinling 86, 87, 183
Gilbert, Sir Alfred 217-18, *219*, 232
Gilbert, Sarah 139, 141
Giovane, Palma 36
Gleichen, Lady Feodora 232
Gleichen, Victor, Count 232
Gloucester, Duke of *see* William, Duke of Gloucester
Godolphin, Sidney, 1st Earl 113-14
Godolphin House, London 8, *77*, 100-1, *112-13*, 113-14, *117*, 187
Gonzaga dukes of Mantua, art collection of 49, 52
Goodison, Benjamin 132-3, 134, 136, 139, 141, 142, 144, 145, 153, 157
Goring, Sir George 31, 67
Goring House, London 31, *66*, 67, 69
Gossett, Charles 190-1
Government School of Design 196
Grammatica, Antiveduto 62
Granville, John, 1st Earl of Bath 72
Great Gatehouse 1, 19, *20-1*, 21, 25, *40*, *112*, 157, *163*, 175, *220*, 242 n. 133, *Plan A*
great halls 23
Great Stairs/Grand Staircase *20*, 25, *208*, 209-10, 213, *213*, *Plans A, C, D*
Green Park, London 63, 77, 146, 147, 187
Greenwich Palace 17, 21-2, 52, 73
Grosvenor estate 65, *65*
Groves, John Thomas 162, 164
guard chambers *20*, 25, 73, *171*, 180, *Plans A, C*
Guard Room 180, 205, *210*, 211, *Plan D*

guard room, Engine Court 160, 161, *161*, 163, *189*, 206-7, *208*, 230, *Plan D*
Gurle, Leonard 78
Gwillim, William 157
Gwyn, Nell 75

Hall, Benjamin 198, 202
Hamilton, Lord Claud 225
Hampton Court Palace, London
 bronzes *49*
 chimneypiece sent to 73
 George I and 6
 Great Hall 23
 holyday closet 27
 nursery 24, 27
 portraits from 210
 Queen's Gallery 35
 tapestries from 143, 200
 tennis court 32
 terracotta roundels 26
 William and Mary at 97, 98
Handel, George Frederick 131, 134, 135, 146, 244 n. 61
Hanneman, Adriaen 156
Harley, Sir Robert 54, 56
Harman, R.S.O. 219
Harrington House, London *189*, 195
Harrison, Thomas 61
Hawksmoor, Nicholas 77, *77*, *106*, 107, 113, *124*, 125
Hayward, Richard 47
Heasman, A.W. 223
heating 178; *see also* chimneypieces; fireplaces
Hedges, Sir Charles 110, *112*, 114, 115
heirs to the throne 4, 7, 11, 19
Henderson, James 183
Henrietta, Princess (dau. of Charles I) 73-4
Henrietta Maria, Queen (wife of Charles I) 4, 5, 43-5, 46-7, 50, 54, 73-4
Henry, Prince of Wales (son of James I) 5, 21, *22*, 31-3, *31-3*, *35*, 46, 66, 68
Henry IV, King 15
Henry V, King 15-16
Henry VI, King 16
Henry VIII, King 4, 17-19, *20-4*, 21-5, 46
Herbert, Sir Thomas 57
Herbert, William, 3rd Earl of Pembroke 38
Heritage, Thomas 19
Herrenhausen Palace (Hanover) 120, *120*
Hervey, John, 2nd Baron 6
Hilens, Shadrick 76, *117*
Hinchliff, Thomas 153, 157
Holland, Cornelius 54-5, 56
Holland, H. & R. 198
Holland, Henry 178
Holland & Sons 204
Hollar, Wenceslaus 21, *21*, 68
holyday closet 27, 45, *Plans A, C*
Hooper, William 6
Hospital of St Giles, London 13, *14*, 66
Hospital of St James, Westminster 13-17, *14*
Houses of Parliament, London 2, 10
Howard, Henrietta, Countess of Suffolk 129, 137
Howard, Philip 79, 80, 81, 82, 95
Howard, Thomas, 1st Earl of Berkshire 31, 67
Howard, Thomas, 14th Earl of Arundel 31, 67
Howard, William, 1st Viscount Stafford 31, 68, *78*
Huddleston, John 78-9, 82
Hunt, Thomas Frederick 176, 178, 180, 189

hunting 65, 66
Hussey, Christopher 232
Huysmans, Jacob 85, 86, 128
Hyde, Edward, 1st Earl of Clarendon 72, *78*
Hyde Park, London 65-6

inner court 19, 24, 25-6, *Plan A*
ironwork 187, 189
Itesamuddin, Mirza Sheikh 149

Jack, J.F.S. 224
James Edward, Prince (the Old Pretender) 95-7, *96*
James I, King 4, 33, 37, 43, 64, 65, 67
James II, King 73, 88-94, *89*, *91*
 childhood 50, 54, 57
 inventories 92-4, 95
 lodgings 74, *84-5*
 marriages 72, 82
 return to London 56
 Roman Catholicism of 82, 94, 95
Jeffrey & Co. 210
Jenkinson, Robert, 2nd Earl of Liverpool 175, 185
Jensen, Gerrit 129
Jermyn, Henry, 1st Earl of St Albans 74
Johnstone & Jeanes 204
Jones, George 183
Jones, Inigo
 chimneypiece 184-5, *185*
 Civil War, during 56-7
 gate, designs for 48, *48*
 Queen's Chapel 39, *39-40*, 40-2, *42*
 as Surveyor of the King's Works 35, 38
Jordan, Mrs Dorothea 188
Justel, Henri 98

Kemp, Thomas 16
Kensington Palace, London
 background 6, *7-8*
 chimneypieces from 177, 180, *180*, 231, *231*
 Edward, Duke of Kent 162, 164
 George I and George II 123, 131
 William and Mary 97-8
Kent, Duke and Duchess of *see* Edward, Duke of Kent; Victoria, Duchess of Kent
Kent, William 131-2, 137, *137*-42, 139, 146, 184-5, *185*
Ker, Jane, Countess of Roxburghe 50
Kielmansegg, Sophia von, Countess of Darlington and Leinster 123
Kielmansegge, Frederick von 148
Kime, Robert 235
King's Closet 146, 167, 183; *see also* Audience Chamber; Royal Closet
King's College, Cambridge 22-3
Kip, Johannes *70*, 75, 111, *112*, 115, *116-17*
Kitchen Court 23, 24, 125, *179*, *Plan C*
Kitchener, Horatio Herbert, Earl 216
kitchens
 King's 125, *125-6*, 163, *Plan D*
 pastry 110, 111, 161, *163*, 247 n. 236
 Tudor *20*, 23, 27, *58-9*, 110, 111, *112*, *Plan A*
Kneller, Sir Godfrey 110, 128
Knyff, Leonard 115, *116-17*
Koopman, Elias 212
Kynwolmersh, William 15

La Rochefoucauld, François de 156
Laking, Guy Francis 214, *215*
lamp posts 187, *187*, *197*
Lancaster House, London 1, 8, 188
laundry 151, *151*, *163*
Lawrence, Henry 62
Lawrence, Sir Thomas 181, *182-3*, 183
Le Sueur, Hubert 49, *49*
Leach, F.R. & Sons of Cambridge 210
Lehmann, E.G. 220
Leicester House, London 7, 31, 66, 67-8, 69, *78*, 124, 143
Leineschloss, Hanover 120
Lely, Peter 93, 156, *156*
leper hospitals 13-17, *14*
Levee Room 145, *172*
levees 10, *10*, 148, 160, 192, 200, 201-3, 212, *212*, 216, 223
Leverton, Thomas 168, *169*
Lewis, George Cornewall 202
Leyburn, John 95
librarians 33-4, 60, 92, 98, 141
libraries
    Commonwealth 60, 61, 62
    of the friary 81, 83, 95
    George I 126
    of Henry, Prince of Wales 5, 33-4, *34*, 99
    public, proposals for 60, 99
    Queen Caroline's 5, 6, 84-5, 131-2, 137, *137-42*, *139*, *141*, *142*, *163*, 180, 188, Plan C
    Restoration 92-3
    of Sir Robert Cotton 99
    William and Mary 98-9
    York House 222, *223*
light fittings 133-4, *133*, 139, 142, 154, 155, 178, 180, 184, 214, *215*, 216
    electric 212, 215
    gas 173, 187, *187*, 200, 205, 212
    oil 180
    see also chandeliers; lamp posts
Llewellyn, Sir William 222
lodgings
    housekeeper's 37-8, *37*, *58-9*
    for James and Anne, Duke and Duchess of York 72-3, *74*
    of James II 74, 95, 98
    keeper's 111, Plan C
    library keeper's *87*, 92, 99, *99*
    of Mary II *20*, 88, *89*, Plan B
    of Mary of Modena 91
    at Newmarket 42, *42*
    of Queen Anne *84-5*, 88-9, *90*, Plan C
    Tudor 23-4, *24*, 25-6, *26*, Plan A
    see also apartments; bedchambers; friary; nurseries; State Apartments; State Bedchamber
Long, Charles, 1st Baron Farnborough 164, 176, 181, 184, 186
Lotti, Ottaviano 36
Louis, Prince (of Cambridge) 236, *237*
Loutherbourg, Philip James de 181, *183*
Lovegrove, William 158
Lozer, Gideon 32
Lumley, John, 1st Baron 33
Lumsden, Archibald 32-3
lying in state 29, 37, 43, 102, 188, *188*
lying-in preparations *see* childbirth

MacEune, Priscilla 157
Mansart, François 81
Margaret, Princess (dau. of George VI) 234
Maria Anna of Spain 38
Marie de' Medici, Dowager Queen of France 26, *26*, 46, 53-4
Marlborough House, London 2, 11, *112-13*, 114, 132, *179*, 190, 196-7, *197*, 198, 214, 218, 225
Marlborough Road 197-8, *197*
Marsh, Thomas B. 168
Mary, Princess (dau. of George II) 134-5
Mary, Princess (dau. of James I) 31
Mary, Queen (wife of George V) 194, *195*, 200, 222, 223-4
Mary I, Queen 28-9
Mary II, Queen *20*, 88, 89-90, Plan C
Mary of Modena, Queen (wife of James II)
    children 89
    conspiracy 95-7, *96*
    marriage 82, 88
    oratory 89, 90-1, 93-4, *94*, Plan C
    at St James's 5
Matilda, Queen (wife of Henry I) 13
Matted Hall 104, 184, 211, Plan D
Maugham, Syrie 220
May, Adrian 76
May, Hugh 71, 76
menagerie 66, 77
military ground 66, 68
mirrors 129, 142, 153, 157, 164, 165, 211, 221, *222*; *see also* pier glasses
Mollet, André 47-8, *47*, 49, 77, *78*
Monck, George 62-3
Moore, Jonas 69, 75, *75*
Morgan, William 46, 77, *78*
Morris, Marshall, Faulkner & Co. 205
Morris, William 180, 183, 185, 208-10, *208-10*
Mountbatten, Louis, 1st Earl 233
mulberry garden *31*, 65, *65*, 69
Musard, Phillipe 192-3, 250 n. 150
music 131, 134, 135

Naish, Katherine 151-2, 153, 154, 157
Napper, John 229, 236
Nash, John 9-10, 168, 170-1, 175-6, 189
Nayler, Sir George 190
Nedeham, James 18, 19
Nemon, Oscar 232
Newcourt, Richard *31*, 32, 46, 63
Newmarket (Cambridgeshire) 42, *42*
Newton, Adam 31, 33
Norden, John 62
Norfolk House, London 143
nurseries 24, 27, 31, 50-1, 88, *89*, 90, 97, 100-1, 143, 157

Office of Works
    Elizabethan 30
    floor plans *193*
    George I, proposal for 121
    and historic remains 219, *220*
    and John Nash 170-1, 175-6
    under Prince Henry 33, 35
    Queen Anne, proposals for 107-8
    Queen Charlotte's apartment 154-5
    records of 2, 25
    Restoration period 72, 74
Ogilvy, David, 13th Earl of Airlie 228, 230

Oglethorpe, Sir Theophilus 77, 113
oratory 73, 89, 91, 93-4, *94*, Plan C
Oratory (Paris) 81, 85
organs 30, 79, 98, 192, 198, 200, 223-4, Plans A, C
Orgrave, Thomas 15, 16
Osborne, Thomas, 1st Duke of Leeds 103
Outer Court *see* Colour Court

paintings
    Charles I collection 51-2, *51*
    Henry, Prince of Wales collection 5, *35*, 36
    history 95, 181, *181*, 183, 205
    overdoors *35*, 36, 90, *184*
    religious 61-2, 93-4, 94-5, *94*, 109, 110, 128, *128*, 172
    Second World War, rehang after 231
    see also portraits
palace, definition of 3-4, 242 n. 156
Palazzo della Cancelleria, Rome 22
Palazzo Te, Mantua 22
Pall Mall, London 63, 75, *75*, 112, 132, 224, 225
Palladio, Andrea 41, 48, *48*
panelling 34-5, 72, 73, 90
Parkinson, John 47, 64, 239 n. 154
Parr, David 210
Parran, Benjamin 160
parterres *see* gardens
pastry house 110, *111*
pastry kitchen 161, *163*, 247 n. 236
Peacham, Henry 49
Peel, Sir Robert 193-4
Peers, Charles 219
'pell mell' 31-2, *32-3*, *58-9*, 64, 75, *117*
Pemberton-Piggott, Viola 232
Penn, Arthur 234
Pennethorne, James 196-7, 198
Pepys, Samuel 76, 79, 80, 81
Percival, L.J. 223
Percy, Algernon, 10th Earl of Northumberland 56, *57*
Percy, Elizabeth, Duchess of Northumberland (wife of 1st Duke) 148-9
Perry, William 178, 180
Peruzzi, Baldassare 22
Peter, Hugh 60
Philip, HRH Duke of Edinburgh 233, *233*
Phipps, John 202, *203*, 204
picture galleries 5, 36, 204
Picture Gallery 211, 214, *215*, Plan D
pier glasses 141, 156, 162, 180, *182*
Place, Francis 168
plays, performance of 35, 38, 51, 88
Ponsonby, Sir Henry 207-8
Ponsonby, Spencer 203-4
Popish Plot (1678) 82, 90-1
Porcellis, Jan *35*, 36
portraits
    Charles I (Van Dyck) *51*, 52
    classical 52
    courtiers 61, 129
    George III hang 155-6, *156*, *171*
    George IV (Lawrence) *182-3*, 183
    Henry, Prince of Wales (Peake) *21*, 22
    historical 205
    military 95
    modern 234
    Queen Anne hang 109, *110*
    Queen Victoria *183*, *184*, 221

royalty, British 181, 184, *201*, 204, 205, 210, 222
royalty, European 5, 25, 128, 146, 172–3
Sarah Churchill's daughters (Kneller) 110, 128
'Windsor Beauties' (Lely) 93
Portuguese community 81, 82
Pratt, Sir Roger 72, *78*
Presence Chamber 20, Plans A, C
 chimneypieces 73
 furnishings 24, 92, 142, 152, 155–6
 paintings *171*, 172
 tapestries 129, 142–3
 terracotta roundels 26, *26*
 see also Tapestry Room
Pride, Thomas 61, 62
priests 43–4
Prior, Matthew 6
Privy Chamber 20, 26, 37, 129, 142, 143, 152, 156, *156*, Plans A, C
privy closet 79, 83
Privy Court 27, 73, *Plan A*; see also Bay Court
Privy Gallery 26–7, *Plan A*
privy kitchen 27, *Plan A*
Puget de la Serre, J. 52, 53
pulpits 30, 80, 83
Pyne, William Henry 171–2, *171–3*, 178

Queen Anne Room 180–1, *180*, 186, 188, *188*, 205, 210, 216, *217–18*, 231, *231*, Plan D
Queen's Chapel 1, 4, 5, Plans B, C
 construction of 38–44, *39–40*, *42*, 54, 106
 dome 84–5, *84–5*
 Georgian period 130
 as German chapel 158–9, 171, *173*, *179*, 197–8, *197*, *199*, 214
 James II 94–5, *94*
 organs 79, 98, 198, 223–4
 Parliamentary reformation of 56
 rebuilding after fire 84–5, 86–8, *86–7*, 100–1
 Restoration period 71, 74, 78–84, *80*
 20th century 223–4, *225*, 227–8
 20th-century 226–7
 weddings 133–4, *133*, 159–60, *159*, 246 n. 214
Queen's House see Buckingham Palace
Queen's House, Greenwich 184–5, *185*
Queen's Stairs see Sovereign's Stairs

Read, Charles 219
Recouchez, Louis 15
Redgrave, Richard 204–5
Reni, Guido 110
reservoir 187, 195, *196*
Richard II, King 13, 15
Richardson, Charles James 192
Richmond Palace 21
riding house 33, *33*, 73, 110, *112*
Robson and Hale 184
Romano, Giulio 22, 52, 62
Rose, John 78
Ross, Thomas *87*, 92, *99*
Rossetti, Dante Gabriel 205
Rotherham, Thomas 71
Royal Closet 200, *201*; see also Audience Chamber; King's Closet
Royal Collection Department 228
Royal Mews *2*, *14*, 33, 63, *66*, 131
Rupert, Prince of the Rhine 77, *112*
Ruskin, John 205

Russell, John 160, 162, 164, 165, 166
Russell, Richard 79
Ryder, Dudley 105
Rysbrack, John Michael 139, *142*

Sackville, Mary, Countess of Dorset 56
St Anne's church, Soho 98
St James's parish, London
 changes in 105
 St James's church, Piccadilly 75
 St James's fair 64, 75
 St James's Field 63–4, *64*, 69
 St James's Park 21, 65, *65*–6, 66–7, 76–7, *76–8*
 St James's Square 74–5
 St James's Street 63, 64, 65
St Martin's parish, London 67, 75
Salviati, Vincenzo 36
Santa Maria Nova, Vicenza 41, *41*
Saussure, César de 127–8
Schiavone, Andrea 93, *94*
Schloss Herrenhausen, Hanover 120, *120*
Schrijver, Herman 220–2
Schulenburg, Ehrengard von der, Duchess of Kendal and Munster 123, 129
sculpture gallery 48–9, *48–9*
sculptures 49, 61
Second World War 224–5, *224*
Sellis, Joseph 168
Serlio, Sebastiano 22
Servi, Constantino de' 36
service court 110, 111, 112, Plan A
sewers 146, 166, 241 n. 55
Seymour, Edward, 1st Duke of Somerset 28
Seymour, Francis, 5th Marquess of Hertford 208
Seymour, Thomas, 1st Baron 28
Sheppard, Edgar 206, 215
Sidney, Robert, 2nd Earl of Leicester 31, 67–8
silk industry 65
Simpson, James 187
Simpson, Wallis 221
Smirke, Robert 187–8, 192, 195
Smirke, Sydney 189, 190
Smith, Consul Joseph 172–3
Smith, William 35
Smythson, John 37, *37*
Smythson, Robert 33, *33*
Soane, Sir John 10, 160–1, *161*, *163*
Somer, Paul van 110, 173
Somerset House, London
 art and furniture to/from 61, 83, 87, 155
 chandelier from 134
 friary 78, 82, 83
 royal use of 7
 see also Denmark House
Sophia Dorothea (wife of George I) 123
Southern, Thomas 105
Sovereign's Stairs *209*, 213–14, *214*
Sprimont, Nicholas 187
stable yard 73, 111, *136*, *163*
Stable Yard House *124*, 125, 228, 230–1
Stable Yard Lodge 195, *196*
Stafford House, London see Lancaster House
staircases 20, 25, 84–5, 178, 202, *202*, 208–9, *209*–10, 213–14, *213–14*, 216, Plans A, C, D
State Apartments 1, Plan D
 George I 121, *121*, 128–9
 George II 141–3, 146
 George III 151–5, *152*, *154*, 170

George IV 176–84, *177–85*
Queen Anne 108–9, *108*
Queen Victoria 201
20th century 212, 216–17, *218*, 231–2
William Morris decoration in 210–11, *211*
State Bedchamber 127, 141–2, 156, *157*
stencilling 180, *183*, 205, 206, *207*, 210
Stephenson, Benjamin 177, 180, 189, 192
Storr, Paul 186, 187
Stuart, John, 3rd Earl of Bute 156
Stuart, Ludovic, 10th Seigneur d'Aubigny 79
Summerson, Sir John 228
supper room 184–5, *184–5*
suttling house 160, *161*, *163*
Sutton, Robert, 2nd Baron Lexington 113
Swift, Jonathan 109
Sydenham, John de 15

tables 32, 129
Taitt, Richard 165, 166
tapestries 53, 56, 92, *93*, 128–9, 130, 142–3, 145, 156, *172*, 200
Tapestry Room Plan D
 fireplace *12*, 24, *24*, 178, 180, 206
 19th-century redecoration 180, 205, 206, *206–7*
 see also Presence Chamber
Tapling, T. & Co. 204
Tapster, Thomas 187
Tart Hall, London *31*, 46, 67, 69
Tatham, Charles Heathcote 178
Taylor, George Warrington 205
Taylor, John 194, 197, 206–7, *208*
tennis courts *31*, 32, *58–9*, 80
terracotta busts 139, *142*
terracotta roundels 25–6, *26*, 73
textiles 79, 92–3, 110, 142, 146, 152, 153, 155, 157, 162, 164, 165, 201, 204, 210, 211; see also tapestries
Thirlby, Thomas 19
Throne Room 180–1, *182–3*, 183, 201, 204, 205, 210, 211, *212*, Plan D
Tiarini, Alessandro 128, *128*
tiles 17, *17*, 219
tiltyard 46, 48
Tite, William 197
Titian 52, 62
Tompion, Thomas 109
Torshell, Samuel 55
Trento, Lodovico 41
Treswell, Ralph 64, *64*
Turner, J.M.W. *181*, 183
Turnor, John 241 n. 75
Tyburn river 13–14

upholstery 92, 102, 109, 139, 142, 152, 162, 164

Vampage, Dame Catherine 16
Van Dyck, Sir Anthony 44, *51*, 52
Vanbrugh, Sir John 6, 71, 121, *121*, 125
Vere, Mary, Lady 56
Vernon, Robert 196
Verrio, Antonio 78
Versailles, Palace of (France) 6
Versailles, Treaty of (1919) 216, *216*
Victoria, Duchess of Kent 194, 195, 202
Victoria, Princess Royal (dau. of Queen Victoria) 199–200, *200*

INDEX   279

Victoria, Queen 193–212
    balls 192–3
    Clarence House 195–6, *196*
    demolition proposed 193–4
    Drawing Rooms 200–2, *201*, 203–4, *203*
    German chapel (Queen's chapel) 197–8, *197*, *199*
    levees *10*, 200, 201–3
    Marlborough House 196–7, 198
    redecoration 204–12, *206–11*
    State Apartments 201
    use of St James's 10–11
    weddings 198–200, *199–200*
    York House 194, *195*
Victoria and Albert Museum, London 196
Vile, William 152, *152*, 153, 154, *155*, 156, 157
Villiers, Barbara, Duchess of Cleveland 75
Vroom, Hendrick 36

Waller, Charles Bullen 195–6
Waller & Sons 195
Wallmoden, Amalie von, Countess of Yarmouth 137
wallpapers *208–9*, 209, 210–11, *211*, 221, *221*
Walpole, Horace 146, 147, 148, 149, 153
Walpole, Robert, 1st Earl of Orford 6
Walton, Parry 87, 129
Warwick, Sir Philip 77
water closets 89, 95, 170
water supply 30, 145, 157, 187
Waterloo, Battle of (1815) 170
Waterloo Room *see* Banqueting Room
Watson, Francis 228
Webb, John 40, 56–7, 92, 239 n. 124
Webb, Philip 205–6, *206–7*
weddings 132–5, *133*, *147*, 159–60, *159*, 198–200, *199–200*, 210, 246 n. 214
Weekes, William 139, 141
Weippert, J.M. 192–3, 250 n. 150
Wellesley, Arthur, 1st Duke of Wellington 196
Wentworth, Peter 109
Wescott, J.B. 213
Westminster Abbey, London 2, *14*, 15, 18–19, 66
Westminster Palace, London 2, 4, *14*, 17, 18, 66
White Allom & Co. 213–14, *213–14*
Whitehall Palace, London
    Banqueting House 35, 40, 45, *50*, 103, 104, 107
    cabinet of Charles I 52–3
    chapel 94, 95
    Charles I, execution of 60
    Commonwealth 60–1, *66*

    Edward VI at 28
    fire 104
    galleries 34
    organ 79
    origins of 4, 18, 19
    parks and gardens 77, 78, 82
    tennis court 32
    William and Mary 97, 98
Whitelocke, Bulstrode 60, 62
Wild, Charles 171–2, *171–3*
Willement, Thomas 187
William, Duke of Cumberland (son of George II) 134, 135–6, 145
William, Duke of Gloucester (son of Queen Anne) 102–3, 104–5, 110
William III, King 90, 97, 104
William IV, King 8, 10, 160, 162, 164, *165*, *174*, 188, 190–3, *190–1*
Williams, Henry 133, 134, 142, 143
windows *40*, 41, 79, 180, 185–6, 187, 194, *194*, 229, 236
Windsor, Duke of *see* Edward VIII
Winter & Hay 162, 165
Wolsey, Cardinal Thomas 17
Woodroofe, Edward *89*, 90
Woodward, Hugh 69, 75
Wootton, John 181, *181*
Wraxall, Nathaniel 159
Wren, Sir Christopher
    ballroom *100–1*, 104
    library 34, *34*, 99, *99*
    Marlborough House *112–13*, 114
    nursery 90
    Queen's Chapel 81, 84–6, 241 n. 75
    Whitehall Palace, chapel at 94
Wyatt, Benjamin Dean 187–8
Wyatt, Edward 180, 183, 184
Wyatt, Edward, jun. 195
Wyatt, James 166, 170
Wyatt, Matthew 189
Wyatt, Sir Thomas 28–9
Wyatville, Sir Jeffry 190, *190–1*, 191

Yeomen of the Guard 158, *158*, 163, 230
York House 11, 160, *161*, 194, *195*, 215, 216, 219–23, *221–3*, 228, *Plan D*
York Place, London *14*, 17–18
Yorke, Jemima, 2nd Marchioness Grey 146
Young, Patrick 33–4, 60, 61
Yusuf Agah Efendi 160

ILLUSTRATION CREDITS

Unless otherwise stated, all works reproduced are Royal Collection Trust / © Her Majesty Queen Elizabeth II 2022

Royal Collection Trust / All Rights Reserved: Figs 4.74, 4.75, 4.76, 4.77, 4.78

Royal Collection Trust / © Her Majesty Queen Elizabeth II 2022. Photographer: Peter Smith: front cover, back cover, p. vi; Figs 1.1, 1.3, 1.21, 3.5, 3.7, 4.10, 4.11, 4.12, 4.17, 4.20, 4.45, 4.46, 4.47, 4.48, 4.59, 4.60, 4.63, 4.69, 4.73, 5.1, 5.4, 5.5; photographer: Mark Fiennes: Fig. 5.9; photographer: Christopher Simon Sykes: Figs 5.10, 5.11

Royal Collection Trust would like to thank Bob Marshall for the creation of Figs 1.33, 2.20, 3.22; all figures are Royal Collection Trust / © Her Majesty Queen Elizabeth II 2022

Royal Collection Trust would like to thank MOLA (Museum of London Archaeology) / Juan Jose Fuldain for producing Figs 0.2, 1.2, 1.36, Plans A–D (Plan D was created from an original drawing by Simon Thurley); all figures are Royal Collection Trust / © Her Majesty Queen Elizabeth II 2022

Royal Collection Trust is also grateful for permission to reproduce the items listed below:

All Souls College, Oxford, © The Warden and Fellows of All Souls College, Oxford: Figs 1.4 (plus key), 2.3, 2.11, 2.23, 2.26, 2.27. The images reproduced in this publication can be viewed on the Bodleian website via the following links:

Fig. 1.4: <http://codrington.asc.ox.ac.uk/wren/st_james_palace.html#250>

Fig. 2.3: <http://codrington.asc.ox.ac.uk/wren/st_james_park.html#412>

Fig. 2.11: <http://codrington.asc.ox.ac.uk/wren/st_james_palace.html#242>

Fig. 2.23: <http://codrington.asc.ox.ac.uk/wren/st_james_palace.html#244>

Fig. 2.26: <http://codrington.asc.ox.ac.uk/wren/st_james_palace.html#249>

Fig. 2.27: <http://codrington.asc.ox.ac.uk/wren/st_james_palace.html#252>

Art Institute of Chicago, Illinois, Gift of Mrs James Ward Thorne (1940.603.26). Chicago (IL), Art Institute of Chicago. © 2022. The Art Institute of Chicago / Art Resource, NY/ Scala, Florence: Fig. 4.1

Bibliothèque de l'Institut national d'histoire de l'art, collections Jacques Doucet, Fol Res 543, <https://bibliotheque-numerique.inha.fr/viewer/10960>: Figs 1.24, 1.25

Birmingham City Council, Benjamin Stone Collection. Reproduced with the permission of the library of Birmingham: Figs 4.27, 4.46, 4.53, 4.55

Birmingham Museum and Art Gallery, photograph by Birmingham Museums Trust, licensed under CC0: Fig. 2.15

Bodleian Library, University of Oxford: Figs 1.23, 2.24

British Library, London, © 2022 The British Library Board. All rights reserved: Figs 1.8, 1.10, 1.31, 1.35, 1.37, 2.1, 2.7, 2.16

British Museum, London, © The Trustees of the British Museum. Figs 0.5, 1.11, 1.29, 2.25, 2.29, 2.30, 3.12, 3.30, 4.4, 4.5, 4.6, 4.18

British School at Rome, © BSR Library, Thomas Ashby Print Collection, tapir-L611.D9.003, <www.bsrdigitalcollections.it/>: Fig. 1.18

Corpus Christi College, Cambridge, © The Parker Library, Corpus Christi College, Cambridge: Fig. 1.32

Country Life / Future Publishing Ltd: Fig. 5.8

Getty Images, © Hulton Archive / Getty Images: Fig. 4.64

Getty Images, © Hulton Archive / Getty Images / Keystone / Stringer: Fig. 4.79

Getty Images, © Keystone-France / Getty Images: Fig. 4.67

Historic England Archive, Swindon, © Crown copyright / Historic England Archive: Figs 4.30, 5.3

Historic England Archive, Swindon: Figs 4.7, 4.30, 4.34, 4.43, 4.50, 4.61, 4.65, 4.70, 4.71, 4.72, 5.6

Illustrated London News, © Illustrated London News Ltd / Mary Evans: Figs 4.14, 4.15

London Metropolitan Archives, © London Metropolitan Archives (City of London Corporation): Figs 1.17, 2.19, 4.16, 4.41, 4.54, 4.56, 4.62

Magdalene College, Cambridge, reproduced by permission of the Pepys Library, Magdalene College Cambridge: Figs 2.9, 2.10

Metropolitan Museum of Art, New York / Creative commons / Harris Brisbane Dick Fund, 1917: Fig. 1.9

Metropolitan Museum of Art, New York / Creative Commons / Purchase, Louis V. Bell, Harris Brisbane Dick, Fletcher, and Rogers Funds and Joseph Pulitzer Bequest and Annette de la Renta and Mr. and Mrs. Richard L. Chilton Jr. Gifts, 2014: Fig. 2.13

Musée Carnavalet, Paris, © Musée Carnavalet / Roger-Viollet: Fig. 2.8

Museum of London, © Museum of London: Fig. 3.32

The National Archives, Kew, © The National Archives: Figs 1.13, 1.34, 2.6, 2.18, 3.14, 3.34, 3.47, 3.48, 4.2, 4.3, 4.22, 4.25, 4.26, 4.29, 4.36, 4.38, 4.40, 4.42, 4.49, 4.68, 5.2

National Maritime Museum, Greenwich, London, Greenwich Hospital Collection: Fig. 4.9

National Portrait Gallery, London, © National Portrait Gallery, London: Fig. 3.10

Parham House and Gardens, West Sussex: Fig. 1.6

Press Association / Alamy: Figs 0.3, 0.4, 5.7, 5.12, 5.13

Private collection, © 2022 Christie's Images Limited: Fig. 4.33

Private collection, © The Picture Art Collection / Alamy Stock Photo: Fig. 2.22

Royal Horticultural Society, London, © RHS Lindley Collections: Fig. 2.5

Royal Institute of British Architects, London, © RIBA Collections: Figs 1.12, 1.15, 1.16, 1.20, 1.27, 4.24

Sir John Soane Museum, London, © Sir John Soane's Museum. Photography by Ardon Bar-Hama: Figs 2.31, 3.15, 3.16, 3.17, 3.18, 3.19, 3.20, 3.42, 3.43

Victoria and Albert Museum, London, © V&A Images: endpapers; Figs 3.38, 4.52, 4.53, 4.57

Wellcome Collection, London / Creative Commons: Fig. 4.21

Westminster City Archives, London, © Westminster City Archives: Figs 3.46, 4.80

Yale Center for British Art, New Haven, © Yale Center for British Art, Paul Mellon Collection: Fig. 3.11

Every effort has been made to contact copyright holders; any omissions are inadvertent, and will be corrected in future editions if notification of the amended credit is sent to the publisher in writing.

Plans

A Plan of the first floor of St James's Palace, *c.*1550

B Ground-floor plan of the palace, *c.*1688

C First-floor plan of the palace, *c.*1688

D Coloured phase plan of St James's Palace today: first floor

Plan A

The first floor, c.1550

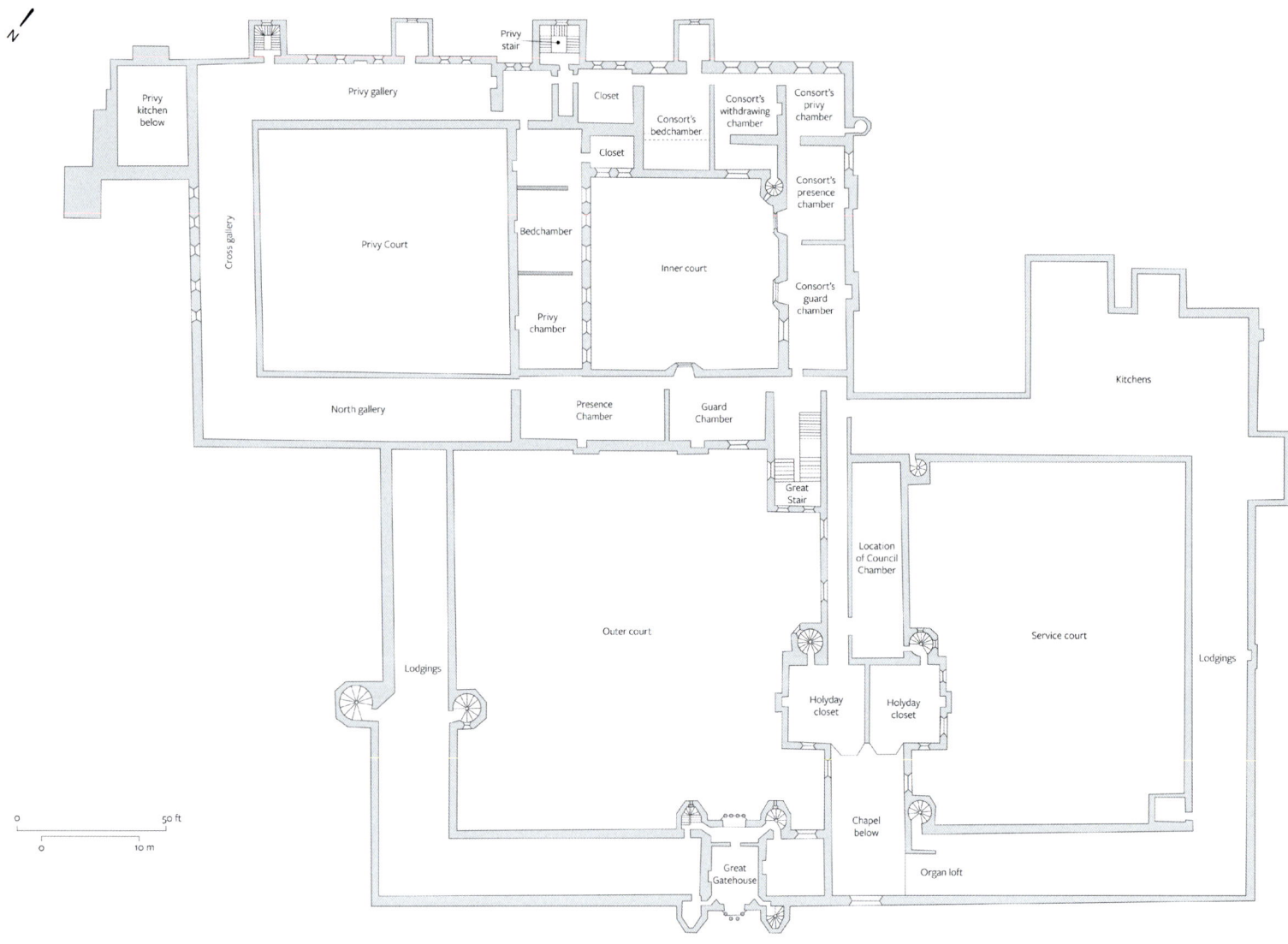

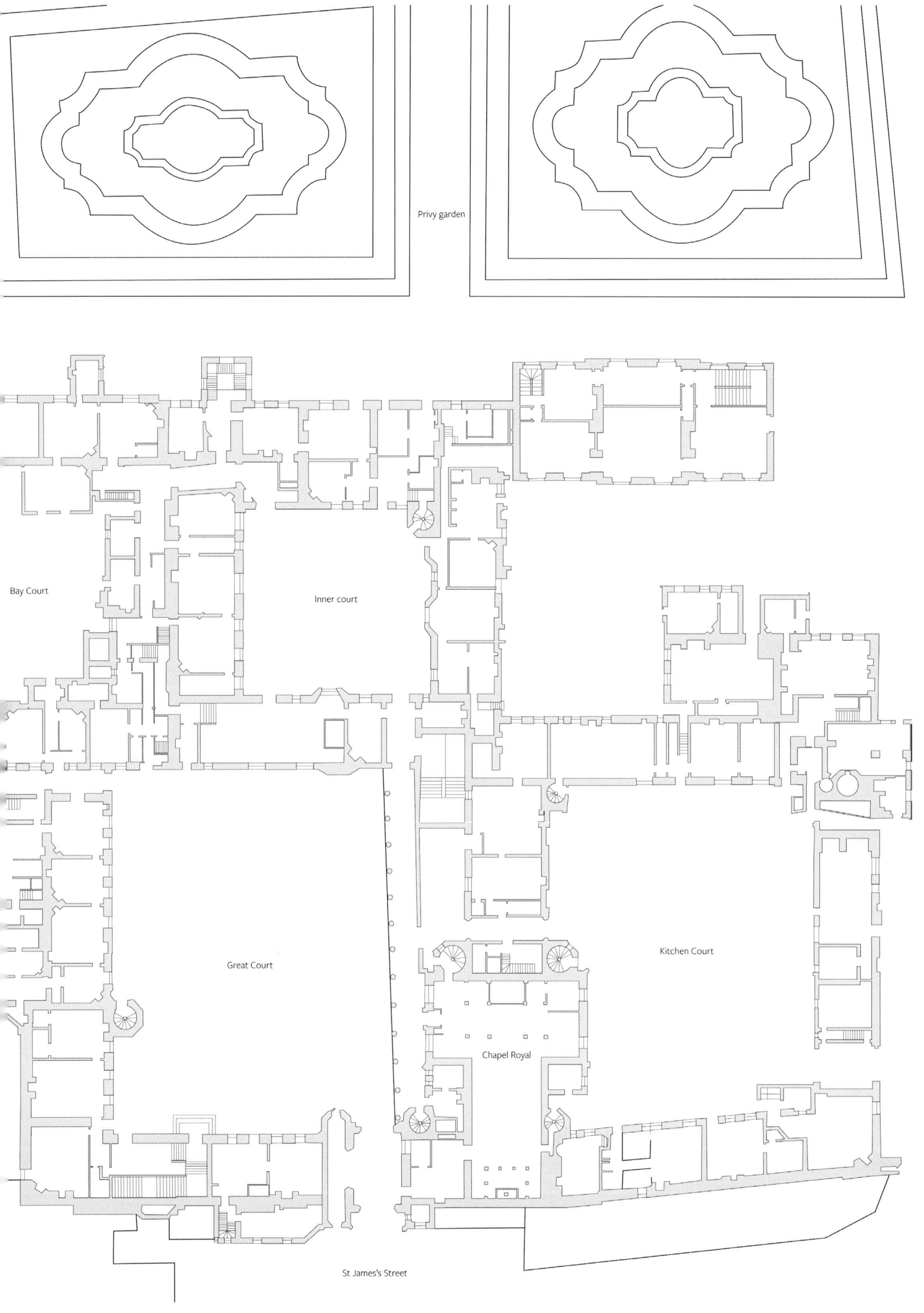

Plan B

The ground floor, *c.*1688

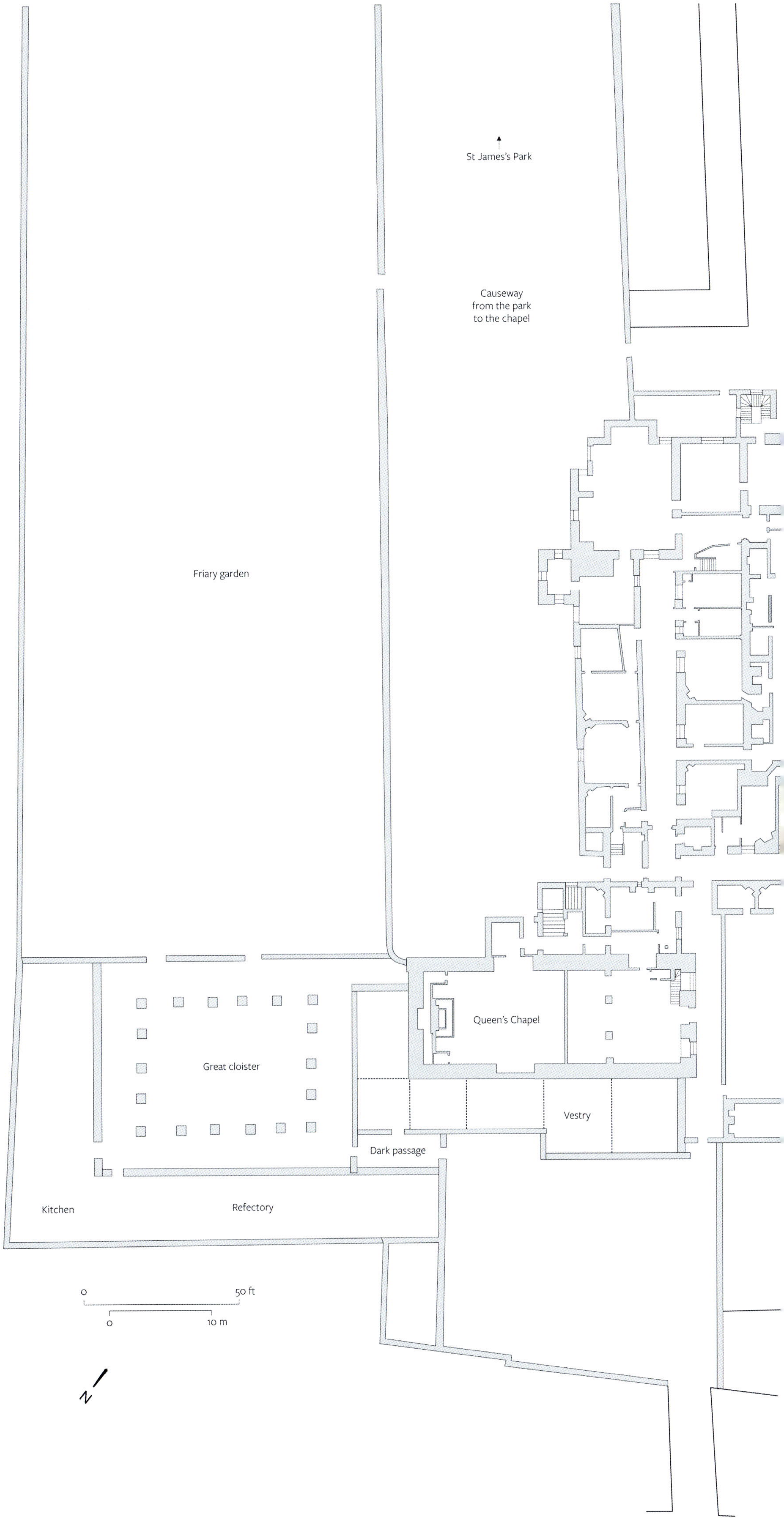

St James's Park

Causeway from the park to the chapel

Friary garden

Queen's Chapel

Great cloister

Vestry

Dark passage

Kitchen

Refectory

0 50 ft
0 10 m

N

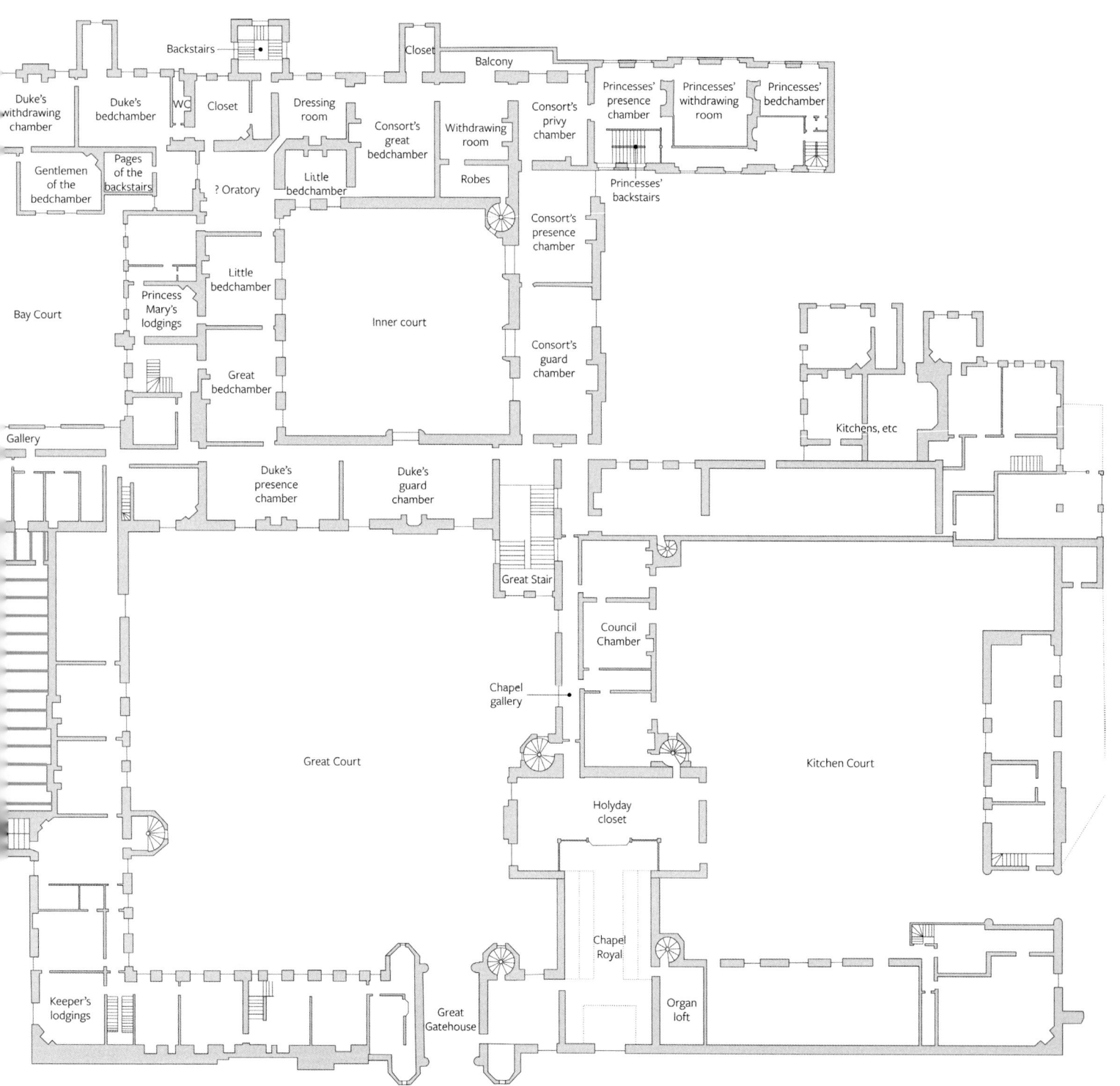

Plan C

The first floor, c.1688

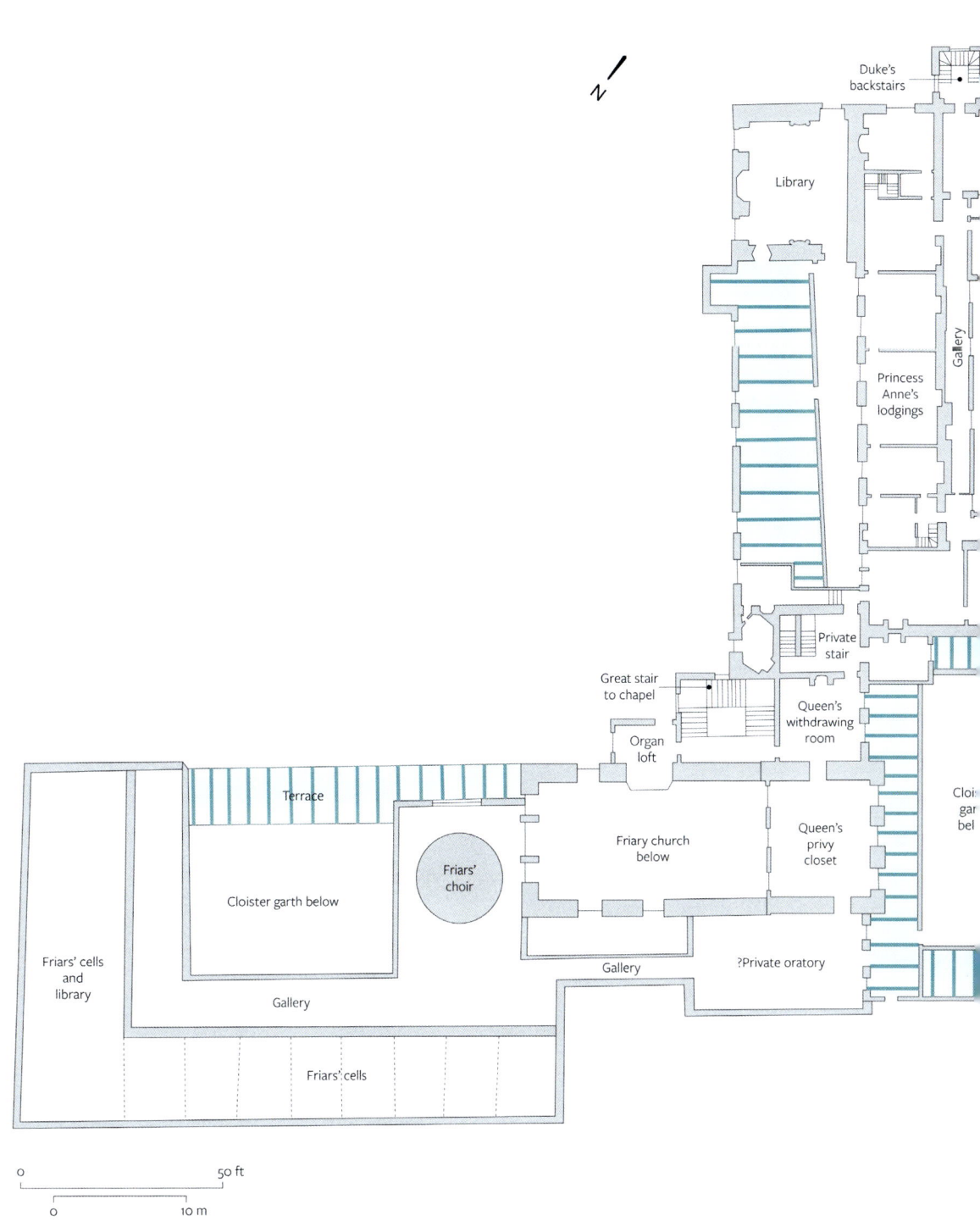